HITLER and the
Beer Hall Putsch

HITLER and the Beer Hall Putsch

HAROLD J. GORDON, JR.

Princeton University Press, Princeton, New Jersey, 1972

Preface

This book arose from a series of questions I asked myself because I am interested in the nature and uses of power. Since Hitler and National Socialism are crucial in any study of power in Germany in the Weimar period, a good number of these questions revolved around the man and his followers. Two related questions led me into this particular project. The first was: Why did Hitler and his party rise from a minor position in a welter of similar leaders and organizations to a position of unquestioned leadership in the Racist Movement? The other question was: Why did Bavaria in the later years of the Republic prove a less fertile field for the National Socialist Party than did much of the rest of Germany?

Increasingly, I came to feel that the years 1923-24 were the decisive years in which the developments occurred that made Hitler central to the Racist Movement and that "inoculated" great numbers of Bavarians against Hitler and Hitlerism. As I worked my way further into the materials, I became increasingly convinced that the story was a complex one and that Hitler and the National Socialists were only one of the more important stones in an intricate mosaic. I also became convinced that my original questions were only a portion of those that needed to be answered to make the period and people intelligible to myself and to the reader.

My book therefore addresses itself to the original questions and others associated with them, within the broader framework of my basic research interests. This broader framework establishes three further goals. The first is the detailed portrayal of a series of developments that determined the political fate of Bavaria for a decade and laid the foundations for Adolf Hitler's rise from the wings to the center of the world stage. The second is the provision of a case study of the roots of power—its development, transfer, use, and abuse—the significance of individuals in the power structure, and the manner in which they can dilute, warp, or concentrate power as a result of their prejudices, strengths, and weaknesses. Finally, this study is intended to serve as one of the probes on which a general analysis of power in Weimar Germany can be based.

In order to achieve these goals, the emphasis in this work is on primary materials. The secondary literature is cited only if it directly contributes facts or ideas not available elsewhere or if a quotation from the work in question is employed. Some further citations are used to correct factual errors or to call the reader's attention to sharp divergences of opinion.

The first chapter presents tentative conclusions about the factors leading to the rise of the Patriotic Movement in Germany after 1918. These conclusions are the results of studying the general background and analyzing the materials presented in the book itself. They help to place the entire study in perspective and to explain the views and aims of the members and leaders of the Patriotic Movement. The remainder of the first portion of the book provides a base for understanding the political situation in Bavaria in the fall of 1923. Political and social analyses of institutions and the presentation of programs are supplemented by the introduction of significant leaders and the consideration of their characters.

Part Two is devoted to the prelude to and the climax of the struggle for power in Bavaria in 1923, the climax being the Beer Hall Putsch.

Part Three is given over to the consideration of the new situation that arose after the Putsch and that situation's significance. Particular stress is laid on those factors that were to have lasting significance, such as the elimination of Hitler's major rivals within the Racist Movement, the decline of Bund Bayern und Reich as a major force within the Patriotic Movement, and the consolidation of the power of the conservative political coalition ruling Bavaria. The true significance of the developments in Bavaria in 1923 and of the Putsch emerge only when one considers the differences between the basic political scene in the fall of 1923 and that at the end of 1924.

In the preparation of this work I was aided by a great number of people to whom I owe a major debt of gratitude. None of them, however, is in any way responsible for the analyses I have made or the conclusion to which I have come.

First of all, I would like to thank my wife for both her patience and her active assistance. She not only lived with this project for nearly a decade, encouraging, correcting, suggesting, debating, and refining, but she also typed the final draft. My children, Betsy, Ned, and Richard deserve special mention for card sorting and musical accompaniment.

The Social Science Research Council, the Fulbright Commission, and the University of Massachusetts Research Council supported the project financially, and without their aid it could scarcely have been completed.

Many colleagues in both Germany and the United States aided greatly in the development of the project by suggesting, discussing, and correcting, as well as uncovering new evidence. In this regard I would particularly like to thank William Bischoff, Karl Bosl, Ernst Deuerlein, Frau Ursula von Gersdorff, Louis S. Greenbaum, Kurt Kolle, Hans Meier-Welcker, Reginald H. Phelps, Robert Potash, and John Zeender. David Danahar and Gilbert E. Southern provided invaluable aid in the preparation of social data and in processing personal testimony of participants.

Many persons who were active in the political events of the period, or who observed them from first hand, assisted me with testimony and advice. I am particularly indebted to those who, like Hans Ehard, Oskar Erhard, Immanuel von Kiliani, Max Lagerbauer, Emil Leeb, Ernst Schultes, and Graf von Soden, again and again came to my aid. I am also deeply indebted and most grateful to all the others who contributed evidence and testimony and only regret that considerations of space make it necessary for me to refer the reader to the Bibliography for their names.

Last, but far from least, I wish to thank all of the many archivists who helped me so much over the years. Gerhard Böhm occupies a special position in his double role of archivist and key figure in the suppression of the Putsch. Among the other archival personnel who devoted much time and energy to aiding me in my research were Richard Bauer, Hermann Goldbeck, and Sergeant Wagner of the National Archives of the United States; Fräulein A. H. Bayer, Hermann-Joseph Busley, Harold Jaeger, Otto Puchner, Otto Schottenloher, Hildebrand Troll, and Eberhard Weiss of the Bayerisches Hauptstaatsarchiv; Cecile Hensel of the Geheime Staatsarchiv, Berlin; Werner Jochmann and Uwe Lohalm of the Hamburg Forschungsstelle für die Geschichte des Nationalsozialismus; Anton Hoch and Thilo Vogelsang of the Institut für Zeitgeschichte; and Friedrich Facius of the Württembergisches Staatsarchiv. A portion of any success this book may enjoy will be the result of such assistance.

Contents

PART THREE: *The New Political Milieu*

List of Illustrations and Maps

INTRODUCTION

1.

THE NEW WIND IN BAVARIAN POLITICS

I. *The Patriotic Movement*

The end of World War I brought with it a "new wind" in politics throughout Germany, but especially in Bavaria, where the natural developments of the postwar era were accelerated by the violent atmosphere of the Räterepublik and the passions it loosed. Therefore, while elsewhere it was still a breeze, slowly growing in strength but fitful and unpredictable, this wind became a tornado in Bavaria.

The wind blew from the trenches, from the schools, from the universities and, to a lesser extent, from other institutions, and it affected all sorts of people, but particularly the young. Fanned by it, a large number of new political and political-military groups and institutions developed in postwar Germany. In general, the new groups and institutions opposed all existing political groups, institutions, and doctrines, and were to a considerable extent mutually competitive and destructive. Taken together, they nonetheless constituted a clearly recognizable political-social-military movement of great potential depth and strength which was in many ways parallel to Marxism as well as being hostile to it. This movement may perhaps be best called, as it usually was at the time, the "Patriotic Movement" (Vaterländische Bewegung).

Most historians and political scientists have devoted practically all of their attention to only one aspect of this movement, the National Socialist German Worker's Party (NSDAP). To the extent that they have looked at the broader movement at all they have done so only in a very narrow context, in which it and its component parts—aside from the NSDAP—were considered only as contributors to or predecessors of National Socialism, or even as "neo-conservatives" who influenced National Socialism. The result is an examination of the whole in terms of one component part, a very clear case of the woods being obscured by the trees. Thus the total picture is distorted.

There have been a number of standard approaches to the problem of the background and theoretical basis of National Socialism. They may perhaps be divided into the moralistic approach, the intellectual approach, and the Marxian-influenced sociological approach. All of them, naturally, shed at least some light on the origins of National Socialism. However, all of these approaches suffer from the same defects. They ignore the broader movement of which National Socialism is only a portion, and until rather late in its development, a fairly small portion. Secondly, they examine the National Socialist Movement in terms that are meaningful to themselves, without seriously examining much of the existing evidence to learn whether or not these terms were meaningful for the persons involved. In other words, they do not, usually, try very hard to place themselves in the shoes of the National Socialists. Instead, they try to fit the National Socialists into shoes which they feel should fit them.

Besides these general criticisms, there are serious specific criticisms which can be made of each of the standard approaches. The first approach, which just says that the National Socialists were bad and that they did bad things because they were bad, does not help the serious historian or political scientist greatly and, to be fair, has largely been abandoned in favor of the other approaches. It is simply recognized that the National Socialists did some very vicious and cruel things, and the question of why and how they got into a position to do them and why and how they performed them is raised. This question is particularly important because it is increasingly clear that many National Socialists were, in their every-day lives, "good people" in the ordinary meaning of these words.

The intellectual approach is weak for a number of reasons. The first and most important is perhaps the fact that the persons who created and led the National Socialist Movement were basically anti-intellectual in the sense that they were men who scorned abstract ideas and interested themselves in practical, down-to-earth matters. They were patronizing or scornful towards their own intellectuals, considering them foolish ranters. Alfred Rosenberg never managed to achieve any real stature in the party and lost all his political battles, except for those against other intellectuals on the periphery of serious politics.[1] Dietrich Eckart was a father-figure without real influence or power. Gottfried Feder was alternately tolerated and ignored.

Secondly, there is very little convincing evidence of serious intellectual influence having been exerted on these leaders by the various key figures who have been seen as their predecessors and teachers—a list which ranges from Martin Luther through Wagner and Nietzsche to Houston Stewart Chamberlain and beyond. There is no evidence that Hitler ever read in the works of these men, and there is a good deal of evidence that far more key National Socialist leaders were influenced by Theodor Fritsch and his pamphlets than were influenced by all of the learned books by great literary and philosophical seers that were ever printed. Certainly some bastardized forms of a great number of people's ideas found their way into the minds of the men who started National Socialism and many more into the minds of those who led the broader Patriotic Movement, but it is scarcely fitting to create a literary circle out of a group of men who scorned literary figures, no matter how eminent, unless they were also men of action. This seems to be another case of intellectuals crediting their "class" with much more influence than it could legitimately claim.

The intellectuals, indeed, often try to make the National Socialists believe things that they did not believe and to represent intellectual movements that were abhorrent to them. For example, National Socialists are seen as a "conservative" force by many historians, but no one to my knowledge has ever produced a single institution that Hitler and his circle wished to conserve. Certainly they used popular symbols of earlier regimes to popularize themselves, just as they used unpopular symbols of earlier regimes to discredit those regimes, but in each case they twisted the symbol and made it into what they wanted it to be. Certainly they showed no real reverence for it.

It is, indeed, impossible to find ideas of the past that the National Socialists wished to conserve. Christianity they tried to replace with various pseudo-religious and neo-pagan rites, which were more inventions than a real return to the Teutonic past. Monarchy they

[1] For Hitler's views regarding Rosenberg's work see Hitler, Adolf, *Hitlers Tischgespräche im Führerhauptquartier 1941-1942*, ed. Dr. Henry Picker, Stuttgart, 1965, 2nd edn., pp. 269-70. Hereafter cited as Hitler, *Tischgespräche*.

loathed, scorning both Hohenzollerns and Wittelsbachs, although they were prepared to make use of any royalty they might be able to win over to their cause.[2] Neither throne nor altar, the standard values of old conservatives, had any real validity in their cosmos. Capitalism came out no better. From the beginning they launched bitter attacks on international capitalism and were, throughout, suspicious of big industry. In his last years Hitler even talked of liquidating much of big industry in postwar Germany. Nor did the old society win their plaudits. Hitler and Ernst Röhm were vehement on the decadence of the old regime from top to bottom, arguing that it would never have fallen without a blow if it were not rotten through and through. To replace it they favored a society with mobility for all who were able and loyal.[3] In sum, they wished to conserve nothing, and therefore cannot be labeled conservatives.

The sociological approach seems to be on firmer ground, and in a way it is. However, the sociological approach that has normally been made to the National Socialist Movement is the sort of sociological approach that was taught to the historical profession by Karl Marx, who was a far better historian and sociologist than he was a political or economic prophet. Marxian (as opposed to Marxist) analysis has been a very important tool of the modern historian, even more for the non-Marxist than for the Marxist. This tool, however, is of most value when applied to a society or group that is basically class oriented or a situation where divisions arise over questions of class. It is least applicable, without drastic modification, to situations where the basic questions at issue are political, religious, or have still other origins, or where class is eschewed. This is the situation in the Patriotic Movement to a considerable extent and in the National Socialist Party to a far greater extent. Furthermore, while there have been a good number of assumptions made about the sociological aspects of the early National Socialist Party, they have rarely been carried further than assumptions and generalizations—and preliminary examination of the facts does not seem to support the basic assumptions made by those using the sociological approach.

The proposition that the party was essentially a class party based on the dissatisfaction of the lower middle class with their position in Weimar Germany is a good example of this approach and is supported by statements in the contemporary Marxist press. It is not,

---

[2] See Chapter III, Section II below; Hitler, *Tischgespräche*, pp. 439-40.

[3] See Chapter III, Section II; and Chapter IV, passim below.

however, supported by any other type of source, including those most interested in the NSDAP and those closest to it. Essentially, the proponents of the sociological approach force the National Socialists to adopt a class position, when really the entire Patriotic Movement and the NSDAP in particular were organized for the specific purpose of destroying the class concept and the class stratification of Germany in the interest of unifying the people both to protect them against the exterior foe and to carry out the manifest destiny of Germany. Therefore, class, which destroys internal cooperation, was no basis for such a movement. It was anathema to the movement and to its members.

The sociological approach seems to have more validity than it does because it was true that a good number of lower-middle-class people moved into the party early, but these people were among those who had the least to lose by losing class. They were not, as were Marxist workers, wedded to their class by a socio-political doctrine that made divorce from that class a sin. Nor were they as fond of their class as were the higher strata of the middle class, who had privileges, social position, and even wealth to lose, or as were the nobility, whose members had by this time become a specially privileged appendage of the upper middle class, with which they were inextricably intertwined. Therefore, of all those groups or individuals active in the prewar world, the lower middle class and the "Lumpenproletariat" (non-Marxist workers) would find it easiest to accept such a movement, and the lower middle class would find it easier than the workers because the unions could not put serious pressure on it to conform to other and older patterns.

However, neither the movement nor the party was essentially lower-middle-class in make-up according to the best available evidence. This sub-class formed an element in the party, but an element apparently no larger than its share in the population—if as large. Instead, it was from the young men that the movement drew a high percentage of its recruits, and the more radically classless the group, the greater was its attraction for youth.[4]

It is far simpler and probably far wiser to use the available sociological evidence, the existing documentation as to the views and attitudes of the members and leaders of the Patriotic Movement and the NSDAP, to create a composite picture indicating their motivations and the origins of these motivations than to force them into

[4] See Chapters III and IV, passim.

a preconceived pattern. One set of factors can then be used as a check on the other, and both together must be solidly grounded on facts rather than assumptions. Yet these facts reach back into the prewar world, which set the scene for the changes that were to revolutionize Bavaria and then Germany. Only against this background do the true significance and origins of the Patriotic Movement become clearer and more understandable.

II. *Prewar Conditions*

Basically, political life in prewar Germany was based on class or on the Catholic religion, and Catholicism had some characteristics of a social class made up of sub-classes, just as does the Negro community in the United States or as did the Jewish community in Germany. Furthermore, the prewar political parties had practically all been founded as defensive groups to protect special interests which had come under attack from one quarter or another. The conservatives saw themselves as defending their just interests against liberals and Marxists. Liberals saw themselves as defending their interests first against conservatives and later against both conservatives and Marxists, and on occasion against the Catholic Church. The Marxists saw themselves as being on the defensive against the vicious machinations of all the others. Each political party represented a clearly defined "in-group" which was essentially interested in serving the interests of that group rather than the community as a whole—and this was true in theory as well as fact. There was no national German party with broad appeal to all Germans. There were only parties representing and perpetuating the division of Germans into mutually antagonistic groups.

The rulers of prewar Germany were drawn from all of these groups. The upper social and economic levels exercised the lion's share of control and enjoyed the greatest prestige, but even the Social Democratic leaders had their sphere of influence, power, and prestige, either as union leaders or parliamentary deputies, newspaper editors or professors. In general, then, it was a paternalistic state, paternalistic in two senses. The leaders came predominantly from the older, established classes and the sharing of power was to some extent on their terms—although their hold on power was thinner each day and, like economic power, political power in 1914 was in far different hands than it had been in 1870, let alone 1848. Within each group, the leaders were old men, as much among the socialists as among the conservatives. To a considerable extent, the men at the top of the government, the unions, the army, and other key institutions were men whose formative years had been lived before 1870, who had grown up in a Germany—or Germanies—where even Bismarckian ideas were new and startling. Many of these men, especially in such states as Bavaria, had come to terms with these ideas only reluctantly and in part. For these reasons, class attitudes and particularism were stronger among those at the top of any institution—taken by and large—than among those lower down, if only because they were from different generations with different basic assumptions of normality.

This was the society that was gradually changing as it was reshaped by explosive economic and social forces stemming from the Industrial Revolution, from unification, and from the existing international situation and Germany's new status as a world power. German society was also gradually changing as somewhat younger men came to power here and there throughout the system. William II is an example—perhaps not the most fortunate one but not the most unfortunate—of a new generation on the contemporary scene, while the substitution of the younger Liebknecht for his father showed that dynastic considerations were important on the Left as well as the Right and that father and son were not necessarily alike in either ideas or abilities. Germany before the war was thus a society and a political system in flux, but in gradual flux. Without the stimulus of the war, it is very likely that the changes in power as well as in attitude would have continued to be gradual and peaceful rather than violent and spasmodic. But the war did come, and it acted both as a catalyst and, to a lesser extent, as a redirector of energies and aims within Germany as elsewhere. The world that emerged from such a war could scarcely emerge unaltered, and it did not, though the effect was greater in the defeated lands than in the victorious.

III. *The Impact of the War*

The impact of the war was essentially twofold. In the first half of the war, old divisions were bridged over and the German people were unified, as perhaps they had never been before. This was the period when the Kaiser's internal political truce (Burgfrieden) was a very real force throughout Germany. Even before the war, there was developing a tendency throughout Europe for nationalism to replace class as an overriding consideration for men of all classes everywhere. The war naturally intensified this tendency. Nationalism became a primary, positive good. It was preached in the press; it was taught in the schools; it was axiomatic in the home. And, war being a breeder of hate as well as patriotism, this nationalism was strongly mixed with hatred of the enemy powers. This was the impact of the coming of the war, and it could perhaps be said to have endured in Germany until the failure of the offensive against Verdun—an arbitrary date, but one useful for symbolic purposes. It was the failure of this offensive that brought Paul von Hindenburg and Erich Ludendorff to the high command, as much to renew confidence by bringing the authors of victory in the east to the overall command as to express confidence in them as the team to win the war.

Thereafter, while Hindenburg remained personally very popular, the strain of war inevitably ate into the sinews of the German nation, as it did, according to various evidence, into the sinews of the other warring powers.[5] Naturally, the older people—who remembered a peaceful world and had in many cases been only superficially touched by the enthusiasm of the war fever—were more susceptible to such pressures than the younger ones who had been brought up in a world of struggling great powers; they were especially more susceptible than the very young ones who came to manhood during the war and for whom the war was increasingly the natural state of affairs between nations. Furthermore, old people felt the impact of the war less directly. For them the enemy was a vague abstraction. Cartoons in the press, stories in the newspapers, were their enemy, and this enemy seemed less real as time went on.

Then too, it was on the home front that the dull daily grind and the privations of war were most felt. The situation was made far worse by the generally liberal attitude of the German government as compared with those of the Allied powers. It did less to enforce some share of the ordinary man's privations on those who were better off or had special access to food, clothing, and other rare goods. The press, although regularly fed official military communiques, was given little general positive propaganda guidance and was subject to no serious control. Even defeatism was tolerated in the press to an extent that would never been thought of in England or America. The home front as a whole, and not just Marxists or workers, grew increasingly weary of a war they could neither fight nor escape. A war that disrupted what they felt was normalcy, was

---

[5] Russia is, of course, the prime example, but pacifism, defeatism, and demands for peace at any price grew everywhere.

galling and increasingly unpopular. The same situation applied increasingly to the noncombat elements of the armed forces, in which older soldiers predominated. The result was defeatism and warweariness.

Meanwhile, the mass of the nation's young manpower was undergoing a quite different experience, which led to quite different attitudes and viewpoints. This meant that in its latter phases, the war worked to split the population, and to split it perhaps more on lines of age than on political lines, although it did both. The young boys and girls in school learned hatred of the foe as a positive virtue, as well as a very fervent patriotism. Their older brothers were literally swallowed up by the war in an intellectual and emotional as well as a physical sense. Just as today in the Negro ghettos of America the authorities find it almost impossible to overcome the influence that elder brothers, who are hostile to authority and organized society, exercise over younger siblings, it was difficult (or would have been, had anybody tried) to undermine the influence of older youths on younger ones in wartime Germany.

For the elder brothers themselves, the war was life. They were at the front, where the war was a real one. The enemy was a man who shot at you if you showed your head. A German was ipso facto a friend; the foreigner was ipso facto an enemy in this situation. While often the men who had been fighting for years were at best bone weary but stolidly determined and at worst broken down and sent to the rear to increase the disquiet there, the young officers and the young men brought vigor and enthusiasm to their tasks. They were too dedicated, too busy, and too emotionally involved, by and large, to be defeatist until the end, and then it was largely very new draftees, troops transferred from the quiescent eastern front, and men scraped up from the bottom of the manpower barrel who proved to be a very serious morale problem. To a considerable extent, the front, and especially the young men on it, never gave up hope of victory and never really accepted defeat.

Whether the revolution came before or after defeat was immaterial to many of them. It was a blow directed against the beloved fatherland; it was a blow against them. They believed, and World War II experience suggests that they were correct here, that Germany could have held out far longer, at the very least. They also believed, and no one will ever know to what extent they were right or wrong on this point, that had Germany held out longer she would have wrung a better peace from the Allies. The rightness or wrongness of this matter is not vital for the historian. The fact that large numbers of German soldiers on the front, including a high percentage of the able-bodied youth of the nation, believed it, was of extreme importance to them and was crucial for Germany.

The latter part of the war had seen Germans drift apart over the question of the war. The revolution dug a deep abyss between at least the active political Left, including portions of the middle-class moderate Left, and the bulk of the front soldiers. Even front soldiers drawn from the Left and belonging to it politically were often not entirely at ease with those who had been at home and made the revolution.

Basically, the war had also done something else to a great many of the front officers and soldiers, to a great number of the school children, and even to a great number of ordinary older Germans: it had changed them from a class orientation to a national orientation. German was good; non-German was bad. In moderate forms this led to a de-emphasis on the importance of class differences, suspicion of foreigners as hostile, and a general sympathy for anyone who put nation before class and resentment of anyone who did not. In its extreme forms this national orientation led to bitter hatred of all foreigners and everyone who did not subscribe to the belief in a united German society in which classes would play, at most, a subordinate role. Most Germans were affected to some extent by this philosophy, as were most nationals of the warring countries. As late as 1969, an English gentleman of that approximate generation, a man with an excellent education and broad experience of the world, could say to the author with transparent sincerity: "Scratch a German and you find a beast." The young were affected most and were affected most deeply.

As a corollary, these men favored social democracy—a baton in every knapsack. Birth was no criterion of importance to them. Any German should be able to climb to the limits imposed by his abilities, as long as he was a true "German"—that is, a nationalist. The National Socialists went farther and demanded that he also accept party discipline and the decrees of the Führer. No one deserved consideration or any post of responsibility who did not meet these qualifications. Just as a Marxist would and did feel that no one who did not represent the proletariat had a right to leadership in a Marxist society, so the patriot felt that only a nationalist should hold such posts. Class consciousness was replaced by national consciousness as a criterion of virtue.

When the troops came home, these notions were still inchoate and often not fully recognized by many of those who carried them. Those who understood and most consciously recognized these new directions were the better-educated youths. What the meaning of this reorientation would be and how it would express itself was still unclear to everyone in the fall and winter of 1918.

IV. *The New Concepts in the New Environment*

Before the new concepts had jelled in any way, the radical Marxists attempted to carry the revolution far to the Left in Bavaria. A tiny minority of the populace favored this extension of the revolution. Kurt Eisner, for instance, has been pointed to as an idol of the poor and disheartened masses. When these masses went to the polls, however, at a time when he headed the government, they gave his political party only 3 seats out of approximately 140, a peculiar way of expressing their enthusiasm and confidence. If Eisner was anathema to a great number of Bavarians, the Communists were more so. The result of the brief period of dominance by the Communists and their allies was therefore—particularly in view of the execution of a number of hostages at the time of their regime's collapse—not merely to freeze most Bavarians into a violently anti-Marxist position, but also to precipitate the new ideas in the minds of many young men, and to inflame others to work actively in spreading the new doctrine. The time and situation were ripe.

As the young soldiers and officers returned from the front to offices, workshops, factories, and universities, they were the natural leaders of the generation behind them. Just as the veterans of World War II set the tone in American universities for practically a full decade, so the new veterans set the tone in German universities and particularly in Bavarian universities in the years right after World War I. The "old men" had, in the eyes of the young, either lost the war and the revolution by weakness and cowardice or, worse, had actively betrayed Germany and supported the revolution. Whether monarchist or merely nationalist these young men were disgusted with the corrupt old men. The natural candidates to take their places were the older students, back from the war with the glamor of heroes and officers and preaching a doctrine that fitted the attitudes to which the new century and the war had "sensitized" the younger students. Some of the older youths were actually teachers and instructors at the secondary and university levels.

Then too, in a period when athletics were weak or non-existent at German universities and nationalism burned high, paramilitary training took the place in the educational system that football games took in contemporary America. Here, again, it was the older youths who were the leaders, and their ideas dominated and permeated the organizations they developed. Rudolf Nissen, later an eminent surgeon, says of this phenomenon, which he observed at first hand:

> [In] 1919 it was interesting to watch the transformation of the political spirit [in the universities] at close quarters. Representatives of liberal and democratic ideas were driven into the minority by a blustering soldier of fortune type, which grew rapidly in numbers, although rational discussions were by no means infrequent. Just as later, before Hitler's rise, antisemitism became the means for separating viewpoints. . . .[6]

This movement was particularly effective in the cities. It was here that patriotism had burned highest among idealistic youth, that the returning apostles of patriotism found masses of possible disciples available, and that these men could study or work. Particularly at first, the movement was strongest outside the working class, but by 1923 the scene had shifted. The older workers were still held in line to a considerable extent, especially in large plants, by union discipline, but many young workers were falling by the wayside.[7] The barriers of Marxist tradition, labor discipline, and ward cohesion acted as checks to some extent, but they did not stop the general flow of young workers to the Patriotic Movement in general and to its National Socialist wing in particular.

The farming population—the peasantry and, to a lesser extent, the farm workers—were at first relatively untouched by the Patriotic Movement, and this continued to be partially the case throughout 1923. By that time a good number of them, particularly younger men, were attracted by the movement, but they tended to move into its most conservative and passive organizations, eschewing the vigorously activist ones. The farmers' primitive patriotism, which had sent their young men out with the simple enthusiasm that had inspired Andreas Hofer to rise against Napoleon, had often not been proof against the trials of five years of a war whose involu-

---

[6] Nissen, Rudolf, *Helle Blätter, Dunkle Blätter*, Stuttgart, 1969, p. 42. Hereafter cited as Nissen, *Helle Blätter*.

[7] See Chapter III, Sections IV and V below.

tions were increasingly incomprehensible to them. The peasants withdrew into themselves. Some of them had been vaguely revolutionary in 1918-19, but the Räterepublik killed this weak spark. They returned to passivity and an equally vague conservatism, which in most areas became increasingly monarchist as the immediate memory of the war waned. Their children received little schooling and that reluctantly, while the Catholic clergy, conservative and largely monarchist by tradition and personal attitude, helped to hold them in the old paths.

Country was thus divided from city and generation from generation by differing attitudes toward and concepts of the proper political course for the future and even by differing ideas about man's relationship to man within Germany.

v. *The Patriotic Movement in Bavaria*

When these young men came back, or came out of school, or became politically conscious, they found no political party or group interested in them or their desires. As far as the parties were concerned, whether they were Left or Right, the revolution was a mere episode that did not turn them one whit from their basic course. None of the existing parties had any appeal for those who believed in the new orientation. Had the Social Democratic Party (SPD) become, as it did to an increasing extent after World War II, a non-Marxist, national socialist party, it is very likely that it would have been here that many young men would have found their political home. Some of them did, indeed, flirt with the SPD or the Independent Social Democratic Party (USPD) before realizing how totally alien to them they were.[8]

Albert Speer, in a passage that seems as applicable to today's intellectual radicals as to his own generation, vividly portrays the spirit of unrest and unease that might have moved these young men to a national, revolutionary Left but instead moved them to a national, revolutionary Right:

So it was not only a welling up of youthful obstinacy, when I was dissatisfied with the luxurious life at home. It was as an expres-

[8] Graf Arco-Valley, who shot Eisner in 1919, was, for example, briefly an Independent Social Democrat and an enthusiastic adherent of Eisner's. The much older National Socialist leader Major Ritter von Bolz also sojourned briefly in the SPD. A good number of other Völkisch leaders of the early period also came over from the Left. Gordon Papers, D, 1 (Personen-Kartei).

sion of definite opposition that I preferred authors critical of society, when I sought my favorite circle of friends in the rowing club or in the huts of the Alpine Club. Even my inclination towards a simple [lower-] middle-class artisan family flew in the face of the custom of finding one's comrades and one's future wife in the sheltered social circle which was associated with one's parents' house. Indeed, I felt spontaneous sympathy for the extreme Left—without this sympathy ever finding concrete expression. I was immune to any form of political engagement. This did not alter the fact that I felt myself to be "national" and, for example, at the time of the Ruhr occupation [in] 1923 was upset by [observing] inappropriate revels or by the threatening coal crisis.[9]

Although he says that he was invulnerable to political engagement, in actual fact Speer's own words make it clear that he was looking for just such an engagement. Equally interesting is the fact that he does not seem conscious of the fact that it was his "national" feelings that stood in the way of such an engagement on the Left. He was a man without a political home but with definite ideas as to the nature of the one he sought. It was not by chance that he was to find his way into the one political organization that offered a program calling for social mobility and national revival.

In the absence of a hospitable existing political organization, it was natural that such energetic, ambitious, and dedicated young men should establish new groups of their own. These groups were often amorphous at first, and they represented many different degrees of nationalism and often advocated divergent paths to the new national and united Germany. They differed from one another in both kind and degree, in size and organization, and in methods and objectives. However, they were all strongly nationalist, favored the militant defense of Germany against her foes both domestic and foreign, and therefore wanted a strong armed force and police. They all demanded a reorganization of Germany to develop greater efficiency, reduce corruption and complacency, and unite all Germans. All were vaguely allied with one another against the Left (of all shades) as traitors and divisive elements in German society and the German nation. To a lesser extent they were all more or less against the "reaction"—the old men of the old regime.

By early 1923 three fairly clear wings of the movement had

---

[9] Speer, Albert, *Erinnerungen*, Berlin, 1969, p. 25.

emerged. The right or nationalist wing was moderate and gradualist in approach. It depended largely on nationalist businessmen, government officials and, traditional veterans' organizations for leadership. It was prepared to accept and even support the existing government and political-social situation in Bavaria, but it was strongly opposed both to any attempt to return to a pre-Bismarck particularism and to even a single step towards the Left.[10]

The center element wanted change but was ready to work for it within the existing system and through legal or semi-legal channels, although it was quite prepared to use lobbying tactics and even implicit blackmail to get its way. A good example of this wing of the movement was Bund Bayern und Reich, with one foot in old Bavaria and one foot in a new, radically-oriented nationalist Reich.[11]

Finally, on the left of the movement, occupying the same relative position as did the Communists in the Marxist Movement, was the NSDAP and its allies. Here was the highly activist element, demanding a violent revolution, a new state, and a drastically modified society. These were the so-called Racist Bands (Völkische Verbände),[12] although some members and groups of the Center also called themselves "racist." These radical groups were of various types, and varying degrees of virulence. Some, like the German Racist Defense League (Deutschvölkischer Schutz- und Trutzbund) or Gottfried Feder's League for the Breaking of Interest Slavery (Deutscher Kampfbund zur Brechung der Zinsknechtschaft) limited themselves almost entirely to the generation of propaganda for the cause. Many were primarily or entirely paramilitary in nature, like Captain (Ret.) Adolf Heiss' Reichsflagge, Lieutenant Commander Hermann Ehrhardt's Wikingbund (called "Brigade Ehrhardt," when mobilized), First Lieutenant (Ret.) Gerhard Rossbach's organization—which changed its name with a

---

[10] See Chapter IV, Section III below.

[11] See Chapter IV, passim; and Chapter VI, Sections I and II below.

[12] I have met with some objection to my translation of "Völkisch" as "racist," but I am inclined to stand by my guns. The chief characteristic of these groups was racism; that is what the word meant to them and what it means literally. The one tenet all Völkisch groups had in common was a belief in the importance of the German race or people. This belief was accompanied by a xenophobic hostility toward other races and peoples, which was particularly characterized by a more or less vigorous antisemitism. We would (and do) say that groups with these characteristics are "racist," and the groups themselves used the word in this sense.

bewildering regularity that baffled contemporary authorities and confuses historians—and Peter von Heydebreck's Silesian organization. However, the one organization in the entire left wing of the Patriotic Movement that enjoyed the advantages of both a paramilitary organization and a propaganda organization was the NSDAP. This organization was also the only one that had begun, by early 1923, the transformation from a more or less amorphous association of like-minded people into a tightly organized political party. It still denounced parliamentarianism and parliamentarians, but it was increasingly prepared to meet them on their own ground, despite its renunciation of participation in parliamentary life.

This meant that the NSDAP enjoyed the tactical advantage of being the extreme radical cutting edge of the movement, with the whole weight of its combined numbers more or less behind some of its activities and clearly opposed to interference with any of them. At the same time, it was the best led, the best organized, and most versatile of all the factions on the left of the movement. Finally, representing the essence of the movement, it attracted the most vigorous activists and a number of youths out of proportion to its size and significance within the total movement.

VI. *The Situation at the Beginning of 1923*

By the beginning of 1923, it was clear that the Bavarian government, while not overtly hostile to the Patriotic Movement, approved of only its most conservative elements and had no intention of allowing the extreme radical wing—which it considered to be national bolsheviks—to have a free hand. The men who ruled in München were now a generation younger than those who had ruled during the war, but they too were essentially monarchist and conservative in outlook. Where their predecessors had been essentially pre-Bismarckian in background and attitudes, these men were Bismarckian. Far from regretting the formation of the Reich, they fully accepted it and the Germany it created. At the same time, they wanted to maintain all those special rights and privileges with which Bavaria had entered the Reich. Here they found the right wing of the movement most helpful, for it reflected these ideas to a considerable extent, as did much of the Center. Therefore, needing support against Berlin and fearing the Marxist Left, the leaders of the government were ready to support those elements of the movement that were loyal to them. Hitler and the radicals had, in their eyes, value only as a "drummer," to win workers away from

Marxism, and this value was rapidly declining as the danger to their system from Hitler's own activities increased. This meant that Hitler and the government were already sparring in the middle of the ring when the year opened.

Simultaneously General Arnold Ritter von Möhl—commander-in-chief of the Bavarian military district of the Reichswehr who had been a friend and a patron of the Patriotic Movement from the very beginning but had kept control of it firmly in the hands of the center organization, Bund Bayern und Reich, by adroit use of patronage and adamant refusal to train or arm any other organizations—was transferred from München by the army leadership in Berlin because of his connections with the movement and his hostility towards the Reich. He was replaced by the intelligent, affable, but weak-willed, General Otto von Lossow, who soon became as much the victim and colleague of the leaders of the movement as their master. As a result of this passing of the reins into less capable hands, the Patriotic Movement in Bavaria began to break up into its component segments with great rapidity and these segments —the wings of the movement—in turn began to splinter. Both centrifugal and centripetal forces were constantly at work within the movement as a whole and within each wing of the movement. In early 1923 the centrifugal forces were clearly in the ascendance, but the nature of the new balance that would develop before the movement achieved its definitive form was still obscure.

Therefore, when the year began, the relations of the movement with all elements of the government and with its traditional political institutions and groups were increasingly hostile. Within the movement itself the last vestiges of unity were disappearing and the struggle for control of the component elements was beginning. All in all, fireworks were indicated.

VII. *Conclusion*

World War I and the early postwar months had precipitated the Patriotic Movement, which reflected the new wind in politics, more fully and rapidly in Bavaria than elsewhere. This movement was extremely diffuse, and its various elements differed from one another in many ways. However, all members of the movement had certain basic attitudes in common, just as did all Marxists. This common denominator was the idea of nationalism or patriotism as the primary, natural, and good moving force in politics. In many ways this movement was the inverse of Marxism. Where Marxism looked to the brotherhood of the international proletariat, after the extermination of the exploiting classes (whether by evolution or revolution), as the eventual, absolute good, so the "patriots" saw the brotherhood of all Germans, after the elimination of the anti-German or non-German elements (by evolution, conversion, or expulsion), as the ultimate good. All members of the Patriotic Movement agreed on the need to eliminate class divisions, religious divisions, and all other barriers between Germans, so that they could weld all Germans together into a single homogeneous body, a great band of brothers. Here again their attitude is startlingly close to that of the Marxists, if one substitutes the word "nation" for the word "class."

The result is that the Marxists were in part right when they believed that the members of the Racist Movement were déclassé; they were déclassé, not because they had lost their class, but because they had rejected it and the very concept of it. They specifically and violently rejected the concept of class as a proper and meaningful way to categorize mankind. If Marx was revolting against the class from which he sprang, these men were revolting against the "class tyranny" that history and Marx had fastened on them. They believed that the meaningful divisions were to be made in terms of national differences, or, as they expressed it, in terms of "race." The categories as they saw them were, roughly: corrupt and debauched races, like the Jews and the gypsies who constituted a dangerous, disruptive, and threatening element in society; less valuable but harmless races; and Nordic races, like the Germans. The Germans were then further categorized into traitors, bad Germans, good Germans, and racists. Seen in these terms, the world had no place for class and class had no meaning for the world. Only insofar as the customs and traditions of a given class made for "good" or "bad" Germans did the National Socialists or other racists have any serious interest in class, and then they were interested in its characteristics rather than in the class itself.

Their quarrel with Marxism was not based on dislike for workers but on dislike for a divisive and international philosophy that tried to turn German against German and to "de-Germanize" the nation. In their cosmos the worker was important not as a worker but as a German, and the racists wished not only to unify but also to improve the lot of all Germans, not just the lot of one class. In a sense they wanted to create a new European upper class including all Germans. This theme persisted, as is indicated by Hitler's comment during World War II on the importance of the Volkswagen as a means for getting every German out into the green countryside.

Hitler's thoughts were not essentially bourgeois, as has so often been argued, although they clearly contained middle-class elements. He adopted ideas just as readily from all other classes: his idea of the superiority of the Nordic races had its origins in the French aristocracy, while his strong distaste for the habits and attitudes of the bourgeoisie seems to blend the prejudices of the working classes with those of the artists' quarter. His personal style of dress also smacked far more of the déclassé artists of Schwabing than of the middle or upper classes. Similarly, his antisemitism was the defensive antisemitism of the poor, who see the Jew as the great exploiter, who fear him and hate him, rather than that of the upper classes, who lump the Jew with the poor and the nouveau riche as unsuitable for polite society. The upper-class antisemite thus sees the Jew as one of a group of unwelcome intruders trying to make their way into the charmed circle. The lower-class antisemite sees the Jew as a monstrous shadow of evil, and this is the vision of Hitler.

Just as Scharnhorst, Stein, and Gneisenau embraced liberalism not merely for itself, but as a force that would defeat the conqueror, so the racists saw the adoption of their concept as a prelude to the liberation of Germany from the new oppressors. Only by liberating the forces of the German people, by welding them into one Volk, could the bonds of Versailles be broken and Germany emerge on the world stage as a superpower. Disunity had been an essential element in the defeat of Germany, and unity must be a factor in her resurgence. Racism was therefore both a means and an end, the touchstone of the new religion. The racists, treading in the footsteps of Mohammed and Marx, were the fanatic purveyors of a new and militant faith. Their introduction to the Bavarian scene in 1919-20 set in motion forces that began to ripen by early 1923 and brought about the political struggle that marked the next two years.

PART ONE

The Contenders in the Struggle for Power

2.

TRADITIONAL PARTIES, POLITICAL PRESSURE GROUPS, AND THE PRESS

1. *Introduction*

In the early Weimar Republic the political parties, political pressure groups, and the press played a less significant role in Bavaria than they did elsewhere in Germany because of the powerful Bavarian organizations, outside the parties themselves, that included great numbers of people, disseminated institutional propaganda, and, in many cases, wielded direct power or influence within the state. Even the government itself, being dependent on the parties rather than simply an extension of them, was less identified with the parties than was the case elsewhere in the *Reich*. Nonetheless, one should not fall into the error of many of their political opponents in 1923 and discount the traditional parties, for, in the end, it was elements of the traditional party system that won the power struggle of that year with the aid of state and national armed forces. It is therefore impossible to consider the balance of forces within the Bavarian state in this period without looking at the parties and pressure groups.

The traditional Bavarian parties, that is those going back to the prewar period, were all essentially special-interest parties based on the support of a limited segment of the population. They were ideological in nature, in that they demanded of their members adherence to a more or less specific theoretical program. The Middle Party, the National Liberal Party, and the German Democratic Party were essentially upper- and middle-class parties appealing to conservative or liberal groups within this class. The Bavarian People's Party and the Center Party were based on the Roman Catholic Church and can be seen as its secular political arm, although the Bavarian People's Party was also strongly representative of Bavarian state interests and of Bavarian monarchism. The Bavarian Peasants' and Mittelstand[1] League was, despite its bow to the Mittelstand, a farmers' party for those peasants who found the Bavarian People's Party too Catholic or too disinterested in farmers' problems. The Social Democratic Party, the Independent Social Democratic Party, and the German Communist Party were Marxist parties of the Right, Left-Center, and Left, appealing almost exclusively, in Bavaria, to the working class and a scattering of left-wing intellectuals who identified themselves with this class.

Bavarian political pressure groups can be divided into two general classes: those with and those without paramilitary auxiliaries. The groups with military auxiliaries will be considered later, since their nature and activities were quite different from those pressure organizations that were purely civilian. The Weimar Republic was characterized by the existence of large numbers of political pressure groups, many of which were highly specialized and small. A substantial proportion of the political pressure groups were sub-organizations of political parties or groups representative of special interests within one or more of the parties. Some of the organizations were, however, quite independent of the parties and, in some instances, inimical to them. Some were ephemeral; others endured throughout the life of the Republic. Multiple membership was common within associated or similar groups.

The political pressure groups worked, either with or without the cooperation of the political parties, to influence the government to accept or support their objectives. They used all of the normal methods of cajolery, threat, and financial pressure or incentive directed at the government, and they mounted propaganda campaigns to win over the public. They used formal and informal lobbyists, and many of the organizations published a newspaper or magazine. Most of these publications were flimsy and enjoyed only a limited circulation, but a few were heavily subsidized and widely distributed.

Most of the press was party-political in nature, with most larger towns and cities having organs of the major parties. München and Nürnberg dominated the press picture, just as they tended to dominate all political life, and of the two, the München press was by far the more significant. Besides the clearly identified party press, there were also independent newspapers in Bavaria, chiefly in München.

[1] *Mittelstand* is a catch-all term of dubious validity. See Chapter III, note 79.

II. *Analysis of the Party Positions*

The Middle Party (Mittelpartei) was a special Bavarian creation. It was really a more or less permanent alliance of the two most conservative parties on the national scene: the German Nationalist People's Party (DNVP) and the German People's Party (DVP), the DNVP being by far the stronger partner. These parties were strongest in north Germany and suffered heavily in Bavaria from their identification with Prussia and with Protestantism, although it was this very identification that brought the Middle Party its clientele. Despite the fact that it was comparatively weak, the Middle Party was needed for the creation of a viable middle-class–peasant coalition after the elections of 1920 reduced the German Democratic Party's strength by half.[2] The coalition assured the party of a seat in the government: the Ministry of Justice.[3] The party's leader, Dr. Hans Hilpert, was a member of the DNVP and a Gymnasium professor. Prominent members also included such Protestant defectors from the Bavarian People's Party as Freiherr Wilhelm von Pechmann and Professor Walter Otto. The party was supported by the Farmers League (Landbund), which, in Bavaria, primarily represented the Protestant peasantry of Franken.[4]

The Middle Party was monarchist and authoritarian in attitude, and it made no attempt to hide these views. The German Nationalists felt that they had neither formed nor desired the Republic and that parliamentary democracy was a form of government ill-suited to the German people.[5] The DVP held the view that, since the first and most important task was rebuilding Germany, it would work within the republican framework, but would not give up its monarchist position or its hopes for a legal return to the monarchy.[6]

The Middle Party looked with favor on the development of the Patriotic Bands (Vaterländische Verbände) in Bavaria, since the Verbände were nationalistic and hostile to Marxism, but the party was not entirely pleased by some of the activities of the Verbände. The party spokesman, Hans Brosius, said in the Landtag in June, 1923:

---

[2] Schwend, Karl, *Bayern Zwischen Monarchie und Diktatur*, München, 1954, pp. 154-55. Hereafter cited as Schwend, *Bayern*.

[3] *Ibid.; MNN*, 73 Jhrg., Nr. 230, 9.6. 1920, p. 1.

[4] Schwend, *Bayern*, pp. 154-55.

[5] *BLV*, 1922-23, 8, 6.6. 1923, p. 340.

[6] B, II, MA103163, Entschliessung des Landesvorstandes.

> *We welcome every movement that is active in a proper manner on the Right.* We therefore welcome also the *movement of the Vaterländische Verbände.* We see in such a movement in a time of party and parliamentary squabbles the dawn of a better future. We devoutly hope that they will not drag themselves into the party bickering or allow themselves to be seized by the spirit of the parties and of disunity. We have indeed seen some developments in this movement of late that have not pleased us, but we see now to our joy clear signs of improvement. . . .[7]

The party wanted the state to keep hands off the Verbände and warned the Verbände that they must not try to establish themselves as a state within the state. It was their mission to encourage the spirit of military defense (Wehrhaftigkeit) and to support the government of the state in its policies. Brosius also warned the Verbände to eschew personal quarrels and jealousies in the interest of the nation.[8] The Middle Party took a similar stand regarding the enfant terrible of the Bavarian political scene, the NSDAP, even after many other middle-class elements had distanced themselves from this party. To quote Brosius's Landtag speech again:

> My party is often blamed, covertly or openly, for not taking a clear position regarding the National Socialist Movement. Although we have no need to defend ourselves against such attacks, I must flatly declare that these accusations are misdirected and false. . . . As I have just said, we have defended this movement in this sense [against unjust attacks], but we have never identified ourselves with it. After all, they have formed a party and we are a party also; therefore differences must exist. . . . The program of the National Socialists has some similarities to that of the German nationalists, especially in the most important points. In part, these are taken practically word for word out of the German nationalist program, as for example, the emphasis on the national idea and the consequences which flow from it. Similarly the demands of the National Socialists are tangential to ours in the German racist question. In these two points one can see a relationship, or rather, perhaps, a lack of ground for disagreement, since the national demands which we raise were stated before there was a National Socialist Party, before their name and existence was known. . . .

[7] *BLV*, 1922-23, 8, 6.6. 1923, p. 345.   [8] *Ibid.*

Or, we are asked, what is *your attitude towards the political terror*, towards the disruption of meetings, which are—according to the leftists—especially the work of the National Socialists? Here also, we have left no doubt that we condemn any political terror, from whatever side it may come, and that we expect the state government to take all steps within its power to prevent it. If the National Socialists have committed excesses, we have never defended them and will not defend them. However, I must say that it is a most unpleasant business, when for the nth time it is again established that the terror acts were initiated by the Left (How true! from the right and center of the hall) and that they still proceed in great measure, if not exclusively, from the Left.[9]

The Bavarian People's Party (BVP), the most powerful party in Bavaria, with 64 out of 129 seats in the Landtag,[10] was an essentially conservative party, but here its similarity to the Middle Party ends. Where the latter was Protestant, secular, and nationalistic, the BVP was Catholic, clerical, and a strong defender of states' rights. Indeed, one of its most prominent figures, Dr. Georg Heim, carried the traditional Bavarian distaste for the north and Prussia to the extent of offering the French a proposal for the division of Germany into two states in 1919,[11] and the suspicion was widespread, both in Bavaria and beyond her borders, that the BVP as a whole was inclined to separatism. However, there is strong evidence that, at least by 1923, the bulk of the party at all levels was nationalist vis-à-vis foreign nations, while remaining "white-blue" in German politics, although, as the situation grew more black for Germany, party voices were heard suggesting separatism not as a "good thing" but as the lesser of two evils and the only way to save Bavaria from disaster.[12]

The BVP's attitude towards Berlin was based on four major factors: suspicion of an attempted take-over by the national government, suspicion of the leftist tendencies of "Red" Berlin, suspicion of a Protestant plot against Catholic Bavaria, and suspicion of an attempt by "big business" to exploit agricultural Bavaria. These

[9] *Ibid.*, pp. 345-46.

[10] NA, T120, 5569, p. K591661; *MNN*, 73 Jhrg., Nr. 230, 9.6.1920, p. 1.

[11] U.S. Department of State ed., *The Paris Peace Conference, 1919*, Washington, 1944-46; 13 vols., v, Appendix I, 906-9.

[12] W, L, E131, C5/25, W.G. 263; W.G. 251; NA, T120, 5569, pp. K591510, K591535, K591494-95.

suspicions were aggravated by a long series of individual quarrels with Berlin over substantive matters of greater or lesser significance, which had a cumulative effect of souring the relations between state and Reich. Typical questions which arose in 1923 were: the centralization of the German financial system, taxes levied in Berlin on farm products, the fiscal policy of the Reichsbank, and the involuntary transfer of officials of the federal government out of Bavaria. Still other questions were exacerbated by the economic crisis. The *Bayerischer Kurier* (the party's München organ) complained that the sum that Bavaria was paid when her railroads were taken over by the Reich would, in mid-1923, be barely sufficient for the purchase of a pig.[13]

On the home front, the Bavarian People's Party favored parliamentarianism, supported the government (which was closely associated with and heavily dependent on it), and opposed Marxism, right radicalism, and political violence.[14] Theodor Auer spoke clearly to the point on the last issue in June 1923:

A sign of the moral decline, I might say, or at least of the painful confusion (of ideas) of our times is the attempt, on a scale not seen since the revolution, of the radical groups on Right and Left *to prevent or disrupt the meetings of their opponents with brute force.* (How true! from the Bavarian People's Party.) . . .

. . . The National Socialists have created combat organizations for themselves. As a result the socialist parties have again organized their security detachments (Sicherheitsabteilungen). Field exercises are held by the storm troops of the National Socialists and by the security detachments of the Social Democrats. The opponents march, with and without weapons, partly to the defense of their own meetings and partly to attack the meetings of the hostile parties. We see how first one and then the other is beaten up. There are serious injuries, indeed even deaths as a result, and even in the past few days we again had such an affair in Feucht near Nürnberg, where there was also a death.[15]

Unlike the Middle Party, which also deplored violence, if in a less convincing tone, the BVP made it clear that it considered the

[13] *Ibid.* pp. K591220, K591222, K591465-66, K591472, K591502, K591583.
[14] *Ibid.* pp. K591348, K591477-78.
[15] *BLV*, 1922-23, 8, 5.6.1923, p. 320.

NSDAP to be a serious menace to law and order and to the Bavarian state, although it was inclined to see the Social Democratic chicken as coming before the National Socialist egg, as is indicated by Joseph Graf Pestalozza's remarks. "He [Interior Minister Franz Schweyer] would have to say the same thing here that the former Minister-President Dr. Gustav von Kahr has said: If there were no Left-oriented antinational radicalism, there would also be no Right-oriented nationalism. The one is the result of the other, and the moral responsibility for the latter and its deeds can therefore be placed with far more justice on antinational radicalism than on the government."[16]

In general, the BVP became less and less enthusiastic about all of the Verbände as the year rolled on. As early as January, a party leader complained to the Württemberg envoy in München that the party did not trust the present leaders of the Verbände and feared that they would fall into Hitler's lap. What Bavaria needed was a state-financed legal self-defense force that could be tightly controlled, so that it would neither become a menace to the state nor be an instrument for a war of revenge, which was out of the question. The party chief, Dr. Heinrich Held, who had broken with Kahr, had even visited the latter, since he would be needed if the Home Guard (Einwohnerwehr)[17] was to be revived. In February, the party organization for Oberbayern debated an open stand against Bund Bayern und Reich, the paramilitary organization nearest to the BVP in program and composition. In the same month, Dr. Held supported the Verbände as being necessary for the security of the state but warned that they must be watched with care in view of the inclination of their leaders to see themselves as German messiahs. Later, in the spring, the BVP refused to support the demands of the Verbände that right radicals should be protected from the National Political Supreme Court (Staatsgerichtshof) and chided them for their threats against the Bavarian government in this matter.[18]

Even in early 1923 the BVP's complaisant attitude towards the Verbände did not extend to the NSDAP. In 1922, Graf Lerchen-

---

[16] *Ibid.*, p. 304.

[17] Dominated by the government, it had been dissolved at the insistence of the Allies and the federal government.

[18] B, IV, BuR, Bd. 34, Item 17, Zimmerer an Schonger; W, L, E131, C5/25, W.G. 20; W.G. 74, Beilage "B.K." *BLV*, 1922-23, 8, 5.6.1923, p. 319; NA, T120, 5569, p. K591363.

feld, the retiring Bavarian minister-president, favored the development of a radical opposition party on the extreme Right in order to rid his party and the Middle Party of their radical fringes. In the same letter, he added: "The *National Socialists* play the greatest and most dangerous role among the right radicals, under the leadership of an exceptionally energetic and, in his own way, significant young man named Hitler. One cannot really talk any more of right radicalism, since it is really a form of Bolshevism that glorifies antisemitism and nationalism. . . ."[19]

In February, Dr. Held accepted the idea that the NSDAP had a sound national core, but he attacked its vague and dangerous economic and social programs.[20] The activities of the National Socialists during the spring of 1923 sharpened the antagonism felt toward them by the BVP. Dr. Heim told Professor Paul Cossman, the publisher of the *Süddeutsche Monatshefte*, that Hitler was more dangerous than Eisner had been.[21] In April another BVP leader, Sebastian Schlittenbauer, attacked the NSDAP in a public meeting in Dingolfing. This distaste for the NSDAP extended in still sharper form to Hitler's ally, the aggressively Prussian and anti-Catholic General Ludendorff. This hostility continued right up to the Putsch, being expressed by Graf Lerchenfeld at a party rally in Kronach in October.[22]

The Center Party played a very minor role in Bavaria, depending on the Palatinate (Bavaria left of the Rhine) for its support. Even here, though, it did not garner enough votes to make it a serious power. The same is true of the German Democratic Party, particularly after it dropped out of the government coalition in 1922. The Democrats, whose liberal-democratic position and willingness to cooperate with the Social Democrats had cost them dearly in Bavaria, were strongest in Mittelfranken, where one of their number, Dr. Hermann Luppe, was mayor of Nürnberg. Even here, their position was heavily assailed and depended in considerable part on Luppe's alliance with the SPD. In general, the Democrats sided with the Reich in its quarrels with Bavaria, and this posture further weakened them. In domestic matters, however, they could be counted upon to support the Bavarian government against the ex-

[19] B, II, MA103163, Brief-Entwurf, Lerchenfeld an Ebert, 1.9.1922.

[20] W, L, E131, C5/25, W.G. 74, Beilage "B.K."

[21] B, I, Kahr MS, p. 1177.

[22] B, II, MA102140, HMB 2201, Ofr., p. 1; NA, T120, 5569, pp. K591345-47, K591358-59.

tremists of both Right and Left, despite their opposition to much of the regime's program.[23]

In general, the Peasants and Mittelstand League[24] was preoccupied with the specific economic interests of the peasantry, especially as taxes were increased and the effects of the economic crisis became heavier. However, aside from the possibility of a "taxpayers' strike," the League was not a direct threat to the security of the government and, indeed, sided with the authorities against the NSDAP and other groups that wished to introduce brute force into politics.[25]

The Peasants' League favored Georg Escherich, the former leader of the Einwohnerwehr (EW), as a man of common sense, but said regarding the NSDAP and its allies:

> . . . We take the stand that the sword must rest in the hands of the state, because otherwise chaos develops in the state and the state is lost. We have already, more than a year ago, pointed out from this floor that handgrenades and storm troops are not the tools with which the fatherland can be revived. From this floor both my colleague Engelsberger and myself have more than once pointed out the agitation that right radical circles, especially the National Socialists, conduct, and to what end this leads. Things cannot go on as they have been going. The people must gradually lose faith in the power of the state, if the government does not find the strength to take action. Unfortunately, however, the government has, in our eyes, let things ride for too long and *acted far too late.*[26]

At the same time, Anton Staedele said that the only peasants who supported the right radicals were those who stemmed from the north and had spent most of their lives running around barrack squares with monocles in their eyes. The real Bavarian peasants would stand by the legal government if and when trouble came.[27]

[23] *BLV*, 1922-23, 8, Th. Auer (BVP), 5.6.1923, p. 323; Hübsch (DDP), 7.6.1923, pp. 363-64; B, II, MA99521, 11.5.1923; MA100445, 15097, Knilling an Luppe; MA103281, Telefonat von Preger (Berlin); MA103458, Landtagsfraktion DDP an Staatsregierung, 22.10.1923; Brief: Rothmeier an Oswald, 22.10.1923.

[24] This party was a member of the Wirtschafts-Vereinigung, a loose association of minor parties.

[25] B, I, GSK 43, pp. 300-302; II, MA102140, HMB 257, N/B, p. 5; HMB 800, p. 2; MA103261, ca. 24.7.1922.

[26] *BLV*, 1922-23, 8, 7.6.1923, p. 365.   [27] *Ibid.*

The left-wing parties had a quite different outlook on the world, on the Reich, and on Bavaria than did the non-Marxist parties. Despite their bitter grievances against one another they had a number of positions in common and at times cooperated against the Right, at least on the local level. The most important of these common positions were their common theoretical goal of the proletarian state, their dislike and distrust of the Bavarian government, and their hatred of rightists of all shades and types, especially monarchists and right radicals. The result of these common attitudes was the adoption of similar programs and the use of similar tactics in at least some instances, which in turn led many persons of other parties and classes to minimize the differences among the parties of the Left, which were actually deep and broad.

The largest of the Marxist parties was the Social Democratic Party.[28] The SPD was also the most moderate of the Marxist parties, with its insistence on the achievement of a classless society by democratic and peaceful means. However, in Bavaria, even this party had been affected by the trend towards violence and militarism in politics to the extent of indulging in guerrilla warfare with its rightist opponents. It was further plagued by the same division into left, right, and moderate factions that caused the party so much grief at the national level.[29]

The relations between the SPD and the Bavarian government are probably best highlighted by an emotional address by Johann Vogel, a member of the Reichstag and key leader in northern Bavaria: "We Social Democrats have only two foes: the French in the Ruhr and the royal Bavarian government in München. The German Republic is only endangered by Bavaria. . . ."[30] Similarly, Reichstag Deputy Richard Meier accused Bavarian Interior Minister Dr. Schweyer of being an abettor of the Nazis who should long since have been tried.[31] The *Bayerisches Wochenblatt*, the sister organ of the main SPD newspaper in Bavaria (the *Münchener Post*) made the same accusations against the Bavarian government as did the National Socialists. It claimed that French money was

[28] Also known as the Majority Social Democratic Party (MSPD) or the United Social Democratic Party (VSPD). The first name was applied to it primarily during the short life of the USPD. The second reflected the claim that the SPD was the successor of the USPD, despite the fact that the bulk of the electorate of that party had clearly gone over to the KPD.

[29] B, I, GSK 43, pp. 45, 137-38, 244; GSK 44, pp. 82-83.

[30] B, II, MA102160, HMB 532, Opf., p. 2.

[31] B, II, MA102140, HMB 1716, M/F, p. 2.

behind the government, that Minister-President Eugen von Knilling was involved in plans for a "bloodbath" of republicans and workers for the purpose of setting up a dictatorship of militarists and big business, a goal that would be reached by means of a "Danube monarchy."[32] At the same time, the SPD in the Palatinate aggravated the Bavarian government and called the patriotism of the party into question in many eyes by demanding independence from Bavaria in the midst of the French occupation. Even though this demand, which apparently raised a storm in the Palatinate, was almost immediately withdrawn, it hardly acted like oil on troubled waters.[33]

Erhard Auer, speaking for the SPD, admitted the need for a paramilitary organization in Bavaria but was opposed to the existing rightist organizations. His solution was the creation of a force like Austria's socialist-dominated Republican Defense Force, but this was not likely to be any more palatable to the majority in Bavaria than were the Verbände to Auer. Unlike the middle-class and peasant parties, the SPD lumped all of the Verbände together and identified them with the National Socialists, even when the leaders of the Verbände were at loggerheads with one another.[34]

The SPD mounted a vigorous campaign against the NSDAP, not only in the public press and parliament, but also among its own followers, which lends weight to the belief of local officials that the party was losing strength to the Nazis. However, this campaign's impact outside the Marxist Movement was greatly weakened by attacks on broad groups of the populace at large and on the government, by the SPD's obvious lack of knowledge of the basic nature of the Nazi Movement, and by palpable misstatements of fact. For example, a Social Democratic leader in Würzburg said that the Racist Movement (Völkische Bewegung) ". . . in the last analysis was aimed at overthrowing the Republic and re-establishing the old state of the monarchistic oppression again."[35]

Thus the SPD was, at least to some extent, against the NSDAP for the wrong reasons, since the NSDAP was not seeking to do what the Social Democrats had accused it of desiring. On occasion, the SPD press accused the National Socialists of attacking the SPD

[32] B, IV, BuR, Bd. 34, "Bayerisches Wochenblatt," 22.9.1923.
[33] B, II, MA103458, Telefonat aus Heidelberg, 26.10.1923.
[34] *BLV*, 1922-23, 8, E. Auer (SPD), 6.6.1923, pp. 334-36; B, IV, BuR, Bd, 35, Akt 4, item 41, "Fränkische Tagespost"[?], ca. 27.8.1923.
[35] B, IV, BuR, Bd. 34, item 41, Reg. Obb. 541, p. 3.

in cases where the shoe was clearly on the other foot. The *Münchener Post* accused a Nazi in Lichtenfels of intimidating a Jewish merchant, whereas it was the Jewish merchant who had been convicted of conspiring against the National Socialist. On other occasions, the SPD refused to present evidence supporting their accusations. Again, the *Münchener Post* printed an allegation that the National Socialists had threatened Erhard Auer at one of their open meetings, whereas investigation by the police led to the admission by the reporter that the threat had been made by an unknown person in the audience, rather than by the party speaker. Finally, such claims as that of the former Bavarian minister for military affairs, Ernst Schneppenhorst, that he was behind all of the discord in the Racist Movement was not likely to impress a critical and informed mind.[36]

Why the SPD chose to use absurd or unsupported charges against the NSDAP and to mix these with real evidence regarding the activities of this party is unclear. They should have realized, if they did not, that such wild accusations would be likely to throw doubt on their best evidence. Probably the answer is that their press was directed primarily at their own followers and that they believed any weapon was a good one in a just struggle.

The SPD did not confine its battle against the Right to the printed or spoken word. It created two major and several smaller paramilitary organizations of its own. These were the Storm Troops (Sturmabteilungen)—known like their Nazi counterparts as the "SA"—and the Socialist Order Service (Sozialistische Ordnungs-dienst—SOD). The SA, which was banned by the Bavarian government before it reached maturity, was largely concentrated in Oberbayern, although it had offshoots in other provinces. This organization, despite the official pacifism of the SPD, indulged in the same kind of "militaristic" play-acting, based on the ceremonies of the prewar German army, as did the right radical Verbände. Its members wore a prescribed uniform, held drill periods and field exercises, and formally and ceremoniously presented standards to new units. Some 1,200 men attended such a ceremony in Holzkirchen in July 1923. Like the rightists, they also ignored legal curbs on their activities. On 8 June 1923, despite the ban on open-

[36] *BLV*, 1922-23, 8, E. Auer (SPD), 6.6.1923, pp. 332-33; B. I, SA 1, 1475, PDM 228/vid; 1477, Gend. Hptst. Lichtenfels 430; 1486; PDM via-F-1442/23; IV, BuR, Bd. 34, Item 41, Reg. Obb., 541.

air parades with banners, the Sendlinger unit of the SA marched
in formation without seeking a police permit. However, the Social
Democratic SA was never more than a pale and mild shadow of its
Nazi counterpart and disappeared completely when it was banned,
despite vague talk of going underground.[37]

The other SPD paramilitary organization, the SOD, was not as
much in evidence as the SA, although the authorities were aware
of its activities in many areas. Associated with the SOD were other,
overt SPD organizations, such as the Socialist Bicycle League "Solidarity," (Radfahrerbund Solidarität) which allegedly was the
"cavalry" of the SOD, and the Workers' First Aid League (Arbeit-
er-Samaritenbund), which served as its medical corps. Workers'
Defense Forces (Arbeiterwehren) and "Proletarian Hundreds"
(Proletarische Hundertschaften), both apparently associated with
the SOD, were to be found throughout Bavaria. To what extent the
SOD became more than a paper superstructure above the local
defense organizations is unclear, as is the question of the effectiveness of its intelligence organization. In any case, like the SA it
seems to have collapsed as soon as it was banned.[38]

Despite the existence of these paramilitary organizations in the
SPD, the evidence strongly suggests that the brunt of the guerrilla
war with the right radicals and conservatives was borne by impromptu groups of rank and file members under local leaders. The
struggle was carried on in two ways: by means of economic pressure and black lists on the one hand and by actual combat with
National Socialists and other anti-Marxists on the other hand. Evidence regarding the existence of black lists and economic pressure
is sparse but persuasive. For example, Neustadt district headquarters reported in May 1923 to the Police Directory in München that
the National Socialist leader in Weiden had been removed from his

[37] *BLV*, 1922-23, 8, Dr. Schweyer, 8.6.1923, p. 382; B, I, GSK 9, p. 6;
GSK 43, pp. 8, 11-12, 45-46; M. Inn. 73441, HMB Miesbach, 17.7.1923;
II, MA102140, HMB 385, Obb., p. 2; HMB 473, Obb., p. 3; HMB 763,
Obb., pp. 5-6; HMB 837, Obb., p. 6; HMB 927, Obb., p. 6; HMB 1040,
Obb., pp. 9, 11-12; HMB 1167, Obb., p. 11; HMB 1857, Schw., pp. 1-2;
HMB 313, N/B, pp. 2-3; HMB 1716, M/F, p. 1; Vo., 40 Jhrg., Nr. 445,
23.9.1923, p. 3.

[38] B, I, GSK 43, pp. 1, 3, 10, 110ff; II, MA102140, HMB 1813, M/F,
p. 2; HMB 588, Ofr., p. 4; HMB 816, Ofr., pp. 1-2 (unnumbered); HMB
1979, Ofr., pp. 2-3; IV, BuR, Bd. 34, Item 41, Reg. Obb. 541, pp. 1, 3,
5, 7-9; Bd. 35, Akt 3, Answers to Fragebogen 2.

post by the Factory Council because of his political activity. In early November 1923 another worker was allegedly dismissed because he belonged to Jungdo[39] after the Factory Council exerted pressure. In July the Erlangen chapter of Bund Bayern und Reich reported to Bund headquarters that eight workers belonging to various Verbände had been beaten up or locked out of their jobs because they had attended the Deutscher Tag—a rightist patriotic celebration—in Erlangen. In September a member of Bayern und Reich in Schwarzenbach was beaten up and forced to leave his union and job. In August Rosenheim district headquarters reported that there were eight or ten cases of dismissals of workers belonging to Verbände at the instance of Factory Councils, and as early as November 1922 an SPD leader told Captain Truman Smith of the United States Military Attaché's Office that while Hitler was making some progress in workshops and smaller factories, the unions were able to hold the line pretty well in the larger factories.[40]

Actual combat between the socialists and the rightists varied from gang attacks on one man to large-scale encounters between hostile groups. These larger "battles" usually resulted from one side or the other's trying to break up a hostile meeting or parade. The honors for aggression seem to be reasonably evenly divided in 1923, although there are indications that while the socialists had been more on the offensive in the past,[41] the balance was gradually shifting the other way, particularly in the south of Bavaria. In a SPD meeting in May 1923 Matthias Kern of the Würzburg SOD said, in explanation of the building up of paramilitary forces: ". . . As time passed, however, the party, throughout Germany but especially in Bavaria, had to go over to copying the enemy's militarily organized troops, if it does not wish to run the danger that one day the reactionaries with their trained troops will go over to the offensive while the workers, disorganized and aimless, must go onto the defensive, as has already occurred on occasion. Should the reactionaries go over to the offensive, they must come up against

---

[39] See Chapter IV, Section III, for a discussion of Jungdo.

[40] B, I, SA 1, 1486, p. 173, BA Neustadt an PDM, 16.5.1923; II, MA102140, BA Rosenheim, Abschrift zu HMB 1093, Obb., p. 3; IV, Lapo, Bd. 17, Akt 4, PNB Ofr., Abschnitt Kühme, 2.11.1923; BuR, Bd. 35, Akt 4, Item 13 g-u; Akt 5, Item 4; Y Report of Captain Truman Smith, 25.11.1922.

[41] See, for example, Hoegner, Wilhelm, *Der schwierige Aussenseiter*, München, 1959, pp. 18-19.

organizations that will never allow a military dictatorship to be set up. . . ."[42]

Examples of the sort of clashes that occurred with monotonous regularity in Bavaria during 1923 indicate the problem facing the authorities in maintaining law and order, especially in the smaller towns of the countryside, where only a handful of policemen were normally on hand. In late 1922 a typical affray took place in München. An armed force of Nazis escorting several party members home through a workers' section, fought a pitched battle with pistols, clubs, and knives with organized workers. On 4 January 1923 Social Democrats shouted down Nazi speakers and broke up a meeting in Rothenburg, having done the same thing in Weiden a few days before. In February Nazis tried to break up an SPD meeting in Nürnberg but were foiled by the police. In mid-March there was a sharp clash in Immenstadt that was largely the fault of imported Nazi storm troopers, and in Neu-Ulm the National Socialists broke up a meeting of a peace society associated with the Left. In Ingolstadt, SPD and German Communist Party (KPD) members so disrupted a Nazi meeting that the police had to break it up. The same forces later tried to break up a meeting where Hitler spoke but were beaten up and ejected from the hall. In early April a Social Democrat wounded two Nazis in Kulmbach, and in early May, Anton Drexler was allegedly assaulted at work. In June a member of the SPD had his finger broken in a scuffle with a Nazi in München, but finally admitted that they were both at fault. In July a number of SA (NSDAP) men in München complained to their headquarters of being beaten up by Social Democrats, and a Nazi was badly injured by workers in Ingolstadt. In September a group of Nazis returning from the Deutscher Tag in Nürnberg came to blows with workers in Regensburg and some eight persons were slightly injured. In Rothenstadt a number of Nazis were stabbed after a violent speech by an SPD leader—although the offenders were apparently Communists. In Würzburg only police intervention prevented Social Democrats from attacking Nazis headed for the Deutscher Tag. These incidents indicate how endemic violence was and how varied it was in nature.[43]

---

[42] B, IV, BuR, Bd. 34, Item 41, Reg. Obb. 541, p. 2, Protokoll-Notizen.
[43] Z, 207/52, ED7, Fasc. III, Bericht, ca. Ende 1922, 20.6.1923, 7.7.1923; *BLV*, 1922-23, 8, Dr. Schweyer, 8.6.1923, p. 380; B, II, MA102140, HMB 6, N/B, p. 3; HMB 198, M/F, p. 2; HMB 563, Schw., pp. 1-2; HMB 288, Obb., p. 2; HMB 3, Opf.; HMB 385, Obb., p. 3; HMB 258, Opf., p. 3;

The violence was not limited, though, to Nazi-SPD clashes. Socialists fought at one time or another with members of the most important Verbände: Bund Bayern und Reich, Reichsflagge, Bund Oberland, and others. Most of these clashes were minor, but occasionally, as on 3 June 1923 in Feucht, where Social Democrats, Reichsflagge, and the State Security Police (Landespolizei) tangled, there was real fighting and a number of dead and wounded. In some of these affrays the Social Democrats clearly took the initiative, as was remarked by the Reich's diplomatic representative in Bavaria, Edgar Haniel von Haimhausen, an acute and dispassionate observer, who witnessed an Oberland-SPD skirmish in mid-September.[44] Leftist workers also, on occasion, attacked rightist-oriented schoolboys and even members of Catholic religious organizations. While it is doubtless true that such attacks were made without any sanction from above (at least on the part of the SPD), it is equally true that they helped to poison the political atmosphere and sour still further the relations of the academic youth with the political Left.[45]

Unlike its healthy rivals on the Right and Left, the Independent Social Democratic Party (USPD) was by this time largely limited to its fraction in the Landtag, as was indicated by its showing in the next Landtag elections (1924), where it polled 2,393 votes in Bavaria. A number of its leaders had gone over to the SPD, but election statistics indicate that the bulk of its rank-and-file members passed to the Communists when the party collapsed in 1922. It is therefore not worthwhile considering this party as a political factor in the Bavaria of 1923.[46]

By contrast, in 1923 the German Communist Party, having ab-

HMB 588, Ofr., p. 6; HMB 927, Obb., p. 6; HMB 717, Opf., pp. 2-3; HMB 1368, Pfr., p. 1; I, SA 1, 1486, PDM, Abt. VI-N 289/23, p. 191.

[44] *BLV*, 1922-23, 8, Th. Auer (BVP), 5.6.1923, p. 320; E. Auer (SPD), pp. 336-37; Hüsch (DDP), p. 356; Dr. Schweyer, p. 368; B, II, MA102140, Abschrift bei HMB 1093, Obb.; HMB 1400, Schw., p. 3; HMB 678, Opf., p. 3; HMB 717, Opf., p. 2; HMB 754, Opf., pp. 2-3; HMB 834, Opf., p. 1; HMB 1815, Ufr.; HMB 721, Ofr., p. 3; HMB 1187, Ofr., p. 1; HMB 1460, Ofr., pp. 1-2; MA100411, M. Inn. 2032 z 108; Brief: Zwosta an Staatsregierung, 11.9.1923; IV, Lapo, Bd. 26a, Akt 3, Items 34 & 36; BuR, Bd. 35, Akt 4, Item 13, passim; Item 15; Item 26a; NA, T120, 5569, pp. K591518-19.

[45] B, II, MA102140, HMB 403, Opf., pp. 2-4; HMB 1400, Schw., p. 2; HMB 585, Opf., p. 4; Personal testimony of a former Lapo officer.

[46] NA, T120, 5570, p. K591752.

sorbed much of the USPD, was a fairly healthy, if extremely unpopular, party. During the course of the year it apparently grew still more, largely at the expense of the SPD, because of the ever-deepening economic crisis. Despite increasingly repressive measures on the part of the authorities, the party was very active during the period leading up to the Beer Hall Putsch. The ban on the party's paramilitary organizations and press in the fall of the year weakened it somewhat, since these bans were rigidly enforced by the police. In the north, however, where contact with the rampant Communist organizations of Saxony and Thuringia was possible—and where asylum across the border was easy to reach—the party continued its open defiance of the authorities.

Nonetheless, short of successful revolution there was no possibility of the KPD's influencing Bavarian policy or seriously inconveniencing the government. And revolution was hopeless in Bavaria, for a small portion of the right radical paramilitary forces, let alone the armed forces of the state, was doubtless capable of handling any force the KPD could raise. Until the collapse of the united front coalition in Saxony the Communists apparently had strong hopes for a Communist invasion of Bavaria from Saxony and Thüringia. Thereafter all doors were closed.[47]

KPD propaganda was based on the party's theoretical goals and took little account of political and military realities. Ignoring the bad scare they had given the middle class and peasantry in 1919, the Communists demanded economic and police powers for their workers' committees and prepared for a general strike, although the SPD controlled the bulk of the work force. The party openly accused the police and army of being hand in glove with the National Socialists while seeking to win over policemen and soldiers. Like the Social Democrats, the Communists were not very well informed on the aims and activities of the NSDAP or on their relationship with other rightist organizations. For example, the Communists saw Hitler and Ludendorff as rivals rather than allies, while they saw Bund Bayern und Reich as sailing in Hitler's wake. Despite their activity and the reams of propaganda that they distributed broadside, there is not much evidence that the KPD won many converts except for other Marxists. Its great public appeals

[47] B, I, GSK 3, p. 6; GSK 6, p. 10; GSK 43, pp. 1, 26, 48; II, MA102140, HMB 1040, Obb., pp. 9-10; HMB 520, N/B, p. 1; HMB 670, N/B, p. 2; HMB 719, N/B, p. 2; HMB 765, N/B, p. 1; HMB 795, Opf., pp. 2-3; HMB 1642, Ofr., p. 1; MA103458, GSK Pol./488.

fell flat. The "Antifascist Day" it proclaimed found very little response even among foes of fascism, and its attempt to hold a congress of Factory Councils was still-born.[48]

Despite their mutual hostility, the SPD and KPD cooperated in some matters. For example, in Bavaria they usually held joint May Day celebrations, as they did in 1923. They also closed ranks to fight right radicals in many cases, and in some instances, especially in the smaller towns of the countryside, where KPD organizations were nonexistent or weak, Communists actually joined SPD paramilitary organizations, despite the SPD leadership's warning that they would help to put down a Communist revolt.[49] The Communists had some paramilitary organizations of their own, called "Proletarian Hundreds," until they were banned, in addition to the ones in Thüringia that Bavarians joined. On the whole, however, they seem to have been vestigial and poorly armed.[50]

As in the case of the Social Democrats, most of the actual fighting seems to have been done on an impromptu, locally-organized basis, although in theory at least, the district headquarters (Bezirksleitungen) were responsible for seeing that "fascist" organizations were unable to meet. In February Communists, using iron rods and a pistol, tried to disrupt a meeting in Eichstätt at which Hitler spoke, but they were defeated and driven out of the hall by Nazis using heavy walking sticks. Ten persons were injured. In March the same pattern unfolded in Gunzenhausen. In these and other cases, the Communists picked areas with a Marxist superiority in strength and then imported workers to reinforce the local Communist organization. Since these areas were usually weak in police, the Communists often succeeded in breaking up Nazi meetings completely. Sometimes, however, the shoe was on the other

[48] *BLV*, 1922-23, 8, Gahr (KPD), 7.6.1923, p. 369; B, I, GSK 43, pp. 13, 46, 140-41, 168ff; GSK 44, pp. 34-35, 41, 63-66, 70, 129; GSK 99, pp. 7, 60; II, MA102140, HMB 683, Ofr., p. 3 (unnumbered); HMB 487, Opf., p. 1; Misc. HMB, ca. 29.7.1923 (Antifaschistentag); IV, Lapo, Bd. 26a, Akt 5, Gr. Sch. IIIc, Erfahrungsbericht, Lapo Bamberg, St. V. Nord, p. 3; St. V. Süd, p. 3.

[49] B, II, MA102140, HMB 169, Obb., p. 5; HMB 1246, Obb., p. 7; HMB 1153, M/F, p. 1; HMB various Reg. Präsidien, May 1923; NAT120, 5569, p. K591555; B, I, GSK 43, p. 25.

[50] B, II, MA102140, HMB 346, Opf., p. 3 (unnumbered); HMB 370, Opf., pp. 2-3; HMB 1187, Ofr., p. 2; HMB 1400, Schw., pp. 2-3; IV, Lapo, Bd. 26a, Akt 5, Gr. Sch. IIIc, Erfahrungsbericht, Lapo Bamberg, St. V. Nord, p. 2.

foot. In May a group of Nazis invaded a Communist meeting in Neukirchen-Salzbach and precipitated a fight, which the gendarmery broke up. So it went, through summer and fall, with the Communists often on the offensive. These fights were not exclusively with National Socialists. Bund Bayern und Reich, Blücherbund, and Reichsflagge were also involved in this see-saw guerrilla war.[51]

III. *Political Pressure Groups*

The political pressure groups can be broken down roughly into five categories: right radical, conservative, moderate, leftist, and professional. On the whole, the pressure groups on the extremes of Right and Left were the most active, although not necessarily the most effective. The conservative organizations probably had the most money and certainly had the best contacts in government circles, as well as the largest sympathetic audience.

The Pan-German League (All-Deutscher Verband) was a national organization that was weak in Bavaria except for its connections with important figures, such as Dr. Gustav von Kahr, the provincial president of Oberbayern and "dictator" of Bavaria in the fall of 1923. The league, led by Heinrich Class, was essentially a pan-German propaganda organization dedicated to ultraconservatism, especially the promotion of a narrowly oligarchic government. In many ways, it was more an organization of the past than of the present, and Class appeared to be far more influential than he actually was.[52]

Another organization of moderate significance was the Bavarian Order Block (Bayerische Ordnungsblock). This was an umbrella organization of patriotic groups with a general program based on the struggle against Marxism. In a way it was, like the Pan-German League, an organization of the past, but had right radical overtones.[53]

The German Racist Defense League (Deutschvölkischer Schutz- und Trutzbund) was a more typical right radical organization than

[51] B, I, SA 1, 1474, p. 123; II, MA102140, HMB 1060, Schw., pp. 1-2; HMB 1749, p. 1; HMB 370, Opf., p. 2; HMB 487, p. 2; HMB 532, pp. 2-3; HMB 795, p. 1; HMB 1195, Ufr., p. 1; HMB 359, M/F, p. 2; HMB 474, pp. 1-2; HMB 2201, Ofr., p. 1; MA101249, RK, In 84, p. 4; IV, Lapo, Bd. 26a, Akt 3, Item 3, Reg. Ofr., 2198.

[52] B, I, M. Inn. 73685, PDM, Abt. VID 1637. For further information see Kruck, Alfred, *Geschichte des Alldeutschen Verbandes*, Wiesbaden, 1954.

[53] B, I, M. Inn. 73685, Abt. VID 1637.

either of those above. Its primary program was a vigorous anti-semitism which it promoted by means of incessant propaganda. Despite some duplication of membership, it was not specifically allied with the NSDAP, and it did not enter into politics on a broad front as did Hitler's party. One of the chief Bavarian leaders of the league was the attorney Willibald Freiherr von Zezschwitsch, a perennial defender of right radicals before the courts. Although it was banned for the virulence of its antisemitism in a number of German states, the league was legal in Bavaria, where the Law for the Defense of the Republic was not popular with the authorities. The league was not an organization that would take violent action against the state, but its propaganda was certainly aimed at winning over Germans to a philosophy that was likely to lead them into potentially revolutionary organizations that made hatred of the Jews a major point of doctrine.[54]

Another significant right radical pressure group was the Academic League for German Culture (Hochschulring Deutscher Art). This was a radical association of university students who were ultranationalist and racist in attitude. It was not officially coordinated with the NSDAP, but it clearly followed the same course towards the same goals and saw Adolf Hitler as the political messiah of Germany. Although it was apparently largely Bavarian, the Academic League had affiliated chapters in other states. In Bavaria it was extremely active and influential among students, leading them to defy existing laws and authorities in pursuit of a "higher law" that it—and Hitler—identified for them. Aggressive and activist, if helped both to create a racist elite and to provide soldiers and leaders for immediate revolution.[55]

Among the conservative pressure groups, one of the most important was the Bavarian Christian Peasant Union (Bayerischer Christlicher Bauernverein). Dr. Heim was the leader of this organization, which was associated very closely with the Bavarian People's Party. It represented the extremely strong Catholic and conservative element among the Bavarian peasantry. Its voice re-

[54] *Ibid.*; B, I, GSK 100, p. 16; II, MA102140, HMB 99, Ofr., p. 3; MA104393, BG in St. 492, T 986; IV, BuR, Bd. 36, Akt. 4. See also Lohalm, Uwe. *Völkischer Radikalismus.* Hamburg, 1970 (Leibniz Verlag) for the history of the *Deutschvölkischer Schutz- und Trutzbund.*

[55] B, I, M. Inn. 73685, PDM, Abt. VId 1637; NA, T84, 4, p. 3784; T120, 5569, p. K591657.

inforced that of the party in the press, on the streets, and in the beer halls, as well as in the government.[56]

Another active conservative organization was the Bavarian Homeland and King's League (Bayerischer Heimat- und Königsbund) which represented a monarchism too blatant and quixotic to suit the taste of many Bavarians, including possibly the crown prince himself. It seems to have been more noisy than influential, but should not be ignored in a survey of organizations seeking to influence the public with some degree of success.[57]

The Bavarian League (Bayernbund) was the Bavarian branch of the German League (Deutscher Bund). It was a federalist organization that was prepared to accept the social progressiveness of the Weimar Constitution but deplored its centralism. Its lack of party affiliation and the existence of rivals with such connections undoubtedly played a role in keeping the size of this group down, although the police were inclined to see the NSDAP's vigorous physical and propaganda assaults on the league as the decisive factor stunting its growth. Not surprisingly, it fell into Kahr's wake as the year wore on and was friendly with the Bavarian Homeland and King's League.[58]

The Farmers' League (Bund der Landwirte or Landbund), which was dominated by large-scale farmers and Junkers, was relatively weak in Bavaria, where it could not compete with local, Catholic peasants' organizations for religious, regional, and social reasons. Nonetheless, because of its ties with Dr. von Kahr and its desires for south German allies, it came to play, briefly, a minor but crucial role on the Bavarian scene in 1923. The Landbund was ultraconservative and hostile towards the Republic. In the fall of 1923 it hoped for the creation of a national directory to replace the parliamentary government of the Reich, and it worked actively in Bavaria for support for this solution to the German problem.[59]

In the center of the political spectrum there were the Free Peasants (Freie Bauernschaft) and the Republican National

[56] B, II, MA102140, HMB 226, Obb., p. 2; W, L, E131, C5/25, W.G. 18, p. 292; NA, T120, 5569, pp. K591411-12.

[57] B, I, M. Inn. 73685, PDM, Abt. vid 1637; II, MA102140, HMB 927, Obb., p. 4; IV, BuR, Bd. 35, Akt 3, p. 36; Bd. 36, Akt 4.

[58] B, I, M. Inn. 73685, PDM, Abt. vid 1637; II, MA103160, Entschluss von 25.8.1921; MA103458, Brief: Ballerstedt & Bäcken an Kahr, 3.10.1923.

[59] B, I, M. Inn. 73685, PDM, Abt. vid 1637; II, MA103476, p. 696; MA104221, Seisser Besprechung, 3.11.1923, p. 2.

League (Republikanische Reichsbund Bayern). The first was a peasant organization well to the left of either Dr. Heim's group or the Peasants' and Mittelstand League. The government watched it with considerable suspicion because of its candid hostility toward the government, and its attempts to organize farmers' strikes and to form its own paramilitary organization, but even more because some of its leaders were suspected of separatism and dealings with the French in the Palatinate and in München. Its greatest influence was among peasants disgruntled over rising taxes and the economic uncertainties of 1923, caused by swiftly rising inflation. The Free Peasants were thus one more divisive force in a time and place where there seemed more divisive forces than the political, social, and economic fabric could contain.[60] The Republican National League is an example of the feeble republican organizations active in Bavaria. In the face of disinterest or hostility on the part of the general public, stiff competition from specifically Marxist organizations, and the coolness or hostility of most government officials and parliamentarians, this organization was peripheral to the political life of Bavaria. Only in the Nürnberg area, where Dr. Luppe was one of its patrons, did it carry any weight at all. Ironically, by 1923 one of its early leaders, Adolf Schmalix, was already a rabid Nazi.[61]

On the Marxist Left, the pressure groups were primarily close to the parties. Like the parties, they worked against the government as well as against the radical Right and were influential only among that minority of the population that was socialist or communist in inclination. The most significant of these leftist pressure groups were the Unions of White Collar Employees (AFA Bund) and Workers (Freie Gewerkschaften—ADGB) and the Factory Councils (Betriebsräte). These organizations, theoretically free of political affiliation, were vital to the socialist parties, and, to a much lesser extent, to the KPD.[62] On the national scene these organizations were a power with which every politician must reckon. In Bavaria they made little progress against a solid front of government, middle class, Catholic Church, and peasantry. The most they

[60] B, I, GSK 43, p. 300; II, MA102140, HMB 670, N/B, pp. 2-3; HMB 871, N/B, p. 3; HMB 800, N/B, p. 2; MA100446a, A.Z. xxII 75/1922, P.R. 4321, 1922, p. 24.

[61] B, I, M. Inn. 73685, PDM, Abt. vId 1637; NA, T120, 5569, p. K591312-13.

[62] B, I, M. Inn. 73685, PDM, Abt. vId 1637.

could do was to help the left-wing parties maintain the hostility of the "class-conscious" worker towards other elements of society and their political representatives.

IV. *The Press*

Most of the Bavarian newspapers were small, catering to a small city and the adjacent countryside, and many of them were weeklies. A considerable number of little magazines supplemented the newspapers. Sometimes these magazines were associated in one way or another with newspapers or with the various political organizations, but sometimes they were completely independent. If a Bavarian was uninformed about politics, it was not for want of a politically active press.

On the extreme Right, the most important paper was the National Socialists' chief organ, the *Völkischer Beobachter*, published in München. Other active Nazi papers were the *Deutscher Volkswille* (after October 1923, *Die weisse Fahne*) in Nürnberg and the *Sturm-Glocke* in Augsburg, which was used as a substitute for the *Völkische Beobachter* when that sheet was banned for the violence of its attacks on the Bavarian government or other breaches of official regulations. Besides the Nazi press, a number of more or less independent racist papers followed the same general line. One such sheet was the *Miesbacher Anzeiger*, whose owner, Professor Bernhard Stempfle, might have been less of a thorn in the flesh of the Bavarian authorities had he known that he was destined to die before SS guns in the "Blood Purge" of 1934.

The most important of the conservative newspapers was the independent *Münchener Neueste Nachrichten*, which had been democratic in the early years of the Republic but leaned towards Hitler early in 1923 and supported Kahr during the fall. It was under the direction of Dr. Fritz Gerlich, who later shared Professor Stempfle's fate. The *Münchener Zeitung*, a consistently and strongly conservative newspaper was also pro-Nazi early in 1923 but cooled off markedly in the course of the year, supporting Stresemann's government in October. Another of the major papers in München, the *München-Augsburger Abendzeitung*, was the house organ of the German Nationalist People's Party, while the *Bayernblatt* represented the German People's Party. The most important organs of the Bavarian People's Party were its Münchener organ, *Der Bayerische Kurier*, and Dr. Held's mouthpiece, *Der Regensburger Anzeiger*, although Dr. Heim's *Bayrisches Bauern-*

blatt should not be forgotten. *Die Bayerische Staatszeitung* was the official organ of the Bavarian government but was able, to some extent, to follow an independent editorial policy, much to the annoyance of Minister-President von Knilling.

There was no significant representation of the middle-class Left in the Bavarian press, but there were several important Marxist papers. The *Münchener Post* was far and away the leader among these sheets, followed by the *Fränkische Tagespost*, which represented the strong local party organization in Nürnberg. The Communists' central Bavarian organ, *Die rote Bayernfahne*, collapsed in July 1923, and thereafter the party had to rely on its central organs in Berlin and on intermittent broadsheets.

The Bavarian press was clearly a political press, following the major parties or active political pressure organizations. Not even the few allegedly independent newspapers took an objective view of the political scene. As is so often the case in crisis situations, cool observers were in a very small minority and were popular with none of the contenders.[63]

v. *Summary*

Bavaria had all of the usual political organizations and propaganda outlets normally found in a democratic state, and these organizations and organs played a key role in her political life. However, they were by no means the only politically active forces in Bavaria in 1923. Willingly or reluctantly, as the case might be, they shared the stage and practical power with paramilitary organizations and with the official police and military organizations of the state. Living in crisis conditions, where the man on the street was bewildered and frightened by remorseless political and economic phenomena that he did not understand, the political organizations and organs were only too well aware that the old adage, "The pen is mightier than the sword," is not always true.

[63] GP, D, 3 (Presse Kartei).

3.

THE NSDAP

I. *Introduction*

In many ways, the NSDAP was the most important single element in the political spectrum in Bavaria in 1923. It was important less because of its size and power than because of its nature and potential. Most of all, it was important because it was a catalyst that brought a comparatively stable system into violent if brief motion and both rationalized and polarized the political positions of individuals and groups. The reason that the NSDAP played such a role was threefold.

First, the NSDAP occupied in the Patriotic Movement the same position that the Communist Party occupied in the Marxist Movement. It was the most radical as well as the best organized and most determined element in the movement. Therefore, it operated like the cutting edge of a heavy cleaver, since in many situations it could depend on support from more moderate elements of the movement and even from the conservative Right. These other groups might not like the NSDAP, but they felt sufficiently hostile to the party's enemies, sufficiently sympathetic with at least some of the party's professed aims, and sufficiently hopeful of inheriting some of the party's glamor and most of its followers that they would rarely disavow it and would invariably side with it against any element of the Left. Just as a Social Democrat bristled when a German Nationalist attacked Communists—even though he himself might hate his proletarian rivals—so would a German Nationalist react to a Social Democratic attack on National Socialists. In both cases this reaction was intensified by the tendency of the attacker to lump everyone on the other side of the political spectrum together.

Secondly, as the most vigorous element in the only new movement to develop in Germany after World War I, the party attracted the most activist groups and therefore enjoyed an impetus far out of proportion to its size. Most of the traditional political parties and groupings were largely involved in protecting a position already conquered. The National Socialists, like the Communists, enjoyed the advantage of the offensive, since they had yet to win any position for themselves and represented forces that desired to overturn the existing political, economic, and social system by any means available.

Thirdly, the NSDAP had as its leader one of the three great "common men" of the first half of the twentieth century. Henry Wallace on occasion called the twentieth century the "century of the common man," and there was a great deal of truth in this adage. However, insofar as political power and leadership is concerned, it was in the autocracies and not the democracies that common men like Hitler, Stalin, and Mussolini rose to the top of the heap and directed the destinies of millions. Hitler, the man who, once aroused from his political lethargy by the revolution and its aftermath, had seized control of the German Workers' Party and transformed it into the NSDAP, was an incomparable asset to any political organization. He was a spell-binder who could conquer the emotions and loyalties of masses of men. He was also a cunning plotter of Byzantine skill and, last but not least, a man who did not know when he was beaten—and historically the fool who doesn't know when he is beaten has more than once crushed the over-whelming powers arrayed against him. Hitler thus united in his physically insignificant person the talents and characteristics of Demosthenes, Ferdinand of Aragon, and Robert the Bruce; and he added to them the ambition and sweeping aims of Alexander or Napoleon. He was just the man to make the most of the party.

The rapid growth of the movement as a whole and of the party in particular during the year 1923 was a sign of the growing impatience of many elements in the population, especially the young, with the existing situation and the existing political "system." Even without the tremendous pressures generated by the economic tragedy of 1923, there is good reason to believe that the Patriotic Movement and the NSDAP would have gained ground. The "hot-house" atmosphere caused by inflation resulted in extremely rapid growth and in a premature "ripening," really a false ripening of both movement and party. The Hitler Putsch was a symptom of the dangers and weaknesses attendant upon such forced and unsound growth. The Putsch thus ended an epoch in the development of the party. Indeed, it saw the end of the "first NSDAP"—or, perhaps more properly, of the "second party."[1]

The NSDAP of 1923, characterized as it was by rapid growth, by greatly increased "militarization," and by an assault on the existing political powers of all shadings, must be scrutinized carefully by anyone who wishes to understand the events of late 1923 and the Putsch that crowned them and set the balance of power in Bavaria for a decade.

II. *Program and Objectives*

By 1923 Hitler was the leader and ruler of the party to such an extent, that it was his ideas and his aims exclusively that shaped the party's actions. The official party program, which was largely the work of such men as Anton Drexler and Gottfried Feder, contained elements that were either of no interest to Hitler or in conflict with his own ideas. Characteristically, Hitler handled the program as he did the men who wrote it. He used it where it was tactically advantageous to do so and ignored it otherwise.[2] For the rank and file of the party and for its key leaders, Hitler was already the central factor in the political cosmos, and SA members, at least, were already being required to swear an oath of allegiance to him.[3]

In essence, his basic program and plans were threefold. First, he would destroy the "November criminals" who had emasculated Germany and the evil Jews and Marxists who were the masters of these traitors. He would then build a new, national Germany. Finally this new, national Germany would reconquer its proper place in the world.[4] He had thus a great advantage over the other right radical foes of the Weimar Republic. Men like Gerhard Ross-

---

[1] It can be argued that the party after Hitler took over was a far different organism than it had been earlier, and that, therefore, the two epochs may be considered to constitute two parties differing with one another in regard to goals and personnel.

[2] See, for example, Maser, Werner, *Die Frühgeschichte der NSDAP-Hitlers Weg bis 1924*, Frankfurt, 1965. pp. 274ff. (hereafter cited as Maser, *Frühgeschichte*); and Phelps, Reginald, "Hitler and the *Deutsche Arbeiterpartei*," *American Historical Review*, LXVIII (1963), pp. 976-86, passim.

[3] B, I, GSK 60, p. 26.

[4] Evidence regarding this program is manifold. See Hitler, Adolf, *Mein Kampf*, München, 1942, passim; for Hitler's speeches at his Trial in 1924; and pp. 53-54 below; see EAP 105/7, *passim*; for contemporary evidence. See also B, II, MA103476, pp. 608-15.

bach, Hermann Ehrhardt and Erich Ludendorff had purely negative programs. They wanted to destroy the Republic, but they had
no positive program for the future once the Republic was gone.
Hitler, on the other hand, had a program for a "brave new world"
that would replace the corrupt "system" of the old men whose
weakness and veniality had destroyed Germany's power. Without
a positive program, rebels are merely dissidents; with one, they
have the possibility of becoming serious revolutionaries. One must
be prepared not only to destroy but also to create, if one is to gain
serious political momentum.

Besides the negative political aims to which Hitler himself gave
primary importance, the party recognized, with his acquiescence
if not positive support, the deep economic resentments by all other
classes and groups—from the rich landowner, through the intellectual, to the "little man" on the street—of the great moneyed powers, which they saw as authors of, or at the very least profiteers
from, the misery of the great majority. In a National Socialist meeting in Augsburg, in December 1922, Heinrich Dolle, a miner and
former Communist, sounded this note clearly:

> You are becoming impatient and wish at last to strike. Be
> patient! We will call you up against the white and black Jews,
> when the proper time comes. Be patient for only a little while!
> Then, though, when we call you, spare the savings banks
> [Sparkassen], for there we proletarians have our few pennies, but
> storm the great banks; take all the money that you find there and
> throw it in the street and burn the great pile! And hang the
> white and the black Jews on the gallows of the streetcar [tracks]!
> And if you want land and no one will give it to you, then do as
> I did in my home village with my cooperative: Take it and build
> houses on it. We did that and the government did not dare to
> take from us what we had taken against their will.[5]

Here sounds a spirit of rebellion far older than Marxism and much
deeper rooted in the hearts of mankind, to judge by history. This
is a cry not for the destruction of private property but for a more
equitable distribution of it. That this echo of the Bundschuh leaders' demands was not alien to Hitler is indicated by the denuncia-
tions and threats against the capitalists that he himself made at the

[5] Z, Akten, aus d. Hpt. Archiv. d. NSDAP, Mappe 99, Bericht d. M.
Inn. von 1.12.1922.

height of his power, as well as by his comments on the middle class and his World War II plans for the postwar era.[6]

As to his short-term program, Hitler presented it to his SA leaders on 26 October 1923. The official SA summary of the speech reveals his hopes, fears, and plans:

> The narrow-visioned policy, centered purely on the defense of Bavarian interests by the powers behind the Bavarian "dictatorship" [Kahr], has resulted in Bavaria appearing today throughout Germany as the "separatist" state, seeking a break [from Germany], deserted by all allies, dependent upon itself! The Bavarian Reichswehr General von Lossow stands there as a "mutineer," to proceed against whom is the soldierly duty of the remaining Reichswehr, a duty which already today is recognized by all other Wehrkreise (1-6). In other words, a complete morass seen from the German standpoint.
>
> Bavaria has three paths before her:
>
> 1st Path: "Marxistization" of Bavaria by the non-Bavarian forces directed from Berlin. Thus the last bulwark against the Bolshevization of Germany falls!
>
> 2nd Path: Bavaria fights against this Marxistization under its present defensive and petulant party, so that, in the end, foreign aid must be "thankfully" accepted, because Bavaria alone is too weak. Who does not see here Poincaré's friendly-helpful face? And there are circles in Bavaria which say: "Better even this than Prussian-Bolshevik."
>
> 3rd Path: Roll up the German problem in the last hour from Bavaria. Call up a German army of liberation under a German government in München. Raise up the black-white-red swastika banner as the symbol of struggle against everything non-German, of struggle, in the last analysis, against the symbol of the Soviet Star, which today still partly hides itself behind [the] black-red-gold. Carrying the struggle throughout Germany and hoisting the black-white-red Swastika on the Reichstag building in Berlin as a sign of the freeing of greater Germany.[7]

Here, in a few simple paragraphs is the analysis of the German problem—compounded of shrewd insights and foolish assumptions

[6] Hitler, *Tischgespräche*, pp. 138, 208, 261, 318, 403, 440-41; Goebbels, Joseph, *The Goebbels Diaries, 1942-43*, Garden City, 1948, passim. See also the remainder of this chapter.

[7] NA, SA Rgt. München. 230-a-10/3 1, 26.10.1923.

—that was to lead him to the Feldherrnhalle in November 1923, to the Reichstag building in 1933, and to suicide in the Führer-bunker in 1945 just before the Soviet Star replaced the Swastika atop that edifice. First clean up Germany and create a new order. Then settle with her enemies, especially the arch-enemy, Jewish-Bolshevism. This was the situation as Hitler saw it throughout his political career, and, seen in this light, many otherwise inexplicable moves become natural and logical. Few men follow a single goal unswervingly throughout an entire political lifetime. Those who do are rarely quite sane and nonetheless are often amazingly successful. Hitler was such a man, and the NSDAP was his tool for accomplishing his ends.

Hitler was never in any doubt as to how his goal must be reached. He did not believe that a miracle would bring him to power and his ideas to fruition. He was deeply scornful of a Bavarian crown prince who would only take back his throne by acclamation. Hitler expected to have to take anything he wanted by force and was quite prepared to do so. He believed fully and passionately in the "triumph of the will" as expressed in violent action.[8] The end justified any and all means that he might use. Here, then, was a policy and a will that, given the proper instrument, could and would shake the world.

In 1923, as later, Hitler used primarily two weapons. The first was propaganda, which was one of the main tasks of the "civilian apparatus" of the party, and the second was force, which was the province of the "military apparatus." Hitler himself put the matter succinctly at his trial: "Our viewpoint is: for those who are minded to fight with intellectual weapons, we have the struggle of the intellect, and for those who are minded to fight with the fist, we have the fist. The movement has two instruments, the propaganda machine and at its side the SA. . . ."[9] These two weapons he used brutally and more effectively than did any of his opponents or competitors. One might be superior to him in the use of one or the

---

[8] See Chapters VIII-XIV below, passim.

[9] EAP 105/7, I, pp. 43-44. Even the SA was, in part, a propaganda weapon as Hitler later pointed out: "5. Er habe politische Gegner durch Saalschutz stets so unsanft hinausbefördern lassen, dass die gegnerische Presse—die die Versammlungen sonst totgeschwiegen hätte—über die Körperverletzungen bei unseren Versammlungen berichtete und dadurch auf die Versammlungen der NSDAP aufmerksam machte." Hitler, *Tischgespräche*, p. 261.

other, but by inspired manipulation of both he was again and again to stave off impending disaster and win victories.

Hitler's aims and his tactics determined his relations with all other elements of the Bavarian political scene. His aims determined his attitude towards them and his views on tactics determined his manner of dealing with them. Even within the Patriotic Movement and its racist wing, these rules held good. Neither sympathy with fellow racists nor agreement with vigorous nationalists on the role of Germany in the world moved him one iota from his path. If they stood in his way, they must be brushed aside. If they resisted, they must be smashed. If they compromised, they must be used ruthlessly and discarded whenever they became restive.

In discussing the manner in which other Verbände would be dealt with when the great day of the march on Berlin came, Hermann Göring, the former ace and new leader of the SA, said, on 23 October 1923: ". . . The trained men of our organizations' troops will be assigned to the Reichswehr. With regard to the remaining V[ölkische] V[erbände], which do not belong to the Kampfbund, it was arranged therein, that these Verbände would not again appear as organized units. . . ."[10] A decade later, one of the first moves of the triumphant National Socialists was to eliminate all such rival groups.[11] In their eyes there was only one organization worthy of saving Germany and destined to do so.

In the same meeting, Göring told his SA leaders that it was their duty to locate the arms caches of other Verbände and to seize them on the "day of revolution." He even spoke of arresting the leaders of rival Verbände. Nor were these orders wasted on the SA leaders. In a number of instances, the National Socialists did try to seize arms caches of other organizations with varying success, even before the Putsch.[12]

Finally, this hostile attitude towards all patriotic and racist rivals was clearly behind Hitler's order of 29 September 1923 that no National Socialist could belong to any Wehrverband that did not belong to the Kampfbund. This order was applied not only against groups like Bund Blücher, which was outspokenly hostile to Hitler, but also against Bund Frankenland, whose leader was a National

---

[10] B, II, MA103476, p. 1148.

[11] See, for example, the elimination of the Stahlhelm by absorption into the SA. The Bavarian Archives (Ministry of the Interior) contain extensive data on the elimination of other Verbände after the Machtergreifung.

[12] B, II, MA103476, p. 1148; IV, Lapo, Bd. 26a, Akt 3, Item 56.

Socialist[13] and which cooperated closely with the Kampfbund. Hitler recognized that he would lose party members because of his decision and that he would be blamed by many right radicals for increasing the disunity in the Patriotic and Racist Movements, but —like Lenin—he preferred a small and disciplined party to a large and heterogeneous one, and here the forces of history seem to side with him. It has been the tightly-organized and intolerant rebel movements that have tended to have the most success. The loosely-organized and tolerant ones are usually much larger but rendered impotent by their own internal quarrels, indecision, and lack of control over their followers.[14]

If the attitude of the leaders of the NSDAP towards other racist and patriotic groups was that of a vigorously expansive church towards its rivals, their attitude towards the established institutions of the state was that of the same church towards pagans. The institutions must go and the masses be won over to the true faith. Although the relation of the NSDAP to the regular political parties has already been considered,[15] its relations with the other institutions of the old regime (whether the Weimar Republic or the monarchy) has not. Hitler's hostility towards the Bavarian government, despite all of Minister-President von Knilling's attempts to mollify him, is clearly expressed in a laconic remark at his trial. In considering his actions had the Putsch succeeded, he said: "First, there was the possibility of a thoroughgoing purge in Bavaria. Then a man of iron energy would replace Knilling."[16] Here there was no sympathy or admiration for those who had created and maintained the "cell of order" in Bavaria; only contempt for a man who, in Hitler's eyes, had failed to follow the right direction and who was too weak to sweep away his foes.

Max von Scheubner-Richter, one of Hitler's closest colleagues in the months before the Putsch, was equally frank on the subject of the government in a conversation with Graf Soden, Crown Prince Rupprecht's "cabinet chief." " 'My conversation with Scheubner now moved to the relationship of the National Socialist Party to the Bavarian government. Scheubner remarked that it was incomprehensible that the Ministers Schweyer and Wuzlhofer

[13] Dr. Otto Hellmuth. He eventually became a Gauleiter.
[14] NA, SA Rgt. München. 230-a-10/3 1, 26.9.1923; B, iv, BuR, Bd. 35, Akt 5, Item 52; and Akt 3, Fragebogen 2; Alter, Junius, *Nationalisten*, Leipzig 1930, pp. 132-33.
[15] See Chapter ii above, passim.   [16] EAP 105/7, i, p. 124.

[sic] were still in office although he, as political manager of the Kampfbund had already, some days earlier, demanded from the minister-president the resignation of both ministers.' "[17] Göring carried this contempt even further when he admitted in testimony before the public prosecutor in the summer of 1923, that he was prepared to defy the Bavarian government in the interests of the fatherland—as he interpreted them.[18]

The Bismarck Reich fared little better than the Weimar Reich in the eyes of Hitler and his inner circle. In November 1922, Hitler told Captain Truman Smith, the American assistant military attaché in Berlin, that monarchism was nonsense. The rulers had lost any claim to their thrones by running away in 1918. Should the people want a monarchy, they can always decide for one later. In 1924, at his trial, he reiterated this stand in somewhat softer words.[19]

In September 1923, Hitler's secretary, Fritz Lauböck, wrote in Hitler's name to a monarchist who had requested a clear declaration in favor of the monarchical cause:

> . . . Good. We also hold the monarchical state form for the better, because it provides a stronger order than the democratically inclined republic. Never, though, will you find that the National Socialist German Workers Party will make the slightest attempt to bring the completely degenerate house[s] of Hohenzollern and Wittelsbach together with their whole band of horrid toadies to take over the government of the German people. We have respect for Frederick the Great, William I, for Ludwig II and I; we will never minimize the services of these rulers for our German people. But a president, who has the necessary capabilities for a ruler is, to be honest, more welcome to us than a degenerate ruling house that was not able to maintain the inheritance of its fathers before the people.[20]

On occasion, when talking to monarchists or when trying to win the support of princes, the National Socialists could take a somewhat different tack, but even here their real views were only imperfectly concealed behind the veneer of friendship and deference. For example, the words in which Scheubner-Richter assured Graf Soden

[17] B, II, MA103476, p. 1131.   [18] *Ibid.*, p. 204.
[19] Y, Truman Smith Notebook, pp. 72-73 (unnumbered); EAP 105/7, I, p. 102.
[20] NA, T84, 4, pp. 2958-59.

of Hitler's support of the crown prince were more a threat than an expression of devotion to the dynasty:

> . . . I [Soden] asked, whether a government would be [considered] as such [acceptable] which had the confidence of the crown prince. Scheubner-Richter rejoined: "If the crown prince joins the Racist Movement, Hitler, who is in his heart a monarchist, will have, himself, nothing against a Bavarian monarchy. On the contrary, the movement will carry the crown prince upwards and he will be its highest leader. Otherwise, the movement will march over the crown prince."[21]

Even the former officers in the Hitler Movement, who often claimed that they were personal monarchists, adopted a very loose interpretation of their obligations to their "monarch." Ludendorff, for example, admitted to the ring-leaders of the rebellious cadets of the Infantry School that Hitler was not a monarchist but claimed that he was.[22] Yet some months thereafter, Ludendorff said, in public, according to a police report: "that there was no longer a class-community but only a people's community, in which the salvation of the fatherland was to be found. The time when kings could defame [others] unjustly was gone. The honor of every German man is worth as much as that of a king."[23] Ernst Röhm spoke of himself as a monarchist, but in discussing the Hitler Putsch he said that Hitler had proclaimed a "national republic" rather than, like most reporters of the event, that he had proclaimed a "national revolution." This seems a significant slip of the tongue and one that a fervent monarchist would scarcely make.[24] The situation was perhaps best summed up by a racist officer who said, in a discussion of the differences between Putschists and anti-Putschists: " 'There are two viewpoints regarding these events. We want a great German republic and the others want a south German Catholic monarchy.' "[25]

---

[21] B, II, MA103476, p. 1402.   [22] B, II, MA103476, pp. 782-84.
[23] B, II, MA101248, PDM 19, p. 10.
[24] Röhm, Ernst, *Die Geschichte eines Hochverräters*, München, 1934 (5th ed.), p. 232. Hereafter cited as Röhm, *Geschichte*.
[25] B, IV, BuR, Bd. 36, Akt 1, Item 33. This remark was, like so many NSDAP statements only half true, since "the others" had quite different aims than those ascribed to them here. See Chapter IV below, passim.

Similarly, using the argument that the present crisis situation was no time to divide the German people by raising the question of monarchy versus republic, the National Socialists tried to discredit the monarchists by cast-

There was also a very strong anti-clerical and anti-Catholic bias to the party, although, in Catholic Bavaria it was played down until the time of the Putsch, when it burst out vigorously in the most inflammatory attacks on both the Church and the higher clergy. Although Hitler himself did not attack the Church frontally and, as late as 1936, gave his religion as "Catholic" in *Wer Ist's*, neither did he disavow the attacks made by his party press organs or by party speakers against higher clergymen, against the Jesuit Order, or against "Rome." It therefore seems safe to say that the National Socialist attitude towards the Church was one of measured hostility, held in check by the desire to win over as many Catholics as possible to their banner.[26]

III. *Organization*

The control of the party lay completely in the hands of Adolf Hitler by early 1923. In theory, rule by committee continued, but, in fact, and by statute, Hitler occupied the same position in the NSDAP that Bonaparte had enjoyed as first consul. He was first among unequals. He made all important decisions either entirely on his own initiative, or after consultation with members of the official hierarchy of the party, or, more often, after consultation with members of his large, active, and amorphous "kitchen cabinet" of personal cronies, party leaders, and administrators. Therefore, the organization of the high command of the party was not too important, especially since men more or less outside the formal structure of the high command, such as Putzi Hanfstaengl, Theodor von der Pfordten, Hermann Esser, and Max von Scheubner-Richter were far more influential than were Anton Drexler, the founder of the party and its honorary chairman, and Hans Jakob, the second chairman of the party.

Typical of this personal rule of the party was the control of its finances, which Hitler apparently handled to a very large extent on an informal basis. There is good reason to believe that he kept much of the pertinent information—particularly regarding the

---

ing doubt on their patriotism. B, I, GSK 43, p. 122; II, MA103476, p. 1230; NA, T84, 4, p. 3745; T120, 5569, p. K591529.

[26] B, I, GSK 43, pp. 76-77, 122, 133; GSK 90, pp. 151-52; II, MA101248, PDM21, 16.12.24; MA102140, HMB 3073, Ofr., p. 1; MA103457, *Völkisches Nachrichtenblatt*; MA104221, Hüfner Bericht, 7.12.23; Ludendorff, Erich, *Auf dem Weg zur Feldherrnhalle*, München, 1938, pp. 10-22 and passim. Hereafter cited as Ludendorff, *Feldherrnhalle*.

sources of funds—only in his head. While Max Amann, his wartime sergeant major and close confidant, and Franz Xaver Schwarz, the senior party treasurer, may have been more or less aware of the financial situation, there is very little indication that anyone else was. Schwarz, always a shadowy background figure in party history as he was in official photographs, was tight-mouthed and completely dominated by Hitler. Amann was a more vigorous, independent personality, but he, too, was loyal to Hitler and constitutionally averse to showing anyone his financial cards. Allegedly, Amann physically threw Jakob out of his office for merely asking to see the account books.[27] During the bad times of 1923, it was Hitler who adopted priorities and dispersed money as he saw fit. The sources of some of these funds are known, but most of them are not. It is not even clear as to whether the money came mostly from small contributors or large ones. It is clear only that it flowed to Hitler and from Hitler.[28]

Below Hitler, the party divided into separate organizations, one civil and one military. The civilian organization was still primitive and München-oriented, although the party was now spreading rapidly throughout the entire Reich. Control of the civilian organization remained tied to the leadership of the München municipal party organization (Ortsgruppe). This municipal organization was headed by a committee (Ausschuss) elected by the members. The committee consisted of a first and second chairman, two treasurers and secretaries, and presided over a series of subcommittees. The first chairman was entrusted with all real authority and stood above the committee. Since 29 July 1921, Hitler had occupied this post.[29]

Below the central high command, the party was divided into state (Landgruppen), area (Gaugruppen), and municipal (Ortsgruppen) organizations. At this stage, the municipal organizations were often in direct contact with Hitler and the central apparatus of the party, while the intermediate headquarters seem to have been rudimentary. The authority of state and area leaders must have depended to a considerable extent on their personal drive and initiative, since the chain of command was so indistinct. A strong re-

[27] B, II, MA103473, *Bayerischer Kurier*, 29.10.1924.

[28] B, I, Kahr MS, p. 1341; SA 1, 1943, A, pp. 223-24; II, MA103476, pp. 77-78, 85-90, 113-14, 777, 1481-82; Müller, Karl Alexander von, *Im Wandel einer Zeit*, München, 1966, p. 143. Hereafter cited as Müller, *Wandel*.

[29] B, II, MA100425, Entschl. St. G. Hof, pp. 231-32.

gional leader like Julius Streicher or Gregor Strasser might still operate to some extent on his own, while others, especially in the newly "colonized" north, seem to have been effectively by-passed from below and above alike.[30]

Officially, Ortsgruppen had to have at least fifty members. Smaller groups were attached to a nearby Ortsgruppe and were apparently called "chairmanships" (Obmannschaften). An Obmannschaft had little direct contact with München and was not considered to be an autonomous entity. Despite these official arrangements, however, smaller groups formed on local initiative seem to have called themselves Ortsgruppen with impunity, even if they had less than the official minimum membership.[31] Most Ortsgruppen seem to have been headed by a single executive officer, who at this time was sometimes termed Ortsgruppenleiter and sometimes Ortsgruppenführer. Some Ortsgruppen, though, like the one in München were subordinated to a committee, and at least a few were headed by a manager (Geschäftsführer) in the absence of a regular leader.[32]

Finally, attached to the civilian organization was the Jugendbund or Jugendabteilung, the ancestor of the Hitler Jugend and Bund deutscher Mädel. This organization, led by Adolf Lenk, a working-class youth, was already a center of recruiting efforts by the party. SA members were ordered to have their children join the organization and vigorous recruiting was carried on both before and after the Putsch.[33]

The military organizations were completely separate from the civilian apparatus,[34] but worked in coordination with it at all levels,

[30] There are indications of tension, for example, betweeen Streicher in Nürnberg and the central party leadership in München. Streicher does not seem to have reported all new Ortsgruppen to München, and he apparently fought off attempts by München appointees to build up rival centers of power in his satrapy. There is a hint that Hitler was attempting the tactics he later used to destroy Gregor Strasser's hold on Berlin. Walter Kellerbauer, his Nürnberg envoy, was, however, no Goebbels, and Streicher was far too strongly entrenched to be brought completely to heel in a short time. In any case, the Putsch and its aftermath changed the picture so completely that the struggle was not continued on the same basis thereafter. B, II, MA101325, Anlage zu PDN-F 1531 (Extrablatt d. *Völkischen Echos*).

[31] B, I, SA 1, 1486, passim. See also II, MA102140 & MA102141, passim.

[32] GP, D, 1 (Personalities); B, I, SA 1, 1486, passim.

[33] B, I, SA 1, 1635, pp. 758-61; GSK 90, p. 308; NA, SA Rgt. München, 230-a-10/4 3, 3.7.1923, 25.7.23, 13.8.23; Maser, *Frühgeschichte*, p. 307.

[34] B, I, SA 1, 1486, passim.

although not without some friction.[35] The party's major military organization, the Sturmabteilungen, or SA, might perhaps claim a literary origin, since it was apparently formed in a printing house, but its mission was a militant one. Initially formed to protect the meetings of the party from hecklers and opposition paramilitary groups, by 1923 this organization had grown to such an extent that in at least some areas it was able to go over to the offensive against the foes of the party. It had also become sufficiently militarized to constitute a clear revolutionary threat to the power of the state.[36]

The SA had not developed fullblown like Venus from the foam. It began with the formation of a sports organization (Turn- und Sportabteilung) in the fall of 1920. By the summer of 1921 the name Sturmabteilung—probably derived from the crack assault battalions of the German army in World War I—had become common. A regular military structure was adopted in May 1922, and further reorganizations occurred in 1923 as a result of Göring's accession to command of the SA and as a result of the spectacular growth of the force during the year.[37]

Late in 1922 and early in 1923 there was a change of the guard in the SA. Hitherto, Hans Ulrich Klintzsch had been leader of the SA. Klintzsch was a former naval lieutenant and an Ehrhardt man, as were a number of other key officers of the early SA. In fact, the Wikingbund and the SA were, on the testimony of both Lieutenant Eberhard Kautter and Captain Göring, at one time closely related. By the beginning of 1923 this relationship was clearly souring and the appearance of Göring at the head of the SA was probably either a symptom or a cause of the breach—for which each organization blamed the other.[38] Thereafter, the only naval officer in a senior post in the SA was Lieutenant Senior Grade Alfred Hoffmann, and

[35] Indications of this friction are to be found throughout the documents dealing with the early party. They especially come to the fore in the period following the Putsch. An anonymous letter published in the *Bayerischer Kurier* by a contributor who clearly knew where the bodies were buried, sums up the quarrel in terms that are probably generally correct. D, II, MA103473, *Bayerischer Kurier*, 29.10.1924. See also NA, SA Rgt. München, 230-a-10/3 1, 26.10.23.

[36] See Chapter II above and Chapters VIII-XIII below, passim.

[37] B, I, SA 1, 1771, PDM VI N/521/23 v. 30.11.1923; II, MA100425, PDM 1159 vid, p. 198.

[38] B, I, SA 1, 1474, pp. 111, 120; 1475, p. 142; II, MA100425, pp. 247-48; IV, BuR, Bd. 35, Akt 4, Item 31 (*MP*); NA, T84, 4, p. 3165; Hanfstängl, Ernst, *Hitler: The Missing Years*, London, 1957, pp. 76-77. Hereafter cited as Hanfstängl, *Hitler*.

he was eased out of his central position into a peripheral one in the early fall.[39]

Göring controlled the SA through a headquarters (Oberkommando), which was organized along the lines of a German army general staff. Attached to this headquarters was a special guard unit, the Stabswache, which was originally commanded by Klintzsch and which wore black caps adorned with deaths-head insignia—which suggests that it was either a predecessor of the SS or that it provided inspiration for the later SS uniform.[40]

The SA itself was divided into regiments, battalions, and hundreds (companies in later 1923). These units, as was almost always the case with the paramilitary organizations of the Weimar Republic, were upgraded in title. In other words, they were far smaller than were parallel units in the Reichswehr, or in other contemporary armies. This practice had the double advantage of allowing the paramilitary groups to upgrade their leaders in rank and also gave the impression of far greater strength than they really could muster. In München the SA also boasted a transportation battalion (Verkehrsabteilung), which consisted largely of party members who owned or drove vehicles that they were prepared to use for party purposes on demand, although it also included a transport detachment, which drove vehicles provided by the party.[41]

Characteristically, at the same time that he was tightening his hold on the SA and improving its discipline and responsiveness to command authority, Hitler undermined it in another direction. Right after the May Day affair, a new National Socialist paramilitary organization was authorized. This was the Stosstrupp Adolf Hitler, which seems to have vague ancestral connections with the SS. Certainly the Stosstrupp had parallel responsibilities and rights and even wore similar insignia to those of the SS in the new party of 1925. This organization, which was approximately the strength of an infantry company (100 men more or less) was apparently the brain child of Julius Schreck, Hitler's personal chauffeur, who became its first sergeant and selected its first members. Command of the new force was given to Lieutenant (ret.) Josef Berchtold, a

---

[39] B, I, SA 1, 1493, A, p. 223.

[40] B, II, MA103476, pp. 1103-4; NA, SA Rgt. München, 230-a-10/4 2, Oct. 1923; 4, 4.5.1923.

[41] B, I, SA 1, 1477, Christian Weber, pp. 464-68; 1494, p. 372; NA, SA Rgt. München, 230-a-10/4 4, 14.4.23, 14.4.23.

tobacconist, who devoted much of his time and energy to it. The men were given special training and the unit would seem to have been more heavily armed than regular SA units. It was to be assigned special missions, apparently by Hitler himself.

The SA had no control over the Stosstrupp and the München SA regiment at least, reacted with suspicion and jealousy towards the new organization as early as mid-summer. Stosstrupp Hitler died stillborn, since it was destroyed by the Putsch and never resurrected in the same form. However, it seems significant because of the role it played in the Hitler Putsch, because of the precedent it seemed to establish for the SS and because it showed Hitler playing the game of establishing parallel and overlapping authorities that he could use one against another, and perhaps already toying with the thought of an elite organization to balance the mass SA. In any case, the entire development was an example of the Hitlerian system of checks and balances and personal control of independent elements within the party, which marked his operations to the end of his days.[42]

IV. *Strength*

A consideration of the strength of the party may well be introduced by Captain Truman Smith's remarks on this subject at the end of 1922:

> It is very difficult to gain an impression of the total party strength. Opponents of Hitler estimated it as high as 200,000, other neutral observers as 35,000. It is not easy however to distinguish between actual party members and Hitler sympathizers, who as yet take no active part in the movement. These were found in the army, the government, and among the press. It was stated that the larger part of the Munich police was entirely in sympathy with the National Socialists.[43]

An official police report issued in the summer of 1923 estimated the party as numbering 35,000 members in München and approximately 150,000 in Bavaria. This estimate clearly threw together party members and sympathizers.[44] Other, fragmentary evidence

---

[42] B, I, SA 1, 1494, pp. 244-45; NA, SA Rgt. München, 230-a-10/4, 2, 18.8.1923; Kallenbach, Hans, *Mit Adolf Hitler auf Festung Landsberg*, München 1939, pp. 11-14. Hereafter cited as Kallenbach, *Mit Hitler*.

[43] Y, Official Report of Captain Truman Smith, 25.11.1922.

[44] B, I, M. Inn. 73685, PDM, vid 1637. Party members' official numbers

would suggest that Smith's higher figure was probably a reasonable estimate for party members and sympathizers in Bavaria and that his smaller estimate was probably not too far off regarding actual party members.

Far more important than the question of the numerical size of the party was the extent to which it was a growing organism, and on this the evidence is unequivocal. It is true that here and there during 1923 the party lost both members and supporters. The events of May Day, for example,[45] caused some fall off, as did Hitler's order that party members leave other Völkische Verbände. On the whole, though, the trend is markedly upward. Nor was this growth limited to Bavaria. New Ortsgruppen were appearing throughout Germany and new members were entering the party in some numbers—despite the indifference of Hitler and his deputies towards the party outside Bavaria, and particularly outside the south.

The growth of Ortsgruppen during 1923 is extremely impressive. Werner Maser records that in the middle of 1922 the NSDAP had approximately 45 Ortsgruppen in Bavaria.[46] By the time of the Putsch, there were at least 100.[47] The growth of the party was, of course, not to be measured in terms of new Ortsgruppen alone. In many instances the existing nuclei drew ever larger numbers of members to themselves—although there were certainly cases of almost moribund local organizations, like those in Schliersee or Zwiesel,[48] and of comparatively resistant areas, such as Schwaben.[49]

Where the Ortsgruppen were active, and vigorous speakers—like Frau Andrea Ellendt, Dolle, Streicher, or Hitler himself—were available, growth was rapid, and it was not only the people on the fence who were won over. Just as Adolf Hitler had been won over when he came to investigate the nature of the old German Workers' Party for suspicious military authorities, and just as more than

---

do not seem to be a very reliable index of the size of the membership in view of the large number of members who seem to have dropped out or been expelled during the course of 1923 and earlier years.

[45] See Chapter VIII, Section II below, passim.

[46] Maser, *Frühgeschichte*, pp. 319-20.

[47] Based on extremely diverse data. Appendix Ia provides a list of the towns concerned.

[48] B, I, SA 1, 1486, Gend. Stat. Schliersee 724, p. 160; BA Regen. D49, pp. 189-90.

[49] B, II, MA102140, HMB 883, Schw., p. 3.

one policeman set to watch the NSDAP had become an ardent member,[50] so other scoffers were roped in. Dr. Friedrich Trefz, the business manager of the *Münchner Neueste Nachrichten* and a liberal of the old school, told Truman Smith in 1922 of sitting at a Hitler meeting between a retired general and a Communist. Both explained to him before the meeting began that they had come out of mere curiosity. Afterwards, both enrolled themselves as party members.[51]

Such conversions were not by any means unusual. Reports from all parts of Bavaria make the trend clear. Even the Social Democratic leader Kern, rejoicing in the temporary drop-off of National Socialist expansion following the May Day affair, warned that all the other racist organizations continued to grow,[52] and the other Verbände were also recruiting grounds for the NSDAP. In Erbendorf the later Gauleiter Adolf Wagner persuaded most of the members of Bayern und Reich to join the NSDAP, and in Roding the local SA unit was formed almost exclusively of recently recruited Bayern und Reich members.[53]

As early as January 1923 the provincial president (Regierungspräsident) of Oberfranken reported:

> The National Socialist Party has recently won further ground. Its newly formed Ortsgruppe in Kulmbach numbers something over 300 members. In the Münchberg district they will soon build groups. In Coburg the movement of the National Socialist Workers Party has already taken on firm form. The group presently counts 25-30 members, who meet every Thursday in the Schinzel Inn, Judengasse 36. . . .[54]

And three days before the Putsch he was reporting similar gains in the Münchberg-Stadtsteinach vicinity.[55] In October, the provincial president in Augsburg, who had been pleased at the slow progress the Nazis were making in his satrapy, had to admit that ". . . the

---

[50] See Chapter xx, Section vi, for general mention of policemen in party. Josef Gerum was an example of those policemen who entered the Hitler circle as police agents but were converted to National Socialism. B, ii, MA103476, p. 1195.

[51] Y, Truman Smith Papers, Notebook, p. 46.

[52] B, iv, BuR, Akt 34, Item 41, p. 3.

[53] B, ii, MA102140, HMB 717, Opf., p. 3; HMB 795, p. 3.

[54] B, ii, MA102140, HMB 99, Ofr., p. 3.

[55] B, ii, MA102140, HMB 2407, Ofr., p. 2.

unrest among the unemployed is exploited not only by the Communists but also [by] the National Socialists. The former Communist Eichberger carries on a vigorous agitation for the National Socialists along these lines. . . ."[56] And the testimony is not confined to officials. A leader of the Wanderverein, an especially militant and youthful organization within Bund Bayern und Reich, reported in September from the area of Naila: "The spirit and ideas of the National Socialists are gaining ground here. As a result there are constant demands for cooperation with them."[57]

Such reports poured in during the course of the year from every province and district. Some groups, like that in Birnbach, were reported to have only five or six members, but a membership of 200 to 300 men was not exceptional, and the Ortsgruppenleiter in Kronach claimed, in a letter to Hitler, to have almost 2,000 members in his Ortsgruppe.[58] In short, even before the November Putsch and Hitler's Trial in early 1924 gave fresh impetus to the party, it was clearly expanding rapidly throughout Bavaria.

In much of the rest of Germany the party was banned. It was forbidden in Prussia, in Württemberg, in "Red" Thüringia and Saxony, in Hamburg, Bremen, and Baden. But as early as January 1923 the party was growing wherever the ban did not hold it under.[59] And even where the ban was in existence, the authorities found that although they could hold down the numbers of the National Socialists and could dissolve their organizations, they could not effectively prevent the NSDAP from forming new organizations again and again or from picking up tough-minded recruits.[60] The upshot was the same as that in the case of the Social Democrats under the Bismarck ban. The ban was effective enough to keep down the party's numbers but at the same time soft enough to allow determined followers to hold on and even to build up re-

---

[56] *Ibid.*, HMB 1984, Schw., p. 2.

[57] B, IV, BuR, Bd. 35, Akt 5, Item 6.

[58] B, I, SA 1, 1486, p. 19; II, MA102140, passim; NA, T84, 4, pp. 3034-36.

[59] B, II, MA101249, Rk. O. In. 84, p. 15.

[60] B, I, SA 1, 1474, pp. 78-79; 1477, p. 256; II, MA100411, BG in St. 1029 v. 4.10.1923; MA100425, BG in St. 121 Tgb. 292 v. 7.3.1923; MA101249, Rk. O. In. 83, pp. 10-11; GP, D, 1 (Personalities); Jochmann, Werner, *Nationalsozialismus und Revolution: Ursprung und Geschichte der NSDAP in Hamburg, 1922-1923*, Frankfurt, 1962. Hereafter cited as Jochmann, *Hamburg*. See also *Das Deutsche Führerlexikon, 1934-1935*, Berlin, 1934, passim. Hereafter cited as *Führerlexikon*.

sentments and techniques that would make them more formidable later.[61]

v. *Social Composition and Attitudes*

It has long been an article of faith among many of those who talk or write about the early National Socialist German Workers' Party that this party was essentially a lower middle-class party, manned by persons driven off the edge into "classlessness" by economic pressures. Moreover, the contemporary statements of such politically engaged observers of the National Socialists as the editors of the *Münchener Post*, who saw the movement through specifically Marxist glasses, albeit slightly corrected to meet revisionist standards, support the general tendency. A typical statement of this type and vintage is that of an editor of that paper, Heymann, who asserted that the National Socialists drew their recruits " '. . . from the déclassé, many former officers, and from the dregs of the proletariat.' "[62]

Although questioning this myth may be regarded as heretical, it seems to rest on no better a factual foundation than the allied myth that the National Socialists were, from the beginning, the darlings of German capitalism.[63] Neither the persons most involved in the critical examination of the National Socialist Party at the time nor the information available regarding the members of the early National Socialist Party and their attitudes seem to support these assumptions.

The most striking single social fact about the National Socialist Party is that it was a party of the young. Both followers and leaders tended to be far younger than their opposite numbers in the traditional political parties and remained so throughout the period of the Weimar Republic, as is indicated by the fact that the mass entry of National Socialists into the Reichstag in 1932-33 reduced the

---

[61] The National Socialists apparently drew from this experience the conclusion that a ban must be rigidly enforced and absolutely without loopholes to be effective, and that it must be accompanied by the elimination of activists and leaders among the opposition. Operating in this manner, Hitler maintained bans which were very effective, even if some shadow organizations lived half-lives despite these measures.

[62] B, II, MA100425, p. 325.

[63] Professor Henry Turner of Yale University has recently been examining this theory critically. See Turner, Henry, "Big Business and the Rise of Hitler," *American Historical Review*, October 1969, pp. 56-70.

average age of that august body by a full decade.[64] Both the general information available from contemporary sources and the specific information on individuals belonging to the NSDAP before 9 November 1923 clearly supports the thesis that youth was the outstanding characteristic of the party.

Truman Smith reported in November 1922 that students were one of the prime elements of the NSDAP.[65] The Bavarian Minister-President Graf Lerchenfeld stated specifically: "The active members [of the NSDAP] consist primarily of young people of all classes (Erwerbsstände), including students. . . ."[66] This story is fully supported by authorities on the local level and even in other states. The Lindau authorities reported that the National Socialists there were ". . . mostly very young party members."[67] The reports from Augsburg noted the feverish and fanatic energy of the NSDAP's members, most of whom were, like members of the rest of the *Kampfbund*, mere youths.[68]

Otto von Strössenreuther, the Regierungspräsident of Oberfranken and himself somewhat sympathetic with the Patriotic, if not the Racist, Movement, reported immediately after the Putsch: ". . . The N[ational] S[ocialists] carry out in the cities as well as in the smallest villages an extremely vigorous agitation by personal contact, leaflets, and placards, mostly with falsified news. The official proclamations are often destroyed. The culprits, who are apparently mostly half-grown youths, are extremely hard to identify. . . ."[69] In Günzburg, students from the university in München were recruiting for the NSDAP in their home town.[70] In Staffelstein the district authorities reported in February that the NSDAP was recruiting actively "with the result that the young go over to them in droves."[71] Freiherr Franz von Gagern, the Kreisleiter of Bayern und Reich for Oberfranken and a bitter foe of the NSDAP, reported to the assembled leaders of the Bund that the Kampfbund

[64] *Kürschners Volkshandbuch des Deutschen Reichstags 1933*, Berlin, n.d. (1933). Foreword. Hereafter cited as *Kürschners Volkshandbuch 1933*.

[65] Y. Truman Smith Papers, Official Report of 25.11.1922, pp. 43-44.

[66] B, II, MA103163, Letter: Lerchenfeld an Friedrich Ebert, 1.9.1922, p. 2.

[67] B, I, SA 1, 1486, p. 94.

[68] B, II, MA102140, HMB 1231, pp. 1-2.

[69] B, I, GSK 44, pp. 17-19.

[70] B, II, MA102140, HMB 563, Schw., p. 3.

[71] B, II, MA102140, HMB 186, Ofr., p. 6.

had only youths without military service, whereas all the veterans of World War I were in Bayern und Reich.[72] The same story was true in Oberbayern, where the leader of Bayern und Reich in Bad Reichenhall explained that his unit was understrength because "most of the young people are with B[un]d Oberland (twenty-three men) and the National Socialists (nineteen men)."[73]

There were so many young activists and they were so active that they were sometimes an embarrassment to the party or its elements. The SA regiment in München complained, for example, that the Jugendbund insignia was so similar to that of the SA that the regiment was often blamed for activities of the Jugendbund. This complaint is significant not merely because it shows the activity of the Jugendbund, but also because it indicates that many of the SA men were also very young—otherwise how could they be mistaken for school children?[74] A similar report comes from Karlsruhe, where the police reported that approximately one-third of the audience of approximately 350 persons at an NSDAP rally were under twenty years of age, and this evaluation was echoed by General Reinhardt of the Reichswehr in Stuttgart.[75]

These generalized reports are strongly supported by statistical data. The statistics here presented are based on a file containing data regarding 1,672 persons who were members of the NSDAP before 9 November 1923.[76] The information available on these persons varies from individual to individual. However, birth data is available for 994 of them, and this sample includes a very considerable proportion of the leaders and activists of the movement. The sample fully confirms the testimony regarding the youthful profile of the party. Of these 994 members, 195 were 21 years of age or less. Almost two-thirds, 610 persons, were under 31 years of

---

[72] B, IV, BuR, Bd. 35, Akt 5, Item 35/2, Sitzungsbericht, 6.10.1923.

[73] B, IV, BuR, Bd. 34, Item 139, Wirsing an Schonger, 2.11.1923.

[74] NA, SA Rgt. München, 230-a-10/4, 3, 25.7.1923.

[75] B, I, SA 1, 1474, Meldung d. Fahnungsabtg. Pol. Karlsruhe, 23.3.23; M. Inn. 73696, BG in St. 699 Abschrift, p. 3.

[76] GP, D, 1 (Personalities). In perhaps ten instances the persons involved may not at that time have been official members of the NSDAP, but they were vigorous activists on behalf of the party. Members of the SA are considered to be members of the party in view of their clear commitment to Hitler and the movement as well as because, in theory, no one was allowed to join the SA unless he also belonged to the party. (In practice, this rule does not seem to have been strictly applied.) These persons would therefore seem to be at the very least de facto National Socialists.

age. These figures are given added weight by the strong evidence that other persons in the larger sample, for whom there were no specific birth dates available, were also well below 30,[77] and that a number of other persons, who had probably—but not demonstrably—been National Socialists before 9 November 1923 were also very young.[78]

The same youthful profile is clearly apparent at the leadership level as well. Out of a group of 45 Ortsgruppenleiter whose ages were known, 2 were under 21, 24 were under 31, 38 were under 41, and only 7 were over 40. Out of a group of 25 local SA leaders, 3 were under 21 years of age, 17 under 31, and 5 over 30. Out of a group of 16 leaders at the provincial or central party apparatus level, 3 were under 21, 6 were under 31, 4 were between 30 and 40, and 3 were over 40 years of age. The SA side of the picture was equally clear. Here were no aging colonels and generals, but young and active representatives of the "new generation." Out of a group of 15 SA leaders in key positions at the provincial or central level, one was under 21, 8 were under 31, and the remaining 6 were under 39.

It therefore seems safe to say that in many ways the NSDAP represented a rebellion of dissatisfied youth against an elder generation that had not only stumbled into a war but had failed to win it, and that had equally failed to create a world with which these young men could sympathize. At this time these adherents did not represent more than a small fraction of Germany's youth, but the party's nature, as the vehicle of the young against the old, the new and innocent against the old and corrupt, was already clearly established, at least in the eyes of many of its members and in those of increasing numbers of other youths. It was a party of impatience and enthusiasm for simple solutions to complex problems—both age-old characteristics of younger generations.

To what extent, however, was the NSDAP a class party within the terms of reference established for us by Marx and applicable with considerable success to the various traditional political parties of Germany and Bavaria (except for the Center-BVP parties, which defied Marx in honoring an older political determinant—religion)? Who were the members of the early party? And who, in particular, were the party members of the year 1923? Which were

[77] Many persons for whom birth data were not available were students, had been lieutenants in World War I, were apprentices, etc.

[78] See Appendix 1b for Age Charts.

the groups most attracted by the siren song of Hitler and his fellows?[79]

[79] The traditional division of German society into an upper class, Mittelstand, and Arbeiterschaft was orginally conceived in a semi-industrial period and is strongly influenced by Marxist theories. It does not have any very clear relevance in a modern industrial society, even one at the stage that Weimar Germany represented—if indeed this system ever really reflected an existing situation rather than academic and political theories. Particularly weak is the concept of the Mittelstand, which emerges not as a recognizable social or political entity but as a grab-bag consisting of those elements that the inventors of the system did not wish to include in either the "Herrscherklasse" (Obrigkeit usw.) or the Arbeiterschaft. For the purposes of this book a more flexible system, representing modern society, is needed to fit actual social conditions and the attitudes of the groups and individuals involved. Therefore society is broken up into groups that represent social connections, occupations, and social cohesion, as well as political-social development.

The nobility having been, to all intents and purposes, absorbed into one or another of the strata of the middle class, the old "ruling class" falls away. The middle class is divided into an upper middle class, a middle middle class, and a lower middle class. The working class is divided into a "white collar" (Angestellte) group and a "blue collar" (Fabrik- und Handarbeiter) group. Finally, there is the peasantry, with its close if sometimes ambivalent connections with portions of the agricultural nobility.

The upper middle class contains those persons who have large fortunes, or control large fortunes—for today, on both sides of the Iron Curtain, the men who administer and control money are often far more important than the people (or institutions) who own money—or occupy leading positions in the government, the Church, and other major institutions and organizations. The most important, wealthy, and successful members of the free professions and the wealthier nobility fall into this category, as do the higher nobility whether wealthy or not.

The middle middle class contains those administrators, government officials, members of the free professions, etc. who occupy responsible and/or well paid positions, and have some influence on policy or direct the operations of considerable numbers of men. It also contains small factory owners, the owners of medium-sized businesses, and independent professional men who have achieved reasonable stature in their home communities if not in a wider circle. Socially, the middle middle class is interlocked with the upper middle class and passage back and forth is frequent.

The lower middle class includes the shopkeeper-owner, the middle-level government official, the artisan who owns his own shop, foremen, chief clerks, and other persons of their general income and occupational level. The lower middle class in the Weimar period was also clearly marked, as it often is today, by a far lower educational level than either of the other two segments of the middle class.

The "white collar" segment of the working class includes those of the German "Angestellte" who are at a level where they have relatively low salaries, very little influence on policy, and less than a Gymnasium education. They are, in effect, simply clerical workers with nothing ,to offer in the labor market beyond their bodily energy and simple acquired skills. Some members of this group perform far more complex functions than others, but fall well within the general range of income, training, and occupation. Store clerks, lower government officials, and similar groups also fall naturally into this sub-class, as do waiters and similar service personnel.

The "blue collar" workers are essentially those who work with their hands rather than with paper or by performing service for others. These workers (called Arbeiter in my classification) can be further divided into skilled workers, semi-skilled workers, and unskilled workers, but all fall into the same broad sub-class. They bring primarily physical strength, tempered to a greater or less extent by skills, to the labor market and have an income that places them well below the bulk of the middle class's lower levels—although in the shadow areas on the borders, income is not the best determinant of class. An example is the fact that Bismarck's pension was lower than that of a brewmaster from a famous Dortmund brewery, according to their advertisements. Often occupation, spending habits, and attitudes are more significant.

The attempt of Marx and others to make a distinction between "artisans" and workers made sense in the middle of the nineteenth century, when one group clearly represented a dying and the other a new, rising proletariat. Well before the Weimar period, however, this distinction had little left to recommend it. The artisan now had the same training as did many skilled factory workers. Also, to judge by a number of individual cases, the same man often went back and forth between factory work and independent work as an artisan. The decision to drop the term and concept "artisan" is further reinforced by the fact that, at least in the Racist Movement, a good number of these persons—in defiance of Marxist theory—do not strive desperately to join the middle class, but describe themselves as workers. Unionization and the disappearance of any true mass artisan organizations doubtless played a role in this shift, as did the drift away from the concept of class that began even before World War I. The change was accelerated by the abhorrence of class barriers that marked the attitudes of many young men after the war. A final contributory factor was, undoubtedly, the rising social value given to "work" and the "worker" in a day and age when it is increasingly realized that even the millionaire or the ruler is a "worker" in many senses of the term if he has a regular occupation.

All social determinations in this book are in accordance with this social scale. It is, naturally, far from perfect, but seems to be much more practical and representative of the existing situation than a semi-artificial nineteenth century system. In an article in *Vierteljahrshefte für Zeitgeschichte*, 19, Jhrg./Heft 2 (April 1971), pp. 124-59, Michael H. Kater comes to different conclusions using different categorizations and a different (larger) sample of Party members, all of whom seem to have joined the NSDAP in the months of economic pressure immediately preceding the Putsch. In view of all of the available evidence, I still hold to my views. However, the divergences indicate the need for more detailed social analysis of the early Party based on broader data.

Here, too, the Social Democrats, who claimed that the National Socialists held no terror for them and could attract only a handful of workers, seem poor guides for the serious inquirer into the facts, especially since, in private, the Social Democrats sometimes sang a quite different song. Captain Truman Smith noted in his official report on the NSDAP in November 1922: "The actual party membership and the members of the Stosstruppen [*sic*] have been recruited to date almost entirely from south Bavarian cities, and have been drawn from two widely differing classes of the population, the students and the middle class on the one hand, and the radical Social Democrats and Communists on the other hand. Hitler's conversions in the latter class are admitted on all sides to be numerous, but it was pointed out that they were employees of either small factories or stores. In the larger factories, it was stated by a Social Democrat, the strong labor discipline had resisted any serious inroads."[80] It is very significant that this Social Democrat indicated that "labor discipline," by which he clearly meant both expulsion from work and physical punishment,[81] was the force that held the workers away from the party, rather than its lack of appeal to them. This admission also suggests the existence of an unorganized National Socialist "fifth column" within the ranks of the unions, which would help to explain a number of later developments.[82]

We are not, however, dependent on casual remarks for evidence regarding the worker and the NSDAP. Here, too, both contemporary local reports and the analysis of personnel data play an important role in developing the picture of the relationship of the workers to the party.[83] Graf Lerchenfeld is again the first witness.

[80] Y, Truman Smith Papers, Official Report, pp. 43-44.

[81] The Bavarian police records contain a good number of accounts of such attacks on rightest workers by their fellows, and there are numbers of complaints regarding such cases in the Hauptarchiv der NSDAP (B, I, SA 1). Individual instances are mentioned elsewhere in this book.

[82] Such incidents as the mass defection of a workers' Turnverein to the NSDAP immediately after the Hitler Putsch strengthen this supposition. B, I, GSK 101, BA Selbitz, 3.1.1924.

[83] Here, for the sake of clarity, I will again warn the reader that when I speak of a "worker" I mean a "blue collar worker," whether skilled or unskilled, and when I speak of an "employee" I mean a "white collar worker." The German equivalents are respectively "Arbeiter" and "Angestellter." I will also, in those instances where the distinction is possible, indicate whether the workers are factory workers or not. Unfortunately, but significantly, this distinction is not often possible because neither workers nor the various tabulators seem to have thought in these terms.

In his letter to President Friedrich Ebert concerning the party he stated: "Above all, many workers have joined this group [NSDAP], who were previously socialists or Communists. . . ."[84] This is the testimony of a man who thoroughly detested the National Socialists and who had available to him all of the official data regarding them.

The Prussian government, controlled by Majority Socialists and, to judge by evidence uncovered by the Bavarian government, maintaining its own secret agents in Bavaria, also seems to have believed that the National Socialists were having far too much success with workers, for it officially protested to the Bavarian government in early November 1923 that 1,000 trade unionists in Bamberg had been forced to join the NSDAP. Since the Bavarian government and the dominant Bavarian political parties were at this time at drawn daggers with the NSDAP and the trade unions were controlled by Social Democrats, it is a little difficult to understand who was in a position to put such pressure on the workers. However, the protest certainly suggests cries of anguish from Bavarian trade union leaders to their comrades in the north about sizeable losses to the National Socialists.[85]

The federal government's envoy in München also testified to the participation of large numbers of workers in the NSDAP. On 15 April 1923 he reported:

. . . As I was able to ascertain for myself, there were in the estimated 5,000-6,000 man [strong] force of Hitler's besides the National Socialist Assault Troops, the Blücherbund, Reichsflagge, the Bund Oberland, and some smaller organizations. The marchers represented all classes of the population. Besides a large number of workers, former soldiers dominated, partly equipped with steel helmets, though otherwise unarmed. Also some National Socialist Storm Troops from the Oberland were in Tracht in the parade. The tight military discipline of the men must be stressed.[86]

From Augsburg came the remark that the National Socialists seemed to be winning more followers from Left radical groups than from the Right.[87] The district chief in Naila reported:

[84] B, II, MA103163, Brief Abschrift: Lerchenfeld an Ebert, 1.9.1922, p. 2.
[85] B, II, MA104381, ca. early Nov. 1923.
[86] NA, T120, 5569, p. K591365.
[87] B, II, MA102140, HMB 1984, p. 3.

In Red Selbitz the MSP[D] and the USP[D] have their backs to the wall. Whether the heavy transfer of Socialists into the National Socialist German Workers' Party is the result of conviction or rather has the aim, in the present difficult times, of getting weapons from the National Socialists in order to join the Thüringians in attacking Bavaria, is not yet clear. . . .[88]

Here is a clearly honest report of the winning over of workers, as is indicated by the pained and disbelieving tone. For the district chief, the anti-nationalism and class-consciousness of the Social Democratic worker had become as much an article of faith as it was with the SPD leaders, and he resented its overturning as much as they did. In Unterfranken the story was the same. At the end of December 1922 the provincial president said:

> The *German Racist and National Socialist Movement* is expanding more and more in Unterfranken, especially at the expense of the VSPD. The middle-class parties see these losses of the Social Democrats without sorrow and most of them generally swallow for this reason the antisemitism which is bound up with the movement. However, sensible elements of the middle-class parties still show a strong distrust of the movement, because they are in doubt as to whether in the end patriotic, or as seems more likely from the former party background of most of the followers of the movement, the socialist ideas hostile to the present state system will gain the upper hand.[89]

Here one finds a different suspicion of the converts from socialism, a suspicion that they will destroy the nationalism in the movement —whereas, as subsequent events have clearly demonstrated, actually the nationalist motif was the most important positive motif in the movement and was probably one of the main forces leading the workers into new political paths.[90]

In at least one district of Oberfranken even the apparatus of the SPD proved unreliable in the fall of 1923:

[88] B, IV, Lapo, Bd. 26a, Akt 3, Item 23.

[89] B, II, MA102140, HMB 1815, Ufr., pp. 1-2.

[90] The remark that the middle-classes were ready to tolerate antisemitism in view of the National Socialist impact on the Marxists suggests that here, as elsewhere, there is reason to believe that the virulent antisemitism that dominated Hitler's negative program was more of a hindrance than an aid to the spread of his political doctrine, at least among the educated classes.

The National Socialists have mounted an astonishingly vigorous propaganda campaign in Oberfranken recently. The response of left-oriented workers is remarkable. In Reha[u] two Ortsgruppen were formed in the last weeks, as also in the Land district of Bayreuth, where the leaders of the VSPD also joined the Ortsgruppen. . . .[91]

In reporting on the composition of the party the München police also stressed that, while it was made up of all classes of the population, it included "very many workers."[92] Captain (Ret.) Rudolf Schonger, a leader of Bayern und Reich in Oberbayern, explained his cooperation with the local National Socialists by saying: "We are grateful to them because they bring us the workers. Without them the Bund could never penetrate workers' circles."[93] In May 1923, the leader of the SA in Forchheim explained that he could not bring his men to München for May Day as ordered because in Forchheim there was work in the factories on 1 May, and he didn't wish to tear his men from their work.[94]

The Ortsgruppenleiter of Kronach, who claimed 2,000 followers, begged for financial aid for his people. Three-fourths of them were jobless because almost all of the factories had closed down, and there was no hope for aid from the local employers since they were all BVP men. As a last argument he added that his people were almost half former Communists and therefore without financial resources to fall back on.[95] In Erding the Ortsgruppe consisted mostly of workers and employees from the Middle Isar region. Workers wrote to Hitler assuring him of their faith in him, and they filled the ranks of the SA. A former Freikorps officer found to his surprise that the local SA was led by the same men he had disarmed when they led the local Red Guard.

The reports coming from outside Bavaria play the same score. The *Karlsruhe Zeitung* stressed that a great number of the former Communist rowdies now belonged to the NSDAP. In Hirschberg in Thüringia twenty-five National Socialist workers were arrested at their factory benches in November 1923. In Altensteig/Württemberg, the police reported many workers at an NSDAP rally.[96]

[91] B, IV, Lapo, Bd. 26a, Akt 3, HMB 2408, Ofr., Item 565.
[92] B, I, SA 1, 1474, PDM 1687 vid.
[93] B, IV, BuR, Bd. 34, Item 27.
[94] B, I, SA 1, 1486, p. 46 (Schutzm. Forchheim 1480).
[95] NA, T84, 4, pp. 3034-36.
[96] B, II, MA100425, BG in St. 351 Tgb. 812; IV, Lapo, Bd. 26a, Akt 5,

It would, nonetheless, be an error to think of the NSDAP as a "workers' party" in a Marxist or even Marxian "class determinist" sense. All reports, while stressing the heavy influx of workers, a shocking novelty in a non-Marxist party, indicate that these workers are only one element in a very rich and varied "mix." In Oberfranken, Protestants clearly joined to protest the "black clericalism" of the ruling parties in München. Employees, students, members of all strata of the middle class were to be found in considerable numbers; this is the balance of the general reports.

Two significant social groups, however, are notable for their relative coolness toward the NSDAP in 1923. The first of these is the peasantry and the other is the nobility. There is, with a few local exceptions, as much unanimity on the disinterest of the peasantry in the NSDAP as there is on the enthusiasm of the workers. Agriculture Minister Johann Wutzlhofer and Anton Staedele, key peasant leaders, boasted of the immunity of their class to Nazi wooing. Wutzlhofer told the Cabinet: ". . . the land and the peasant organizations as well as the agricultural chambers (Landwirtschaftskammern) are outspoken foes of the Hitler Movement. If it came to a Putsch, we would not merely act by means of an immediate producers' strike, but, above all, would march against Putschist München."[97] Staedele said in the Diet: ". . . The right radical circles must not forget that *München is not Bavaria,* . . . and that the land will not stand by idly if the radicals ever decide to exchange their agitation for 'action.' "[98]

These men were both outspoken foes of Hitler, and it might be argued that they misrepresented the attitudes of their constituents, but the local officials solidly support their view. The National Socialists who marched in local costume through the streets of München came from the "Oberland" all right, but they came from the little towns that dotted it and not from its farms. The Rosenheim district chief noted in his report of 19 November 1923: "The peasantry of the district has never shown any sympathy for the Hitler Movement, and I did not fail to mention here and there that the Hitler program, which also calls for the socialization of real property, is not very attractive to the landowner. . . ."[99] From Aichach

---

Gr. Sch. iiic, Erfahrungsbericht St. V. 1 33, p. 2; W, E131, s16/2, O. St. an M. Inn., 24.3.1923.

[97] B, ii, MA99521, 26.1.1923, p. 4.

[98] *BLV*, 19, 22-23, 8, p. 365.   [99] B, i, GSK 44, pp. 78-80.

came the same report, and from Fürstenfeldbruck, Starnberg and Traunstein.[100] Nor was this indifference a phenomenon restricted only to Oberbayern. The provincial president of Niederbayern reported immediately after the Putsch: "The country folk stand overwhelmingly on the basis of the constitutional government and sharply condemn Hitler's and Ludendorff's actions, the latter of whom they regard in any case with suspicion as a north German. . . ."[101] Oberfranken noted also that the peasants, especially the older ones, adopted a very sensible attitude after the Putsch. The district chief in Miesbach/Oberbayern, long a close but hostile observer of the party, sang the same tune:

> . . . The supporters of the Hitler Movement, who are still strong among the local youths and workers, carry on even here in the countryside a raging propaganda. The agitators, apparently [operating] under a common set of instructions, now leave even Hitler's person in the background and attract the young people, who are always susceptible to an activist propaganda, by telling them that no improvement can be expected from Kahr: he is dealing with the foreign foe, forwards Bavaria's separation from the Reich, etc. The peasantry on the other hand still stands true to Kahr, as was pleasantly illustrated last Sunday by a heavily attended rally of the Bund Bayern und Reich.[102]

From the far north of Bavaria—Bayreuth—a battalion commander of Bayern und Reich had the same story to tell as the Miesbach official. A fifth of his men in the city had gone over to the Kampfbund after the Putsch, but the units based in the countryside remained intact. By and large, the peasantry was not yet ready to accept National Socialism.[103]

There were, of course, some exceptions to this rule. In Pfefferhausen the SA members were mostly either peasants or agricultural laborers. They may well have been the latter, for there is other evidence, from Weissenhorn, of farm workers joining the party in some numbers.[104] These exceptions, though, seem rare enough

[100] *Ibid.*, pp. 74-80.
[101] B, II, MA102140, HMB 1102, N/B, p. 3.
[102] B, I, M. Inn. 73694, BA Miesbach an Reg. Obb., 14.12.23.
[103] B, I, GSK 43, p. 157, Reinhard an Kahr, 28.11.1923.
[104] Out of 200 approached, 25 joined up, which is a fair number for an agricultural locality.

merely to underline the rule. National Socialism was still essentially confined to the towns and cities.[105]

The nobility also do not seem to play a very considerable role in the party and very few, indeed, of the party leaders, even at local levels, were nobles, except among the students. There were some nobles in the party, but apparently proportionately far fewer than were in other non-Marxist parties. Out of the sample of 1,672 party members, only 31 were members of the nobility.[106] These men seem to have been either eccentrics or youths.

The data from the specific sample of party members strongly confirm the reports of the local observers regarding class as well as age. In this case, class will be determined largely by occupation.[107] The 1,126 persons for whom occupational data were available represented practically every occupation and profession from the most honorific and best paid down to the humblest and worst paid. Twenty persons were professionally trained teachers at the university (technical university) and university preparatory secondary-school level, with the bulk being Gymnasium professors. Six were lawyers by profession and 3 were clergymen. One was a professional economist. Eighteen doctors of medicine, 8 dentists, 8 veterinarians, and one nurse represented the health professions. Students, the second largest single category, were represented by 104 at the university level, 3 "work students" at the same level, one instructor (Assistent), one student each from a Bauschule and a Technikum,[108] 8 secondary school pupils, one music student, and one student at a teachers' college (Lehrerseminar). At the base of the educational pyramid, the party boasted 27 grammar-school teachers.

Another 27 persons were editors or professional writers of one sort or another, mostly political pamphleteers and propagandists. In the business end of the writing profession were 5 publishers and 8 bookdealers. The arts and crafts were well represented with 13 painters, 3 sculptors, an art historian, 7 musicians, 2 photographers, a dramatic director, and 6 full-time actors, 3 poets (or artistic writers), and 5 craftsmen devoted to art.

---

[105] B, I, SA 1, 1486, p. 136; II, MA102140, HMB 246, Schw., p. 7.

[106] Twenty-three members of the lower nobility, 6 barons, 1 count, and 1 prince.

[107] For a chart of occupations see Appendix IC.

[108] Institutions that, although basically "blue-collar" in nature, prepared students for degrees in engineering and allied disciplines.

In the world of industry, business, and agriculture the members of the party were also active on all levels and in all branches of endeavor. Factory owners (almost all on a small scale) were 13 in number. Senior industrial and business administrators numbered 8. Sixteen National Socialists owned shops of one kind or another, of which half were the socially acceptable and financially remunerative pharmacies. Another 11 owned small businesses of various kinds, including bars, boarding houses, and a technical business of undisclosed nature. Fourteen National Socialists were landowners, mostly on a small scale. Four others were professionally trained agricultural specialists and 2 were senior farm administrators. Two more rented farms. Perhaps the one real estate dealer and 3 persons who lived on their personal fortunes also fall into this category.

The largest category of all was that of "white collar workers," for into this group fit best the many persons who called themselves or were called merchants (Kaufmänner). A good number of these could undoubtedly more accurately be termed "sales personnel," being employees rather than independent merchants. There is good evidence in at least some cases of such an upgrading of occupation, and there is also reason to believe that in some cases this designation was a genteel pseudonym for "unemployed." Altogether the "white collar" workers of all levels totalled 242 (121 Kaufmänner).

Skilled workers, particularly strong in the metal trades, came to 230, while unskilled workers numbered 25, and semi-skilled workers came to only 7. Five workers were referred to as factory workers and another 14 were reported simply as "workers." Another 13 were chief clerks or foremen of various kinds, and 22 were semi-professional technicians of varying types.

Twenty-eight engineers and 11 architects belonged to the technical elite of the party with, like the other learned professions, many more to come from the ranks of the students. The official bureaucracy was represented, despite vigorous discouragement on the part of the various governments concerned, by 13 members of the lower bureaucracy, 36 members of the middle bureaucracy, and 21 members of the higher bureaucracy (including judges and judicial apprentices). Another 16 officials, whose level was not indicated, probably belong in the lower categories.

Despite the suggestions from various quarters that many policemen were party members or sympathizers, not many could be positively identified. Only 26 policemen, police employees, or former policemen were present in the sample. Four foresters of various types, 3 employees of the *Reichswehr*, and 20 employees of the NSDAP itself make up a category of special employees, while 22 apprentices of various trades and professions close out the list of masculine members of the party.[109]

Only 32 women were included in the sample, which suggests that women were neither very numerous nor very active in the early party. This conclusion is given further weight by the fact that a good number of the women seem to have been wives of party members, while only 3 were actively involved as agitators or leaders. The women seem to have been mostly either quite elderly or very young. The sample was, however, too small and the accompanying information regarding them was too slight to permit of any serious analysis or comment.

It is clear from all of the above evidence that it is very difficult indeed to see the National Socialist Party as a "one class" party. Instead it emerges as a heterogeneous mixture of people of all classes and all professions and trades.

Both at the time and since, there has been much talk of the role played by military officers in the National Socialist Party, and it therefore seems worthwhile to consider this aspect of the situation in 1923. First, however, terms must be defined and the general situation examined. The basic question is, Who is an officer? This seems foolish, but it is not. Germany had just gone through a world war during which she had mobilized a proportion of her population that has not since been surpassed in size. A very high percentage of the mobilized manpower served in the German army. As a result, practically anyone of moderate intelligence, good health, and education at the high-school completion level (Obersekunde) had a chance at a commission. The opportunities for young men from new social groups to obtain commissions, even in the regular army, had been increasing regularly since at least 1848 and very rapidly in the twentieth century. The mere size of the army ensured this development. The war destroyed all barriers except education and warped this one since a good number of young men without the

---

[109] The occupations of party leaders present the same wide variation as does the membership itself. The 73 Ortsgruppenleiter for whom occupational information is available are, to put it mildly, a "bunte Mischung," and the 30 SA leaders also represent a broad spectrum of occupations. For detailed data on these groups see Appendix id.

proper educational requirements were commissioned for bravery in the field, and a good number more were sent to special short-term courses to complete their secondary education so that they could be commissioned. Therefore, calling a man an "officer" simply because he had been commissioned as a war lieutenant makes as much sense as the American military government's decision to deny a widow a pension in 1945 on the grounds that her husband —who died in the early summer of 1914—was a German general staff officer and therefore a National Socialist.

Consequently, in speaking of officers in the National Socialist Party one must, to inject meaning into the discussion, separate in so far as possible the career officer from the civilian who received a commission during the course of the war and never considered himself to be a soldier as far as his basic career was concerned. Associated with this question is the equally interesting one of the enlisted men in the National Socialist Party, which has never been discussed in any serious way, although it is very significant in any consideration of the National Socialist Party's class composition and its social attitudes. To what extent were enlisted men present and active in the party and what was their status?

Statistics on military status are incomplete but suggestive. First of all, it can be stated on the basis of age alone that very few National Socialists in the sample used were regular officers in the army before World War I. Perhaps 20 fall into this category, out of 162 officers who can be specifically identified. Thirty-nine of the remaining 142 officers are specifically identified as reserve officers, while 103 are of unknown status. The ranks of the National Socialist officers suggest that a high percentage of the remaining 102 were also reservists, since, in view of the many officers accepted into the regular army in the earlier years of World War I, there seems to have been a tapering off of firm commitments in the latter part of the war. Further, simple logic indicates that a good number of these men would have other careers in mind.

A coolness of attitude on the part of regular officers toward the party is also indicated by the rank profile of the former officers in the party. There were in the sample 5 cadets, 67 second lieutenants, 35 first lieutenants, 36 captains, 16 majors, 3 lieutenant-colonels, and no officers above that rank.[110] It therefore seems that glib generalizations about the number of officers in the early party should

[110] Bruno Heinemann, a long-retired general, is an exception here. See Chapter IV for the quite different situation in Bund Bayern und Reich.

be avoided until more serious work is done on the question. At the same time, it is safe to say that officers of field grade rank and even captains did not feel the attraction of the party nearly as strongly as did very junior officers.

The number of identifiable enlisted men in the National Socialist Party and the role they played there is probably more significant than is the role of the officers, because of the fact that the officers were drawn from groups with a leadership tradition as well as considerable advantages in education and morale, and the fact that they received both training and, more important, experience in leadership during the world war. What about the enlisted men and non-commissioned officers? Since men who did not have commissions often said little about their war service or avoided comment on their rank, it was not easy to identify enlisted men, but the ones who were identified are particularly significant, because almost all of them were either leaders in the early party or became leaders in the later party. Thirty-four men were identified as being "other ranks," that is, enlisted men who did not attain the rank of sergeant (Unteroffizier) or higher. Forty-three non-commissioned officers were identified. It is.interesting, but not surprising—when one considers the matter seriously—that these men were not discriminated against in any way, but after all, Adolf Hitler himself had never reached the rank of sergeant and his close companion and financial advisor Max Amann had been a sergeant. It is even more significant, though, and illustrative of the spirit of the NSDAP, that even in the SA former enlisted men were being given officers' posts as early as 1923, despite the presence of officers of the old army in lower posts, and the ex-officers clearly accepted this arrangement. The commander of the SA regiment in München was a former first lieutenant. The commander of the First Battalion was a former lieutenant; his adjutant was a former naval NCO, while his aide (Ordonnanz-Offizier) was a former major. Rudolf Hess, a former lieutenant, was a battalion commander, while his aide was a first lieutenant. Six company commanders were former NCO's and one was a former private, while officers served as platoon leaders, or even in the ranks. Here was an Alice-in-Wonderland world from the viewpoint of a regular army officer, and especially for one of World War I vintage.[111]

These examples, which are not isolated, introduce another aspect

---

[111] NA, SA Rgt. München, 230-a-10/4 2 passim.

of the question of the social composition of the party. This question is: What was the attitude of the party leaders regarding class? Hitler himself was never able to hide his distaste for the upper-middle and noble classes, and it shines through not only in *Mein Kampf* and *Table Talks*, but also in his dealings with persons who were emotionally identified with these classes. Ernst Röhm, himself bourgeois by birth, made no bones about his contempt for the old upper classes,[112] and he was equally frank in his belief in social mobility. In his autobiography he wrote: "If a non-commissioned officer distinguishes himself through exceptional bravery and is able to lead a troop, he should become an officer. These men do not undermine the unity of the Officer Corps. A promotion after the war or on discharge is of value neither to the army nor to the non-commissioned officer."[113] Hitler had a similar positive attitude. In a letter of 13 October 1923, for example, he assured two former Social Democrats that they were welcome in the fold. It was not the misled, but those who misled them who had committed a crime against Germany.[114]

Major Hans Baumann, formerly a battalion commander in Hitler's regiment, accepted the former corporal as his leader as well as his Kriegskamerad—scarcely a caste-oriented view.[115] Similarly, "Böse Christian" Roth, in a speech to a group of former officers in Bamberg immediately after the Putsch, stressed that in the armed forces of the future there would be no place for class privileges, class quarrels, or "court rank" precedence.[116] In the SA oath, each member agreed to eschew class distinctions:

> I promise that I will see in every member of the Sturmabteilung without thought of class, occupation, wealth or poverty, only my brother and true comrade, with whom I feel myself bound in joy and sorrow.[117]

Both the evidence regarding the social composition of the party and that regarding the social attitudes of the leaders indicates clearly that the Social Democrats were partly right when they said that the NSDAP was a party of the déclassé. It was precisely this, but not in the way the Social Democrats meant. The NSDAP was

---

[112] See Chapter IV, Sections I and III above, passim.
[113] Röhm, *Geschichte*, p. 47.   [114] NA, T84, 4, pp. 3652ff.
[115] B, II, MA100425, p. 344.   [116] B, I, GSK 90, pp. 407-08.
[117] Z, 207/52 ED 7, Fasc. III, 23.2.1923.

a party *against class*. For the National Socialists, the German people (Volk) was the primary good and therefore class, which divided or tended to divide the Volk, was bad. Despite their opposition to political democracy, they favored social democracy, and their attitude towards both was shaped by their view of Volk and Reich and by their plans for the future.[118]

VI. *Conclusion*

The NSDAP was something completely new in German history. It was the first political party to seek to appeal to the entire German people regardless of class, religion, or region—and to date it has been the only party to avoid these self-imposed barriers to growth. The National Socialists invited every German to join them, excluding only the half million German Jews—and this exclusion was made on the basis of the National Socialist belief that they were not Germans. Catholic or Protestant, rich or poor, worker or employer, Bavarian or Prussian, all were welcome if they accepted the doctrines of the party and the authority of its leader. Such a party had great natural appeal in a nation welded together against the hostile foreigner by war and defeat, and this appeal was naturally greatest among those whose entire politically-conscious life had been spent in the post-Bismarckian, post-particularist atmosphere of the war and postwar years.

Here was a party that looked to the future, that ignored or denounced all those barriers that had long separated German from German, a party that promised to unite all Germans and lead them into a new and better world, where they would regain what they had lost in the old world and force their enemies to recognize the German place in the sun. It is not surprising that, faced with traditional parties preaching the same divisive doctrines that they had preached in prewar days and concentrating on quarrels that had

---

[118] Ernst Jünger testified in this regard: "Wenn ich den Eindruck hatte, mich in einem Schmelztiegel, an einem Ort der nationalen Einigung zu befinden, so war das nicht unrichtig. Aber es wirkte dahinter noch etwas anderes: die Entdeckung der klassenlosen Gesellschaft mit ihren Konsequenzen, ihrem ungeheuren Anfall an Energie. Sie verwischt die Palette, zerstört die Hierarchien, befreit die einzelnen von ihrer Bindung und saugt sie in ein dynamisches Gefälle ein. Die Masse erkennt ihre Einheit, ihre Gleichheit und sogar ihre Freiheit in einem einzelnen. . . ." Jünger, Ernst, *Jahre der Okkupation*, Stuttgart, 1958, p. 248. See also Hitler on the irrelevance of class (Hitler, *Tischgespräche*, p. 170) and Gürtner on the social heterogeneity of the party (B, II, MA103476, p. 254).

lost their meaning for many Germans, a new party, led by young men and concentrating on problems arising out of the war and postwar world, proved irresistible to large numbers of youths. At the same time, many older men who had changed their outlook during and after the war were also attracted, although they, more cynical and more dubious of easy solutions, did not come to the party in such numbers or with such enthusiasm as did the young men of all classes.

Hitler was, essentially, a new Peter the Hermit, leading his youthful followers on a new crusade against a new heathen—and it was thus that German schoolbooks were later to depict him. As possessed as Joan of Arc he set himself the same task with the same merciless, humorless, desperate enthusiasm and confidence, and, equally enthusiastic, his disciples followed him to the Feldherrn-halle in November 1923 and, ranks thinned temporarily by the loss of waverers, through the lean, hard years that followed.

1. SA demonstrators in early 1923

4.

THE PATRIOTIC BANDS

I. *Introduction*

While the National Socialist Party was the most active and rapidly growing element in the Racist Movement, which formed the center and left of the Patriotic Movement, those elements of the movement outside the NSDAP were much more numerous than those within it, and before the Putsch it was far from clear that the NSDAP would be able to dominate even the left wing, let alone the entire movement. The various elements of this movement, including the SA of the NSDAP (and sometimes the party itself), were grouped together in the eyes of Bavarians of all shades into the Patriotic Bands (Vaterländische Verbände) and the Racist Bands (Völkische Verbände). These Verbände constituted a major force on the Bavarian political scene in 1923.

The Patriotic Bands were basically political paramilitary organizations, although some of them had purely civilian branches, and theoretically one of the most important, Bund Bayern und Reich, was divided into more or less autonomous military and political sub-organizations. In fact, however, the significance of all of them, aside from the NSDAP, lay predominantly in their military potential. It was their military coloration that gave them character and it was their military organization and arms that gave them a political weight well beyond that which their numbers alone would have brought.

There were two basic types of Verbände in Bavaria. The first was native Bavarian organizations, the second was Bavarian branches of national organizations. The first category was the more numerous and significant, but some of the national Verbände also played a very important part in the tumultuous events of 1923 in Bavaria. The most important of the Bavarian organizations were Bund Bayern und Reich, Reichsflagge, and Bund Oberland. The most vigorous and powerful of the national organizations were the

Viking Band (Bund Wiking) and the Young German Order (Jungdeutscher Orden). The Bavarian Verbände had a common origin.
They can all be traced back to the various irregular or semi-official
organizations that suppressed the Communist–Independent Socialist Republic of Councils in Bavaria in the spring of 1919, or to
organizations established to prevent a revival of revolution from
the Left.

Since the more important Bavarian Freikorps, with the partial
exception of Freikorps Oberland, furnished the cadre for the
Reichswehr, the Freikorps were less important in determining the
shape and nature of the Verbände than were the local paramilitary
organizations such as the Home Guard (Einwohnerwehr) or the
Temporary Volunteer Corps (Zeitfreiwilligenkorps). However,
former Freikorps members who were unable to enter the Reichswehr, or refused to do so, helped to flesh out the Verbände and
provided a portion of the leadership.[1] Therefore the Bavarian
Verbände can be seen as the lineal descendants of the Bavarian
Einwohnerwehr, which had been dissolved at the insistence of the
Allies in 1921.[2] The national Verbände were simply the Bavarian
branches of organizations with a broader territorial base. Most of
them suffered in membership and significance because they were
"foreign" and, far more, because the native Verbände had soaked
up most of the available manpower before they arrived on the
scene.

Originally, there was only one Bavarian Verband or Wehrorganisation (Defense Organization), which came to be known as Bund
Bayern und Reich.[3] Dr. Otto Pittinger, a Regensburg physician,
took over the leadership of the new organization, which was
created on the dissolution of the Einwohnerwehr. Apparently the
old leaders, such as Dr. Escherich and Lieutenant-Colonel (Ret.)
Hermann Kriebel, felt that they were too conspicuous and wanted
a "straw man" to head the new organization. Pittinger, however,
had no intention of playing second fiddle to anyone, and, with the
continuing patronage of Dr. von Kahr, he soon made himself the

[1] For the Bavarian Freikorps see Gordon, Harold J., Jr., *The Reichswehr
and the German Republic, 1919-1926*, Princeton, 1957, pp. 42-49, 70-75,
436-38. Hereafter cited as Gordon, *Reichswehr*. B, IV, BuR, Bd. 36, Akt 2,
Anon. Denkschrift (Schad ?), Item 59, p. 1; Item 29, Brief: Pittinger
an Tutschek, 3.1.1924; NA, EAP 105/7, III, pp. 14-15, Kriebel.

[2] Heiden, Konrad, *Der Führer*, New York, 1944, pp. 104-5. Hereafter
cited as Heiden, *Führer*.

[3] Aside from Bund Oberland.

real master of Bayern und Reich. Pittinger was able to maintain the unity of the Wehrorganisation largely because of the insistence of the shrewd and politically acute General von Möhl, commanding general of Wehrkreis VII (Bavaria), that the Reichswehr would deal with only one organization.[4] However, at the end of 1922 Möhl was "kicked upstairs" by the military authorities in Berlin because of his political activities and general intransigence. Without his restraining hand, the vigorous centrifugal forces in Bayern und Reich could no longer be penned up. The result was a rapid secession of significant elements, which became rivals of the mother organization and sometimes of each other.

The immediate cause of the break was a quarrel between Dr. Pittinger and Captain Ernst Röhm, an officer in the headquarters of the Bavarian Reichswehr who occupied a quasi-political, quasi-extra-legal position between the army and the Verbände.[5] The real causes, however, were far deeper and essentially unbridgeable. Then and now, the quarrels among the leaders of the Verbände have often been portrayed as being primarily the result of petty jealousies, greed for power, and personal clashes. Certainly these quarrels and personalities played an important and sometimes unsavory part in the story of the Verbände, but they were really far less significant in splitting the movement asunder than the differences in political outlook, because the latter affected all members, high and low alike. Despite complete agreement on such issues as the primacy of the nation over other values, the evils of parliamentary democracy, the importance of military preparedness, and the need to crush Marxism, and despite at least partial agreement on antisemitism, a wide gulf separated the two poles of the movement, and, as always, an uncertain middle group drifted between them, pulled first this way and then that. The essential difference between the conservatives and moderates in the Verbände and the right radicals was nicely expressed by Lieutenant Colonel (Ret.) August Schad, one of the key military leaders of Bayern und Reich:

Even within the Defense Organization itself a wing soon developed—as early as the summer of 1921—whose political ex-

[4] B, IV, BuR, Bd. 36, Akt 2, Item 59, Anon. Denkschrift (Schad ?), p. 1; Item 29, Brief: Pittinger an Tutschek, 3.1.1924; NA, EAP 105/7, III, pp. 14-15, Kriebel.

[5] See discussion of Reichsflagge and Reichskriegsflagge below for further information on Röhm.

ponents were Röhm-Heiss-Hofmann and Pöhner.[6] This group is distinguished by its inner conviction regarding means. For them revolution is an article of faith. Their slogan is the ending of revolution by counter-revolution.[7]

From the right-radical side, Captain Ernst Röhm agreed:

The "nationals" see in the restoration of the conditions that existed before November 1918 their ideal and their final goal. A "middle-class" government without obvious Marxist influence, the tried and true generals and excellencies in splendid positions, and finally again a king behind whom one may stand (but not before him), in whose sun so many can bask, for whom there is today no place in the state. . . .

In short, that is the dream world of the "nationals." A true idyll for the garden bower! . . .

We nationalists can have no ties with these circles. A world separates us from them.

First, the November Revolution of 1918 is one of the greatest crimes, if not the greatest, that was ever committed in Germany. However, it could not have come if the responsible men had been and remained at their posts. It could not have come had the representatives of the old system not collapsed completely. There can never be a return to the days before 1918 in Germany. . . .

Further, for five years now all the elite excellencies, ministers etc. have been activated to resuscitate Bavaria. The result: confusion and deprivation through the land. We have sunk even deeper.

So, now we revolutionaries say: not the return of the old, the reactionaries, not the musty excellencies and generals can rescue us; we can only be helped by men of action out of all classes, especially the young, the front veterans, who are ready to fight and are filled with patriotism and fanaticism.[8]

An eventual break was natural and, especially from the viewpoint of the right radicals, desirable as well as necessary. However,

---

[6] Pöhner was a former police president of München and a vigorous, though relatively conservative, right radical. Röhm, Heiss, and Hofmann will be discussed later in this chapter.

[7] B, IV, BuR, Bd. 36, Akt 2, Item 59, p. 2 (Schad ?).

[8] Röhm, *Geschichte*, pp. 278-80.

it seems to have come prematurely as a result of the intrigues of that indefatigable but cautious revolutionary, General Ludendorff, who had taken up his abode in Bavaria after the collapse of the Kapp Putsch.[9]

Ludendorff's influence on the right radicals laid the groundwork, but the actual break arose over problems of money and competence. Pittinger accused Röhm of misappropriating goods and monies which he was administering for the Bavarian state, the Reichswehr, and Bund Bayern und Reich.[10] Röhm riposted with accusations of cowardice and unpatriotic behavior against Pittinger. The upshot was that by early 1923, Röhm and his friend Captain Heiss had taken their followers out of the Bund and formed them into an independent organization, Reichsflagge. Their ally, Alfred Zeller, followed suit with his Patriotic Ward Organizations of Munich (Vaterländische Bezirksvereine Münchens—VVM), while Lieutenant Colonel Hofmann officially remained in Bayern und Reich but declared his provincial organization, Niederbayern, to be autonomous. The division of the Racist Movement in Bavaria had now been accomplished along ideological lines, setting the stage for a struggle that would continue in one form or another for years to come.[11]

II. *The Verbände Groupings in 1923*

After the split in Bund Bayern und Reich most of the Verbände fell into one of two categories, right radical or right monarchist (whether reactionary or moderate), although there were some groups that did not fit clearly into either category, such as Stahlhelm or Orgesch. The right radical organizations fell into the sphere of influence of one of two umbrella organizations, or associations of Verbände: the Working Group of the Combat Organizations (Arbeitsgemeinschaft der Kampfverbände) and the Ehrhardt organization, which had no specific name. Bund Bayern und Reich was its own umbrella organization, as a result of its size and the na-

---

[9] B, IV, BuR, Bd. 36, Akt 2, Item 59, Anon. Denkschrift (Schad ?), pp. 2-3; Bd. 35, Akt 3, Item 21, Brief: Pittinger an Kahr (?), 9.2.23; NA, EAP 1-e-16/4, Epp Denkschrift, 22.3.23; Frank, Walter, *Franz Ritter von Epp*, Hamburg, 1934, p. 108. Hereafter cited as Frank, *Epp*.

[10] For further information on this matter see Chapter VI, Section VI, below.

[11] B, IV, BuR, Bd. 36, Akt 2, Item 59, anon. Denkschrift (Schad ?), *passim*; NA, EAP 1-e-16/4, Epp Denkschrift, 22.3.23; Section III below.

ture of its organization. Finally, the United Patriotic Bands of Bavaria (Vereinigte Vaterländische Verbände Bayerns—VVVB) operated as a competitive organization, seeking to unite all patriotic rightist organizations, whether paramilitary or civilian. The VVVB was founded in the summer of 1922. By early 1923, it was clear that it had very little serious power and not too much influence. As compared with the Verbände organizations or the NSDAP it was too weakly organized and its membership too disparate to be much more than a propaganda organ. Dr. Hermann Bauer, its leader, was the reverse of President Theodore Roosevelt: he walked and talked loudly and carried a very small stick. He was not able to take any action without the assent of the leaders of his organizations, which were unlikely to agree on many theoretical or practical points, since they covered the entire spectrum of the Racist Movement.[12] As a result, the VVVB played a noisy but insignificant part in the political struggle for power in Bavaria in 1923-24, even though some of its constituent organizations were both active and important.[13]

The most important right radical roof organization was the Arbeitsgemeinschaft, the name of which was later changed to Kampfbund. The Arbeitsgemeinschaft was apparently formed in January 1923, shortly after the NSDAP left the VVVB as a result of Hitler's refusal to support the Reich government's passive resistance to the French occupation of the Ruhr. The Arbeitsgemeinschaft included the NSDAP, the Patriotic Ward Organizations of München (Vaterländische Bezirksvereine Münchens—usually referred to as VVM), Bund Oberland, Reichsflagge, Bund Unterland (or Niederbayern), and the Zeitfreiwilligenkorps München

---

[12] In April 1923, the following organizations belonged to the VVVB: Alldeutscher Verband, Andreas Hoferbund für Tyrol, Bayerischer Heimat- und Königsbund, Bayerischer Kriegerbund, Bayerischer Ordnungsblock, Bund Bayern und Reich, Deutschnationaler Jugendbund, Deutscher Offiziersbund, Deutschvölkische Arbeitsgemeinschaft, Düll-Verband (VV Schwabing-Ost), Eichheimer Ärztebund, Frontkriegerbund, Hochschulring Deutscher Art, Interessengemeinschaft deutscher Heeres- und Marineangehöriger, Jung-Bayern, Nationalverband deutscher Offiziere, Reichsverband akademischer Kriegsteilnehmer, Verband bayerischer Offiziers- und Regimentsvereine, Verband nationalgesinnter Soldaten, Schutz- und Trutzbund, Zentralverband deutscher Kriegsbeschädigter.

[13] B, I, M. Inn. 73685, PDM, Abt. vɪd 1637; GSK 101, p. 24; GSK 100, p. 24; ɪɪ, MA100425, Brief: 19.7.1923; MA103476, pp. 56, 1033; ɪv, BuR, Bd. 35, Akt 3, Neue Heimatlandsbriefe, 20.4.1923.

(sometimes called Organisation Lenz). The organization of the Arbeitsgemeinschaft was loose and decisions were made in conferences of the leaders, which took place regularly. Former Justice Minister Roth, unkindly dubbed "Böse Christian" by his foes, was the propaganda chief, while Lieutenant Colonel (Ret.) Hermann Kriebel, the former chief of staff of the Einwohnerwehr, was the military leader. Walther Hemmeter, of Bund Wiking, was appointed second secretary with the right to speak at meetings but not to vote (apparently because Wiking was not a member of the Arbeitsgemeinschaft). Captain (Ret.) Wilhelm Weiss was also included in the Arbeitsgemeinschaft leadership council, apparently because his periodical, *Heimatland*, was to be the official press organ of the group.[14]

After the May Day debacle,[15] several organizations dropped out of the Arbeitsgemeinschaft. The guiding committee of the VVM was forced to resign because the bulk of the district leaders would not accept its right radical policy. The main body of the organization then left the Arbeitsgemeinschaft, while a rump group, led by Alfred Zeller, remained under the name Kampfbund München.[16] The Zeitfreiwilligenkorps was so badly divided over the May Day affair that its leader, Colonel (Ret.) Lenz, resigned, and the organization dropped out of the Arbeitsgemeinschaft, changing its name to Hermannsbund.[17]

The remaining, hard core Verbände stayed in the Arbeitsgemeinschaft until it was replaced by the Kampfbund in September 1923. The Kampfbund (or Kampfgemeinschaft Bayern) was a narrower and tighter organization than its predecessor and reflected Hitler's rise within the organization. It originally contained only Oberland, Reichsflagge, and the SA of the NSDAP. The directory of the Kampfbund consisted of Captain Heiss, Hitler, and Dr. Weber of Oberland. Kriebel was still military leader. Dr. Max von Scheubner-Richter, a member of the NSDAP, was general manager (Bevollmächtiger), Captain Weiss was business manager. Hitler was soon officially appointed political leader. Since the Kampfbund was exclusively a paramilitary organization, the NSDAP as such

---

[14] B, II, MA103476, pp. 51, 95-101; *BLV*, 1922-23, 8, Auer, Th. (BVP), 5.6.23, p. 319.

[15] See Chapter VIII, Section II.

[16] B, II, MA103476, p. 1390; NA, T120, 5569, pp. K591396-97.

[17] B, II, MA103476, pp. 129-31; NA, Epp Papers, EAP 1-e-16/4, Lenz Erlass, 14.5.23.

did not belong to it; only the SA did. Thus Hitler was in a position to wield decisive influence within the Kampfbund, while the Kampfbund exercised no direct influence on his party.[18]

In early October, after Hitler refused to support Generalstaatskommissar von Kahr,[19] serious tensions developed within Reichsflagge which resulted in a geographical split. The north Bavarian Reichsflagge remained loyal to Captain Heiss, withdrew from the Kampfbund, and supported Kahr. The southern Bavarian organizations remained in the Kampfbund, with Captain Röhm as their leader, and adopted the name Reichskriegsflagge. Meanwhile, Kampfbund München entered the Kampfbund, which had now achieved its final form.[20]

Less significant in Bavaria was the Ehrhardt group of Verbände, which was apparently rather loosely integrated. The primary organization of the group, the Wiking Bund, served as the central organization. The group consisted of Wiking itself, the Blücher Bund, Bund Frankenland, and the Bavarian branch of Jungdo. The unifying factor here was the person of Lieutenant Commander (Ret.) Hermann Ehrhardt. The other Verbände of his group were all small and only Blücher had a claim to being more than local in nature.

III. *The Verbände*

Below the roof organizations came the individual Verbände, most of which jealously guarded their individuality and reserved the right to secede from the various groupings at will.

Next to the SA of the NSDAP, Bund Oberland is the most important Kampfbund group. It was a paramilitary Verband descended from the Freikorps of the same name. Like the Freikorps, Bund Oberland had a checkered career. In late 1922, Dr. Friedrich Weber, an instructor in veterinary medicine at the university in München was appointed leader of the Bund by court order after an acrimonious struggle for control of the organization. Brigadier General (Ret.) Aechter was the military leader of the Bund, while General Ludendorff stood in the wings with advice and counsel. These leaders brought Oberland into a close alliance with the

[18] NA, T84, 4, p. 3183; NA, EAP 105/7, II, pp. 3, 5; Röhm, *Geschichte*, pp. 210-13, 215.

[19] See Chapter IX, Section II, below.

[20] B, I, GSK 43, p. 17, BuR Intelligence Report; NA, T120, 5569, p. K591551; NA, SA Rgt. München, 230-a-10/3 1, RKF Mitteilungsblatt 1.

NSDAP, which endured until after the Beer Hall Putsch.[21] Other important figures in Oberland were Eugen Meyding, a legal interne; "Captain" Ludwig Oestreicher (a former protégé of the SPD leader, Alwin Saenger), whose background and right to the rank he claimed were both somewhat cloudy; and Professor Dr. J. V. Mulzer, a former captain in the army.[22]

Oberland was controlled by a board of directors (Vorstand) and a number of central officers. Its political organization broke down into district offices (Kreisstellen in Bavaria, or Landesstellen elsewhere), county offices (Bezirksstellen),[23] and local groups (Ortsgruppen). The military organization went from the central headquarters (Militärische Leitung) to battalions, companies, platoons, etc. München boasted four (very understrength) battalions by October 1923, while most contingents elsewhere seem to have been far smaller, although Bamberg had a battalion.[24]

It is difficult to get a clear picture of the size and distribution of a secret or semi-secret organization like Bund Oberland. However, it is clear that it had members and Ortsgruppen throughout Germany and Austria, and that the areas of main concentration were Bavaria and Upper Silesia.[25] Figures from Oberland records in 1922 indicate a membership of only a few hundred men, but they probably refer only to Bavaria, or, very possibly, only to München. In any case, the Bund grew rapidly in 1923 and certainly must have numbered some 2,000 men in Bavaria by November 1923.[26] It seems to have been particularly strong in the Bavarian highlands south of München.[27]

---

[21] B, I, SA 1, 1662, Amtsgericht Aktenzeichen 1989/21; II, MA100428, *MAA* 23, 24.1.1925; NA, EAP 105/7, II, p. 4, Dr. Weber.

[22] B, I, GSK 43, p. 281; SA 1, 1493, p. 52; II, MA100423, p. 8; MA100428, *MAA* 23, 24.1.25; IV, OPA 1190/I "Akt Oestreicher"; NA, EAP 105/7, II, pp. 8-9, Dr. Weber.

[23] A number of the Verbände reflect in their organization the old Bavarian administrative system, where the Kreis was on a level with the Bezirk in north Germany.

[24] B, II, MA103476, pp. 1122-23; IV, Lapo, Bd. 26a, Akt 3, Item 8.

[25] For the purposes of this study the Upper Silesian contingent is irrelevant.

[26] Spotty reports from BuR sources indicated 772 members of Oberland in Bavaria outside Oberbayern.

[27] B, I, SA 1, 1662, Bd. Oberland Tgb. 89/22; Brief: Dahn an Amtsgericht München, 8.9.1922; GSK 44, p. 190; II, MA101249, Rk. O. In. 99, p. 22; MA102140, HMB 11, 3.1.1923, p. 2; HMB 816, Ofr., pp. 9-10;

The social composition of Oberland is also difficult to ascertain with any certainty. The very scanty data at hand, however, suggest that there was at least some truth to Dr. Weber's claim that it united men of all classes of society, and also that, as he did not indicate, it united honest and enthusiastic men with others of criminal tendencies. In speaking of Freikorps Oberland as it was in 1919, General Ritter von Haack, to whom it was then subordinated, later wrote:

This Freikorps had an unusual composition at the time of the München fighting. In large part it consisted of educated and generally unexceptionable young people, who had joined up for idealistic reasons, but in part it consisted of criminals who wanted nothing more than plunder. . . .[28]

This odd mixture seems to have continued to exist to some extent in the successor organization, a situation to which the participation in 1921 of Oberland in the campaign against the Poles in Upper Silesia contributed, since here, too, students and working-class youths found themselves cheek by jowl with hardened adventurers and professional freebooters, the sort of carrion hunters who are always attracted by disorder and are to be found—especially in the rear echelons—in any army in the field. Dr. Weber, not an entirely unprejudiced witness, described this "melting pot" in glowing terms at his trial after the Putsch:

. . . We were then greatly surprised, indeed shaken, when we found in the ranks of Oberland miners from the Ruhr in peaceful cooperation with Bavarian and München workers and Bavarian and München students. It was a revelation for us that something like this was again possible in 1921, after two and a half years of revolution. . . .[29]

The less fortunate side of this phenomenon was seen by the state commissioner for public security, who remarked in December of 1923 that in Upper Silesia a good number of these men later committed crimes (probably a good portion of which were political in

HMB 763, Obb., pp. 4-5; MA103476, pp. 1025-26; IV, BuR, Bd. 35, Akt 3, Fragebogen.
[28] B, IV, Handschrift 428 (Haack).
[29] NA, EAP 105/7, II, p. 4, Dr. Weber.

nature). Since he noted that many of the workers in Oberland were former Communists, it seems safe to say that the violence advocated by extreme leftists helped hone a still sharper edge to the radicalism of the extreme Right.[30]

In 1923, Oberland still seemed strong on students and their butterfly form, the free and learned professions, as well as on government officials of all levels, and on white-collar workers (especially bank clerks) together with some workers.[31] Most of its military leaders were young former officers, many of whom were students in 1923. Higher officers were few and far between. Only three nobles and two Protestants were among its easily identified members. The age pattern of the organization seems similar. Aside from such patriarchs as the military leader, General Adolf Aechter, and the publisher, J. F. Lehmann, the father-in-law of Dr. Weber and a probable financial angel of the Bund, even the highest leaders were only in their mid-thirties or younger and the largest concentration of ages was in the twenties. Here, as in the Nazi Party, one can almost hear the warning of today's New Left: "Don't trust anyone over thirty!"[32]

A good number of Oberländer had had combat experience either in World War I, or in Bavaria in 1919, or in Upper Silesia in 1921, Practically all of the Oberland officers had been officers during the war, although the younger ones had probably been commissioned less than a year in November 1918. On the other hand, despite various efforts to train and exercise their "week-end warriors," the disagreements on this score with the military authorities and the Bavarian government[33] greatly complicated the officers' problems. Then too, Oberland apparently, like most of the Verbände, suffered seriously from a shortage of specialist officers and key non-commissioned officers. It therefore seems safe to say that the Oberland

[30] B, II, MA101249, Rk. O. In. 99, p. 22.

[31] This statement and the following remarks are based on fragmentary data on approximately 125 Oberländer, mostly leaders, as well as on widely scattered evidence and the testimony of Professor Hans Fehn, then a student at Erlangen.

[32] Among those on whom appropriate information is available, there was one brigadier general, one colonel, two lieutenant colonels, nine majors, nine captains, nine first lieutenants and thirteen second lieutenants. This list includes most of the senior officers in the organization but only a small fraction of the junior ones.

[33] See Chapter VI, Section V, below.

troops were not prepared either psychologically or militarily for heavy combat.

Where weapons were concerned, Oberland apparently was comparatively well off, especially in the south, since there were great numbers of weapons stored in Oberbayern, which was the Bund's home base. However, there is good reason to think that many of these weapons were not usable and that many types needed for arming modern military units were not present in suitable numbers. Also, it is clear that in some areas—Bamberg for example—the Bund was short of weapons in general. On the other hand, the Oberländer claimed to have heavy artillery pieces and ammunition, which the army did not possess.

A further limitation on the armament of the Bund was the fact that, in München, by the fall of 1923, many of Oberland's arms were in the hands of the Reichswehr in view of the need for maintenance and security. In general, it seems safe to say that Oberland had enough arms to be able to wage war against leftist rebels or against other Verbände, or to support a low level guerrilla war against regular troops, but that shortages of heavy weapons and, especially, ammunition, would make protracted heavy combat impossible without effective support from the Reichswehr, even if other factors were favorable. This liability would be greatly increased if the Bund were unable to recover possession of the arms held by the Reichswehr.[34]

Where aims are concerned, Oberland fell clearly into the ranks of the right radical organizations, which did not want to turn back the clock or even to maintain the existing situation, but to create a new Germany in which class distinctions would fade before national unity. The Bund was "grossdeutsch" rather than particularist in outlook and saw the salvation of Germany in the destruction of Jewish and Marxist influence and the smashing of the Treaty of Versailles by means of a reckoning with France.[35]

Reichsflagge, because of its division into two organizations in the

[34] B, ɪɪ, MA103476, pp. 1005-6, 1021-22; ɪv, Lapo, Bd. 26, Akt 1, Stadtkomm. Bamburg 497 DJ, p. 7; Bd. 26a, Akt 3, Lapo Kdo. Bamberg 2866, Item 8; Akt 5, Gr. Sch. ɪɪɪc, Erfahrungsbericht Lapo Coburg, Chef J 361g, Beilage 1, pp. 1-2; BuR, Bd. 35, Akt 5, Items 35/2, 50/4; Bd. 36, Akt 2, Item 42, pp. 5-6.

[35] NA, EAP 105/7, ɪɪ, pp. 4-7, Dr. Weber; T84, 4, pp. 3369; B, ɪɪ, MA102140, HMB 11, Ofr.; ɪv, BuR, Bd. 35, Akt 3, Brief: Oberleitung an Iversen, 7.6.1923.

fall of 1923, is considered after the split, since some of the different social characteristics within its diverging segments probably helped to create the tensions leading to divorce. Captain (Ret.) Adolf Heiss, who had left the army in early 1923 rather than give up his political activity, was the dominant figure in Reichsflagge. Not surprisingly, he ran it on military principles and with a staff composed largely of former officers, of whom Major (Ret.) Gross was the military specialist and Major (Ret.) Knoll the political specialist. Under this staff, the Verband was divided into local political groups (Ortsgruppen), which were subdivided into military units, student organizations, and youth organizations.[36]

Reichsflagge was limited to north Bavaria after the loss of Röhm's southern contingent. Ortsgruppen were to be found in the provinces (Regierungsbezirke) of Oberfranken, Mittelfranken, and Oberpfalz, with a particular concentration in Mittlefranken, where Reichsflagge was probably the strongest Verband, a position it clearly held in Nürnberg.[37] Some indication of the strength of Reichsflagge is provided by contemporary estimates that it had 3,500 men in the Erlangen area (probably including Nürnberg) and 462 in the Oberpfalz.[38]

Specific information on the social composition of Reichsflagge personnel is difficult to uncover. There are, however, enough scattered materials to indicate that Reichsflagge was considerably different in make-up than Oberland or than its own daughter, Reichskriegsflagge (RKF). In 1924 Police Director Gareis of Nürnberg indicated that Reichsflagge had "very many officers," giving this as one of the reasons why right radical elements broke away from it during 1923. Another indication of social composition is found in Major (Ret.) Karl Winneberger's plaint that all the patriotic industrialists in Nürnberg were members of Reichsflagge and that his Ortsgruppe of Bayern und Reich was therefore left with practically no money sources. Both of these statements carry with them the implication that Reichsflagge represented the upper middle class and the more conservative elements in the Racist Movement, and they also carry implications that the membership was older than that of Oberland or the SA. However, until more data on the

---

[36] NA, EAP 105/7a, RW Bericht vom Putsch; Epp Papers, EAP 1-e-16/2, Org. Skizze und "Reichsflagge"; B, I, SA 1, 1450, Item 100.

[37] B, II, MA102140, HMB 87, M/F; 1153; 1501; 1963; HMB 2201, Ofr.; 2407; HMB 194, Opf.; 346; 795; IV, BuR, Bd. 36, Akt 1, Item 14/3.

[38] B, IV, BuR, Bd. 35, Akt 3, Antworten auf Fragebogen 2.

membership of Reichsflagge in this crucial period become available, the extent of these differences can only be a matter of speculation.[39]

Reichsflagge, which had close ties with the local police authorities and the provincial president in Mittelfranken, had large stores of arms and found it relatively easy to keep them. Little information is available on the character and condition of these arms. It must, in general, be assumed that they were mostly infantry weapons, since the location of heavy weapons was watched with considerable interest and some apprehension by both military and civil authorities.[40]

In aims, Reichsflagge straddled the conservative and right radical positions. On the one hand it wanted the re-establishment of a German empire under the colors black-white-red, while on the other it subscribed to a number of right radical views, opposing party politics, emphasizing the value of the nation and German unity, and accepting an antisemitic, racist position. It was grossdeutsch, rather than Bavarian particularist in tone. The anti-Catholic tendency, natural enough in Protestant Franken, was as characteristic of the right radicals as it was of traditional Protestantism, and this aspect of the position is given additional weight by the linking of Catholicism with separatism in the Reichsflagge propaganda against Bund Bayern und Reich.[41]

Unlike Reichsflagge, Reichskriegsflagge was a veritable prototype of the right radical paramilitary organization. It was formed when Captain Heiss, apparently rather reluctantly, decided to leave Hitler's Kampfbund and support Kahr in October 1923. The real leader of Reichskriegsflagge was Captain Röhm, but, since increasing pressure was being placed on army officers, even in Bavaria, to get out of politics, he operated through straw men. Captain (Ret.) Joseph Seydel was his closest and senior representative in the Verband, as he had been in Röhm's armament activities. Lieutenant (Ret.) Karl Osswald, the leader of the assault detachment of the München Ortsgruppe, was another key figure in Reichs-

[39] B, II, MA101235, PDN-7 3822/II, p. 33; IV, BuR, Bd. 36, Akt 1, Item 35, Brief: Winneberger an Reinmöller; GP, D, 1 (Personalities).

[40] B, II, MA100411, PDN-F 319/II Abschrift; MA102140, HMB 2174, M/F; IV, BuR, Bd. 36, Akt 1, Tr. Insp. an Bdltg., 25.11.1923.

[41] NA, Epp Papers, EAP 1-e-16/2, "Reichsflagge"; B, II, MA102140, HMB 11, Ofr.; IV, BuR, Bd. 35, Akt 3, Zur Lage, 22.3.1923; Bd. 36, Akt 1, RF Ldltg., Item 35, Tagesbefehl, 16.11.23.

kriegsflagge. In the "provinces," Künanz was the Augsburg leader, and Emil Bäuerle led in Memmingen, while Heinrich Himmler's friend, Heinrich Gärtner, was the chief in Schleissheim.[42]

Reichskriegsflagge was organized into units by function. The men of fighting age with some military training were organized into a Sturmabteilung, the active fighting force of Reichskriegsflagge. Within the assault detachment, Gruppe Stark, led by Captain Wilhelm Stark of the Landespolizei, was made up primarily of active soldiers and policemen. Young men without military training were placed in the Rekrutenabteilung and were trained together. Older men were gathered together in Captain (Ret.) Freiherr Hildolf von Thüngen's Stammabteilung. Finally, a semi-autonomous organization, Battery Lembert, which had seceded from Oberland, was included in RKF. It was led by Lieutenant (Ret.) Walther Lembert, who had been commissioned in 1919 by the Social Democratic war minister, Schneppenhorst.[43]

RKF was a comparatively small organization. It had four Ortsgruppen: München, Augsburg, Memmingen, and Schleissheim, and only a few hundred members. Exact figures for the Verband are not available, but Captain Röhm claimed over 300 members for the München Ortsgruppe in October of 1923. A membership list captured by the police after the Beer Hall Putsch, however, suggests that he padded its strength, since the card file held only 170 names. The Ortsgruppe in Memmingen was later reported to have had 70 members in November 1923, while no figures are available for either Augsburg or Schleissheim. It therefore seems that the strength of the Verband was between 250 and 500 men.[44]

Although Röhm claimed that RKF was a healthy mixture of all classes and social groups, the fragmentary evidence available re-

---

[42] NA, SA Rgt. München, 230-a-10/3 1, RKF Mitteilungsblatt 1, 15.10.23; B, I, GSK 43, p. 17, BuR Intell. Bericht; Röhm, *Geschichte*, pp. 219-24. Hofmann errs in his identification of Seydel as an active Reichswehr officer in 1923. (See Hofmann, Hanns Hubert, *Der Hitlerputsch*. München, 1961, p. 75. Hereafter cited as Hofmann, *Hitlerputsch*.) Like most FZ employees he was a former officer. B, I, GSK 7, pp. 5ff; GSK 90, pp. 8-9; Reichswehrministerium, ed. *Rangliste des Deutschen Reichsheeres. Nach dem Stande vom 1. April 1923*, Berlin, n.d. (1923) p. 137. Hereafter cited as *Rangliste 1923*.

[43] B, I, SA 1, 1493, pp. 46-48; 1633, p. 514; II, MA103476, p. 1315; Röhm, *Geschichte*, pp. 222-23.

[44] B, I, SA 1, 1634, pp. 603-4; 1635, PDM via 2410/24, p. 765; Röhm, *Geschichte*, p. 222.

garding it does not support this claim. These figures, and such testimony as exists on the nature of the organization, indicate that RKF was one of the most homogeneous of the Verbände, and that its social base was perhaps the narrowest. The members were primarily young men of the middle class. In the 40 cases where the occupations of individuals (mostly leaders) can be ascertained, the distribution confirms this general impression: 3 professional officers (still serving or with most of a career in the army), one non-commissioned officer, 4 members of the middle middle class, 4 members of the free professions, 6 officials (including policemen), 8 white collar workers (mostly bank clerks), one worker, 12 students, one large landowner, and one unemployed bank clerk. In the 47 cases where the ages of RKF men are known, 33 are in their twenties, 7 in their thirties, and only 5 are older, although the group includes the bulk of the senior leadership. Naturally enough, a good proportion of these men seem to have been unmarried. Equally naturally, while a good number of the leaders of Reichskriegsflagge had been officers during the war, very few of them held high rank: one lieutenant-colonel, 2 majors, 5 captains, 12 lieutenants and first lieutenants, one cadet.[45]

Captain Röhm was enthusiastic about the training and discipline of his organization and claimed that inspections were held nearly every day. It is probably true that RKF, with its many students and considerable number of military employees working under Röhm's direction, had more chance for drill than did many of the other Verbände, but it is very dubious that this training went much beyond the "school of the soldier" type of individual training in view of the circumstances and the training personnel. Arms and equipment were no serious problem, since Röhm disposed of great quantities of both until shortly before the Putsch and remained in close contact with the secret semi-official ordnance organization even after he ceased to control it directly.[46]

Reichskriegsflagge saw itself as an entirely military organization with nationalist aims. It recognized "no superiority of birth, position, class or possession,"[47] and it adopted the revolutionary position of the Kampfbund as its own.[48]

Very little concrete information is available regarding Kampf-

---

[45] GP, D, 1 (Personalities).

[46] NA, T79, 72, pp. 1075-76, 1142; B, IV, BuR, Bd. 36, Akt 4, Geschäftseinteilung (FZ), Feb. 1922; Röhm, *Geschichte*, p. 223.

[47] *Ibid.*   [48] See Chapter IX, Section I, below.

bund München. In essence, it was identical with the VVM, of which it was so long a part, so that the discussion of VVM covers it—except for the fact that it was slightly more right radical in attitude than the other ward organizations. Formed in the early fall of 1923, it consisted of the former VVM organizations of the seventh and twelfth wards, both political and military.[49]

Almost as radical as the Kampfbund Verbände were those associated with Lieutenant Commander Ehrhardt, which sometimes cooperated with the Kampfbund and were overtly hostile to the Republic. Bund Wiking was the direct descendant of the Second Marine Brigade (or Brigade Ehrhardt), one of the most effective of the Freikorps of 1919-20. After its official dissolution, many of its members held together and continued to serve their "chief" in this paramilitary organization. The Bund was a national organization and was comparatively weak in Bavaria, despite the intermittent presence of its outlawed leader. Commander Ehrhardt had been imprisoned in Leipzig awaiting trial as a Kappist, but on his escape returned to Bavaria in the early fall of 1923, where he was tolerated by the authorities. However, Lieutenant Senior Grade (Ret.) Eberhard Kautter, a student at the University in München, was the man through whom Ehrhardt normally operated in directing Bund Wiking. Most of the other leaders in Bavaria were also apparently students. Certainly, those in München were. Among the most active leaders were Walther Hemmeter, a law student, Hans Engelhardt, an agricultural student, and Major (Ret.) Kurt Kühme, a senior military leader and one of the few non-students.[50]

In theory at least, Bund Wiking in Bavaria was divided into four districts: north, middle, south, and central (München).[51] However, there is little evidence of activity outside of München and the northern border districts during 1923, so that much of this organization may have been a mere skeleton without flesh. This weakness on Bavarian soil was compensated for in a high degree by Ehrhardt's ability to stamp paramilitary units out of the ground wherever he might want them by summoning his lieutenants to

[49] B, I, SA 1, 1633, Zeller, p. 511; GP, D, 1 (Personalities), 2 (Organizations). See also VVM below.

[50] B, I, SA 1, 1665, Auszug vom Sitzungsbericht, 28.4.1923, p. 5; GSK 43, pp. 64ff; Kahr MS, pp. 1266-68; GP, A, Ehrhardt Brief, 25.11.1958; Freksa, Friedrich, Hsg, *Kapitän Ehrhardt*, Berlin, 1924, pp. 214-31, 319-46. Hereafter cited as Freksa, *Ehrhardt*.

[51] B, IV, Lapo, Bd. 17, Akt 4, Befehl, 6.12.1923.

bring their contingents to a designated spot, and by his ability to gather volunteers by the magic of his name. Since Wiking included a high percentage of officers with combat experience, the individual volunteers could be absorbed with ease to form a relatively effective paramilitary force considerably larger than the basic organization.[52]

Since the organization was banned in much of the Reich and frowned upon even in Bavaria, precise data on its strength and social composition are not readily available. From general information and from data on 110 specific members (mostly leaders) of Wiking, it seems safe to say that the basic cadre of the organization still consisted of former naval officers and enlisted men, but a very considerable number of right radical former army officers and students had been added since 1919, so that in the lower leadership army officers outnumbered naval officers in the available sample. The almost strictly paramilitary nature of the organization is indicated by the fact that although only fragmentary data are available for the sample of 110 members, 69 can be identified as former officers. It was also an organization of young men, with only 10 members clearly identifiable as being over 30 years of age, while 45 were almost certainly younger. Most of the identifiable members were drawn from the upper or middle classes, with an occasional worker as leaven, but since these men were mostly leaders of the Bund, the social composition at lower levels remains unclear. Ehrhardt himself said, many years later, that he had approximately 10,000 men in his national organization in 1923, but this probably includes allied Verbände and may well be somewhat inflated.[53]

Bund Wiking was armed only with light weapons, most of which came from hidden arsenals of the organization, although Lieutenant Commander Wilhelm Canaris, already active in naval intelligence and similar areas, provided further weapons and money when necessary. Ehrhardt also collected money from industrialists, allegedly for Kahr, but Kahr and company claim not to have received it.[54]

Ehrhardt's aims and those of his organization are not entirely clear, but it is certain that he still took a right radical position in

[52] See Chapter IX, Section VI.
[53] NA, EAP 105/7a, WKK 34375/Ib 6285 v. 27.11.1923; GP, A, Ehrhardt Brief, 25.11.1958; Freksa, Ehrhardt, passim. GP, D, 1 (Personalities).
[54] GP, A, Ehrhardt Briefe, 25.11.1958; 4.5.1959; B, II, MA103476, pp. 758-60.

1923 and was hostile to the Republic and all its works. Wiking was therefore anti-Marxist and anti-republican, and there is a good deal of evidence that Ehrhardt was planning a revolt against the Republic throughout the summer and fall of the year, although nothing came of these plans.[55]

Bund Blücher was originally formed in August or September of 1922 as "Bund Treu-Oberland," as a result of differences of opinion and the clash of personalities in Bund Oberland. Early in 1923, it adopted the name "Blücher." Rudolf Schaefer, a government architect, was the key leader of Bund Blücher and effectively dominated it.[56] The other leaders of the organization stood very much in his shadow.[57] Blücher was never a large organization and seems to have been confined chiefly to the provinces of Oberbayern, Mittelfranken, and Oberfranken.[58] Fragmentary evidence suggests that its leaders were mostly drawn from the middle class, especially small tradesmen. A number were former officers.[59]

Blücher, like its parent organization and like the other Ehrhardt organizations, was racist and activist, as is indicated by the following excerpt from a statement of purpose issued in September 1923:

The Bavarian proclamation of the state of emergency undoubtedly was aimed at preventing a special Bavarian revolt and had this temporary result. This is doubtless to be welcomed in view of the general Bavarian governmental relationships, under which the Patriotic Movement can in general grow and develop undisturbed. For the *undisturbed* and powerful development of the armed Patriotic Movement in *Bavaria* offers the most dependable basis for a successful rising throughout Germany.

Such a rising is, as should be generally known, the first and foremost aim of our formation. We want, and the state of emer-

[55] Blome, Dr. Kurt, *Arzt im Kampf*, Leipzig, 1942, pp. 156-61. Hereafter cited as Blome, *Arzt*. B, II, MA103476, pp. 758-60, 861, 896; Freksa, *Ehrhardt*, pp. 213-14.

[56] A dissident group that resented Schaefer's dominance formed a very small organization called Landbund Blücher in 1923, but it never had any significance. B, II, MA100411, PDM to Reichskomm., 11.9.1923; MA102140, HMB 837, Obb., p. 4; *BLV*, 1922-23, 8, pp. 334-35, Auer (SPD), 6.6.1923.

[57] B, II, MA100446, Anz. Verz. XIX 73/23, Proz. Reg. 468/23, pp. 1, 17, 128-29; MA102140, HMB 226, Obb., pp. 1-2.

[58] Only in these provinces did the Reg. Präsidenten report Blücher activity during 1923.

[59] Gp, D, 1 (Personalities).

gency does not prevent us from so declaring, a *German* up-
heaval, a racist revolution throughout Germany.[60]

It is thus clear that Blücher took a national rather than particularist
position in the fall of 1923. However, its national credentials were
not entirely clear and unequivocal. Leading figures of the Blücherbund were involved in the Fuchs-Machhaus "Danube monarchy"
plot,[61] and it is not absolutely certain that, as they claimed, they
were involved merely to obtain evidence against the plotters—or
even to get money from the French government, although they
seem to have tapped French intelligence funds fairly successfully.
Ernst Röhm, not always a dependable witness, has accused
Schaefer of being prepared to go ahead with the separatists until he
found that he had "blown their cover" in approaching Röhm and
Freiherr von Freyberg of the Bavarian Ministry of the Interior.
However, after the separatist debacle in the summer of 1923, there
is no doubt that Blücherbund stood squarely on the program stated
above.[62]

Bund Frankenland, another of Ehrhardt's satellite organizations,
was a small, local group. Confined to the area around Würzburg
(Marktbreit), it was headed by Dr. Otto Hellmuth, a dentist who
was already a member of the NSDAP in 1923. No clear data on the
size of the organization are available, but it claimed to have a regi-
mental-size paramilitary unit. Such fragmentary data as are available suggest that this "regiment" was very understrength and probably had little military significance even in terms of the rather
elastic yardstick used by the Verbände. Certainly, it played no independent role in 1923.[63]

Far more important than Frankenland was the Jungdeutscher
Orden, usually called Jungdo. Jungdo was a national, relatively
moderate, rightist paramilitary organization that was led by Artur
Mahraun. However, the Verband had only local importance in
Bavaria, being limited to the area around the city of Coburg. Hans
Dietrich, a school teacher, and Hellmuth Johnsen, a Protestant
minister, were the leaders of the Bavarian Jungdo and determined

---

[60] B, ɪ, GSK 100, p. 4.

[61] See Chapter vɪɪɪ, Section ɪɪɪ, below.

[62] B, ɪɪ, MA100446, passim; Röhm, *Geschichte*, pp. 179-80; *BLV*, 1922-
23, 8, Auer (SPD), 6.6.1923, p. 330.

[63] B, ɪɪ, MA102141, HMB 350, M/F, p. 2; MA101235, PDN-F 2743/ɪɪ
24, pp. 12-13; GP, D, 1 (Personalities), 2 (Organizations); Degener, H.A.L.
Hrsg, *Wer Ist's 1935*, Leipzig, 1935. Hereafter cited as *Wer Ist's 1935*.

its policies—apparently without reference to those of the national organization. It was they who allied themselves with Ehrhardt.[64]

The general organization of Jungdo was territorial and was, in terminology, modelled after that of the Teutonic Knights and similar groups. The provincial organization was the Ballei, which was divided into Bruderschaften, which in turn controlled some eight Gefolgschaften. The Bavarian province was Ballei Franken (more properly Oberfranken). For paramilitary purposes Ballei Franken created an infantry regiment, many of whose officers were drawn from the Ehrhardt organization. Hans Ulrich Klintzsch, who had been the first leader of the SA of the NSDAP, was a battalion commander in this regiment.[65] The precise size of Ballei Franken is uncertain, but some 6,000 men appeared at one of their rallies in July of 1923. At another rally near Staffelstein in the same month some 3,000 members appeared. The organization grew more in the fall. In the Coburg area Jungdo was even larger than Bayern und Reich. As far as social composition was concerned, Jungdo appealed primarily to very young men, especially the sons of peasants, and had a strongly Protestant character. As a paramilitary organization it was far less efficient than Bayern und Reich because it lacked both trained and experienced enlisted men and senior officers, since Wiking provided primarily subalterns.[66]

The level of military training of Jungdo was very low, as became apparent when the regiment was called up to help guard the frontier in the fall of 1923. The lack of trained men, of NCO's, and of officers, showed up here starkly. How many arms the Ballei had is not clear, but Ehrhardt and the Bavarian authorities were able to supply small arms as and when they were needed. Jungdo was, however, very short of all other types of military equipment.[67]

The aims of Jungdo in Bavaria were determined by its local leaders. It was therefore strongly antisemitic, anti-Catholic, and racist

[64] B, I, GSK 43, pp. 217-18; II, MA101249, Rk. O. In. 99, p. 21; IV, Lapo, Bd. 26a, Akt 5, Gr. Sch. IIIc, Erfahrungsbericht Lapo Coburg, J Chef 361g, Beilage 1, p. 1.

[65] B, I, GSK 43, pp. 214, 217-18; IV, Lapo, Bd. 17, Akt 4, Jungdo Regt., B.E.J. Nr. 29/23.

[66] B, I, GSK 43, p. 211; II, MA102140, HMB 1269, Ofr., p. 2; HMB 897, p. 4; HMB 1187, p. 2; HMB 1642, p. 2; IV, Lapo, Bd. 26a, Akt 5, Gr. Sch. IIIc, Erfahrungsbericht, Lapo Coburg, J Chef 361g, Beilage 1, p. 1.

[67] B, IV, Lapo, Bd. 26, Akt 1, Stadtkomm. Bamberg 497DJ; 26a, Akt 3, Item 59, 2454, Ofr.; Akt 5, Gr. Sch. IIIc, Lapo Coburg, J Chef 361g, Beilage 1, pp. 1-6.

in orientation, tendencies that the alliance with Ehrhardt and the use of Wiking officers intensified. Hans Dietrich, one of the two mainsprings of the Bavarian Jungdo, was also area leader (Gauleiter) of the German Racist Defense League. His colleague Parson Johnsen made no bones about his strong antisemitism and vigorously attacked the Bavarian People's Party and the Bavarian government as being separatist in sentiment and dominated by Rome. Thus the Bavarian Jungdo, far more than the mother organization, bore the stigmata of racist right radicalism.[68]

In the center of the Patriotic Movement stood the largest and richest of the Patriotic Bands, Bund Bayern und Reich. Despite the splintering off of such groups as Reichsflagge and VVM and the defiant autonomy of Hans-Georg Hofmann's Kreis Niederbayern (later Bund Unterland), Bayern und Reich remained far and away the Verband with the largest membership and the most significant position in the state. At the head of this organization stood Dr. Pittinger. Initially he had clearly controlled both the civilian and military activities of the Bund, being advised in military matters by Lieutenant Colonel (Ret.) Paul Schmitt. As the paramilitary activities of the Verbände became increasingly important, however, a more elaborate military apparatus and a more exalted leader were needed. By early 1923, General of Cavalry (Ret.) Otto von Stetten was military leader of the Bund, with Lieutenant Colonel Friedrich Preitner as his chief assistant.

In June, still another change occurred. Major General (*Generalleutnant*) (Ret.) Ludwig von Tutschek replaced Stetten and brought in Lieutenant Colonel (Ret.) August Schad as his chief of staff. The precise relationship of the military leader to Dr. Pittinger, as leader of the Bund, was never satisfactorily delimited, and friction developed over matters of competence as well as over personality questions during the course of 1923. Pittinger saw himself as the single responsible leader of the Bund, while Tutschek insisted upon his autonomy in all military matters. This uneasy marriage of convenience contributed significantly to the difficulties of the Bund and made mastery of the provincial and local organizations difficult to attain and harder to maintain.[69]

[68] B, II, MA101249, Rk. O. In. 99, p. 21; MA102140, HMB 99, Ofr., p. 3; HMB 1187, Ofr., p. 2.

[69] NA, Epp Papers, EAP 1-e-16/4, Auftrag von Major Adam; B, IV, BuR, Bd. 34, Item 45; Bd. 35, Akt IV, Item 18 and passim; Bd. 36, Akt 2, Items 30 and 41.

Like a number of the larger Verbände, Bayern und Reich had parallel civilian and military organizations, which cooperated closely and overlapped to some extent. The civilian organization followed the pattern of governmental organization, with Kreisleitungen, Bezirksleitungen (apparently sometimes called Gauleitungen), and Ortsgruppen. Alongside the regular civilian structure in Mittelfranken there was the Hiking Club (Wanderverein), which was more militant and active than the basic organization and had some of the characteristics of a youth organization.[70]

The military organization was headed by the military chief in the Bundesleitung in München. Apparently for reasons of distance and efficiency, an intermediate headquarters was established for northern Bavaria, headed by Brigadier General (Ret.) Wilhelm Kaiser, which was later transformed into an "inspectorate of troops." Below this level, the Bund followed the standard military organization from regiment downward.[71]

On 1 July 1923, Bayern und Reich had 56,715 members, of whom 37,649 were fit for military service. These members were scattered throughout Bavaria in 1,054 Ortsgruppen. Even Hitler's order of late September that all National Socialists must leave other Verbände did not hurt Bayern und Reich, since aside from a very few Ortsgruppen no sizeable losses were reported and at least 2,700 new members joined the Bund in the three weeks that followed. It therefore seems likely that an estimate of 60,000 members and 1,100 Ortsgruppen would be justified for November 1923.[72]

On the military side, Bayern und Reich could boast of the following "complete units":[73] 6 infantry regiments, 10 signal troops, 12½ artillery batteries and one platoon, 20 infantry battalions, 65 infantry companies, as well as practically the same number of "cadre" units requiring considerable numbers of further personnel to bring them to a reasonable strength. This was, without question,

---

[70] B, I, GSK 43, p. 313; GSK 99, p. 27; IV, BuR, Bd. 35, Akt 3; Fragebogen 2, Opf.; Deutscher Wanderverein; Akt 4, Item 43; Akt 5, Items 6 and 35/1.

[71] B, IV, BuR, Bd. 35, Akt 3, Nordbayern an Bayern, 14.4.1923; Akt 5, Item 65; Bd. 36, Akt 2, Item 30; Lapo, Bd. 26a, Akt 5, Bericht von Ostfränk. Volkswehr-Rgt., 23.11.1923.

[72] B, IV, BuR, Bd. 36, Akt 3, Übersicht; Bd. 35, Akt 5, Item 35/2-3; II, MA102140, passim.

[73] Almost certainly well below regular army strength levels and short of some special personnel.

a force far larger than any other Verband could raise and was probably nearly equal to all other armed forces, official and unofficial, in Bavaria, at least in numbers.[74]

It is clear from the available information that Bayern und Reich differed in social make-up from the more radical Verbände. Its leaders seem to be much older and much better established in life, both on the civilian and the military side. Out of a sample of 156 men, mostly leaders, 11 clearly belonged to the upper middle class, 6 were mayors or aldermen, 37 belonged to the higher civil service, 19 were members of the free professions (including pharmacists), 7 belonged to the middle reaches of the middle class, 9 were university or secondary school (Gymnasium) professors, while 24 were grade-school teachers. Eight belonged to the middle or lower civil service, one was a white collar worker, one a blue collar worker, one a Protestant clergyman, and one was a student. The group also included one large landowner, 11 peasant proprietors, and 19 members of the lower middle class (including shopkeepers and independent master craftsmen). Its former officers included 10 general officers, 65 field grade officers, and 71 company grade officers,[75] indicating a far greater participation of former senior officers than was to be found in the other Verbände.[76]

Even where followers were concerned, Bayern und Reich seems to have appealed to a more solid and dependable type of citizen than did most of the other Verbände. It also had a good deal more drawing power among the peasantry than did the right radical organizations,[77] and workers were not necessarily immune to its lures. A local leader in the Erlangen area reported, for example, that one Ortsgruppe was composed almost entirely of basket weavers. In another town, although the left parties had ordered the workers not to attend Bayern und Reich rallies: " '. . . A number of workers, among them former members of the USP[D] have joined the Ortsgruppe. It is recommended that still more recruiting rallies be held in this area in order to counter the hostile propaganda, [which claims] that Bund Bayern und Reich is the bitterest foe of the workers.' "[78] In October, the president of the Oberpfalz

---

[74] B, IV, BuR, Bd. 36, Akt 3, Übersicht.

[75] There were, of course, far more junior officers in the Bund, but this many were clearly identified.

[76] GP, D, 1 (Personalities).

[77] B, IV, BuR, Bd. 26a, Akt 3, Item 16; Bd. 34, Item 33.

[78] B, IV, BuR, Bd. 35, Akt 4, Egerer an Nord, 14.8.1923.

reported: "The patriotic celebrations . . . recently held by Bund Bayern und Reich have reawakened patriotic thoughts in broad groups of the population, especially among the workers, and begin to counteract the leftist endeavors effectively."[79]

The appeal of the Bund to veterans is attested by a number of sources. Major Arno Buttmann of Bayern und Reich, for example, made the following comparison of the men in his regiment and those in the regiment raised by Jungdo in the fall of 1923:

> . . . Almost the entire active and reserve officer corps stands in our ranks. War lieutenants and reserve officers up to first lieutenant are battalion commanders in Jungdo. I see the difference between our battalions, built entirely after the old pattern, and this formation, which lacks all leadership material, with more than mixed feelings. . . .[80]

Buttmann's remarks, which might otherwise be dismissed as partisan, were confirmed by the Landespolizei report on the respective units.[81] The Bayern und Reich leader in Bad Reichenhall reported in early November that his troops were largely war veterans:

> . . . It is always the same ones who volunteer, people who fought through the entire war, were wounded three or four times and, further, are married. Hopefully these men will later be granted preferment over the "draft-dodgers," otherwise even these men are likely to lose their enthusiasm for constantly pulling the chestnuts out of the fire for the others.[82]

Freiherr von Gagern, Bayern und Reich Kreisleiter in Oberfranken, confirmed these local impressions at a general meeting of Bund leaders: "Gagern speaks about the Kampfbund and us. The Kampfbund has only young people, who have no [military] service, whereas the veterans are with us. . . ."[83] In general, the level of training in Bayern und Reich was far better than that in the other Verbände, as is natural not only because they had far more officers and non-commissioned officers, but because many of their men

[79] B, II, MA102140, HMB 795, Opf., 17.10.1923.

[80] B, IV, BuR, Bd. 35, Akt 5, Brief: Buttmann an Schad, 22.10.1923.

[81] B, IV, Lapo, Bd. 26a, 9kt 5, Gr. Sch. IIIc, Erfahrungsbericht Lapo Coburg, Chef J 361g, Beilage 1.

[82] B, IV, BuR, Bd. 34, Item 139, Brief: Wirsing an Schonger.

[83] B, IV, BuR, Bd. 35, Akt 5, Item 35/2, Sitzungsbericht, 6.10.1923.

needed, at most, only mild refresher training in view of their previous service.[84]

Bayern und Reich undoubtedly had far more arms than any other Verband, although Oberland may well have been proportionately better off. In the summer of 1923, an inventory revealed that the Bund had on hand 65,469 rifles and carbines, 1,280 machine guns, 1,552 light and medium artillery pieces,[85] and 15 heavy ones. The ammunition problem was more difficult, with an overall shortage of all types except rifle ammunition, although some areas were reasonably well off. Further, in theory, the Bund had influence over (and access in time of emergency) to the Bavarian government's illegal arms, munitions, and equipment caches. In fact, the situation was worse than it appeared on paper. Many of the weapons held by the Bund were inoperable. There were no readily available sources of resupply for ammunition and, after the quarrel between Pittinger and Captain Röhm, the latter was able briefly to deny to the Bund all access to the official caches. In the eyes of men who were, like the leaders of the Bund, used to having access to a vast, national resupply system, the situation seemed most unsatisfactory, leading General Kaiser to say to General Tutschek in later October that Bayern und Reich was the worst armed of the Verbände, a statement that expressed his dissatisfaction at existing shortages rather than reflecting an existing situation.[86]

Financially, as in other respects, Bayern und Reich was probably the best situated of the Verbände, as a result of its close ties with the wealthier elements of the state and the individual communities. Apparently it relied very little on money from members, but gathered large sums from wealthy sponsors. Such gifts were, however, not sufficient for the great and growing needs of the Bund, and it was therefore increasingly in the business of selling protection from leftist rioters to industrialists, business men (large and small), and farmers. Those who paid up would be protected by the

[84] B, IV, Lapo, Bd. 26a, Akt 5, Erfahrungsbericht Lapo Coburg, Chef J 361g, Beilage 1; and other sources cited above.

[85] Most of these artillery pieces are reported from one area, the Chiemgau, and may possibly represent an error. However, a great proportion of the concealed material in Bavaria seems to have been hidden away in the southern mountains, so this figure is probably correct.

[86] B, IV, BuR, Bd. 35, Akt 3, Antworten auf Fragebogen 3; Akt 5, Item 28; Item 61/2; Item 65; Bd. 36, Akt 1, Item 14; Akt 2, Item 42/5-6; Lapo, Bd. 17, Akt 4, Itzgrund Btl. an Buttmann und Hptm. Bernhardt.

troops of the Bund. Those who did not would be left to the mercy of looters. No exact figures are available to show the income of the Bund or its expenses, but its wealth is indicated by the fact that it contributed heavily to the maintenance of the Bavarian government's weapons and materiel caches in 1922 and met the heavy expenses of maintaining and expanding its own organization in 1923. Nevertheless, especially in this year of economic crisis, the Bund was always on the edge of destitution and some local organizations were desperate for cash.[87]

Bund Bayern und Reich was essentially a conservative organization with right radical overtones, which grew stronger as one proceeded down the hierarchical ladder and were strongest in the local military organizations, which were composed of the younger men in the Bund. There were further divergences of opinion between military and civilian leaders as blocs and among individual leaders at the state, provincial, and local levels. However, certain basic views were characteristic of the Bund, and it pursued a number of clearly defined ends. The Bund was essentially monarchist and maintained close touch with the House of Wittelsbach. It opposed parliamentary government. It supported a united Germany organized on a federal principle, with considerable autonomy for Bavaria. Despite the accusations of Hitler and the Social Democrats and despite some suspicion at lower levels within the Bund, there is no persuasive evidence that the Bund was ever separatist or involved in the vague plans, which the press brought forward from time to time, for the creation of an Austro-Bavarian Danube monarchy under French sponsorship. Indeed, the Bund was strongly hostile to the former Allied powers. It also apparently excluded Jews from membership, and some of its members were very clearly antisemitic. However, next to nationalism the strongest theme in the Bund was hostility towards Marxism, usually a corollary to strong nationalism.

The primary aims of Bayern und Reich were the maintenance of (or establishment of) a thoroughly nationalist, conservative, and anti-Marxist government in Bavaria, the defense of Germany against foreign foes (which some leaders put first), and the suppression of internal uprisings against the Bavarian government. However, there was some difference of opinion within the Bund as to how national and conservative the successive governments of

[87] B, IV, BuR, Bd. 35, Akt 4, Item, 35; Bd. 36, Akt 1, Item 35.

Bavaria were in the years 1922-23, and there is some reason to believe that Dr. Pittinger himself toyed with the idea of a Putsch in the summer of 1922. On the question of maintaining order within Bavaria, the senior leaders, both civilian and military, insisted that rebellions from the radical Right must be fought as well as those from the radical Left, whereas such significant local leaders as Dr. Johannes Reinmöller of the Wanderverein and Captain Schonger of Chiemgau West were flatly opposed to any action against the right radicals, to whom they felt strongly drawn by common interest and views and by local cooperation.

The military leadership was increasingly repelled by the extent to which the Bund and the other Verbände became involved in politics and wanted the creation of a single military organization (based on Bayern und Reich) dedicated to the preparation of national mobilization. In July this dissatisfaction had proceeded so far that Lieutenant Colonel Schad proposed to Kriebel that the military forces of the Bund and the Arbeitsgemeinschaft should unite in defiance of the political leadership of both organizations. Nothing came of this suggestion, but it is symptomatic of the desire of many "simple soldiers" in the Bund to set aside political differences in the interest of military efficiency, patriotic duty and—ironically—political influence.[88] Therefore it may be said that the Bund's aims and interests ran roughly parallel to those of the Bavarian government but that there were sufficient divergences of view to make for mutual unease.[89]

On the military side, however, the leadership clearly recognized the primacy of the Reichswehr and Landespolizei. A memorandum of May 1923, stated:

a.) Any *military* action is doomed from the outset to failure without the closest cooperation with Reichswehr and Polizeiwehr, not to speak of an action against RW and PW

[88] One of Schad's chief aims was to get rid of Interior Minister Dr. Schweyer and Police President Mantel of München.

[89] B, II, MA99520, 26.8.1922, p. 10; IV, BuR, Bd. 35, Akt 3, Item 9/2 Brief: Reinmöller an Schad, 3.2.1923; Item 37/4, Denkschrift d. Mil. Obltg., ca. May 1923; Item 41, Appendix; Akt 4, Item 3, Erklärung (Hofberger), July 1923; Item 18, Brief: Schad an Kriebel, 20.7.1923; Akt 5, Item 13, Meldung Ortsgruppe Kipfenberg, 25.9.1923; Bd. 36, Akt 2, Item 30, Brief: Tutscheck an Pittinger, 2.3.1923; Item 59/1-2, Anon. Denkschrift (Schad ?), ca. Jan. 1924; Akt 4, passim; *BLV*, 1922-23, 8, Rosshaupter (SPD), 12.6.1923, pp. 403-4; Röhm, *Geschichte*, pp. 149-50.

b.) Without the means and the support of the state every organization is in the long run unable to maintain its units, its *armament* and its training. The need to depend on the state is increased by the continuing devaluation of the currency.[90]

To carry out their policies, the Bund leadership laid plans for four military eventualities:

1. National war (Reichskriegsfall). The Bayern und Reich Volkswehr does not appear as such but is absorbed into national military organizations as cadre. Reichswehr handles the matter and all materiel is turned over to the military authorities. Local units of older men will perform home guard functions.

2. Minor internal disturbances. The Volkswehr will reinforce the Reichswehr and Landespolizei, and will form the core of the police auxiliary force (Polizeiliche Nothilfe Bayern—PNB).

3. Civil war in the Reich. The suppression of Bolshevism.

4. A combination of the above three.[91]

The main thrust of the Bund's military effort was in the direction of the support and defense of the Bavarian state and its armed forces, rather than in the direction of revolution against them. As long as this organization was more or less autonomous, however, there always remained the possibility that it could become a threat to the existing government, especially in view of the existence of strong right radical dissenting elements within the Bund.

Similar to Bayern und Reich was its München offshoot, the VVM. Situated in München, the center of Bavarian right radicalism, it was more sympathetic towards the Kampfbund than was the parent organization. Essentially, VVM was the old Einwohnerwehr organization in München. Its membership was surprisingly large. Thirty thousand members is one informed estimate. However, the great bulk of the members were passive, and many were probably well over military age. After the splitting away of Kampfbund München, it wavered vaguely between the two poles of the movement, generally settling, in decisive moments, on the side of conservatism and the existing government, in practice at least, although not always in theory.[92]

[90] B, iv, BuR, Bd. 35, Akt 3, Denkschrift, Item 37/3.
[91] B, iv, BuR, Bd. 35, Akt 3, Item 37/3, Denkschrift; Akt 4, Item 14.
[92] B, i, SA 1, 1817, PDM 1840, 3.5.1923, p. 2; ii, MA103476, pp. 94-95; iv, BuR, Bd. 35, Akt 3, Item 36.

The central leadership of the VVM lay primarily in the hands of its first chairman, Max Kühner, a factory manager and reserve officer from Württemberg, and in those of its business manager, Major (Ret.) August Semmelmann. Real power in the organization seems to have lain in the hands of the leaders of the individual ward organizations, so that united action in a troubled and uncertain situation was more a hope than a reality.[93] Each ward had a separate name, and each in turn had a "sport" organization, which was its military arm. The ward leader and sport leader were usually the keys to the control of the ward organization. Like Bayern und Reich, VVM apparently appealed most to men twenty-five or over, while the young hotheads flocked to the Kampfbund. A good number of its members were government officials of one kind or another, and quite a few were policemen. These factors helped to determine the nature of the VVM's military effort. It was essentially a home defense organization intended to operate as a police auxiliary in case of civic disorder or war, although there was a good deal of doubt regarding the readiness of some ward organizations to fight right radical rebels.[94]

Considerably more right radical than Bayern und Reich was Bund Unterland, or Kreis Niederbayern of Bund Bayern und Reich as it was variously styled. In theory, Niederbayern remained within the Bund. In fact, it insisted on complete autonomy, and the Bund sought to build up an obedient replacement organization in Regierungsbezirk Niederbayern. Neither side, though, pushed the schism to its ultimate and logical conclusion until after the Hitler Putsch, so that Niederbayern lived in a shadow zone which enabled it to take advantage of the relative respectability of Bayern und Reich while enjoying all the advantages of complete independence and cooperation with the Kampfbund.[95]

The true leader of Niederbayern was Reichswehr Lieutenant Colonel Hans-Georg Hofmann,[96] who was known in the Racist Movement as "Trotsky" because of his appearance, vigor, and in-

---

[93] B, II, MA103476, pp. 1052-54; W, L, E131, C5/25, p. 208; GP, D, 1 (Personalities), 2 (Organizations).

[94] B, II, MA103476, pp. 147-48, 205, 1052-54; IV, BuR, Bd. 35, Akt 1, V.V. Schw.-Ost an PDM, 5.6.1923; Röhm, *Geschichte*, pp. 170-71, 174.

[95] B, IV, BuR, Bd. 35, Akt 3, Items 41-42; Akt 4, Item 5; Akt 5, Item 23/3; Item 23/4; Item 35/3-4; Item 37; NA, T79, 72, pp. 1240-41; Röhm, *Geschichte*, pp. 174, 182.

[96] Later an influential leader of the NSDAP.

clination towards intrigue. In view of the growing pressure on Bavarian Reichswehr officers to withdraw from politics, he increasingly left the official representation of his organization vis-à-vis other groups in the hands of his deputy, Lieutenant Colonel (Ret.) Wilhelm Willmer, the official political leader.[97] In organization and composition, Niederbayern was identical with the rest of Bayern und Reich, but in political orientation it was closely allied with the Arbeitsgemeinschaft and Kampfbund, on the radical edge of the conservative portion of the Racist Movement.[98]

Besides the foregoing organizations, a number more existed in Bavaria in 1923, but were of little importance. Stahlhelm, an activist veterans' organization with racist overtones and some of the characteristics of the Verbände, was only beginning to get a foothold in Bavaria.[99] Organisation Escherich and the Einwohnerwehr still existed in ghost form, but, despite their control of many weapons and a lingering reputation of power among leftists (always the last to learn what was happening on the Right), they were unable either to influence or to compel the flow of events.[100]

IV. *The Clashes with the Left*

Throughout 1923 and 1924 there were continual clashes between the members of the various Verbände and the militant left organizations. In general, all paramilitary organizations of the Racist Movement cooperated with one another against the leftists, although, on occasion, they sometimes scuffled vaguely with one another. There can be no question that for members of any of these Verbände the enemy stood left—or over the frontier. Being militant, military, and armed, the Verbände, wherever they felt themselves to be strong, went on the offensive against the Left. Especially where they were relatively weak they cooperated with one another and massed their forces for spectacular demonstrations calculated to bring out the Reds to attack them.[101]

---

[97] B, IV, BuR, Bd. 35, Item 42; NA, Epp Papers, EAP 1-e-16/4, Brief: Loeffelholz (Curt) an Epp, 4.2.1923; T79, 72, pp. 1238-39; Röhm, *Geschichte*, pp. 174, 182.

[98] *Ibid.*   [99] B, I, M. Inn 73685, PDM, Abt. vid 1637.

[100] B, II, MA99521, 20.4.1923, p. 6; IV, BuR, Bd. 35, Akt 4, Item 37, Obb. 335g3598AI; Akt 5, Item 5; Röhm, *Geschichte*, p. 151; RV, 358, p. 9536, Remmele (KPD), 26.1.1923.

[101] The evidence here is so diffuse and the incidents so numerous that, especially since a good number of them have already been discussed with regard to the NSDAP or to the left-wing parties, the reader is referred only

v. *Summary*

The tendency now is to look back on Bavaria in 1923 and see only the NSDAP as representative of the Patriotic and Racist Movements. In fact, the NSDAP was a relatively small component of those movements. For every National Socialist and especially for every SA man, there were hundreds of members of other organizations (although plural membership blurs the picture a bit at the edges). Furthermore, even the relatively informed reader today is inclined to think of the National Socialists and their "allies" as representing a single viewpoint and standing together against all comers, or at most being divided by the personal ambitions of a few leaders. In truth, the Racist Movement was deeply divided within itself, with the most serious cleft being that between the Right and the Left, rather than among individual leaders. In 1923 the divisions were not as yet sharply drawn and many persons within the movement had not yet clearly chosen their true places in the ranks. The Hitler Putsch was to be the catalyst that would split the movement asunder and begin the re-evaluation of ideas and the clarification of personal stands.

---

to the biweekly reports of the Interior Ministry's provincial officials and to those of the PDM and PDN-F in the Bavarian Hauptstaatsarchiv.

2. Minister President von Knilling

3. Dr. Otto Pittinger, leader of Bund Bayern und Reich

5.

THE BAVARIAN POLICE AND THE POLITICAL SITUATION

In Weimar Germany, basic control of the police lay in the hands of the state, rather than the national government. Bavaria was particularly jealous of her "police sovereignty" (Polizeihoheit) and deeply resented the mildest infringement of her rights, although she was ready to allow the Reich to pay a portion of the costs. This attitude was stiffened by evidence, which came to the surface in 1922, that the Reich had agents in Bavaria (as well as other states) to keep an eye on the state governments, as well as by difficulties over the investigation of political crimes against the Reich in Bavaria by Reich officials. Therefore the Bavarian police were not merely independent of Berlin, but suspicious of Berlin.[1]

The Bavarian police were, as is normal in modern society, the chief internal support of the Bavarian government against political unrest and the primary instrument used by the government to maintain law and order as well as to combat crime. However, in Weimar Bavaria a portion of the police fulfilled yet another function, unlike similar forces elsewhere in Germany. The Landespolizei Bayern was in many ways not merely a riot police organization but a Bavarian army, a substitute for the lost but deeply regretted military autonomy under the Second Reich. The Reichswehr, albeit manned almost exclusively by Bavarians in Bavaria and commanded by officers and NCO's most of whom had served in the royal Bavarian army, was none the less looked on with some suspicion in Bavaria, even in Bavarian government circles, as a representative of "foreign" (that is, north German) interests. In the light

---

[1] B, I, M. Inn. 71490, Niederschrift von Polizei Treffen, 8.5.1922; II, MA99516, 23.2.1920; MA99520, 5.7.1922, p. 10; 7.11.1922, p. 4; MA-100466a, p. 440; MA103161, Knilling an Heinze, 15.3.1923, pp. 14-15; MA103163, Lerchenfeld an Ebert, 1.9.1922, pp. 3-4; BLV, 1922-23, 8, Dr. Schweyer, 8.7.1923, p. 378.

of this "states' rights" climate and of the prevailing monarchism in Bavaria, it is not surprising that the Landespolizei was more military than elsewhere in the Reich and that the House of Wittelsbach took a strong interest in this force.[2]

In view of the central position of the police in the political power structure, and of the comparatively strong police forces available to the government, no picture of the Bavarian political situation can be complete without a serious consideration of the Bavarian police. Usually the police are ignored or passed over lightly in historical studies, but while historians have relegated them to obscurity, the political figures of the time did not do so. The position of the police was of vital importance in the plans and actions of all of the key figures in Bavaria in the crisis years 1923-24.

I. *Control of the Police*

Basic control and responsibility for the police lay with the Ministry of the Interior, although the Cabinet, acting as a whole, could and did establish general policy and direct the minister of the interior to take certain actions. Even in such cases, the orders of the government were channeled through the Ministry of the Interior. In theory, the police organizations were an entirely passive system responding to the will of the minister of the interior.[3] In fact, the situation was not so simple, nor was the control of the minister (or the ministry) so direct and undisputed as the theory indicated. For one thing, local police authority in the cities and towns—aside from München and Nürnberg—had been delegated to the local authorities, which sharply reduced the minister of the interior's influence and led to a campaign for the absorption of the municipal, or "blue," police (so called for the color of their uniforms) into the service of the state. In the early Weimar period, however, the scheme fell through, apparently primarily for financial reasons, and the larger towns remained masters in their own houses.[4]

---

[2] See Chapter VI, Section III, below. Also typical of the special "Bavarian" nature of this "second army" was the fact that the crown prince personally welcomed every candidate for a commission in the Landespolizei, congratulating him on entering a career as a future officer of the Bavarian army. GP, B, Colonel Emil Schuler.

[3] B, II, MA103476, p. 583; NA, Lapo Bekanntmachungen, 174; T120, 5569, pp. K591371-72; GP, I, General von Kiliani, 18.9.1960; General Christian Pirner, 26.9.1960.

[4] B, II, MA99521, 11.5.1923, pp. 5-6; MA99522, 14.3.1924, pp. 6-7, 11; 17.3.1924, pp. 5-8.

Far more significant was the position of semi-autonomy achieved by the Landespolizei. Officially, the chief of the Landespolizeiamt, Colonel Hans Ritter von Seisser, had no command authority over the Landespolizei units. This lack of command responsibility derived primarily from Allied objections to earlier arrangements, as did Seisser's relatively low rank—for which he was partly compensated by higher pay and allowances and by an understanding that his rank was really that of a major general. In practice, the lack of command responsibility made for difficulties and was largely ignored, with the silent consent of a succession of ministers of the interior, who were content to let Seisser run the Landespolizei. Seisser—shrewd, ambitious, and tenacious—carefully built up a personal position that, as the governments of Minister-Presidents von Knilling and Held were to find to their sorrow, was practically unassailable. Seisser himself said of this development:

> Not surprisingly, at the beginning the task of employing a [militarized police] force was somewhat alien to a succession of civilian authorities. The Entente forbade [the creation of] a central organization. Since organization, training, personnel matters, and administration were my primary spheres of concern, I helped to insure, despite the pressure from the Entente, with much difficulty and with the consent of the then minister of the interior, often in direct contradiction to regulations issued with an eye to the Entente, that the Landespolizei was not broken up into localized police [organizations] but became the tightly organized and effective police troop it has since proven itself to be.[5]

However, it is clear that other factors played a role in leading Seisser to develop this special position for himself in the Landespolizei. He was a brilliant young general staff officer with great drive and a thirst for power. Recognizing the limited opportunities in the new army, he carved out a new military career for himself in the postwar world. In order to do so, he was forced to divorce himself from the Ministry of the Interior to some extent, since his one serious rival, another former general staff major, Christian Pirner, was entrenched in the ministry as its specialist (Referent) for Landespolizei matters. Pirner worked hard to hold Seisser under the ministry's thumb and Seisser worked even harder—and

[5] B, ii, MA103457, Denkschrift, 10.12.1923.

more successfully—to get out from under Pirner, and therefore the ministry. Here, he had the advantage of the commander over the staff officer. He had, in fact if not in theory, command of the Landespolizei and, probably even more important, control of its personnel policy. He used this position to surround himself with bright young staff officers too young to hope to overturn him before his normal retirement age (but hopeful of succeeding him) while filling higher troop command positions with sound but uninspired colonels, whose only ambition was to remain in service and command their regiments well. These two groups Seisser welded into a solid phalanx which supported him loyally and developed a "Seisser mystique" which can be seen as paralleling the "Seeckt legend." This mystique was so powerful that it reached into and beyond the Third Reich, so that—ironically—there are today many former policemen who still honor the old man in the Bad Brunnthalstrasse long after Hitler's myth has been shattered.

Further, as the city commandant of München in the crucial period following the liberation of the city from the Republic of Councils, Seisser had become one of the darlings of the middle class and the political Right, and he consolidated his position through the effective use of the Landespolizei against left rioters. With such a powerful base, he could pretty well defy Pirner or even break a lance with a minister of the interior, as he did in 1923.[6]

This assumption of independence by Seisser does not seem to have worried Dr. Schweyer, who was Knilling's minister of the interior, until the spring of 1923 or later, when the question of a right radical insurrection became acute. Although the evidence is not clear, and—at least where Schweyer is concerned—stems from a much later time, it seems that the minister was increasingly troubled after the affair of May Day 1923[7] as to whether Seisser and the Landespolizei would obey orders to fight the right radicals,[8] a question that was answered at the Feldherrnhalle on 9 November. By that time tensions within and without the Bavarian government had grown greatly and Seisser had come to loom ominously in the eyes of the government. As a result, there were serious attempts to dislodge him, and to sharply reduce his power, but these came to nought.[9]

[6] B, II, MA99522, 28.8.1924, pp. 2-3; GP, B, Colonel Ernst Schultes. See also Chapter XIX, Section I, below.

[7] See Chapter VIII, Section II, below.   [8] See Section IV below.

[9] See Chapter XIX, Section I, below.

Even with regard to the state police in München and Nürnberg, the minister of the interior did not always find smooth sailing. He was overruled by the minister-president and other Cabinet members regarding the appointment of the police director in Nürnberg, while in München he found himself forced to replace the police president in May because of the latter's failure to obey specific orders stemming from the Bavarian Cabinet. The Nürnberg problem was, however, the more acute. The minister could keep close check on the police president in München and was usually supported by the Cabinet in his attempts to hold the reins tightly there. Police Director Heinrich Gareis of Nürnberg, however, protected by distance and strong voices in the Cabinet, could, and did, follow a policy not entirely in consonance with that of Dr. Schweyer. So here, too, the theoretical power of the minister of the interior was sharply curtailed by political and administrative problems which he could not entirely master.[10]

II. *Organization of the Police*

The Ministry of the Interior was the headquarters of the entire police system, much of which was administered directly by the civilian elements in the ministry or by its subordinate agencies in the provinces. The primary exceptions were the Landespolizei, which had its own headquarters and whose chief was directly subordinate to the minister of the interior, and the municipal police of towns and smaller cities, which were autonomous at the convenience of the Bavarian government.

Central to the entire system was the Landespolizei (often called the "green" police because their uniforms were green and black). Not only was it by far the largest single element of the Bavarian police system, but also it controlled access to the lower rungs on the ladder of the rest of the system, since recruits for most of the other elements of the system had to have police experience as a prerequisite for employment and the Landespolizei (Lapo) was the only place where a novice was accepted. Even the autonomous municipal police forces normally required Landespolizei experience of recruits.[11] Only personnel entering the higher administrative

[10] B, I, GSK 43, p. 230; II, MA99521, 30.7.1923, pp. 3-5; 17.8.1923, pp. 8-9; Röhm, *Geschichte*, p. 174.

[11] NA, Lapo Bekanntmachungen, 194, 7.12.1921; 9, 21.1.1922; 17, 6.2.1922; 20, 11.2.1922; 58, 12.5.1922; 51, 13.4.1923; GP, B, Colonel Ernst Schultes.

levels of the blue police as officials came through other channels, that is, academic training and appointment as officials of the higher civil service.[12] Police officers of the blue police themselves came from the Lapo.

The headquarters of the Landespolizei was the Landespolizeiamt, which maintained liaison with the Lapo specialist (Landespolizei-referent) in the Ministry of the Interior. All units and schools of the Landespolizei were administratively subordinated to the Landespolizeiamt, and, as we have seen, looked on its chief as their commander-in-chief. In normal times, most of the troop units were placed under the operational orders of the provincial administrators of the Ministry of the Interior or of the police president of München or of the police director of Nürnberg-Fürth. In times of serious emergency, they were usually concentrated as needed and employed under the command of the chief of the Landespolizei or of a commander delegated by him.[13]

The Landespolizei was essentially the equivalent of an infantry division in strength, plus schools and special institutions. It was organized in roughly the same manner as an infantry division, minus artillery but including armored car units and three air squadrons (with the camouflage name Luftfahrtüberwachungstelle). A regiment (Grosses Landespolizei Kommando) was stationed in München and another in Nürnberg-Fürth, while a third had its headquarters in Augsburg with subordinate units in Augsburg and two other cities. München-Land (the designation for the Bezirk around München) had an independent infantry battalion (Abschnitt), which was directly subordinate to the Landespolizeiamt, and a reconnaissance battalion (Streifstaffel). Another source of police troops in an emergency was the Police Basic Training School (Polizei-Vorschule) in Eichstätt, whose units could— and did—operate as a tactical battalion if necessary.[14]

The municipal state police were limited to two cities in 1923-24: München and Nürnberg. Operating directly under the Ministry of

[12] See, for example, the careers of such men as Pöhner, Frick, Pirner, Nortz, Mantel etc. GP, D, 1 (Personalities).

[13] NA, Lapo Bekanntmachung 186, 9.12.1925; GP, D, 1 (Personalities), 2 (Organizations).

[14] B, II, MA104221, Bericht Salbey, 10.11.1923; IV, Lapo, Bd. 26a, Akt 1, Abt. A, Lapoamt Chef Nr. 451; Sagerer, G., and Schuler, Emil, *Die bayerische Landespolizei von 1919-1935*, München, n.d. (1954), pp. 14-15. Hereafter cited as Sagerer & Schuler, *Landespolizei*; GP, B, Colonel Ernst Schultes.

the Interior these two police headquarters were independent of the municipal government, and, in the case of Nürnberg, clearly at odds with it.[15] The police president of München and the police director of Nürnberg-Fürth occupied essentially the same position. Each of them normally had operational control of a regiment of Landespolizei, as well as of a regular force of blue police for uniformed duty and the usual criminal and administrative work to be found in any major city. They also had, however, a civilian element consisting of legal officials to control and direct the force and subordinate officials associated with the Blue Police, who performed detective and other plain clothes duties. An important part of this civilian element was a "political police" to keep in touch with the political situation, to oppose subversives, and to detect revolutions in their early stages.[16]

The municipal police of the smaller cities and the towns of Bavaria were organized on the same basis and had the same functions as the state municipal police, but their forces were much smaller and were only augmented by Landespolizei at the discretion of the provincial authorities. In such cases of augmentation, command was usually delegated to the Landespolizei commander rather than remaining in local hands, although no standard procedure had been laid down at this time.[17]

The final organization in the regular Bavarian police system was the rural police or gendarmery. The gendarmery was centrally organized but widely dispersed over the countryside in small packets. Frequently only one or two policemen were available in case of need to villages and farm districts. The result was that the gendarmery was in a position to deal with rural crime and problems of order in normal times but in case of serious trouble or political riots could do nothing but call for Landespolizei aid.[18]

III. *The Police and the Reichswehr*

As in the other political problems and situations involving the police, the Landespolizei determined the relation of the police to the army, and Seisser determined the stand of the Landespolizei. The other police forces had only peripheral and usually indirect

---

[15] B, I, GSK 57, Tel 2693; NA, T120, 5569, p. K591, p. K591406.

[16] B, I, M. Inn., Misc. Files; GP, D, 2 (Organizations).

[17] B, I, GSK 3, GSK Abt. A/Nr. 2724, 19.11.1923; Chapter XIII below, passim.

[18] B, II, MA102140, HMB of Reg. Präs., passim.

dealings with the Reichswehr, whereas Seisser dealt with the Bavarian state commandant (Landeskommandant) regularly in matters of state and national security, regarding mobilization, etc. Fortunately for the relation of the two forces, Colonel Seisser and General von Lossow, the commandant of the Bavarian Reichswehr, were clearly compatible and cooperated with one another very closely. Indeed, the closeness of their cooperation appears to have given some of the senior officials and ministers of the Bavarian government food for thought, especially in the fall of 1923.[19] Moreover, Seisser felt himself to be still an army officer and was an admirer of General Hans von Seeckt, who allegedly referred, on occasion, to the Landespolizei as the Reichswehr's eighth division. This cooperation went so far that Seisser even agreed to subordination of Lapo to Reichswehr in case of serious unrest.[20]

Relationships between Landespolizei and Reichswehr officers and men were on the whole cordial, since they shared a common military tradition and many of them came from the same general social milieu. Most of the older officers and men had served in the same army together and many knew each other well from the "old days." On the other hand, especially where the officers were concerned, there were some sources of uneasiness which chilled relations a bit. A large number of the Landespolizei officers had been rejected for service with the Reichswehr, and it is clear that some of them resented their "selection out" bitterly. An example is a field grade officer who so vigorously attacked those superiors whom he blamed for his exclusion, that one of them wished to bring him before a court of honor (Ehrengericht).[21] This resentment must have been fanned and in some cases created in at least some Landespolizei officers by the faint tinge of condescension one can sometimes discern in the attitude of Reichswehr officers towards them, an attitude reminiscent of the relations of the West Point officer with the ROTC officer in the United States army. It is hard to pin

[19] Details concerning their cooperation will emerge in the course of succeeding chapters.

[20] GP, D, Colonel Schultes, whose father was a member of Seisser's staff. NA, Epp Papers, EAP 1-e-16/3, Epp an Möhl, 3.8.1922.

[21] Courts of Honor were instituted to prevent duels and to keep the army's dirty linen from being washed in civilian courts. These courts came under heavy attack in the first years of the Republic and were officially abolished. In fact, however, they lived on in a slightly different form in Reichswehr, Landespolizei, and veterans' organizations. Gordon, *Reichswehr*, pp. 155-56, 189 (German edn.: Ss. 162-64, 192).

down such vague attitudes, but hints may be found scattered here and there throughout the documents of the Wehrkreiskommando and in the Bavarian Archives. One point where this feeling surfaced was the sharply negative reaction of the Reichswehr to the Bavarian government's suggestion that all Lapo and Reichswehr officers should be placed in a common pool from which appointments in both services would be made.[22]

IV. *The Police and the Radicals*

Interior Minister Dr. Schweyer's attitudes were, to a very considerable extent, decisive in official police policy—although opposition within the Cabinet, opposition on the part of Colonel Seisser or Gareis, or foot dragging at lower levels could undermine his policies. Schweyer, a former protégé of Kahr, was, like any Bavarian minister of the Weimar period, cold towards the Majority Socialists and strongly hostile towards the Communists, whom he kept under constant pressure.[23] With regard to the Verbände his feelings were clearly mixed. He made it clear that he preferred the defunct Einwohnerwehr to the plethora of Verbände that succeeded it and that he did not entirely trust the leaders of some Verbände, but he considered that, in view of the limitations put on the official armed forces by the Allies, the Bavarian state needed the Verbände for defense against leftist revolutionaries and as a military reserve.[24]

Where actual dealings with the Verbände were concerned, Schweyer was less and less cooperative as 1923 progressed and as their attitude towards the government became more obscure or, in some cases, openly hostile. As early as the end of 1922, he publicly denied supporting Bund Bayern und Reich, but, in fact had just arranged to pay for the maintenance and repair of their secret weapons caches since their funds and the Reichswehr funds for this purpose had run out. Yet this move could have been politically neutral or even hostile to the Verbände, since, in return for his money, the weapons and equipment concerned were recognized as the property

---

[22] B, I, M. Inn. 71771, akt w/w4b, Bericht, p. 16; NA, Epp Papers, EAP 1-e-16/4, Adam *Auftrag*; T70, 50, p. 1017; GP, A, Josef Lehmann, 13.8.1955; B, Colonel Ernst Schultes.

[23] B, I, M. Inn. 70708, 6.9.1923.

[24] B, I, M. Inn. 71708, 14.9.1923, Reichsrat; NA, T120, 5569, p. K591391; *BLV*, 1922-23, 8, p. 378.

of the Bavarian state.[25] However, since he was unpopular with the Verbände, most government negotiations with these organizations were carried on through other channels.[26]

Schweyer made it very clear that he did not approve of violence or of ostentatious parades and demonstrations, which was one of the main reasons the leaders of all the Verbände disliked and distrusted him.[27] His chief target was the NSDAP and its SA. As early as 1921 he had warned of the "National Socialist danger,"[28] eliminated Ernst Pöhner as police president,[29] and ordered the München police to take sharp action against antisemitic vandals:

> Recent events, such as the defamation of the synagogue in the Herzog Rudolfstrasse here, but especially the ferocious attacks [which marked] the last lecture of the "Gnosis" Society, seem grounds for underscoring the orders [contained in] the directive of 5 October 1920 Nr. 2304 d 29. The Police Directory will continue to pay particular attention to the Antisemitic Movement and will strive to counter its excesses ruthlessly. If it is impossible under the existing conditions to prevent the repetition of such actions, at least every effort must be made by means of the infliction of heavy penalties to suppress the enthusiasm for such outrages, so that even the appearance of taking outrages of antisemites less seriously than those from the Left radical side will be avoided.[30]

Although, according to Kahr, Schweyer felt at the beginning of 1923, that the time was not opportune for acting against Hitler, he continued to stand against the NSDAP and to attempt to hold them in check throughout the year, and he used the München police to execute this policy.[31]

[25] The existence of this Bavarian state property was to play a considerable role in the relationship of the Bavarian government and the Reichswehr with the Verbände during 1923. See Chapter VI, Section VI, below.
[26] See Chapter VII, Section II.
[27] NA, T120, 5569, p. K591372; *BLV*, 1922-23, 8, 8.6.1923, p. 383.
[28] B, II, MA99519, 17.12.1921, p. 4.
[29] *Ibid.*, 17.9.1921; 3.10.1921, pp. 8-9; MA103476, pp. 56-57; Röhm, *Geschichte*, p. 136.
[30] B, II, MA100403, M. Inn. 2304 d 3 to PDM, 3.5.1921.
[31] B, I, Kahr MS, p. 1169; II, MA103476, pp. 586-87; NA, T120, 5569, p. K591391; *BLV*, 1922-23, 8, Staedele (DBMB), 7.6.1923, p. 365; see also succeeding chapters.

Aside from the minister of the interior, Colonel Seisser was the most important single factor in determining the position of the police regarding the Verbände, and, in view of the striking power of his organization, and the weakening of Schweyer's position as the year wore on, Seisser may have been a good deal more important than Schweyer. It is not, however, easy to portray Seisser's position, since it was not entirely clear. In times of crisis key persons rarely take positions that are quite as clearcut as they appear, and they are often themselves uncertain of their own next moves, sometimes for reasons of principle, sometimes for reasons of tactics, and sometimes out of the instinct for political survival. There is no doubt that Seisser sympathized, to some extent, with some of the official aims of the Verbände, that he felt that they were needed as a reserve for the Lapo and the Reichswehr and that he was impressed by their ability not only to hold the radical Left in check, but also to win over numbers of workers for the nationalist cause. At the same time, there is clear evidence that he did not trust some of the leaders, and he does not seem to have shared their antisemitism.[32]

Of all the Verbände leaders, Seisser seems to have been closest to Hermann Ehrhardt of Bund Wiking, and the available evidence indicates that it was Seisser and not Kahr who was Ehrhardt's sponsor and defender in Bavaria in 1923, although, according to Ehrhardt, Kahr was far more friendly than he later admitted. Seisser was certainly responsible for the central position accorded to the Wiking Bund in the Grenzschutz Nord, which was established against Saxony and Thüringia in the fall, and he provided arms for Ehrhardt's units while cold-shouldering other Verbände.[33]

In evaluating Seisser's relations with the other Verbände, it is necessary to realize that, during much of 1923, Seisser wore two hats and, in the fall, four. He was, throughout, the Chef des Landespolizeiamts and therefore very involved in the maintenance

---

[32] In 1919, for example, Seisser vigorously defended the Eastern Jews in München when Pöhner, the police president, sought to have them expelled from Bavaria. Seisser ratified only 185 of the 900 rejections of application for continued residence which Pöhner submitted to him, and accused Pöhner of seeking to expell the Ostjuden en masse, although they were politically harmless. B, IV, GM99902, M. Äussern, 35555, pp. 317-24.

[33] B, II, MA103476, pp. 861, 870; MA104221, Unsigned Denkschrift (Seisser ?), 28-29.9.1923; IV, Lapo, Bd. 17, Akt 4, Lapoamt an Chef Lapo Coburg, 16.10.1923; NA, EAP 105/7, II, Pöhner, p. 89; GP, A, Ehrhardt, 25.11.1958.

of law and order in Bavaria. He was also, as the chief of a military force of significance, heavily involved in the pre-mobilization measures authorized by the Reich government and executed by the Reichswehr and state governments, as well as the pre-mobilization measures authorized by the Bavarian government (or the Generalstaatskommissariat), which went well beyond those of the Reich. These measures called for Lapo supervision of the military training of the Verbände and therefore brought not only Seisser but many other Lapo officers into close contact with the Verbände on a regular and more or less cordial basis. From the middle of September forward, Seisser was also the military advisor to Generalstaatskommissar von Kahr and in this capacity dealt with the Verbände for Kahr in military and military-political matters. As a result of these complex and overlapping responsibilities and duties, it is very hard to say when Seisser was acting in any particular capacity or even whether he was acting on his own or with the authorization of either Kahr or Schweyer. Finally, as a member of the committee established by Minister-President von Knilling to represent the government in dealing with the Verbände, Seisser also operated as a direct agent of the minister-president. It is therefore not surprising that Seisser became more and more a law unto himself in the course of 1923. Whether he wished to do so or not, he was in a position where he had to play off his "masters" against one another and against the leaders of the Verbände with whom he was dealing, and even against General von Lossow of whom he was at the same time an equal and a subordinate (according to the hat he was wearing).[34]

A man of independent mind and strong character, Seisser undoubtedly made good use of his autonomous position and operated a "free-wheeling" dialogue with the Verbände leaders, including Hitler. There is no indication in his dealings with Hitler, however, of any of that warmth that he appeared to feel for Ehrhardt, or which characterized the dealings of Lossow with Hitler before the Putsch. With Hitler, Seisser was all business and from the beginning of the year both sides were aware that they could well find themselves in sharp conflict, although they would clearly have pre-

[34] For discussion of the mobilization problem see Chapter VI, Section IV, below. For Seisser's membership on the government commission dealing with the Verbände see B, IV, BuR, Bd. 35, Akt 3, V.V. Schwabing an PDM, 5.6.1923; for Seisser's position on Kahr's staff see B, I, Kahr MS, pp. 1256-57; II, MA103476, p. 585; NA, Lapo Bekanntmachung 144, 27.9.1923.

ferred to avoid such a clash. When in January the Bavarian Cabinet considered the use of force against Hitler, Seisser's position was presented as follows:

Colonel Seisser assures [the Cabinet] that the Landespolizei is accustomed to obedience. That is the case even for those whose feelings are with the other side. When one leads such an organization, one must not set it tasks that it is not capable of solving. As leader one must not abuse their obedience. Their use to protect the Entente commissions has already embittered the men. The new task is similar, for the men see in the Hitler Movement only the national [position], not the errors and tremendous dangers. Colonel Seisser is convinced that the National Socialist Movement must be chastened, considers it dubious, however, that this is the moment for a test of strength between the government and the National Socialists. In the end, all patriotically organized men will support Hitler. If one wishes to attack someone militarily, one does not choose the moment when he has concentrated all his strength.[35]

To judge by his later actions, this is a fair exposition of Seisser's position regarding the NSDAP. Confirmation of Seisser's distance from Hitler and his colleagues is provided by General Ludendorff, who was certainly in a position to know who was close to the movement and who was not. In speaking of the situation in October, Ludendorff complained: ". . . How strained were the relations between the Landespolizei and the Völkische Verbände in München at that time is clear from the words of Colonel Josef Banzer of the München Landespolizei to his subordinates: 'Whoever does not wish to fire at the National Socialists should resign.' "[36] This statement is also a clear indication of Seisser's attitude, since Banzer was not a man to expose himself by taking a position contrary to his chief's—as became only too clear in the Putsch and afterwards. Kriebel, the military leader of the Arbeitsgemeinschaft, also confirmed the tension between the Lapo and his "troops" as early as April: he declared that, "as a result of the attitude of the Landespolizei, negotiations with the Landespolizei were broken off."[37]

[35] B, II, MA99521, 26.1.1923, Notizen, Min. Rat Sitzung.

[36] Ludendorff, *Feldherrnhalle*, p. 54.

[37] B, II, MA103476, Extract from *Protokollbuch der Arbeitsgemeinschaft*, 16.4.1923.

While Seisser steered a careful course among the Verbände without committing himself irrevocably for or against them, the police presidium in München was seriously divided on the question of the National Socialists. The police president and the majority of his senior officials, especially those who had the most contact with the National Socialists, were hostile to the movement and followed the lead of the minister of the interior, or, in some cases, sought to move him further in the direction of restrictive measures against Hitler. However, a minority, mostly officials who had been close to Pöhner during his tenure as police president, were led by Dr. Wilhelm Frick in opposition to the official policy. Ironically, also included in the opposition were some policemen who, like Josef Gerum, came to know the NSDAP by being placed in its ranks as spies and "went native."[38] This minority was unable to make policy, but it could and did obstruct policy execution, especially since a number of its members were in the political police, despite their gradual exclusion from key posts. Frick, in particular, was to play a significant role in the Putsch.[39]

Ministerialrat Josef Zetlmeier, the senior police expert (Referent) of the Ministry of the Interior, rode close herd on the Police Directory in München (Polizeidirektion München—PDM), and his position is succinctly expressed in a memorandum of 22 December 1922:

The line of development of the National Socialist Movement is further made clear by these ten meetings. The movement is, despite its nationalistic drive, negative in content and is moving rapidly towards a revolutionary explosion, even though perhaps a portion of the leadership may not wish this [result]. This [tendency] was also expressed in the ten meetings and is also *psychologically* necessary. Where else could they be moving? They do not wish to take part in the parliamentary [system] and speeches alone have no value. The movement is therefore without doubt a danger for the state, not merely for the present state

---

[38] The loss of secret agents, and even diplomats, to the other side is a standing problem in the shadow world of intelligence activities. For the Gerum case see B, ii, MA103476, p. 1195.

[39] B, i, SA 1, 1474, PDM 1341 vid, 22.6.1923; Denkschrift, PDM vid, 16.3.1923, p. 136; vid 2136, 27.10.1923, pp. 147-48; ii, MA103476, pp. 189, 1195; GP, D, 1 (Personalities).

form, but for the state system itself. For if they intend to carry out even in part . . . the dark ideas they harbor against Jews, Social Democrats, banking capital, there will be much bloodshed and disorder. . . .[40]

Friedrich Tenner, the chief of the political section of the PDM, was inclined to take a more philosophical view than Zetlmeier and saw the increasing violence in the streets in terms of a long career as a policeman. In commenting on a Socialist protest at Nazi attacks on leftists, he said:

Actually provocative National Socialist troops or "interception patrols" were not found at all. If Storm Troops took action, it was in reply to earlier individual clashes with Socialists. . . . Most of these skirmishes go back to grudges between individual districts and wards, as they have always existed, even in prewar days, and [which] are typical occurrences among the youths of all major cities. In those [prewar] days youths fought each other only as the result of local jealousies and had no interest in political hostilities. As a result of the revolution and of the competition among all political parties for youths under the slogan: "Whoever has the youths, has the future" these normal skirmishes have been given a political tone and the less dangerous hazelnut rods, riding crops and [fence] palings have given way to more modern weapons, such as firearms, blackjacks, truncheons, etc.[41]

This resigned and philosophical evaluation by the professional policeman helps to place the street battles in perspective and to indicate that traditional rivalries helped to bring many "soldiers of the streets" to the ranks of the contending political extremists. The police, however, while they rarely succeed in completely stamping out crime of any kind, are not primarily philosophers or detached observers. Therefore, the PDM did take practical measures to maintain order in the streets, as the many arrests following clashes with Nazi storm troopers and the PDM request for the dissolution of the Nazi SA in May testify. These incidents make it clear that not merely the policy makers but also many policemen wished to do their duty vis-à-vis all comers. For example, on 8 June, when a group of SA men leaving a Nazi meeting at the Zirkus Krone tried

[40] B, ɪɪ, MA100425, Zetlmeier Denkschrift, 22.12.1922.
[41] B, ɪ, SA 1, 1783, PDM vɪd 1174/23, p. 232.

to march home in ranks, they were twice dispersed by patrols of the blue police. In early July, Josef Berchtold, a battalion commander in the SA, was jailed eight days on political charges. On 14 July there was a vigorous scuffle between the blue police and SA members who tried to march into the inner city in formation with banners after a party rally. A good number of men were injured on both sides, and a number of arrests were made, including a pro-Nazi Landespolizei officer. Feelings ran so high that the SA regiment in München felt it necessary to warn its members against alienating the blue police. Again, on 3 October, nine National Socialists were arrested for carrying arms in the streets, and during the Putsch itself a policeman was "arrested" by Putchists for trying to defend a critic of the Putsch.[42]

In Nürnberg, Gareis was clearly friendly to the Verbände, including the National Socialists, but his reports on their activities seem to be sound and dispassionate, and he was careful never to slip over the line into overt opposition to his superiors. As a result he rode out the storms of 1923 and remained in office after the Putsch.[43]

Only fragmentary evidence is available regarding the autonomous municipal police and the gendarmery, but it indicates that they, too, did their best to maintain order, even when the offenders were from the political Right. In any case, they were too weak and too bogged down in day to day affairs to have any serious impact on the course of events.[44]

Where the mass of the police were concerned, aside from some isolated socialists or left-wing democrats, mostly at lower levels, hostility towards the political Left and a strong feeling of nationalism were dominant. Most of them seem to have been very little interested in politics beyond these general sentiments. There were, however, especially among the younger men who made up the bulk of the Landespolizei a good number of officers and men who were committed to the radical Right. Schweyer, Regierungs-Präsident Paul von Praun of Schwaben, and even Seisser worried about the

---

[42] B, I, SA 1, 1490, Pol. Komm. Freisleben, Bericht, III, pp. 15-16; GSK 43, pp. 10, 180ff; *BLV*, 1922-23, 8, Dr. Schweyer, 8.6.1923, p. 382; NA, SA Rgt. München, 230-a-10/3 3, Befehl 28; 230-a-10/3 2, 1-15.9.1923.

[43] See Gareis Berichte, z. B., B, II, MA101235, MA103473, passim.

[44] B, I, GSK 44, p. 34; SA 1, 1474, Stadtrat Erlangen, Tg. B. 17, 3.1.1923, p. 74; II, MA100401, p. 4; MA102140, passim; IV, BuR, Bd. 35, Akt 5, Item 17 Bericht Ortsgruppe Rosenheim.

impact of these personal views on the actions of the police should the Verbände revolt against the government. When the Putsch came, however, all but a handful of policemen carried out their orders to the letter.[45]

v. *Polizei Nothilfe Bayern*

Still seriously frightened by the brief Left radical reign of terror in München and other Bavarian cities in 1919, the Bavarian government—and the majority of Bavarians—could not believe themselves safe from the threat of serious revolution, especially in view of the constant agitation and empty boasts of the Communists and the more radical of the Independent Socialists. Looking back now, we can see that there was little or no base for a Red revolution in Bavaria, but this was not clear to the men of the time, especially in view of the coming to power of Red-tinged governments in neighboring Saxony and Thüringia.

One of the results of this fear of revolution, and of a defensive war with France and her eastern allies, was the creation of a Police Reserve Force (Polizei Nothilfe Bayern), which was usually referred to as the PNB. The PNB was intended to provide the government and the police with a reliable force, independent of the Verbände, that could be used as a local anti-riot organization in case of minor trouble or as a home guard to maintain order in case a major crisis or war made necessary the withdrawal of the Landespolizei units from their garrisons. The PNB could also be used to provide reinforcements for Lapo units. They were to be employed under Lapo control and in coordination with Lapo units, rather than independently.

The Bavarian government undertook to pay the costs of the PNB but was determined to keep them to a minimum, which is one reason why the force did not prosper and why it was not possible to maintain state control to as great an extent as Schweyer had hoped. The men were badly armed and badly equipped in many instances —apparently being largely dependent on their own resources or those of the Verbände for such items. They were, however, covered by insurance when on duty and received an allowance based on the

[45] For Schweyer and Seisser see above. For Praun see B, II, MA102140, HMB 246, Schw., p. 6; GP, B, Lieutenant Colonels Max Lagerbauer and Otto Muxel.

expense account of the lowest rank of officials. Full-time employees received pension credit.[46]

The PNB was organized in local groups, under the supervision of district leaders appointed and paid by the Ministry of the Interior. Individuals, not groups, were taken into the PNB in an only partly successful attempt to reduce the power of the Verbände in the organization and to emphasize duty to the state.[47] Despite the attempt to set up the PNB on a basic pattern and to keep firm control of it, the make-up of the force differed sharply from area to area and from one village or town to another, reflecting the local situation. In some portions of Oberbayern, for example, the peasants were hostile to the Verbände and saw the PNB as a vehicle to enmesh them with the Verbände. The result was that only as the economic and social crisis deepened and theft from the fields and fear of the Left grew, did peasants join up in any numbers. In Niederbayern, most of the persons who signed up were known to be sympathetic with Hitler, which cast doubt on their loyalty in case of a clash between Hitler and the state. In another area, the PNB was reported to be nothing but the old Einwohnerwehr under a new name. So there was no unity of purpose and leadership beyond the elemental aim of guarding against Communist attack. Further, many employers, including the national and municipal governments, were not keen on having their employees join the PNB, apparently partly for political reasons, partly because of annoyance at absenteeism.[48]

From the very beginning, the PNB was torn by a vigorous struggle for control of the organization, which prevented it from growing into an effective and dependable organ of the state. Not surprisingly, the Verbände saw the PNB as a vote of "no confidence" in themselves. Some of them reacted sharply and directly, with actions like the NSDAP's refusal to have anything to do with the PNB. Others, like Oberland and Bayern und Reich, sought to enter the

---

[46] B, IV, Lapo, Bd. 26a, Akt 1, Items 19-20; Akt 3, Item 51; BuR, Bd. 35, Akt 3, Item 5, M. Inn. 2036 b 164, 6.12.1922; M. Inn. 2503c/II, 18.6.1923.

[47] B, II, MA102140, HMB 1040, Obb., 27.7.1923; IV, BuR, Bd. 34, Items 40, 91.

[48] B, I, GSK 60, p. 20; II, MA102140, HMB 695, Obb., p. 3; HMB 1040, pp. 5-6; HMB 1093, Appendix; HMB 1167, p. 3; HMB 1310, p. 9; HMB 1370, p. 3; HMB 1531, p. 2; HMB 871, N/B, p. 1; IV, BuR, Bd. 34, Item 13.

new organization and take it over. By October 1923 Bayern und Reich, Reichsflagge, Oberland, Wiking, Frankenland, Stahlhelm, and Jungdo had accepted, in theory at least, the government's demand that such members as joined the PNB would fight any and all foes of the government, whether from the Right or the Left, just as they accepted in theory the government's insistence on enlisting individuals rather than groups. In practice, the struggle for control of the PNB continued. In February, Oberland claimed to have a monopoly on providing members for the PNB until Schweyer flatly denied this rumor. Various Verbände tried to recruit unorganized members of the PNB. Bayern und Reich tried, in the fall, to incorporate their entire "defense organization" into the PNB and established General Kaiser as commander of the Grenzschutz Nord (that is, the mobilized PNB), a move that Seisser promptly countered. The Frankenländer avoided taking the required oath to serve the state government, as did some members of Bayern und Reich. As a result, no one fully trusted the PNB and no one was interested in seeing it develop too rapidly. Aside from local importance in the areas where Verbände units were mobilized under this rubric, contrary to the spirit of its founders, the PNB never was a real power in Bavaria.[49]

vi. *Conclusion*

The Bavarian police were an effective and well organized body, capable of defeating any possible leftist uprising in Bavaria and probably capable of handling an attack by all of the Vaterländische Verbände. The key elements governing its employment were the aims of the government in power; the personal decisions of key leaders, especially Colonel von Seisser; and, to a much lesser extent, the personal political convictions of other leaders and men. All the evidence available indicates that the first two factors were the truly significant ones. Therefore, the stand of Colonel Ritter von Seisser became increasingly important as the situation in Ba-

[49] B, i, GSK 3, Kommission für PNB, 10.10.1923; GSK 43, pp. 52ff.; ii, MA100411, p. 25; MA102240, HMB 1246, Obb., p. 3; HMB 871, N/B, p. 1; HMB 2201, Ofr., p. 1; HMB 2407, p. 1; iv, Lapo, Bd. 26a, Akt 1, Lapoamt A/Nr. 449, 19.10.1923, p. 6; BuR, Bd. 35, Akt 3, Item 25, Abschrift v. V.O. Bl. 2, 6.2.1923; Brief: Schweyer an Pittinger, 28.2.1923; Akt 4, Item 12, Vaterl. Kampfverbände B. Der Mil. Führer 102; Bd. 36, Akt 2, Item 20; NA, T84, 4, pp. 3081-82; Röhm, *Geschichte*, pp. 181-82.

varia grew more tense. More and more responsibility and power were delegated to him and more and more pressures placed on him from all sides, a process which continued until the Putsch of 8 November forced him to show his hand once and for all, by committing the Landespolizei.

MAP 1. Provinces of Bavaria

6.

THE REICHSWEHR AND
THE POLITICAL SITUATION
IN BAVARIA

I. *Introduction*

The Bavarian Reichswehr grew out of the Bavarian army and maintained its tradition in many ways. Like the Bavarian army, it was of the German army, but different from it in a number of minor ways. Also, like the old Bavarian army, the Bavarian Reichswehr enjoyed a number of rights that the other contingents of the Reichswehr had lost, or of which they did not avail themselves to the extent that Bavaria did. For example, by law the Bavarian Landeskommandant was at the same time the commanding general of the Bavarian formations (unless the Bavarian government consented to other arrangements) and therefore had responsibilities far beyond those generally laid down for the Landeskommandant in other Länder. Yet even these general provisions authorized, in backhanded fashion, the Landeskommandant to stand between Reich and Land governments,[1] which indicated some jurisdiction over him on the part of the state government.

The Bavarian units were to constitute a complete formation under unitary command. Exceptions to this rule were subject to agreement of the state government, as was the employment of Bavarian troops outside Bavaria for extended periods in peacetime. Even the question of the right to select the commander of the Bavarian division was thrown into question by the special status of Bavaria, for the Reich government had the right to appoint general officers to posts in Bavaria, including the commander of the Bavarian division, after consultation with the state government, but the Bavarian government had the right to nominate the Landeskommandant. Since in Bavaria these two persons were identical,

---

[1] *Reichsgesetzblatt*, 31.3.1921, Wehrgesetz, Paragraph 12.

the Bavarian government's rights were considerably reinforced, and those of the Reich, called into question. Furthermore, the state governments were promised the right to use the troops in their states for police duties and to suppress public disturbances, another concession that called the rights of the Reich and even the function of the Reichswehr into question. Did the troops have an obligation to perform police duties at the behest of the state authorities, whatever the Reich government and the army leadership (Heeresleitung) might direct? Was defense of the nation against foreign enemies or the defense of the state (and national) governments against internal foes its primary mission? These issues were raised by concessions made to the states in the Wehrgesetz and by the preceding agreements between the governments of the Reich and the larger states in 1919.[2]

The compromise solution sketched out above, which, probably intentionally, left a good deal of room for each side to maneuver, was hammered out in a series of meetings between state and national representatives in the spring of 1919. The Reich accepted the compromise reached in the conferences even though its sovereignty in military matters was partially undermined by the demands of the states.[3] It was almost certainly accepted only because it was the maximum that the state governments would accept and because it seemed unwise to try to dragoon them in the intensely uncomfortable and precarious political situation in which the Reich was enmeshed in the summer of 1919.

From the very beginning the Bavarian government clung doggedly to the remnants of military sovereignty that remained to it. Ironically, the left radical governments of Eisner and his successors took essentially the same position in this matter as did the right socialist-monarchist coalition that succeeded them. In late 1920 and early 1921, when the Reichswehrgesetz was being considered by the Reichstag, the Bavarian government demanded complete adherence to the Weimar Agreements of 1919, and thereafter proved ever-vigilant in defense of all its prerogatives.[4]

[2] *Ibid.*, Wehrgesetz, passim; NA, H1/360, Krgs. Min. 562/19 Wei; H1/360 II 2, Anlage 1.

[3] NA, H1/360, Krgs. Min. 562/19 Wei.

[4] B, II, MA99517, 14.12.1920, pp. 2-3; MA99518, 29.1.1921, pp. 3-5; MA103595, Eilmitteilung, 8.3.1919, Nr. 29085A; Reichsarchiv (später Reichskriegsministerium und Oberkdo. d. Wehrmacht), ed. *Darstellungen aus den Nachkriegskämpfen deutscher Truppen und Freikorps*, Berlin, 1936-40. 9 vols., IV, pp. 13, 101. Hereafter cited as *Nachkriegskämpfe*.

In this situation of uncertainty, mutual suspicion, and continuous attempts by each side to improve its position, the character of the Bavarian Landeskommandant became crucial. The original Bavarian choice, General Arnold Ritter von Möhl, had proven to be strongly "white-blue" and a very determined personality.[5] He had continually crossed swords with his superiors in Berlin on matters of policy and personnel, and had ignored or given only lip service to orders with which he was not in agreement. Since the Bavarian government supported Möhl in this policy and he was thus more or less immune to direct attack, the Heeresleitung finally got rid of him in December 1922 by promoting him to the command of Reichswehr Group II, in Kassel, where he was surrounded by officers loyal to the Heeresleitung and isolated from his military and political base.[6]

II. *General Otto von Lossow*

The Heeresleitung then appointed, to replace Möhl, General Otto von Lossow, a Bavarian officer who had served mostly in north Germany since the end of World War I and who had a reputation for being a man of moderate views and one who was friendly towards the Reich. In making the appointment the Reich government ignored Bavaria's exclusive right of recommendation. The Bavarian reaction was automatic:

> Minister-President Dr. von Knilling informed [the Cabinet] that Major General von Lossow had been appointed as Bavarian Landeskommandant to succeed General von Möhl, without Bavaria having made the proper recommendation. The appointment of the new Landeskommandant was thus illegal in this respect. The Reichswehrminister has already apologized in this matter, admitting that he had made a grave mistake. As far as the person of General von Lossow is concerned, the Minister-President can only approve his appointment.
>
> The Cabinet agrees that a protest be made against the manner and the appointment, but that it should be added that Bavaria has no objections to nominating Major General von Lossow and

---

[5] As late as the end of the 1920's, General von Möhl still hoped for the establishment of a Bavarian Kriegsministerium. GP, B, General Emil Leeb.

[6] B, II, MA99518, 18.6.1921, p. 5; RV, 347, Ersing (Z), 27.1.1921, p. 2202; Gordon, Harold J. Jr., "Ritter von Epp und Berlin," *WWR*, June 1959. p. 336; Frank, *Epp*, p. 105.

that it [the affair] can be treated as if Bavaria had made the recommendation.[7]

The affair was typical of Bavarian-Reich relations. Berlin, not for the first or the last time, showed a surprising insensitivity towards Bavarian feelings and had clearly violated Bavarian legal rights. The Bavarians, on the other hand, who, as Ritter von Haack once remarked, "could rarely see beyond the white-blue border markers," not only over-reacted to slights from Berlin, but also failed to see anything but their own rights and interests. It was typical that throughout 1923-24, in their dealings with one another regarding Lossow, the Bavarian government always referred to him as the "Landeskommandant" (thus stressing his responsibility and subordination to Bavaria) while the Heeresleitung and Reich government referred to him as commander of the Reichswehr (Befehlshaber der Reichswehr) or military district commander (Wehrkreisbefehlshaber) or division commander (stressing his responsibility to Berlin). Caught in the middle of this continual crossfire, the Bavarian commander needed to be tough and resilient and something of a military diplomat. Lossow, unfortunately, was none of these things, with the result that he found himself continually squirming on a hot griddle, under fire from at least two directions. There is something plaintive and bewildered in the note he wrote to Knilling in October 1923 about a newspaper article condemning "political generals": "What can we poor generals do when we are placed in positions where we must play politics?"[8]

General von Lossow is almost invariably portrayed as a power-hungry soldier, seeking to make himself independent of all restraints, a man of overweening ambition and ruthless determination who ignored the orders of his superiors callously and with impunity. This is not, however, the General von Lossow who emerges from the documents,[9] nor was this the Lossow his subordinates saw, as the following characterization indicates: "Lossow, as a result of his character and his experiences in Turkey, inclined more to compromise than to energetic action."[10] This Lossow is quite the reverse of the forceful and ruthless figure of "historical fiction." He

[7] B, II, MA99520, 23.12.1922, p. 16.

[8] B, II, MA103458, Handwritten Note, Lossow an Knilling, 25.10.1923.

[9] Unfortunately these official documents can probably never be supplemented by personal ones since, according to the testimony of a neighbor, Lossow burned seven chests of documents shortly before his death.

[10] GP, A, Leuze, 11.4.1960.

is both less significant and more likeable, more honest and less imposing.

As a man, Lossow had courage and a touch of humor. When the men who had put down the Hitler Putsch were living in barracks in the midst of largely hostile München, he showed both traits. A butcher sent the triumvirs (Kahr, Lossow, Seisser) Weisswürste, rare as hens' teeth in that spartan autumn and beloved of all true Bavarians, to brighten their breakfast table. As they were about to eat, the specter of poison arose. Was the butcher friend or foe? The others hesitated, but Lossow resolutely stuck his fork in his sausage with the remark, "I'm going to eat it." This was a tiny episode, but a revealing one.[11] Another reveals shrewdness and a wry humor. In discussing Hitler with Dr. Hans Ehard, the junior prosecutor at the Putsch trial, Lossow had said that the Nazi leader was both a brutal and a sentimental man. When, during the trial Hitler accused Lossow of lying, Ehard asked the General if this was the sentimental Hitler or the brutal one. Lossow replied: "This is neither the sentimental nor the brutal Hitler. This is Hitler with a bad conscience."[12]

As a soldier, Lossow was apparently efficient and respected. However, it seems apparent that he had reached his level as a military district commander, for the whole pattern of his activity indicates that he was not capable of independent action, lacking both initiative and the determination needed to adopt a course and carry it through to its logical conclusion. During the year 1923, Lossow found himself in a position roughly analogous to that of Seisser, but, where Seisser made the most of the situation and remained independent of all of his titular masters, Lossow became the servant and later the victim of first one and then another of his masters.

As military district and divisional commander, Lossow was the subordinate of the Heeresleitung or, in terms of people, of Reichswehrminister Dr. Otto Gessler and General von Seeckt. As Landeskommandant, Lossow was the subordinate of the Bavarian government or of Minister-President von Knilling, until September 1923. Thereafter he was also the subordinate of Dr. Gustav von Kahr, the Generalstaatskommissar (commissioner with dictatorial powers for security purposes). As Landeskommandant and as military district commander, Lossow was also responsible for pre-

---

[11] B, IV, HSIV, EE7, Endres MS, p. 65.
[12] GP, B, Justizminister a. D. Dr. Hans Ehard.

mobilization measures and was therefore entrusted with dealings with the Verbände and their leaders, including Adolf Hitler. Finally, since both he and the Bavarian government emphasized the internal security aspect of the mission of the Reichswehr over its mission of national defense, Lossow was also a key figure in the maintenance of law and order in Bavaria, and he negotiated with the Verbände leaders in this capacity. All was well as long as his masters were in general agreement. Once they clashed, however, the fat was in the fire.[13] A man who wanted no trouble with anyone, he soon found himself, as is so often the case, in trouble with everyone. In the words of Mao Tse-tung, Lossow was a paper tiger.

Not only was Lossow directed by his superiors and influenced by his partners in negotiation, but he was also frequently swayed by his subordinates. Testimony by members of his staff makes it clear that his chief of staff, Lieutenant Colonel Otto Freiherr von Berchem, was very close to him, and the right radicals, too, saw Berchem as influencing Lossow against them. Lossow was also clearly influenced by the general officers subordinate to him.[14] Even the unruly Captain Röhm, before he discredited himself by open insubordination in May 1923, was able to persuade him to rescind —temporarily—an order against political activity on the part of officers.[15]

Because of his character, Lossow's appointment was not a success from Berlin's standpoint. After arriving in Bavaria, he soon took on a white-blue coloration (tinged with the red-white-black of the right radical nationalists). Within three months, the Heeresleitung was disenchanted with him and had begun its campaign to bring him back into line with national policy, but their efforts were in vain. Seeckt, Gessler, and Lieutenant Colonel von Schleicher were in Berlin; Knilling, Seisser, Kahr, and Hitler were in München with direct access to Lossow; and it was to the voices directly in his ear that Lossow reacted most vigorously.[16]

The primary problems existing between Berlin and München

---

[13] See the discussion of the relations of the Reichswehr and the Bavarian government above and Chapters VIII-XIII below for detailed information on the role Lossow played up to 10 November 1923.

[14] See Chapters XI-XII below.   [15] Röhm, *Geschichte*, pp. 177-78.

[16] Seeckt Papers, Stück 281, Lieber Notes based on the Hasse Diaries, pp. 5, 13, 17; Rabenau, Friedrich von, *Hans von Seeckt, Aus seinem Leben, 1918-1936*, Leipzig, 1941, p. 337. Hereafter cited as Rabenau, *Seeckt*.

in the military sphere were mobilization, particularism, and political activism. The Heeresleitung believed that Lossow was going too far with mobilization preparations, and—more important—that he was being far too obvious. However, here, as in other matters, Lossow remained obstinately on the course set by the Bavarian authorities.[17] Far more sensitive was the matter of particularism. The Heeresleitung position was clear-cut and determined:

> . . . Seeckt also sharply rejected all desires for the creation of Bavarian military sovereignty. [Otto] Hasse says that Lossow himself takes a conciliatory stand, but the bulk of his Bavarian compatriots did not. . . .[18]

However, the question of particularism came up in the end as a clash not so much between military authorities as between the Reich and state Governments.[19] Therefore the major problem that troubled direct relations between Lossow and Seeckt was the question of the Reichswehr and politics. This matter had two facets. First, there was the question of relations with the Patriotic Bands, and second, the question of the political activity of individual Reichswehr officers.

Dr. Gessler, General von Seeckt, and Schleicher, already the political expert of the army, all opposed the relations that Lossow openly maintained with the Verbände. Seeckt was persuaded by Lossow, when the former was in München, to see Hitler, and was very impressed by the abilities and energy of the rising politician. He did not, however, make any agreement with Hitler or even reach a meeting of the minds, as Hitler notes in *Mein Kampf*.[20] According to Hans-Harald von Selchow, Seeckt's aide, the interview ended when Seeckt, after being treated to a typically violent and bloodthirsty Hitler tirade, said coolly: "From today forward,

---

[17] See below, Section IV; Seeckt Papers, Stück 281, Lieber Notes, p. 5.
[18] *Ibid.*   [19] See Chapter IX, Section IV, below.
[20] Hitler, Adolf, *Mein Kampf*, Berlin, 1942, pp. 773-74. Hereafter cited as Hitler, *Mein Kampf*. ". . . Ich habe sie [nationale Kreisen] immer wieder gebeten, dem Schicksal freien Lauf zu lassen und unserer Bewegung die Möglichkeit einer Auseinandersetzung mit dem Marxismus zu geben; aber ich predigte tauben Ohren. Sie verstanden es alle besser, einschliesslich des Chefs der Wehrmacht, bis sie endlich vor der erbärmlichsten Kapitulation aller Zeiten standen." See also Seeckt Papers, Stück 281, Lieber Notes on Hasse Diary, p. 5; Stück 289, von Selchow, p. 8; GP, A, Oberst a. D. Hans-Harald von Selchow, 15.10.1956.

Herr Hitler, we have nothing more to say to one another."[21] Throughout the year, Lossow was ordered, urged, and cajoled by both Seeckt and Gessler to keep his distance from the Verbände.[22] Instead Lossow, seeing himself as the Bavarian commander in chief, followed the direction indicated by the Bavarian government, and as long as they did not wish to provoke a national crisis the Berlin leaders had to allow Lossow his head.[23]

In theory the same thing was true with regard to the political activity of individual Bavarian officers, but in fact the situation was quite different. Quite obviously, even before General von Möhl's translation, the Heeresleitung had decided that the simplest and most effective way of coping with the Bavarian right radical officers was by indirect attack. The central authorities had basic control of the personnel apparatus of the entire army, and it was this apparatus, always a crucial weapon in non-violent struggle,[24] that they used with marked success in bringing the Bavarian officer corps to heel.

One after another, the politically active officers were eliminated by General Heye's personnel office. Hauptmann Hans Streck, who refused to accept the new republican colors, was one of the first to go. He was forced to resign in September 1922.[25] Next came the three most active political figures, men who were actually Verbände leaders: Lieutenant Colonel Hans-Georg Hofmann, Captain Heiss, and Captain Röhm, as well as Major Hühnlein, a less obvious activist. First, in early 1923, two of these men were ordered transferred from one garrison to another. When, in the case of Heiss, Lossow tried to intervene, Dr. Gessler made it plain that either Heiss moved or Gessler resigned as minister. Heiss, refusing the transfer, resigned from the service.[26] Hofmann was transferred from his post as battalion commander in Passau, where he was head of the Bayern und Reich organization, to Ingolstadt as commandant of

[21] *Ibid.*

[22] Seeckt Papers, Stück 281, Lieber Notes, pp. 5, 13, 17, 27-28; Rabenau, *Seeckt*, pp. 348-49; B, I, SA 1, 1477, p. 259.

[23] B, II, MA103476, p. 54. In talking about the events of May Day in München, Lossow said: " 'Ich . . . als oberster Träger der Machtmittel des Staates. . . .' "

[24] Stalin, after all, came to power largely through his control of the personnel apparatus of the Soviet Communist Party.

[25] NA, T79, 72, p. 692; Röhm, *Geschichte*, p. 159.

[26] B, I, SA 1, 1493, p. 100; NA, T79, 31, p. 1053; 72, pp. 1363-65; 82, p. 148; Röhm, *Geschichte*, pp. 160-61.

the more or less non-existent "fortress" there. This was a transfer away from the scene of his political activity and, even more significant, a transfer from a post with a future to a deadend post— since commandants of fortresses and cities were usually retired at the end of their tour of duty. This move did not prevent Hofmann from continuing his political activity and making himself a thorn in the flesh of the Bavarian government, as well as the national authorities, but it did set a term to his career.[27] Hühnlein was retired.

Captain Röhm was a more difficult problem. Initially, he had the protection of General Ritter von Epp, although they fell out in the course of 1923.[28] Nonetheless, he was transferred from Epp's staff to Lossow's, where his wings were somewhat clipped and where he brought down upon himself the wrath of both the chief of staff and the commanding general. Berchem on one occasion flatly asked Röhm if he was trying to replace Berchem as chief of staff, while Lossow accused Röhm in a letter of 25 June 1923 of not being in his right mind. Nonetheless, Lossow intervened to prevent Gessler from accepting Röhm's first resignation, so that it was only Röhm's own inability to operate within the framework of the army that resulted in his second resignation, despite the best efforts of Berlin to eliminate him.[29] Even so, the writing was on the wall for the right radicals, and it was underlined by the defeat and "expulsion" of their chief guardian angel, General Ritter von Epp, who retired (after violent recriminations) in the fall of 1923. The mills of the Personnel Office ground slowly, but they ground inexorably.[30]

Generally speaking, until the development of the "Lossow affair" in September, the Heeresleitung seems to have felt that in the long run things would work out in Bavaria. Seeckt found Los-

[27] It is clear that someone must have been protecting Hofmann from direct disciplinary action, in view of his retention in the army during the post-Putsch period despite the number of influential persons, including Bavarian Cabinet ministers, who wished to see him dismissed. There is, however, no hint in the documents as to the identity of this person, although Ritter von Epp, an old friend and commander, seems a likely possibility.

[28] NA, Epp Papers, EAP 1-e-16/4, Brief: Loeffelholz (Curt) an Epp, 4.2.1923.

[29] NA, T79, 72, pp. 1182-83; 73, pp. 7-19; B, IV, HSIV, EE7, Endres MS, pp. 25-26; Röhm, *Geschichte*, pp. 200-203, 275.

[30] Gordon, Harold J. Jr, "Ritter von Epp und Berlin," *WWR*, June 1959, pp. 336-41.

sow pleasant and even compliant in personal conversation—very typical—and was probably more worried about the separatism of the Bavarian conservatives than he was about the right radicals, a view in which the Heeresleitung was encouraged by the visits of Scheubner-Richter, one of the more presentable and impressive Nazis, to Berlin.[31] Then too, Prussians found it a little hard to take Bavarians very seriously. Seeckt gives clear indications of this attitude in letters to his wife. On 20 September he wrote:

> You will hear more complaining and croaking than elsewhere, but I can't alter that any more than the inflation. . . . I was very pleased with what I saw and heard in Bavaria: soldiers, populace, surroundings—and even food and drink. The days were full and left little time for other thoughts. . . .[32]

In essence, the Heeresleitung, feeling that the Bavarian troops were not entirely dependable and too involved in politics, tried to bring them to accept national policy, without, however, any great sense of urgency, which is not surprising in view of the other problems facing the Reich and the political obstacles to any course of action other than the use of attrition to solve the problem.

III. *The Bavarian Reichswehr and the Bavarian Government*

To a considerable extent the special character of the Bavarian Reichswehr resulted from the fact that it, far more than any other component of the Reichswehr, was created to fight a civil war rather than to defend the frontiers. Both civilian and military leaders in Bavaria looked on the army as an instrument of internal policy, whereas in Berlin both the civilian government and the Heeresleitung looked on the army as an instrument primarily for national defense. There is little indication in the papers of Wehrkreis VII that either Möhl or Lossow were ever very interested in the problems of the defense of Germany, whereas Seeckt's papers reveal a much different view, and Lossow's successor, General Friedrich Freiherr Kress von Kressenstein, from his advent turned his attention to the Czech borderlands and away from the politics of München.[33]

[31] Seeckt Papers, Stück 281, Lieber Notes, pp. 5, 14, 26.
[32] Rabenau, *Seeckt*, pp. 337-38.
[33] NA, T79, 72 and 73, passim; B, II, MA99522, 27.10.1924, pp. 2-5; MA102141, HMB 789, Opf., p. 5.

The Bavarian government looked on the Bavarian Reichswehr as a tool that should be entirely subordinate to its desires and wishes, which were devoted to the maintenance of law and order at home. The Bavarian minister of the interior believed that the Reichswehr should obey him as unquestioningly as did the Landespolizei. At the same time, he and his colleagues were quick to resent the least interest of the national government in the Bavarian police, even though the Reich paid most of the costs of the Landespolizei. Like so many people, the Bavarian ministers wanted to have their cake and eat it too.[34] The Bavarian government was aware, though, that the Reichswehr was not entirely at its beck and call. The result was an odd mixture of confidence and distrust. The distrust stemmed from two sources. First, Hasse is probably right in believing that the Bavarian government felt that the Bavarian Reichswehr was not entirely dependable because it would very possibly not always support Bavaria against the Reich, a suspicion that included the officials of other Reich agencies as well, even though they were born Bavarians. Certainly, there was suspicion of the non-Bavarian divisions of the Reichswehr.[35] Second, there was also suspicion that the Reichswehr was too friendly with the right radical Verbände, and not only the minister-president but other ministers expressed doubts in 1923 as to whether the troops would be dependable in case of a right radical revolt. Yet the same ministers encouraged the maintenance of ties between the Reichswehr and the Verbände and blandly denied to the Reichswehrminister that they had any doubts as to the willingness of the troops to obey any and all orders.

Finally, in September 1923, the Bavarian government supported Generalstaatskommissar von Kahr in his decision to make General von Lossow the executive officer of the Bavarian government under the state of emergency that they had proclaimed. Throughout the year, the government used and even exploited Lossow, but never fully gave him its trust. In the end, it dropped him without a qualm. If there is any complaint to be made about their relations with one another, it would seem that Lossow had more right to complain

[34] B, II, MA103476, pp. 373, 583; T120, Ministerratsitzungs-Protokolle 1920-1924, passim.

[35] The provincial president of Oberfranken, for example, warned the Bavarian central authorities that the troops of a Württemberg Reichswehr Regiment, which had just passed through Bavaria en route to Saxony, could eavesdrop on Bavarian troops with their radios.

than the government that led him into unenviable situation after
unenviable situation, that encouraged him to disobey his superiors
and then suspected him more than ever because he had done so.[36]
It would seem from the uncertainty of the Bavarian government
regarding the Bavarian Reichswehr that the government had few
if any private sources of information in the army. Otherwise, it
could have satisfied itself regarding the military situation at least
in part through such channels. As it was, the relationship between
the Cabinet and Lossow was a close but uneasy one, made more
difficult, but at the same time cemented, by the stresses of the times
and the several crises they faced together.

IV. *The Reichswehr and Mobilization*

Throughout the year 1923, the German nation faced the possibility
of war against France, civil war resulting from left radical revolution, and civil war resulting from right radical revolution. The
Bavarian government and Reichswehr were deeply apprehensive
on the latter two scores and the German government and Heeresleitung on all three. The result was that a good deal of attention was
given to the problem of mobilizing Germany's and Bavaria's forces
to meet the three emergencies.

The Reich's mobilization preparations were the most widespread
and were aimed at the possibility of war with France. Neither the
government nor the Heeresleitung was enthusiastic about the prospect of war and neither saw victory as even a remote possibility.
However, especially after the French began to move beyond the
Ruhr, steps were taken to prepare for a bitter resistance, which
might hold up the French until their own allies could halt them.
The Bavarian division was involved in these plans as were all the
others. Lossow, however, entered into them with an enthusiasm
and lack of secrecy that appalled his superiors. The level of these
national preparations was, however, very low. They involved
preparations for mobilization rather than mobilization itself, and
the only very visible aspect of the program was the training of individuals for short periods.[37]

---

[36] B, II, MA99521, 26.1.1923, pp. 2-3; MA100425, pp. 286-87; NA, T79,
82, p. 74; T120, 5569, pp. K591351, K591407, K591563-65, K591571,
K591582; Seeckt Papers, Stück 281, Lieber Notes, p. 5; Stresemann, Gustav,
Vermächtnis, Berlin, 1932, 3 vols., I, p. 169. Hereafter cited as Stresemann,
Vermächtnis.

[37] Seeckt Papers, Stück 281, passim; Stück 289, Selchow (II), p. 5; FH,

Far more conspicuous and far more risky politically were the mobilization preparations made by the Bavarian Reichswehr in cooperation with the Bavarian government and the Landespolizei. For a number of reasons, partly political, partly practical, the Bavarian Reichswehr, unlike the Heeresleitung, concentrated on the integration of entire Verbände, rather than individuals, into the armed forces. This decision was based partly on a belief that the right radicals were really not bad fellows, even if they talked irresponsibly. It was also based on the recognition that it would be very hard to build up a large reserve force for the Reichswehr without the Verbände, since they had cornered a large percentage of the available manpower, and particularly those men and youths who were best prepared to undergo military service. Further, any attempt to build up a reserve system without the Verbände would unite them against the government and the Reichswehr, which was precisely what these authorities wished to avoid. The result was an attempt to create a system that would integrate the Verbände into the official system and subject to them to the control of the authorities.

It has usually been believed that these measures were military measures taken by General von Lossow without the knowledge or consent of the civilian authorities and indeed in defiance of their wishes. This assumption is, however, untrue. There was some difference of opinion as to whether or not the military authorities were carrying out their mission in the most effective and wisest manner, but there does not seem to have been any difference of opinion regarding the broad outline and purposes of the program. The minister-president himself was in the chair at least during some of the meetings of military and police authorities with the Verbände for mobilization purposes, and when he was not present, his personal deputy, Oberregierungsrat Stauffer of the Justice Ministry, apparently was.[38]

Stauffer was also one of the members of the government commission for Verband affairs. There is little concrete information available concerning this commission, but a letter from General

---

Allg. Akten 1923, Hamb. Gesandtschaft J-No. 2307; NA, EAP/7, xi, Lossow, p. 006710; Stülpnagel, Joachim von, *75 Jahre meines Lebens*, Düsseldorf, 1960 (private edn.), pp. 205ff. Hereafter cited as Stülpnagel, *75 Jahre*. NA, T79, 82, pp. 72, 79.

[38] B, ii, MA103476, pp. 817-26, 1026-27; W, L, E131, C5/25, W.G. 64, p. 265; NA, T79, 72, p. 1268; Röhm, *Geschichte*, p. 188.

(Ret.) Karl Düll of the VVM to the Police Directory throws some light on the commission and the confusion that existed regarding competence even within informed circles:

> I might [also] mention that according to information given to us, the state government has given to the commission formed of Colonel von Seisser, Oberregierungsrat Stauffer, Regierungsrat Balss[39] a completely independent position parallel to the state Ministry of the Interior, whereas according to the Polizeidirektion this commission has only a consultative position in the ministry. This uncertainty has completely shattered the already wavering faith [of Düll's Verband in the government].[40]

This letter may leave the precise powers of the commission unclear, but not its official character. Further evidence of the agreement of the government with the scheme for enlarging the Bavarian division is to be found in a letter from Justice Minister Gürtner to Minister-President von Knilling, in which Gürtner asks Knilling if Lossow's plans have been abandoned or if they will be carried out.[41] Finally, on the very day of the Beer Hall Putsch a representative of the Bavarian Finance Ministry was conferring with Reichswehr representives on the question of the costs involved in the army expansion program.[42]

What, then, was this program, or, more accurately, these programs? The basic plan called for the expansion of the Seventh Division into two or three divisions. There were also loose arrangements for filling up vacant places in the Reichswehr, which resulted in over 2,000 men being taken into the army on a part-time basis during the fall of 1923. Individuals were hired to serve within active companies. Whole units were organized in a few instances. For example, Company Werner was raised from members of München Verbände through the VVM to replace a machine gun company that had been ordered to Berlin to perform guard duty. Other small groups were hired at various times to occupy barracks when the regular troops were ordered out of them, as was the case in early May or at the time of the Putsch.

The Beer Hall Putschists have often claimed that the program for expanding the Seventh Division was a part of the plan of Gen-

[39] An official of PDM.
[40] B, IV, BuR, Bd. 35, Akt 3, V. V. Schwabing-Ost an PDM, 5.6.1923.
[41] B, II, MA100411, Brief: Gürtner an Knilling, 23.5.1923.
[42] NA, T79, 48, p. 1017.

eralstaatskommisar von Kahr for a "march on Berlin," but it seems probable that the official explanation is the correct one. According to Seisser and Lossow, and on the basis of interoffice communications of various kinds, the plan was set up—as an alteration of earlier mobilization plans—to meet the possibility of civil war in Germany or an uprising in Bavaria when Bavarian troops were out of the state.[43] Aside from the political crises brought on by the more radical of the Verbände, it was very largely in connection with this Bavarian mobilization plan that the Reichswehr and the Bavarian government dealt with the Verbände during 1923.[44] It was also these mobilization preparations that brought the army and the personnel of the Verbände together, and led many of the lower ranking members of both groups, especially younger men, to feel that they stood for a common cause, and therefore made the danger in case of a right radical Putsch greater than it had been initially. One can scarcely order men to cooperate with one another for months and then suddenly order them to fire on one another without some questions being asked and some defections. Yet, it is clear that it was not merely the military leaders who made the decision to cooperate with the Verbände but the political leaders of the state, just as it is clear that both groups were aware of at least some of the dangers attendant upon their course of action. To some extent they were the prisoners of past decisions and to some extent they were choosing what they considered to be the lesser of two evils. Fearing the Left more than the Right, and hoping that their mobilization measures would even help them to cope with the right radicals, they went ahead.

v. *The Reichswehr and the Verbände*

The Reichswehr's relations with the Verbände were governed to a considerable extent by factors we have already noted: Lossow's

[43] During October the Reich alerted Bavarian troop units for possible use in the occupation of Saxony and Thuringia, but it was later decided that it was unwise to use troops from one rebellious state against other rebellious states. Seeckt Papers, Stück 281, Lieber Notes, pp. 27-28; NA, T79, 48, pp. 938-40; EAP 105/7, XI, pp. 006713, 006716. For the "march on Berlin" see Chapters, IX, X, and XIV below.

[44] B, I, SA 1, 1494, p. 335; GSK 59, p. 2; II, MA103476, pp. 992-93, 997, 1022, 1024, 1053-54, 1314-15; IV, BuR, Bd. 36, Akt 1, Item 12; Akt 4, FZ, Anon. Anordnung; NA, T79, 48, pp. 918, 936, 946-47, 981, 1014-15, 1029-33; Z, Akten aus Hauptarchiv d. NSDAP, Mappe 125, Besprechung d. Kdrs. RW I.R. 20.

character, the established policy of the Bavarian government, and the mobilization preparations. They were further affected by the tendency of most soldiers to sympathize with the nationalist tone of the Verbände and with their hostility towards Marxism. Finally, family and class ties, as well as the fact that many of the leaders (and followers) of the Verbände were former soldiers, played a role. The result was a generally friendly atmosphere, which, for many on both sides, had worn somewhat thin by November.

Working against this generally friendly atmosphere was the increasingly clear divergence between the objectives and methods of the active soldiers and those of the Verbände, and a gradually developing suspicion on both sides. Many soldiers came to see the members of the Verbände as irresponsible and undisciplined pseudo-soldiers following leaders of doubtful wisdom. Epp spoke of their leaders as "Balkan irregulars"[45] (Komitadschi). The "political soldiers" saw the regular soldiers as stodgy, dull, and obedient servants of an outworn and corrupt system, as defenders of parliamentarianism and Marxism, as men who had sold their souls and the rights of their countrymen for pay and privileges. The soldier placed obedience and courage above personal inclinations. The members of the Verbände put personal political beliefs (or, as they phrased it, "conscience" or the "future of the nation") above obedience to any laws—shades of Thoreau in another land and a turbulent time.

Aside from these imponderables, there were very clear-cut matters of policy at stake. Both sides wanted cooperation between the armed forces of the state and the Verbände, but both wanted this cooperation on their own terms. The result was a prolonged tug of war. Lossow, Dr. Schweyer, and Knilling wanted reserves on whom they could count unquestionably for support. Bayern und Reich and the other more conservative Verbände were prepared to support the government, as long as it stood Right, against the militant or moderate Left. In return they wanted aid and assistance from government and armed forces. The right radical Verbände wanted to win over the Bavarian government and armed forces for a crusade against "Red Berlin," and, if the government would not go along, hoped to be able to use the armed forces against the government. Finally, should this not work, they were prepared to try to turn the "young men" (junior officers) against the "old men" (field

[45] B, IV, HSIV, EE7, Endres MS, p. 18.

grade and general officers) in order to carry out their "revolution of the future."

The points at which these attitudes most clearly clashed were problems regarding the organization, training, and arming of the Verbände. The government and the army wanted to break the Verbände up into small groups, if not to absorb their personnel individually,[46] thus assuring obedience and greater military efficiency. The Verbände leaders, on the other hand, were determined to maintain their units intact, within the expanded armed forces, to the greatest extent possible not only to salvage their own power and influence but also in order to defend their political beliefs. Only in case of a major war were the conservatives prepared to be completely absorbed into the Reichswehr, while the right radicals would not accept this fate even in such a crisis. Some of them even saw themselves—-as Röhm and his circle were later to see the renascent SA—as the core of the army, with the Reichswehr as a mere appendix.

Möhl had kept the Verbände reasonably well in hand by refusing to deal with more than one organization—Bund Bayern und Reich. Lossow, in his soft and pliant fashion, allowed the single organization to become a hydra and found himself dealing with dozens of leaders over whom he had less and less influence.[47] Lossow could not even keep his own right radical officers in hand and gave many junior officers reason to believe that he was very sympathetic towards the right radicals and would support them in a crisis.[48] His personal friendship with Hitler, for example, worked in this direction, as did the concessions he made to the Verbände during the course of 1923, to say nothing of the fact that he allowed officers and men to belong to the Verbände until the May Day affair.[49]

However, even Lossow, stiffened by the government, was determined to maintain the primacy of the Reichswehr and the government, as is clear from the following proposal he made to the Verbände (Kriebel, von Stetten, and von Lenz) in April 1923:

[46] For example, persons included in the PNB program could not be accepted into the Reichswehr expansion program. Yet some Verbände were involved in both programs. B, IV, BuR, Bd. 35, Akt 3, WKK VII Ia Nr. 295/23 Geheim.

[47] See Chapters VIII-X below.

[48] B, IV, HSIV, EE7, Endres MS, p. 60.

[49] NA, T79, 72, p. 1255; Röhm, *Geschichte*, pp. 177-78.

Now that there is substantial agreement among the Reichswehr, the Polizeiwehr, and the Verbände regarding military missions and goals, I ask myself if it is not now possible to organize all of the military bands into an association for purely military matters on the following basis.

1. The so-called Severing Agreement[50] does not apply to the Bavarian government and the Bavarian Landeskommandant.

2. The Landeskommandant directs, in consultation with the organizations, the registration, storing, security, administration, and maintenance of the war materiel. The war materiel hidden and administered by the organizations remains under their protection until mobilization, subject to redistribution to meet mobilization requirements, which will be made in agreement with the organizations.

3. All Bavarian troops will be organized as a Bavarian contingent under the command of the Bavarian Landeskommandant in case of mobilization. They will be distributed throughout Bavarian regiments, etc. and will swear allegiance on the Bavarian flag to the Bavarian government. The [mobilization] call will come from the Bavarian government.

4. The military leaders of the organizations pledge themselves to obtain the materials necessary for the mobilization preparations, to take part in these preparations, and in the case of mobilization to place the military portions [of their organizations] at the disposal of the Landeskommandant.

5. Costs which arise from the maintenance and administration of the war materiel will be borne by the Landeskommandant from the funds at his disposal.[51]

Even more indicative of the attempt of the military authorities to gain control of the members of the Verbände trained by the Reichswehr is the pledge categorically demanded of each volunteer:

In return for training in arms by the Reichsheer I agree:

a) To respond to the call of the Landeskommandant to armed service without reservations.

---

[50] One of a series of agreements between Seeckt and Severing regarding military relations with Prussia. This one concerned the relationship of the Reichswehr with the Verbände. Severing, Carl, *Mein Lebensweg*, Köln, 1950, 2 vols., II, p. 117. Hereafter cited as Severing, *Lebensweg*.

[51] NA, T79, 82, p. 75.

b) [When] not called up, to take part in no hostile or violent actions against the Bavarian Reichsheer or the Landespolizei.

c) That I will not speak of being trained by the Reichsheer, so that no foe of the [Bavarian] state will learn of it.

d) To obey the orders or directions of the training leader and his superiors implicitly in matters concerning training and during training periods.

e) As a mobilized soldier, to accept the existing military regulations and punitive laws.[52]

The opposition of the Verbände, especially the right radical ones, to these arrangements emerges clearly from a confidential letter sent by Lieutenant Colonel (Ret.) Kriebel to the military leaders of the Verbände of the Arbeitsgemeinschaft on 25 June:

The continued spreading of rumors that individual Verbände have accepted the Individual Obligation Forms (Einzelverpflichtungsscheine), which are doubtless set afoot by those who wish to sow disunity and mistrust among the Verbände, lead me to take the following position on this matter.

1. His Excellency von Kleinhenz, the leader of the *Hermann-Bund* [sic] (former Zeitfreiwilligenkorps), also rejects the Einzelverpflichtung absolutely. He has forbidden his members to sign the Verpflichtungsschein. All contrary rumors are outright lies.

2. The Reichswehr goes so far that it continually seeks to persuade individuals or leaders of subordinate units to independent action on the threat of refusing to train them, simply in order to destroy the Verbände. . . .

3. I stand by the wishes of the Verbände, and in accordance with my convictions, on the position that the Einzelverpflichtung must not be accepted. I will fight out this battle together with His Excellency von Kleinhenz. I must then demand that no one will take a contrary position. I am no friend of "questions of confidence." However, in this question I must declare that I cannot further remain in my post if an organization deviates from the common stand. . . .[53]

---

[52] NA, SA Rgt. München, 230-a-10/4, Abschrift vom 20.10.1923, OK d. SA an Bez. Führer. For Lossow's insistence on the acceptance of these conditions see B, II, MA103476, p. 805.

[53] NA, SA Rgt. München, 230-a-10/4 3, Kriebel an Mil. Führer.

On 14 July—the very day of a pitched battle between the München police and the SA—a compromise was reached at a meeting where Lossow represented the Reichswehr; Seisser, the police; Stauffer and Baron von Freyberg of the Ministry of the Interior, the government. The Arbeitsgemeinschaft, Bayern und Reich, and the Hermannsbund were the Verbände involved. According to Kriebel, the Verbände were informed by Stauffer that if they accepted neither the Notpolizei obligation nor the Reichswehr Verpflichtung they would be considered foes of the government and their weapons would be seized by the authorities. Willingness to fight against a foreign foe was not enough to exempt an organization from this fate. As a result Kriebel found it necessary to accept the Reichswehr Verpflichtung after Lossow explained that he had only established these terms in order to be able to include the SA of the NSDAP in the training program.[54]

The result of this sparring was that the training of the Verbände was intermittent. For example, the training of the München SA began right after the French invasion of the Ruhr. It was then interrupted, only to recommence in early April. By early May the training had been halted again. On 5 June it was announced by the SA high command that training would resume, but three days later the München regiment of the SA was still complaining about the failure of the Reichswehr to resume instruction. In July the Reichswehr was again running courses. Another break occurred sometime later, and it was early October before full training was resumed. It is interesting that much of the training for officers of the Verbände was at the enlisted level, indicating the general preparedness of these organizations. Then, with the Putsch, the entire scheme broke down. All in all, the training program had been a military farce— the cheap and easy things had been done and the rest ignored— and a political disaster from the viewpoint of government and Reichswehr. It had even had disadvantages from the viewpoint of the Verbände, since many of their men became restless when they saw how well the Reichswehr soldiers lived.[55]

Other Verbände, of course, were trained in München and some training—though far less, apparently—was undertaken in some provincial towns. The relations of the Reichswehr with the Kampf-

[54] B, IV, BuR, Bd. 35, Akt IV, Item 12, V. Kampfverbände Bayerns, Der mil. Führer 102.

[55] NA, EAP 105/7, III, p. 35, Hitler; SA Rgt. München, 230-a-10/3 4, passim; B, II, MA103476, pp. 750-51, 1020, 1044.

bund and with the SA, however, give a general picture of the situation.[56]

VI. *The Reichswehr and the Feldzeugmeisterei*

The question of the armament of the Verbände caused even more trouble and concern for the authorities—as well as for the Verbände—than did the general problem of relations with the Verbände and their training. It was, after all, the arms that made the Verbände a possibly decisive force in Bavaria and that were therefore crucial not only for them but also for the authorities. However, the question of arms for the Verbände is inextricably interwoven with the history of the immediate postwar era and with that of a peculiarly Bavarian institution, the Ordnance Headquarters (Feldzeugmeisterei).

At the end of the war, the revolutionary era had seen the war materiel of the Bavarian army scattered far and wide. Individuals had come into possession of large quantities of armaments by one means or another. Organizations—Right, Left, and Center—had acquired more. The state and what was left of the army had considerable stocks still under their control. With the end of the Republic of Councils in München, the authorities mounted a double arms campaign. They painstakingly disarmed the city workers, and kept them pretty well disarmed by a continuous campaign of searches. At the same time, determined not to fall victim to another tyrannous leftist minority, they armed the bourgeoisie and the peasantry by way of the Einwohnerwehr. With the dissolution of the Einwohnerwehr, the government collected some of the weapons involved and turned them over to the Allied-supervised institutions, set up under the Treaty of Versailles for destruction. They did not, however, collect large quantities of materiel—partly as a matter of policy, partly because the material was concealed from them. Thus by early 1921 large quantities—by some estimates more than half the available stocks—of arms and equipment were in the hands of private citizens and paramilitary organizations. The remainder were in the hands of the government and army, which could not admit their existence.[57]

[56] B, I, SA 1, 1477, p. 456; II, MA102140, HMB 613, Obb., pp. 2-3; MA103476, pp. 1020-21, 1035, 1042-43, 1157-59; *BLV*, 1922-23, 8, Gahr (KPD), 7.6.1923, p. 369; Z, Auszüge aus den Akten d. Hauptarchivs d. NSDAP, Mappe 125, Röhm an Kdo. Augsburg, RKF.

[57] The material on which this paragraph is based is so diffuse that it

Since the Bavarian government and the Reichswehr had, under the treaty, no right to possess these stocks of war materiel, and since they had no intention of giving them up, the authorities were in a difficult position. Reichswehr installations were in danger of inspection at any time by Allied inspection teams. On the other hand, for a number of reasons the authorities did not wish to turn over all of the illegal stocks to the Verbände. First, the Bavarian government looked on the war materiel almost as much as a financial resource (or at least as a valuable possession) as a rearmament base, and the Reichswehr wished to retain basic control of the resources needed for a considerable expansion of its size. Furthermore, both authorities wished to have the use of certain types of items, particularly vehicles, for day-to-day purposes. Increasingly, neither the government nor the Reichswehr trusted the Verbände enough to wish them to increase their holding of small arms or to acquire large stores of crew-served weapons. Finally, whether or not they trusted the Verbände, it soon became apparent that war materiel in the hands of the Verbände was only very loosely under official control, was liable to unauthorized sale, and, even more important, was often so badly maintained that it was soon either useless or in need of major overhaul.

As a result, the Bavarian government, and the Reichswehr resorted to a technique that has become increasingly popular in recent decades with the governments of nations where greater flexibility of operation and less direct popular control and inspection seems useful for practical purposes (or even as a shield for corruption). They created two publicly-owned corporations, one as a dependent of the other. The basic corporation, the very existence of which was officially a secret—and a rather well kept one at that— was the Feldzeugmeisterei, which was usually referred to by its initials "FZ." The other, a "daughter organization" of the Feldzeugmeisterei, was Faber Motor Vehicle Rental Service (Mietautogeschäft Faber), operated openly as a business by Major (Ret.) Wilhelm Faber. It was, however, officially owned and used military vehicles exclusively. Its employees, including Faber, were civilian employees of the Reichswehr. Theoretically, it served only official

---

cannot be adequately documented in small compass. However, the following citations bolster up the basic statements. B, ɪɪ, MA99518, 9.5.1921, pp. 4-5; Z, ᴍs 28e, Schober ᴍs on Einwohnerwehr, passim; Rabenau, *Seeckt*, pp. 348-49; *Nachkriegskämpfe*, ɪᴠ, pp. 168-69.

ends, but, as time went on, it fell increasingly into the service of the Kampfbund, despite the disapproval of senior officers of the Reichswehr. In turn, this whole system was tied in with the official army ordnance system in Berlin through Colonel Freiherr von Botzheim.[58]

Crucial to the problems of the Bavarian government and the Reichswehr in 1923 was the history of the Feldzeugmeisterei, which was Captain Röhm's power base and therefore a threat to Lossow and Knilling alike, although they did not realize this until after the May Day confrontation with the right radical wing of the Verbände. As far back as 1919, the problem of supervising the armaments lay in the hands of Colonel von Epp. When the Reichswehr became stabilized with Epp as Infantry Chief VII (Infanterieführer VII), the armaments function remained in his hands. He then assigned the function to his second general staff officer, Ernst Röhm, who retained it until May 1923. Röhm turned his amazing energy and very considerable organizational and political talents to building up a formidable and effective Feldzeugmeisterei. As he became more and more involved with "political soldiering," he increasingly staffed this organization with men from his Reichsflagge or allied organizations, or won over the men assigned to the FZ. The result was the creation of an organization more centered on and loyal to him personally than to the Reichswehr, from which most of its personnel stemmed, or to the state. All of the key men in the FZ, Captain (Ret.) Joseph Seydel, Major (Ret.) Faber, and Major (Ret.) Streck were his personal friends and disciples.[59]

Röhm had a practically free hand with the FZ partly because of Epp's disinterest and patronage, but also because, as was so often the case in Bavaria in 1923, the lines of authority were loosely drawn. By 1923, as a result of a series of agreements, the war materiel in the hands of the FZ and the Verbände was agreed to be the property of the Bavarian government, whose Finance Ministry sometimes showed an embarrassing interest in its welfare. At the same time, the war materiel in the possession of the FZ was entrusted to the Landeskommandant for control and maintenance.

[58] B, IV, BuR, Bd. 36, Akt 4, FZ Akt, Geschäftseinteilung, Feb. 1922; Anon. Denkschrift; NA, T79, 72, p. 1228.

[59] NA, Epp Papers, EAP 1-e-16/4, Denkschrift, Spring 1923; Brief: Röhm an S.C. München and Epp, 19.6.1922; T79, 72, pp. 1075-76 etc.; B, IV, HSIV, EE7, Endres MS, pp. 24-25; Röhm, *Geschichte*, pp. 130-31, 197-98, etc.

However, the Verbände, and particularly Bayern und Reich, which for some time had provided much of the money for maintenance, had certain residual rights—never clearly specified—in the FZ materiel. Furthermore, one of the duties of the FZ was to keep lists of and to maintain such materiel as was in the hands of the Verbände, and, by the middle of 1923, the government and Reichswehr were threatening to confiscate all arms and other materiel not reported to the FZ.[60]

Under these circumstances, Captain Röhm soon learned to play off one of his superiors against another and to achieve such complete autonomy that it is clear from his correspondence and even from his autobiography that he came to feel that the FZ was his personal fief. For a considerable time he was able to hold his position against all challengers. However, in the first half of 1923 he went too far. After successfully eliminating Dr. Pittinger's influence, Röhm quarrelled with Epp and then, in defiance of orders, allowed his subordinates to alienate the government and the Reichswehr alike by providing arms and vehicles for the right radical Verbände on May Day. On 3 May Lossow informed Röhm in the presence of Epp, Danner, Kress, and Berchem, that he had been relieved from his post. The resignation from the FZ of most of Röhm's immediate entourage followed in the next few days, and the episode was essentially over, as was the autonomy of the FZ. Röhm's successor showed no such messianic tendencies, and the few remaining right radicals in the organization were apparently no longer able to play a serious role, but much damage had already been done.[61]

Before and after Röhm's departure, the FZ, acted both as a bridge and a wall between the Reichswehr and the Verbände. The Verbände needed the Reichswehr and the FZ to store weapons properly, to repair them, and even to teach their men how to use them effectively. On the other hand, they did not trust the Reichswehr to return weapons given over to it, especially since the right radical groups, at least, might well wish to use them to defy the government. These fears were realized both in May and in Novem-

---

[60] B, I, M. Inn. 66135, RWM, Abt. VIII B, Nr. 3114 E, 7.8.1919; IV, BuR, Bd. 36, Akt 4, FZ Akt, Anon. Denkschrift, 1923; Anon. Anordnung, ca. 16.3.1923; NA, T79, 82, pp. 74, 116-17; Epp Papers, EAP 1-e-16/4, Epp Denkschrift on Röhm-Pittinger clash, 22.3.1923.

[61] *Ibid.*; NA, T79, 72, pp. 1224-27; Epp Papers, EAP 1-e-16/4, Brief: Epp and Lossow, 23.4.1923; Röhm, *Geschichte*, p. 200.

ber when Lossow or other officers refused to release stores of their "own" weapons to the Verbände. Even the conservative Bayern und Reich, with its relatively *staatstreu* outlook, had none too much faith in the army in such matters. At one stage Lieutenant Colonel Schad wanted the Bavarian government to tighten its control over the Reichswehr in FZ questions, and in the middle of 1923 the military leadership of the Bund stated firmly that no arms were to be given up to the FZ except with the express consent of the military leadership. Local groups were informed that the Reichswehr had no right to confiscate weapons; only the Landespolizei had such authority.[62]

Thus the illegal arms constituted an apple of discord among government, Reichswehr, and Verbände. All agreed on the need for the arms; all agreed that they were the property of the Bavarian state; but the question of actual possession and control was never satisfactorily resolved before the Beer Hall Putsch.

VII. *Summary*

Throughout the year 1923, the Reichswehr occupied a difficult and uneasy position, caught between the Reich government and the Bavarian government on the national front and among a host of contenders for power on the Bavarian front. Even a strong man of genius could probably not have led the Bavarian Reichswehr through the resulting storm of conflicts without difficulty. General von Lossow, a "Gummi Löwe," was completely incapable of mastering the situation. Instead, he tacked to every nearby wind and, ironically, brought the Reichswehr and Bavaria home free with far less immediate bloodshed than might have resulted from a more consistent policy in the hands of a more resolute and balanced man. Although, who knows but what more bloodshed in 1923 might have meant far less bloodshed between 1933 and 1945? As it was, a competent military technician without an effective will of his own followed the orders of his civilian masters, who, themselves, roughly followed the wishes of a parliamentary majority elected by the people. Thus we have a perfect picture of how an army should in theory function in a democratic republic—except for the fact that none of the principal actors were republicans and most of them, including the parliamentarians, were highly suspicious of parliaments, democracy, and their electors.

[62] B, IV, BuR, Bd. 36, Akt 5, FZ, Grundsätze; Anon. Denkschrift (Schad ?).

7.

THE BAVARIAN GOVERNMENT

1. *Introduction*

The Bavarian government in the Weimar period was a typical continental parliamentary government in which the legislature (Landtag) was elected by universal suffrage. The election system was based on proportional representation, which reduced wastage of votes but magnified the influence of smaller parties. The executive branch of the government was a joint executive consisting of the Cabinet. The minister-president had more prestige than his colleagues but, as Knilling bitterly complained, practically no institutionalized authority over them. The Cabinet was elected by the Landtag and was responsible to it. However, in the early Weimar period the Landtag allowed the Cabinet pretty free rein within the limits established by the ruling coalition. Bavaria also retained the royal Bavarian tradition of "bureaucratic rule," generally appointing professional officials to the Cabinet. The result was that in 1923 the Cabinet, while responsible to the Landtag, and sensitive to the will of the majority parties, was essentially a government of technical experts, rather than full-time politicians.[1]

The Landtag was dominated by a conservative coalition led by the Bavarian People's Party, which was the largest single party in Bavaria but needed the assistance of the Bavarian Middle Party to stay in power. The Left, radical and moderate alike, could boast only 46 seats, as opposed to the 86 of the ruling coalition, which was a clear and safe majority. Hence, even if the leftists had been united, which they were not, they would have been completely helpless to influence policy.[2]

The judiciary did not play a very significant role in Bavarian politics, although on occasion the courts handled cases and pro-

[1] B, II, MA103473, Knilling an Held, 22.2.1924; *MNN*, 12 & 19.8.1919; GP, D, 1 (Personalities), 2 (Organizations).
[2] *MNN*, 9.6.1920.

claimed verdicts that had political significance. Most of the judges were, not surprisingly, older men, with strong roots in the Bavarian kingdom, who were both monarchist and conservative. In general, however, they executed the law fairly and effectively, except for some clear evidence of prejudice in political trials, where they tended to be "soft" towards the Right and harsh towards the Left. Even here, though, it is important to note that the extraordinary People's Court (Volksgericht), which contained lay as well as professional judges, was more likely to err in this way than courts manned entirely by jurists.[3]

Below the level of the state government, Bavaria was administered, like France, by officials of the Ministry of the Interior. The cities and larger towns were at least semi-autonomous but could be taken over in times of emergency by appointment of "city commissars" who were responsible to the ministry or the general state commissar (Generalstaatskommissar). Other ministries, like the Finance Ministry, had offices scattered throughout Bavaria, but it was the network of the Ministry of the Interior that was responsible for local government and security.[4]

A provincial president (Regierungspräsident) directly subordinate to the Ministry of the Interior administered each of the seven provinces of Bavaria "right" of the Rhine: Oberbayern, Niederbayern, Schwaben, Oberpfalz, Unterfranken, Mittelfranken, and Oberfranken. The Pfalz, Bavaria "left" of the Rhine, also had a provincial president. These provinces were officially entitled administrative districts (Regierungsbezirke), but in the Weimar period they were still often referred to by their old title—circle (Kreis). The provinces were in turn broken down into districts (Bezirke), headed by a district officer (Bezirksamtsvorstand) who was subordinate to the Regierungspräsident. Through this chain of command, the minister of the interior or the Cabinet could administer the entire state and exert political influence at all levels.[5]

II. *The Knilling Cabinet and the Domestic Scene*

The Knilling government, which succeeded that of Graf Lerchenfeld in September 1922, was typical in its conservative cast and

---

[3] B, II, MA99519, 27.9.1921, p. 5; MA99518, 4.6.1921, p. 6; GP, B, Minister a. D. Hans Ehard; Professor Karl Loewenstein.

[4] B, II, MA102140, passim.

[5] For an example of this system in operation see B, I, GSK 43, Reg. Präs. 129, Ofr., 17.1.1924. For the old nomenclature see the *Hof- und Staatshandbuch des Königreichs Bayern 1890*, München, 1890, pp. 390ff.

bureaucratic background. All its members except the minister-president had belonged to the Lerchenfeld government,[6] and to a considerable extent they carried on its tradition, although the new minister-president was more acceptable to the right radicals than Lerchenfeld had been. Like most of the Cabinet, Knilling was a member of the BVP. Its allies were represented by Johann Wutzlhofer of the Bavarian Peasants' League (Bauernbund) and by Franz Gürtner of the Middle Party.[7]

Despite his protests against the impotence of his office, Knilling gave his stamp to the entire government and directed its policy effectively, periodically overriding complaints from some of his colleagues, especially Dr. Schweyer and Wutzlhofer. A shrewd, incisive, and devious man who had been minister of public worship and education (Kultusminister)[8] during World War I, he continually sought to balance and counterbalance the forces striving for control of Bavaria in such a manner as to preserve the essence of the status quo. A choleric man, he reacted sharply and directly to resistance within his Cabinet, although he tended to meet strong resistance elsewhere by oblique methods. In foreign policy, he was a realist, as is indicated by a report written by Moser, the Württemberg envoy to München, in February 1923:

> Herr von Knilling also deprecated the constant talk of war and [the belief] that in case of a further advance of the French one could and should meet them in arms. "The conduct of a war is entirely out of the question for us on two grounds: first, we lack the technical weapons and, second, a unified will among the people. The days of the wars of liberation, when everyone hung a rifle over his shoulder and marched to meet the enemy, are over."[9]

These remarks, which Knilling would never have made publicly in Bavaria, were, characteristically, made to a German envoy to Bavaria with whom he was on friendly terms. He often told his troubles and his plans to Moser or to Edgar von Haniel, the Reich envoy to München, when he would not reveal them to his own Cabinet, and the evidence indicates that he was, generally, honest in his

---

[6] Schweyer, Matt, Gürtner, Krausneck, Oswald, and Wutzlhofer.

[7] B, II, MA99519, 23.9.1921; MA99520, 11.9.1922, p. 1.

[8] Then called Staatsminister des Innern für Kirchen- und Schulangelegenheiten.

[9] W, L, E131, C5/25, W.G. 64, 23.2.1923, pp. 267-68.

dealings with both diplomats, although he certainly made efforts to use them to persuade their governments to accept Bavarian policies.[10] He apparently felt that he could speak more safely and freely with them than with anyone who was involved in the witches' cauldron of Bavarian politics.

Yet his private opinions did not prevent Knilling from making speeches in which he attacked the French in such terms that the strongly nationalist *Münchener Zeitung* could refer to his having sounded a trumpet call for all good Germans.[11] Like many a good American politician he was quite prepared to "get the corn down where the hogs can reach it" without necessarily altering his policy a single millimeter.

At the beginning of the year 1923, Knilling was inclined to be friendly towards the Verbände, believing that there was much good in the movement and hoping to swing it behind himself and the Bavarian state. Ludendorff, the "great Prussian" and priest-baiter, was an anathema to Knilling, who neither liked nor trusted him.[12] Hitler, on the other hand, made a rather good initial impression on the older man, an impression that the events of the early months of the year were rapidly to destroy.[13] Knilling's statement to the Landtag in early February regarding the Verbände probably expresses his true opinion at that time:

> I am extremely anxious that the patriotic bands, who are the bearers of the national liberation movement, should also have absolute confidence in the national attitude and posture of the government. On the other hand, I wish to express the expectation that the patriotic bands on their part will stand as firm supporters behind the government in its duty to maintain public order and national unity, even if the threat to public order and national unity comes from a movement, which itself follows patriotic aspirations, but also special aims, which are as suspect with regard to social and cultural policies as they are from the standpoint of the federalist view of the state.[14]

Here Knilling lays down a policy he was to follow until the Putsch. By this open call for the other Verbände to support the government

[10] See Moser dispatches: W, L, E131, C5/25, passim; NA, T120, 5569, passim.
[11] *Ibid.*, p. K591422. [12] W, L, E131, C5/25, p. 295.
[13] *Ibid.*, p. 294.
[14] B, II, MA100425, Bayr. Landtag, Beilage 3281, p. 290.

in case the NSDAP went over to violent revolution, he undoubtedly hoped to force the National Socialists to abandon any such plans or, at worst, to save the government from having to fight the united Verbände.

While he refused to speak on the same program with Hitler, he was prepared to speak to other Verbände. Although he had no intention of accepting the honorary presidency of the Kampfverbände, which was proffered him, he carefully waited for a favorable opportunity before informing them of his refusal.[15] There is also good reason to believe that Knilling was sincere when he argued, vis-à-vis the Reich, in early May:

. . . The selfdefense organizations can be dissolved only on paper. [They would] be more dangerous if they continued to exist in secret and followed their goals in darkness. Bavaria is also in favor of stronger protection for [political] rallies and therefore supports the bill lying before the Reichstag in this regard. One must not forget that the selfdefense [organization] in Bavaria developed at a time of great governmental weakness. It was created as a means of maintaining law and order. Now, unfortunately, the selfdefense [organization] has in part entered the political arena. One cannot sweep it away overnight. . . . Even in the patriotic bands calm will reappear. The Bavarian government is not weak, but on the contrary strong enough to remain master. It can rely implicitly on the Reichswehr and the Landespolizei.[16]

This speech reflected his hope that if the crisis were staved off long enough it would disappear, and his belief that in case of a miscalculation he held trumps in the form of the armed forces.[17]

Opposed to this cautious and indirect strategy was the more direct and volatile Dr. Schweyer, who was also the minister most exposed to the Verbände and the most aware of the threat they posed to state and government. Even he, however, drew a sharp distinction between NSDAP, against which he wanted to move firmly, and the more moderate Verbände. In September he said in the Federal Council (Reichsrat):

[15] W, L, E131, C5/25, p. 193, W.G. 184; W.G. 64; NA, T120, 5569, p. K591289.

[16] FH, Allg. Akten 1923, Hamb. Gesandtschaft J-No. 2307, p. 8.

[17] W, L, E131, C5/25, W.G. 126.

... The Bavarian government assumes the position that, because the state presently lacks the power to perform all [its] tasks, it is desirable to have volunteer forces available to serve the state, naturally under the understanding that they subordinate themselves completely to the state. No state within the state must develop. . . .[18]

Even though he made this distinction, which Knilling admitted to be justified, Schweyer was unable to win over the bulk of his colleagues. It is important to recognize, though, that their differences were not so much a question of viewpoint regarding the National Socialists as they were a question of which tactics would be most effective in holding the Nazis in check and preventing them from winning new support.[19] Schweyer's difference of opinion with Knilling developed into a personal feud, which Knilling pursued with vigor and gusto, while Schweyer played the part of a dourly silent, but obstinate, opponent, who refused to cry quits although often defeated in detail.[20]

Franz Gürtner, the justice minister, was a key figure in the Cabinet because he represented the Middle Party, the most difficult and uncertain element in the ruling coalition. This meant that he carried weight far beyond his personal influence in the Cabinet, and even Knilling hesitated to break with him on any important issue. At the same time, he is the most difficult figure in the Cabinet to evaluate. At times he initiated complaints or attacks against the SA or other Verbände, while sometimes he defended them. In practice, there is good reason to believe that he protected them by placing his thumb on the scales of justice. After the events of May Day it was common gossip in the prosecutor's office that it was Gürtner who quashed the subsequent proceedings. Later, though himself imprisoned by the Putschists and allegedly angered by at least some of their actions, his handling of the legal proceedings against the Putschists was suspiciously ineffectual. He thus presents the picture of a man who sympathized with the Nazis in many ways but was not yet overtly and uncritically identified with them, as he was to be later.[21] If many members of the moderate Left in Berlin believed

[18] B, I, M. Inn. 71708, pp. 5-6.
[19] For Schweyer's viewpoint on the NSDAP see B, II, MA99521, 5.1.1923, p. 3; MA103476, p. 254.
[20] B, II, MA103473, Knilling an Held, 22.2.1924; NA, T120, 5569, p. K591637.
[21] He was Hitler's justice minister in the Third Reich.

that the enemy stood Right, Gürtner was equally sure that the foe stood Left and could always find excuses for the excesses of the right radicals. Yet, more than once the Verbände expressed distrust of him. He was not their man—then.[22]

Johann Wutzlhofer, the agriculture minister, was a shrewd and determined man, a prosperous peasant, whose sausages were justly famous. He was primarily the watchman of the Peasants' League in the Cabinet and increasingly sided with Schweyer in pressing for action against the NSDAP, which he disliked and distrusted, for Knilling brackets him with Schweyer in his complaints against the latter.[23]

Heinrich Oswald, the minister for social care, was a tough-minded conservative belonging to the Bavarian People's Party. In the general discussion of the NSDAP on 5 January, he "agreed with the remarks of the other ministers regarding the serious threat from the National Socialist Movement. A surprising number of people belonging to it were also active earlier in the Councils Movement. The Communists gain arms through entry into the movement."[24] For him, therefore, the danger was essentially still from the Left, and he recognized the attraction that the NSDAP was developing for Marxists of all colorations, but, like a good number of policemen, he saw here an attempt by Marxists to infiltrate the movement and exploit it. Entertaining a linear rather than a circular concept of the political spectrum, he failed to realize that the distinctions between Right and Left tend to fade away into nothingness at the far edges of the range, where common belief in violent means and common enemies increasingly obscure the differences of utopian vision impelling such radicals. While his political vision might have been slightly blurred, Oswald was clearly not blind and demanded tougher police action against the Nazis.

Dr. Wilhelm Krausneck, the finance minister, was obviously primarily interested in his own ministerial sphere and continually worked to keep standing expenses and new expenses down to a minimum. He, too, was no friend of the National Socialists, as he

[22] B, II, MA99521, passim; MA100411, Gürtner an Knilling, 23.5.1923; MA103476, pp. 59, 1377-78, 1389; NA, T120, 5570, p. K591843; Müller, Karl-Alexander von, *Im Wandel einer Zeit*, München, 1966, pp. 176-77. Hereafter cited as Müller, *Wandel.*; GP, B, Minister a. D. Hans Ehard.

[23] B, II, MA99521, passim; NA, T120, 5570, p. K591843; Müller, *Wandel*, p. 176; GP, D, 1 (Personalities).

[24] B, II, MA99521, 5.1.1923, p. 6.

made clear throughout the year and in the Putsch crisis. A conservative with a strong stake in the existing system, he was also a man with an orderly mind and a bent for careful calculation. His every instinct must have been horrified at the looseness of talk, vagueness of planning, and violence of manner displayed by the Nazis—to say nothing of his opposition to their basic beliefs.[25]

Dr. Franz Matt, the Kultusminister, was another Bavarian People's Party stalwart. He was strongly "white-blue" in political coloration and suspicious of Prussia and Prussians, although he denied—probably honestly—being a separatist. He liked and trusted neither the government of the Reich nor the right radicals and was prepared to stand up to either of them if necessary. He was not, however, a "strong man" in the Cabinet and tended to go along with Knilling in most matters.[26]

Dr. Ritter von Meinel, the minister of commerce, another old-line civil servant, is the most obscure of the Cabinet members. In general, he was in agreement with his colleagues on political questions, whether regarding the Reich or the Verbände. For example, in January he volunteered to work among Bavarian industrialists, whom he felt had been supporting Hitler to some extent, in order to lead them away from the National Socialists. Like the other ministers, he rejected the Beer Hall Putsch sharply and helped Matt in his preparations to set up a "government in exile" in Regensburg.[27]

Why, if the Cabinet was so solidly opposed to the National Socialists, did it cooperate with them and with the other Verbände to a greater or lesser extent until the Beer Hall Putsch, despite slights and direct attacks from this quarter? The answer seems to be twofold. The government feared the Left more than it feared the Right and wanted to be able to put down a possible Red revolution. Secondly, the government was not entirely sure it could suppress the National Socialists effectively, and certainly not without a serious battle, in which even the more moderate Verbände might support the Nazis. The result is that there was a good deal of truth to the boast of Professor Schmidt that "they [Reichsflagge] and other Verbände had forced Graf Lerchenfeld out of office. Knilling had taken the office only after being assured of the cooperation of the Verbände. . . ."[28]

---

[25] B, II, MA99521, passim; NA, EAP 105/7a, Reichswehr Narrative of Putsch; Chapters XI-XII below.
[26] *Ibid.*   [27] *Ibid.*
[28] B, II, MA102140, HMB 11, Ofr., p. 2.

Interestingly enough, while uncertainty regarding the position of Lossow and the Reichswehr was one of the reasons for the government's "softness" towards the Nazis and the Verbände, a good number of key Reichswehr officers were obviously unhappy with the government's relations with the Verbände. Men like Generals Kress von Kressenstein and Ritter von Danner, Lieutenant Colonel Freiherr von Berchem, Colonel Loeffelholz von Colberg of Artillery Regiment 7, Colonel Etzel of Infantry Regiment 20, Lieutenant Colonel Wenz zu Niederlahnstein, Acting Commander of Infantry Regiment 19, Lieutenant Colonel Endres, and Majors Hanneken and Loeffelholz von Colberg of the Wehrkreis staff were among those whose words and actions before and after the Putsch clearly indicated their hostility or coolness towards the right radical Verbände.[29] At the time, being serving officers and loyal ones, they said little, but in his memoirs Endres sums up their views quite clearly—if more forcefully than some of the others would have phrased them—in a sweeping indictment of the failure of the government to attempt to halt terror either from the Left or from the Right:

> Why did they not employ the police and even the Reichswehr against the boundless terror [tactics] of the Communists at rallies? Why did they not introduce draconic punishments? Nothing happened and one cannot be surprised that the conduct of the struggle and the [maintenance] of freedom in rallies and on the streets fell more and more into the hands of the illegal Verbände, especially the young National Socialist Movement. Force calls forth counterforce. The right of the strongest begins. Hitler organizes the Hall Guards, forms Storm Troops, and travels, when his followers are too weak outside Munich, with trainloads of combat-ready youths to cleanse the land, as for example, in Coburg in 1920.[30] The battles in the halls weld the Nazis together. Blood has always been a good cement. The government forbids and prevents the railroad and truck excursions, without providing as a substitute against the leftist terror its own armed forces. Communism triumphs; the anger of the rightists more and more concentrates on the government and Hitler, as the man of action, wins the sympathies of the upright.[31]

[29] See below, Chapters XI-XIII.

[30] Endres undoubtedly refers here to the rally in Coburg in October 1922. See Hitler, *Mein Kampf*, pp. 614ff.

[31] B, IV, HSIV, EE7, Endres MS, pp. 9-10.

Later, he turns to the other side of the coin and remarks, regarding the probability that the Putschist leaders would have escaped punishment had they not marched on the Feldherrnhalle on the second day of the Putsch, ". . . The Bavarian government was at that time so indulgent towards the Right Verbände that it would have yet built for the rebels golden bridges [to immunity]. . . ."[32]

The government thus occupied a most unenviable middle position. Failing to keep peace and order in the streets, it was—as Endres and more than one policeman noted—forced to witness the sliding of power into the hands of those who could hold it rather than those who were authorized to hold it. The government then took just enough action to annoy the Verbände, but not enough to keep them in hand, and certainly not enough to pacify the Left or even to satisfy those moderates on the Right who wished the right radicals to be bridled or disbanded. Even for a circus acrobat, riding two horses bareback is a difficult feat. The government found it an excruciatingly painful and embarrassing position, but one which was nearly as hard to abandon as to maintain. Yet, in the end, with more agility than grace, Knilling brought off the trick.

III. *The Knilling Government and the Reich*

Knilling and his Cabinet inherited a long, bitter, and involved feud with the Reich when they came into office. This feud had destroyed both Bavarian governments since Hoffmann fell victim to the Kapp Putsch in 1920. Kahr had fallen because he had promised more than he could deliver in this quarrel. Lerchenfeld fell because he did not promise enough. Knilling was threatened with the same fate should he not be able to maintain Bavarian interests, or, indeed, perhaps if he could not win a famous victory over the federal government.

Unfortunately, neither in Berlin nor in München was the feud observed with clear eyes and cool heads, nor was it seen in clear and concise terms. Further, neither party to the feud was entirely honest in negotiations, magnanimous in victory, or noble in defeat. The real bone of contention was the equitable division of power, pomp, and wealth between federal and state governments in a federal system. The Bavarian leaders were unhappy about the division that had been forced on them in 1919 and looked back on the Bismarckian system—which their fathers had denounced vigorously

---

[32] *Ibid.*, p. 51.

in its day—with nostalgia. At the same time they believed, with very considerable reason, that the Reich was interpreting its powers under the Weimar Constitution more and more broadly. The capstone of their pyramid of grievances was their resentment of the failure of successive Reich Governments to live up to the commitments to Bavaria made by their predecessors. Essentially the Bavarians wanted redress in three areas: the army, finances, and matters concerning the police and justice. The Bavarians were particularly sensitive about the police question because the basic police power was the greatest power still left to the states, and they deeply feared that it was being eroded, particularly because of recent proposed federal legislation regarding the criminal police, the dispatch of federal and Prussian police and court officials into Bavaria on investigative missions, and because the Reich seemed to be trying to gain a hand in control of the Landespolizei in return for its large contribution to its budget.[33]

Finally, divergences over the Bavarian government's relations with the Verbände were often a major stumbling block in the way of smooth relations with Berlin. Many petty matters soured even day-to-day relations between agencies not directly involved in matters of policy. For example, the studied Bavarian refusal to celebrate "Constitution Day" annoyed avowed republicans (especially the Social Democrats), while Bavaria was outraged when the Reich planned to regulate the wearing of the uniform of the old Bavarian army. Such questions may seem petty, but in the atmosphere of mutual suspicion and irritation that marked Bavarian-federal dealings, it is not surprising that some of them were blown up out of all relation to their significance.[34]

However, neither side really wished the feud to get out of hand, and various agreements had been reached between the two governments. An example is that of 11 August 1922:

> As a result of the political development of the last year, especially through the passage of the Law for the Protection of the Republic, the apprehension has arisen in individual states that

---

[33] B, II, MA99520, 5.7.1922, p. 10; 7.11.1922, p. 4; MA100446a, p. 440; MA103161, Knilling an Dr. Heinze, 15.3.1923, pp. 14-15; NA, Epp Papers, EAP 1-e-16/3, Gürtner an Knilling, 15.3.1923; *BLV*, 1922-23, 8, Dr. Schweyer, 8.7.1923, p. 378.

[34] B, II, MA99520, 7.11.1922, p. 3; MA99521, 1.6.1923, p. 9; 1.8.1923, pp. 11-12; MA100411 R.M. Inn. VII4355, 1.8.1923; MA103456, Reichskanzler Rk. O. 4440, 3.4.1923.

the policy of the federal government is specifically directed at the progressive reduction of the competence of the states, to, in the end, divest them of their character as states and to form the Reich increasingly into a unitary state.

This apprehension is baseless. The facts of life of our Reich, driven under exterior pressure towards internal unity, have made a broadening of the competence of the Reich necessary. This development has, however, as far as one can judge, reached its end. The restriction of the police power and judicial power by the Defense Law is limited in duration.

The federal character of the Reich and the individual characteristics of the states are recognized in the federal constitution. The federal government does not intend to seize for itself sovereign rights of the states beyond the constitutional rights of the Reich. It is convinced that the organization into individual states expresses the multiplicity of the Germans' character and German culture, and that the cultivation of the tribal consciousness within the living narrower community is the best security for voluntary integration in the nation as a whole.[35]

To this pious declaration of principle was appended a firm set of concessions on the part of the Reich government. With regard to the Defense of the Republic Law, the Reich promised that only the most important cases would be sent to the Staatsgerichtshof;[36] all other cases would go to state courts. Cases primarily of interest to or concerning one Land were to go to its courts. In exercising his police authority the federal attorney general (Oberreichsanwalt) was to use the police of the Land concerned. Other police would be brought in only with the consent of the state authorities, on the assumption that the states would not try to thwart the Reich. Judges would not be chosen on a political basis. Several senates (individual courts) would be created within the Staatsgerichtshof, and both the manning and distribution of cases would take into account the locality of the offense. Similar concessions were made with regard to the Federal Law Concerning Officials (Reichsbeamtengesetz) and the Federal Criminal Police Law (Reichskriminalpolizeigesetz), but it was the agreement regarding the Law for the Protection of the Republic that was most significant.[37]

[35] B, II, MA103163, 11.8.1922.
[36] Supreme political court of the Reich in Leipzig.
[37] B, II, MA103163, Denkschrift, 9-10.8.1923, pp. 1-5.

In December 1922 the Cuno government confirmed the concessions made by the Wirth government. In April 1923, the Bavarian government officially accepted its obligations with regard to the Defense of the Republic Law, with the official comment that it disapproved of the law. Cuno assured the Bavarian government that he believed in strong states and cooperation between Reich and Länder.[38] It was therefore with a muted optimism that the Bavarian government entered upon 1923, and its very sharp reaction to the position of the Reich in the fall of 1923 should be seen in this light. When matters they believed had been settled in 1921 and 1922 returned to plague them, the Bavarian ministers determined to fight the matter out once and for all. Separatism and Nazism were not, for them, the issues of greatest significance. They were fighting for autonomy and, with luck, a revision of the constitutional division of spoils between state and Reich.[39]

IV. *The Bavarian Government and the Other States*

Traditionally, relations between Prussia, the largest and dominant state, and Bavaria, the next largest and the leader of the opposition, had been bad. Just as even today in the south of the United States, there are doubtless children who do not realize that "Damn-Yankee" was originally two words, there were certainly many Bavarian children who, more than twenty years after the dissolution of Prussia, believe that "Saupreissen" ("Prussian Pig") is one word. This traditional hostility received heavy reinforcement after 1919 with the development of a ruling coalition in Prussia in which the Majority Socialists were the dominant element, so that "godless Marxist internationalists" faced conservative Roman Catholics in any Prussian-Bavarian negotiations or confrontations. The result was that relations were, at best, cool and distant; at worst, bitterly acrimonious.

By 1923, a number of specific grievances had grown up between the two states. The Prussians pressed so hard for the dissolution of the Verbände in Bavaria that the Bavarians accused them of interfering in Bavarian affairs, while the Prussian leaders, seeking to fight the Communists despite opposition within their own party, deeply resented Bavarian charges that they were soft on Com-

[38] B, II, MA99520, 11.12.1922, p. 2; 27.11.1922, p. 2; MA99521, 20.4.1923, p. 5.
[39] See Chapter IX, Section IV, below.

munism. The Leoprechting Case,[40] with its implications of Prussian spies operating in Bavaria, and the Bavarian request for the recall of the Prussian envoy in München left sour tastes in mouths on both sides. Therefore, despite an occasional closing of ranks to protect states' rights, the Prussians and Bavarians looked askance at one another.[41]

Bavaria had very little to do with most of the other north German states, except for the border states of Saxony and Thuringia, and here the relations were uniformly bad. In 1923 the governments of "red" Saxony and Thuringia had little sympathy with the Bavarians, who in turn heartily detested and feared their neighbors. The readiness of both sides to support the radical opposition in the other state did nothing to ease relations, and by late 1923, Saxony and Bavaria had broken off diplomatic relations with one another and a state of siege, broken by minor forays on both sides, reigned along the Thuringian-Bavarian border.[42] Only in one respect was there the least Bavarian sympathy in regard to either Saxony or Thuringia, and here self-interest was the motivation. The Bavarians watched with mixed emotions the increasingly bitter quarrel between Saxony and the Reich during 1923. Although they were in full agreement with the Reich regarding the iniquity of the Saxon government—and indeed considered the Reich to be too "soft" in this regard—when federal troops actually marched into Saxony they suddenly realized the possible implications for themselves in their own quarrels with the Reich. The minutes regarding Knilling's remarks on this event in the Bavarian Cabinet are revealing of his ambivalent position in this affair:

> The minister-president sketched briefly in this connection the action of the Reich in Saxony. "What was done here against Communism could only be welcomed, in itself. The events illus-

[40] Hubert Freiherr Leoprechting von Ober-Ellenbach was tried and convicted of espionage for the French in 1922. In the course of the investigation and the trial it became apparent that he was also closely associated with the Prussian and federal intelligence networks and had had contacts with the Prussian minister in München. B, II, MA100446, passim.

[41] B, II, MA99520, 10.1.1922, pp. 9-11; 4.3.1922, pp. 8-9; MA100425, pp. 318, 320; MA100446a, pp. 441-43; FH, Allg. Akten 1923, Hamb. Gesandtschaft J-No. 2307, p. 9.

[42] For the "little war" between Bavaria and Thuringia see Chapter IX, Section VI, below. For Saxon-Bavarian relations see B, I, M. Inn. 71708, Reichsratssitzung, 14.9.1923, p. 6; II, MA99521, 17.8.1923, p. 5; 17.10.1923, p. 10; NA, T120, 5569, pp. K591498, K591547, K591556; 5570, p. K592136.

trated clearly, however, to what a pass the position of the states has come within the Reich."[43]

Bavarian relations with the other south German states—Baden, Württemberg, and to a lesser extent Hessia—were closer, but also complex and ambiguous. There can be no doubt that the three large south German states and Hessia felt that they had some interests in common, and that they represented somewhat different policies than did Prussia, and the Reich. On the other hand, it cannot be denied that the others were all inclined to look askance at Bavarian internal policy, which represented a far more conservative line than their own. Too, even before the Revolution of 1918 there had been a certain feeling that the Bavarians wanted to be a little more equal than their fellows. This resulted in foot-dragging in their relations with Bavaria. As Graf von Moy, Bavaria's last royal envoy to Stuttgart saw it, the Württembergers were for anything the Bavarians were against.[44]

On the subject of the Reich, however, there was a good deal of agreement among these south German states. In August 1922, for example, Otto von Brentano di Tremezzo, the Hessian justice minister, wrote to Lerchenfeld:

> You will know my position on the Reich-Bavarian conflict from your envoy to the present ministerial conference. Unfortunately I couldn't go to Bruchsal, because the [state] presidents preferred to make our policies alone.
>
> It is obvious, that I have considered this exceptionally serious problem [the Law for the Defense of the Republic] from all angles. The events in Berlin mean, I am firmly convinced, a major victory for Bavaria and the states which stand upon the federal viewpoint. Though the Berliners may have won in a formal sense, in the matter itself Bavaria has held its own in a way I would not have believed possible.
>
> Should further efforts be made later to infringe upon the remaining sovereign rights of the Länder, the declarations and concessions of the Reich provide so strong a defensive position that, without *force* it will be *unbreachable*.
>
> And that would then give the opportunity to step in with force.
>
> In my opinion, this viewpoint *cannot* be refuted.

[43] B, II, MA99521, 30.10.1923, p. 3.
[44] B, II, MA103281, BG in St. 169.

In Bavaria they should be grateful to you and your colleagues for your brilliant tactics.

There is no denying that in far wider circles than Berlin suspects sympathies are on the side of Bavaria.[45]

Similarly, when the chiefs of state and party leaders of Baden, Württemberg, and Hessia met in October 1923 to consider their position regarding the new Bavarian-Reich conflict, their suspicion of Berlin surfaced again. Before agreeing to condemn Bavaria in the particular question at issue—military discipline and federal control of the army—they bewailed the aggressiveness of the Reich:

At first the conference concerned the *general* questions raised by the conflict between the Reich and Bavaria. In this regard the conviction was expressed from all sides, including the two Social Democratic state presidents, that the intensified centralism or unitarianism which had been pursued by Berlin for three or four years and especially recently must go no further. The viewpoint was unanimous that the Länder must again be given back more rights, if the question is not finally to end with damage to the entire Reich. Far less unanimous were the views on how to achieve this goal. . . .'.[46]

Thus, despite all disagreements regarding liberalism and conservatism, National Socialists and Communists, there was a strong base for general south German support of Bavaria in any conflict with the Reich in 1923, assuming that this conflict was over matters of common interest to all the south German states. Ironically, and, in fairness to the Bavarian government, accidentally, the conflict arose over a matter involving the NSDAP and then became a struggle over Bavaria's residual military rights, a question in which none of the other German states had the most remote stake, since they had all voluntarily handed over these rights to the Reich either in 1918 or before. So the Bavarian government stood alone.

v. *The Generalstaatskommissariat*

In the fall of 1923 the Bavarian political scene was complicated by the introduction of yet another power factor, the Generalstaatskommissariat. As in the Kapp Putsch, in September 1923 the Ba-

---

[45] B, II, MA103163, Brief: Brentano an Lerchenfeld.
[46] B, II, MA103457, BG in St. an M. d. Äuss., 23.10.1923, 591T Nr. 1118.

varian government, with the consent of the Landtag majority, decreed a state of emergency and appointed a Generalstaatskommissar, Dr. Gustav von Kahr. Kahr, unlike Theodor von Winterstein in 1920, did not merely take over the security powers of the state for the period of the emergency but created an administrative structure responsible to him. In this manner a "government within the government" arose, which operated parallel to the elected government throughout the next five months.[47]

Kahr's "Cabinet" consisted of Seisser as his deputy for military and police matters; Regierungsrat Freiherr Hubert von und zu Aufsess for general administration; Freiherr Karl von Freyberg as liaison with the Ministry of the Interior; Lieutenant Colonel Forster of the Landespolizei (Seisser's chief of staff) as chairman of the economic committee; Oberregierungsrat Stauffer (on loan from the Justice Ministry); Oberregierungsrat Schuler, the chairman of the justice committee; Adolf Schiedt, press officer; and Major Heinrich Doehla (Landespolizei), chief of the intelligence service. Besides these key men, there were other officers and officials to aid them and further liaison officers from other ministries. In October, Knilling also appointed a number of deputies to the Generalstaatskommissar, with power to make arrests and to order limitations on the movement of suspected persons. These were the police president of München, the chief of the state police office (later police director) in Nürnberg-Fürth and the Regierungspräsidenten. On 6 October 1923, Kahr was also given the power to create deputies, but apparently made no actual use of this authorization despite consideration of Eduard Nortz, the former police president of München, as Kommissar for North Bavaria, and a brief but disastrous—from the point of view of propaganda—flirtation with Ernst Pöhner.[48] The Volksgerichte were given juris-

[47] See Chapter IX, Section I, below.

[48] Pöhner went to talk to Kahr about the possibility of becoming his deputy for northern Bavaria. According to Pöhner, he went at the instance of Crown Prince Rupprecht among others. All accounts, on both sides, agree that the talks were inconclusive. Pöhner claimed at his trial, however, that they revealed Kahr's intention to "march on Berlin." The existing documents stemming from the pre-Putsch period do not support this statement. It is also extremely unlikely that the conversation proceeded along the lines Pöhner described because Kahr and Knilling were then negotiating with Nortz concerning the post in question, which, in the end, was never created. For Pöhner's account see NA, 105/7, III, Pöhner Testimony. See also Chapters IX and X below.

diction over offenses against orders and decrees of the General-staatskommissar.[49]

Kahr had broad, and not clearly defined, powers under the State of Emergency Law and had his own executive and judicial channels through which they could be exercised. In theory he was subordinate to the Cabinet, which in turn was dependent on the Landtag, but in practice such a parallel structure and such broad powers made Kahr's position a very powerful one. He was limited by his own character, by his dependence on the Finance Ministry for funds, and by the fact that he could be removed from his post should he sufficiently irritate the Cabinet or the minister-president.[50]

VI. *Summary*

The Bavarian government enjoyed the support of the elected representatives of the bulk of the Bavarian population throughout the stormy year 1923, and there is good reason to believe that it also enjoyed the support of the majority of the population. Nonetheless, faced with the vigorous demands of a militant and armed minority at home and by the power of the federal government "abroad," it occupied a very dangerous and precarious position. The creation of the Generalstaatskommissariat relieved some of the direct pressure on the government but also created another competing power factor and a more involved situation. Only great luck coupled with considerable skill saved Knilling and his Cabinet from shipwreck on several occasions. Nonetheless, although they failed to make the most of some of their opportunities, the Cabinet stood the one political test that counts: it endured, at least through the greatest crises of the first decade of the Weimar Republic.

[49] B, II, MA103457, 42218, 4.10.1923; M. Pr. 1438 an GSK, 10.10.1923; 20464; M. Inn. 3064 a 7; MA103476, pp. 866-67; I, Kahr MS, pp. 1256-63, 1268; NA, Lapo Bekanntmachung 144, 27.9.1923.

[50] For Kahr's personality and political activities see Chapter IX, passim.

PART TWO
The Conflict

MAP 2. Central München, 1923

8.

THE OPENING VOLLEYS—JANUARY TO SEPTEMBER

I. *The Parteitag of the NSDAP*

On 3 January, when the Bavarian Cabinet discussed the National Socialist Party, its members all agreed that the fledgling political organization was a very real menace to law and order and to the existing state. At the same time, in the way of men from time immemorial, they decided to do nothing about this menace, apparently hoping that it would either abate or disappear. This natural reaction is particularly strong among men in high political office, where action against a menace must often be drastic and on occasion is dangerous for those who undertake it. It is undoubtedly fortunate that this reaction exists, for many menaces do disappear when ignored and many unnecessary battles are avoided in this manner. Unfortunately for Bavaria in 1923 and for many other people and lands in later years, the NSDAP was not a menace that was fated to disappear quietly and calmly from the scene.[1]

Indeed, within a few weeks, the National Socialists made it clear that they could not be ignored and that they would be most difficult to pacify. January was, in any case, a turbulent month. The French invasion of the Ruhr raised nationalism in Germany to fever pitch. In Bavaria, the peasants were relatively untouched by this emotion, but München was boiling over. The growing inflation and unemployment gave an added edge to the unrest in the city. The recent conversion of several of the more important papers, especially the formerly democratic *Münchner Neueste Nachrichten*, to an aggressively nationalist posture, was both a symptom of the times and a spur to further unrest. Even the Majority Socialists attacked the French for "imperialism." On 14 January a "national day of mourning" rally was held by the VVVB and was attended by a crowd estimated at 100,000. Knilling, Schweyer, Gürtner, and

[1] B, II, MA99521, 5.1.1923, passim.

Landtag President Heinrich Königbauer, spoke, as did Professor Bauer of the VVVB, Dr. Pittinger, and the fiery Jesuit Rupert Mayer. Hitler, however, loudly contemptuous of the idea of "passive resistance" and of the seriousness of a "national front" that included Marxists, held aloof.[2]

A few days later, on 18 January, the University held two celebrations of the founding of the Reich. Patriotic fervor was high and the mood was red-white-black rather than white-blue. Even the rector, Father Georg Pfeilschifter, spoke in an almost belligerent tone. Kahr, who had put up the money for one of the meetings, also spoke. Ludendorff was present as a guest of honor and was loudly cheered, the only one the students so honored.[3]

On 22 January the VVVB celebrated the Reichsgründung with three mass meetings in München beer halls at which Crown Prince Rupprecht, Professor Bauer, Kahr, Königbauer, and the second mayor of München spoke. After the meetings crowds cheered Rupprecht at the Leuchtenberg palace and then demonstrated in front of the Inter-Allied Military Commission's headquarters.[4]

In this supercharged atmosphere, it is not surprising that the National Socialists, never renowned for their self-restraint, sought to expand the scope and visibility of their activities. The occasion for this upsurge of activity was the Party Day of the NSDAP, which was not yet held in the fall or identified with Nürnberg. The plans in 1923 were a long way from the "spectaculars" staged by Goebbels in the days of the Third Reich but they were impressive—and ominous—enough by the standards of early Weimar Germany. By itself the Party Day would not have been a matter of serious concern had it not been for the recent "militarization" of the NSDAP, in the course of which the Storm Troop units had been greatly strengthened in number and size.[5]

Rumors of a National Socialist Putsch were rife, as they were to be so often during 1923, and even penetrated to Berlin.[6] National Socialist activity in München had been greatly stepped up. Plans had been laid for the Party Day, and all seemed well. Then the government decided to place definite limitations on the festivities.

---

[2] B, II, MA102140, HMB 6, N/B, p. 3; HMB 226, Obb., pp. 2-3; HMB 288, pp. 1-3; HMB 385, p. 5; NA, T120, 5569, pp. K591231-37, K591248-49, K591260, K591263; Röhm, *Geschichte*, p. 163.
[3] NA, T120, 5569, p. K591245.   [4] *Ibid.*, pp. K591246-47.
[5] See Chapter III, Section III, above.
[6] B, II, MA101249, Rk. O. In. 84, 24.1.1923, p. 15.

Police President Eduard Nortz had the unenviable task of informing Hitler, on 25 January, two days before the Party Day, that his wings were to be clipped. Hitler reacted predictably and violently when his twelve rallies and his massed marches were banned. He stressed the patriotism of his party, and called down the maledictions of future historians on the small-minded who did not recognize the way of destiny. Nortz suggested to the ranting Hitler that he should take his objections to the Ministry of the Interior, but the Nazi leader rejected the suggestion with contempt. He said that he had carefully held his men, especially his Storm Troops, in check. Now he would give them their heads and see how the authorities liked the result. He would hold his dedication of standards (Fahnenweihe) in any case. The government could call up police and soldiers. They could shoot if they so wished. He would place himself in the front ranks. The first shots would release a red deluge. Two hours later the government would be swept away.[7]

Hitler was now desperate. He, the self-proclaimed "man of action" could not turn back now and expose himself to the ridicule of his enemies and the disillusionment of his followers. However, his military allies rallied to his support. At a conference called by General von Lossow, who tended to operate as a committee chairman more than as a commanding officer, General Ritter von Epp and Captain Röhm strongly defended Hitler's position and ridiculed the idea of a Putsch. By his own admission, Röhm, whose credit was still undamaged in the eyes of his new commander, took so strong and emotional a stand that one of his fellows on the general staff suggested to him that his conduct was incompatible with his position as an officer. Apparently Lossow was not convinced, but Epp and Röhm visited him again after the meeting and persuaded him to talk to Hitler. Hitler promised that he would see to it that the meetings went off without disorder, and Lossow promised to ask the government to modify its ban. He then sent Röhm off with Hitler to see Gustav von Kahr, the provincial president of Oberbayern (which surrounded München), and Kahr, always soft towards nationalists of any hue, also agreed to speak for reconsideration of the decree.[8]

Meanwhile, the government, under pressure of various sorts to reconsider, sounded out members of the majority parties and lead-

[7] B, II, MA99521, 24.1.1923, pp. 10-11; MA100425, Bayr. Landtag, Beilage 3281, Ausschuss für Staatshaushalt, pp. 288-89.

[8] Röhm, *Geschichte*, pp. 164-65.

ers of the Verbände, and discussed the matter with Nortz and Lossow. Lossow said he favored giving Hitler his head, but keeping the army and police ready for action and using them firmly if Hitler violated his promise to maintain order. He said that if a state of emergency were declared, he thought that he would be able to keep the Reichswehr, its reinforcements from the Verbände, and the police in hand, although one couldn't wean away those who sympathized with Hitler overnight. Apparently his tone as well as his words indicated that he would do what he was ordered to do, but that he wasn't enthusiastic about the idea of a confrontation without a clear violation of the law by Hitler. The party leaders agreed to go along with the government on a state of emergency decree. Schweyer refused to go back on his earlier decisions, and it was decided to meet Hitler head on. Pirner reported that police reinforcements had been ordered to München, and the government requested that Reichswehr reinforcements also be ordered to stand by.[9]

By the time Kahr, Grainer, and Keller (VVM), Colonel von Lenz, Dr. Pittinger, and Professor Bauer were called in to speak to the ministers, the decision had been made. Grainer said that he did not have the impression that Hitler wanted to revolt and warned that the Verbände couldn't be used against Hitler because too many of their young members supported him. Lenz, whose organization was made up largely of students, said that he was a soldier and would obey. He had called up his unit and was sure that the leaders, at least, would come, even the National Socialists among them. He doubted if Hitler could be called off. Pittinger said that, although a good number of his followers were influenced by Hitler and some of the younger men, especially students, might not oppose him, Bund Bayern und Reich would stand by the government. Pittinger also promised to try to work through the Verbände on Hitler. Professor Bauer didn't believe Hitler was planning to revolt, but promised that the Verbände to which he, Bauer, was close would support the government. Yet he would not promise to act against Hitler with armed force. There was no direct response to Schweyer's demand for a proclamation by the Verbände attacking Hitler.[10]

[9] B, II, MA99521, 26.1.1923, Notizen für Ministerratsitzung, pp. 2-7; NA, T79, 48, p. 1000.

[10] B, II, MA99521, Notizen für Ministerratsitzung, pp. 7-11; IV, BuR, Bd. 36, Akt 5, "Zur Lage" n.d. (Jan. 1923).

Before the Cabinet meeting, Schweyer had been approached by Lieutenant Hans Ulrich Klintzsch, the former naval officer who led the National Socialist Storm Troops, with a request for permission to allow at least processions to the quarters assigned to visiting party members from outside München. Schweyer refused, pointing out that the Cabinet decree could not be rescinded by him and that, in any case, the party representatives from the Reich, with whom he had just met in Mannheim, had insisted that common action against the French was only possible if the Bavarian government stood firm against the NSDAP. Klintzsch or his companion replied, " 'If blood flows tomorrow, then it flows. There won't be any cowards there. The Ruhr resistance will break down anyway.' "[11]

In the end, although the government had screwed up its courage to action, the action never came. Nortz had been full of fight earlier in the day. Although he estimated that some 15,000 party members and 25,000 supporters were gathered for the Party Day, no more than 4,000 need be considered in a fight. Out of another 12,000 from outside, no more than another 4,000 could be seen as possible combatants. He would answer for the loyalty of the city police. Even those who favored Hitler would do their duty. Colonel Banzer of the Landespolizei and Lieutenant Colonel Thenn of the blue police had assured him that they could depend on their men. He wanted to use large numbers of men to insure that there would be no bloodshed. If there was to be shooting, a small detachment could do the job. He wanted no retreat before Hitler and recommended that the twelve proposed rallies be included in the ban.[12]

On the evening of 26 January, however, Hitler came to see Nortz in a very chastened mood. He claimed that it was technically impossible for him to call off the Fahnenweihe with so little notice, but he would restrict it to a half hour instead of the planned two hours. By the time the conference was over, the police president had, on his own initiative, agreed that the Fahnenweihe could be held in the Zirkus Krone—a favorite rallying point of the National Socialists because the manager, a member of the party, allowed them to use it without charge.[13] All that Schweyer could do when he heard about the concessions the next day, was to reduce the number of rallies to six, and even this was futile, because Hitler

---

[11] B, ii, MA99521, Notizen, 26.1.1923, pp. 1-2.
[12] *Ibid.*, pp. 3, 6.
[13] NA, SA Rgt. München, 230-a-10/3 2, 13.9.1923.

quite correctly pointed out that on such short notice there was not time enough to change the arrangements.[14]

The Party Day went off without any serious incident, although Hitler characteristically violated the terms of his agreement with Nortz in detail, by holding his Fahnenweihe outside rather than inside the Zirkus Krone, in defiance of the ban on meetings "under the open sky" in the state of emergency regulations. He did, though, stay outside the "Bannmeile," a circle around the center of the city where marches and demonstrations were forbidden. All in all the affair was an anticlimax.[15]

The repercussions of the Party Day were, however, significant. For one thing, it smoked out a number of hitherto unrecognized Hitler supporters. Among these were Alfred Zeller, the leader of VVM, whom both Schweyer and Knilling had believed to be in their corner, and the elusive student leader Walther Hemmeter, who was to play an active, indeed violent, role in the following months. Dr. Christian Roth, a former justice minister, also deserted the position of the Middle Party to support Hitler and attack the government.[16] The Party Day clash of interests also precipitated the break away of various right radical elements in Bund Bayern und Reich, a break which had been pending since the transfer of Möhl and Ludendorff's encouragement of the "separatists."[17] Furthermore, the January confrontation led to a greater radicalization of the students at the University and the Technical University (Technische Hochschule). Disgruntled by the pro-government position adopted by Colonel von Lenz and Pittinger, as well as by the success of the rector of the University in keeping the students quiet, Hemmeter and Dr. Roth now began organizing the students militarily outside of Bund Bayern und Reich and without dependence on the Reichswehr.[18]

In the government camp the repercussions were equally as strong. Knilling and his colleagues, although they had apparently asked for Lossow's advice, had found the advice they received decidedly unpalatable, even though he tempered it by making it clear

---

[14] B, II, MA100425, Bayer. Landtag. Beilage 3281, p. 290.

[15] *Ibid.*

[16] B, I, Kahr MS, pp. 1170-73. See Hofmann, *Hitlerputsch*, p. 71, for a differing account of these January events, based largely on memoirs and secondary materials.

[17] See Chapter IV, Sections I-II, above.

[18] B, I, Kahr MS, pp. 1172-73; II, MA102140, HMB 169, Obb., p. 3.

that he would follow any orders they gave him. However, as in the Kapp Putsch, the civilians resented the advice for which they had asked and blamed the military leaders for being unreliable—without having asked them to do anything! Knilling was also soured by Hitler's threats of violence. Dr. Schweyer, although he publicly assumed the responsibility for the concessions made by Nortz, was clearly angered at assuming the blame for decisions contrary to his express orders, and Nortz had a black mark against him for the future.[19]

In addition, the Reich government, usually anxious, at least in theory, to see the Bavarians take a firm hand with the Verbände, now stepped in—reflecting questions in the Reichstag—with a decision that Bavaria had no right to declare a state of emergency without consulting the Reich and a demand that she rescind it.[20]

Finally, adding insult to injury, Hitler, who had managed to hold his rallies only by means of abject pleadings and by stressing technical difficulties in calling them off, boasted during the Party Day that he had defied the government successfully:

> The gentlemen of the government cling too tightly to their ministers' chairs to take the responsibility for firing on defenseless men. . . . This evening shows us that we have triumphed. Despite exceptional law and state of siege our rallies take place, and our Fahnenweihe will be held tomorrow.[21]

He also accused Schweyer of lying in his account of the events leading up to the state of emergency. All in all, Hitler could be content, and the government discontent, with the events of January. May was to show, however, the weakness that Hitler revealed many times in his career. Having found a solution that worked in January, he applied it again in a situation changed by his own triumph and was soundly drubbed as a result, just as in the Russian winter of 1942-43, the tactics that had been successful the year before no longer worked.

II. *The Arbeitsgemeinschaft and May Day*

The Arbeitsgemeinschaft was formed in late January, probably on the twenty-sixth. Dr. Christian Roth and Captain Ernst Röhm both

[19] NA, T120, 5569, pp. K591255-59.
[20] *Ibid.*, 1745, p. D754273.
[21] B, II, MA100425, Entschluss des Staatsgerichtshofs, p. 239. Quoted from *Völkischer Beobachter*, 31.1.1923.

claim the credit for having founded it. Roth, at the time, asserted that it controlled a large number of north German organizations, but there was no reality behind that assertion. Essentially, it was a coalition of those groups that were prepared to ally themselves with Hitler in the pursuit of a right radical program.[22] At a meeting on 4 February 1923, Röhm declared the goals of the new alliance to be: the struggle against Marxism, the creation of a powerful military force, and the production of propaganda through *Heimatland*. Hitler stressed the struggle between parliamentary and nonparliamentary power. The Arbeitsgemeinschaft would support the Bavarian government as long as it remained "national."[23]

On 5 March 1923, Kriebel was appointed "military leader" for all of Bavaria. On the same evening, the coalition took its first move towards becoming a "state within the state." At Hitler's suggestion, a committee consisting of Kriebel, Dr. Weber of Oberland, and Hemmeter was sent to Knilling to demand that a speech by Captain Hermann Schützinger of the Prussian police be canceled. They were successful, but it seems unlikely that any pressure was needed, since Schützinger was *persona non gratissima* in Bavaria and at least one speech by him was banned in 1925.[24] The sequel suggests that the Arbeitsgemeinschaft, at least, interpreted the ban as an indication of fear or favor on the part of the government.

In April the leaders of the Arbeitsgemeinschaft, whose spirits and aggressiveness seem to reflect—perhaps not entirely by coincidence—the appearance of the strong spring beers so beloved of Müncheners, began to bait the government directly. On 7 April they decided to march through the "Bannmeile" during a "military exercise" which appears to have been a combination of propaganda march and Bierabend. It was here, too, that Hitler made the suggestion that led to the May Day debacle: that the Arbeitsgemein-

---

[22] NA, Epp Papers, EAP 1-e-16/4, 11.5.1923, Denkschrift von Hptm. Daser; Röhm, *Geschichte*, pp. 170-71; Chapter IV, Sections I-II, above.

[23] B, II, MA103476, Auszüge aus Protokollbuch der Arbeitsgemeinschaft, p. 96.

[24] Schützinger was a former Bavarian army captain who joined the SPD and became a Prussian police officer. In mid-1923 he left the Prussian service and entered the Saxon police as a colonel as a result of Zeigner's campaign to find Left-inclined officers. He was later a leader of Reichsbanner, the socialist paramilitary organization. GP, D, 1 (Personalities). For the speech incident see: B, II, MA103476, p. 97; NA, T120, 5569, pp. K591312-13.

schaft should sponsor a national celebration on 1 May.[25] Finally, Captain Heiss was able to inform the group that he had returned from Berlin with the information that he and Hitler were planning a Putsch in a few days. The Secretary, Hemmeter, humorlessly wrote in this regard: "Was noted for the record."[26]

However, it was on 12 April that the next confrontation with the government began. The Staatsgerichtshof in Leipzig had summoned two members of the NSDAP, Dietrich Eckart and Hermann Esser, to appear before it for judgment, and summonses for Hitler and Captain Wilhelm Weiss were pending. Hitler told his colleagues in the Arbeitsgemeinschaft that he would not permit the arrest of any of his men. Dr. Roth suggested a demand that the Bavarian government not permit the arrests, and this course of action was adopted. Hitler, Kriebel, and Lenz visited Knilling on Friday, 13 April, and gave him an ultimatum, demanding that the Cabinet reject the arrest orders and that it insist upon the nullification of the Law for the Defense of the Republic in the Reichsrat.[27] Should the Reich refuse to act, Bavaria must unilaterally reject the law. They wanted a reply the next day.[28] Knilling told the delegation flatly that there was no hope that the government would comply with this demand, but that he would present it to the Cabinet. The Cabinet agreed with Knilling and decided to ignore the ultimatum. Nortz and Lossow, when consulted as to means of enforcing the arrest orders, both promised their full support to the government.[29]

Meanwhile, Lossow and other unofficial representatives of the government worked on the Verbände, with the result that they saw the folly of their ways. This was particularly important, because a "military exercise" of the Arbeitsgemeinschaft Verbände was scheduled for Sunday. As it happened, the "exercise" went off without demonstrations against the government, and on Monday, two days after the expiration of the ultimatum, Knilling received the leaders of the Arbeitsgemeinschaft again. Without mincing words, he told them that he was no friend of the Law for the Defense of

[25] B, II, MA103476, Protokollbuch, p. 99.
[26] *Ibid.*, "Wird zur Kenntnis genommen."
[27] First chamber of the German Parliament, representing the state governments.
[28] B, II, MA103476, pp. 101-02; NA, T120, 5569, pp. K591360-62.
[29] *Ibid.*

the Republic, but that it was nonetheless the law and he would enforce it. Kriebel said, " 'That means, then, a declaration of war by the government on the Arbeitsgemeinschaft.' " Knilling countered with the reminder that it was the Arbeitsgemeinschaft and not the government that was on the offensive. In discussing the matter, Knilling shrewdly remarked, " 'The enemy stands Left, but the danger on the Right.' "[30] Then, with the typical civilian viewpoint, he added that it was the former officers, like Kriebel, who were the most incorrigible elements, thus ignoring the far more vociferous civilians Hitler and Roth as well as the men whose violence had led to their indictment and the ultimatum, the most unmilitary Eckart and the former revolutionary, Esser.

The whole affair was a slap in the face for the Arbeitsgemeinschaft and should have been a warning to them that the authorities were in no mood to be bullied. However, their reaction was quite different. They swept the matter under the rug with no more comment than complaints by Kriebel over the conduct of the Landespolizei, where he had apparently hoped in vain to find support, and some discussion of the intricacies of the legal situation. Then, on 26 April, having achieved on paper a consolidation of power through a vague alliance with the hapless VVVB, whose wily leader was not prepared to get himself out on a limb of Hitler's choosing, the Arbeitsgemeinschaft turned its attention to Hitler's proposal for a "national demonstration" on May Day.

This proposal was at once shrewd and dangerous, the sort of *coup* that always attracted Hitler. In Bavaria May Day was fraught with possibilities for conflict far beyond those to be found elsewhere in the Reich. To the Center and Right it was the day on which München had been rescued from the Republic of Councils. To the Left it was the sacred holiday in honor of Marxism and organized labor. The resulting tensions were similar to those one might find in Belfast if the anniversary of the Battle of the Boyne fell on the day Eire became independent. Should the Arbeitsgemeinschaft organize a demonstration, the government would be placed in a most unpleasant dilemma. If the authorities allowed both celebrations there would undoubtedly be bloodshed, plus the danger of a two-front battle by the police against both groups of celebrants. If the government gave way to the right radical demands it would give the latter an unearned victory while exposing

[30] *Ibid.*, pp. K591369-70.

itself to violent protests from the Marxists and official recriminations from Berlin. If, on the other hand, the government banned
the right radical demonstration and permitted the Marxists to
march, it would be supporting Marxists against nationalists in a
strongly nationalist state, where Marxists were thought of not in
terms of utopian idealism, but in terms of the detested Republic of
Councils and the "hostage murders." Even many moderates would
condemn such a position. Needless to say, banning both demonstrations would enrage all concerned, invite flagrant violations of
regulations, and very possibly lead to confused fighting.

After some debate, the Arbeitsgemeinschaft leaders decided
that they should march and that they should prevent the "Reds"
from marching. The government should be warned that the Reds
were armed and aggressive. Lossow should be confronted with a
fait accompli, an adamant decision.[31] The extent to which they had
already seen through the general's firm exterior to the pliable personality beneath is indicated by Hemmeter's confident evaluation
"that Lossow will not thus cross the Rubicon."[32] The resulting
audience with Knilling and Schweyer was heated. Knilling was
apparently inclined to give way and ban the Majority Socialist
demonstration—very probably more because of his distaste for
Marxists than because of his desire to placate the Verbände.
Schweyer, however, stood firm despite sharp attacks from Roth,
who was the Arbeitsgemeinschaft spokesman.[33]

At the Cabinet meeting the next day, though, a new element was
introduced into the picture. The Communists had announced that
they would take part in the May Day parades in full force and had
called out their members. The Cabinet might be prepared to see the
SPD and union members parade, but not the Communists. The
ministers were especially uneasy because of recent gunplay between workers and right radicals in Neuhausen and Schwabing.
The result was a banning of the planned massed march of the
Marxists. Instead, they were to be permitted to hold seven smaller
parades. A question of competence was also involved. The police
president had given the original permission for the leftist celebrations without consulting the government. Knilling was annoyed at

[31] B, II, MA103476, Protokollbuch, pp. 104-109; NA, T120, 5569,
K591380.
[32] B, II, MA103476, Protokollbuch, p. 107.
[33] B, II, MA103476, pp. 52-56.

this presumption, especially since he was afraid it might lead to the police having to defend Reds against nationalists.[34]

In a sense, the Arbeitsgemeinschaft had won their point regarding the Red mass demonstration, but their leaders were not satisfied. They were obviously steering a collision course with both government and Marxists, but it is not clear which was their primary target, although Hitler disowned any hostility towards the government even in Arbeitsgemeinschaft meetings. They now demanded that the government ban even the seven small parades, but their ranks were not entirely united. On the night of 28 April the district leaders—and real masters—of the VVM voted not to attack the Marxists on May Day. Zeller, the titular head of the organization, defied this decision and agreed to go along with Hitler.[35]

The final decision, however, was put off to 30 April. Then, at a full Arbeitsgemeinschaft meeting, after considerable discussion, it was agreed that the Red demonstration would be attacked and that the Verbände would appear under arms. Roth wanted to try to arrange for the Verbände to be called up as Notpolizei, but Hitler, his mask slipping a little, argued that this would oblige them to protect those whom the government wished protected. There must be "aggressive action with the use of armed force," he said. Lossow was to be informed of their decision.[36]

The right radicals were extremely active that day. They visited Lossow to seek his support and to demand "their weapons" which were in his care. They received cold comfort, for the general turned a deaf ear to Hitler's plea that Lossow was obligated to support the Verbände. Röhm, often not too trustworthy a witness,[37] claimed in his autobiography that Lossow admitted this stand to be a violation of confidence, but Endres, Lossow's operations officer, paints a different and more likely picture of Hitler threatening violence and Lossow trying to soothe him. With regard to the arms, Lossow was equally firm. He wrote shortly thereafter: " 'I would have to have been a fool or a criminal, if I, as the highest bearer of the power of the state,[38] had given arms in this moment into the hands

[34] B, ii, MA99521, 28.4.1923, pp. 3-4. The ban itself may have been issued on the twenty-seventh. See MA103476, pp. 377-78.

[35] B, ii, MA103476, pp. 51, 138. [36] Ibid., Protokollbuch, pp. 109-10.

[37] For example, in Geschichte eines Hochverräters, p. 197, Röhm says that he was not present when the Arbeitsgemeinschaft planned the May Day affair. The rosters of the key meetings, however, carry him as present.

[38] Note that here, too, Lossow speaks more as a Bavarian than as a German soldier.

of men who wished to move against the state on the next day. . . .' "[39] In assessing Lossow, the Verbände had assumed that he would never cross his Rubicon, and in this they were quite right. What they failed to realize was that for him, crossing the Rubicon meant disobeying his legal Bavarian superiors. Any soldier in a quandary is likely to obey the orders of his direct superiors; a weak-willed soldier is practically certain to do so. In this case there is no serious suggestion that Lossow wished to take any other course.[40]

Kriebel also visited Nortz, but was warned by him that in case of fighting between Right and Left, the police would "fire in both directions." Seisser also was unhelpful. Matt was approached that evening and agreed to call a special meeting of the Cabinet to consider the question of the seven Marxist parades. Captain Hermann Göring was in his usual flamboyant form, threatening that if the SPD marched through the streets with red flags they would be fired upon. Nonetheless, the ministers, meeting in Knilling's absence decided not to alter their decision: the seven parades were legal.[41] With this decision the die was cast. Both sides now began preparations for the encounter on the morrow, while would-be neutrals sought safe ground where they could weather the storm without alienating either the government or the Arbeitsgemeinschaft.

No one on the government side, including Justice Minister Gürtner, believed that the Majority Socialists or the unions were planning trouble for May Day, although they did shrewdly—and accurately—assume that the leaders could not keep all of their followers in line, especially with the Communists seeking to infiltrate the demonstrations. Therefore, their primary attention was directed towards keeping the right radicals away from the Marxists on the Theresienwiese, which was where their seven parades culminated.

Gürtner, Nortz, and Matt, at the police presidium, received all sorts of alarming and harrowing reports during the course of the evening. A typical example dealt with the progress of an armored car though the city to join the Verbände. The result, largely because of the dependence on telephone communication and policemen on foot or bicycles, was a comedy chase. After wandering about during most of the night—and breaking down twice—the

[39] B, II, MA103476, p. 54.
[40] B, II, MA103476, pp. 129-31; IV, HSIV, EE7, Endres MS, p. 20; Röhm, *Geschichte*, pp. 197-98.
[41] B, II, MA103476, pp. 53-55, 130.

armored car finally returned to its base in the dirigible barracks area, which was one of Röhm's Feldzeugmeisterei depots (for Faber's rental service). The episode illustrates the difficulties facing the authorities in keeping their fingers on the pulse of a large city at night in the days before radios and patrol cars, as well as the vagueness and inefficiency with which the Verbände went about their preparations.[42]

Meanwhile, army and police units from outside München had been ordered into the city, and at 9:00 a.m. General von Danner, the army commandant of München, took over control of defense measures. Lossow was now sufficiently suspicious, partly because of Verbände use of Lossow's name during the course of the night in order to gain military or police cooperation, that he ordered Major Artur Matthiess to remain in the telephone switchboard room of the Wehrkreis headquarters throughout the morning to prevent unauthorized use of the telephones. Lossow later denied that this measure was aimed specifically at Röhm, but it would seem that he and his comrade Adolf Hühnlein were the logical suspects.[43]

The Arbeitsgemeinschaft had been primarily active in the attempt to obtain arms and had had moderate success. At the engineer barracks, they succeeded in collecting a large store of their own arms despite Lieutenant Colonel von Wenz's ban on distribution. Lieutenant Hans Hoeflmayr, himself a member of Röhm's Reichsflagge, gave out the arms, but it is possible that he did so with permission of his commander, Lieutenant Colonel Josef Königsdorfer, who had right radical ties. In any case, the confusion attendant upon the fact that the battalion was out on an exercise made pinpointing the responsibility very difficult.[44] At the barracks of the first battalion of the Nineteenth Infantry Regiment, the Verbände suffered a setback. Entering the barracks with their training passes and a permit made out by Major (Ret.) Faber for their leader, Captain (Ret.) Richard Kolb, the SA men took weapons from a storage shed belonging to Röhm's Feldzeugemeisterei. However, before they could get them off the post, an officer alerted

[42] B, I, SA 1, 1493, Laberger, p. 145; II, MA103476, pp. 62, 180-93, 240-42.

[43] *Ibid.*, p. 186; MA102140, HMB 883, Schw., pp. 1-2; NA, T79, 72, pp. 1152-53, 1172, 1217-19, 1229.

[44] B, I, SA 1, 1817, PDM via 1106 I/23; Hitler Aussage; II, MA103476, pp. 193-94, 201-2.

by Hugo von Wenz discovered them, and made them return the weapons to the shed. Violent protests by Göring to both the lieutenant and to von Wenz had no result. The troops then built a barbed wire barricade in front of the gate. At 9 a.m. Göring returned but had no better luck with Major Karl Freiherr Loeffelholz von Colberg, the battalion commander, than he had had with von Wenz. Earlier, even a Landespolizei officer who had wished to use the telephone had been turned away from the barracks as a suspicious character.[45] The Nazis did get some arms from a house on the Schellingstrasse and, not surprisingly, succeeded in taking a good supply of arms and ammunition out of the dirigible barracks. Even here, however, a Reichswehr artillery sergeant noted the activity and reported it to division headquarters. The soldiers there were then ordered to allow no more arms to be removed and to lock all doors. Major (Ret.) Streck got away with several trucks and the ubiquitous armored car, but Göring, late as ever, was turned away when he tried to get several artillery pieces.[46]

Originally the Arbeitsgemeinschaft troops were to assemble in the Englischer Garten, in the center of München, along with the trade unionists, a plan sure to lead to conflict. When it became clear that the VVM and Lenz's Zeitfreiwilligenkorps had dropped out of the action, the assembly area was moved to the Oberwiesenfeld, a military exercise ground in the garrison quarter of the city. Assembled there by mid-morning were the Storm Troops of the NSDAP, including some small contingents (about 250 men) from other cities and towns; Röhm's branch of Reichsflagge; Organization Lembert (1 field artillery battery), Bund Blücher; and some small groups from Lenz's organization and from Bund Wiking. Altogether there may have been some 1,200 to 1,300 men, according to Josef Zetlmeier who was sent to estimate their numbers, and his figures are undoubtedly far more accurate than the rumors of thousands that were current in the city that day or that were spoken of by Leftists (who were not present) later.[47]

The Oberländer assembled at the Maximilaneum in central München, where they were held in check by Lapo units. By a local arrangement they were allowed to remain assembled during the

[45] B, II, MA103476, pp. 186, 194-95.
[46] *Ibid.*, pp. 184, 189-93.
[47] B, I, SA 1, 1486, passim; 1817, PDM 974 vid; II, MA103476, pp. 121, 161-65, 170, 179, 195; NA, T120, 5569, pp. K591394-95.

4, 5 (OPPOSITE PAGE BELOW). SA men on the Oberwiesenfeld during the 1 May demonstration

6. Oberlander at the NSDAP Party Standard dedication ceremony in München

Marxist May Day celebration and then dispersed about 2:00 p.m.[48] The main force on the Oberwiesenfeld did no more than the Oberländer. After standing around for hours holding their rifles and facing the Landespolizei, they tamely handed over their weapons again and marched off the field in small groups. Some had started drifting away well before the general capitulation. As a result the only violence that day was a few vague scuffles between small groups of Marxists and right radicals on their way home. Apparently there were no serious injuries on either side.[49]

Serious bloodshed, though, nearly occurred. Nortz, apparently in a panic, had called the Reichswehr headquarters at 8.30 a.m. and demanded that the Reichswehr clear the Oberwiesenfeld, by force if necessary. Lieutenant Colonel Endres asked if the Landespolizei had been committed. Nortz replied negatively. Endres said that, in that case, he could not order the troops to move without confirming orders from his superiors, pointing out that, unlike the Landespolizei, who were trained to handle mobs with truncheons, the Reichswehr was trained to shoot. If it marched, it would shoot and shoot to kill in case of resistance. Nortz then phoned General Jakob Ritter von Danner and got the same answer: the Reichswehr was the trump and should not be played too soon.[50]

The major impact of the incident on the Marxist celebrations was that the police more or less ignored their activities and the celebrants were able to violate the terms of their marching permits by marching with unfurled red and Soviet flags. The Württemberg envoy noted that the Marxists seemed to be trying to outdo the Nazis in military falderal. Some were in uniforms with steel helmets and they marched to military commands.[51]

The aftermath of the May Day demonstration for the Verbände was far more significant than the events of the day itself. The appearance of the Verbände under arms in opposition to the wishes of the government helped to bring the dangers of the situation home sharply to the authorities. However, Gürtner succeeded in persuading the none too reluctant Cabinet that it would be unwise

---

[48] B, II, MA103476, pp. 198-99.
[49] B, I, SA 1, 1817, WKK Ib 495 Geh.; II, MA103476, pp. 61-62, 180, 187-89, 1382; NA, T120, 5569, pp. K591387, K591392; B, IV, HSIV, EE7, Endres MS, pp. 20-23; Röhm, *Geschichte*, p. 199.
[50] B, IV, HSIV, EE7, Endres, MS, pp. 20-23.
[51] *Ibid.*, p. 22; W, L, E131, C5/25, W.G. 149, p. 230.

to ban the Storm Troops. While agreeing with Knilling in theory on the need to show that the government was master in the state by means of extraordinary measures akin to a state of emergency, he favored half-measures in practice:

> Minister Gürtner remarked first that the state prosecutor's office was already investigating the events on 1 May. The government must now consider measures for the future. What can be expected of it is an offensive against the Storm Troops. This is possible in three ways, either: like Severing, dissolving them by name, whether the Partei itself or, as in other states, merely the Storm Troops, on the basis of the decision of the Staatsgerichtshof of 15 March 1923; or, after the example of the Württemberg government's decree on the basis of Article 48 of the R.V.,[52] which, however, places the judge in an unfortunate situation; or by means of establishing a legal basis for dissolution in case of offenses against definite regulations. This way recommends itself for Bavaria. One would reintroduce the requirement that all meetings and processions under open skies need [official] permission. An organization that violates this provision or paragraph 127 R. St. G.[53] could be dissolved.[54]

The justice minister had hit upon a scheme calculated to get the Cabinet out of its embarrassing situation with the least unpleasant public repercussions—and with the least damping effect on the Racist Movement. His subsequent activities clearly suggest that this was the carefully planned trap of a wily jurist rather than the bumbling of an ineffectual or short-sighted man. Gürtner's scheme offered the government a weapon against the Verbände that could be used without recourse to the authority of the Reich or to the detested Law for the Protection of the Republic. Further, it was a selective weapon that the government could use as a sword of Damocles over Hitler without being committed to cutting the cord should the moment seem inopportune. Equally important, it was a weapon that could be used against the Left as well as against the Right and could be defended against rightist attacks in these terms. It was a wonderful solution, which salvaged their prestige without danger, gave them a weapon against the right radicals

[52] Federal Constitution.
[53] Reichsstrafgesetzbuch (Federal Penal Code).
[54] B, ii, MA99521, 8.5.1923, pp. 2-3.

in case of future need, and placed the onus of taking serious action against the Verbände on the judiciary rather than on the Cabinet.[55]

Unfortunately for the effectiveness of this solution, the judicial authorities did not carry out their share of the program. They started out energetically enough, collecting evidence to prepare indictments. During the course of the summer, however, the process was halted and no further action was taken, since, when interest was reawakened by the Beer Hall Putsch, the more recent events naturally took the spotlight. It is not absolutely certain who was behind the quashing of the indictments, but the evidence that Gürtner was the man is strong. He had the position from which this action could have been most easily taken, and it was commonly believed in administrative circles and in the office of the prosecutor that he had given the orders. There is also some evidence suggesting that Knilling himself may have agreed to this decision, which would fit in with his policy of avoiding a direct confrontation on difficult ground. And in this case the ground would be very difficult, since Hitler threatened to bring out into the open the agreements of the Verbände with the authorities, including the Reichswehr, and a direct attack on Hitler for opposing Marxists would be likely to lead even Bund Bayern und Reich to side with him.[56]

At first the May Day affair tended to increase government suspicion of the Reichswehr leadership. After the investigation had been made, however, Knilling decided that these suspicions were unjust —as they were.[57] Within the Reichswehr the repercussions were more significant. May Day brought Röhm to the end of the road as a free-wheeling politician operating from a safe and influential base. On 4 May[58] Lossow called Röhm to him and in the presence of Generals von Epp, von Danner, and von Kress and Lieutenant Colonels von Berchem and Meier relieved him of his post and

[55] *Ibid.*, pp. 1-4. Haniel predicted that some such solution would be found because he believed that the Cabinet feared to meet the Verbände head on. NA, T120, 5569, p. K591381.

[56] B, I, SA 1, 1817, M. Inn. 1028 b 2; II, MA103476, pp. 65, 72, 238, 245-51, 288; MA100411, 23.5.1923, Brief: Gürtner an Knilling; I, Kahr MS, p. 1183; GP, B, Minister a. D. Hans Ehard.

[57] B, I, SA 1, WKK VII 573g Ib 549 Geh.; II, MA99521, 1.6.1923, p. 4; MA103476, pp. 373-74; NA, T120, 5569, pp. K591407-9.

[58] Röhm says 3 May, but I use the date in Lossow's statement written on 14.5.1923.

announced his transfer to a rifle company.[59] Lossow stated the reasons for his action:

1.) The events in the dirigible barracks on the night of 30 April–1 May, which indeed were not instigated by Captain Röhm[60] but also were not prevented by him. Captain Röhm, as section chief of the Feldzeugmeisterei, was responsible in part for the grave derelictions of the Transport Section München, [which was] subordinate to him.

2.) The misuse of the offices of the Feldzeugmeisterei, in which, not only on the afternoon of 30 April, although I had expressly rejected the plans of the Kampfverbände, but also frequently during the preceding weeks, meetings of a purely political character had been held, by means of which the Wehrkreiskommando was compromised. It is an erroneous assumption that such purely political conferences could have taken place in our offices with my consent in view of the existing relations between the Wehrkreiskommando and the patriotic Verbände.

3.) The developments in the Kampfverbände in the weeks before 1 May, where, frequently in a manner contrary to discipline, positions were taken against the Landeskommandant or the government in memoranda with the character of [an] ultimatum. The signatures "Reichsflagge" and "Org. Niederbayern" were in these instances equivalent to those of the Reichswehr officers leading these organizations. The holding of militarily useless large-scale field exercises including Reichswehr officers, although it must have been evident that I opposed such exercises.

4.) The decision that arose from the above, to forbid Reichswehr officers to belong to the Kampfverbände in question. His very transfer should make it simpler for Captain Röhm to withdraw from Reichsflagge.[61]

To complete the clean-up of the Feldzeugmeisterei "empire" of Captain Röhm, Lossow also took over the "Transport Section" and removed Major (Ret.) Streck from his post as its chief after having given Röhm a decent opportunity to explain the peculiar events

[59] NA, T79, 72, p. 1229; Röhm, *Geschichte*, p. 200.

[60] In fact, they probably were, but conclusive evidence to this effect is not available.

[61] NA, T79, 72, pp. 1222-23.

in the dirigible barracks. Together with the resignations of such Röhm cronies as Captain (Ret.) Seydel and Major (Ret.) Faber from their positions as civilian employees of the Reichswehr, these actions returned control of the Feldzeugmeisterei to the military and civilian authorities and eliminated a right radical stronghold at a sensitive and important pressure point.[62]

Finally, the May Day affair led Lossow to take a much less rosy view of the leaders of the Arbeitsgemeinschaft. He cut off relations with Kriebel and was more careful in dealing with the others. He also found himself involved in a conflict of honor with Röhm, which was eventually resolved by a Court of Honor but undoubtedly left scars. General von Epp, too, lost some of his enthusiasm for the right radicals as a result of honor conflicts not only with Röhm but also with "Böse Christian" Roth. In any case, Epp and Röhm had come to a temporary parting of the ways when Epp upheld Kahr and Pittinger, and therefore the government, after the cleavage in Bayern und Reich as well as on May Day.[63]

The Reichswehr was not the only institution in which there were recriminations and in which heads rolled. Police President Nortz, who had once again made concessions to uncertain elements in the course of the evening of 30 April without consulting the government, now paid the penalty for his readiness to seek compromise in crises. The Cabinet agreed that he was loyal and hard-working and that he deserved well of the government. They were also agreed that he was not tough enough to hold the post of police president of München. He was therefore transferred and his post given, first on a temporary and then on a permanent basis, to Karl Mantel, whom Knilling thought an experienced and calm man. Mantel wanted the SA dissolved, but was unable to get permission to take so drastic a step. The police were, however, in accordance with Gürtner's proposals, given extra authority by a special decree of 11 May, which gave Mantel more power than Nortz had had.[64]

According to his later testimony, Schweyer was annoyed at Seis-

[62] B, IV, BuR, Bd. 35, Akt 4, Kriebel an Hermannsbund, 11.7.1923; NA, T79, 72, pp. 1224, 1228-29.

[63] NA, Epp Papers, EAP 1-e-16/4, Epp an Lossow, 23.4.1923; Epp an Danner, 12.5.1923; B, I, Kahr MS, p. 1183.

[64] B, I, SA 1, 1817, PDM vid 974g and via 1120/23, PDM 1840; GSK 43, p. 180; II, MA99521, 8.5.1923, p. 5; MA102140, HMB 982, Schw., p. 1; MA103476, p. 408; NA, T120, 5569, pp. K591409-10, K591414; W, L, E131, C5/25, W.G. 159, 14.5.1923; *BLV*, 1922-23, 8, Schweyer, 8.6.1923, pp. 375-76.

ser for his conduct in the May Day affair.[65] The fact that there is no indication of an attempt by Schweyer to reprimand Seisser or to remove him suggests that this question did not arise until later, when Schweyer and Seisser were at odds over the Beer Hall Putsch. In any case, the question at issue was clearly one of competence and not one of Seisser's loyalty to the government, since Schweyer does not attempt to deny that Seisser reported the incident in question to Nortz.[66] However, the seeds of future conflict were to be found here.[67]

Gustav von Kahr, the provincial president of Oberbayern, who played an active but unclear role in the May Day conflict, claimed in 1924 and in his unpublished memoirs that he took a stand in favor of the abolition of the Nazi Storm Troopers and all other paramilitary political Verbände in May. It would seem that Kahr's memory betrays him here, for, not only did he insist in late March on the need for the Storm Troops as a reply to socialist terror, but as late as July his comments on May Day were ambiguous at best. Later, he strongly defended the SA against the München police. Very clearly, his conversion into an opponent of Nazism had not yet begun in the summer of 1923.[68]

Other groups formerly sympathetic with the right radicals, however, did begin to veer away from them. The *Münchner Neuesten Nachrichten* began a reversal of policy that led to sharper and sharper criticism of the NSDAP. Even the German Nationalist newspapers like the *München-Augsburger Abendzeitung* favored the tightening of police restrictions, perhaps partly because they could strike Left as well as Right, which is clearly why the socialist *Münchener Post* was cool towards these restrictions.[69]

[65] Seisser allegedly did not immediately report the tenor of a conversation with Hitler on 30 April to Schweyer, although he did report it to Nortz, as the police official most directly involved. Seisser claims that Schweyer was then told about the matter by Nortz in Seisser's presence.

[66] Seisser does not seem to have reported that he and Lossow talked to Hitler that day, whether at this meeting or another. Again, his loyalty to the government vis-à-vis Hitler is not brought into question, but there is a suggestion that he was concealing the extent to which the Reichswehr and Landespolizei chiefs coordinated their actions and attitudes.

[67] B, II, MA103476, pp. 382-83, 468-70, 582-84.

[68] B, I, Kahr MS, p. 1184; II, MA102140, HMB 385, Obb., p. 3; HMB 613, Obb., p. 11; HMB 1040, Obb., p. 8; MA103476, pp. 386-87.

[69] NA, T120, 5569, pp. K591393, K591403-4; Bennecke, Heinrich, *Die Reichswehr und der "Röhm Putsch,"* München-Wien, 1964, p. 87. Hereafter cited as Bennecke, *"Röhm Putsch."*

Two of the Verbände in the Arbeitsgemeinschaft withdrew and a third drifted away from formal association with the National Socialists and their allies, while maintaining friendly personal relations. The VVM had been bitterly divided on May Day between those who would have liked to fight the Marxists but who would not do so in opposition to the government, and those who were prepared to defy the authorities. The result was a partially successful attempt to get Nortz to call up the VVM as police auxiliaries. Under pressure from the VVM Nortz called them up. Under pressure from Schweyer, when the latter found out about his action, Nortz then cancelled the mobilization order. The result was complete confusion and violent recriminations. In the end Alfred Zeller and the governing committee of the VVM resigned and a more moderate committee was elected, which supported the government. Zeller took his people, as Kampfbund München, over to Hitler, which enraged Knilling, who had hitherto been rather approving of Zeller.[70]

As a result of the influence of Father Pfeilschifter of the University, the students of Lenz's Zeitfreiwilligenkorps refused to take part in the May Day demonstration of the Verbände and von Lenz resigned in anger. He was succeeded by General Karl Ritter von Kleinhenz, under whom the organization became known as the Hermannsbund and moved closer to Bund Bayern und Reich. Kleinhenz maintained vague relations with the right radical Verbände but stayed out of their orbit.[71]

Bund Niederbayern also moved away from the Arbeitsgemeinschaft after May Day. The reasons are not at all clear, but they probably include the difference of opinion between the München leaders and Hans Georg Hofmann regarding Hofmann's refusal to permit the Ingolstadt Storm Troops to go to München and the warning that must have gone out to Hofmann from Lossow—if one is to judge from the parenthetical remarks regarding Hofmann in Lossow's criticism of Röhm.[72] In any case, Hofmann did stay out

[70] B, I, Kahr MS, p. 1181; SA 1, 1817, PDM VIa 1105/23, p. 523; PDM VIa, Glonner an von Tutschek; Glonner an PDM, 5.5.1923; 404 VVM an Knilling, 8.5.1923; A. Holl an Knilling, 22.5.1923; II, MA103476, pp. 138-39, 143-51, 154, 160, 205; T120, 5569, pp. K591396-97; *BLV*, 1922-23, 8, Dr. Schweyer, 8.6.1923, p. 378.

[71] B, I, Kahr MS, p. 1179; II, MA103476, pp. 131-32, 137-44; NA, SA Rgt. München, 230-a-10/4 3, 25.6.1923; Epp Papers, 1-e-16/4, 14.5.1923, Lenz Erlass; GP, B, Colonel Ernst Schultes.

[72] See p. 203 above.

of the new organization set up by Hitler and Kriebel and kept his skirts officially clean during the fall of 1923, although he was in touch with Hitler and other right radical leaders. "Trotsky" played the game carefully until the Putsch.[73]

The National Socialists themselves reacted with bravado to their check at the Oberwiesenfeld. That very night they held a rally in the Zirkus Krone, where Hitler was his aggressive self and where many of his followers openly carried weapons. The right radicals also tried, as they did in November, to implicate the government, the Reichswehr, and the police in their demonstration, and insisted that they had really been acting in the best interests of the government. Hitler, who had reportedly told Heinrich Class, the leader of the Pan-German League (Alldeutscher Verband), in late April that in three days he would have München, in three weeks, Bavaria, and in three months, the Reich, merely shifted his timetable a little. With the tenacity that he showed throughout his life, he refused to be cowed by defeat or daunted by odds. On the other hand, he apparently admitted to a tactical error, telling Zeller that had he known that the police and Reichswehr were to be reinforced from outside München he would not have pushed matters to a crisis.[74] Yet, as the Beer Hall Putsch was to show, he himself did not draw any of the obvious conclusions from this error. He does, however, seem to have agreed with Captain (Ret.) Wilhelm Weiss, the later editor-in-chief of the *Völkischer Beobachter*:

> I am of the opinion that the Kampfverbände cannot afford another First of May. For in essence the First of May was nothing more than an orderly retreat of the Kampfverbände and a retreat not, naturally, before Marxism, but before the armed forces of the state.[75]

The National Socialists and their allies were not, of course, the only ones to try to make political capital from the events of May Day. The Marxists also mounted a propaganda offensive based on these events. This was almost entirely an SPD action because the Independent Socialists were to all intents and purposes a dead party and the Communists were primarily involved in plans for an

---

[73] B, II, MA103476, pp. 812-16; NA, T84, 4, pp. 3349-52.

[74] B, I, Kahr MS, p. 1179; SA 1, 1486, PDM Abt. VI-N-289/23, 16.5.1923, p. 192; II, MA103476, pp. 134, 204-5; IV, BuR, Bd. 35, Akt 4, Item 41; NA, EAP 105/7, I, p. 49; Röhm, *Geschichte*, p. 199.

[75] B, II, MA103476, p. 623.

armed revolution.[76] As a badly outnumbered faction in the Landtag, the Social Democrats were condemned to legislative impotence, but here was a chance to lambaste the Bavarian authorities and they made the most of it. Very little of their energy was expended in attacks on the Verbände. The main target both in the Reichstag and the Landtag was the Bavarian Reichswehr and, in Bavaria, the Landespolizei and the Bavarian government. Unfortunately, from their own viewpoint, the Social Democrats warped the facts—whether through ignorance or malice is unclear—too much to have any impact on even the reasonably informed Bavarian bystander. For example, Bund Bayern und Reich, which remained completely quiescent during the May Day demonstration, was accused of being involved, although the very evidence cited indicated its disengagement. Dr. von Kahr, Dr. Pittinger, and General Ludwig Ritter von Tutschek[77] were all making speeches in far away Lichtenfels. Had they been involved it is unlikely that all three of them would have been so far away, and unbelievable that none of their forces would have been committed. Similarly, Colonel Josef Banzer of the Landespolizei was accused of negotiating with the Verbände on the Oberwiesenfeld, although he never left his office during the period in question. In any case, negotiations, to the extent of arranging the terms of the surrender or withdrawal of the Verbände, were essential if the possibility of large-scale bloodshed was to be avoided. In fact, such negotiations as were conducted were officially ordered by General von Danner, an anti-Nazi, and were conducted by a Reichswehr officer, Major Baumann of the Wehrkreis headquarters.[78]

The Social Democrats also made other surprising factual errors, which leads one to wonder how much they really knew about either the Reichswehr or Verbände. They identified Lieutenant Colonel Kriebel as commander of SA Regiment München although he not only did not hold this post but was not a member of the SA, being instead commander-in-chief of the military forces of the Arbeits-

[76] Angress, Werner T., *Stillborn Revolution: The Communist Bid for Power in Germany, 1921-1923*, Princeton, 1963, Chapter XII. Hereafter cited as Angress, *Stillborn Revolution*. Gordon, Harold J., Jr., "Die Reichswehr und Sachsen, 1923," WWR Dec. 1961, passim.

[77] Who was peripherally involved in the prelude to May Day while wearing his VVM hat (as a ward leader).

[78] Otto Baumann was personally friendly to the Kampfverbände and was later to be in some difficulties on this score, although he did not clearly commit himself to Hitler as did Röhm and Hühnlein.

gemeinschaft and a member of RKF.[79] Further, Erhard Auer's *Münchener Post* claimed that the Nazis had aimed artillery pieces at their building, but the National Socialists had had no artillery on the Oberwiesenfeld. The only guns there were those of the fifth battery of the Seventh Artillery Regiment of the Reichswehr (an orphan unit, whose headquarters was in Nürnberg) which was carrying out routine drill in one corner of the area. The reports of any observer who could not tell the uniform, materiel, deportment, and activities of a regular army unit from those of badly trained political irregulars in the remnants of half a dozen styles of outmoded uniforms deserve no serious consideration. Such attacks were merely certain to increase the distance between government and opposition rather than to lead to changes favorable to the SPD. If politics is the art of achieving the possible, the SPD leaders were playing some other game.[80]

III. *The Lull in the Political Storms*

After the flurry in early May, things settled down somewhat and the reports of local officials throughout Bavaria indicate a relaxation on the political front and a decline in popularity of Hitler and his cohorts. Economic matters were eclipsing politics, but men were not yet desperate enough to embrace radical politics as a solution to economic woes. As a result there was comparatively little significant political activity until fall.

Although not too significant in itself, the first political development of the summer provided fuel for political propagandists and particularly for those of the radical Left and Right. The plans of Professor Georg Fuchs and Hugo Machhaus to overturn the Bavarian government, lead Bavaria out of the Reich, and form a Danubian monarchy under French protection had all the elements of a bad musical comedy crossed with a confidence game. Fuchs, in his role as a drama critic, would undoubtedly have panned a play on these lines. Apparently no one of any stature in Bavaria was involved, although the conspirators managed to talk to various persons in positions of power at one time or another, including General von Möhl, but not necessarily about their schemes. They did,

[79] First Lieutenant (Ret.) Wilhelm Brückner was the Commander of SA Regiment München. NA, SA Rgt. München, 230-a-10/4, 12.4.1923.

[80] B, II, MA103476, pp. 174, 197, 488; IV, HSIV, EE7, Endres MS, pp. 20-23; *BLV*, 1922-23, 8, Dr. Schweyer, 8.6.1923, p. 379; E. Auer (SPD), 6.6.1923, p. 331; *RV*, 360, pp. 11053-54, Henke (SPD), 14.5.1923.

however, get into contact with Bund Blücher and with the French intelligence service, through Colonel Augustin Xavier Richert, who seems to have been an energetic but bumbling secret agent right out of a New Left attack on the CIA.[81] The whole affair merely shows how little interest in separatism and how little love for France there really was in Bavaria, but, because of the general atmosphere of mutual political hostility and the many secret activities taking place in Bavaria at the time, it was possible for Hitler and the Left to claim that the Bavarian government was involved in the plot and that Machhaus had been murdered by government agents.[82] There seems to be no other connection between serious political events in Bavaria and this incident.[83]

More directly pertinent to the main chain of events was the clash between police and National Socialists in München on 14 July 1923. The German Turnerschaften were convening in München that week, and the National Socialists held a giant rally at the Zirkus Krone, which attracted many of the right radicals attending the convention. After the meeting, in defiance of police regulations, a section of the audience, including various SA units, attempted a march into the center of the city with banners unfurled. They were halted by the police near the railway station and a sharp skirmish developed in which the police were the victors. The clash was minor, but it indicated clearly that the police were prepared to do their duty vis-à-vis the National Socialists and that the National Socialists were still not prepared to obey the ordinances and laws established by the Bavarian authorities.[84]

Thereafter München was relatively quiet until the collapse of the Cuno government. The entry into office of the Stresemann government, with its Social Democratic members, was greeted without great enthusiasm in Bavaria and led to a general tightening of relations between Bavaria and the Reich, while the abandonment of

[81] B, II, MA100446, passim; NA, T120, 5569, pp. K591309, K591320, K591325, K591334-35, K591409, K591415-17.

[82] He committed suicide in his cell.

[83] B, I, GSK 43, p. 122.

[84] B, I, SA 1, 1756, Anz. Verz. XIX 241/23 PR904/23; II, MA100411, Brief: Frhr. von Rotberg an VVVB, 2.8.1923; MA100425, PDM 1503c/vid, Abdruck, 26.7.1923, pp. 204-8; MA102140, HMB 1040, Obb., p. 8; MA103476, p. 1219; NA, SA Rgt. München, 230-a-10/4 3, 18.7.1923, and 3.8.1923; NA, T84, Brief: L. Schubert an Hitler, 28.8.1923; Z, Auszüge v. Akten d. Hptarchiv d. NSDAP, Mappe 2, Brief: Ernst Graf zu Fischler v. Treuberg an Hitler, 30.7.23; 207/52, ED7, Fasc. III, pp. 00029-32

the passive resistance policy in the Ruhr brought tempers to a fever pitch even in moderate nationalist circles. The stage was thus set for the traumatic and violent events of the fall.[85]

IV. *Summary*

During the first nine months of the year 1923 the situation that would lead to a series of violent explosions in the fall had developed. In every case, the government had been able to avoid the confrontations with the Reich and with the Verbände that were clearly in the wind, but in each case they paid in political leeway for the boon of peace. This meant that when they were faced with trouble in the fall there would be little room to maneuver and that they would also be facing opponents at least as desperate and distracted as themselves. The lightning was still building up and everyone concerned was aware, with pleasure or with fear, that it would soon break loose.

[85] NA, T120, 5569, Haniel's reports for August and September, passim; W, L, E131, C5/25, Preger an Moser, pp. 136-37.

9.

KAHR AND HIS FIVE-FRONT WAR

I. *The September Crisis*

A new wave of vigorous activity on the part of the right radical Verbände was inaugurated on "German Day" in Nürnberg, 2 September 1923. At this nationalist celebration, dominated by the more radical Verbände, the hard-core members of the Arbeitsgemeinschaft formed a new organization, the Deutscher Kampfbund (apparently originally also called Kampfgemeinschaft Bayern). Its first members were the SA of the NSDAP, Oberland, and Reichsflagge.[1] This German Day also gave further impetus to radicals on both the Right and Left through the violent clashes between them on that day and the guerrilla warfare that followed. The Marxist workers who sought to disrupt the nationalist convention were defeated but took revenge later by beating up and expelling right radical workers and employees from their posts in various factories. Finally, the employers and the police expelled the most vigorous of Marxist activists from the plants, and the antagonisms dropped to a simmering level. The entire affair indicated, however, the revival of political activism. A hot autumn was to follow a cool summer.[2]

The Kampfbund was brutally frank about its aims from the beginning. Its initial pronouncement proclaimed its opposition to Marxism, internationalism, pacifism, and Jews, as well as parliamentarianism, the Weimar Constitution, international capital, and the class struggle.[3] However, this proclamation—drawn up by Gottfried Feder, the fading economic theoretician of National Socialism, and Captain Weiss, the editor of *Heimatland*—was much less important than the "action program" that Weiss, at the direc-

[1] See Chapter IV, Section II.
[2] B, I, GSK 43, p. 4, Kdo. d. Lapo PDN-F, Abt. Pol. 81 Geh./23; NA, T84, 4, Brief: Klotz an Hitler, 7.9.1923.
[3] Röhm, *Geschichte*, pp. 210-13.

tion of Scheubner-Richter, drew up for the new organization on 24 September 1923, the day before Hitler officially became its political leader. The action program clearly stated the immediate political objectives the leaders wished to pursue and reflected the general atmosphere within the Kampfbund. The essential question was that of power:

> "The struggle for political power in Bavaria therefore reduces itself in practice to a struggle over possession of executive power and the organs and means for its expression. That is, the Kampf-verbände will first be able to undertake their basic mission, the crushing of Marxism, with success if they are in control of the state power in Bavaria, i.e., that the most important ministry of Bavaria, as in every other state, the Ministry of the Interior, must be in the hands of an ally of the Kampfverbände. The situation is therefore this: the national revolution in Bavaria must not precede the assumption of political power. Rather, the possession of the police power of the state is the prerequisite for the national revolution. That is, the attempt must be made to obtain the police power in an at least apparently legal manner, although admittedly this legal path must be taken while employing more or less illegal pressure."[4]

Weiss then went on to propose that the Kampfbund press for the establishment of an economic tsar, since the man in the street was primarily interested in the price of beer and bread and had been disillusioned with the recent measures the government had taken in this regard. The government should be given a free hand to name anyone it liked in the hopes that the appointee's failure would discredit both the government and, with luck, the BVP. At the same time the Kampfbund was to demand the dismissal of the minister of the interior, on the grounds that the creation of an economic tsar would lead to trouble with the Reich, which, together with the need to inforce economic decrees, would call for a man with the support of the nationalist Verbände in control of the police. This demand would put great pressure on the government. The Verbände should also insist on a new police president for München, and here too the arguments should be economic, but the motivation was control of the blue police. Then would come a Generalstaatskommissar who would use his dictatorial powers to lead the national revolution in

---

[4] B, II, MA103476, pp. 623-24.

concert with the Verbände. Dr. Christian Roth should be minister of the interior and Pöhner, Generalstaatskommissar, although Weiss apparently foresaw objections to these men even within the Kampfbund. Dr. Wilhelm Frick, Pöhner's old right-hand man, would become police president. The memorandum stressed the danger that Kahr and Pittinger would take action if the Kampfbund did not, and argued that the Kampfbund with a stronger power base in München was ideally situated to take the comparatively minor risks of pushing for its plan. There was risk, but there always would be risk, and it could be greatly reduced by popular support and by the appearance of legality.[5] Here then was the skeleton of the Kampfbund's fall program although Captain Weiss was to resign his post as "business manager" of the Kampfbund two days later in reaction to Hitler's appointment as political leader. Personalities shifted, the plan was embroidered, tactics were flexible, but the aim remained that laid out by Scheubner-Richter and Weiss in September.[6]

Hitler's appointment as political leader of the Kampfbund was a reply to the official abandonment of the policy of passive resistance against the French in the Ruhr. Although Hitler had opposed this policy from its inception, he now used its collapse as an occasion for stepping up his political war on the Republic. Taking advantage of the bitter disillusionment and despair in nationalist circles he called fourteen political rallies for the evening of 27 September, and the Kampfbund organizations issued recruiting appeals for their military organizations. Once again the government faced the menace of massed demonstrations of the National Socialists and their allies in an atmosphere of utmost tension.[7] It was the call for the fourteen rallies that set in motion the chain of events that led to the clash at the Feldherrnhalle on 9 November, but, in view of the determination of the Kampfbund to seize power, it is almost certain that had this match not set the trail of powder afire another would have been struck.

The Bavarian government, like the Bavarian public, had been hit between wind and water by the end of passive resistance. Knilling made no bones about his displeasure and his fear that the Stresemann government would accept any terms the French might

---

[5] *Ibid.*, pp. 624-28, 1458.

[6] NA, T84, 4, Brief: Weiss an Hitler, 26.9.1923.

[7] T120, 5569, pp. K591520-26; Ludendorff, *Feldherrnhalle*, p. 51; Röhm, *Geschichte*, pp. 215-16.

care to present. Haniel and Konrad Ritter von Preger, the Bavarian envoy in Berlin, were both fearful that the Bavarian official reaction would be violent.[8] However, the Bavarian government was too preoccupied by the reactions at home to give much attention to the cause. As early as the beginning of September there had been talk in BVP circles of a commissar for Bavaria and of closer identification of the government with the monarchy, a typical political attempt to take shelter in the lee of a popular institution in turbulent times. Dr. Schweyer approached Kahr on this subject at about the same time. By 18 September Moser reported to Stuttgart that Held was negotiating with Crown Prince Rupprecht regarding Kahr's appointment, although Knilling was not enthusiastic at the prospect. He didn't care for Kahr and increasingly distrusted the Verbände.[9]

On 21 September, Knilling informed the Cabinet that the coalition parties had decided at their last meeting that a commissar should be appointed to maintain order. This decision was not to be acted upon at once, partly because the question of finding the proper man was not easy.[10] The next evening, Knilling and Kahr, whom both Kultusminister Dr. Matt and General von Lossow allegedly wanted as commissar, met under the auspices of Crown Prince Rupprecht. Nothing was said directly regarding the commissar's post, but both the prince and Knilling asked Kahr to help rein in the Verbände. Kahr later claimed that he told them he favored curbing the National Socialists, but if he did, his conversion to this position was very recent indeed.[11]

Hitler's mass meetings now forced the hand of the government. Warnings poured in from all sides that the Nazis were preparing a revolution. A leader of Wikingbund, probably Kautter, warned Knilling early in September that Ludendorff was planning a Putsch with the aid of the Kampfbund. Even Gürtner apparently told members of Reichsflagge that the government had evidence that the National Socialists were planning a Putsch following the rallies. Professor Hermann Bauer of the VVVB, who knew Putsch preparations from long personal experience, also testified later that he thought the National Socialists had planned to use the rallies as a

[8] NA, T120, 1748, p. D756734; 5569, pp. K591520-26; W, L, E131, C5/25, pp. 136-37, Brief: Preger an Moser.

[9] *Ibid.*, W. G. 263, pp. 139-40; B, I, Kahr MS, pp. 1246-48.

[10] B, II, MA99521, 21.9.1923, p. 7.

[11] B, I, Kahr MS, pp. 1249-51, 1395-96.

launching pad for a Putsch. Scheubner-Richter, one of Hitler's closest associates, in talking to a government official and to Graf Josef Maria von Soden-Fraunhofen, Crown Prince Rupprecht's cabinet chief, on the eve of the rallies, went so far as to admit that while the leaders had no actual plans for a Putsch they would lead it if one developed spontaneously.[12]

The result of all these rumors was that Knilling decided to act immediately, and on 26 September proposed Kahr to the Cabinet as Generalstaatskommissar, since the appointee must have at least a portion of the Verbände behind him. Schweyer pointed out that the appointment must go along with the declaration of a state of emergency. Lossow assured the Cabinet that the Reichswehr was well in hand and that he had already ordered the recall of men on leave. He could bring two infantry battalions and two mountain batteries into München immediately. The commissar must call on all the Verbände to support him and those that did not agree were to be treated as insurgents. Seisser also guaranteed the loyalty of his forces and offered to bring in contingents from Augsburg, Landshut, and Ingolstadt to be placed at the disposal of the police president.[13]

Knilling then asked Kahr if he would take the post of commissar. Kahr made a long speech on the difficulties of the situation—which seemed aimed largely at showing his nobility of spirit and self-lessness—before accepting. Then, without further ado, he got down to brass tacks.

> In reply to his [Kahr's] question concerning the nature of his position, he received the answer that the Generalstaatskommissar was subordinate to the Cabinet but would have a free hand in the exercise of the executive power. The impression that he is merely a tool of the government must be avoided. His responsibilities are not purely of a police nature but embrace also the post, communications, economics, food supply, etc. Officials would be placed at his disposal on request, who would act as liaisons with their ministries.[14]

In other words, the government wanted Kahr to take the responsibility for actions that were bound to be more or less unpopular

---

[12] B, I, Kahr MS, pp. 1251-52; II, MA103476, pp. 852-54; W, L, E131, C5/25, W.G. 255, p. 150.

[13] B, II, MA99521, 26.9.1923, pp. 2-4. [14] *Ibid.*, pp. 4-5.

while it maintained control behind the scenes. His leash might be loose and invisible, but it was there and would chafe increasingly as time proceeded. However, Kahr wanted power and prestige and the government offered him an avenue to them which, to judge by his actions, he hoped to be able to make real rather than illusory by means of public pressure to give him a free hand. Knilling, meanwhile, had come to see in Kahr not only a buffer against the winds of public displeasure, but also the man who could keep a large portion of the Verbände away from Hitler.[15] For these reasons, and very possibly because he felt that Kahr would destroy himself as a political force, Knilling had given way to the pressures for the appointment of Kahr as the savior of Bavaria, although he neither liked nor trusted him.[16]

Kahr thus started off his crusade against the foes of Bavarian conservatism with the support of the powerful influence wielded by the crown prince, Lossow, and Seisser, and with a grudging promise from the government that it would support him to the hilt. He had broad but undefined powers. It was up to him to fashion from these raw materials a force that would enable him to carry through successfully his program for Bavaria's salvation. Unfortunately, having achieved power, Kahr found his seat slippery and the sword of executive authority a two-edged one. Truth to tell, neither the man nor his "program" were calculated to galvanize Bavaria to new life or to save her from the wiles of Hitler or the dangers of inflation.

II. *Gustav von Kahr*

Gustav von Kahr was the descendant of a middle-class Protestant family that had risen to prominence in the nineteenth century, and he was the third member of the family to receive personal nobility as a reward for his services to crown and state. A career civil servant, he became Regierungspräsident of Oberbayern in 1917. After the revolution he became a hero and a leader of both the conserva-

---

[15] On 9 October Knilling told Haniel that if he gave in to the Berlin government's demands, the Verbände that Kahr had won to his support would shift to Hitler. Haniel, who kept in close touch with Knilling throughout this period, believed that the minister-president had evaluated the right radical Verbände and the political situation correctly and manipulated Kahr with dexterity. NA, T120, 5569, pp. K591548, K591594, K591536-37.

[16] W, L, E131, C5/25, 14.5.1923, W.G. 159, pp. 220-21; 16.6.1923, W.G. 184, p. 196.

tive monarchists and the Catholic Church in Bavaria. A strong personal monarchist, he never pretended to have any love for the Republic, and he detested Marxism and Marxists bitterly.[17]

Kahr never ceased to be a bureaucrat. He believed that action consisted of drawing up memoranda and proclamations, and his sense of his own infallibility kept him from seeing that he often mouthed empty phrases or failed to arrange for the machinery that would translate theory into practice. There is much truth in Röhm's bitter gibe that Kahr was the man of "eternal preparations"—although Röhm and Hitler were not always truthful in their accusations against the Generalstaatskommissar. Unfortunately, Kahr's characterization of Dr. Schweyer as "the man with ten thumbs" also applies remarkably well to Kahr himself. Despite the homespun touch provided by his conspicuously patched and shabby trousers, it is hard to see how this stiff, highly opinionated, old-fashioned man with his obvious pompousness and lack of "political style" became for so long a time the paladin of the youthful right radicals as well as the elderly conservatives. Yet, he had unquestionably held the center of the stage both officially and unofficially during his period as minister-president and, despite the disenchantment of the most activist elements among the right radicals, much of the old magic was still alive in 1923. He believed himself to be a great man; he talked in grand terms; he supported the right people and causes. Hence he must be a strong man.[18]

Kahr's program was vague and disjointed. In fact, it is hard to discern any coherent program behind the activities of the Generalstaatskommissar and equally hard to distill one from the torrent of words flowing from his pen and lips. Some elements or planks of a program were certainly discernible. He wished to crush Marxism, and especially Communism, in Bavaria. He wanted to turn the clock back to the Bismarck Reich where a strong Bavaria could live within a strong Germany. He wanted to lead Bavaria to prosperity again and, like many other Bavarians, was inclined to feel that the loosening of the Reich's economic grip on the state was a step in the right direction, but initially his positive economic ideas do not seem to have gone much beyond a vague belief that the firm han-

[17] B, I, Kahr MS, passim; Wulz, Georg, *Die Familie Kahr. Archiv für Rassen- und Gesellschaftsbiologie*, B. 18, Heft 3 (Sept. 1926), pp. 249-53.

[18] B, I, Kahr MS, passim; NA, EAP 105/7, I, p. 52; II, pp. 13-14; III, p. 27; GP, A, Graf Soden, 6.8.1966; B, Professor Karl Loewenstein; Röhm, *Geschichte*, p. 218.

dling of profiteers would roll prices back towards normal levels, and he soon lost his faith even in this panacea. Perhaps most of all, he would have liked to reintroduce the monarchy, but he seems to have realized that neither the times nor the situation were right— even if the crown prince had been willing to ascend the throne. Thus, without a serious positive program, and with the Cabinet watching his moves with a vigilant eye, Kahr was reduced to essentially negative measures. Instead of leading Bavaria in new directions, he was kept busy preventing the existing regime and society from being swept away. He was more a policeman than a political leader.[19]

Kahr's most significant supporters were the Crown Prince and the monarchist-conservatives; Bund Bayern und Reich, whose leadership, both local and central, tended to identify itself with him; such state's rights organizations as the Bayernbund; the veterans' organizations, which were largely royalist and conservative in nature; and the middle-class München press, with the bulk of the business and industrial communities of München and Nürnberg apparently behind it.[20]

Commander Ehrhardt and his allies took a less clear position. Various sources indicate that Ehrhardt himself was none too keen on Kahr, largely because he was increasingly inclined to doubt that Kahr would lead a crusade against Berlin. Lieutenant Kautter shared these doubts. In a memorandum regarding the "Kahr dictatorship," Kautter indicated that Hitler understood the needs of the present and the essence of the nationalist movement better than Kahr:

> While Hitler, in ignorance of the historical, living prelude, paid no attention to these feelings and thus closed the avenue to the broader public, Excellency von Kahr is today seen as the exponent of this viewpoint, since he is thereby more "folksy" and more easily understandable. Or, in other words, the Kahr dictatorship also rests on "antisemitism, nationalism, and acti-

[19] See B, I, GSK Akten, passim; and the remainder of this chapter.

[20] B, I, Kahr MS, pp. 1246-81, 1395-96; GSK 43, p. 17; GSK 73, p. 66; GSK 99, pp. 1, 5; GSK 100, p. 15; II, MA102140, HMB 1370, Obb., p. 4; MA103458, Brief: Bäcken and Ballerstedt an Kahr, 3.10.1923; MA103476, pp. 767-68, 778, 832-33, 1397; IV, BuR, Bd. 34, Item 104, 28.9.1923; Bd. 35, Akt 5, Item 16; Bd. 36, Akt 1, Item 4, Brief: von Glass an Schad, 3.11.1923; GP, A, Graf Soden, 22.7.1966 and 6.8.1966; NA, T120, 5569, pp. K591531-32.

vism["] in truth and if Kahr does not bear these forces in mind, the apparent forces on which he bases himself, "monarchical, religious, and federalistic forces" will become mere empty shells incapable of bearing him up. In reality the Kahr dictatorship is based on weakness rather than strength. The parliamentary system could no longer bear the pressure from the national-activist Hitler Movement and called on the Kahr forces, which seemed to them the lesser evil, to exorcise these wicked spirits.[21]

Despite such a biting—if largely accurate—analysis of the situation, Ehrhardt and his allies remained on Kahr's side. They owed to Kahr-Seisser their protection from the legal officers of the Reich, and they were doubtless well aware of their very small following within Bavaria. Then too, Ehrhardt and Hitler were essentially rivals for the leadership of the right radical movement against the Weimar Republic. Finally, the former naval officer was neither as radical nor as brutal as the National Socialist and instinctively disliked and distrusted him as a person. Ehrhardt wanted to march on Berlin, but he wanted to do so on his own terms and for his own ends.[22]

Not surprisingly, the sharpest reaction to Kahr's appointment was that of the Kampfbund. The Kampfbund had hoped to force its own candidate for "dictator" on the Bavarian government, but was aware that plans were afoot to bring Kahr to the fore. At the end of August, Kriebel had been approached by Dr. Pittinger regarding the possibility of a directory headed by Kahr and including Hitler and Pöhner. Kriebel, at the Hitler Trial, claimed piously that the Kampfbund refused to go along with the plan because of its "separatist" overtones, such as a Bavarian "tax strike,"[23] but the true reason is revealed by a contemporary Kampfbund memorandum, dating from the time of Kahr's appointment. The author of the anonymous document, captured after the Beer Hall Putsch, was apparently Scheubner-Richter, which indicates that it reflected Hitler's views. The tone of rage and disappointment at being outmaneuvered rings clearly through the angry words of the prelude:

[21] B, ɪ, GSK 98, pp. 2-3.

[22] B, ɪ, GSK 100, pp. 3, 5ff; NA, EAP 105/7, ɪɪ, pp. 89-90; Pöhner; GP, A, Captain Hermann Ehrhardt, 25.11.1958 and 4.5.1959; Carl Tillessen, 19.6.1960.

[23] B, ɪɪ, MA103476, pp. 832-33.

The sudden dictatorship of Kahr is a severe blow for all racists. For, on the one side, even if he wished to act, Kahr is not the man in whom one can place trust in this decisive time. He has already failed completely in a similar situation.[24] On the other hand, there is the well-based suspicion that he is being used by his clerical masters only as a buffer. Since, unfortunately, the name Kahr still has a strong resonance in patriotic circles, the announcement of the Kahr dictatorship is calculated to weaken and confuse the racist camp. As bright as the possibilities for the seizure of power by the Kampfbund looked in the eyes of the people twenty-four hours before [the announcement], assuming that one decided to take immediate positive measures, the political climate is reversed by the cleverness of our opponents in seizing time by the forelock. It is now possible to undertake something against Kahr, in view, above all else, of the declarations of loyalty of most of the patriotic Verbände, only when and if his conduct of Bavarian policy is publicly branded as being contrary to racist interests. At this time a number of demands must be made of him in full public view, the fulfillment of which will decide whether the Kampfverbände can support him. If he wavers or opposes them, then the Kampfverbände will wage the most vigorous campaign against him and it will then be supported by public opinion.[25]

Röhm later testified that Hitler saw Kahr's appointment as a declaration of war on the Kampfbund and, at the time, Heiss warned Kahr that Hitler wanted to appoint Pöhner to his post.[26] Bund Oberland took the same hostile view as the Kampfbund.

In Reichsflagge, however, the situation was very different. Although initially Heiss agreed with the policy of standing aloof from Kahr until it was safe to attack him, he soon found himself under severe pressure in Nürnberg to alter this course. On the very day that the Kampfbund's neutrality announcement was made, Police Director Gareis of Nürnberg, whose ear was always to the ground, reported: "Reichsflagge, Ortsgruppe Nürnberg, is in difficulties now that the Kampfbund has refused to place itself behind Gen-

[24] This is apparently a reference to the Einwohnerwehr crisis of 1921.

[25] B, II, MA103476, pp. 628-29; I, Kahr MS, pp. 1285-86; Röhm, *Geschichte*, p. 217. See also Graf Treuberg's letter to Glaser: B, II, MA103476, pp. 1460-68.

[26] B, I, GSK 43, p. 14; II, MA103476, pp. 833-34.

eralstaatskommissar von Kahr. It is not impossible that a revision of the policy followed in the last few days by the leadership of Reichsflagge is in the wind."[27] This observation proved to be prophetic. A number of key leaders of the Nürnberg Reichsflagge, who represented the conservative business community, had won over the membership for Kahr. At first it seemed that Heiss would nonetheless seek to hold to the Kampfbund policy. However, when the federal supreme court sought to arrest him and Kahr refused to allow the warrant to be served, Heiss gave way and went with the bulk of his organization into the Kahr camp. The south Bavarian portion of Reichsflagge remained in the Kampfbund under Röhm, who, having submitted his final resignation from the Reichswehr, now openly flaunted his leadership of Reichskriegsflagge.[28]

The public reaction was, in general, very favorable to Kahr. Graf von Spreti, the newly appointed Regierungspräsident of Schwaben stated the matter succinctly when he said:

". . . The appointment of Herr von Kahr as Generalstaatskommissar has hardly been criticized, even among the workers, as one would have expected. The people expect the impossible of him. He should not only maintain peace and order but also reorganize the currency [situation], provide jobs and normal prices. In short, he should rescue them from all need. That he will definitely not be able to do. . . ."[29]

The acting Regierungspräsident of Oberbayern, Loritz, reported that at first the activists were happy and the leftists alarmed at the appointment of Kahr, but that, as the smoke settled, the situation reversed itself. A majority of the populace welcomed the development and looked to Kahr for relief. In Mittelfranken, the Right was keen on Kahr and the Left disapproving. The Regierungspräsident of Unterfranken reported support for Kahr from all but the leftists, although this support was clouded somewhat by concern over relations between Bavaria and the federal government. A similar situation existed in Niederbayern. The Generalstaatskommissar clearly

---

[27] B, I, GSK 43, p. 4, Kdo. d. Lapo, PDN-F, Abt. Pol. Nr. 81 Geh./23, Monatsbericht.

[28] B, I, GSK 43, p. 17, BuR Intelligence Report, early Oct. 1923; SA 1, Aufklärungsblatt d. aufgelösten Kampfbundes, Dec. 1923; NA, T120, 5569, p. K591551; Epp Papers, EAP 230-a-10/3 1, RKF Mitteilungsblatt 1, 15.10.1923; Röhm, Geschichte, pp. 219-21. See also Chapter IV, Section III.

[29] B, II, MA102140, HMB 1857, Schw., p. 2.

had broad popular support, but it was based on the expectation of rapid, drastic, and effective solutions to Bavaria's political and economic problems.[30]

The government had prevented the National Socialists from attempting a Putsch, if they had planned to do so, which Kriebel officially denied in a letter to Knilling. By its military measures for the defense of München, the government had served warning against rebellion.[31] At the same time it had not only widened the growing chasm between the less radical and more radical wings of the Völkische Bewegung, but also succeeded in splitting the Kampfbund itself. In the end, though, it had only bought time. Unless Kahr was able to improve the situation or it improved of its own accord, the crisis between the supporters of the *status quo* and the right radical revolutionaries was almost certain to result in an explosion.

III. *Kahr's General Activities*

The primary emphasis in Kahr's term of office as Generalstaatskommissar was on the maintenance of law and order. He approached this problem from both positive and negative sides, with the greatest emphasis on the negative. On the positive side he distributed propaganda widely through his official channels and through those Verbände friendly to him. Here the stress was on rallying the Bavarian community against the Marxist Left. Other propaganda was channeled through the regular press by his press chief, Adolf Schiedt, the chief editor of the *Münchener Zeitung*. Another positive measure was the payment of temporary pensions to the dependents of Germans placed in protective custody by his orders. This helped to take the sting out of the security measures and at the same time to protect the innocent.[32]

The major emphasis, however, was on directly repressive measures, and, in order to apply these measures effectively, Kahr established an intelligence reporting system based on the political agencies of the Ministry of the Interior as well as on the police. In times of trouble, reports were to be made daily by telephone to

[30] B, II, MA102140, HMB 1370, Obb., pp. 3-4; HMB 1716, M/F, p. 3; HMB 871, N/B, p. 1.

[31] B, II, MA100411, Brief: Kriebel an Knilling, 3.10.1923; NA, Epp Papers, 230-a-10/3 2, 25 and 27.9.1923; T79, 33, p. 1156; 56, p. 1206.

[32] B, I, GSK 43, pp. 156-59, 180ff; Kahr MS, p. 1263; II, MA103458, GSK R/Nr. 3216, 8.12.1923; MA103474, 8-9.11.1923.

Kahr's headquarters in the government building of Oberbayern, where Major Heinrich Doehla served as chief intelligence officer.[33] The actual security measures themselves consisted largely of protective arrests or the restriction of the movements of potentially or actively dangerous persons, the deportation of non-Bavarians, and the control of public assemblies. In the ensuing weeks protective custody was used often, first against the members of the left radical movement and then, during and after the Beer Hall Putsch, against right radicals.[34]

Kahr's deportation policy was one of the most controversial of his activities. To some extent, it expressed his personal anti-semitism,[35] but it was far more a sop thrown to the National Socialists and their allies. However, the policy seems to have been used sparingly. United States Consul General Robert Murphy reported to the State Department in January 1924 that apparently about thirty families of foreign Jews had been expelled and twelve other families had won appeals against deportation orders. Some further appeals were being considered. To judge by the few records that survive,[36] at least some investigation of the cases was made and a number of the persons involved had records of criminal offenses —usually minor, economic crimes. On the other hand, this weapon was not used only against Jews. One of the first persons to be expelled under this system was a violent antisemitic orator, Dr. Arnold Ruge, a former instructor at Heidelberg University. Knilling later stated that the number of expulsions was less than 100 and claimed that they had been discussed with the local consuls of the countries involved and that no case had been officially contested.[37]

Nonetheless, if Kahr believed that this policy would calm the antisemites without making much trouble for himself, he was mistaken. While Knilling more or less supported him against protests and questions from the Reich, Dr. Schweyer completely disassociated himself from the deportations. The Archbishop of München

[33] B, I, GSK 3, p. 11; GSK 4, pp. 2, 7; GSK 43, p. 4.

[34] See below. For regulations regarding protective custody and restriction of movement see B, I, GSK 7, p. 1, GSK R/Nr. 610, 13.10.1923; GSK 90, pp. 16ff.

[35] Kahr seems to have been an antisemite of the "old," social-aversion, selective school rather than the new, rabid, racist school, for he was friendly with conservative Jews, such as his press chief, Schiedt.

[36] The records of the Bavarian Ministry of Justice were among the victims of U.S. strategic bombing.

[37] B, II, MA103458, passim; IV, Lapo, Bd. 26a, GSK R/806.

Michael von Faulhaber wrote a public letter to the German Chancellor which said, in part: " 'How can we master the enormous, everincreasing economic distress, the misery that unemployment will cause this winter, if all moral forces without distinction of creed or party do not work together? How can we otherwise hope to soften the blind hatred with which our Jewish fellow-citizens and other circles of the population have been attacked and condemned wholesale without proof of guilt?' "[38] The München Catholic Central Committee also attacked antisemitism at this time, and Murphy was told that the Cardinal's intervention apparently stopped the expulsions. American Jewish organizations complained, and several foreign governments allegedly submitted formal démarches. The Bavarian Industrialists' Organization also registered a formal protest. Kahr had stirred up a violent storm over a policy about which he was clearly less than lukewarm, since he pursued it so haphazardly.[39]

Despite the problems regarding other security measures, much of the day-to-day work of the Generalstaatskommissariat dealt with the question of political assemblies, since all public assemblies that did not obtain a special permit from the police were banned. The control of the permit system and the final court of appeals for all such decisions was the GSK.[40] Meetings open only to members of political parties were not subject to this ban, and non-political youth organizations could receive blanket permits for meetings. The purpose of the decrees limiting meetings was threefold. The authorities wished to prevent the National Socialists and Communists from organizing mass rallies, which might prove to be the take-off point for riots or revolution. They wished to prevent the exploitation of the difficulties of the government by hostile orators, which would increase the already dangerous level of political tensions. And they wished to discourage "conspicuous consumption" in the midst of economic misery.[41]

The result was a reduction in the number and size of political assemblies, although a good number were allowed to take place despite these limitations. From time to time the restrictions were

[38] M336, 79, p. 0385.
[39] *Ibid.*, pp. 0383-86; B, II, MA102140, HMB 1531, 6.11.23, p. 5; MA103458, passim.
[40] B, I, GSK 73, p. 53, GSK R/Nr. 1667; p. 74, GSK R/Nr. 5; M. Inn. 73695, GSK 1665.
[41] B, I, GSK 71, p. 59; GSK 73, p. 69; GSK 101, p. 12.

violated in detail, and there were some minor skirmishes between partisans of Left and Right, but, on the whole, the ban imposed by the GSK seems to have had a damping effect on political violence. Both Left and Right were hit by the ban on assemblies. The Communist metal workers were refused permission to hold a meeting on 8 October, and the SPD was refused permission to hold a "German Day" in Bayreuth, although the rightists had just been permitted to hold such a celebration. On the other side, a number of National Socialist and Kampfbund celebrations and assemblies were also forbidden, as for example in Augsburg on 6 October, Regensburg on 17 October, and Neumarkt (Oberpfalz) on 22 October. Even Kahr's own allies in Bayern und Reich were hit occasionally by the ban, as in Erlangen on 18 October, when their radical wing, the Wanderverein, was refused permission to hold a patriotic celebration.[42]

Although economic problems were perhaps more pressing than any others during his term as Generalstaatskommissar, Kahr did very little in this area. Economic reports in September were crowding political reports out in the official communications of the provincial authorities, but clearly Kahr still thought in traditional political terms. He was not an "economic man" and apparently neither felt at home in economics nor had much understanding of economic problems. He issued economic decrees here and there, but they seem to be more in the nature of stopping leaks in the dyke than expressions of any clear plan or doctrine. For example, he refused to order the collection of new federal taxes in Bavaria in early October, but it is not clear whether this was a weapon in his quarrel with the Reich or an economic measure for the benefit of Bavaria. He made attempts to prevent profiteering, but apparently only sporadically. He banned the free export of dairy products from Bavaria in late October.[43] Yet, in early November he still seems to have had no clear idea of what he planned to do to fight the runaway inflation that grew from day to day. This is indicated by the vagueness of his letter of 1 November to the minister-president and by his suggestion of simple charity and harder work as an economic panacea:

The fatherland is threatened by the ruin of its economy, a con-

[42] B, ɪ, GSK 71, passim; GSK 73, passim.
[43] B, ɪ, GSK 4, p. 5; GSK 44, p. 41; ɪɪ, MA103458, *MNN* Announcement, 26.10.1923; NA, T120, 5569, p. K591541.

sequence of the lost war, the tribute based on the Dictate of Versailles, the theft of German wealth, soil, and human resources. But the ruin is made unbearable by the teachings of false prophets that German men can be made more happy with less work. Already hunger and cold rampage [garbled word]. Only through the thorough reorganization of the entire economy can lasting help be brought about. In the meantime German men, women, and children [will] starve or freeze, if immediate measures are not taken to meet at least the most pressing needs of the suffering segment of the population. . . .

Therefore I request that the Bavarian government immediately take up the battle against hunger [with] one million gold marks. Fair distribution and special protection for the dying children will be assured.[44]

This is clearly no monster of indifference, but a worried man who wants to aid the suffering, but this is also a man who after six weeks of dictatorial power is no closer to a grasp of the basic economic problem than he was at the beginning. Kahr was clearly no Moses who would lead his children out of the wilderness.

However, in fairness to Kahr it is also true, that, had he been an economic genius on the scale of Keynes or that ill-fated Scotsman, John Law, he could scarcely have done much more than he did. He might have known what to do, but he could not have done it. The Bavarian economy was fully integrated into the German economy and could only have been disengaged at the cost of still greater misery and dislocation—and even then the prognosis for the future would have been dim. If the economy was to be cured it would have to be cured by economic surgeons in Berlin, and in fact they were even then whetting their scalpels. The leaders in Bavaria were, at best, onlookers and, at worst, distractions to the surgeons. Perhaps in the end, by doing practically nothing, Kahr did what was best for the Bavarian economy and made recovery easier than it would have been had he proceeded in a more knowledgeable and effective manner. Sometimes ineptitude and ignorance succeed where skill and knowledge are helpless.

IV. *Kahr's Greatest War*

Almost immediately upon being appointed Generalstaatskommissar, Kahr found himself "at war" with the Reich government. There

---

[44] B, I, GSK 6, p. 15, Pol/1854, 1.11.1923.

is no indication that either he or the Bavarian Cabinet desired or sought this confrontation, although the Cabinet members certainly wished to win before long a favorable accommodation with Berlin on a number of issues. The appointment of Kahr, though, was made in response to a local crisis and seems to have been made without any thought of Berlin. The Berlin government, always suspicious of Bavaria, saw the appointment of Kahr as an act aimed against the Reich and as a threat to the rights of the federal government. The president and Cabinet therefore immediately set up a federal "dictator," Dr. Otto Gessler, as a countermeasure.[45] The Berliners seem to have had no idea of the reasons for the Bavarian action and to have made no attempt to find out. At the same time, despite a good deal of indignation against the Bavarians, there was little agreement on what concrete action the Reich should take.

Dr. Radbruch, the justice minister, seems to have been more annoyed at his colleagues for infringing on some of his prerogatives in the matter than he was at Knilling. His party colleague, Sollmann, the minister of the interior, saw the appointment of Kahr as a "strong provocation of all republican circles," meaning his own Social Democratic Party. He demanded that the Reich force the Bavarians to withdraw their emergency decree. This question was first considered from the legal viewpoint, where it was agreed that federal law overrides state law. It was then considered from the practical point of view when the chancellor announced that Knilling had said that he would reject any such argument. In the end, it was agreed that, for the time being, federal and state decrees could operate side by side in Bavaria.

Had both sides been extremely circumspect and understanding of one another's views, this parallel operation might have succeeded. Since the opposite was the case, it broke down almost immediately over a trifling affair. On 27 September Dr. Gessler, as the Reich's dictator, ordered the banning of the *Völkische Beobachter* for attacks on Seeckt and Stresemann. He passed this order on to General von Lossow, who had been appointed, like all other Wehrkreis commanders, executive officer for the federal state of emergency. Lossow, who was also one of the executive officers for the Bavarian state of emergency, reported the receipt of this order to

45 Gordon, *Reichswehr*, p. 232.

Kahr. Kahr forbade him to execute it. Kahr's order placed Lossow in an impossible situation. As the chosen instrument of each of the contending dictators, he could do nothing that would not be in defiance of the orders of one of them. He had to choose to obey either the Reichswehrminister or the Generalstaatskommissar. Gessler was in Berlin at the end of a telegraph wire, while Kahr was in München. In view of Lossow's background as a Bavarian officer and of his personal character there could be no serious question as to his decision. He chose to obey the master at hand.

Since by chance the quarrel broke out over a question involving the National Socialists, it has usually been portrayed as a simple case of a "pro-Nazi" Bavarian government protecting the National Socialists from the just wrath of the federal government. This was not the issue. The Bavarian government was feeling extremely hostile towards the National Socialists, and neither it nor the federal government were very interested in the National Socialist aspect of their quarrel. It was a simple confrontation over the relative powers of the two governments. The extent to which the specific question of the *Völkische Beobachter* was a side issue is indicated by the reversal of the two governments' positions regarding it within the first three weeks of the "Lossow affair," and by the fact that the fight went on long after both sides had forgotten all about the newspaper. Originally, the Reich banned the paper, while Kahr, not prepared for a direct confrontation with Hitler and still hoping to win over all "national" forces, refused to allow the execution of the order. Lossow then reported to Berlin, and his envoy was apparently told by Gessler to avoid a direct clash with Kahr. However, before the officer had returned to München, the Berliners had changed their minds. The order to ban the *Völkische Beobachter* was renewed by telephone. Lossow and Kahr again protested. Berlin stuck to its guns and the Bavarians, supported by the Cabinet, refused to budge. From that moment forward the basic issue had changed. The quarrel was now over Lossow's survival, which meant that it was over Bavaria's right to retain a Landeskommandant in the face of federal rejection of this officer. The *Völkische Beobachter* is scarcely mentioned again in the quarrel. However, on 5 October, Kahr himself banned it for ten days for publishing recruiting advertisements and calls for civil war. Hitler had not been idle during this time. He sent Scheubner-Richter to Berlin to seek a settlement. Learning that the offending article attacked Seeckt and claimed that his wife was Jewish,[46] Hitler ordered the printing of an apology—but only after obtaining assurances that the ban would be lifted as a result. The federal ban was ended on 20 October, and since the Bavarian ban had already expired, the newspaper was no longer proscribed by either party to the quarrel, but the feud ran hotter than ever.[47]

In truth, the whole Lossow affair was only peripheral to the development of the internal Bavarian situation and to the coming of the Beer Hall Putsch, although in a way it could be said to have acted as a trigger by encouraging the Putschists to believe that the Bavarian government and the Generalstaatskommissar were sufficiently embroiled with Berlin over matters of competence that they would support the "march on Berlin," which the Putschists wished to make for quite different reasons. While welcome to the Putschists tactically, the Lossow affair was at the same time painful and disruptive for them, since in the basic questions at issue they agreed with Berlin: Hitler, Ludendorff, Dr. Weber, and the rest were all supporters of the idea of a centralized German state and deplored the federalism of the Bavarian government and Kahr, which they, with characteristic unfairness, denounced as separatism. Only their intense hatred of the "traitors" in power in "Red Berlin" made it possible for them to accept grudgingly the idea of a Bavarian quarrel with the federal government, and then only for the sake of seizing the federal government and making such revolts impossible in the future.[48]

The Lossow affair and its implications, however, absorbed much of the time and energy of the Generalstaatskommissar, although it was really the Bavarian government that called the tune to which he danced. This does not mean that the Cabinet or its members approved of each move he made, but they did take the same basic attitude towards the conflict. Bavaria must hold out and win. Proceeding on this basis, Knilling and Kahr moved closer and closer to a complete break with Berlin. They stopped gold shipments from

---

[46] An allegation that was half-true, since Frau von Seeckt was half-Jewish. See Meier-Welcker, *Seeckt*, p. 23.

[47] B, I, GSK 83, p. 24; II, MA103458, 513 B.G. in Berlin, 25.10.1923; NA, T120, 5569, pp. K591540, K591558; EAP 105/7, I, p. 72; Seeckt Papers, Stück 155, unpublished interview for MNN; T120, 1749, Sept.-Oct. 1923, passim.

[48] See Hitler Manifesto draft of 19.4.1923 (never released) in B, II, MA103476, pp. 608-15; NA, EAP 105/7, I, pp. 58ff.

Bavaria to the north, they swore the Bavarian Reichswehr into the service of the Bavarian state and generally defied the authority of the federal government to intervene in Bavarian affairs.[49] As a result, in early November both the government and Kahr were preoccupied with Bavaria's "external relations" just as her internal affairs reached a crisis.

v. *Kahr's War Against the Bavarian Left*

Far more to Kahr's taste than the struggle with the Reich was his offensive against the Bavarian Left. Two days after his assumption of office he banned the paramilitary organizations of the Majority Socialist and Communist Parties, and ordered their weapons confiscated. The Landespolizei as well as the local police were used to search for concealed weapons, and Kahr showed a consistent interest in the success of this campaign. Early in October Kahr banned all Communist publications. Later in the month he ordered their youth organizations dissolved and forbade students in secondary schools to belong to Communist organizations. On 17 October Kahr ordered the northern provinces of Bavaria to watch for arms shipments to the states of Saxony and Thuringia.

This anti-Marxist campaign was none too successful, primarily because it was largely directed against mirages. The socialists were neither organized for nor interested in anything more than local skirmishes with the right radicals, while the Communists, who would have liked to have been dangerous, were too weak and too carefully watched to have any hope of developing real strength. Even the arms collection campaign was not very successful. There apparently were not many arms in leftist hands, and those which they did possess were small and easily hidden. Neither socialists nor Communists in Bavaria were in any position, either before or after Kahr's offensive, to undertake major armed action against the state. They were outgunned and outmanned by trained and experienced men both among their political foes and in the armed forces of the state.[50]

Here again a good deal of Kahr's energy was expended in more

[49] See Chapter x, Section iii, below.
[50] B, i, GSK 3, pp. 46-47; GSK 60, p. 30; GSK 83, p. 6; M. Inn. 71537, 1680 in Staatsanzeiger, 1.10.1923; ii, MA102140, HMB 1979, Ofr., p. 1; HMB 2201, Ofr., p. 2; HMB 1030 N/B, p. 2; HMB 2150, Schw., p. 1; MA103458, GSK Pol./Nr. 540, 11.10.1923; *Vo.*, 40 Jhrg., Nr. 457, 30.9.1923, p. 1.

or less pointless activity, although, to be fair to him, most men in Bavaria in 1923 believed that there was far more danger from the Left than really existed, and an ultraconservative monarchist who had seen the revolution and Republic of Councils sweep across the face of Bavaria could scarcely be expected not to fear the menace of the Left.

VI. *The War Against the Left Outside Bavaria*

At the time when Kahr became Generalstaatskommissar the eyes of many Bavarians were turned in anguish and hatred towards their northern frontiers, where "Red" Saxony and "Red" Thuringia seemed poised to unleash a wave of revolution over the rest of Germany. In both states coalitions including Communists had taken over the state governments, although their enemies were strong and their legislative majorities were paper thin. In normal times the idea of an attack by states so much smaller than Bavaria would have carried little terror and might indeed have been cause for mirth in München's myriad beer halls. In the fevered fall of 1923 this was not the case. Rightist refugees from Communist terror told exaggerated tales of Red armies forming on Bavaria's borders. Half in fear, half in indignation, Bavarian right radicals demanded a counter-offensive against the Reds, while even moderates demanded protection against the Red flood. The result was Kahr's "Thuringian War." He called up a portion of the PNB, primarily units of Bund Wiking, Bund Bayern und Reich, and Jungdo. These units were sent to the Thuringian border to form a defensive bulwark against the "Red Hundreds" and Thuringian Landespolizei drawn up along the Bavarian border. The Bavarians were armed with small arms from secret caches in the south and were placed under the command of the Landespolizei commander in Bayreuth, Lieutenant Colonel Georg Häublein.[51]

The aim of the Generalstaatskommissar and the police in calling up the PNB was the defense of the Bavarian frontier. Most of the men who were called up or turned up on their initiative seem, however, to have expected to march on Berlin and overthrow the Weimar Republic. Certainly, this is what they would have liked to

[51] B, I, GSK 3, pp. 10, 13; GSK 44, pp. 53, 57; GSK 90, p. 458; II, MA99521, 17.10.1923, pp. 8-10; MA104221, Unsigned Grenzschutz Denkschrift (Seisser or Doehla); IV, Lapo, Bd. 26a, Akt 1, Vereinbarung, p. 1; Akt 3, Item 3, 2198 Reg. Ofr., 22.10.1923; Item 15, 2224, Ofr.

do. On the other hand, they were clearly incapable of such action under any conceivable circumstances. They were too few in number, they were too badly trained and supplied, and they lacked effective sources of support in north Germany. Without the active support of the Bavarian government, Reichswehr, and police their march would have broken down in twenty-four hours without opposition—and we now know that the northern Reichswehr and the Thuringian Landespolizei were prepared to fight them. Even the Kampfbund leaders showed no interest in the Grenzschutz at the time, although at their trial after the Beer Hall Putsch[52] they tried to claim to have been involved in it.

There were probably a total of 2,500 men involved in the Grenzschutz in one way or another. These included several companies of Bavarian Landespolizei, some 500 to 700 PNB members, up to 1,000 other men from Verbände involved in the call up of the PNB, and several hundred men from organizations not involved in the official Grenzschutz, who appeared without any authorization in comparatively small groups. A considerable number of these men were disorganized political refugees from Saxony and Thuringia rather than organized paramilitary groups.[53] The rumors current in north Germany of many thousands of men marshalled on Bavaria's border were compounded of equal parts of hysteria and propaganda.

The upshot of the matter was a series of vague border clashes, mostly between irregulars, in which there was a good deal of wild firing which resulted in one death and a few arrests of policemen, alleged spies, and political extremists on each side of the border. Although the Communists may well have had fond hopes of invading Bavaria in the course of their projected "revolution," the "Red hordes" of Thuringia and Saxony were an even less real menace than the right radical army opposing them. Kahr was still shadowboxing with his fears of Red revolution, while the Bavarian Cabinet, which seemed to disapprove of his activities far more on fiscal

---

[52] For Kampfbund attitudes see B, ıv, BuR, Bd. 35, Akt 5, Dt. Kampfbund, Mil. Führer 227, 13.10.1923; NA, T120, 5569, p. K591586; EAP 105/7, ııı, p. 29.

[53] B, ı, GSK 60, p. 5; ıı, MA99521, 3.11.1923, p. 3; MA102140, HMB 1358, Ofr., p. 3; MA104381, Bev. Pr. in München an M. Äuss., 14.11.1923; IV, BuR, Bd. 36, Akt 2, Item 33/4; NA, T120, 5569, p. K591581; 52 Jhrg., Nr. 489, 18.10.1923, p. 3.

than political grounds, clucked disapprovingly in the background but did not tighten his leash.[54]

VII. *The War Against France*

If several of Kahr's other campaigns featured greatly inflated foes, this struggle was more in the nature of a flea attacking a giant. It is doubtful if the giant even knew it was being attacked. Here, as elsewhere, Kahr was not entirely a free agent. The French military governor in the Pfalz, General de Metz, was one of the most active of those French officers who were attempting to foment revolution and support separatism in the occupied areas of Germany in 1923. The imprisonment and harassment of Bavarian officials, the expulsion of many citizens from the Pfalz, and similar developments distracted Kahr from more important matters.

In this situation, since the French controlled the Pfalz by force of arms, there was little that Kahr could do, but he did press the government to provide funds for "intellectual resistance" to support the Pfälzische Kampfbund and the Akademische Rhein-pfalzausschuss, propaganda organizations opposing French policies and propaganda. Even had he wished to ignore the French question entirely, it would have been very difficult to do so, for the issue was so hot in Bavaria and in the highly patriotic Pfalz that individual Frenchmen and persons who associated with them were in considerable personal danger, and official disinterest would have been construed as treachery or an expression of separatism.[55]

VIII. *The Guerrilla War with the Kampfbund*

The relations between Kahr and the Kampfbund can perhaps best be described as similar to those of two strange tomcats on their first encounter with one another: they were cautiously hostile without (until the Putsch) committing themselves irrevocably to battle. The same factors prevented the Kampfbund from launching an all-out attack against Kahr during the weeks preceding 8 November that had prevented them from attacking his appointment unequivocally. Also, they hoped to win over many of his followers. The result was that they followed a zig-zag course calculated to discredit and

[54] For the Bavarian government attitude see B, II, MA99521, 3.11.1923, pp. 2-5.

[55] B, I, GSK 43, pp. 7, 119, 220; GSK 100, pp. 13, 17; II, MA99521, 19.11.1923, pp. 2, 8; MA102140, HMB 1716, M/F, p. 2; HMB 99, Opf., pp. 3-4; NA, T120, 1748, p. D756734.

undermine him without exposing themselves to a serious riposte. Kahr, on the other side of the table, had similar problems. While he probably despaired of Hitler himself, he was clearly hopeful of winning over many of the Kampfbund rank and file at least. This he could only do if he could place the onus for the friction between the Kampfbund and himself on the Kampfbund leaders. At the same time, he did not wish the Kampfbund to get completely out of hand. Therefore he met their most vigorous sorties with counterattacks, but the sorties, like the attacks, were limited in aim and scope. The fight was with gloves and by Marquess of Queensberry rules, insofar as it was conducted in public.

Both Hitler and Kahr were under heavy pressure from within their own camps to reach an accord, since many of the lesser leaders believed that the only chance for a racist triumph was to be found in the unification of all branches of the movement. Both Hitler and Kahr received letters from various individuals urging cooperation, some of them from men of considerable influence in the Racist Movement. Even Kampfbund members took this viewpoint. Lieutenant Colonel Hofmann went so far as to suggest that Hitler cooperate with Crown Prince Rupprecht, which implied friendship with Kahr. Such pressures also help to explain the tentative nature of their confrontation in this period.[56]

The pin pricks began early and continued, alternated with conciliatory gestures from one or the other side, throughout October. Hitler started off the series by sending Dr. Scheubner-Richter, in place of himself or Kriebel, to a meeting called by Kahr for all Verbände leaders. Two days later, the *Völkische Beobachter* attacked Kahr as a monarchist. At the same time, the Kampfbund began the program of trying to force or induce Kahr to share his power with Pöhner, a scheme with which they were to make no progress in October. Hitler then took offense at the Verbände that had supported Kahr, and he decided to remove all of "his people" from the debilitating influence of such leaders. He issued an order that National Socialists must resign from any Verband that was not in the Kampfbund. This order was a first major step towards the sorting out and subsequent estrangement of radicals from moderates within the Racist Movement.[57] Similarly, Dr. Frick of the München

[56] B, I, GSK 9, Dr. M. Holl an M. Kühner, 1.10.1923; NA, T84, 4, pp. 3349-52, 3392-95, 3482-85, 3506-7, 3575-76, 3614, 1641-42.
[57] Not all National Socialists were prepared to accept dictation on this

police praesidium, a close friend of Pöhner and an ally of Hitler, refused to join the staff of the Generalstaatskommissar. Kriebel flatly refused to obey Crown Prince Rupprecht's order to all former officers to support Kahr, and subsequent negotiations by Graf Soden aimed at winning Kriebel over proved fruitless. Captain Göring, who never had his tongue under any more effective control than he did his various voracious appetites, went so far as to threaten General von Lossow's life in the course of a quarrel with the operations officer of Wehrkreis VII over limitations placed on National Socialist paramilitary activities.[58]

Kahr fought back largely with bans on meetings and newspapers, such as the *Völkische Beobachter* ban, the ban on *Heimatland*, and that on Helmut Klotz' *Weisse Fahne* in Nürnberg.[59] He, Lossow, and Seisser also made it very clear that they did not intend to let their "triumvirate" be broken by attempts to deal with them individually.[60]

In response to this strong stand, Hitler and his allies, particularly Oberland, decided to try honey instead of vinegar, with the result that Dr. Weber allowed Oberland to continue in the PNB, despite its membership in the Kampfbund and assured Seisser that he would consider his obligations to the Bavarian government to be primary and those to Hitler secondary in case of conflict. Within Bund Oberland, Dr. Weber tried to smooth over the tensions between Kahr and Hitler and even cast doubt on their existence.[61] On 18 October, even the high command of the SA of the NSDAP denied that the SA was committed to hostility towards the Generalstaatskommissar.[62] Hitler himself took a similar tack in dealing with Seisser. In a report of 26 October, Captain Adolf von Bomhard of the Landespolizei, who headed the intelligence system of the government of Oberbayern, wrote:

> Hitler keeps himself very much in the background since the state of emergency. He has admitted that he cannot undertake a spe-

---

point, and some left the NSDAP rather than their other organizations. See Chapter IV, Section III.

[58] B, II, MA103476, pp. 767-68, 859-66, 1365, 1398-99; IV, HSIV, EE7, Endres MS, p. 23; NA, T120, 5569, p. K591532; Röhm, *Geschichte*, pp. 216-19.

[59] B, I, GSK 83, pp. 3-8; NA, T120, 5569, pp. K591549-50.

[60] On this point see Chapter XI, passim.

[61] B, II, MA103476, pp. 1118-22, 1154.

[62] NA, Epp Papers, 230-a-10/3 1, ca. 18.10.1923.

cial action since the R[eichs]W[ehr] and the L[andes]P[olizei] are too powerful, [so that] he can do nothing against them, [and] that he will also not be able to undertake any special action against Berlin without the cooperation of the other Verbände. These assurances he gave Colonel von Seisser in a conversation last night. He thus gave up his own struggle against Kahr, even though he still holds himself in the background.[63]

This evaluation indicates not only how much the authorities misjudged Hitler and his real mood, but also the very real dilemma in which the Nazi leader found himself. It was this dilemma as much as their misreading of his character that led the authorities astray. In the face of such hopeless odds they believed that he had no choice but to fall into line. A man of reason and common sense would doubtless have agreed with them. Hitler, however, was neither, but a gifted revolutionary secure in an unshakeable belief in his own destiny and borne forward by the storms of his own wild emotions. For such men, from Alexander the Great to Castro, every day realities are meaningless, odds are meaningless. They believe in what Goebbels was later to call the "triumph of the will," and surprisingly often the will does triumph, at least for a time. Certainly in this period of crisis it triumphed briefly in Hitler and in the councils of the Kampfbund, just as it was later to triumph first in Germany and then in much of Europe. Even as Bomhard wrote his complacent words, the planning for a Putsch was underway.

[63] B, IV, BuR, Bd. 34, Bomhard Lagebericht, 26.10.1923.

10.

THE COMING OF THE PUTSCH

I. *The Economic Pressures*

One of the most important factors in bringing on the Beer Hall Putsch was the disastrous economic situation that developed in Germany in the fall of 1923. The German economy had never recovered from World War I and from the losses and dislocations caused by the Treaty of Versailles. Massive unemployment, reduced resources, reduced foreign trade, tremendous internal war debts (although these had already been partly repudiated), reparations, and extremely heavy social disbursements had proven more than the postwar German economy was able to bear without readjustment and sacrifices. The result was that the economy was already staggering drunkenly by the end of 1922. The additional cost burden of the passive resistance policy in the Ruhr was apparently the last straw and the economy broke down. A racing inflation of disastrous scope ensued.

Unfortunately, the official reaction in both the Reich and Bavaria was neither determined nor informed. By the middle of the year, drastic action would have been needed to prevent disaster, if in fact this end could still have been achieved. In September the federal finance minister, Dr. Rudolf Hilferding[1] stated succinctly: "One must clearly recognize that in the immediate future it will not be possible to cover the expenses of the Reich by income or credits. As a result one must reckon on a certain further development of the inflation under all circumstances. . . ."[2] This cool and accurate evaluation of the situation, however, was only part of what the nation needed. The other, and far more important need, was for strong action to bring the disastrous inflation to a halt as soon as possible. Here, the omens were none too good, since the economic experts, not surprisingly, differed sharply in their diagnosis of the

---

[1] Formerly USPD, then SPD.   [2] NA, T120, 1748, p. D756619.

case and in their prescriptions for a cure. In part these differences seem to have resulted from different doctrines and approaches to the study of economics, and in part, from concern as to which elements of the population should bear the bulk of the burden. Even the Reichsbank and the government were at odds over the solution of the problem. The end result was delay when delay was least tolerable to the great bulk of the German people, who stood with their backs to the wall and expected the financial marines to arrive in time to save them from disaster.[3]

The cause of the man in the street's distress is easy to understand when one looks at the decline in value of the mark. On 18 August the dollar was already worth 1,100,000 paper marks, but by 27 August the value of the mark had dropped to 2,200,000 to the dollar. In ten days the purchasing power of the mark had declined by exactly half, and this was just the beginning.[4] By October, the value of the mark had reached such an ebb that Ernst Röhm reports paying one billion[5] marks for a simple lunch.[6] Under these conditions it is not surprising that many men lost their heads completely and that critics of the government came to feel that revolution was their only hope. Even the federal minister of the interior, Wilhelm Sollmann (SPD), warned his colleagues as early as the end of August:

> Under certain circumstances a form of dictatorship cannot be avoided. All responsible people are agreed that this Cabinet, built on the broadest parliamentary base, will be the last constitutional Cabinet of the German Republic if it does not succeed in bringing the Ruhr question to an end.[7]

When democratic members of the government took this line—and Sollmann was not rebuked for his remarks—it is not surprising that radicals of Right and Left alike believed that their hour had come, while many moderates had their own schemes for the rescue of the ship of state. Disaster leads many men to despair, but it also raises up many self-appointed saviors of the people, some of whom are pathetically ludicrous, while others are convincing and collect large followings. Sometimes they really do become saviors. Thus crises lead both the masses and the elite to seek a strong figure to lead them, and this search for a strong man was important on the German political scene in the fall of 1923.

---

[3] *Ibid.*, pp. D756619-7515.
[4] *Ibid.*, p. D756701.
[5] U.S. billion, European milliard.
[6] Röhm, *Geschichte*, p. 230.
[7] NA, T120, 1748, p. D756442.

While the leaders of the Reich wrestled with the problems of economic revival, French pressure, the Ruhr struggle, and the incipient revolutions in Saxony, Thuringia and Bavaria, the Bavarian economic and political situation deteriorated rapidly. At the end of September the chief of the Bayreuth Lapo reported:

The *feelings of the populace* [are] extraordinarily irritable. As a result of rising prices and increasing unemployment the workers are bitter. The patriotic bands are at fever pitch because of the foreign policy of the Reich government, the abandonment of the Ruhr resistance, and the negotiations with the Entente. The peasants are working in every way against the new tax laws. The well-known Freiherr von Gagern[8] indeed called for open tax sabotage and for resistance against enforced collection in a peasant meeting. The resolution of the peasants was also sent to the other peasant chambers as an example. All circles are, each according to its interests, unhappy with the government and desire a change of relationships. In the last days before the proclamation of the state of emergency the National Socialists and the Kampfverbände indulged in a particularly harsh tone. The exacerbation of political differences increased rapidly as a result of the holding of "German Days," which are now held primarily in the strongholds of Social Democracy.

Unemployment has increased sharply.

The morale of the third battalion of the [Twenty-first] Infantry Regiment and of the Landespolizei is good.[9]

Despite the pressures of events, everyone was still inclined to see the situation through his own special glasses. Employers, especially the brewers, were seeking to reduce wages as a result of the crisis and Kahr's appointment, while many workers with jobs worried primarily about the possibility of losing the eight-hour day. The average consumer was becoming increasingly restless and incipient or actual riots took place in the München food market (Viktualienmarkt) on 12 and 18 October. The Communist Party, needless to say, took advantage of the situation where a worker might well earn as much as two billion (Milliarden) a week and still not be able to do more than purchase bread and potatoes. And

---

[8] A leader of Bayern und Reich and a strong foe of National Socialism. See, for example, B, IV, BuR, Bd. 36, Akt 1, Item 18.

[9] B, I, GSK 43, p. 1, Bayreuth Lapo 835.

the fact that bank employees seemed to fare quite well helped to build up resentment against "finance capital" at both ends of the political spectrum, for National Socialist theorists, like Gottfried Feder, had little more love for bankers than did the most radical of Communists.[10]

Men were hungry enough that mass theft of potatoes from the field was commonplace and only widespread use of the Landespolizei to protect the crops ensured the survival of seed potatoes for the future. The peasants, who had been enjoying unaccustomed prosperity from the end of World War I until September 1923, continued to react violently against the new taxes, which bore down on them so heavily, as well as against the bewildering decline in the value of the currency. When a sum of money that seemed adequate to buy a farm was paid the peasant for a hog, but a few days later would no longer purchase a liter of beer, he was both frightened and angry. On 19 October, the acting Regierungs-Präsident of Oberbayern reported:

The tax calamity, which stands in the center of all interest, is, in part, blown up and turned to political advantage. In Landsberg an assembly of the Christian Peasants' Association (Christlicher Bauernverein) took place which demanded that the tax laws be immediately altered and be reduced to a bearable level. Demands were also made that the states, especially Bavaria, should again be given the political and economic autonomy of a confederated state (Bundesstaat).

The rising prices have influenced the mood of the population to such an extent that, according to the report of a district office (Bezirksamt), it is close to the mood of the November days of 1918 and April 1919. Remarks to the effect that it doesn't matter if everything is smashed are, as the chief of a purely agricultural district reports, not uncommon. The populace is particularly disturbed about the question of the distribution of potatoes. In this regard the Bezirksamt München reports:

"It is certainly deeply to be deplored that at the very time in which the raids on the potato fields (Kartoffelfrevel) are being strongly curbed, the official potato distribution system in München has broken down completely. In all of München (including the food market) absolutely no potatoes have been available

[10] B, I, GSK 43, pp. 9, 12-13, 24, 46.

for days, which, in view of the fact that potatoes are naturally the cheapest food, is particularly tragic at this time."[11]

Things were no better in other parts of Bavaria. The Regierungs-Präsident of Oberfranken reported on 23 October that four pounds of black bread cost over four billion (Milliarden) marks and that he was awaiting riots at any moment. Unemployment was growing by leaps and bounds and local industry had few orders on hand. Large elements of the population simply could not feed themselves. Demands for price control measures on the part of the General-staatskommissar were heard on every hand.[12] By the end of the month the government was not even able to pay its own employees in Oberfranken, let alone lend aid to the poor and the unemployed.[13]

In this situation, there was undoubtedly a great deal of truth in the report of the Regierungs-Präsident of Niederbayern for 4 November:

> The general situation in the Regierungsbezirk has not changed greatly. The greatest portion of the population is so concerned with the economic distress that even the political events of the last [few] days have played no important role in the consciousness of the people. Even among the Left parties there is no indication at present of vigorous activity, for which, of course, the state of emergency may be partially responsible. The existing irritability of the workers has far more an economic than a political basis.[14]

However, such terrific economic pressures were bound to have their political repercussions soon, and these political repercussions, naturally enough, appeared first among the active groups of the opposition. The Communists tried to fish in troubled waters, but much more significant for Bavaria were similar activities on the Right.

II. *Pressures for Political Action*

In the fine old, largely mythical, conspiratorial school of historical interpretation, Hitler and his entourage are often envisaged as sitting down and coldly planning a Putsch in a situation that left

---

[11] B, I, GSK 43, pp. 52ff, HMB 1437, Obb.
[12] *Ibid.*, GSK 44, p. 47.   [13] *Ibid.*, pp. 31-34.
[14] B, II, MA102140, HMB 1030, N/B, p. 1.

them entirely free to decide their best possible course of action. In some ways it is perhaps truer to see them hurried into a smoke-filled room from which they did not dare to emerge without having decided to go ahead with the Putsch. They were by no means free agents, as such men rarely are in troubled times. The leaders of revolutionary movements are men who have harnessed the whirlwind. They can, at best, hope to guide its direction. They cannot halt it without destroying it or themselves or, more probably, both.

Inside the Kampfbund there were most insistent demands for violent political action that would ease the economic distress of its members. The social and economic motif appeared again and again in the course of the prelude to the Putsch and in the course of the Putsch itself. For example, when Wutzlhofer was led out of the Beer Hall under arrest he was pursued by threats and curses, and one Putschist remarked: "He has three farms. He should be hanged."[15] Economic revisionism was by no means a monopoly of the political Left. The leaders of the Kampfbund were well aware of the misery of many of their followers and sought to alleviate it. The demand for an army to liberate Germany from Marxism and Allied pressure was at least partly economic. Thus, when Dr. Weber of Oberland ordered the formation of companies to be integrated into the Reichswehr in case of mobilization, he said: " 'In the choice of the men [for these formations] the largest possible number of unemployed is to be included.' "[16] Similarly, as early as June, SA Regiment München had stressed that men who volunteered and were accepted for machine-gun training by the Reichswehr would receive free travel, clothing, food, and training. The pay and perquisites of a private soldier may not mean much to an American or a German today, but in 1923 they were most attractive to many penniless and hungry Germans.[17]

Leaders at all levels echoed the demands of their subordinates. Wilhelm Brückner, the leader of SA Regiment München, testified:

"I also said to Hitler personally: 'The day is coming when I can no longer hold my people. If nothing happens now the men will sneak away.' We had very many unemployed men among us, men who had expended their last garment, their last shoes, their last ten pfennigs on training, as they said [because] we will strike

[15] B, II, MA103476, pp. 1370-71.   [16] *Ibid.*, p. 1157.
[17] NA, Epp Papers, SA Rgt. München, 230-a-10/3 3, 22.6.1923.

soon. Then we will be taken into the Reichswehr and will be out of the entire mess."[18]

Fürst Karl von Wrede, the leader of a National Socialist cavalry unit, confirmed the pressures on Hitler and added that they came not only from the rank and file but also from leaders:

> . . . Beyond these circumstances, Hitler was driven into his actions of 9 November because his lieutenants (with the single exception of the R[eichs]K[riegsflagge] leader) gave him to understand that their formations could no longer be held back and were determined to strike. . . .[19]

Captain (Ret.) Graf Wolf von Helldorff, later a leader of the SA and of the 20 July 1944 plot who was still a Stahlhelm official at the time, provides further evidence of the extent to which Kampfbund leaders felt the pressure from below:

> "I also spoke with Scheubner-Richter about the National Socialist Storm Troops. Scheubner-Richter declared: 'It is difficult to hold the people together. The men are undernourished, badly clothed, and receive no pay for their activities. They make comparisons with the Reichswehr, which is well fed, well clothed, and well housed. The people will not be content any longer with mere parades before a row of generals and with pretty speeches. In order to keep the men together, one must finally undertake something. Otherwise the people will become Left radicals. . . .' "[20]

Perhaps the National Socialist non-commissioned officer who remarked to a policeman during the Putsch, " 'We have overthrown the rotten government that let us all starve. We don't need a Catholic government any more,' " summed up the views of the rank and file of the Verbände quite well, if the word "Catholic" is interpreted as "old fashioned."[21]

Besides the demands of his followers, there were other severe pressures that acted on Hitler, primarily those resulting from the cold logic of the situation and those emanating from within himself. As far as the logic of the situation was concerned, Hitler had placed himself at the head of a revolutionary movement and had preached the need for violent action for years. He had accused Kahr and Dr.

---

[18] B, II, MA103476, p. 1020. [19] NA, T79, 82, p. 210.
[20] B, II, MA103476, pp. 750-51. [21] B, I, SA 1, 1490, III, p. 15.

Pittinger of inaction and indecision, of futility. Now, with the economic, political, and social structure of Germany and Bavaria visibly wobbling and with no salvation from the existing authorities in sight, how could he, either in his own eyes or in the eyes of his followers, defend the failure to practice what he preached? Only if he were a hypocrite, or a man of empty words, could he fail to see that his own doctrine, his own existence, called for the passage from words to deeds.

Finally, Hitler's own character pushed him forward. A man like Stalin was undoubtedly sincere in his devotion to the doctrines he espoused and preached, but Stalin was essentially a cold man of reason, a man whom Machiavelli would have understood, though probably not have loved. However, Savonarola was a leader who would have understood Hitler and who shared his characteristics. Hitler was a man of keen if untrained intelligence—as most men who came into close contact with him have admitted, including, surprisingly, Arnold Toynbee[22]—but one who consciously subordinated his intelligence to his emotions. Whereas Stalin placed his emotions at the service of reason (within his own context), Hitler placed his reason at the service of his emotions, which provided the direction as well as the motive power for his career. Had reason been pleading against emotion, it would not have gotten far with Hitler, but when, as in the question of a Putsch, reason and desire worked together, Hitler was driven inexorably in the direction in which they pointed him. Here we see him, perhaps for the first time, launching one of those headlong expeditions that characterized his political life, where he was whipped along by his emotions like a ship scudding before the hurricane. He was determined to act; all that remained to be set was the date and the conditions. Hitler might have been dominated by his emotions, but he was not entirely blinded by them. Therefore he was determined to establish the best possible situation before acting. Essentially, in the fall of 1923, this meant that he wished to neutralize or to win over the Bavarian Reichswehr and the Landespolizei. Then he would be able to march with a light heart. Apparently he had become enough of a Bavarian that he, too, could not yet see beyond the white-blue border posts, for he later admitted that he thought little, if at all, of the situation beyond those symbolic barriers.[23]

[22] For Toynbee's remarks see Toynbee, Arnold J., *Acquaintances*, London, 1967, pp. 280-81.
[23] B, I, Kahr MS, pp. 1178-79; GP, A, General Pirner, 26.9.1960.

III. *The Struggle for the "Weather Gage"*

Like fleets in the days of sail, the opposing forces in Bavaria maneuvered for position in the last weeks before the Putsch, each seeking a decisive or at least a tentative advantage. The Bavarian government still lurked silent in the background, while the Kampfbund leaders and the triumvirate (Kahr-Lossow-Seisser) circled each other warily. Meeting after meeting, conference after conference, was held. Tentative agreements were made and abandoned, and all of the time the two contenders sought their own advantage. The Kampfbund wished to commit the triumvirate to its plans or at least to prevent them from following another course, while the triumvirate hoped to hold the Kampfbund in play until their own plans had ripened and it was too late for the Kampfbund to move.

From the beginning of Kahr's term as Generalstaatskommissar he seems to have been well aware that Bavaria's problems would, in the end, be solved in Berlin, if they were solved at all. He therefore turned his attention to finding allies in the national capital. Since he represented the political Right, he naturally turned to that end of the spectrum in his quest. After tentative negotiations with various groups he, together with Lossow and Seisser, fell under the spell of Friedrich Minoux—the recently discharged former right-hand man of Hugo Stinnes, one of Germany's key industrialists—who planned the creation of a directorate to take over from Stresemann's government when it collapsed. Minoux envisioned a plural dictatorship of the Right for the salvation of Germany in a crisis where democracy seemed to have admitted bankruptcy. This directory was to consist of Minoux himself; General von Seeckt; Dr. Otto Wiedfeldt, the German ambassador to the United States, who was a man with broad governmental and economic administrative experience; and Henrich, the general director of the Siemens Corporation.[24] The available evidence indicates that Kahr, Lossow, and Seisser hoped not to act themselves, but to second the actions of their north German friends.[25]

The other contacts that Kahr and his colleagues maintained in

[24] Seeckt saw this group as forming part of a Cabinet, according to Hasse, as an alternative to the directorate. See Meier-Welcker, *Seeckt*, p. 394.

[25] B, I, Kahr MS, pp. 1274-80, 1295-1300; II, MA103476, pp. 688, 691, 700-701; MA104221, Seisser Besprechungen in Berlin, 3.11.1923; Klass, Gert von, *Hugo Stinnes*. Tübingen, 1958, p. 340.

Berlin were with the right radical Verbände associated with Heinrich Class's Alldeutscher Verband (although relations with Class himself seem to have been vague and unsatisfactory)[26] and led by General (Ret.) Otto von Below, on one hand, and with the Landbund on the other. Graf Behr of the Landbund was apparently the link between the Landbund and Below. The relation among these groups is not entirely clear—and probably was not clear at the time —but there can be no doubt that, to some extent, at least, the Landbund-Below clique was working at cross purposes with the legal-minded and more moderate Seeckt-Minoux "directorate group." Furthermore, Kahr and his colleagues seem to have been rather more in the former camp than in the latter, since they wished to push General von Seeckt and Minoux into action. Ironically, they played in Berlin, on a smaller and milder scale, the very game that Hitler was playing against them in München. Very possibly they played this game in part because of the pressure they themselves felt. They did not wish to act, but they would welcome action on the part of the Berliners and were prepared to support the Berliners.

After various general negotiations, Major (Ret.) Emil Vogts visited München to see Kahr, Lossow, and Seisser on 28 October, apparently representing both Below and Behr. He warned Kahr, according to the latter, that in Graf Behr's opinion, the northern Verbände had no real military significance. Therefore a directory could only be based on the support of the legal armed forces, the Reichswehr.[27] This account is probably true, for an apparent Landbund reaction to this situation is to be found in Seisser's notes for his report on his subsequent visit to Berlin, and the report was, in general, true enough. According to Vogts he proposed in the name of the northern Verbände that they follow the example of the trade unions in past years and put heavy, but legal, pressure on the federal government to give way to one more in tune with their desires. They hoped to exert this pressure through the leaders of the armed forces, big business, and industry.[28] Phrased more bluntly than Vogts cared to do after the Putsch, what they wanted was for Seeckt to threaten a military coup if the government did not give way to one favored by the Below-Kahr-Landbund constellation. The Bavarians rejected the idea that Kahr should head the direc-

[26] B, I, Kahr MS, pp. 1280-81; II, MA103476, p. 683.
[27] B, I, Kahr MS, p. 1302.   [28] B, II, MA103476, pp. 737-38.

torate, pointing out that his name held no magic in the north, and that it could suggest a Catholic plot. It seems equally likely, however, that this refusal was in line with their general determination not to put themselves in a position that would be opposed by the Bavarian government.[29]

Then, on 3 November 1923, Colonel von Seisser went to Berlin as the representative of the triumvirate. There he spoke with Seeckt, Minoux, and various Landbund leaders, among others. Minoux was of the opinion that the new Stresemann Cabinet would soon fall, but he was also inclined to believe that Seeckt would never bring himself to form a directorate. Minoux added that he would have no hand in a Putsch. He remained unenthusiastic about Hitler and Ludendorff and unready to go along with them regarding the Jewish question. Graf Behr had lost faith in the plans for the directorate. When he visited the Landbund leaders, Seisser found that they, like Minoux, had lost hope that Seeckt would break with Ebert and Stresemann. Speaking for the leaders, Director Kriegsheim said that they would try to push him in this direction, since they must have the Reichswehr. If he would not go along, he must be replaced by Berendt. Kriegsheim then added that Berendt and Möhl were ready to go along.[30] Further conversations, including one with Lieutenant Colonel Fedor von Bock, the Stabschef of Wehrkreis III (Berlin), who warned that the Verbände must not act without the Reichswehr and added that he did not believe that the Reichswehr would move without Seeckt, were capped by his conference with Seeckt, where, according to Seisser, the latter said, "The legal road must be followed."[31] While Seeckt was friendly and said that he had the same goals as did the Bavarian leaders, his refusal to pursue these goals by any but legal means was a serious blow to the plans of the triumvirate, and it seems to be true, as the

---

[29] B, ii, MA103476, pp. 739-41.

[30] This statement, upon which, in the end, all of the accusations of disloyalty against Berendt are apparently based, seems to rest almost entirely on wishful thinking. For a discussion of Berendt's stand see Chapter xvii, Section iii, below. Möhl, on the other hand, was clearly hostile to Seeckt, but there is no evidence that he had close ties to the Landbund. See B, i, Kahr ms, pp. 1324-26; NA, T79, 73, p. 398; GP, A, General Walter von Unruh, 13.3.1955.

[31] B, ii, MA104221, Seisser Besprechungen in Berlin, 3.11.1923. Seisser's testimony at the Hitler Trial passes over this portion of his conversation with Seeckt, mentioning only their discussion of the Bavarian Grenzschutz question. NA, EAP 105/7, xiii, pp. 006895-96.

Putschists later claimed, that Seisser at least saw the situation through new glasses after his return from Berlin.[32]

Negotiations continued, despite the disillusionment attendant on Seisser's Berlin conversations, and reached an acute stage just prior to the Beer Hall Putsch. According to Major Vogts, on 6 November the triumvirate agreed to accept the Berlin proposal that Kahr be included in the directory. At last the München group was prepared to accept some of the public responsibility. On the other hand, such conditions were attached to this concession that its practical value was sharply reduced. The Berliners must produce men capable of serving in this directory and ready to do so. A firm, unanimously acceptable program must be worked out, and assurances must be provided that the establishment of the directory would not lead to disunity and conflict within the Reichswehr. Talking vaguely about saving him for a "more important" role later,[33] both sides agreed that Ludendorff should be excluded from the directory, but they wanted his consent and support for propaganda reasons. Hitler had apparently been sounded out through Lieutenant Colonel (Ret.) Kriebel and was not prepared to cooperate. By this time he had his own plans for action and, in any case, he neither trusted the conspirators nor was prepared to be overshadowed by them or anyone else. Vogts accepted the terms and promised to bring several northern leaders to München on 9 or 10 November to discuss the directory with Kahr.[34]

Thus, in theory, the triumvirate had moved nearer to action, but, in fact, it had shoved action aside, for it was very unlikely that the "northerners" could produce either men of stature to man the directory or guarantees that the Reichswehr would support the "action," whatever it might be. If the triumvirs' terms could be met, they would be taking little risk; if their terms could not be met, they would have kept their skirts clean. The Berliners faced whatever dangers and difficulties there might be, while Kahr and his friends would share in any success that might be achieved.

[32] B, I, Kahr MS, pp. 1305, 1335-39; II, MA104221, Seisser Besprechungen in Berlin, 3.11.1923; NA, EAP 105/7, I, pp. 11-12, 82; XIV, pp. 007082ff; GP, B, Colonel Ernst Schultes; Ludendorff, *Feldherrnhalle*, pp. 58-59, 141-42.

[33] Probably as chief of staff of the army of liberation which the right radicals planned to create. It is not, however, entirely clear whether they were really saving the general for greater things or whether they were pushing him gently aside.

[34] B, II, MA103476, pp. 741-42.

The triumvirate was, meanwhile, also negotiating with other dissidents, who were equally cautious. These were the leaders of Stahlhelm in central Germany, Lieutenant Colonel (Ret.) Theodor Duesterberg, and Graf Helldorff. Duesterberg arrived in München on 28 October and visited General Ludendorff, with whom he had been closely associated in World War I. Ludendorff and Duesterberg were in agreement on the need for a rightist Government in Berlin, which would be independent of Parliament. Ludendorff sent the Stahlhelmer on to Lossow. Duesterberg told Lossow that he did not believe that the north German Reichswehr would fire on the Bavarian Reichswehr if it invaded the north, but admitted that he was not sure what the troops would do if Bavarian Verbände tried to move north. However, while Lossow admitted his agreement with Duesterberg on the need for a rightist directory and even spoke of an "Ankara government,"[35] the general would not commit himself to action. Like most strong individuals who dealt with Lossow, Duesterberg left with the impression that Lossow favored his scheme for the establishment of a national directory in München. Duesterberg therefore came to the same conclusion as Hitler —that a careful shove would convert Lossow into a revolutionary —and, again like Hitler, he went off determined to find a way to apply this pressure. Two days later he sent Lossow a letter assuring him that the Reichswehr units in Saxony would not try to stop the Bavarian Reichswehr, although the senior officers were "dubious." Since Duesterberg was admittedly seeking to push Lossow into action, and in view of the speed with which he came up with his answers, his assurances must be taken with a good deal of salt.[36] Interestingly enough, Graf Helldorff, who was in München again just prior to the Putsch, tells us that the Duesterberg letter had a depressing effect on Lossow. Perhaps he doubted if lieutenants could be depended upon to face down majors and generals, or perhaps he feared that he would, in the end, be forced to move. Helldorff also visited Seisser again and received soothing answers but nothing more.[37]

---

[35] A reference to the revolutionary national government set up by Kemal Ataturk in Ankara.

[36] For a Saxon captain's views on the Saxon Reichswehr and Bavaria in September see B, IV, BuR, Bd. 35, Akt 5, Item 11.

[37] B, II, MA103476, pp. 730-36, 744-46, 749. Ludendorff later claimed that Duesterberg reported to him that Lossow took a much stronger line than Duesterberg's testimony indicates. However, Lossow's character, Ludendorff's tendency to twist everything he heard to suit his own fantastic

On 8 November, the situation remained unchanged. There was no news from the north. Graf Helldorff testified that he had had to admit to both Ludendorff and Lossow that the northerners had not been able to find prominent leaders for the directory and that he did not believe that they would find them. He even admitted that he probably pressed for action by the Bavarians alone. Lossow, faced with the prospect of exposing himself or giving up his hopes for a "turn to the Right," raged against the northern eunuchs. He still demanded at least three northern leaders from agriculture, industry, and the government before he would consider action, and even then he hedged with reservations regarding the northern Reichswehr. Helldorff confessed that he came away from their conversation with the conviction that Lossow would not act, because he did not have the strength of character to reach a decision. Helldorff also talked to the Kampfbund leaders, who were cordial but preoccupied. They pumped him about Lossow and told him of their own dealings with the triumvirate, but allegedly said nothing at all about their own Putsch plans. It seems that neither the northern Verbände nor the Putschists entirely trusted the Stahlhelm leaders, and it is very dubious if the triumvirate did.[38]

Meanwhile, and far more significant in view of coming events, the triumvirate was conducting parallel negotiations with the Kampfbund. A mere five years ago, such conferences might well have seemed incredible to Americans. Today, though, when conferences between local and federal authorities and radical leaders openly dedicated to the violent overthrow of the existing government are commonplace, they fall into perspective much more easily. The Kampfbund existed. To some extent its leaders represented ideals attractive to large segments of the population, and, even more significantly, they represented an uncomfortably strong and militant revolutionary movement. They were therefore alternately consulted, cajoled, and threatened by the authorities. This is a pattern constant in history from ancient Rome to modern Detroit or Columbia University. In the Bavaria of October and November 1923, the situation was made more critical by economic disaster and the clearly impending fall of the existing federal government, as well as by the ambiguous position of the Bavarian lead-

---

dreams, and the course of Lossow's parallel negotiations with the Kampf-bund lead me to accept the Duesterberg-Helldorff testimony as being roughly accurate. For Ludendorff's version see *ibid.*, p. 754.

[38] B, II, MA103476, pp. 744, 747-51, 756.

ers, especially General von Lossow, in whose hands lay the chief
responsibility for the maintenance of law and order.

In mid-October, in a statement to his officers at a meeting in the
Wehrkreis headquarters, Lossow criticized the National Socialist
Movement sharply and ordered them to remain strictly aloof from
it—while training its members! Captain Röhm, naturally, went to
Hitler with news of this meeting, and Hitler visited Lossow and
bathed the susceptible general in a flood of fiery and persuasive
words, with the result that Lossow, surprisingly democratic for a
man who disapproved of parliamentarianism, agreed to give Hitler
"equal time" to defend his movement. He not only allowed Hitler
to speak to the officers of the Wehrkreis headquarters,[39] but reversed himself in a second officers' conference, telling his listeners
that the Reichswehr would support the sound national efforts of
Hitler, although he added that he (Lossow) had warned Hitler that
the Reichswehr would put down any Putsch the National Socialists
might attempt. In view of this typically wavering policy it is not surprising that on the day of the Putsch some officers were unsure
where their commander stood and therefore acted on their own interpretation of his position.[40] Lossow did not neglect Ludendorff
either. When the Bavarian Reichswehr was officially sworn into the
service of the Bavarian state, Lossow twice assured Ludendorff that
his motives were national and not particularist.[41]

October twenty-fourth was another busy day. Hitler gave Seisser
a four-hour lecture on his aims, in the course of which he underscored his awareness that he could take no action without the support of Kahr, the Reichswehr, and the Landespolizei. As usual,
Hitler painted himself as the "selfless drummer" who would bring
the masses to the "national idea." Allegedly, in the end Seisser cut
Hitler off and told him that his plans were fantastic, but a speech
of four hours can scarcely be said to have been "cut short," nor
would Hitler be discouraged by mildly phrased dissent from a man
who had listened to him so patiently.[42]

That same day, General von Lossow called a conference of the
Verbände. As usual, Karl Freiherr von Freyberg was present for
the government and Generalstaatskommissar, and Major Franz

---

[39] Possibly including other officers of the München garrison.
[40] GP, A, General Schwandner, 23.1.1960.
[41] Ludendorff, *Feldherrnhalle*, pp. 55, 133-35.
[42] B, I, Kahr MS, p. 1333.

Hunglinger was there for Colonel von Seisser, while the military leaders of the Kampfbund (Kriebel), Bayern und Reich (Tutschek), Hermannsbund (Kleinhenz), VVM (probably Kühner), Wiking (probably Kautter), Niederbayern (Willmer), and Stahlhelm (Wenninger) provided the rest of the audience. General von Lossow and Major von Hösslin spoke to them about the possibility that the Reichswehr would be expanded,[43] by absorbing personnel and sub-units of the Verbände, and about the technical problems involved. During the discussion, Lossow indicated that two or three possible situations might call for the mobilization of extra forces: primarily, either the establishment of a rightist dictatorship or directory in Berlin, or a deterioration of the present situation and mass riots. It is also clear that Lossow spoke of the first possibility as desirable. Thereafter, the available reports on the meeting are not in close agreement with one another. Leaders of the Verbände that took part in or sympathized with the later Putsch claimed that it was clear that Lossow was talking of leading a revolution, although only one claims that there was talk of a "march on Berlin." The Reichswehr minutes of the meeting, as later reported by Lieutenant Colonel Wilhelm Ritter von Leeb, who had no personal axe to grind,[44] indicated that Lossow was much more circumspect, and Lossow himself denies many of the allegations of the Putschists. Most significantly, all witnesses are agreed that Lossow did stress that the participation of the Verbände in the mobilization would be permitted only within the ranks of the Reichswehr and the Landespolizei. Independent units on the Freikorps model would be prohibited. In the end, all of the leaders accepted the plan in principle, although Kriebel, as always, made it clear that he had reservations and could not commit himself until he had clearance from Hitler.

It seems likely, in view of his usual performance both before and after this conference, that Lossow was circumspect rather than overbold. On the other hand, since one of the reasons for calling the meeting was to keep the Verbände in check, there is little doubt that he phrased his presentation in such a manner as to lead them to believe that he was going their way and that they could follow him. In other words, Lossow bought time at the cost of the prob-

---

[43] See Chapter IV, Section IV, for information on the mobilization plans.

[44] Having been rejected by Lossow as chief of staff, he was in Stettin at the time. GP, A, Field Marshal Ritter von Leeb, 8.3.1954.

able later disillusionment of the more radical leaders. This is a typical tactic of the born temporizer and of the harried politician in a tight place.[45]

On the next day Hitler and Dr. Weber conferred with Seisser and Lossow, trying to persuade them that Kahr was unfit for dictatorial powers and a mere pawn of the Bavarian government and the BVP. Here Hitler presented his slate for a federal directory, which had to be formed in München and forced on Berlin: Hitler, Ludendorff, Lossow, Seisser. When Seisser and Lossow said that such a slate was impossible, especially because of Ludendorff's impact on foreign nations, Hitler stuck to his guns. He needed Ludendorff, he said, to win over the Reichswehr. The generals, naturally, would be against Ludendorff, but the officers from major downwards would disobey them.[46] At the same time, Hitler once again assured Seisser that he knew he could take no steps without the Reichswehr and Landespolizei.[47]

During the next few days, Ludendorff and Hitler also spoke with Minoux under the auspices of Lossow and Seisser. These conversations tended more to drive the two groups apart than to bring them together, since they tended to talk around one another, revealing the deep differences that divided them. Minoux was interested mostly in economic recovery, while the right radicals were primarily interested in matters of political control at home and in breaking the fetters of Versailles.[48]

On 26 October, in a secret conference that was reported to selected Verbände leaders by his intelligence network, Seisser, apparently wishing to satisfy the Verbände, announced that the Stresemann government would soon fall and be replaced by a nationalist dictatorial government, which would not be trammeled by Parliament. How this government was to be set up, whether in the south or north, by peaceful means or by struggle, was of secondary significance. Then, a reflection of the extent to which the crisis was economic, he went on to assure his listeners that the new finance minister had already agreed to abolish all taxes introduced since

---

[45] B, I, SA 1, 1493, A. Hoffmann, p. 221; II, MA103476, pp. 997-98, 1003-4, 1036-39.

[46] B, I, Kahr MS, p. 1328; II, MA103473, GSK Denkschrift on Putsch; MA103476, pp. 1139-40.

[47] B, IV, BuR, Bd. 34, Item 133, Bomhard Lagebericht.

[48] B, I, Kahr MS, pp. 1300-01; II, MA103476, pp. 700-01, 1139.

the end of World War I and to replace them with a simple and easily collected tax.[49]

Despite all of the talk, the situation remained essentially the same at the end of October as it had been at the beginning, in so far as the achievement of an understanding between the triumvirate and the Kampfbund was concerned. Kriebel's remark to Helldorff summed up the Kampfbund problem neatly: "Hitler has repeatedly believed that he had brought Lossow into line. However, something always went wrong."[50]

In November, the circle of meetings began all over again. On the first, Seisser met Hitler and Dr. Weber at the latter's house at Hitler's request. Hitler again trotted out his arguments of 25 October, according to Dr. Weber's pre-trial testimony.[51] Seisser said that he was going to Berlin to find out what the situation there was. Hitler replied: " 'Colonel, I will wait until your return, but act then and persuade the Generalstaatskommissar to act. It is high time. Economic pressures drive our people so that we must either act or our followers will swing to the Communists.' "[52] Dr. Weber claimed at the trial that he believed Hitler and Seisser were in full agreement, but his own statements and those of Hitler make it clear that, in fact, they had made no more progress than they had the week before.[53]

The crucial meeting, though, was that of 6 November, when Kahr, Lossow, and Seisser spoke to the assembled leaders of most of the Bavarian Verbände. Kriebel, Dr. Weber, and General Aechter were present for the Kampfbund; Ehrhardt and Kautter represented Wiking and its allies; and Dr. Pittinger and Tutschek of Bayern und Reich, Heiss of Reichsflagge, Kühner and Mayerhofer of VVM, General von Kleinhenz of the Hermannsbund, and Colonel von Tannstein of the officers' organization stood for their groups. Oberregierungsrat Stauffer and Freiherr von Aufsess represented the Generalstaatskommissariat and, to a lesser extent, the Bavarian government, whose civil servants they were. The twelve

---

[49] B, IV, BuR, Bd. 34, Item 133, Bomhard Lagebericht.

[50] B, II, MA103476, p. 745.

[51] This initial testimony differs significantly in some places from his testimony at the trial, particularly in tone and detail.

[52] B, II, MA103476, p. 691.

[53] B, II, MA103476, pp. 690-91, 1085, 1140; NA, EAP 105/7, II, pp. 16-17, 19, 45.

accounts, some rather sketchy, that have been provided by participants agree to a surprising extent on what was said at the meeting,
despite some apparent and understandable distortion in the reports
of those participants who were Putschists. All agree that Kahr told
the assembled leaders that the establishment of a nationalist government in Berlin, independent of the Reichstag, was imperative.
He said that this government might be established in the normal
manner, and that this was preferable. He added that it was possible
that it must be created in an abnormal manner.[54] In this case, it
might be necessary to support this government by force of arms,[55]
and preparations must be made for this contingency. If it arose—
and here there is general agreement among the sources—he said
he would give the signal for action and would meanwhile tolerate
no independent action on the part of any organization. He then
passed on to a description of the political situation as he saw it and
to details of finances and personnel.

Lossow and Seisser spoke after Kahr and each underlined his
determination to support Kahr and his readiness to put down any
Putsch by force. Lossow stated, "I am ready to support a rightist
dictatorship if the affair is likely to succeed. If we are merely to be
harassed into a Putsch, which will come to a sorry end in five or six
days, I will not cooperate."[56] Both Seisser and Lossow put emphasis on warnings to the Verbände, by which they clearly meant the
Kampfbund, and they specifically denounced the placards calling
for revolution that had appeared in the last few days, allegedly
signed by members of the triumvirate. The meeting was as much
a dressing down for the Verbände leaders as a preparation for future cooperative action.[57]

[54] Here the Putschists claim that Kahr said "illegal," but this is denied
by the majority of the accounts by participants and seems unlikely in view
of Kahr's tendency to avoid blunt words, even when he meant them.

[55] The Putschists state that Kahr spoke of a "march on Berlin," but
the other participants either insist that he spoke of aiding the Berlin government or do not touch on this point at all. The interpretation in the text
is certainly the one that seems to coincide best with his established aims
and reservations.

[56] B, II, MA103476, p. 1113.

[57] B, I, SA 1, 1450, PDN-F, Abt. II, 9.4.1924; Kahr MS, pp. 1342-44;
II, MA103476, pp. 666, 764-70, 897, 1071, 1086-87, 1090, 1113; IV, HSIV,
EE7, Endres MS, p. 35NA, EAP 105/7, II, pp. 22-23. Hofmann (*Hitlerputsch*, p. 136) and Carsten (*Reichswehr*, pp. 201-2) differ here but seem
to be based on very thin evidence.

Therefore the later Kampfbund claim that essential unity on goals had been reached, even if the time of action was still up in the air, was untrue. The triumvirate clung to its determination to support a directorate to be established in Berlin, excluding Hitler and Ludendorff, while the Kampfbund still stood for the creation of a directory in München, including Hitler and Ludendorff, and for carrying the power of that directory to Berlin by force. Later the Putschists also claimed that they did not realize that this difference existed or that they had anything to fear from the Reichswehr and the Landespolizei if they carried out their Putsch. This statement is also untrue as is indicated by the following letter sent by Lieutenant Colonel Kriebel, obviously in a towering rage, to the other Verbände, on 7 November:

> The Conference on the evening of November 6 with the Generalstaatskommissar shows that he counts on disunity among the Verbände.
>
> The Generalstaatskommissar has declared flatly, through the Landeskommandant and Colonel von Seisser, that he is firmly determined to move with armed force against any Verband that attempts to unleash a violent change on its own initiative.
>
> As military leader of the Kampfbund, I formally declare that differences of viewpoint, no matter how great they may be, that may make cooperation with the individual Verbände impossible, cannot hinder me from placing myself with the full military might of the German Kampfbund on the side of the Verband against which the Reichswehr and Landespolizei are called out in arms.[58]

Here is clear evidence that the Kampfbund knew that the Reichswehr and Landespolizei commanders had ranged themselves against a Putsch and that the Kampfbund was, despite all later denials, prepared to fight the armed forces of the state at the time of the Putsch.[59]

---

[58] NA, EAP 105/7a, Reichswehr Official Bericht, Appendix 3a. At the Hitler Trial, Kriebel admitted writing the letter, but suggested that he was really only giving Kahr a friendly hint and that it was all fun among friends. See NA, EAP 105/7, IV, pp. 00517-18. However, the tone of the letter gives him little support.

[59] The decision to strike had already been taken when this letter was written. It is therefore, in part, probably an attempt to show the other Verbände that the Kampfbund was ready to defend them against the

This conference was the final meeting between the Kampfbund leaders and the triumvirate, although Ludendorff met with Kahr on 8 November, the day of the Putsch. Ludendorff claims that Kahr, Lossow, Seisser, and he were clearly in general agreement at the end of their conversation, but this is not borne out by the fact that Kahr flatly refused to see Hitler. It is much more likely that the interview ended on the same note as the conference of the sixth. Ludendorff demanded action in München and, as Kahr maintains, the triumvirate insisted upon waiting for action in Berlin. Further weight is given to this interpretation by the fact that even Ludendorff notes the urgency with which Kahr complained of the lack of news from the north.[60]

Meanwhile, the Berlin government had also been trying to deal with both the triumvirate and the Kampfbund through unofficial channels, since the official ones were clogged by the "Lossow affair" recriminations and negotiations, and since the federal government could not afford direct and open negotiations with the Kampfbund. These negotiations came to nothing, though, for neither Kahr nor the Kampfbund leaders and Ludendorff were ready to cooperate with Stresemann on any terms. Kahr refused to see one of Stresemann's emissaries, despite the urgings of the crown prince that he do so, and did not take the other one seriously. On the right radical side, while Ludendorff talked with Admiral Scheer, who came to him from Stresemann, he did not budge from his hostility towards the "Red" government in Berlin. On the third side of the triangle, talks between Major Vogts and Ludendorff also rapidly led to a morass of disagreement. On the eve of the Putsch there was no real sign of agreement among the various factions in any quarter. An impasse had been reached.[61]

IV. *The Putsch Develops*

While the last negotiations were still underway between the triumvirate and the Kampfbund, the die was already cast. Hitler, and his

---

authorities and that they should therefore support the Kampfbund. See Section IV below.

[60] B, I, Kahr MS, p. 1345; II, MA103476, pp. 740, 750-57, 529, 1040; NA, EAP 105/7, I, p. 92; II, pp. 23-24; Ludendorff, *Feldherrnhalle*, pp. 143-44.

[61] B, I, Kahr MS, pp. 1299-1300, 1304, 1339, 1347; GSK 43, p. 100, Meldung Ob. Reg. Rat Dr. Fritsch, 4.11.1923; II, MA103476, pp. 689-96, 743, 754-57, 953-54; Ludendorff, *Feldherrnhalle*, pp. 142-43.

inner circle of advisors, had been thinking of a Putsch ever since the galling failure of their May Day demonstration. They had been planning this action in a more or less desultory manner at least since the appointment of the Generalstaatskommissar. It is, however, only in the first days of November that these plans begin to take on immediacy. There are indications, although slim ones, that the Kampfbund leaders, or some of them, may have planned to kidnap the leaders of the Bavarian state and armed forces during the parade on 4 November celebrating the laying of the cornerstone of the memorial to München's war dead in the Residenz Gardens. One such indicator of trouble was the absence of Ludendorff, who was always careful to be away from the scene of active rebellion when the outcome was unclear. (He later explained that he had had an auto accident.) In any case, nothing happened on this day, which the biographer of one of the alleged plotters, Captain (Ret.) Wilhelm Freiherr Marschall von Bieberstein, ascribes to the large numbers of Landespolizei units guarding the Bavarian leaders.[62]

Whether or not there was anything more behind the plans of 4 November than the beer hall boasts of SA men years later, the plans of 6 and 7 November were serious ones made by Hitler himself.[63] The decision to move immediately was a reaction to the Kahr conference of 6 November. It was allegedly made by Hitler and two other leaders (whom he refused to name) that same evening. Since he said at the trial that the two men were dead, they must have been Dr. Scheubner-Richter and one of the most significant of the "back-room boys" of the early movement, Theodor von der Pfordten. Pfordten kept himself very much in the background, so that even some people who did not like him believed that he had not been involved with Hitler.[64] It is very possible that others were present, whom Hitler wished to protect, but no evidence exists on this score.[65]

Then, on the morning of the seventh, a meeting of the senior

[62] B, I, GSK 71, p. 48; II, MA103476, pp. 1145-48, 1215-16, 1406; NA, T120, 5569, pp. K591582-84; Epp Papers, SA Rgt. München, 230-a-10/3, 2-3.11.23; Pölnitz, Gotz Freiherr von, *Emir: Das tapfere Leben des Freiherrn Marschall von Bieberstein*, München, 1938, pp. 124-25 (hereafter referred to as Pölnitz, *Emir*); Hanfstängl, *Hitler*, pp. 89-90.

[63] There was allegedly an alternate plan to move on 10 or 11.11.23. B, I, SA 1, 1493, A. Hoffmann, pp. 223-24.

[64] See, for example, B, IV, HSIV, EE7, Endres MS, pp. 57-58.

[65] B, I, SA 1, 1491, p. 4; NA, EAP 105/7, pp. 89-90; Coblitz, Wilhelm, *Theodor von der Pfordten*, München, 1937, p. 17.

Kampfbund leaders was held to confirm this decision. Although he denied being present and is not mentioned among the participants by Dr. Weber, it is almost certain that Ludendorff was there.[66] The others present included Hitler, Dr. Weber, Göring, Dr. Scheubner-Richter, and Kriebel. Röhm apparently was missing, and Prince Wrede has suggested that Röhm opposed the idea of a Putsch at this time. This may explain his apparent absence.[67] The plotters agreed on the plan that they executed on 8-9 November and also agreed, at Hitler's insistence, to keep the number of persons with prior knowledge of the Putsch to the absolute minimum. This arrangement had the double advantage of reducing the number of serious offenders in case of failure and of reducing the chance of compromise before the event. By noon of 7 November, the Putsch was on, although the orders could still have been revoked up till the last minute.[68] The Putschists' plans called for them to take control in the major cities and towns of Bavaria: München, Regensburg, Augsburg, Ingolstadt (which they considered already secure), Nürnberg, and Würzburg. In each of these towns the Verbände were to seize the railroad station, the telegraph office, telephone office, the radio station, public utilities, town hall, and police headquarters, as well as the installations of hostile groups. Communist and socialist leaders were to be arrested, including trade union leaders and shop stewards.[69]

As early as 6 November, plans had been made for assembling various Kampfbund groups for training or propaganda meetings. Now these assemblies were used for the purposes of the Putsch. Units were ordered to hold themselves ready for action. Such orders were issued periodically and did not mean very much to

[66] During Ludendorff's interrogation after his arrest, he was shown several documents pertaining to the Putsch which had been captured by the police in the course of the uprising. He denied having seen these papers. However, when the deputy prosecutor asked him if certain marginalia on these documents were in his hand, he replied in the affirmative. Because the documents had been in the hands of the police since the Putsch, his notations could only have been placed on them before the Putsch, in which case he had known about it beforehand. However, Ludendorff ignored logic and contradictions alike and refused to alter either statement. GP, B, Minister a. D. Hans Ehard.

[67] It is possible that he was present but was not named in view of his status as an army officer, since this status could have placed him in heightened jeopardy if he were identified as one of the planners of the Putsch.

[68] NA, T79, 82, p. 210; EAP 105/7, I, pp. 90-92; II, pp. 25-27.

[69] B, II, MA103476, pp. 1159-60.

many of the men who received them. On the night of the seventh and morning of the eighth orders were sent to Kampfbund military leaders in Oberbayern and in key cities throughout the state, often by motorcycle courier. In some cases, the telephone was used, but in such cases, the speakers were discreet (in case their telephones were being tapped by the authorities). The written orders were sealed and were not to be opened until late on the eighth.[70] Some of the leaders were ordered to report to München with their men, while others were ordered to take control of their own localities.[71] The same morning most of the military leaders at regimental and battalion levels were told of the Putsch. These in turn assembled their officers and men, telling them of the Putsch only when it was necessary for them to know it in order to prepare effectively. Those who were going to the Reichskriegsflagge beer party at the Löwen-bräukeller were mostly left in ignorance of impending events until the official announcement was made during the course of the evening.[72]

Dr. Wilhelm Frick had been chosen well before the Putsch to succeed Mantel as police president, while Major Hühnlein, who was apparently on terminal leave from the Reichswehr,[73] was to replace Colonel Banzer as commander of the München Landespolizei. These men were to ensure that the police did not interfere with the Putsch in its early stages and to direct the police thereafter for the new government. Frick clearly knew of the coming of the Putsch—although, of course, he later denied this knowledge.[74] Apparently, even if the authorities went along with the Putsch, some senior officers and officials were to be replaced by more reliable or more worthy aspirants for their posts, a sign of how little love and trust

[70] In at least some instances these preliminary orders contained the statement that Kahr, Lossow, and Seisser supported the Putsch—a flat lie!

[71] For examples see B, I, GSK 90, p. 312; II, MA103476, pp. 1052, 1208, 1243-44, 1328; IV, BuR, Bd. 36, Akt 1, Item 31/1, Hofberger an Bezirksver-bände; NA, EAP 105/7, II, p. 27. See also Chapter XIII, below, passim.

[72] B, I, SA 1, 1491, Ebenböck, pp. 25-26; II, MA103476, pp. 1204, 1208, 1226, 1280-81, 1328-29, 1332, 1338, 1348; NA, Epp Papers, SA Rgt. München, 230-a-10/3, 6-7.11.23; Pölnitz, *Emir*, pp. 124-26.

[73] He had orders to retire as of 16 November 1923, orders which had been issued before the Putsch after extension from an earlier deadline in the spring (possibly for pension purposes). NA, T79, 31, p. 1053.

[74] This knowledge is indicated by his activities that evening and by the code telephone message he received from Kriebel as soon as the Bürger-bräukeller was secured. B, II, MA103476, pp. 1131, 1225-26.

the Putschists had for those they later claimed as allies who had fallen away.[75]

Meanwhile, First Lieutenant (Ret.) Gerhard Rossbach, a hard-bitten veteran Putschist, was to take over the Infantry School.[76] Other military installations were to be occupied by groups of Putschists in an obvious attempt to neutralize the Reichswehr should it prove impossible to win over Lossow and the other generals.[77] Plans were also laid for securing the chief government buildings and public utilities in accord with the overall scheme. The second battalion of Oberland under Captain (Ret.) Max Ritter von Müller was assigned the chief responsibility for this task.[78]

The collection of arms was one of the most pressing and difficult questions facing the Putschists, and one that they never solved entirely. They did possess a very considerable number of weapons and had plans to confiscate far more. Some weapons were brought in from caches in the country, others were taken, apparently, from other Verbände. Röhm obtained some arms for his organization by pretending that his Verband was going on a night exercise. Since no ammunition was requested, the request aroused no suspicion. Lieutenant Colonel Hofmann of Ingolstadt sent arms from there, and plans were laid for getting still more from the Reichswehr and the police. This was one problem that had been considered seriously, although not in all of its aspects as the Putschists were to learn to their sorrow.[79]

Transportation was supplied by Christian Weber's National Socialist organization supplemented by rented trucks and even taxicabs. Some of the vehicles were owned by the party. Others were placed at its disposal by their drivers, or simply rented.[80] Where population control was concerned, the Putschists had prepared

[75] *Ibid.*, pp. 1205, 1215-16, 1406.

[76] This institution was the Infantry's Officer Training School, which also received the officer candidates from other armed services for basic officer training. In 1923, besides training cadets to be officers, the school had the additional temporary function of giving remedial training to those second and first lieutenants who had been commissioned during the war and therefore had never had proper preparation. These were the "officer students" who participated in the Putsch.

[77] See Chapters XI and XII below.

[78] B, II, MA103476, pp. 1163, 1406; NA, EAP 105/7, II, p. 32.

[79] B, I, SA 1, 1490, Tröger, p. 53; II, MA103476, pp. 8, 1198-1202, 1204, 1332-34, 1341, 1457; GP, A, Eberhard Dennerlein, 29.2.1960.

[80] B, II, MA103476, pp. 1044, 1107, 1110, 1204.

both the carrot and the stick. They had plans for drumhead courts martial to deal with political enemies in summary fashion, but they also set up a propaganda office to influence the population. They even arranged for printers to stand by to produce material for the Kampfbund during the night, although allegedly they did not tell the printers what their work would be.[81] Finally, the Putschists arranged for the establishment of recruiting stations for all of their organizations and printed placards directing the public to them.[82]

Ironically, there were also personal preparations for the Putsch on the part of those "in the know." It is always hard to keep insiders on the stock market from taking advantage of their knowledge to help themselves. The Putschists apparently faced the same problem, since, despite the danger of alerting the authorities, Gottfried Feder tried to withdraw his securities from his bank the day of the Putsch and made a most surprising commotion when informed that this would be impossible. Since he had in his pocket a decree written by himself freezing all bank accounts on behalf of the new government, his actions are perhaps understandable, but not easily condoned in one who bled so vigorously over the financial corruption of the Republic. The other, and more successful, Putschist was Ludendorff, who cleaned out his account two days before the Putsch. The general was cautious with his funds as well as with his political commitments.[83]

At the same time the Kampfbund adopted confusion tactics aimed at misleading both its opponents and the general public. For example, plans for Adolf Hitler to speak in Freising on the night of 8 November were not cancelled, although, of course, he planned to be elsewhere at the appointed hour. A proclamation signed with Lossow's name attacked the Berlin government and called mutiny against it an act of patriotism. This document, dated 7 November, was distributed widely throughout the Reich and was accepted by many of Lossow's foes as genuine. In fact, it had been denounced by the triumvirate in the *Bayrischer Kurier* of 7 November as a forgery and was probably one of the false documents of which Lossow complained in his speech to the Verbände leaders on the sixth. Similarly, proclamations informing the public of a Hitler-Kahr-Lossow national government were printed long before Hitler con-

---

[81] B, I, SA 1, 1492, PDM, Abt. viaF, p. 32; ii, MA103476, pp. 1045, 1179-80.

[82] *Ibid.*, pp. 1023, 1246.

[83] B, ii, MA99522, 17.3.1924, p. 11; MA103476, pp. 1248-49.

fronted the triumvirate in the Bürgerbräukeller, which is one reason that the Putschists' side of the story was the one carried in the press on the morning after the Putsch. The adoption of the offensive has its advantages, especially in the initial phases of a conflict.[84]

v. *The Aims of the Putschists*

"The German problem will be solved for me only when the black-white-red swastika banner floats on the Berliner Schloss. There is no retreat, only an advance. We all feel that the hour has come and therefore we will not shirk its demands, but, like the soldier in the field, will follow the order: Keep in step, German people, and forward march!"[85]

So Hitler summed up his drive for power to the thundering applause of his audience in the Zirkus Krone on 30 October, and here is embalmed his essential aim—the attainment of power in Germany by his party and therefore himself. All other aims were subordinate to this one and, in fairness to him, most of them were attainable only if he did come to power.

These other aims were, if one cuts through forests of verbiage and analyzes the various theoretical and practical plans of the Putschists, few, simple, and drastic. Once power was attained the next step would be to "sweep out the pigsty," which in practical terms meant the elimination from office of active political opponents, men suspected of lack of patriotism or of profiteering, and the assumption of their positions and other key posts by men drawn from the party and its allied organizations. The next step was the creation of a tightly-organized, centralized German state responsive to the commands of its new master or masters. The final step, as it was clearly envisaged at that time, was the creation of "Grossdeutschland," a Germany that would include Strasbourg and Vienna and would therefore have sweeping overtones for the future of Europe.[86] This new state would be characterized by dictatorial rule from the center (which later came to be known as the Führer-

[84] B, I, SA 1, 1492, III, p. 13; GSK 43, p. 142; GSK 73, p. 49; NA, EAP, 105/7a, Official Reichswehr Bericht, Anlage 2; FH, S. Hamburg, A.I., Lit. No. 1, Vol. 57, Fasc. 13.

[85] Röhm, *Geschichte*, p. 229.

[86] B, II, MA103476, pp. 608-15, 1169-79; NA, EAP 105/7, I, pp. 119, 124.

prinzip), independent of parliamentary interference. The economy was to be improved, simplified, and freed of international, "parasitic" elements. Social security would be extended and liberalized. Citizenship would be limited to Germans of "Nordic" stock. Strong emphasis would be placed on the maintenance and expansion of a strong peasantry. Justice would be faster, more honest, and much more stringent. A powerful armed force would protect the system and the German people.[87]

In order to carry out this program Hitler and his entourage had already worked out a system of controls. The basic ideas behind the techniques they were to use when they came to power a decade later were already formulated in 1923. A first preventive measure was the exclusion of Jews from political life, and these Jews were already seen as a possible hostage group which could and would be destroyed in time of war. Hermann Esser said at a meeting in December 1922: " '500,000 Jews as hostages carefully guarded, who will be ruthlessly dispatched, if even a single enemy crosses the German frontier.' "[88] While it would probably be incorrect to take literally words spoken in a beer hall by a wild and flamboyant youth, it is equally true that the germ of ideas later carried into practice is found here and that doubtless countless repetitions of this sort of oratory made the adoption of the "final solution" simpler and almost natural for hard-bitten, veteran National Socialists.

Equally significant for the future relations of the party with the state were the remarks of Graf Ernst zu Fischler von Treuberg, one of the few higher nobles to join the early NSDAP, in a letter to a friend.[89] In this missive he not only talks of arresting Kahr and Dr. Pittinger and other rivals of the party but, much more significantly, speaks of the problem of the career official in the National Socialist state:

". . . In view of the mentality of the bureaucrats, most of whom fear to accept responsibility, one must above all consider care-

---

[87] B, ii, MA103476, pp. 608-15, 1169-79.

[88] Z, Akten aus d. Hpt. Archiv d. NSDAP, Mappe 125, M. Inn. Bericht in re NSDAP.

[89] Treuberg later claimed that this letter was far more representative of Captain Weiss' ideas than of his own, but, had he not accepted these ideas, it seems unlikely that he would have passed them on in so positive a manner to Glaser. B, ii, MA103476, p. 1474.

fully the Bezirk offices, which besides their adminstrative activities will exercise police power in the countryside, which especially in those first weeks [will be] extremely important. If one wishes success there in general and wishes to see the decrees of the authorities actually carried out everywhere, then state commissars must be appointed, who must never be officials, for officials mostly carry within themselves a ballast of 'doubts, calculations, and precedents' which is harmful and obscures the grand line of a clear, unwavering will and clouds the open vision for necessities. These state commissars must under all circumstances work without a penny of pay, [although] they may be recompensed for their actual expenses in return for precise receipts. . . . These [state commissars] are to operate under precise directives and to press the chiefs of the Bezirksämter to insure that everything is accomplished that is necessary. . . . It is completely out of the question that the officials who rule by routine can bring themselves to actual deeds. Only men like our commissars, in whose breasts burns the fire of our national-racist movement and who have sound common sense, untroubled by long calculation and an iron will can do that—[men] who are ready at any time to expose their own person, without thought of wife or child, serving only one thought: what is best for the state and its greatness!"[90]

In this plan the impatience of the political amateur, the reformer, is clearly visible, as is the naïveté of the well-to-do amateur who believes that large numbers of men will serve the state selflessly without pay over extended periods. Equally clearly visible is the determination of the National Socialists to force the bureaucracy into their political mould, and their anticipation of the "concealed resistance" which was to be so significant in the Third Reich. Finally, in the state commissars one finds the basic concept behind the Reichsstatthalter and Gauleiter of a decade later, who supervised, competed with, and spied on the officials of the state.

Even the essential idea of the concentration camp system is to be found in the draft constitution that Theodor von der Pfordten drew up and cleared with Hitler in the summer of 1923 and that the authorities found in the pocket of his suit on 9 November:

[90] B, I, M. Inn. 71708, Loritz, 3.3.1924; II, MA103476, pp. 1463-64.

Article 16

"The Viceroys will take measures promptly under Article 9[91] for the cleansing and relief of cities, spas, and tourist areas, especially for the removal of all persons dangerous to security and useless eaters. These [persons] are to be brought together, as needed, in concentration camps (Sammellager) and, where possible, turned to labor productive to the community.

Whoever evades or seeks to evade these measures will be punished by death. The same punishment applies to anyone who gives aid or comfort to them."[92]

Today it is hard to read these simple and superficially colorless lines without realizing that they led to Dachau and to Auschwitz. It is, though, dubious if the middle-aged jurist who took such a firm line with "useless eaters"—although allegedly he had stolen food from prisoners of war in the camp he administered during World War I[93]—fully realized the road on which he was embarking. More important, even if the bloodstained document containing these lines had not mouldered in musty files until it was apparently casually destroyed either by the National Socialists or by Allied airmen, few persons in Germany or elsewhere would have taken seriously the grandiose scheming of a dead revolutionary belonging to a discredited and splintered political movement. Even fewer of those who might have read this constitution would, in view of the bloodlessness of the Putsch, have placed much emphasis on this single paragraph. Certainly, the investigating committee of the Bavarian Landtag did not do so, even though at least two of its members were seeking clubs with which to beat Hitler. It is only long afterwards, in most cases, that we can see the acorns from which the oaks grew. At the time, there are too many acorns for us to be sure which will survive. It is important for the historian to be able to trace the development, to follow the patterns, for the sake of truth and in the hope that, since human beings tend to react in similar patterns to similar stimuli, in time we will be able to identify some of the more dangerous trends before they develop menacing proportions. Without such guide posts we will be no better off than the investigators of 1927.

[91] Martial law.
[92] B, II, MA103476, p. 1174. See also Müller, *Wandel*, pp. 151-53.
[93] B, IV, HSIV, EE7, pp. 57-58.

VI. *Conclusion*

In October and early November three groups of political leaders faced one another in Bavaria. The first was composed of conservative ministers representing a democratically elected Diet. The second group, appointed by the first to stand between them and disaster, represented a mixture of ultraconservative and right radical values and preferred the administrative paternalism of a narrow oligarchy to any democratic system, however conservative. The third group consisted of outspoken radicals who wished to create new patterns and to follow new paths. All three groups sought to reach some form of understanding with the others—on their own terms. None of these groups gave up its essential stand before the Putsch. The Bavarian government wished to maintain its basic control of Bavaria and insisted on the pre-eminence of the Landtag and the political parties. The triumvirate sought to become autonomous and to support a rightist directory in Berlin, which they doubtless expected to support them in Bavaria. The National Socialists and their allies wished to establish a new national government in which they would hold the key posts, although they were ready to take in members of the triumvirate as junior partners. Since none of the groups was prepared to give way to the others, the situation was almost certain to lead to a dangerous confrontation unless events outside of Bavaria changed the balance decidedly in favor of one group or another. The only group that could hope for such a change was the triumvirate, since only they could even hope for serious support from the north.

The triangle was, however, not a stable one, since the government and the triumvirate could come to terms without serious damage to each other, should the hopes of either one for dominance be dashed. They were the same sort of people and had come up through the same system. They wanted to preserve the same general society and political system. Also, they were compromisers. Kahr could, would, and did, give up his hopes with a sigh and return to harness as a bureaucrat, when his dreams collapsed. It is very likely that the government and the Landtag could have made some accommodation had Kahr—contrary to all likelihood—really produced a rabbit from the Berlin hat. They could hope, with justice, that the wheel would soon turn their way again.

The Kampfbund, the spearhead of a revolutionary movement, could not compromise and survive, and standing still was a compromise. Time played for its opponents in two ways. It raised the spectre of a Berlin directorate, which would take all of the wind from the Kampfbund's sails and provide Kahr with the power and impetus to sink it. Should this spectre not come to life, the group faced either the desertion of its followers in disgust at its inactivity or the disappearance of the crisis that brought it many of these followers. Only in a desperate bid for power was there hope for the future. Hitler had made his reputation as the apostle of action. Sooner or later the apostle of action must become the man of action or his movement would collapse. Hitler, who really *was* a man of action, neither could nor wished to hold back the fomenting forces in himself and his movement. He wished merely to pick the best moment to strike. He was therefore in that most dangerous of positions—for his opponents—the desperate man with a cliff at his back. Like Conrad von Hötzendorff in 1914 or Tojo in 1941, Hitler opted for action rather than gradual but ignominious defeat.

11.

NIGHT OF CONFUSION

I. The Opposing Forces

The Putschists could count on very considerable numbers of men from München and were also bringing in men from much of southern Bavaria to strengthen these local forces. They also had the advantage of a great deal of popular support in the city. Yet, many of the members of their organizations and many of their supporters were not of any immediate military value. In terms of actual troops their strength was roughly as follows:

SA of the NSDAP
    SA Regiment München—1,500 officers and men[1]
    Stosstrupp Hitler—about 125 officers and men[2]
    SA units from southern Bavaria—about 250-300 men[3]
Bund Oberland
    3 battalions, undoubtedly understrength—perhaps 2,000 officers and men[4]
Reichskriegsflagge
    2 infantry detachments, 1 machine gun detachment, and 1 artillery battery—about 200 officers and men[5]
Kampfbund München
    approximately 2 infantry companies—about 150 officers and men[6]

[1] NA, SA Rgt. München, 230-a-10/3, Rgt. Befehl 78; 4, Stärkemeldung, 21.8.1923; Schema, 6.11.1923; Brückner an O. Kdo. d. SA, 10.10.1923; Bennecke, Heinrich, *Hitler und die SA*, München, 1962, p. 78. Hereafter cited as Bennecke, *SA*.

[2] Kallenbach, *Mit Hitler*, pp. 11-14.

[3] B, IV, BuR, 35, Akt 3, Antworten auf Fragebogen 2 and estimate based on fragmentary reports. This estimate may be quite inaccurate.

[4] At the trial, Dr. Weber claimed about 4,000-5,000 men (EAP 105/7, II, Dr. Weber) but this number probably referred to all Putschists and was exaggerated.

[5] See Chapter IV, Section III, above.   [6] Section II, below.

In other words, the Kampfbund had a maximum of some 4,000 armed men available for use in the Putsch. They were opposed by the government forces (in men available for combat) as follows:

Blue Police
  about 250 officers and men[7]
Landespolizei München
  headquarters and general staff (Landespolizeiamt) in Armee-museum
  regimental headquarters (Polizeidirektion München) on Ett-strasse
  First Battalion (Erster Abschnitt)—about 400 officers and men (headquarters in Residenz)[8]
  Second Battalion (Zweiter Abschnitt)—about 400 officers and men (headquarters in Max II Kaserne, at the corner of Leonrodstrasse and Dachauerstrasse)
  Third Battalion (Dritter Abschnitt)—about 400 officers and men (Maximilianeum and Türkenkaserne)
  approximately 1 motorized company (Kraftfahrbereitschaft) —about 75 officers and men (Türkenkaserne)
  1 armored car detachment with 12 obsolete armored cars— about 75 officers and men (Türkenkaserne)
  1 communications technical battalion (Türkenkaserne)
  1 Battalion, Lapo Münchenland—about 400 officers and men (Max II Kaserne)
  1 mounted reconnaissance squadron (Streifstaffel)—about 50 officers and men (Max II Kaserne)
  (Besides these units in München itself, there were available approximately two more regiments, a battalion at the Polizei-vorschule in Eichstätt, and miscellaneous smaller units scattered throughout the state.)[9]
Reichswehr
  headquarters of Wehrkreis VII and the Seventh Division (Ludwig- and Schönfeldstrassen)

---

[7] Rough estimate, which probably errs on the low side. There were about 1,500 men in the blue police, but most were tied down by routine duties. B, I, M. Inn. 72175, *MNN* 3, 4.1.1927.

[8] These strength estimates take into account the normal contingent of men on leave, sick, or detached for special service.

[9] Sagerer & Schuler, *Landespolizei*, pp. 14-15; GP, A, General von Kiliani, 5.9.1960; B, Colonel Ernst Schultes; Lieutenant Colonel Max Lagerbauer; Wachtmeister Hermann Ruhland.

First Battalion, Nineteenth Infantry Regiment[10]—about 300 men (Oberwiesenfeldkasernenviertel)

headquarters of Infanterieführer VII and Artillerieführer VII (Ludwig- and Schönfeldstrassen)

Seventh Engineer Battalion—about 225 officers and men (Oberwiesenfeld, Pionierkaserne I and II)

Seventh Signal Battalion—about 150 officers and men (Oberwiesenfeld, Nachrichtenkaserne)

Seventh Motor Transport Battalion, headquarters and first company—about 100 officers and men

Seventh Transport Battalion (horse-drawn), headquarters and first and second companies—about 125 officers and men

Seventh Medical Battalion

Fifth Battery, Seventh Artillery Regiment—about 90 officers and men (Oberwiesenfeld)

city commandant's headquarters (Armeemuseum)

Infantry School—about 350 officers, cadets, and men[11] (Blutenburgstrasse at Marsplatz)

(The remainder of the Seventh Division and the Seventeenth Cavalry Regiment were also under the command of General von Lossow and were available for use against rebels within twenty-four hours, assuming that the railways continued functioning.)[12]

It is clear that the Landespolizei was far stronger in München than was the Reichswehr, and the disparity in strength is much

[10] Minus M.G. Company. The Fourth Company was in Berlin on special assignment—guard duty. It was temporarily replaced by Company Werner, a unit made up of short-term volunteers drawn from various Verbände. Since many of these volunteers were students, the size of the company had declined sharply at the beginning of the semester at the university and Technische Hochschule. GP, A, Kurt Pflügel, 11.1.1966.

[11] The schools were subordinated not to Lossow but to the Heersleitung in Berlin. The number of personnel at the schools is a very rough estimate based on fragmentary data. Data on Reichswehr units in München is drawn from *Rangliste 1923*; GP, A, General von Kiliani, 5.9.1960; Kurt Pflügel, 11.1.1966; B, Colonel Ernst Schultes, etc.

Rossbach estimated Infantry School strength at between 500 and 600 men. However, since the entering junior cadet class was 167 strong, the estimate above seems reasonable. DSZ, Nov. 1956, p. 11; GP, A, Rossbach, 15.11.1951.

[12] *Rangliste 1923*, pp. 17-19.

greater than it appears to be on the basis of mere numbers when one considers that a large portion of the Reichswehr personnel in München were assigned to headquarters units or to noncombat units, while the Infantry School, and its appendage, the Engineer School were not only noncombat units but were not under Bavarian control. The Landespolizei boasted some 1,800 men in combat units in München, while the Reichswehr had approximately 800, out of a total strength of some 1,500 men. Therefore, some 2,600 government troops and approximately 4,000 Putschists were in München on the evening of 8 November 1923. The Putschists, however, had few reserves, and these were weak numerically and badly organized, while the government forces had strong reserves, most of which were available for rapid commitment.

Yet numbers alone mean little in any military problem, unless considered in relation to a number of other factors, which are often decisive. The posture of the two forces was at least as important as their numbers and was probably far more significant. The Putschists, since they took the initiative, had the advantage of surprise and therefore of position. Even though many of their troops had no idea that there was to be a Putsch on the evening of 8 November, they were psychologically prepared for, indeed eager for, such a move, and a good proportion of them were physically assembled at key points at the time of the outbreak of the Putsch or shortly thereafter.[13] The government forces were caught by surprise, at least in a tactical and technical sense, although they were aware of the possibility of a Putsch. There had, however, been so many alarms and excursions in the past few months, that few persons took the warnings of trouble seriously. Certainly the eve of the anniversary of the Revolution of 1918 was an ideal moment for the Putsch of men dedicated to undoing the work of the revolutionaries, but other anniversaries almost as emotionally satisfying had passed without serious incident. There had been reports, some from multiple sources, of National Socialist revolts on 25 August (Ludwigstag), on 2 September (Sedantag), and on 27 September. Nothing had come of any of these rumors, so that 8 November seemed no more serious a threat than earlier national anniversaries. Warnings continually repeated soon fall on half-deaf ears unless they are rein-

---

[13] Some of these units were badly understrength, even by Verbände standards, on 8 November. For examples of weak units see B, I, SA 1, 1493, Lembert, pp. 47-48; 1494, O. Fiehler, pp. 104-5.

forced by eternal vigilance on the part of senior authorities, as the American disaster at Pearl Harbor in December 1941 attests.[14]

The result was that the leaders of the government security agencies and forces took only half-measures or no measures at all against the possibility of a Putsch on the evening of 8 November. General von Lossow took the most decisive steps, rather surprisingly in view of his character. He called a conference of his senior commanders on 7 November and clearly informed them that the Reichswehr would put down any Putsch attempt that might be made. He then ordered these officers to inform all of their subordinate officers of the position that he had assumed.[15] In this conference Lossow specifically named Hitler as the likely Putsch leader.[16]

[14] B, I, GSK 43, pp. 180ff; II, MA99521, 21.9.1923, p. 10; MA102140, HMB 678, Opf., p. 2; MA103476, pp. 836-37; NA, T120, 5569, pp. K591579-80.

[15] Apparently one of the chief reasons why Colonel Leupold was dropped from the Reichswehr after the Putsch was because he had failed to inform the officers of the Infantry School of this conference. In theory, the Infantry School was not under Lossow's command, but, as Landeskommandant and commander of the Seventh Division, the general was in a position to take decisive action regarding the career of any Bavarian officer in any but the most exceptional circumstances.

[16] In view of the strong position taken by Hofmann and Carsten that Lossow was at this time prepared to cooperate with a Hitler Putsch, I will spell out the available evidence to the contrary in some detail here. There is both evidence later presented to the public and evidence not intended for the public eye available regarding this conference. One of the most persuasive statements, because it was clearly not aimed at the public but simply to explain why an officer was less culpable than might seem apparent on the surface, was that made by Lieutenant Colonel von Wenz to Colonel Mittelberger, who had just taken over the Nineteenth Infantry Regiment from him: "[Lieutenant] Rossmann, who, because on leave, did not take part in the acting Regimental Commander's [Wenz's] conference on the afternoon of the seventh, therefore was not aware of the clear position taken by General von Lossow before the Putsch. . . ." (NA, T79, pp. 1064-65.) Colonel Etzel testified in March 1924, at a time when Lossow had already attempted to have him cashiered or at least retired prematurely, that Lossow had warned that the Reichswehr would act against Hitler if he "losschlägt." Etzel's statement is further supported by the prompt action he took against the Putschists in Regensburg on the night of 8 November 1923 before receiving any orders from München. (See Chapter XIII, Section V, below.) For Lossow's own testimony see NA, EAP 105/7, X, pp. 006529-30; and B, II, MA103476, pp. 1087ff. Captain Uhde of the Infantry School told Putschists that he had been officially informed of the warning issued at

Colonel Seisser was, it would seem, a good deal more trusting than Lossow, since, only a few days before the Putsch he flatly rejected the suggestion of the representative of Polizeidirektion München that Hitler and Ludendorff seemed to be moving towards violence, on the ground that " 'General Ludendorff does not lie.' "[17] Seisser allegedly did warn his senior commanders on 8 November of the possibility of a Putsch, but the indecision of such a senior police officer as Colonel Banzer in the early hours of the Putsch suggests that Seisser did not take as clear a position as Lossow in this matter.[18]

Kahr was the least suspicious of the triumvirate. On 7 November he assured Count Soden that Hitler and Ludendorff would not do anything without informing Kahr beforehand, and on 8 November the Generalstaatskommissariat apparently agreed that the security precautions at the Bürgerbräukeller should be as small and inconspicuous as possible.[19]

The Putsch leaders encouraged this confidence by maintaining contact with the triumvirate on a friendly basis after deciding to act, and they even used this friendly intercourse to ensure that the members of the triumvirate would fall into their trap. Ludendorff artlessly asked Lossow in the late afternoon of 8 November if he would be at the Bürgerbräukeller that night, while Dr. Weber telephoned Seisser and asked him the same question at noon.[20]

Whether because of faith in the Putschists, confidence in their own strength, or mere inertia, the triumvirate took no further measures and as a result the army forces were, as is to be expected on

---

this conference. (B, II, MA103476, pp. 1264-65.) General Endres, who was then operations officer of WWK VII, testifies to the tenor of this conference. (B, IV, HSIV, EE7, pp. 38-40.) The secret Denkschrift issued by the GSK on the Putsch fleshes out the story a bit, but agrees with the other existing testimony. (MA103473, Denkschrift, p. 6.) Captain Leuze testified that he was annoyed to learn that garrisons outside München had been warned, but not the officers of the Infantry School. (GP, A, Leuze Brief, 11.4.1960.) For the presentation of Lossow's position as described by Hitler and accepted by Hofmann and Carsten, see Carsten, F. L., *Die Reichswehr und Politik*, Köln-Berlin, 1964, pp. 201-2 (hereafter cited as Carsten, *Reichswehr*); and Hofmann, *Hitlerputsch*, p. 136. Here the Putschist version of the 6 November meeting is given without consideration of the other versions, and the 7 November meeting is completely ignored.

[17] B, II, MA103473, Mantel Bericht, 5.4.1924, p. 3.
[18] B, II, MA103476, pp. 6, 689-90, 1087-92.
[19] B, I, Kahr MS, p. 1340; II, MA103476, p. 1153.
[20] *Ibid.*, p. 1198.

an evening in peacetime, in disarray when the Putsch broke out. Under such circumstances, anywhere from half to three-fourths of the lower-ranking enlisted men will be off post, while the percentage is far higher for higher-ranking non-commissioned officers, many of whom are married, and for officers. The München garrison was no exception to this rule. At 8:30 p.m. on 8 November, for example, one officer, one sergeant, and six men were present for duty in Pionierkaserne I. Many of the others had been invited to a party by Putschists who never appeared.[21] At the First Battalion, Nineteenth Infantry Regiment, the only officer on duty was a senior cadet (Oberfähnrich)[22] serving the dual functions of duty officer and drillmaster for members of the Hermannsbund.[23] Lossow, Berchem, Hösslin and other key officers were in the Bürgerbräukeller. Generals Danner, Ruith, and Kress were obviously found at home or in the city, for they were in civilian clothes in the initial phases of the Putsch. Major Schwandner, Kress's general staff officer, was attending a lecture on German trade with the United States.[24] Major Karl von Loeffelholz was at home.[25] Hitler, who believed—according to his friend Hanfstaengl—that all Putsches should be launched on weekends, at least chose the right hour of the day for his venture, although Thursday was not the best day of the week. Under optimum conditions, it would be midnight before the majority of the officers and men could be brought to their posts and organized for action.

The Landespolizei seem to have had more men and units ready for action than did the army. This was natural enough, since they formed the first line of defense in any civil emergency. But, even so, officers and enlisted men continued to straggle in to their units all night.[26] The higher officers of the Landespolizei were quite a dif-

[21] NA, EAP 105/7a, Cantzler Bericht.

[22] A cadet who had completed his formal training but had not yet been elected to the officer corps and commissioned.

[23] B, iv, HSIV, EE7, Böhm Bemerkungen, between pp. 46-47; NA, 105/7a, Reichswehr Bericht vom Putsch.

[24] GP, A, General Max Schwandner, 23.1.1960.

[25] *Ibid.*, Freiin von Loeffelholz, 21.11.1965.

[26] This is an estimate based largely on general statements scattered throughout the documents regarding the Putsch, rather than on any single reference. These statements strongly indicate that there were considerable forces in the Türkenkaserne and the Max II Kaserne from the outset of the Putsch. The statements of General von Kiliani, Lieutenant Colonel Lagerbauer and Colonel Remold confirm these indications. GP, A, General

ferent matter. A number of them, like Seisser, Banzer, and Hunglinger were at the Bürgerbräukeller. Major von Imhoff was lecturing young officers on tactics.[27] Lieutenant Colonel Muxel was at home with his family.[28] This meant that, although far more men were probably present for duty, there was less early activity on the part of the Landespolizei than on the part of the Reichswehr, where senior officers were contacted early and took strong stands.

Therefore, for a potentially crucial four hours a mobilized Putschist force faced a disorganized, greatly understrength opposing force, temporarily robbed of many of its leaders. However, this advantage was destined to be only temporary and *could* only be temporary unless the Putschists were able, by rapid and ruthless action, to destroy or win over the opposing forces in München within this narrow time span. By 12:30 a.m. the tide would have turned. The enlisted men would be back in their barracks, the bulk of the officers and non-commissioned officers recalled or brought in by the news of the crisis, and the numerical superiority of the Putschists would be offset by the superior discipline, organization, armament, and leadership of the government troops.

Popular historical accounts are full of triumphs of ragged, disorganized irregulars over organized regulars. Serious studies have relegated most of these soul-stirring triumphs to the dust heap or have drastically revised them. The "hordes" of Genghis Khan were more carefully organized and had better officers and tactics than the forces they encountered. The Americans who won battles from the British in the American Revolution were almost always regulars drilled in the European manner and scornful of their own militia. In the same way, effective guerrilla forces are well organized and, even so, usually suffer serious reverses in their early ventures, until they have attained experience and steadiness. With very, very few exceptions, regular troops, under reasonably intelligent leadership, defeat irregulars in any pitched engagement, most especially in the opening engagements of any conflict. The reason is simple. The regular has the advantages of a professional dealing with an amateur; and he usually has better tools than does the amateur. This was certainly the situation in München on 8 November 1923. The Reichswehr and the Landespolizei had selected their officers care-

---

von Kiliani, 5.9.1960; B, Lieutenant Colonel Max Lagerbauer; Sergeant Hermann Ruhland.

[27] GP, A, General von Kiliani, 5.9.1960.

[28] *Ibid.*, B, Lieutenant Colonel Otto Muxel.

fully and had trained their non-commissioned officers and men regularly and well. Officers and men had worked together for years in most instances—although changes in key assignments had just taken place in the Reichswehr—and knew what to expect of one another. Many Reichswehr soldiers, most non-commissioned officers, and most officers were veterans of World War I. Finally, the troops were well armed with weapons kept in excellent condition.

What was the condition of the Putschist troops? Fully-trained, partly trained, and untrained men were thrown together, if not within individual small units, at least within larger ones. Most of the Putschist leaders had had little formal military education and little experience above the company level. Despite all their talk of representing the "front generation," comparatively few veterans were to be found in the Kampfbund ranks. Large numbers of their "enlisted men" were too young to have fought in World War I and a very considerable number were secondary-school or university students. Such "training" as they had had amounted to little more than basic training administered sketchily in the evenings and on weekends. Even Captain Röhm was prepared to admit that most of the Kampfbund's military exercises had no military merit whatsoever. In everything but the most superficial appearance, these men were nearer to being a mob than to being an army.[29]

Where arms and equipment were concerned, the Putschists were in even worse shape than they were with regard to manpower. They had a few artillery pieces, but practically no ammunition, let alone specialized equipment, such as field telephones, aiming circles, and the like, without which artillery units can scarcely function. They had rifles and machine guns in large quantities, but many of these weapons were completely useless. As early as the demonstration on 1 May, there were complaints within the SA regarding the weapons that they were issued. The commander of the Third Hundertschaft of SA Regiment München wrote to Hitler: " 'The issued weapons were in terrible condition. Eight-tenths of the machine guns were not in condition to fire. Yet we have armorers in the SA.' "[30] The official report on the arms captured from the Putschists may be inaccurate regarding the fate of the weapons and may, for foreign policy reasons, exaggerate the extent to which the weapons of the Putschists were damaged, but the general picture it conveys is confirmed by other sources and agrees with Lemke's remarks:

[29] See Chapters III and IV above.   [30] B, II, MA103476, p. 175.

. . . The bulk of these weapons came into the hands of the state as a result of the large-scale disarmament program initiated and executed energetically after the Putsch. The weapons, which had suffered severely as a result of years of improper storage and neglect whereby a high percentage had become entirely useless, were turned over to the Landespolizei to be scrapped.[31]

One further factor remains to be thrown onto the scales, and that is morale. Here, both sides had their problems. The Putschists had a force that was certainly anxious to overthrow the existing civil authorities, but it was not a force that was very anxious to quarrel with the Reichswehr and Landespolizei. A good number of the poorer Putschists dearly desired to enter the armed forces as soldiers, and a clash with these forces must have seemed, at least to some, to be a poor start for such a career. Many of the officers and students in the Kampfbund were relatives and friends of officers in the Reichswehr and Landespolizei or had served in the same units with them in World War I, which was another deterrent to combat with the armed forces. Again, the basis of the Putschists' political philosophy was to be found in the idea of nationalism and the basic unity of all Germans of all classes. While they might, and did, fight Marxists with enthusiasm as traitors to the nation, they did not feel any such enthusiasm for fighting fellow Germans who were not merely representatives of the nation, but, by and large, nationalists. There had, in fact, been much pressure within the Kampfbund for the organization of all national Germans behind the armed forces. Finally, there can be little doubt that many of the more sophisticated among the Kampfbund's officers and men must have felt to some extent as did General Kaiser of Bayern und Reich, who remarked on 31 October that he doubted if the Reichswehr could find among the Verbände five machine gun companies fit to perform duty in the Reichswehr.[32] Captain Heiss of Reichsflagge summed up the relative effectiveness of the two forces neatly in an order of the day issued to his Verband shortly after the Putsch:

"The outcome of such a battle was clear to us. The state leadership [of Reichsflagge] could not deceive itself regarding the combat value of its own formations. (Young and old, veterans and

[31] B, II, MA103472, M. Inn. 2004 kaa 438. See also B, I, M. Inn. 73694, Notiz für Akt 2004 kaa, n.d. (ca. May 1924).
[32] B, IV, BuR, Bd. 35, Akt 5, Item 65 Kaiser an Tutschek.

recruits, all arms and services mixed together; shortages of weapons, equipment, discipline, and leaders.) Speed and difficulty of mobilization without the aid of the state is left out of account here."[33]

Such thoughts are cold comfort on the eve of battle.

If the leaders of the Kampfbund had morale troubles in a struggle against the legal forces of the state, the commanders of the Reichswehr and the Landespolizei also had serious headaches—mostly of their own making. Throughout the year 1923, the leaders of the armed forces had, with the full consent of the government, not merely encouraged but ordered close cooperation between the Verbände, including the Kampfbund organization, and their own München units. It is easy to see why junior officers and enlisted men often interpreted this policy as representing acceptance of the aims of the Kampfbund leaders, and in a number of cases close personal relationships developed between trainers and trainees. Since these relationships were, despite quarrels at higher levels, kept up until the very moment of the outbreak of the Putsch, soldiers and policemen faced the prospect of a fight with the Kampfbund with very little enthusiasm.[34] In view of these circumstances and the general atmosphere in the city, the triumvirs were far from happy regarding the reliability of their local units and clearly looked on units from outside of München as more reliable than those immediately at hand.[35]

II. *The Putschists on the Offensive*

Gustav von Kahr had agreed to give a speech on the evening of 8 November concerning the aims of his "regime." The arrangements for the speech were made by commercial councilor Eugen Zentz, a tobacco merchant with many nationalist and right radical

[33] B, IV, BuR, Bd. 36, Akt 1, Item 35.

[34] The problem was the officers. By and large, although the Heeresleitung was at this time somewhat worried about them, the enlisted men would—as the events in Saxony, Thuringia, and Bavaria were to demonstrate—take their cue from their officers. See below.

[35] See below. It is interesting to note which troops are chosen for active fighting against the Putschists and which are held in reserve, even though they might seem better trained for serious combat operations. Information on the attitudes of the troops and, especially, on the attitudes of the officers is scattered throughout the official documents as well as in the testimony contained in the Gordon Papers and in the personality card files. Specific cases will be dealt with and documented below.

ties. Zentz was approached on 4 November by supporters of Kahr and asked to arrange for the speech. He agreed to do so and was told on 5 November that Kahr had accepted the idea. Zentz then contacted the various rightist political and paramilitary organizations, including the Kampfbund. Zentz had originally wanted a smaller hall, but the Bürgerbräukeller, one of the largest in München, was the only one not already engaged for that evening. Invitations were sent directly to a large number of persons prominent in government, business, industry, and the free professions. The list of invitations was apparently largely drawn up by the Jewish nationalist, Professor Paul Cossmann, who was the publisher of the *Süddeutsche Monatshefte* and the "strong man" of the *Münchner Neueste Nachrichten*, München's most important newspaper.[36] Cossmann and his friends, Adolf Schiedt[37] and Dr. Fritz Gerlich, the chief editor of the *Münchner Neueste Nachrichten*, allegedly wrote Kahr's speech.

Zentz has been accused of having laid a trap for Kahr and the Bavarian government in collaboration with Hitler. However, the evidence tends strongly in the other direction. Not only did Zentz himself energetically deny any such intentions, but, more important, his collaborators, the Cossmann circle, had been increasingly disillusioned with the Kampfbund in recent months and would have been unlikely to assist Hitler and his friends. Most persuasive are the series of attacks launched against Zentz in the National Socialist broadsheets and newspapers after the Putsch, in which he was accused of having, at the instance of a Jewish-Jesuit conspiratorial circle, set a trap for the good, simple, and honest German, Adolf Hitler. On this basis, it seems fair to assume that Zentz acted in good faith towards Kahr.[38]

The authorities were aware of the significance of the meeting in the Bürgerbräukeller and initially planned to place a company of Landespolizei in the building. The final decision was that this would look as though Kahr were afraid of the citizens of München and the police troops—forty-five men—were therefore tucked out of sight in the old Schwere Reiter Kaserne[39] at least a quarter of a

[36] The predecessor of the *Süddeutsche Zeitung*.
[37] Schiedt was, like Cossmann, a nationalist and a Jew.
[38] B, I, Kahr MS, pp. 1349-51; GSK 43, p. 91; II, MA99523, 27.5.1925, p. 7; MA103476, pp. 970, 1220-30, 1376-77; IV, BuR, Bd. 34, Item 175; Bd. 36, Akt 1, Items 33, 36; Müller, *Wandel*, pp. 102, 109ff.
[39] The headquarters of the München mounted police detachment. It was near the Ludwigsbrücke.

mile from the beer hall. The two blue police stations nearest to the beer hall were reinforced by thirteen additional men each to help them to perform security duties with regard to the assembly and a general reserve force (Hauptwache) was provided. Finally, twelve officials of the criminal police were placed in the hall itself and on the balconies to prevent disorder and heckling.

After the street outside of the beer hall filled up with disappointed men who had been refused admittance to the overflowing hall, thirty members of the Hauptwache were sent to help keep order in the small square in front of the beer hall and in the Rosenheimerstrasse itself. At least 150 policemen, including the mounted police detachment, were available to protect and control the meeting, in addition to the many policemen who were in the audience. Therefore, sufficient measures had been taken to handle anything short of a major attack on the meeting.[40] Nor were the police to have the entire responsibility for the maintenance of order. Arrangements had been made for members of the VVM to police the hall itself, but they never appeared.[41]

The crowd in the hall was a surprisingly large one, although the talk had originally been intended for a small but select group. As events developed, the crowd was a thoroughly mixed one. It included many ordinary members of the public as well as the bulk of the most important men in political München. Most of the members of the Bavarian government were present, as was Graf Soden, the Crown Prince's Cabinet chief. The police president of München was there with several of his deputies. The triumvirs were present, each with a small entourage. Bankers, businessmen and manufacturers, newspaper editors, leaders of the Verbände came to hear Kahr elucidate his program, or perhaps take a more positive step towards dictatorship. The hall was closed to all but a few important personages by 7:15 p.m. because it was already jampacked. Some key persons were missing, though. Perhaps the most significant absentee was General Ludendorff, who did not want to be present during the necessarily embarrassing opening scene of a Putsch.[42] The general later claimed to have known nothing of the

[40] B, I, SA 1, 1490, Bericht, Hptm. d. Lapo Müller, p. 8; Bericht of S. Hermann, pp. 10-11; GSK, pp. 180ff; II, MA103476, pp. 1-5, 1209-10, 1227.

[41] Ibid., p. 1298.

[42] Witness his "chance" meeting with Kapp and his Cabinet at the Brandenburger Tor in March 1920 and his failure to appear at the ceremonies on 4 November 1923, where there was a good chance of trouble.

Putsch until it had occurred, but his stepson, Lieutenant (Ret.) Heinz Pernet, an active Putschist, admitted to a friend that his father " 'had stayed away from the meeting intentionally.' "[43]

The speeches were predictably strongly nationalistic, but neither very specific nor exciting. Zentz's introductory oration apparently attacked the Reich government overtly and the Bavarian government covertly. Kahr's contribution, which was never finished (but was printed intact in various newspapers), was a rehash of earlier oratory together with a strong denunciation of Marxism. It was the sort of speech which, delivered in England, would lead the less patient members of his audience to mutter, "How long till the port?" In Bavaria, where the listeners could console themselves with beer and where Marxism was anathema, it seemingly went over reasonably well.[44]

While Zentz and Kahr spoke, events had been moving rapidly. The Kampfbund troops were assembled, for the most part in ignorance of what the night was to offer. Security was carried so far that they were "alarmed" by use of white notices (indicating training sessions) instead of red ones, which were to be used in cases of emergency or serious action. This may be one reason for the high incidence of absenteeism in some units. Stosstrupp Hitler was assembled in the bowling alley of the Torbräu, their home bar, where they were told by their leader, Lieutenant Josef Berchtold, that Kahr and Hitler had reached an understanding and that the Stosstrupp was to strike the first blow for the "new government."[45] SA and Oberland units were similarly assembled at predesignated points and then marched or transported by truck (in the case of units needed for immediate action) to the Bürgerbräukeller, the Löwenbräukeller, or various barracks throughout the city. Some of the units were armed, while others received weapons from Kampfbund caches outside München after assembling or depended upon caches in the city held by the Reichswehr, the police, or other organizations.[46]

Hitler himself, after a last briefing of his SA leaders, arrived at the beer hall a trifle after 8:00 p.m. Finding the street in front of the Bürgerbräukeller clogged with a milling herd of curious citi-

---

[43] B, II, MA103476, p. 1198.

[44] B, I, Kahr MS, pp. 1352-53; II, MA103476, p. 1220; 308, 9.11.1923 (Richter, Zeitungsnotizen-Buch).

[45] Kallenbach, *Mit Hitler*, p. 24; B, II, MA103476, pp. 1196-97, 1338.

[46] See below.

zens, he was worried for fear all of his plans would go awry because his troops might not be able to get their cars and trucks to the hall. He was also worried by the presence of considerable numbers of policemen. Therefore, with characteristic impudence, he suggested to the police that they should clear the streets, since otherwise panic could develop among the audience. The police, who had recognized Hitler and let him in because they had orders that he should hear Kahr's speech, adopted his suggestion. Using the reinforcements that had just arrived, they cleared away the crowds, which departed more or less quietly. Since all was quiet, the reinforcements were then released and marched away. They were scarcely out of sight when the first trucks full of SA men arrived at 8:10 p.m. Since the Stosstrupp was the key element in the action against the Bürgerbräukeller, the SA men remained quietly in their trucks. At a minute or two after 8:30, the Stosstrupp arrived and the National Socialists poured forth from their vehicles to surround the Bürgerbräukeller. The handful of blue police who faced them were confused and helpless. Some of them thought that the newcomers were Reichswehr soldiers because they wore steel helmets and carried army rifles. The others, unprepared for a fight against heavy odds in men and weapons, simply gave way. The first step in the Putsch was a success and a high percentage of Bavaria's leaders were prisoners.[47]

Hitler's bodyguard, Ulrich Graf, informed his master, who was waiting in the antechamber of the hall in which Kahr was speaking, as soon as the Stosstrupp arrived. Hitler now began his famous action. Throwing away with a grand gesture the half-liter beer glass he had reluctantly been nursing, he drew his Browning pistol and advanced into the hall surrounded by armed men. This little phalanx of revolutionaries was an odd lot by any standards. One was his bodyguard, the butcher Graf. Next came Max Amann, his former sergeant-major and business manager, no stranger to violence, but at his other side was Putzi Hanfstaengl, Franklin Roosevelt's Harvard classmate, who was far more at home with a piano or a work of art than with the pistol that had been thrust into his hand. Another of the group was Josef Gerum,[48] and Rudolf Hess, Hitler's later deputy, made up the number. Welded together as

[47] B, I, SA 1, 1490, pp. 33, 37; 1493, Rosenberg, p. 214; II, MA103476, p. 1221; Kallenbach, *Mit Hitler*, p. 25; Pölnitz, *Emir*, pp. 125-26.
[48] For Gerum see Chapter V, note 38, above.

much by Hitler's personality as by their belief in elements of the dogmas he preached, they symbolized the breadth and disparateness of his support.

Hitler's entrance lost much of its planned dramatic effect because he could not simply stride into the hall, but had to fight his way forward painfully (with much use of elbows and pistol) through the tightly packed crowd, which, with the best will in the world could scarcely make way before him. Machine pistols are remarkably effective persuaders, however, and Hitler made steady progress, arriving at the podium without incident, although Hanfstaengl claims that a Reichswehr major (perhaps von Hösslin) along his path tried to shoot the future Führer, a contingency which Hitler claims to have foreseen.[10]

By the time Hitler reached Kahr, the audience was in a state of alarm and confusion. A number of armed men and a machine gun had appeared at the entrance to the hall, and all other exits were blocked. Men who tried to leave were turned back and some, who were persistent, were struck or kicked by the Storm Troopers, accustomed to the rough give and take of political warfare. Although Hitler later claimed that the machine gun was entirely for "morale" purposes, another was set up behind it and out of sight of those in the hall, which covered the exit.[50]

To quell the tumult, Hitler or one of his entourage,[51] fired into the ceiling and silence descended on the hall. Hitler claims that Kahr seemed frightened and derided him for his "fear," in view of the fact that the hall was largely filled with Kahr's followers. Since Hitler and his men were heavily armed and almost all of Kahr's people were disarmed and crowded together in a trap, the allegation of cowardice seems unfair, but the accusation is important since, if Kahr were in fact afraid, the probability increases that his account of his aims and motivations during the evening are true and that Hitler's are false. As usual Hitler wanted to have his cake and eat it, too. Hitler's actions were certainly not such as to give the

[49] B, II, MA103476, pp. 1216-17, 1221-22, 1383; NA, EAP 105/7, I, pp. 94-97; Hanfstaengl *Hitler*, pp. 95-98; Müller, *Wandel*, pp. 161-62. See also other accounts in Protocol of Hitler Trial (EAP 105/7).

[50] B, I, GSK 43, pp. 180ff; SA 1, 1490, II, p. 27; NA, EAP 105/7, I, p. 123.

[51] Testimony diverges here, and, since the point is not significant, there seems no reason for close examination.

triumvirate great confidence in his friendship and stability. Not only did he wave his pistol around in a far wilder manner than usual, but, when Major Hunglinger approached him with his hand in his pocket, Hitler himself said: "I had the feeling that he was drawing a pistol. I held my pistol against his forehead and said, 'Take your hand out.' "[52]

Hitler then invited the triumvirate to join him in a side chamber, which Hess had hired for this purpose earlier in the evening,[53] assuring them that he would guarantee their security. He led them into the anteroom, which he ordered his men to clear of spectators and policemen. Once they were in the side chamber, Hitler apologized for his action: "Please forgive me, for proceeding in this manner, but I had no other means. It is done now and cannot be undone."[54]

There has been a good deal of debate as to what went on in the side chamber, much of which centers around the atmosphere. The Putschists insist that the atmosphere was friendly and warm, while the triumvirate and their supporters claim that it was threatening on the side of the Putschists and cool on their own. We will probably never know precisely what occurred or understand all of the nuances of the attitudes and reactions of the participants, but it is clear even from the testimony of the Putsch leaders that the atmosphere was not as friendly as they asserted. Hitler claims that Kahr was a broken man when he went into the side chamber; this scarcely augured well for friendly conversations. Hitler further admits that the accusation that he threatened the triumvirate with his pistol was true, although he explains that he was only jesting: "I answered Kahr by indicating the pistol in my hand, and, smiling, 'There are five rounds in it: four for the traitors, and, if it fails, one for me.' "[55] These were scarcely reassuring words from an armed man to his prisoners, even if he did, as he claims, hand over the pistol to Graf immediately after this little scene. Nor was the presence of the burly butcher and his machine pistol an indication of a friendly and free conversation, an impression which was heightened by the presence of armed guards at the window. Similarly, although Hitler and Dr. Weber claimed that they wished to place no pressure on the triumvirate and to let them make their own decisions, the Putschists would not let Lossow talk with Hunglinger and

---

[52] NA, EAP 105/7, I, p. 97. [53] B, II, MA103476, p. 1383.
[54] NA, EAP, 105/7, I, p. 98. [55] *Ibid.*

later forced both Hunglinger and Major von Hösslin to leave the room.[56]

For some fifteen minutes Hitler wrestled with the triumvirate for their political souls. Here, too, the exact course of the discussion is unclear. Hitler claims that their objections were purely tactical. The members of the triumvirate and their aides claim that they were fundamental. Be this as it may, at the end of fifteen minutes, Hitler had not succeeded in bringing the triumvirate to the point of accepting his proposals, and he therefore returned to the main hall, where the restless crowd, which had been promised that he would return with an acquiescent trio in ten minutes, were beginning to get out of hand, despite, or because of, the attempts of Captain Göring and other Putschists to win them over by plea or threat. En route, Hitler stopped long enough to say a few encouraging words to his followers at the entrance to the hall: " 'It will succeed. Even now the other section of the city will be occupied.' "[57]

The historian Karl-Alexander von Müller, an eye-witness, graphically describes the triumph of the master orator over this difficult audience:

> . . . The wavering general attitude was, seen from my observation point, still against the enterprise. "Theater!" "South America!" "Mexico!" were the commonest cries which one heard. A number of members of Kahr's staff whom I knew were sitting not far from me. Schiedt and Aufsess [were] very pale; Stauffer excited; Gerlich stared grimly and [was] introspective.
>
> The ten minutes must have been just passed when Hitler returned—alone. He had not succeeded, as he had promised, in winning over the others. What would he say? A dangerous wave of excitement rolled up to him as he again climbed the podium. It did not subside as he began to speak. I still see clearly how he drew the Browning from his rear pocket and now himself fired a shot into the ceiling. If silence is not restored, he shouted angrily, I will order a machine gun placed in the gallery. What followed then was an oratorical masterpiece, which any actor might well envy. He began quietly, without any pathos. The enterprise was not directed against Kahr in any way. Kahr has his full trust and shall be regent in Bavaria. At the same time, how-

[56] B, IV, HSIV, EE7, Endres MS, p. 43; NA, EAP 105/7, II, pp. 52-53, 63-64, 94-96.

[57] B, I, SA 1, 1490, pp. 29 and 32.

ever, a new government must be formed: Ludendorff, Lossow, Seisser, and himself. I cannot remember in my entire life such a change in the attitude of a crowd in a few minutes, almost a few seconds. There were certainly many who were not converted yet. But the sense of the majority had fully reversed itself. Hitler had turned them inside out, as one turns a glove inside out, with a few sentences. It had almost something of hocus-pocus, or magic about it. Loud approval roared forth, no further opposition was to be heard. Only now did he say, in deep earnest, with emotion in his voice: "Outside are Kahr, Lossow, and Seisser. They are struggling hard to reach a decision. May I say to them that you will stand behind them?" "Yes! Yes!" swelled out the roaring answer from all sides. "In a free Germany," he shouted passionately out over the crowd, "there is also room for an autonomous Bavaria! I can say this to you: Either the German revolution begins tonight or we will all be dead by dawn!"[58]

While Hitler spoke, Hess and Graf were left, by Hess' own testimony, to keep Kahr, Lossow, and Seisser from leaving the side chamber.[59] Hitler, having won over the crowd, returned to the side chamber and worked on the triumvirate, assuring them that the audience would greet their agreement to join the Putsch with acclaim. Here, though, he did not achieve that instant success which had marked his address in the main hall. Then Ludendorff, brought by Scheubner-Richter, arrived in full uniform of the imperial army. After a short conference with Hitler, during which he agreed, according to his account, to help win the triumvirate for the Putschists, Ludendorff entered the side chamber and added his blandishments and entreaties to those of Hitler. Ernst Pöhner, who was the Bavarian minister-president-designate of the new regime, also worked on Kahr, his old superior. Hitler sketches a touching scene of emotional togetherness among the soldiers, while the triumvirate take the line that the atmosphere remained cool and uneasy. In the end, first Lossow and Seisser and then Kahr agreed to cooperate with Hitler. The second round was won.[60]

The entire party then trooped back into the hall, where Kahr, speaking first, announced that he had agreed to serve Bavaria as

[58] Müller, *Wandel*, pp. 162-63.   [59] B, ii, MA103476, p. 1383.

[60] NA, EAP 105/7, i, pp. 100-103; ii, pp. 29-31, 96-101; 105/7a, Official Reichswehr Bericht vom Putsch; Ludendorff, *Feldherrnhalle*, pp. 61-62, 146-47.

the regent for the monarchy. Here he was interrupted by violent applause, the loudest of the evening, according to Karl-Alexander von Müller. Hitler stepped forward and pressed Kahr's hand in his own in a theatrical clasp which reminded many of the witnesses of the "Rütli Oath,"[61] as Hitler may well have meant it to do.

Hitler then took up the thread of the meeting, announcing that, until the settlement with the criminals who were running Germany, he would conduct the policy of the new Reichsregierung—no indication here of the retiring "drummer" of legend. Ludendorff then said a few words, not forgetting to mention his surprise at the entire affair. Then came Lossow and Seisser, after Hitler pressed them hard to speak. Lossow rose in his place and made a short and vigorous speech, but one which did not seem to touch his emotions. After him came Seisser, who, on the contrary, was clearly in the grip of strong excitement, but who did little more than echo Lossow. Both made vague allusions that could be taken to refer to a war of liberation, and Seisser spoke of the Landespolizei in clearly military terms. Pöhner brought up the rear with a promise of cooperation with Kahr. Then Hitler shook hands with them all again. Throughout he had dominated the scene. This was his night and here was its climax. He was in his element as a political dramatist.[62]

The audience, as a whole, was clearly overjoyed with the turn of events and roared its approval again and again. Whatever they may have thought after they got out of the hot air of the beer hall and away from the contagious excitement and enthusiasm that dominated it, the bulk of the audience accepted the scene at face value and supported the "new government."[63]

It was now that Hitler made his first major tactical error, although its importance has sometimes been overestimated. Hearing of difficulties between Putschists and Reichswehr troops at the Engineer Kaserne (which he later confused with I./I.R.19) Hitler, who had just given his own forces a pep talk, and Dr. Weber went to straighten out this problem, leaving General Ludendorff in charge at the Bürgerbräukeller. Ludendorff allowed the triumvirate their freedom, and first Kahr, then Lossow and Seisser,

[61] A reference to the oath of the Swiss rebels against the Habsburgs.

[62] NA, EAP 105/7, I, p. 104; 105/7a, Official Reichswehr Bericht vom Putsch; B, I, GSK 43, pp. 140ff; II, MA103476, p. 1231; Müller, *Wandel*, pp. 164-65; Stresemann, *Vermächtnis*, I, p. 204.

[63] B, I, SA 1, 1490, II, pp. 12-25.

left the beer hall, passing out of the ken and control of the Putschists.[64]

Before the audience was released, Rudolf Hess, acting on instructions from Hitler, arrested a number of key hostages. The pencilled list given him by Hitler contained the following names: Knilling, Wutzlhofer, Gürtner, Bernreuther, Zetlmeier, Berchem, and—lined through—Banzer.[65] The names of Police President Mantel and Graf Soden were added later in ink, apparently by Hess. Hess climbed up on a chair and called the roll of the hostages, all of whom dutifully surrendered except for Justice Minister Gürtner, who made a vague attempt to escape and Lieutenant Colonel von Berchem and Zetlmeier who were not present. These hostages were first held in an upstairs room and then transported, at Dr. Weber's suggestion, to the villa of the publisher Julius F. Lehmann, a member of Oberland and Weber's father-in-law.[66] Here they were held until the late afternoon of the next day when their guards fled. In this manner most of the members of the legal government and a number of the most important München policemen were taken out of circulation for the duration of the Putsch.[67]

The remainder of the audience was now allowed to go home, although a vague control was maintained at the door to stop persons probably inimical to the Putschists. Several policemen took part in this operation, claiming later that they did so to prevent the Putschists from doing it in a much rougher manner. This fear was not entirely an empty one, since the door was held by Berchtold and his Stosstrupp, who boasted of the fact that they were not distinguished by gentleness and consideration for their foes. Even so, there were complaints that members of the crowd were roughly treated. Major von Hösslin testified on this score: " 'Meanwhile an elderly white-moustached man of about sixty years came out of the hall, who apparently expressed his disapproval of the seizure. He was mishandled in the roughest manner by armed men and finally thrown against the wall.' "[68] By 10:30 p.m. the hall was empty of specta-

[64] B, I, SA 1, 1494, pp. 186-88; NA, EAP 105/7, I, pp. 105-06; Ludendorff, *Feldherrnhalle*, p. 62.

[65] The name "Vallentin Ham" was also on the list, but no such person could be identified as having been seized or as being prominent on the Bavarian political scene.

[66] Lehmann remarked in this regard: "This cuckoo's egg was laid in my nest by my dear son-in-law." NA, EAP, Epp Papers, EAP 1-e-16/4, Lehmann an Epp, 20.11.1923.

[67] B, II, MA103476, pp. 1366-89.   [68] *Ibid.*, p. 1222.

tors. There remained only the Putschist leaders, who made it one of their two major headquarters,[69] and the Putschist troops held back to guard it or as a reserve force.[70]

While Hitler performed his coup de theatre in the Bürgerbräu-keller, large numbers of Kampfbund troops gathered at the Löwen-bräukeller on the Stiglmaierplatz to drink beer and listen to speeches by Hermann Esser and Ernst Röhm, interspersed with Blasmusik by two bands. By 7:45 p.m. about 1,800 Kampfbund members were present, of whom about a third were in uniform. By 8:15 more SA men had arrived. Kommissar Altmann of the blue police, who was assigned to watch the meeting, became uneasy and, shortly after 8:00 went to the police station in the Dachauerstrasse and called the PDM to warn of the heavy concentration of uni-formed men and his suspicion that they had not gathered together merely to make a parade. The government might well be over-turned.[71]

The authorities took no apparent alarm at this report and the meeting went on uninterrupted, with more and more Kampf-bündler, now mostly Oberländer, arriving. At about 9:00 p.m., in-formed by the innocent-sounding telephone message, "Safely deliv-ered,"[72] Röhm announced the creation of the new government amid thunderous cheers from the audience, and then proposed a march on the Bürgerbräukeller. This suggestion, or command, was im-mediately put into action.

Reichskriegsflagge, led by the Ortsgruppe commander, Lieu-tenant Osswald, collected its arms at Korpshaus Palatia,[73] where Röhm had had them delivered on 6 November, and then marched on to the Wehrkreiskommando building, to which a portion of Röhm's force had been diverted by orders from the Bürgerbräukel-ler.[74] Alfred Zeller's Kampfbund München marched with Osswald.

The Third Battalion of SA Regiment München proceeded to St. Annaplatz, where they took from the basement of the monastery a cache of some 3,000 rifles, which had formerly belonged to the

---

[69] The other was the Wehrkreis headquarters, still generally known in München as the Kriegsministerium from its previous function. It now houses Abtg. II, BHSA.

[70] B, I, SA 1, 1490, pp. 3-4 1/2, 9-11, 46; II, MA103476, p. 1338.

[71] B, I, SA 1, 1490, pp. 1-2, 8; II, MA103476, p. 1215.

[72] "Glücklich entbunden!" B, I, SA 1, 1494, Simmerding, p. 241.

[73] House of a student corps (the German equivalent of a fraternity).

[74] Röhm said that these orders came from Ludendorff. Ludendorff, of course, later denied having issued any such orders.

Einwohnerwehr. The battalion then marched to Giessing and settled down by the Wittelsbacherbrücke, where they spent a quiet and comfortable Putsch. Only one platoon, which accompanied the battalion commander, Hans Knauth, on a currency raid,[75] took a more active part in the revolt.[76]

The First Battalion of Oberland, commanded by "Captain" Oestreicher,[77] marched from the Löwenbräukeller to the Bürgerbräukeller, where it arrived at approximately 10:45 p.m. The battalion then established its headquarters in the Hofbräuhauskeller—completing the rounds of the most famous beer halls in München—although the bulk of the men were retained at the Bürgerbräukeller during most of the night as a part of the Putschists' general reserve.[78]

The police, who had been observing the meeting in the Löwenbräukeller, meanwhile were reduced to taking a streetcar to the Police Directory to report.[79] As the Putschists marched off to the Wehrkreis headquarters, they passed the policemen, peering into the gloom for the lights of a tram. Mack Sennett could scarcely have created a more ludicrous situation, but the policemen had no other transportation available.

In these first hours of the Putsch, the rebels also made inept and feeble attempts at securing for themselves the key installations of the city: military and police barracks, government buildings, transportation centers, communication centers, and the press. Some of these ventures were successful, others were dismal failures. All were characterized by the reluctance of everyone concerned to initiate a bloody struggle.

The most successful move was the seizure of the Wehrkreis headquarters by Putschists under the leadership of Röhm. Flushed with the enthusiasm generated by the coming of the long-awaited revolt, and by the wild enthusiasm of the crowds that had cheered his column as it marched from the Stiglmaierplatz through the Briennerstrasse to the Wehrkreis building, at approximately 10:00

---

[75] See below.

[76] B, I, SA 1, 1490, pp. 1-2, 53-54; 1491, pp. 25-26; II, MA103476, pp. 1198-1201; IV, OPA 73930, Urteil; Röhm, *Geschichte*, pp. 233-35.

[77] See p. 96 above for comment on Oestreicher.

[78] B, I, SA 1, 1490, pp. 49-55.

[79] A number of the policemen released from the BBK also reached their posts by the unromantic "electric"—as the Münchner called their trolley system.

p.m. he demanded entry into the building where he had worked for so many years. The sentries threatened to shoot and were only persuaded to surrender with difficulty, although they were badly outnumbered. The duty officer declared that he yielded to superior force, but remained at his post at Röhm's request, with the understanding that he would attempt to reach General von Lossow and to answer the questions of troop units.[80]

Shortly after the seizure of the headquarters, Major Schwandner of the artillery commander's general staff arrived, after hearing rumors of the Putsch. Schwandner, who, according to Röhm, was hostile to the Putschists and sought to spy upon them,[81] draws a vivid picture of the situation he found:

I . . . hurried immediately to the Wehrkreis headquarters in order to orient myself and to inform General von Kress. The Wehrkreis headquarters had [as reported] in fact been seized by Röhm's SA [sic].

First I sought out the duty officer, then Captain Daser, and asked him what was happening. Captain Daser could only tell me that the affair was extremely unclear and fishy. Hitler and Ludendorff were in General von Lossow's office and were waiting there for General von Lossow and Police Colonel von Seisser, who were expected at any moment.

While we spoke, Captain Röhm stormed into [the room] in full uniform of the old army with all [his] medals and asked for General von Lossow. I immediately told Röhm that this Putsch was in clear violation of yesterday's understanding with von Lossow.[82] Röhm replied in a voice vibrant with sincerity that everything was all right. Von Lossow, Kahr, and von Seisser had all declared themselves in accord with everything and would now come to Hitler in the Wehrkreis headquarters. I said only that that was something different. Röhm then left the room to return to Hitler. . . .

. . . As I returned to Captain Daser (Duty Officer), who had the telephone constantly at his ear, he signalled to me and said

---

[80] One of the Putschists later claimed that the Reichswehr personnel welcomed Röhm and his men with open arms, but all other sources, including Röhm, disagree. B, II, MA103476, p. 1256. See also B, IV, BuR, Bd. 34, Item 145; Röhm, *Geschichte*, pp. 234-36.

[81] NA, EAP 105/7, v, p. 005996.

[82] Actually, he was apparently referring to the meetings of 6 November, although he may have meant Lossow's Reichswehr conference of the seventh.

softly, the affair is crooked. Von Lossow is with Kahr and Seisser, General von Kress and von Ruith in the Infantry Kaserne and will definitely not come here. Shortly thereafter, Daser received from the chief of staff of General von Lossow, Colonel Freiherr von Berchem, from the Infantry Kaserne, orders to bring the nearest Reichswehr battalions in Augsburg, Kempten, Ingolstadt, Amberg, Regensburg, and Landshut to München by rail with the aid of the transport officer. I then arranged with Captain Aschenbrenner [Transport] which battalions he would call and which I [would call] by telephone. We could do this undisturbed since Röhm had failed to take over the telephone switchboard of the Wehrkreis headquarters.[83]

However, this phase of the occupation of the Wehrkreiskommando soon ended, for when Major Karl von Loeffelholz, an old personal friend but political opponent of Röhm's, arrived sometime in the early morning to see what was happening, Röhm told him that he was under arrest and sent him to his office. Loeffelholz then changed into civilian clothes and walked out of the building unchallenged to report to General von Lossow at the Infanteriekaserne where he spent the next few days.[84] Too, telephone service was soon monitored and limited to Putschist traffic. This measure was adopted too late—around 11:30 p.m.—to be fully effective, but indicates Putschist distrust of the army.[85]

An hour or so after securing the Wehrkreiskommando, Röhm attempted to duplicate his exploit at the Stadtkommandantur, which was located in the Army Museum in the Residenz Gardens. Accompanied by his faithful aide, Captain Seydel, and a troop of men, he demanded entrance. The gates were, however, locked. Captain Renz, who was in charge in the absence of his superiors, refused him admittance and warned that he had set up a machine gun (requisitioned from First Battalion, Nineteenth Infantry Regiment) behind the gate and that he would fire if Röhm attempted an assault. Röhm left discomfited.[86]

The Putschists had, in general, no better luck at the various barracks complexes than they had at the Stadtkommandantur. At the

[83] GP, A, General Max Schwandner, 23.1.1960. "Aschenbrenner" is apparently properly "Aschenbrandt." See *Rangliste 1923*.

[84] GP, A, Freiin von Loeffelholz, 21.11.1965; B, Archivdirektor a. D. Gerhard Böhm.

[85] B, I, SA 1, 1493, pp. 23-28, 48-49.

[86] GP, A, Frau Lisa Renz, 2.2.1960; Röhm, *Geschichte*, pp. 235-36.

barracks of the First Battalion of the Nineteenth Infantry Regiment, Senior Cadet Gerhard Böhm was training members of the Hermannsbund when Kampfbund units began to arrive in considerable numbers with various excuses to explain their presence. The first of these was a battalion of Oberländer under the leadership of Captain (Ret.) Hans Oemler, which was soon followed by the First Battalion of SA Regiment München under Lieutenant (Ret.) Karl Beggel.[87] Apparently neither Putschist unit had been effectively alarmed, and Beggel claims that his battalion, which should have been some 600 men strong, had only about 60 men on hand initially, although it built up strength during the course of the night.[88] Böhm confirms the gradual build-up of the Putschist groups during the evening, until they numbered some 250 men by 8:00 p.m., a force formidable enough to give the Oberfähnrich cause for alarm, but no more than a fifth of the theoretical strength of the two Putschist units involved. Despite steady later accretions they must have been woefully understrength throughout the Putsch.

Böhm, puzzled and uneasy about so many unannounced "guests," sought to contact his superiors and succeeded in reaching several, including the commander of the first company, Captain Eduard Dietl, and the acting regimental commander, Lieutenant Colonel von Wenz. However, before these officers arrived, at about 8:30 p.m., two trucks full of weapons arrived in front of the Kaserne and the Putschists attempted to arm themselves. Böhm prevented the issue of arms by threat of force and was holding the Putschists in check when Dietl arrived. Dietl, who handled most of the training of National Socialists for the First Battalion, was very close to them and had, indeed, been in conference with Hitler that very afternoon.[89] He therefore soon reached an understanding with Beggel and was preparing to cooperate with the Putschists when von Wenz arrived. The latter immediately took charge and gave Dietl orders to supervise the return of weapons to the trucks, the driving of the trucks into the Kaserne, and the expulsion of the National Socialists and Oberländer. Dietl, obviously unhappy,

---

[87] Beggel was a former career NCO of the Second Company of the Nineteenth Infantry Regiment, who had, in accordance with a new practice, been given a lieutenant's commission on retirement. B, I, SA 1, 1493, pp. 1-4; GP, D, 1 (Personalities).

[88] B, I, SA 1, 1493, Beggel.

[89] Hanfstaengl reports that he could not get in to see Hitler because Dietl was with him. Hanfstängl, *Hitler*, p. 95.

clicked his heels and replied: "Zu Befehl, Herr Oberstleutnant!" and presided over the destruction of the Putschists' hopes regarding the Nineteenth Infantry Regiment's Kaserne. Empty-handed and, in the words of one of their leaders, "confused,"[90] the Putschists left for the Bürgerbräukeller, having failed to occupy what was to be the headquarters of the opposition to them or to obtain arms.[91]

The rebels were also frustrated at the Engineer Kaserne. Here, too, Kampfbund units were ordered to assemble, apparently without realizing that a Putsch was in the offing. A contingent of SA men from Eduard Heines' Third Battalion of SA Regiment München were to take physical examinations that night to determine their fitness for possible absorption into the Reichswehr should the limited expansion plans with which Lossow and the government were toying be implemented. Captain (Ret.) Max Ritter von Müller's Second Battalion of Oberland had been ordered to meet at the Pionierkaserne for a night exercise.[92]

Captain Oskar Cantzler, the commander of the first company of the Seventh Engineer Battalion, found himself in much the same situation as Oberfähnrich Böhm and reacted in much the same manner. That afternoon Cantzler had, in inspecting his installation, found several members of Oberland who were loading live ammunition into machine gun belts without his permission. Cantzler stopped this activity and became a bit suspicious of the Verband. He did not, however, revoke his permission to Captain von Müller for a night problem on the Oberwiesenfeld in return for a promise that there would be no foolishness regarding the weapons for which Cantzler was responsible.

However, on second thought, when the Oberländer arrived for training at 8:00 p.m. Cantzler informed Ritter von Müller that, in view of this violation of confidence, he could not allow weapons to be taken out of the compound. The Oberländer could either leave immediately without weapons or, as usual, drill under Cantzler's supervision in the field house with weapons. Müller, always an excitable man, insisted heatedly that all he wanted the weapons for was to train his unit, and the argument waxed hot as the two offi-

---

[90] "Ratlos." B, I, SA 1, 1493, Oemler.

[91] B, I, SA 1, 1490, p. 52; 1493, Beggel, Böhm, Oemler; IV, HSIV, EE7, Böhm *Bemerkungen*, between pp. 46-47; NA, EAP 105/7a, Official Reichswehr Bericht vom Putsch; GP, B, Archivdirektor a. D. Gerhard Böhm.

[92] B, I, SA 1, 1493, pp. 168ff (Heines), 349ff (Humbs); II, MA103476, pp. 1020, 1056, 1280-82.

cers fought it out in the midst of Müller's battalion, which stood, fully equipped for active service, in the barracks square. Finally, Müller, feigning acceptance of defeat, agreed to training in the field house. He wanted the arms to be issued in the yard. Cantzler refused, insisting that the battalion enter the field house and doff its field equipment before rifles were issued. After further bitter debate, Müller gave in and the training began.

Cantzler meanwhile left the field house and found a group of Oberländer trying to break into the armory. He confronted Müller with this incident and demanded that he and his unit leave the compound. In reply, Müller drew up his companies and announced the creation of the new government. Under these circumstances Captain Cantzler would certainly issue arms to his men. Cantzler replied that he would give out the arms only if he knew precisely what was going on and if he had orders from his superiors to do so. Müller then threatened to seize the arms, and ordered his men to arrest Cantzler and his seven enlisted men. The result was a quick scuffle at the door which ended with the ludicrously outnumbered regular soldiers holding the closed doors against Müller's 400 men. Cantzler's determination to have them within doors had paid off.

In the end, Müller agreed to guarantee that none of his men would leave the field house while he and Cantzler conferred. They then went to the orderly room to telephone the Wehrkreiskommando. Captain Daser, however, was noncommittal and Cantzler could reach no one at other headquarters. He therefore refused to give out weapons, while secretly ordering the alarming of his company and the placing of two machine guns covering the door of the field house and the barracks square. A runner was sent to find the battalion commander, Major Kuprion.

Hitler and Dr. Weber had meanwhile been turned back from the gate, and the arrival of a Putschist Major, who sought, by appeal or threat, to move Cantzler left the situation unaltered. Müller now agreed to give up and drill his men. Cantzler therefore issued 80 unloaded rifles and began the drill, to gain time for his company to assemble and for the enthusiasm of the Putschists to ebb.

At approximately 10:00 p.m. Major Kuprion arrived and took over. The battalion's non-commissioned officers, who had been invited to the Löwenbräukeller by Rossbach and Lieutenant (Ret.) Heines, also returned about this time, on learning of the outbreak of the Putsch.

Then General (Ret.) Adolf Aechter arrived from the Bürgerbräukeller with a signed note from Lossow, obtained before the latter left the beer hall, ordering the engineers to abandon their state of alarm measures. Aechter also demanded that the Oberländer be issued arms. Once again, as in the case of the telephone control at the Wehrkreiskommando, the Putschists were too late. Kuprion had meanwhile been ordered over the telephone to accept only oral orders and these from General von Danner, the city commandant. After further telephoning, Müller and his troops left the Kaserne without arms and Aechter, enraged, went off to find Lossow and straighten out the misunderstanding. The Kaserne remained in the hands of the Reichswehr, while Müller, alerted to another source of supply, marched to the Annakloster, where his unit picked up weapons. He then marched his men, not to their original goal, the telephone and telegraph building and the railway station, but to the Bürgerbräukeller, which they reached about 2:00 a.m.[93]

No serious attempt was made by the Putschists to take over the other München barracks, but the transportation and artillery units took precautions against attack. The students receiving military training in the Artillery Barracks left as docilely when the alarm was sounded as had those in the I./19 and the barracks were sealed off.[94]

The story at the Infantry School was quite different. The students at the school, both officers and cadets, were mostly recent arrivals to München and intoxicated by the atmosphere of nationalism and rebellion there. Both Classes I and II entered the school on 21 September 1923. The Engineer School students entered even later, on 1 October.[95] The officers were so-called "war officers," who had not received the normal officer candidate training, but were products of greatly speeded up training programs. These men were sent to shortened remedial courses after the war, until all of them had had Waffenschule training. The cadets were divided into two classes, entering cadets taking a general basic course and advanced infantry cadets taking a specialized branch of service

[93] B, I, SA 1, 1493, pp. 73-74 (Schreck), p .350 (Humbs), (Oemler); II, MA103476, pp. 1281-82, 1406; NA, EAP 105/7, II, p. 33; 105/7a, Cantzler Bericht, 19.11.1923; GP, A, General Max Ibel, 30.6.1962; General Wilhelm Ullersperger, 16.8.1962.

[94] GP, A, General Friedrich Sixt, Aug. 1960; General Gottfried Riemhofer, 9.12.1963.

[95] Heeresverordnungsblatt 1923, 15.8.1923, p. 394; GP, B, Anon. Waffenschüler of I. Lehrgang which graduated in early fall 1923.

course. The loyalty and attitude towards discipline of these young men had been shaken in the months leading up to the Putsch not merely by the generally fevered atmosphere in München, but also by the bitter quarrel between Seeckt and Lossow which was the military aspect of the feud between the federal and the state governments. Seeckt was sufficiently worried about the situation (and sufficiently annoyed at Bavaria) that he recommended in the middle of October that the school be dissolved, and gave orders to that effect. These orders were rescinded, as a result of the opposition of Chancellor Stresemann, and the cadets remained in München, with unfortunate results.[96]

Two unscrupulous plotters recognized the vulnerability of the Infantry School to subversion and its potential as a power factor and decided to exploit the situation. Both were flamboyant, aggressive individuals motivated by hatred of the Republic, uncontainable personal energies, and a ravening ambition. Both were popular heroes among nationalist German youths of all shades. Neither had a political or paramilitary power base in Bavaria to enable him to play a serious role in the coming Putsch. Here was a heaven-sent opportunity to seize a ready-made base, which offered the chance not merely for immediate power but for widespread future influence. Forming an alliance, they seized time by the forelock in late October and early November.

Gerhard Rossbach, handsome and with a reputation for personal daring and bold initiative, had come to München to fish in troubled waters on being released from federal imprisonment (on political charges) for lack of evidence. Arrived, he discovered to his consternation that his chief Bavarian deputy, Heines, had gone over to Hitler, lock, stock and Rossbach-Organization, leaving Rossbach only the empty and dubious honor of having an SA battalion named after him. Rossbach's organization in the Reich, a cadre always ready for trouble, remained intact but needed time and a favorable opportunity for fleshing out. More important, it was of no value to him in Bavaria. He therefore turned to Ludendorff, who was the "Grey Eminence" of the Kampfbund, but was apparently beginning to feel the lack of that tight-knit order of supporters[97] which had added so much weight to the opinions of the

[96] Seeckt Papers, Stück 281, Lieber Notes, p. 29; NA, T120, 1749, pp. 281-82; T79, 56, pp. 619, 1113.
[97] The French Capuchins.

original Grey Eminence. Closely associated with Rossbach and Ludendorff in this scheme was Ludendorff's stepson, Heinz Pernet.

Rossbach undertook the active task of winning officer students, the natural leaders of the cadets, to the idea of a Putsch, while Ludendorff assumed the role of patron to give this conspiratorial group a feeling of respectability and of continuity with the revered past. He performed this function partly through Pernet and Rossbach but also by a personal "laying on of hands" at his house on the evening of 4 November 1923. Ludendorff later remembered this event as a cozy fireside chat where he said nothing that wasn't innocent and redolent of violets. One of his audience, however, presents the general as inveighing against the "black menace" of Catholicism, and against Bavarian separatism and hatred of Prussia, and saying that he found himself in conflict with these forces. Ludendorff also directly attacked Seeckt's emphasis on the elimination of party politics from the army by claiming that the old Prussian army was essentially political, since everyone in it was trained to be a monarchist. He touted the "racist" idea as a force destined to weld together the future army.[98]

Rossbach organized the chief conspirators and they, in turn, won over key individuals among the younger cadets. He also met a number of the cadets and student officers himself by frequenting the beer halls and student clubs where they were to be found. By the day of the Putsch he apparently had some twenty officers (almost all students) and eighty cadets clearly lined up. One of these was an instructor, Major Fischach, an outspoken Hitler adherent. One of the senior pro-Kampfbund officers of the school, Colonel Leupold, seems however to have remained outside the circle and may not even have been approached. The Putschists tended to be suspicious of older men in responsible positions.[99]

The commandant of the school, General Tieschowitz von Tieschowa, seems to have heard vague rumors of Rossbach's activities, but he was not the man to counter them effectively even had he not been distracted by the Seeckt-Lossow controversy. Tiescho-

[98] B, II, MA103476, pp. 1186-93; MA104221, Denkschrift, ca. 13.11.1923; Ludendorff, *Feldherrnhalle*, pp. 57, 62-63, 137-39; GP, A, General Walther Leuze, 11.4.1960; General Martin Dehmel, 10.6.1960; Rabenau, *Seeckt*, p. 378.

[99] B, II, MA103476, pp. 1187-91; Bronnen, Arnolt, *Rossbach*, Berlin, 1930, pp. 141-44 (hereafter cited as Bronnen, *Rossbach*); Rossbach, Gerhard, *Mein Weg durch die Zeit*, Weilburg/Lahn, 1950, pp. 80-81 (hereafter cited as Rossbach, *Weg*).

witz was a mild man who had never held a combat command and avoided unpleasantness assiduously. A good staff officer in posts calling for intelligence and dependability rather than a cool head and good nerves, he was lost in a crisis and was not the sort of personality who could rally young men around him by the strength of his character or cow them by his authority. The students simply ignored him and followed their pied piper.[100]

The result was that, when Rossbach arrived at the Infantry School at about 8:00 p.m. on the evening of the Putsch with a handful of SA men borrowed from Heines, everything went off like clockwork. The student officers and cadets already committed to the conspirators had been assured that the Seventh Division, General Müller's Fourth Division, the Landespolizei, and most of the northern Reichswehr were on their side. They now took over with the gusto of students organizing a prank directed against their teachers. They turned out the rest of the students and assigned officer students to command the student companies. They distributed swastika flags, which had been thoughtfully supplied (along with armbands) by Rossbach. Most of the school officers were at their homes in the city, but those who were present were placed under loose arrest when they refused, as almost all of them did, to join the venture.[101]

General von Tieschowitz' own account of his arrest helps to explain why this scheme succeeded where similar attempts on the barracks in the city had failed:

"At 8:30 p.m. on 8 November a delegation of about four armed officer students, with helmets, appeared before me. Their leader, Lieutenant Block, reported to me in military form approximately as follows: A national Reichsregierung has been formed, Ludendorff [is] military supreme commander etc. Lossow Reichswehrminister etc. The I[nfantry] S[chool] is forming up to join General Ludendorff as Storm Battalion Ludendorff under First Lieutenant Rossbach. He asked the Herr General for his reaction

---

[100] B, II, MA103476, p. 1187; IV, HSIV, EE7, Endres MS, p. 40; Bronnen, *Rossbach*, pp. 141-42.

[101] B, I, SA 1, 1493, pp. 168-69; II, MA103476, pp. 1262-68; Bronnen, *Rossbach*, pp. 158-61; GP, E (Akten) Leuze Bericht vom 11.11.1923; A, General Martin Dehmel, 10.6.1960; Oberst Karl Herschel, 11.9.1956; General Walther Leuze, 11.4.1960; General Otto Ottenbacher, 1.5.1960; General Curt Osterroht, 22.3.1960; Gerhard Rossbach, 15.11.1951; General Günther von Uslar-Gleichen, 24.5.1960.

[but warned] further against any attempt to interfere. The I[n-fantry] S[chool] is occupied by Rossbach troops. I convinced myself that I was, at the moment, not in a position to undertake anything. Four armed officers stood before me who would have prevented any action. The same was true of the Rossbach troops in the corridors and courtyard. I therefore said that I was not at the time in a position to undertake anything, since I didn't have any force [at my disposal]. I myself would not join the undertaking but would remain true to my oath. I was then requested not to leave my room."[102]

The school then marched off enthusiastically towards the Bürgerbräukeller. All but a handful of cadets and student officers joined the Putschists. A few missed out on the excitement because they were attending dancing classes in the city, while several refused to go along, one of whom, at least, was briefly arrested by his classmates.[103] Some of the dancers later arrived at the beer hall, while others learned that the Seventh Division was not on the Putschist side and returned to their quarters quietly.[104] En route to the beer hall, an incident occurred which confirmed the students in their belief that the Reichswehr was supporting the Putsch. They saw, or thought they saw, General von Danner—in uniform—and General von Lossow in a passing automobile. Some reported that Kahr was with Lossow. All agreed that General von Danner waved them on approvingly. It is not quite clear whom they did meet, although there is reason to believe that it was General (Ret.) Aechter, who crossed their route at about this time in full uniform. It is quite clear that they did not meet Lossow, Kahr, or Danner. Lossow left the Bürgerbräukeller separately from Kahr and traveled by a route which would not lead him by the Waffenschüler. Danner was at the time in the Stadtkommandantur in civilian clothes. However, the illusion was as effective as a real encounter in confirming Rossbach's claims.[105]

---

[102] B, II, MA103476, p. 1258.   [103] Fähnrich Föst.

[104] GP, A, Oberst Richard Baur, 1.10.1956; Oberst Karl Herschel, 11.7.1956; Gerhard Rossbach, 15.2.1951; Oberst Fritz Teichmann, 17.3.1969; E (Akten), Leuze Bericht, 11.11.1923.

[105] I stress the actual events here partly because of their impact on the Infanterieschüler and partly because Hofmann (*Hitlerputsch*, p. 171) accepts the Putschist account as true, although even Deputy Dr. Hoegner, the most suspicious member of the Landtag investigating committee ad-

The Putschists naturally also sought to gain control of the most important government buildings, particularly the Police Presidency in the Ettstrasse and the headquarters of the Generalstaatskommissar, which was in the building which also housed the Regierung Oberbayern in the Maximilianstrasse. With these installations in hand, they could have made the organization of opposition much more difficult, especially in the early hours of the Putsch. Here, as in the case of the military installations, speed was crucial and here, too, a combination of ineptitude and reluctance to initiate a clash resulted in disastrous delay.

In the case of the Police Presidium the Putschists planned a double-pronged attack. They would seize control of the presidium from within and from without. Dr. Wilhelm Frick, a branch chief who had been shifted from control of the political police because of his close affiliation with the NSDAP, and Ernst Pöhner, who was to be the Putschist minister-president of Bavaria, were to be the key "inside" men, while Oberland was assigned the task of surrounding the building and providing them with reliable armed forces.

Frick played his role to perfection. When the Putsch broke, he was the only senior official immediately available and he used his influence to prevent the Landespolizei duty officer from launching an immediate counterattack against the Putschists with the company at his disposal in the old Schwere Reiter Kaserne. Frick or Police Secretary Rau also drove away Minister-Director Zetlmeier, the Ministry of the Interior's police specialist, by warning him that he was on the Putschists' automatic arrest list. When worried police officers contacted Frick, he soothed them and urged them to do nothing. At the same time he played as safe as possible by pretending to be surprised by the Putsch and by his appointment as police president, although he knew the plans well before the event and

mitted as early as 1927 that the allegation had been proven to be baseless. Testimony of participants on both sides proves the fact that Danner was hostile to the Putsch from the outset and was not present at the point of alleged contact, as well as the fact that he was in civilian clothes. Numerous sources also make it clear that Lossow and Kahr left the BBK separately and did not meet again until much later that night. Lossow did not take a route which would lead him near the Schüler on leaving the BBK. Lossow reported in detail on this question on 9.1.1924. See NA, EAP 105/7a, Bayr. WKK vii, Haupt. Nr. 1459 Geh./iia Nr. 11 pers.; B, ii, MA103476, pp. 1190ff.

had been warned by telephone[106] that it had gone off on schedule.[107]

After the release of the Bürgerbräukeller audience, Pöhner and Colonel Banzer arrived at the Police Directory. Pöhner addressed himself immediately to the problem of propaganda for the press, while Banzer was primarily interested in relieving himself of the company of First Lieutenant Gerhard von Prosch, a Landespolizei officer who had joined the Putschists and had been appointed as Banzer's "guardian angel."[108] Pöhner, after accepting Banzer's allegedly hearty congratulations and assurances of cooperation, ordered Prosch to depart, leaving Major Sigmund Freiherr von Imhoff, Banzer's chief of staff,[109] who had been teaching a class for general staff aspirants and therefore was early on the scene, as the colonel's advisor and guardian. This, too, was at least potentially a crucial decision, since it removed a Putschist check on Banzer and left him in the company of Imhoff, an officer of the old school, who even though he was reportedly personally antisemitic, was no friend of the National Socialists.[110]

Frick and Pöhner then left to consult with Kahr about the question of informing the provincial authorities of the new situation and giving them orders. Arriving at the Generalstaatskommissariat, they had to wait three quarters of an hour for Kahr, who, in apology, explained that he had been talking with Minister Dr. Matt. When they told Kahr of their mission, he informed them that he had already composed a telegram informing all local authorities that he had taken over full control of Bavaria as regent. Pöhner

---

[106] B, I, M. Inn. 73694, Zetlmeier Bericht, 11.1.1924; II, MA103476, pp. 1131, 1225-26.

[107] B, I, M. Inn. 73694, Zetlmeier Bericht, 11.1.1924; SA 1, 1490, pp. 6-8, 12, 15; II, MA103476, pp. 1226-27; NA, EAP 105/7a, Lapo in Putsch, Anlage 4b, Reichswehr Official Bericht.

[108] Apparently the plan of supervising Banzer's activities was adopted as an interim solution to the problem of handling him. Originally he had been on the "automatic arrest" list and Major Hühnlein had already been designated his successor. See above and B, II, MA103476, p. 1205.

[109] Not to be confused with Captain Hugo Freiherr von Imhoff of the Straubing Lapo.

[110] B, I, GSK 90, p. 479; II, MA99522, 14.2.1924, p. 9; MA103476, p. 1218; MA104221, Imhoff Bericht, 13.11.1923; IV, OPA 73930, Abschrift of Imhoff Aussage and von Prosch Bemerkungen vom 4.3.1924; Urteil von Volksgericht, 16.4.1924; NA, EAP 105/7, II, pp. 103-13; GP, A, General von Kiliani, 18.9.1960; B, Lieutenant Colonel Oskar Erhard and Colonel Ernst Schultes.

asked Kahr if he might make use of this telegram in his forthcoming press conference, and Kahr assented. When Frick suggested that they issue propaganda, Kahr pointed out that Hitler had reserved this function to himself. Pöhner and Frick then returned to the Police Directory.[111]

Although the attempt to take over the Police Directory from the inside was initially successful, the other prong of the attack failed. An Oberland unit that sought to replace the Landespolizei cordon around the building was politely but firmly persuaded to give up the project around midnight. Thus, in fact, Banzer, the "outside man," not Pöhner, held the real power in the Police Directory, and his hand had not yet been played.[112]

The major confrontation of the evening was, however, the one at the Generalstaatskommissariat. This was the official center of political power under the state of emergency and therefore its possession seemed crucial to the Putschists and, for a time, to their opponents, although they were later prepared to write it off after realizing that the important thing was to have an impregnable base, rather than an officially recognized one. The Putschists tried hard to occupy the building in the early hours of the Putsch, but ignored it later, when it was abandoned by their foes.

The first attempt to seize the Generalstaatskommissariat was, like the parallel action at the Wehrkreiskommando, tastefully disguised. This time the Kampfbund troops were to form an "honor guard" for Kahr. At about 11:00 p.m. the Second Company of the First (Assault) Battalion of Oberland was ordered by Oestreicher to proceed to the Maximilianstrasse and relieve the Landespolizei on duty there. When Lieutenant (Ret.) Weber arrived with his men, he found that Lieutenant Colonel Wilhelm Muxel had received no orders to accept relief and did not intend to do so. Weber, believing that there had been a delay in the transmission of orders, moved down the street and waited while a messenger reported the situation to his superiors in the Bürgerbräukeller. When the messenger returned, he brought orders for Weber to return to the beer hall.[113]

In recalling Weber, the Putschist leaders had not given up their project. They had decided to bring up their big guns. General

[111] NA, EAP 105/7, II, pp. 103-07.

[112] NA, EAP 105/7a, Reichswehr Official Bericht, Anlage 4b.

[113] B, I, SA 1, 1490, pp. 49; 1493, p. 57; II, MA104221, Hptm. Wild Bericht.

Ludendorff ordered Lieutenant Rossbach to take the Infantry School companies and march on the Generalstaatskommissariat. Although, in theory, the move was a friendly one, Rossbach apparently had orders to take the building by storm if necessary. They even brought a loaded field piece with them, scarcely a sign of peaceful intentions.[114]

The Infantry School units arrived at the Generalstaatskommissariat shortly after midnight. Captain Wild of the Landespolizei, the officer directly in command of the guard on the building, asked Seisser, who was leaving the building as the Putschists arrived, if the building should be held at all costs even after his departure. Major Doehla replied in the affirmative. Meanwhile, Rossbach had drawn up his men, ordered them to fix bayonets and to attack its east facade. The cadets pressed forward slowly across the square until, in places, they were face to face with and even jostling against the members of the Landespolizei cordon surrounding it. Lieutenant Hans Block of the Infantry School and Lieutenant Mahler of the Engineer School, obviously a trifle uneasy about their predicament, asked Lieutenant Colonel Muxel of the police to tell them what the situation was. Muxel, the father of a close friend of Mahler, spoke soothingly, but indicated that Lossow, Seisser, and Kahr were opposed to Ludendorff and Hitler.

Rossbach, meanwhile, had disappeared just as the danger of serious conflict increased, which was held against him later by the no longer so enthusiastic Infantry School students. In fact, he was parleying with Muxel and Wild, attempting to persuade them to yield in the face of superior force. While the conference was going on, a Putschist messenger was sent to the Bürgerbräukeller to report and bring further orders, and Captain Wild called for Landespolizei reserves from the Türkenkaserne. A portion of a company arrived a few moments later under command of Captain Schweinle.

Then came a second order from Ludendorff that the building be taken at all costs and the situation looked really ugly. Cadets and policemen faced each other with loaded, bayoneted rifles at point-blank range all across the street, but it is clear that neither the police nor the cadets really wished to start a bloodbath. The negotiations continued, with each side holding firm orally but taking no physical action. Suddenly, Rossbach reappeared in front of the main body of cadets and shouted: " 'What? Still negotiating here?

[114] B, ii, MA103476, pp. 1270-72, 1363.

You know General Ludendorff's orders. Why the hesitation? Order your men to fire.' "[115]

The Putschist officers moved off to their units, commands were shouted and skirmishers advanced in a semicircular line accompanied by machine guns. Now Muxel invited three of the Putschists into the building. The others halted, but warned that if their delegation did not appear within ten minutes they would attack in earnest. The Putschists edged forward again. The outnumbered policemen held fast.

Then, suddenly and, for the police, inexplicably, the command "Companies withdraw!" rang out across the square, and the Infantry School units disappeared as suddenly as they had appeared. An order, allegedly from Ludendorff, but actually from Dr. Weber of Oberland, had called them off. The Putschists had, although they did not realize it, lost a bloodless Battle of Gettysburg.[116]

The rebels' plans to seize the communication and transportation centers of München had gone awry, too. The fiasco at the Engineer Kaserne cost them dearly. Captain Max von Müller's Second Battalion had been assigned this mission. He was to control communications traffic, to prevent incidents and to keep Jews from fleeing the city. Dr. Weber later claimed that Müller was supposed subsequently to turn over these installations to the Landespolizei, but this is pretty clearly untrue in view of the obvious disappointment of the Putschists when they found that the Landespolizei *was* in control of just these installations. Moving into the vacuum left by Müller's absence, the Landespolizei had, on orders from the Generalstaatskommissariat, occupied these points before midnight, while the Putschists did not try again until after 1:00 a.m., too late to succeed without a battle. Ironically, the government's success here was to some extent double-edged. Kahr ordered that no telephone or telegram traffic be allowed with points outside München except messages of the Reichswehr city commandant or Landespolizei München. He himself then attempted to send messages out through other channels, which were delayed by his own men for hours. Once again he was the man with ten thumbs.[117]

[115] B, II, MA104221, Wild Bericht.

[116] B, I, SA 1, 1493, R. Kolb, p. 143; II, MA103476, pp. 1271-73; MA104221, Wild Bericht; NA, EAP 105/7, II, p. 34; EAP 105/7a, Reichswehr Official Bericht, Anlage 4b; GP, B, Lieutenant Colonel Otto Muxel.

[117] B, I, B. Inn. 73696, Bomhard an GSK, 9.11.1923; GSK 43, pp. 177-82; Kahr MS, p. 1363; II, MA103476, pp. 1294, 1406; MA104221, Wild

Besides arranging for military seizure of the city by physical means, the Putschists also prepared for its conquest by means of propaganda. Hitler was scarcely a man to neglect this aspect of the problem. In this sphere, as in the military, the rebels planned both active and passive measures and were prepared to utilize or replace existing organizations or facilities according to the dictates of the moment. Captain Weiss, the press chief of the Kampfbund, believed that one of the chief reasons for the collapse of the Kapp Putsch had been the failure of the Putschists to arrange for a newspaper to provide propaganda and news and thus counter hostile rumors. He therefore laid plans for the seizure by armed bands of all München newspapers together with their technical and office staffs. Meanwhile the National Socialist organ, the *Völkischer Beobachter* would print an "Extra" to fill the vacuum left by the absence of the other papers.

As late as the evening of 8 November, according to the testimony of a Putschist telephone monitor and the editor of the *Bayrischer Kurier*, the Kampfbund still intended to put this plan into effect. Subsequently they modified their scheme, very probably as a result of conversations between Pöhner and various editors at the Bürgerbräukeller. In the end, only the arch-foe of the National Socialists, the Majority Socialist *Münchener Post* was to be silenced, while the other papers would carry articles approved by the "new government."[118] Almost immediately after the release of the audience at the Bürgerbräukeller, the Stosstrupp Hitler marched to the *Münchener Post* with specific orders from Göring to smash the presses and lay waste to the offices. This they proceeded to do until interrupted by policemen sent by Hitler as a result of reports arriving from the newspaper and of protests from the Police Directory. It is probable that Hitler was quite sincere in his irritation at the senseless destruction, since the plan had been to turn over the entire plant to Captain Weiss for his *Heimatland*. However, before the orders to cease and desist arrived much damage had been done.[119] Even after the destruction was ended, the

---

Bericht; NA, EAP 105/7, ii, pp. 32-34; EAP 105/7a, Reichswehr Official Bericht, Anlage 4b.

[118] B, i, SA 1, 1493, p. 27; ii, MA103476, pp. 1160-62, 1228-29; NA, EAP 105/7, ii, pp. 98-103.

[119] Divided counsels seem to have prevailed here, resulting in wanton destruction which was embarrassing after the collapse of the Putsch, al-

Stosstrupp did not leave until a column of Landespolizei appeared.[120]

Meanwhile, after his return from Kahr, Pöhner held a press conference in the Police Directory, which was attended by the editors of the important non-Marxist papers of München. Here Pöhner established the "line" that he wanted the newspapers to take. They were to publish the events in the Bürgerbräukeller and the establishment of the new government in a favorable light.[121] The Putschists did not limit themselves to feeding their line to the regular press. They also set up their own propaganda headquarters in the confiscated offices of the *Bayrische Siedlungs- und Landbank* in the Kanalstrasse, where Amann, Gottfried Feder, Philipp Bouhler, Anton Drexler, Helmut Klotz, Albert Stier, Julius Streicher, and other important National Socialist propagandists foregathered.[122] Here they prepared placards and decrees for promulgation to the public, as well as announcements of public meetings to be held on the following day. The *Völkischer Beobachter* staff, headed by Alfred Rosenberg, also worked full draft that night, preparing an extra edition.[123]

In the fields of finance and supply, the Putschists were less prepared, less interested, and less effective. Their only serious financial measures consisted of plans to freeze all private economic transactions (undoubtedly with an eye to selective confiscation), of vague schemes for selling München's art treasures to pay for the costs of the invasion of the north, and, on a practical and immediate level, the confiscation of large quantities of paper money from the firms that printed it. Where supplies were concerned, they seem to have had no plans on any broad basis. Even arrangements for food, drink, and shelter during the Putsch itself were extremely impromptu. Individual units simply ordered meals for themselves at various restaurants or beer halls. Units were assigned to sleep in barracks or public buildings, and, most important of all, free beer was served to the Putschists, at the Bürgerbräukeller. A com-

---

though it may well have given the National Socialists some secret satisfaction since it was the only real blow struck against their Marxist foes.

[120] B, I, SA 1, 1494, pp. 224-5, 234; II, MA103476, pp. 1216-17, 1232-34, 1338-40; NA, EAP 105/7, I, pp. 121-22; Kallenbach, *Mit Hitler*, pp. 26-27.

[121] B, II, MA103476, pp. 1230-31, 1458; NA, EAP 105/7, II, p. 107.

[122] B, I, SA 1, 1493, pp. 195-98; II, MA103476, pp. 1242-47, 1250-51.

[123] B, I, SA 1, 1493, pp. 195, 214-15.

bination of concentration on political questions, the experience of making do on a financial shoestring, and a general lack of interest in detailed work characterized the Putschist leaders, especially Hitler, and resulted in very spotty preparations for anything but the actual seizure of power. Thereafter, they expected to use the personnel and expertise of the servants of the state to solve all practical economic and administrative problems—ignoring the fact that it was on these very problems, and on the unwillingness of the bureaucrats to serve the rebels, that the Kapp Putsch had foundered.[124]

While ignoring such immediate bread-and-butter questions as supply sources, the Putschists gave considerable attention to the question of recruiting for the national army which Ludendorff was to lead to new and greater victories. Each of their Verbände arranged for recruiting stations, which were to open on the morning of 9 November, and they printed placards to post around München calling for able-bodied youths to sign up for their various organizations. In practice, nothing came of this planning, but it is significant as indicating the direction of the Putschists' ideas regarding foreign policy and the extent to which they allowed their desires to dictate to their brains. Despite admitting, as they did in calmer moments, that a war with France would be disastrous before Germany had set her house in order, neither Hitler nor Ludendorff could refrain from proclaiming and planning for the execution of the great crusade that would rid Germany of her foreign oppressors.[125]

III. *Midnight—The Putsch at High Tide*

Midnight found the city still in flux. The Putschists had some 2,500 trained men at hand and expected more by morning. Most of these men huddled uncomfortably in the corridors or the halls of the Bürgerbräukeller, trying to snatch a little sleep before they were turned out for action on the morrow. Others were out in the cold, damp wind that presaged rain to come, a threat which apparently explains their theft of bathing suits from the Reichswehr. Others were standing guard at the Bürgerbräukeller or the Wehrkreiskommando, marching towards the Infanterieschule, collecting arms

[124] B, I, SA 1, 1494, pp. 350ff; II, MA103476, pp. 1241-42, 1247-49; NA, EAP 105/7, I, p. 122.

[125] B, I, SA 1, 1493, p. 185; II, MA103476, pp. 1023, 1216, 1246; MA104221, Arnold Rechberg an Ludendorff, 28.10.1923.

at the Anna Cloister, or riding through the night towards München.[126]

Small Landespolizei units marched criss-cross about the city, giving Minister Oswald the impression they did not know what they were doing.[127] Other units guarded key buildings throughout the central city, but the bulk of the Landespolizei troops remained where they had been from the beginning, tucked away out of sight in the compounds of the Max II Kaserne and the Türkenkaserne.

The Reichswehr was hardly in evidence at all, except for guards by the barbed wire entanglements which had sprouted around the gates of their barracks compounds in the course of the early hours of the Putsch. Most of their buildings looked dark and deserted under the dull grey skies, but there was activity inside and couriers moved through the night on deserted roads in the countryside, while far away sleepy troops were loaded onto trains to spend their night lurching towards München.

The Putschist leaders were optimistic. Despite the difficulties at the Pionierkaserne and the Nineteenth Infantry Regiment, and the mysterious disappearance of Kahr, Lossow, and Seisser, they had no serious doubts about the stand of the Landespolizei and the Reichswehr. Ludendorff was enough of an old officer to believe that Lossow would never break his word to Ludendorff—despite the number of times Ludendorff himself had broken or badly bent his own—while Hitler, too much a member of the century of the common man to put any faith in oaths or promises, was buoyed up by his belief in the nobility and infallibility of the instinctive political judgment of the "little man." As he said later at his trial, the senior officers might betray the Putschists, but he was convinced that "the enlisted men stood without exception on the side of Lossow and not of a suddenly surfacing colonel or brigadier general."[128]

There they sat, in Lossow's outer office, waiting for him to come and receive their orders, and as they sat they spun comfortable, fanciful pictures of further successes. A signal non-commissioned officer who passed through the room about midnight reported to his fellows that Röhm and Ludendorff were talking of bringing the Passau Reichswehr battalion to München to help garrison the city

---

[126] B, I, SA 1, 1493, p. 27.
[127] B, II, MA99521, 10.11.1923, p. 4.
[128] NA, EAP 105/7, I, p. 105.

so that the Kampfbund troops could be freed for their triumphant march into Saxony and Thuringia.[129] They seem to have been in the grip of that odd, mesmeric lethargy that so often grips revolutionaries after the first steps of their movement have succeeded. Relaxed and calm they sat quietly when they should have been moving to nail down their successes and reverse their failures. Meanwhile the Passau battalion and many others were preparing to roll towards München but on a far different mission than the Putschists had envisioned. The initiative had slipped from their fingers. The new day belonged to other men.

[129] B, I, SA 1, 1493, p. 28.

7. Party Headquarters of the NSDAP in 1923

12.

DAY OF DECISION

I. *Prelude*

While the basic initiative and the superiority in immediately available strength lay with the Putschists in the period before midnight of 8 November, their opponents had not been idle and their activity, in large part, led to the very rapid shifting of the scales to the disadvantage of the rebels. This activity, however, began only after Hitler had struck. Besides the general rumors of a right radical Putsch that had been endemic for months, there had been specific reports of a Putsch on the night of 8 November. Since these reports came, to some extent, from uninformed persons of the sort that newsmen refer to as "usually reliable sources" and that are known in the intelligence trade as "low-level sources," and since their own spies planted in the Kampfbund reported no Putsch in the offing, it is perhaps understandable that the police put little stock in such vague rumors. Then too, some of these reports never reached Bavarian official channels, and even today it is impossible to estimate the extent to which they reflect mere speculation as opposed to foreknowledge of the revolt.[1]

As for the rumors that flowed around München in the afternoon of 8 November, it is also very difficult to separate guesses from shrewd evaluation of the situation or leaks by the Putschists. It is possible that the Putschists themselves circulated vague rumors that Hitler and Kahr had reached an agreement in order to help prepare the city for coming events, just as they spread false statements purporting to stem from Lossow. Certainly rumors did fly thick and fast. Captain Hermann von Hanneken, a Prussian officer officially on furlough because he would not swear allegiance to Bavaria, was

---

[1] B, I, GSK 43, pp. 98, 180ff; SA 1, 1490, IV, p. 5; 1756, Häublein, Stadtrat Selb, 8601, 7.11.1923; IV, BuR, Bd. 36, Akt 1, Item 44; RV, 361, p. 12260; NA, T120, 5569, pp. K591579-80.

told in the early evening that Hitler would launch the Putsch that night and that Lossow, Seisser, and Kahr would support him. At the same time Hanneken was told that Generals von Kress, von Ruith, and von Danner were determined to put down any revolt that might develop.[2] At about 6:00 p.m. a Reichswehr officer warned Erhard Auer, a leader of the Social Democratic Party, to flee since a Putsch was now certain.[3] Even a street car conductor told a Putschist that Hitler and Kahr had reached an understanding.[4] Putsch rumors penetrated even into the Bürgerbräukeller.[5]

Whatever one may think of the provenance or reliability of these rumors, by 7:00 p.m. much more precise and definite information was flowing in to the police. Josef Gerum, a policeman in the Police Directory, spoke openly at work of being summoned by the party to the Torbräu that evening.[6] Somewhat later, at 5:45 p.m., a policeman reported a body of some 120 storm troopers marching outwards from the inner city. At 6:45 p.m., another policeman reported unusual activity at the National Socialist headquarters in the Corneliusstrasse. A few minutes later, Patrolman Josef Bömerl, who had already reported the statement of a bicyclist, "It comes tonight," to the Police Directory, himself saw Berchtold giving orders to Stosstrupp Hitler. Proceeding to the Corneliusstrasse Bömerl, being in civilian clothes, heard men talking openly of the Putsch. He then called in again but could not reach the Political Section and received a soothing answer from the Day Room official. Finally, Anton Altmann, the chief of the Eighth Criminal District, called the Day Room at about 8:00 p.m. and warned that something serious was in the wind. He had seen armed SA men who were overly enthusiastic for mere routine activities. Fifteen minutes later he reinforced this report with another call regarding the large numbers of National Socialists at the Löwenbräukeller.[7]

In the light of subsequent events, it is very easy to accuse the

[2] GP, A, General von Hanneken, Dec. 1959.

[3] Auer, who was often critical of others for not performing their civic duties, admitted that he did not warn the police, although he seems to have taken the tip sufficiently to heart that he went to ground, since the National Socialists were unable to locate him that night. He later said that he had assumed his informant to have told the authorities. B, I, SA 1, 1493, p. 192.

[4] B, I, SA 1, 1493, p. 33.

[5] *Ibid.*, 1490, II, p. 24; II, MA103476, p. 1224.

[6] B, II, MA103476, p. 1197.

[7] B, I, SA 1, 1490, p. 8; III, p. 5; II, MA103476, pp. 1196-97, 1210-15.

policemen on duty of culpable negligence, and they did show very little sensitivity to the warnings of danger. It is only fair to note, however, that they had not been specially alerted for trouble that night and that there were explanations readily available for the reports that came in to them. They knew that there was a Reichskriegsflagge meeting at the Löwenbräukeller, a "Racist Right-Block" (Völkische Rechtsblock) meeting at the Hofbräuhaus, and Kahr's meeting at the Bürgerbräukeller. There were, therefore, good reasons why great numbers of Kampfbund members should be in the streets. In view of Kahr's recent relaxation of the ban against parading and marching in uniform, it was not surprising that many of them were in uniform. Few recent nights had seen München's streets free from uniformed men wearing the swastika. Therefore it is scarcely surprising that the police hesitated to take decisive preventive action, especially when the only senior official present, Dr. Frick, counseled against such action. The men on duty, with the exception of the Landespolizei officer, were petty officials who had never been encouraged to show initiative or entrusted with much responsibility, and the Lapo man was not only somewhat out of his element but was clearly outranked by Frick. Faced with the choice between having to explain why they had acted precipitately should nothing be wrong and with defending the performance of their duty to the letter in case something was wrong, these men, not surprisingly, chose the latter course. They did try to find one of their superiors in the building, without success, but that was the limit of their daring. They did not wish to disturb them at home.[8]

Once it was certain that a Putsch was underway, though, First Lieutenant Fritz Stumpf, the Landespolizei duty officer, did take action. He accepted Frick's advice against committing the company in the Alte Schwere Reiter Kaserne, because it was so clearly outnumbered, but he did turn his attention to reaching his superiors. Before he succeeded, Major Frhr. von Imhoff appeared and agreed that no attack should be launched. On the other hand, Imhoff ordered the alerting of all Landespolizei units and the warning of the Reichswehr. Stumpf also alerted the entire blue police. This was the first step in organizing resistance to the Putsch and the last to be made from the Police Directory, for with the arrival of Banzer, who remained aloof and uncertain of his course, and Pöhner, who

---

[8] B, I, GSK 43, pp. 180ff; II, MA99522, 17.3.1924, p. 7; MA103473, pp. 1-5; MA103476, pp. 1211-13.

was a leader of the Putsch, the directory passed temporarily out of official control.[9]

In the Generalstaatskommissariat the situation was quite different from that in the Police Directory. Here, Baron von Freyberg was present when the news of the seizure of the Bürgerbräukeller reached that office about 9:00 p.m. He immediately got in touch with Imhoff at the Police Directory, pressing for an attack on the Bürgerbräukeller. Imhoff pointed out that there was not sufficient force at hand for such an attack, whereupon Freyberg ordered the alerting of all Landespolizei units for action. When Captain Wilhelm Daser at the Wehrkreiskommando reported that Röhm had seized the building, Freyberg ordered Major Doehla, who had been summoned from his home, to alert all Reichswehr troops in München and the other garrisons in Bavaria. The police were to take orders only from the GSK.[10]

Doehla, who had arrived by bicycle at about 9:45 p.m., ordered the Landespolizei detachment guarding the building to hold it at all costs, a necessary precaution, since the blue police guarding Kahr's door had been told by their station that the police were neutral in the Putsch. He then gave the order to the telephone and telegraph authorities to prevent all service into or out of the city except for messages of the GSK, an order that Kahr modified later in the night.[11]

At about 10:30 Kahr arrived at the GSK. The police specialist of Regierung Oberbayern, Regierungsrat Habruner, and his intelligence chief, Captain von Bomhard, arrived at about the same time, as did Lieutenant Kautter, the local leader of Bund Wiking. Kahr was evasive about the whereabouts of Seisser and Lossow and soon disappeared into a neighboring room, where he received various of the men assembled in the outer office for individual conversations. Freyberg explained to the newcomers that he had already taken countermeasures against the Putschists as had General von Danner. Kautter then offered to call out the troops of the Ehrhardt Brigade on Bavaria's northern frontier in support of Kahr and, de-

[9] B, I, SA 1, 1490, p. 15.

[10] The messages went out as follows: PDN-F, 10:04; Augsburg, 10:45; Landsberg, 6:46 (?); Landshut, 11:31. B, II, MA103476, p. 1299; MA104221, unsigned, undated, handwritten Doehla Bericht, ca. 13.11.1923.

[11] B, II, MA104221, Wild Bericht; unsigned, undated, handwritten Doehla Bericht, ca. 13.11.1923; NA, EAP 105/7a, Reichswehr Official Bericht.

spite Kahr's denials at the Hitler Trial, received permission to do so.[12]

At about 11:30 p.m. Seisser arrived and shortly before 1:00 a.m. the decision was made to abandon the exposed position they occupied and retire to the center of resistance in the barracks of the Nineteenth Infantry Regiment.[13] Meanwhile the officials of Regierung Oberbayern—apparently unaware of Doehla's orders regarding telephone calls, although they had been in the room when he issued them—tried in vain to reach the various district headquarters in the province. They therefore decided at 11:45 to send off a Landespolizei officer, First Lieutenant Hans Schaumberger, to alert the civil authorities and to order them to obey only the GSK. A few minutes later Dr. Pittinger arrived and, having been briefed on the situation, offered to go to Rosenheim to alert the Chiemgau units of his organization for Kahr, but he did not actually depart until 1:00 a.m., at about the same time Schaumberger left.[14]

After the departure of Kahr, the role of the GSK garrison in the Putsch was finished. The acting Regierungspräsident of Oberbayern, Loritz, and his aides remained behind, but they had taken all the action they could, having read themselves out of any further participation in the Putsch by their orders to the district officials. They seem to have been left unmolested by the Putschists, who were also aware that the center of gravity had shifted to the Infantry Kaserne.[15]

While the civilian authorities were preparing for resistance to the Putsch, similar developments occurred on the military scene. Even before General von Lossow left the Bürgerbräukeller, Generals von Danner, Freiherr Kress von Kressenstein, and Adolf Ritter von

---

[12] It is possible that in the confusion of the moment there was some misunderstanding between Kahr and Kautter, or that the permission came from one of Kahr's entourage rather than from him. However, the order was given and Kahr accepted responsibility for it. He even paid the Verbände members for their services. His later denials, like those of Kautter, were for public consumption. B, I, GSK 49, p. 46; SA 1, 1493, p. 34; M. Inn. 73696, Zusammenstellung der Daten; II, MA103476, pp. 1287-88.

[13] Kahr, Seisser, Doehla, and Hunglinger made up the party.

[14] B, I, Kahr MS, pp. 1363-66; GSK 3, pp. 53ff; M. Inn. 73696, Zusammenstellung der Daten; IV, BuR, Bd. 34, Item 155 Reg. Präs. Obb. an GSK, 13.11.1923.

[15] *Ibid.*

Ruith had, on hearing rumors of trouble, assembled in civilian clothes at the Stadtkommandantur. General von Danner had first proceeded to the Polizeidirektion München where Imhoff assigned Landespolizei Captain Hans Bergen to him as liaison officer. Bergen testified that as soon as Danner met his colleagues they discussed the military measures to be taken against the Putschists. They then confirmed the alert ordered by Baron von Freyberg and warned that only orders from General von Danner, who as commandant of München was commander of all police and army troops in the city in times of emergency, should be accepted.[16]

Lossow arrived in a state of great excitement at 10:45 p.m. and was immediately led aside by the other three generals, according to an eyewitness.[17] Their conference lasted about a half hour. Then Lossow announced to the officers present that he had been threatened by Hitler with a pistol and that his promise was given under duress. He therefore did not feel bound by it. He had no desire to be a follower of Hitler and thoroughly condemned the Putsch, against which he planned to proceed with all available force.[18] Lieutenant Colonel von Saur then reported to Lossow and Seisser, who had meanwhile arrived in his own vehicle, that, in accordance with Lossow's explicit statements regarding his opposition to any Hitler-Ludendorff Putsch, the München garrison had been alarmed, the Augsburg, Kempten, and Landsberg garrisons ordered to München, and the other garrisons informed of the situation. Lossow agreed that these were the proper measures to take.[19]

It was then decided that headquarters should be moved to the Infantry Barracks because the Stadtkommandantur was a dangerously isolated outpost near the Wehrkreiskommando. The four generals, as well as von Saur, Colonel (Ret.) Gustav von Kress, Captain von Hanneken, and Captain Bergen then departed. Captain Renz, who was left behind, had orders to hold the Stadtkommandantur and to inform all officers who enquired, that they were to accept orders only from General von Danner, so that possible

<hr>

[16] B, II, MA104221, Imhoff Bericht; NA, EAP 105/7, XVI, p. 007291; 105/7a, WKK (B) VII 1431 Geh. Ib 1391 Geh.; telephone pad of duty officer at I/19, 8./9.11.23.

[17] Captain von Hanneken, who had joined General von Kress at the Stadtkommandantur shortly before Lossow's arrival. GP, A, General von Hanneken, Oct. 1960.

[18] *Ibid.*; NA, EAP 105/7a, WKK VII 1431 Geh./Ib 1391 Geh.

[19] *Ibid.*

misuse of Lossow's name by the Putschists would be rendered harmless.[20]

Seisser separated from the others. He was to go to the Türkenkaserne to inform the police troops there of the situation and then to get Kahr and bring him to the Infantry Barracks. Seisser did appear at the Türkenkaserne, but, surprisingly, was very uninformative about the situation. He said that the triumvirate had been overpowered at the Bürgerbräukeller, but said nothing about the role of the police in the Putsch, merely ordering the troops to remain on the alert and to defend their installations against all comers. The reason for his reticence is probably to be found in the decision that had been taken not to reveal the defection of the triumvirate from the Putschist camp until the balance of power in the city was in favor of the loyal government forces.[21]

The remainder of the party settled down, at the suggestion of Lieutenant Colonel von Wenz, in the orderly room of the signal officer of the Nineteenth Infantry Regiment within a well-protected building in the center of the regimental barracks complex. For the sake of security the officers had travelled in two parties, but neither had encountered any difficulties. They were joined by First Lieutenant Ferdinand Schörner, who (despite his alleged pro-Kampfbund sympathies) acted as a liaison officer and courier for Lossow throughout the Putsch, and by Lieutenant Colonel von Berchem, who arrived in civilian clothes by way of the Police Directory. Having been at a party, he had been caught off guard like the rest.[22] Schörner was first sent to the adjoining Pionierkaserne to learn what was happening there and was later sent back to summon General Aechter, whom he missed but who came on his own and was promptly placed under arrest, the first Putschist to feel the hand of the law on his shoulder.[23]

Meanwhile, the unexplained delay in the appearance of Kahr and Seisser, which resulted from the siege of the Generalstaatskom-

---

[20] *Ibid.*; GP, A, Frau General Lise Renz, 2.2.1960; General Franz Halder, 23.5.1960.

[21] Seisser knew that a good number of officers and men in the München Lapo were sympathetic towards the National Socialists.

[22] NA, EAP 105/7a, Reichswehr Official Bericht; B, II, MA104221, Imhoff Bericht; GP, A, Marshal Ferdinand Schörner, 20.1.64; General von Kiliani, 18.9.1960. Berchem remarked at the PDM that the report of Lossow as a Putschist was a "Schwindel."

[23] NA, EAP 105/7a, Reichswehr Official Bericht; GP, A, Marshal Schörner, 20.1.1964.

missariat, caused Lossow some uneasiness. Once the triumvirate was reunited, though, the general sent Ruith and von Kress to expedite the concentration of military reinforcements in München. General von Ruith was sent to the southwest to control the movement of, and explain the situation to, the troops moving towards München from Augsburg, Landsberg, and Kempten.[24] Kress was dispatched to Regensburg to take command of the forces in northern Bavaria. En route, he was halted by Julius Schaub, a National Socialist courier, whose truck lights had gone out, marooning him on a bleak country road. After identifying Kress and his adjutant, Hanneken, Schaub waved them on, thus losing the opportunity of capturing a key opponent of the Putsch, albeit after his most significant task had been accomplished. Schaub's failure to recognize the situation and act was symbolic of the manner in which the Putschists sat by while they were outmaneuvered during the cold, wet hours of the early morning. Similarly, Kress' staff car, sweeping along as swiftly as winding roads and nasty weather would allow, symbolized the initiative of the government forces.[25]

The army was in action, but the decision in favor of secrecy caused a good deal of confusion and no little unhappiness for the Landespolizei. At least some of Lieutenant Colonel Julius Stuhlreiter's forces in the Max II Kaserne believed throughout the night that they were on the side of the Putschists,[26] and in fact the bulk of them may well have been under this delusion. Initially, Lieutenant Colonel Karl Schnitzlein, the deputy commander of the München Landespolizei and CO of the Third Battalion, was no better informed than the others, despite the brief visit Seisser had paid to the Türkenkaserne. He was, though, determined to get to the bottom of the matter. Rumors were rife among the troops and orders were lacking, a dangerous combination in an explosive situation. Therefore, as the night wore on, Schitzlein turned to Banzer, his immediate superior. Banzer could easily be reached by telephone, but reaching him was one thing and obtaining orders or information was something quite different, as more than one exasperated officer or official learned. Banzer's own version of his conversation with Pirner, the Landespolizei expert in the Ministry

---

[24] *Ibid.*; B, I, SA 1, 1494, p. 373; NA, 105/7a, Official Reichswehr Bericht; GP, A, General von Hanneken, 10.60.

[25] *Ibid.*

[26] GP, B, Lieutenant Colonel Lagerbauer; B, I, M. Inn. 73696, Reg. Obb. Aufruf.

of the Interior, clearly reveals the reason why Pirner came to doubt
Banzer's loyalty to the legal authorities:

"About 2:30 a.m. Oberregierungsrat Pirner . . . called me from
the First Battalion—Residenz—by telephone and said in brusque,
over-loud tones: 'In the name of the legal government, whose
head at the moment is Kultusminister Dr. Matt, I must declare
to you that all officials who follow the new government do so at
their own risk. Who is presently minister-president[27] of München?' and in reply to my answer, 'Oberamtmann Dr. Frick,' he
continued: 'You must immediately inform me if you recognize
Frick as police president or not.' Since I assumed with certainty
that I was under surveillance in the Police Directory, I hung up
without answering and told the officers in the office with me to
tell Pirner, if he called again, that I had gone off on urgent
business. . . ."[28]

Schnitzlein had, initially, no better luck than Pirner, although he
was one of Banzer's closest colleagues. At 3:00 a.m. Schnitzlein
lost his patience and said to his acting adjutant, Lieutenant Em-
manuel von Kiliani: "This is all foolishness. Take my car and go
to the [München] Command Post and find out what is really
happening."[29]
Kiliani drove through the now empty streets of the inner city
without difficulty but had less luck with his mission. On the steps
of the Police Directory he met Major von Imhoff and asked him for
information, but Imhoff impatiently shook him off with a blunt "I
haven't any time now" and stepped into a waiting police auto. On
the fourth floor, Kiliani found Banzer also preparing to depart. Instead of answering the lieutenant's questions, Banzer ordered him
to remain in the office and tell telephone callers that Banzer was
out. Kiliani, anxious to fulfill his mission, ventured to say again that
Schnitzlein was most anxious for orders and information. Banzer's
reply was "Wait a bit." "Kiliani then said: 'Colonel, can I at least
tell Lieutenant Colonel Schnitzlein clearly whether we should treat
the National Socialists as friends, as foes, or if we should be noncommittal.' " The answer, while illuminating, was not helpful. "The
Colonel stared at me and replied: 'I don't know that myself!' and

---

[27] This obviously should read "*police* president."
[28] B, ii, MA103476, pp. 1237-38. This account of the conversation is
confirmed by Pirner. GP, A, General Pirner, 26.9.1960.
[29] GP, A, General von Kiliani, 18.9.1960.

disappeared."[30] It was 4:00 a.m. before Imhoff, who had been at the Infantry Barracks, came into the room and told Kiliani crisply: " 'Report to Lieutenant Colonel Schnitzlein: Kahr, Lossow, Seisser reject the Hitler Putsch. They hope, with the aid of reinforcements from outside [München], which will arrive in the course of the day, to be masters of the situation.' "[31]

Thus, it was only in the very early morning that the "night of confusion" ended for the largest government force in München, the thousand men in the Türkenkaserne. Had these troops been employed energetically during the early hours of the morning, the course of the day might well have been different. There were, nonetheless, good reasons why no such action was taken.

II. *The Organization of the Counterattack*

The plans of the triumvirate were simple and carefully laid. They took into account the fact that time was on the side of the government forces and the fact that, especially in the early stages of civil war, overwhelming numerical and technical superiority often enables its possessors to win a bloodless or near-bloodless victory. Although there is some reason to believe that Lossow, nettled by the audacity of the Putschists in seizing his headquarters, wanted to storm the Wehrkreiskommando in the early hours of the morning—a move which the evidence suggests would probably have been successful—more cautious counsels prevailed and a two-phase plan was adopted.

The first or holding phase called for defending all important installations in München, while bringing in reinforcements from outside. At the same time, the "safe zone" in the inner city was to be expanded and its perimeter reinforced. During this phase, secrecy would be maintained as far as possible, and no open and obvious moves would be made against the Putschists. In order to maintain this secrecy, Putschists or Kampfbund sympathizers who fell into the hands of the forces in the Infantry Barracks were to be arrested immediately.[32]

However, the period of outward inactivity was not one of idleness. It saw the preparation of the plans for the second phase: the

[30] *Ibid.*

[31] *Ibid.* This account is confirmed in its general outline by the then Lapo First Lieutenant Max Winkler. GP, A, General Max Winkler, 8.10.1960.

[32] NA, EAP 105/7a, Official Reichswehr Bericht (1431), Section on Stab, Wehrkreis VII.

offensive against the Kampfbund. This offensive phase encompassed three distinct actions. The first action was to be political: it consisted of unveiling the opposition of the triumvirate to the Putsch, spreading propaganda against the Putschists, and arresting such Putschists leaders as could be found. This action was to be initiated as soon as the triumvirate felt secure. The military action was to be two-pronged. The major military task force, divided into two detachments or columns made up of both Landespolizei and Reichswehr units, was to be sent against the Wehrkreiskommando. The commander was to provide for strong flanking screens, in case the Putschists in the Bürgerbräukeller should attempt the relief of Röhm's troops. Meanwhile a second force, consisting of the Police Basic School was to seize the Bürgerbräukeller. Before the day was out, the power of the Putschists should be broken and their major strongpoints overrun.[33]

III. *The Government Reaction*

Although Knilling and several other members of the Bavarian government had been arrested at the Bürgerbräukeller, others had failed to attend the gathering and therefore remained free. Dr. Franz Matt, the Kultusminister, who was energetic and tough-minded despite his sixty-three years, took over leadership of the government in the absence of Knilling. Together with the other free ministers, Heinrich Oswald, Dr. Wilhelm Krausneck, and Dr. Wilhelm Ritter von Meinel, Matt retired to the home of Frau Hofrat Amann,[34] somewhat to the consternation of some of his more prudish associates. Here they assembled about them a small staff of reliable officials, especially those concerned with police matters, like Pirner, Zetlmeier, and Captain Hartmann Freiherr von Ow of the Landespolizei, and a number of party leaders. Since Kahr had sounded noncommittal at best when approached by Matt on the telephone sometime before midnight, the ministers decided to act on their own initiative. After much discussion it was decided that the rump Cabinet should withdraw to Regensburg to organize resistance, in view of the strength of the Putschists in München and of the uncertainty regarding the positions of Kahr and Lossow. After formulating a proclamation to be issued to the people of München, Matt, Krausneck, and Meinel left the city, just before

[33] *Ibid.*, 19 I.R., ia Nr. 9013, 14.11.1923; GP, A, General Lehmann, 13.8.1955. The details were worked out by Lossow's and Danner's staffs.
[34] A Landtag deputy of the Bayr. Volkspartei.

Baron von Freyberg arrived with Kahr's assurance that the trium-virate was bent on suppressing the Putsch. Minister Oswald, who had delayed his departure briefly, now decided not to leave München and tried to stop Matt and his companions. They were already out of reach, however, and arrived safely in Regensburg in the early morning, to find General von Kress there before them. In the end, their cross-country dash was, like that of Kress, unnecessary, but both had had great potential significance, since their escape meant that, even if the Putschists had temporarily carried the day in the capital, the legal government would have been in a position to carry on under the protection of the north Bavarian—and north German —Reichswehr.[35]

IV. *The Putschists and the New Situation*

The Putschists leaders seem to have felt quite secure during much of the night. Pöhner, for example, although annoyed at being un-able to locate Lossow, went home to get some sleep, and seems to have been only slightly perturbed to learn at 4:00 a.m. that the Generalstaatskommissar had forbidden the appearance of the morning newspapers.[36] Most of the other senior leaders were still at the Wehrkreiskommando, where they had been since before mid-night. Here, though, the exultation of the midnight hours was slowly being replaced by gloom as confidence leaked out of the room like air from a punctured balloon. Report after report made it clear that the "loyalty" of the triumvirate and, far more impor-tant, of the Reichswehr and Landespolizei was in question. The Putschists later claimed, alternately and volubly, that they did not ever learn that the triumvirate or the armed forces were against them and, on the other hand, that they believed the triumvirate were the prisoners of their subordinates. The course of events in the Wehrkreiskommando makes it clear that in neither claim were they entirely honest.

At 12:30 a.m. Kriebel, still at the Police Directory, could smile condescendingly when Major Doehla sent him the message, " '. . . he can expect nothing from us.' "[37] By 1:00 a.m. the smile was clearly growing forced, for Lieutenant Biechele of the Nine-

[35] B, II, MA99521, 10.11.1923, pp. 2-3; 12.11.1923, p. 16; MA103472, Matt Telegramm aus Regensburg; MA103476, pp. 1284-85, 1300; Müller, *Wandel*, p. 175; GP, A, General Pirner, 26.9.1960.

[36] NA, 105/7, II, pp. 107-09.   [37] B, II, MA103476, p. 1225.

teenth Infantry Regiment had been first arrested and then expelled
from the Wehrkreis headquarters compound when he went there
on a scouting expedition for Lossow.[38] Furthermore, by this time
a friendly Reichswehr officer had informed Röhm that Lossow had
"fallen away."[39] The Reichswehr sentries, who had stood guard
alongside those of Reichskriegsflagge, had already marched back
to their barracks on orders apparently received both through Lieutenant Biechele and their sergeant, who had visited his unit
briefly.[40]

It is clear that the Putschists read these signs correctly, for
shortly after 1:00 a.m. Röhm arrested Captain Daser, who had
been calmly sitting at his desk in the room next to the one that
Ludendorff, Röhm, and their colleagues were occupying. At the
same time, orders were given to arrest all other Reichswehr personnel in the building, for Major Max Schwandner was warned about
2:00 a.m. by a civilian employe of the Reichswehr in time to clean
up his desk and return home, having accomplished his task of organizing the transporting of troops to München.[41]

Somewhat later several Reichswehr officers visited the Putschist
headquarters and their news can have been nothing less than dis-
illusioning, especially since two of them were personally highly
sympathetic with the Kampfbund. First came Lieutenant Michael
Rossmann, sent by Major Hans Schönhärl, the acting commander
of the First Battalion of the Nineteenth Infantry Regiment, to recall the Reichswehr guards. Rossmann told the Putschists that his
unit had been ordered to prepare to defend their Kaserne, which
led Ludendorff to ask sharply "Against whom?" and to send the
lieutenant on to Lossow with a message, which was largely a restatement of the various proclamations of the "new government,"
identifying its members and senior executive officers. Schönhärl
took Rossman to von Wenz, who in turn brought him to Lossow.
Lossow read the message from Ludendorff, remarked "That is all
false,"[42] and told Rossmann that his mission was completed, which
suggests that Rossmann was sent as an unsuspecting intelligence

[38] B, I, SA 1, 1493, p. 112.   [39] B, II, MA103476, p. 1362.
[40] B, I, SA 1, 1493, pp. 49, 112.
[41] B, I, SA 1, 1494, p. 360; II, MA104221, unsigned, undated Denkschrift,
ca. 13.11.1923; GP, A, General Schwandner, 23.1.1960.
[42] NA, EAP 105/7a, 10778 Geh. I./I.R. 19, 13.12-1923. "Das ist ja alles
Schwindel."

agent, having been selected for the warm reception he could expect from Röhm.[43]

The leaders in the Wehrkreiskommando received the same news that Pöhner did about Kahr's ban on newspapers and were also informed that General Aechter had been arrested. Pöhner later admitted at his interrogation that by 4:00 a.m. he knew that the triumvirate opposed the Putsch.[44] The Putschist leaders in the Bürgerbräukeller were also informed of the course of events. Captain (Ret.) Freiherr Marschall von Bieberstein had been sent out by Göring on a general reconnaissance. When he returned shortly before daylight, he reported that while popular feeling was still high in favor of the Putsch, there could be little doubt of the hostile intentions of the armed forces.[45]

At about the same time Colonel Leupold of the Infantry School came to the Wehrkreiskommando at Ludendorff's request. Since Leupold was kept cooling his heels for some time, it was probably 5:00 a.m. by the time he actually saw the general and Hitler. Ludendorff said that he had joined the Putschists because the triumvirate had done so and that he had been waiting for Lossow since 11:00 p.m. Leupold replied that between midnight and 1:00 a.m. Captain Otto Ottenbacher had been sent by Lossow to General Hans von Tieschowitz. He brought with him a written order, signed by Lossow, enjoining him to bring his commander up to date. Leupold was present when Ottenbacher made this official report. Leupold further added that he had personally spoken with Lossow between 2:00 and 3:00 a.m. and received confirmation of his position from the commanding general. Lossow had said that, if necessary, he would put down the Putsch by force. Ludendorff stated that this was the first report he had had of a change of view on Lossow's part. He denied that the consent of the triumvirate had been wrung from them at gunpoint. Leupold replied that he had talked with General (Ret.) Hans Ritter von Hemmer, who had been an eyewitness of the events at the Bürgerbräukeller and who had the distinct impression that the consent of the three was given under pressure.

The conversation ended with Ludendorff requesting Leupold to inform Lossow of Ludendorff's position, and especially to impress on Lossow the impact of his stand on the Vaterländische

---

[43] NA, EAP 105/7, II, pp. 35-36; 105/7a 10778 Geh. I./I.R. 19, 13.12.1923; Reichswehr Official Bericht, Anlage 4a.
[44] B, II, MA103476, p. 1335.   [45] Pölnitz, *Emir*, p. 128.

Bewegung. Hitler reinforced Ludendorff's remarks and ended his long speech with the grandiloquent assertion that he was determined to fight and to die for his cause. Leupold's last words were a warning that he was sure that Lossow would not alter his stand, and that the division would do what its commander ordered it to do. Leupold added that, should Lossow so desire, he would return. At 6:00 a.m. Leupold reported to Lossow, who listened to his report and decided that since Ludendorff had been clearly informed of Lossow's position, there was no purpose to be served by a second visit from Leupold. Leupold was instead sent to the Infantry School with instructions to establish order there.[46]

The decision of the Putschists at approximately 5:00 a.m. to seize the Police Directory by force indicates their recognition of the fact that the authorities had declared against them. If the triumvirate had been on their side, such a move would have been not merely useless, but folly, since it would surely have alienated their allies. Certainly, by 8:00 a.m. the situation was no longer in doubt, since Max Amann was told in the Bürgerbräukeller of the "defection" of the triumvirate. Röhm informed a number of his officers at the Wehrkreiskommando at approximately 10:00 a.m.,[47] although his order to the officer of the guard, Lieutenant Walther Lembert, that Reichswehr personnel were to be refused admittance to the compound and to be arrested if they did enter had been given at around 8:30 a.m. and must have let the cat pretty well out of the bag.[48]

One reason why even many unbiased persons believed the Putschist leaders when they said that they did not know of the "defection" of Kahr, Lossow, and Seisser was because many Putschists could say to their friends and acquaintances with perfect truth that they knew nothing of this development. There was clearly a conspiracy of silence to prevent anyone beyond a very small circle of

[46] B, II, MA103476, pp. 1323ff; NA, EAP 105/7a, Reichswehr Official Bericht, Anlage 4a.
[47] B, I, SA 1, 1493, pp. 48, 185-86; II, MA103476, p. 1247; NA, EAP 105/7, I, pp. 122-23.
[48] This order was largely necessary because 9.11.1923 was payday in the Reichswehr and a steady stream of officers appeared to receive their money. Röhm later claimed that these men wanted to join the Putschists or leaned towards them, but his own officer of the guard testified clearly as to their real objective. General Endres also mentions in his memoirs that the ninth was payday. See B, I, SA 1, 1493, p. 49; HSIV, EE7, Endres MS, pp. 38-40.

the initiated from knowing that things had gone agley. This conspiracy of silence existed not only at the Wehrkreiskommando but also at the Bürgerbräukeller. Further, when silence was no longer enough, it was reinforced by outright lies and by threats against those who tried to spread the truth. Just as before the Putsch the Infantry School students had been assured that the northern Reichswehr was behind the action, they were misled throughout. Lieutenant Block, one of the ringleaders among the students testified on this point:

"I brought to Rossbach's attention with a request for clarification the rumor that the engineers were not going along. He calmed me with the words: 'The battery next door will quickly crush any dissidents.' Later I questioned Rossbach again about the refusal of the engineers, but he gave me his word of honor that all was well. I note here that he twice more in the course of the night gave me his word of honor in support of statements that did not correspond with the facts. . . ."[49]

It is clear that this position of Rossbach's was not taken simply because he was in ignorance of the situation, for, when word came directly from Lossow as to the position of the Bavarian division, Rossbach refused to allow the courier to speak to the students. Another of the student officers, First Lieutenant Müller, testified:

"Towards morning, Lieutenant Spoida came to the Bürgerbräukeller. He came direct from Lossow and informed me. I then went, in my anger over this betrayal, which was now entirely clear to me, to Rossbach and said to him that I would no longer go along. Then I went into the hall and wanted to inform the cadets. Some had already been informed by Lieutenant Volkmann. Rossbach [taking advantage of the] hall full of Hitler troops, forbade Volkmann and me to speak to the company. I then left with Spoida and Volkmann and reported to the colonel [Leupold]."[50]

Even the later Gauleiter of Baden, Lieutenant Robert Wagner, confirms the conscious deception of the students by the Putschist leaders. This attempt was at least partly successful, because while some students learned during the night that the Reichswehr opposed the Putsch, others only heard this news at noon or later the next day.[51]

[49] B, II, MA103476, p. 1274.   [50] *Ibid.*
[51] *Ibid.*, pp. 1268, 1322-23; NA, OKW/857, RWM-Heer-Hrslg. Nr. 335/23g

At the Wehrkreiskommando, too, Röhm tried to keep the news of the opposition of the Reichswehr and Landespolizei from reaching his troops during the night, although, almost inevitably, rumors trickled down to them. By 10:00 a.m., in the face of an impending attack on his position, Röhm gave up the attempt at concealment. By 11:30 a.m. he was openly preparing for defense against the armed forces.[52] It is therefore certain that the Putschist leaders knew that they faced serious opposition and that the armed forces of the state would probably be used against them, and yet they attempted to hide this information from the bulk of their followers. What, then, did they do to meet the crisis?

The leaders found themselves in serious disagreement, and there were vigorous arguments among them both while they were still in the Wehrkreiskommando and after Hitler and Ludendorff returned to the Bürgerbräukeller at approximately 5:00 a.m. It has been stated that the reason Hitler did not deliver the speeches he was planning to give in the morning hours of 9 November was because his nerves collapsed.[53] However, most of the available primary evidence regarding the morning of 9 November suggests that he was in full command of his faculties but far too busy with the problems of command to take any interest in other questions. For example, he not only never went to the propaganda and administrative headquarters set up by Max Amann and Gottfried Feder, but he also refused to take the slightest interest in the question of the disposal of the Jewish hostages held in the Bürgerbräukeller.[54] With the ground quivering under his feet and counsels divided as to what measures should be taken to rescue the situation, it is not surprising that Hitler relegated speechmaking to Streicher, a very effective mob-mover.

It is not easy to piece together a picture of the deliberations of the chieftains, but the general pattern emerges quite clearly. Kriebel, as the military leader of the Kampfbund, reacted in a

---

In. I. Pers (Seeckt Erlass vom 12.12.1923); GP, A, Colonel Richard Baur, 1.10.1956; Colonel Karl Herschel, 1.10.1956; Colonel Fritz Teichmann, 17.3.1969.

[52] B, I, SA 1, 1493, pp. 27-30, 185-86; IV, HSIV, EE7, Endres MS, pp. 49-50; NA, EAP 105/7a, WKK VII 1431 (Bericht).

[53] See Kotze, Hildegard von, and Krausnick, Helmut, eds., *Es spricht der Führer*, Gütersloh, 1966, p. 224. The editors do not, however, indicate any source for their statement.

[54] B, II, MA103476, pp. 1452-53; NA, 105/7, I, p. 122.

clear-cut and militant fashion to the new situation, drawing up a battle plan, which was found among the Putschist papers:

"1) Excellency von Lossow has broken his word of honor. He plans to fight against us.

2) We will defend the 'national federal government' under arms to the bitter end.

3) We will go over to a stubborn defensive and halt every attack.

   a) R[eichs]k[riegs]fl[agge], the Wehrkreiskommando, Captain Röhm

   b) Oberland and Kampfbund München, the Police Directory, Major Hühnlein

   c) Sturmabteilung Hitler, Infanterie-Schule, Sturmabteilung Oesterreich [sic], the Bürgerbräukeller, Captain Göhring [sic]

4) Outposts along the line: Prinzregentenbrücke-Schönfeldstrasse-Ludwigstrasse-Wittelsbacherplatz (inclusive)

   Segment I by Captain Röhm, Briennerstrasse-Maximiliansplatz-Lenbachplatz-Stachus-Sendlingertorplatz (inclusive)

   Segment II Major Hühnlein: Müllerstrasse-Fraunhoferstrasse-Fraunhoferbrücke

   Segment III by Captain Göhring [sic]

5) . . . [Document breaks off!]"[55]

Kriebel thus belonged to the activist camp, although even he opposed the plan of some unknown who wished to use the captured ministers as a human shield behind which they could seize the Police Directory and rescue Pöhner and Frick. Hitler also favored vigorous action. It was he who had insisted that Pöhner recapture the Police Directory and later it was he who, according to Dr. Paul Meinig of RKF, was arguing so strongly for carrying on the resistance that Ludendorff cut his oratory short in mid-flight—one reason perhaps why they never saw eye to eye subsequently. Hitler was sensitive about his speeches as well as his public image—and brusque interruption injured both.[56]

It would seem that Dr. Weber and General Ludendorff were somewhat less bellicose, for Kriebel's plan remained, as he himself admitted, an empty proposal. Only portions of the plan for defen-

[55] B, II, MA103476, pp. 1340-41.
[56] B, II, MA103476, pp. 1315, 1337; NA, EAP 105/7, I, pp. 110-11.

sive dispositions were adopted and this in a more or less haphazard manner. Basically, as adopted, these measures provided for holding the river line against the government forces in the inner city— which, during the later hours of the morning, were already feeling their way forward towards the east bank of the Isar—and for containing the Maximilianeum, which was a strongpoint of the Lapo on the Putschist bank.[57]

Action beyond this point broke down on basic questions of strategy. Kriebel, the determined rebel and professional soldier, thwarted in his original plan, now wanted to withdraw towards Rosenheim in order to gain time and to seek to win over the "Chiemgauer."[58] This decision would have meant the end of the Putsch and would have led either to a serious civil war or to a swift disintegration of the rebel forces. Again he found little support. Ludendorff opposed the proposal on the grounds that he did not wish the affair to choke to death in the mud and slush of a country road.[59] A plan for a long, uncertain guerrilla campaign against overwhelming odds was also unlikely to appeal to Hitler, who had already shown a strong preference for the lightning campaign or military-political tour de force. A typical gambler, his tendency was to take a long chance with dramatic possibilities rather than to embark on a course where victory, if achieved, could come only after long, arduous and grinding effort. Therefore he, too, in the end turned thumbs down on the Kriebel plan. This scheme was now out of the question for, in the long run, Hitler was the decisive force among the Putschists, if only because the bulk of the armed forces were his men.[60]

It was easier to decide what not to do than what to do, for the discussions dragged on for hours and it was only late in the morning that a clear decision was reached. The Putschists had obvi-

[57] B, II, MA103476, pp. 1361-62.

[58] The Chiemgau Regiment of Bund Bayern und Reich, led by Jäger and Schonger, was right-radical inclined and, although officially aligned with Ehrhardt, sympathized with the Kampfbund. It therefore might well have been won over to the rebels had a serious overture been made. B, IV, BuR, Bd. 34, Items 27, 114, 144, 151, 179. See also Chapter XIII, Section II, below.

[59] Müller, *Wandel*, p. 179.

[60] B, II, MA103476, pp. 1361-62; NA, EAP 105/7, I, pp. 110-11. Major Streck, who was present, says that Hitler originally favored the Kriebel proposal. GP, A, Hans Streck, Dec. 1971.

ously not seriously considered alternative action should their first move meet with less than complete success. Now that they were faced with this situation, they did just what they had so often blamed others for doing. They sat about disputing among themselves while their troops lay idle and the irretrievable minutes and hours ticked away.

It is interesting that the rebel high command did not even make any serious attempt to gather more troops to reinforce their dangerously small force. Although there were a good number more SA units in southern Bavaria than had been summoned to München, there is no evidence that even Kriebel sought to gather these in to improve the rebels' position during the coming day. The only attempt to gain outside aid was rather a diplomatic one. General Ludendorff sent Marschall von Bieberstein to Ingolstadt to summon Lieutenant Colonel Hofmann to München, apparently with the hope of using him as an envoy to Lossow, but if the aim was to put pressure on Lossow to return to the cause the scheme was to fail abysmally, for the astute "Trotsky" had no intention of putting himself into direct and obvious opposition to his commander, much as he might be prepared to work against him under cover or even to ignore his orders.[61] Hofmann would seek to avoid bloodshed and to ease the surrender terms offered the Putschists, but he was no John Sobieski come to rescue their citadel.

The result of all these deliberations was inaction and half-measures. For hours no orders at all came from the Putschist high command and the bulk of their troops were left to their own devices. In most cases, this meant that they slept desultorily and argued about the myriad rumors that always attend a fluid political situation. Only "Captain" Ludwig Oestreicher, among the lesser leaders, seems to have seized the initiative during this quiet period and his activities give testimony to his prejudices and energy rather than credit for intelligence and efficiency. He turned his attention to the seizure of Jews and Communists as foes of the "new government," a project that seems to have been executed in a manner as casual as its conception.[62]

Lieutenant Heines distinguished himself by a similarly casual act of initiative. On the way to the Infantry School, where he hoped to find quarters for his battalion, Heines stopped off at the Hotel Vier-

---

[61] Ludendorff, *Feldherrnhalle*, pp. 148-50; Pölnitz, *Emir*, pp. 127-28.
[62] B, II, MA103476, pp. 1235, 1441-42, 1451-52.

jahreszeiten, where, ignoring the handwringing of the proprietor, he seized several Allied officers as hostages, although he finally agreed to leave them under guard in their rooms. Later, when the Putschist high command heard of this affair, Heines was forced to back water. The guard was removed and apologies were offered the French and Belgian officers.[63] Neither of these measures was, of course, calculated to affect in any way the outcome of the Putsch. The fact that they were all that the lesser Putschist leaders came up with during the hours when they were unfettered strongly suggests that they shared the unpreparedness of their high command, and exceeded it in their failure to recognize the need for decisive action.

Later, after dawn and after the weather had improved, more serious measures were undertaken, but they were clearly individual reactions to specific stimuli rather than steps in a regular plan, with the exception of the execution of the one element in Kriebel's plan that had been salvaged—the occupation of the river line.

Around 8:00 a.m. Hitler ordered the seizure of paper money from the Parcus printing press in order to pay the troops and, undoubtedly, to purchase necessities. Here was another problem that could not be ignored and yet had apparently not been considered beforehand. Further sums were later taken from another printing firm, Mühlthaler. The leaders of this operation were themselves bank employees and seem to have taken reasonable precautions to protect the money from unauthorized use, but it was later passed out casually to pay the troops and to prepare for possible expenses, with the result that much of it was never recovered.[64]

There was also a series of other sorties from the two fortresses of the Putschists. The earliest sorties were attempts to seize the Police Directory, the first attempt having been made by Pöhner on orders from Hitler. This action was to be taken by Captain Max Ritter von Müller's Second Battalion of Oberland, but it was entrusted to a portion of Kampfbund München, which left on foot after Pöhner returned to the directory by car. When they arrived at approximately 6:15 a.m., they were turned away by the commander of the Lapo guard unit. Either because they had been, as they claimed, told that they were merely to reinforce the police, or

8. Gerhard Rossbach (center) and other Putschists in front of the
Bürgerbräukeller on 9 November 1923

9. Marxist City Councillors are arrested by Stosstrupp Adolf Hitler on
9 November 1923 (Hans Kallenbach is on the extreme right)

10. Reichskriegsflagge Barricade at the Wehrkreiskommando/Kriegsministerium on 9 November 1923 (Heinrich Himmler is the standard bearer)

11. Julius Streicher speaks to a crowd in the Marienplatz on 9 November 1923

because they had no stomach for a fight, they left docilely after a brief argument. They returned to the Wehrkreiskommando by way of Zeller's warehouse.[65]

The failure of the Kampfbund München "attack" on the Police Directory was followed by a considerable pause. Then, after making a sortie around 8:00 a.m., which netted two München policemen who were "arrested" for tearing down proclamations of the "new government,"[66] the Stosstrupp Hitler was ordered to rescue Pöhner by securing the directory for the Kampfbund. Setting out at 9:00 a.m. it reached the Ettstrasse a half hour later. At the arrival of the Putschists, the Lapo unit holding the gates swung them closed and informed Berchtold that they were holding the building. Berchtold ordered machine guns set up to cover the building and threatened to attack. Some of his men tried to infiltrate the building by way of stores on the Neuhauserstrasse, but they were turned back by Lapo soldiers from the Third Mitte Company. For a few minutes it looked as though an attack would be launched in earnest, but in the end, as was so often the case during the Putsch, the rebels simply withdrew.[67]

Having returned to the beer hall from this expedition, the Stosstrupp set out on a safer and easier mission. On Göring's orders, they were to arrest the Marxists among the city councilors of München for refusing to fly the swastika from the Rathaus. Julius Schaub and Heinrich von Knobloch of the Stosstrupp led the Putschists, who broke into the council chamber, seized the first mayor and the Marxist councilors, and took them to the Bürgerbräukeller to be held as hostages.[68]

Meanwhile, two groups of Putschists had been sent out into the inner city to spread propaganda for the "new government." One detachment drawn from the Second (Rossbach) Battalion of SA Regiment München took with it Julius Streicher, the fluent and passionately antisemitic school teacher from Nürnberg, who made

---

[65] B, I, SA 1, 1493, p. 131; II, MA103476, pp. 1336-37, 1389, 1391; NA, EAP 105/7, I, pp. 122-23.

[66] They were promptly released upon the return of the patrol to the BBK. B, I, SA 1, 1490, IV, p. 14.

[67] B, I, SA 1, 1494, pp. 248ff; II, MA103476, pp. 1337-38; MA104221, Draft Bericht, PDM, Lapo Kdo. M., A Nr. 500 Geh./2300, 17.12.1923; Kallenbach, *Mit Hitler*, pp. 27-28.

[68] B, I, SA 1, 1494, pp. 234-35, 255-56, 294, 373; Kallenbach, *Mit Hitler*, pp. 28, 154-55.

speeches to enthusiastic audiences at regular intervals as they proceeded.[69] Another propaganda team, consisting of three truckloads of Oberländer, was less successful. In the Dachauerstrasse they encountered a column of Landespolizei troops, who took from them the artillery piece they were towing and gave them two minutes to make themselves scarce. Withdrawing, they encountered a less tolerant Reichswehr column at the corner of the Schleissheimer- and Theresienstrassen. Here they were, with the exception of Oestreicher's truck which escaped, disarmed and (if their story is to be believed) treated in a most unfriendly fashion. They were then held as prisoners at the Infantry Barracks until the Putsch was over.[70]

Throughout the entire morning, the only meaningful military measure undertaken by the Putschists unfolded in piecemeal fashion. The First Battalion of Oberland was ordered, at about 3:30 a.m., to hold a number of bridges along the Isar. The Ludwigsbrücke was already held by other Oberland troops, so the First Company was assigned the Bogenhausen Bridge (the Max-Josef-Brücke); the Second, to the Prinzregentenbrücke; and the Third, to the Maximiliansbrücke. The battalion was thus widely scattered and separated by the force at the Ludwigsbrücke, an unpleasant and awkward position in case of combat. One artillery piece was set up at the Friedensengel (behind the force at the Prinzregentenbrücke), while the other was at Am Gasteig, a block further south. The Fourth Company was held at the battalion headquarters in the Hofbräuhauskeller.[71] The Ludwigsbrücke had been seized by Oberland troops at about 8:30 p.m. on the eighth. They were temporarily reinforced by SA units, who arrived at about 11:00 a.m. on the ninth and then joined the march on the Feldherrnhalle.[72] At around 10:00 a.m. on 9 November, Heines was ordered to hold the Corneliusbrücke and Wittelsbacherbrücke with his Second Battalion of the SA. He was to let civilian traffic through, but prevent the passage of enemy troops. By 10:30 he had occupied his new positions without conflict. Most, but not all of the major bridges in

[69] B, I, GSK 90, p. 576; II, MA103476, pp. 1348-50, 1456-57. See also the picture opposite p. 33 in Kallenbach, *Mit Hitler*.

[70] B, I, SA 1, 1493, pp. 57-58.

[71] B, I SA 1, 1490, pp. 50, 55; 1493, pp. 57-58; II, MA103476, p. 1341; MA104221, Schnitzlein: Bemerkungen auf Salbeys Bericht, 24.11.1923.

[72] B, I, SA 1, 1490, p. 52; III, p. 12; II, MA103476, pp. 1222-23, 1341,

downtown München were thus held by the Putschists in the late morning hours, but they could not be said to have established a tightly-knit or even moderately effective defense belt, since not all of the bridges were held, command and communications arrangements were dangerously loose, and, most important of all, their positions could easily be outflanked.[73]

v. The Government Offensive

The first offensive efforts taken by the triumvirate from its base in the Infantry Kaserne on the Oberwiesenfeld were in the realm of police and propaganda action. As soon as they were sure that reinforcements would soon arrive and that the bulk of the München forces were clearly dependable, Kahr gave orders for the arrest of such Putschist leaders as came to hand. General Aechter and his aide, Major (Ret.) Ferdinand Müller[74] had already fallen into the net. Now it was cast wider. At about 3:00 a.m. Major (Ret.) Alexander Siry arrived as an emissary from Ludendorff with the assignment of finding Lossow and learning where he stood. He was given a very cool reception and refused permission to return to Ludendorff. Instead, he was placed under arrest, as was Julius Schreck, Hitler's chauffeur.[75] At almost the same time, Frick was arrested at the Police Presidency, in accordance with directions brought by a courier from the Infantry Kaserne. He had appeared there to urge Banzer to go home and rest.[76]

Since Pöhner's arrest was ordered along with Frick's, and he did not show up at the PDM, a small force under two captains of Lapo was sent to his home. They missed him there, but at about 6:00 a.m., just after they reported his escape, Pöhner walked into Banzer's office and was seized, as was his escort, Major Hühnlein.[77] Major (Ret.) Alfred Zeller, the leader of Kampfbund München, came to the Infantry Kaserne at 7:15 a.m., after the fruitless attempt to take over the Police Directory, and with his companion,

---

[73] B, i, SA 1, 1493, pp. 170-71.

[74] This Müller (almost certainly Ferdinand), a Jäger officer, is not identical with Captain Max Ritter von Müller, the commander of the Second Battalion of Oberland. Testimony of Gerhard Böhm, who was in charge of the arrested men in the Infantry Kaserne: GP, B, Archivdirektor a. D. Böhm.

[75] B, i, GSK 90, p. 152; SA 1, 1493, p. 73; GP, A, Testimony of Maximilian Siry (in a letter from his cousin, Alexander Siry).

[76] B, ii, MA104221, Imhoff Bericht, 13.11.1923.

[77] Ibid.; NA, EAP 105/7, ii, 110-12.

First Lieutenant (Ret.) Altmann, was added to the growing roll of prisoners.[78]

At 4:40 a.m. in response to a rumor that Ludendorff planned to visit the Reichswehr troop units to urge them to join the Putschists, an order was sent to all local units for his arrest. At 6:15 a.m. it was decided that all provincial government authorities should be directed to arrest the Putschist leaders and the border police were ordered to prevent their escape and to control traffic across the border closely—although it was much later before these orders were dispatched.[79]

The arrests were only a nibbling around the edges of the problem, a form of guerrilla warfare, which could be disconcerting to the Kampfbund but not decisive. A more serious counterattack was launched against the Putschists on the propaganda front. It was here, though, that the triumvirate made its greatest and most telling blunders, which helped to turn public opinion against it. The propaganda campaign had both a positive and a negative side: the triumvirate took steps to ensure that Putschist propaganda was crippled, while turning out propaganda of its own. The negative program was only a partial success and hampered the positive program. Since the newspapers had had reporters at the meeting in the Bürgerbräukeller and since Pöhner had set the official line of the "new government" at his press conference before the government forces were organized for action, Schiedt, Kahr's press chief, suggested that all newspapers should be ordered to suspend publication until they could be properly briefed. Schiedt won his battle but lost the campaign. His plan was accepted but received such low priority that he could neither get an automobile nor the use of the single telephone in the headquarters room in the Signal Barracks until 4:00 a.m. He then got through to Hans Buchner, the director of the *Münchener Zeitung* (of which Schiedt was chief editor), who, as chairman of the publishers' organization, seemed the best man to spread the word. Schiedt warned that no papers should be published on pain of death. His efforts and threats were both in vain. Some of the early editions were already on the streets and editor Fritz Gerlich of the *Münchner Neueste Nachrichten*, who was

---

[78] NA, T79, 53, pp. 1146-47; EAP 105/7a, Verzeichnis der vorläufig Festgenommenen.

[79] NA, EAP 105/7a, Reichswehr Official Bericht, Vorgänge beim Stab; Stadtkdtr. M., 9.11.1923, 4.40 Vorm.; Z, Akten Hpt. Arch. d. NSDAP, Mappe 125, Funkspruch Kahr.

to attack the National Socialists bitterly the next day, turned for confirmation of the newspaper ban to Pöhner, who, of course, told him that the story was nonsense. Therefore the early papers carried the Putschists' version of the events in the beer hall and the damage was done. Subsequent editions tailored to official specifications could never wipe out the impression made by those first reports or convince many nationalist Germans that the first story was not the true one.[80]

The confusion was, however, two-edged here as elsewhere. When Dr. Helmut Klotz and Otto May brought two placards to the Police Directory at 4:30 a.m. to be approved before sending them to the printers, they ran into trouble because they had forged Kahr's name at the bottom of one of them—creating what is known in intelligence circles as "black propaganda." The police official recognized that the signature was not in Kahr's hand and insisted on checking. Failing to find any of the members of the triumvirate or Dr. Frick, the policemen called Pöhner. Pöhner agreed to the printing of the placard that announced fourteen Kampfbund public meetings on the ninth, but refused to permit the printing of the "Kahr" placard because no such proclamation had been discussed to his knowledge. Thus one Putschist thwarted his fellows. In any case, when the police were informed that the triumvirate opposed the Putsch, they seized both placards at the printers. The whole episode shows how confusing and confused the situation was to all concerned.[81]

The other negative measures consisted of restricting telephone and telegraph traffic beyond the city limits to the Generalstaats-kommissariat and the Stadtkommandant and destroying Putsch-ist propaganda. The first measure resulted in isolating the Kampf-bund leaders from their organizations elsewhere in Bavaria, but it also resulted in a number of Kahr's own orders and proclamations, which were channeled through the Police Directory after the arrest of Frick and Pöhner, being side-tracked. For example, his order to arrest the Putschist leaders at the border did not get on the wires until after noon. The destruction of Putschist placards also prob-ably had little effect, since many of them were up for a long time before the police began pulling them down after 8:00 a.m. and since the government forces had often regained control of an area before it was possible to remove them.[82]

On the positive side, the government propaganda went better. Even in cases where telegraph and telephone service was denied them by their own measures, the simultaneous use of the radio resulted in the most significant messages getting through on time. As early as 2:00 a.m. radio messages were received in Berlin to the effect that the triumvirate opposed the Putsch and had the situation well in hand. This message was apparently sent out at intervals, for another version of it was marked as being received at an unknown station at 6:46 a.m.[83]

On the other hand, within the city a series of minor delays resulted in Kahr's placards, together with one issued by Dr. Matt before he left for Regensburg, only reaching the public after 11:00 a.m. First, the proclamation reached the police with Kahr's signature in someone else's hand. In view of the Klotz affair, much time was wasted checking to make sure that the proclamation was genuine. Then it was difficult to find a printer who could do the work. Later the printer, who had been fined in 1919 for printing placards for the revolutionary government, had doubts about the wisdom of getting involved. Finally, after all other difficulties were surmounted, there was delay in getting trucks and policemen to paste up the placards, which could at that time, in any case, only be posted on the west side of the Isar.[84]

While these secondary measures were being carried out, the main interest of at least two of the triumvirate was, naturally, focused on the military operations, which would clearly be the decisive factor. Here, too, there were initial difficulties right on the doorstep.

Despite the fact that, generally speaking, the Engineer Battalion was considered to be more sympathetic towards the Putschists than was the Infantry, it was in the First Battalion of the Nineteenth Infantry Regiment that the only serious problem of potential disobedience arose. The battalion had been, for some time, of two minds regarding the National Socialists and their allies. Captain

---

[82] *Ibid.*, pp. 177ff; SA 1, 1490, p. 7; Kahr MS, p. 1363.

[83] B, I, Kahr MS, pp. 1367-68; Z, Akten Hpt. Arch. d. NSDAP, Mappe 125, Funkspruch Lossow; BT, 52 Jhrg. Nr. 52, 9.11.1923, p. 1; Stresemann, *Vermächtnis*, I, p. 204.

[84] B, I, GSK 43, pp. 177ff; NA, EAP 105/7a, Kahr Aufruf, 9.11.1923.

Eduard Dietl of the First Company, who had the task of training the S.A., was a vigorous proponent of National Socialist ideas. First Lieutenant Maxmilian Braun of the Second Company was, in November 1923, as determined a foe of National Socialism as Dietl was its friend—although Röhm later claimed that Braun had once been a member of Reichsflagge. In general junior officers and enlisted men tended to reflect the attitudes of their company commanders, although some of the enlisted men of the First Company were opposed to the NSDAP. There were even fist fights among the enlisted men over the question.[85] The Third Company seems to have fallen somewhere between its sisters in attitude, while the Fourth Company, absent on guard duty in Berlin, had been temporarily replaced by Volunteer Company Werner, which was composed very largely of students and therefore tended towards the Kampfbund.[86]

These clashes of opinion naturally came to a head on the night of the Putsch. Major Schönhärl, the acting commander of the First Battalion, called a meeting of his company commanders at 3:00 a.m. and warned them that it was probable that the Wehrkreiskommando would be stormed in the course of the morning. Dietl said that he would not "fire on Ludendorff." Captain Sigmund von Schacky said that there must be no bloodshed, but that he would defend the Kaserne to the bitter end. Braun said that he would march out of the Kaserne and would shoot, if so ordered. Later, all of the officers of the battalion were informed of the situation with the result that four of them flatly stated that they could not fire on Ludendorff: Captain Dietl and Lieutenants Rossmann, Max Vogler, and Karl von le Suire. All four were obviously in a confused and bitter state, pulled between their sense of duty and their political loyalties. According to Schönhärl, even these four modified their positions as the night wore on and more information was available as to the tactics used by the Putschists in the beer hall and elsewhere. Also, as he pointed out later, none of them refused to obey any orders so that there were no legal grounds for action against them.[87]

An officer from one of the units brought into München to rein-

[85] NA, T79, 53, p. 1143; GP, B, Archivdirektor Böhm.

[86] B, I, SA 1, 1494, pp. 335-36; GP, E (Akten), Aussprache von Kurt Pflügel, 9.9.1963.

[87] NA, EAP 105/7a, Schönhärl an Wenz, 16.11.1923; NA, T79, 53, pp. 1141, 1144; GP, A, General Josef Kammhuber, 8.9.1965.

force the local garrison testifies that when he arrived at the Infantry Barracks he found the officers of the battalion in the midst of a "rather lively" discussion. Interestingly, the emphasis seemed to have shifted from whether or not the Putschists should be attacked to a question of who should attack them, with sentiment strongly in favor of the view that this was the work of the police and not the army, which should not be asked to fire on fellow citizens.[88]

Lieutenant (Ret.) Emil Werner, a graduate assistant (Assistent) at the Technische Hochschule who was the commander of the volunteer company, was apparently not drawn into the various conferences among the regular officers, but was ordered, about 10:00 a.m., to attach two machine gun squads to the Second Company. Werner thereupon asked Schönhärl if there was any possibility that the guns would be fired. Schönhärl replied "Yes." Werner then said he could not give an order that would send his men out to fire on their brothers and friends. He then requested his immediate release from service and permission to disband his company. Schönhärl assented and the unit was immediately dissolved, and left the Kaserne.[89]

On the other hand, the field grade officers of the headquarters of the battalion and of the Nineteenth Infantry Regiment were clearly prepared to carry out their orders without question. Lieutenant Colonel von Wenz' actions throughout the Putsch attest his position, as do remarks made immediately afterwards in his unpublished comments on the Putsch.[90]

The news of this division of opinion seems to have led Lossow to alter his dispositions for the capture of the Wehrkreiskommando, for originally the Second Company was intended to remain in reserve, while the First and Third Companies were to take part in the attack. However, just before the forces marched out of their barracks these assignments were reversed and the Second Company was suddenly released from guard duty and ordered to join von Wenz' detachment. Thus the final test of obedience and loyalty was never applied to the four right radical "resisters."[91] The "crisis

---

[88] GP, A, General Siegfried Rasp, 22.3.1960.

[89] B, I, SA 1, 1494, p. 336; II, MA103476, pp. 1314-15; GP, E (Akten), Aussprache von Kurt Pflügel, 9.9.1963.

[90] NA, T79, 53, p. 1126 and passim; NA, EAP 105/7a, passim; GP, A, General Maximilian Siry, 2.5.1960; E (Akten), persönliche Notizen von Oberstltn. von Wenz zu Niederlahnstein.

[91] NA, T79, 53, p. 1147. See also the handwritten message or memo-

of confidence" in the First Battalion involved far too small a segment of the forces at the disposal of the triumvirate to have more
than a very minor impact on their plans. It caused only a slight re-
arrangement of units within one of their columns, but it was a
warning of the dangers of encouraging politics among soldiers.

The task force was divided into two detachments, led by Lieutenant Colonel Hugo Ritter von Pflügel, commander of the Second
Battalion of the Nineteenth Infantry Regiment (Augsburg) and
Lieutenant Colonel von Wenz. General von Danner was the overall commander of the force, but apparently Pflügel was given operational control of the two detachments.[92] Both forces included
Landespolizei as well as Reichswehr units. Detachment "A"
(Pflügel), which was to approach the Wehrkreiskommando from
the south and west, consisted of the Second Battalion of the Nineteenth Infantry Regiment, two companies (Stations-Verstärkungen)
of Landespolizei, and one platoon of guns from the Fifth Battery
of the Seventh Artillery Regiment.[93] Detachment "B" (Wenz) was
more of a mixed bag. It consisted of the Second Company of the
Nineteenth Regiment, the Second Company of the Seventh Engineer Battalion, the Sixth Company of the Twentieth Infantry Regiment, the Thirteenth (Mortar) Company of the Nineteenth
Regiment, the Fifth Battery of the Seventh Artillery Regiment
(minus one platoon), three companies of Lapo, and two armored
cars (Lapo).[94] Both forces were organized so that the Landespolizei formed an outer ring to protect the flanks and rear of the
detachments, while the Reichswehr elements were assigned to the
actual attack on the Wehrkreiskommando.

One reason for the overwhelming force arrayed against the
Putschists was the desire to avoid bloodshed, a desire that played
a role in all of the triumvirate's deliberations and in the thoughts
of many officers and men. Kahr's orders to Lossow called for sup-

---

randum (on telegraph form) regarding "Ausrückstärken" and "Kasernen-
verteidigung" in NA, EAP 105/7a, 9.11.1923.

[92] Pflügel did all the dealing with the enemy and was later reported to
have taken the Wehrkreiskommando, although the actual units involved were
from Wenz' detachment.

[93] B, II, MA104221, PDM, Kdo. Lapo M., A Nr. 500 Geh./2300v,
17.12.1923; GP, A, General Rasp, 22.3.1960; General Heinrich Greiner,
20.2.1961; General Sixt, Aug. 1960.

[94] B, II, MA104221, PDM, Kdo. Lapo M., A Nr. 500 Geh./2300,
17.12.1923; NA, EAP 105/7a, von Wenz an Gruppe B, 9.11.1923; 19(b)
I.R. Ia Nr. 9013, 14.11.1923.

pressing of the Putsch swiftly, but, if possible, without bloodshed. Such a mission calls for creating a situation where the enemy can readily see that his position is hopeless, and thus requires a major show of force.[95] The operation proceeded with a slow and careful deliberation consistent with the desire to save lives and take no chances of giving the enemy an opportunity for a surprise blow. It may also have been meant to give him time to contemplate his awkward position. Even the preparations were very deliberate. The order for the attack was issued at 7:40 a.m., but it was 11:30 a.m. before the two detachments began to move out—not an unusual time-lag as most old soldiers can testify.[96]

Even at the very last moment there was another little flurry of pro-Kampfbund opposition from junior officers of the First Battalion of the Nineteenth Infantry Regiment. As Lieutenant Braun's company marched out of the Kaserne, Lieutenants Vogler and von le Suire shouted to the troops: "Don't shoot! Don't shoot!" Braun, who did not understand what was said, inquired of his men what had happened. He then said: "What, not shoot? Where a Braun faces a foe he will fire."[97] That must have settled the matter because the men apparently paid no attention to the dissenters, although one of them was an officer of the Second Company.[98] This seems to have been the only sign of indiscipline in the Reichswehr during the operation.

The advance proceeded in two stages. In the first phase, the troops marched to assigned stations in a rough circle around their objective. After all units had reached these stations, they moved forward slowly into the immediate vicinity of the Wehrkreiskommando. The units had orders neither to parley nor to open fire unless they were fired on first. By noon, the forward elements of the task force had reached the assault positions, although some of the succeeding waves were still closing up. The Landespolizei of Wenz' force were drawn up along Königinstrasse with elements in the

[95] *Ibid.*; B, I, Kahr MS, p. 1371; NA, EAP 105/7a, passim; Hartenstein, *Der Kampfeinsatz der Schutzpolizei bei inneren Unruhen*, Charlottenburg, 1926, passim. See also U.S. military doctrine covering civil disturbances. In general, a four-to-one to a five-to-one ratio is striven for in any offensive situation—at the point of main effort.

[96] B, II, MA104221, PDM, Kdo. Lapo M., A Nr. 500 Geh./2300, 17.12.1923; NA, EAP 105/7a, Reichswehr Official Bericht, Stab.

[97] NA, T79, 53, p. 1141. See also pp. 1067-68, 1144.

[98] *Ibid.* passim for accounts of this incident collected for the official enquiry into Braun's conduct.

Veterinärstrasse and Schönfeldstrasse. They faced east and north. Captain Konrad's mortar company was drawn up along the Kaulbachstrasse facing the Wehrkreiskommando. Braun's company was gathered in a courtyard beside the Staatsbibliothek (just off the Ludwigstrasse), while the Sixth Company of the Twentieth Infantry Regiment had not yet arrived. On the other side, facing largely south, the Lapo screening force of Detachment "A" held the area around the Odeonsplatz and the Residenz. A platoon of heavy machine guns from the Eighth Company of the Nineteenth Regiment under Lieutenant Siegfried Rasp was set up at the mouth of the Briennerstrasse covering the Odeonsplatz and the Residenz Gardens, preliminary to moving into the gardens to cover the south side of the Wehrkreiskommando. Two companies of Landespolizei were held by General von Danner in the Türkenkaserne as a ready reserve, while the First and Third Companies of the Nineteenth Infantry Regiment were also held in reserve with the additional mission of defending their Kaserne and the headquarters of the triumvirate.[99]

The movement had been made without incident or losses, although the people in the inner city area, and particularly in the Odeonsplatz, were clearly hostile to the Reichswehr and in favor of the Putschists. They even shook their fists at the soldiers or threatened machine gunners with umbrellas, which suggests not only hostility but confidence in the soldiers' patience.[100]

Röhm, meanwhile, had been preparing for defense. He barricaded the Schönfeldstrasse with chevaux-de-frise (pointed steel obstacles) and the entrance on the Ludwigstrasse with barbed wire supported by a heavy machine gun. In general, it seems that the 150-odd men of his own organization (Reichskriegsflagge) were prepared to fight anyone who opposed them.[101] The enthusiasm of the students who made up the bulk of his men is preserved in a letter written by one of them on 16 November to a comrade who missed the Putsch:

About 10:00 [a.m.] our leaders tell us the facts. We must now

[99] NA, T79, 53, pp. 1152-56; NA, EAP 105/7a, Reichswehr Official Bericht, Lapo in Putsch; 19(b) I.R., ia Nr. 9013 an Kdtr. München, 14.11.1923; GP, A, General Rasp, 23.3.1960. For Röhm's exaggerated account of the strength of the attacking force see *Geschichte*, pp. 239-40.

[100] GP, A, General Rasp, 22.3.1960.

[101] B, I, SA 1, 1493, pp. 21, 186; 1494, p. 385; IV, HSIV, EE7, Endres MS, p. 48.

fight for the black-white-red and conquer or die. Each of us is in his place in accordance with our oath. We tightened the chin-straps of our steel helmets and prepared to take up defensive positions. The Reichswehr advances with armored cars and artillery pieces, armed to the teeth. The buildings opposite the War Ministry are also occupied by the Reichswehr. Machinegun barrels point at us. We have orders not to fire before the Reichswehr does. The order to fire will be announced. . . .[102]

The readiness of the young Putschists to die was doubtless exaggerated by one looking back on the scene, as is indicated by General Theodor Endres' account of seeing young Heinrich Himmler and his companions scuttling for cover when a Reichswehr armored car approached the barbed wire barrier he was guarding.[103] However, the existing evidence indicates that these men planned to stand and fight rather than surrender.

The reaction among the hundred or so men of Kampfbund München was quite different. These men were mostly older and less dedicated to a code of violence. Many of them seem to have been less radical than the RKF men. In fact, they seem to have fallen about half-way between the middle-class home defense force,[104] which they had abandoned because of its passivity, and their new activist allies. They were also men who had other responsibilities and took them seriously. For example, one of the company commanders of Kampfbund München simply walked out in the middle of the Putsch because he was a teacher and it was time for his classes. Many of these men were apparently ready to go home when they learned that the triumvirate opposed the Putsch. It is very unlikely that they would have proven reliable in a serious conflict.[105]

Nonetheless, Röhm, who had been ordered by Ludendorff[106] to hold the building, was determined to fight rather than surrender without orders, although he was not anxious to enter so uneven a struggle as long as it could be avoided. The result was a short

---

[102] B, I, SA 1, 1493, p. 153.

[103] B, IV, HSIV, EE7, Endres MS, pp. 49-50.   [104] VVM.

[105] B, I, SA 1, 1493, pp. 123-25, 127; II, MA103476, p. 1336; Röhm, *Geschichte*, pp. 242-46.

[106] Röhm stated in his pre-trial interrogation that the order was "im Auftrage des Generals Ludendorff" and told the Reichswehr officers during negotiations that Ludendorff was the source. See B, II, MA103476, p. 1362. In *Geschichte*, p. 243, he modifies this claim, but the earlier statement is probably the true one. See also Chapter XI, Section II.

period of calm as the two forces faced each other across the street or stood on opposite sides of the same wall. In the meantime, a number of self-appointed saviors attempted to prevent bloodshed. Major Friedrich Haselmayr, the commander of the Second Battalion of the Twentieth Infantry Regiment, visited Ludendorff about 10:00 a.m. with Captain Friedrich Ritter von Krausser of the division staff, a staunch Hitler supporter, and then hastened to Lossow to try to persuade him to enter negotiations with the Kampfbund. This plea had no effect, but shortly before noon, Lieutenant Colonel Hofmann, the commandant of Ingolstadt, won reluctant permission from Lossow to offer Röhm honorable withdrawal if his unit would surrender and turn in their arms. Then Haselmayr and Hofmann hastened to see Röhm, finding the recently retired General von Epp and Lieutenant Colonel Franz Ritter von Hörauf already with him.[107]

The visitors pressed on Röhm the hopelessness of his situation and urged him to surrender, but he stood firm. Hofmann claimed that there was a new government in Berlin and all was well. Röhm then agreed to a two-hour armistice while he negotiated with General von Danner. Hofmann, on his own authority, ordered a cease-fire. A little later, Pflügel, informed of the situation, confirmed the cease-fire, which accorded with his orders that he formally demand the surrender of the garrison before mounting an attack.[108]

Epp then led Röhm to Danner in the Türkenkaserne, where a highly charged emotional scene was played out.[109] Röhm had brought his closest collaborators, Captain Joseph Seydel and Graf Karl Max du Moulin-Eckart, with him. Captain Bergen of the Landespolizei, another old friend, came along to show his friendship (according to Röhm). Danner, surrounded by staff officers, met them quietly and coolly and said that there was nothing to negotiate. Röhm was surrounded by superior forces and must surrender. If he refused, the subsequent bloodshed would be on his head. Röhm replied: " 'I have orders from General Ludendorff to

[107] NA, T79, 82, pp. 95-97; Röhm, *Geschichte*, pp. 242-43.

[108] NA, 105/7a, Zettel, von Danner an von Wenz, received at 1:00 p.m., 9.11.1923. Hence, certainly in the hands of the executing officer (Pflügel) much earlier. See Röhm, *Geschichte*, p. 243.

[109] In this account, I follow the story as told by General Endres, a participant, rather than Röhm, because Röhm's account is clearly self-serving and politically oriented, while Endres seems to have no reason to lie and is generally accurate in his accounts of events which he himself witnessed. For Röhm's version see *Geschichte*, pp. 243-44.

occupy the Wehrkreiskommando and, as a soldier, I cannot evacuate it unless General Ludendorff revokes his order.' "[110] Danner replied that Ludendorff had no right to give orders to Röhm, who was, of course, still officially in the Reichswehr. Röhm then requested that a messenger be sent to Ludendorff requesting him to rescind his order.

At this moment a police officer brought news of the clash at the Feldherrnhalle[111] and a false report of Ludendorff's death.[112] This news, naturally, resulted in great excitement. Endres, however, insisted that Röhm and Hofmann were lying when they later claimed that this excitement was an expression of sympathy with the Kampfbund and opposition to the government. The Reichswehr officers' anger was directed against the men who had rebelled against the government after having been given such friendly treatment. A second report following close on the heels of the first cleared up the misunderstanding, indicating that Ludendorff was alive and a prisoner. Röhm later claimed that he left as soon as this news arrived without waiting for the final decision of Lossow and Danner regarding terms, and events suggest that he is correct here, since the terms were later conveyed to him by Captain Wimmer under a flag of truce.

During Röhm's absence matters had proceeded apace at the Wehrkreiskommando resulting in the only clash between soldiers and Putschists. He was scarcely gone before two shots rang out from the besieged fortress, wounding two soldiers, an engineer and a rifleman. Immediately, this fire was returned by a machine gun manned by Sergeant Ertel of the Second Company of the Nineteenth Regiment, who was stationed in a neighboring building where he could command a portion of the Wehrkreiskommando courtyard. Since Ertel was separated from his unit, Senior Cadet Gerhard Böhm had ordered him to open fire if the enemy fired. Ertel's bullets killed one Putschist, Martin Faust, and mortally wounded another, Lieutenant (Ret.) Theodor Casella. These casualties were clearly a great shock to the Putschists, who apparently had briefly believed—as did the staff officers of my battalion in Normandy—that they were immortal. Thereafter, despite

[110] B, IV, HSIV, EE7, Endres MS, p. 53.

[111] See below, Section VI.

[112] A result of witnesses mistaking von der Pfordten for Ludendorff because of similarities of build and dress. See Ludendorff, *Feldherrnhalle*, p. 69; GP, B, Sergeant Hermann Ruhland.

Röhm's denials, it is clear from the immediate post-Putsch inter-rogations, as well as from the course of events, that much of their enthusiasm and confidence leaked away with the life of Casella. For many of the students, this was the first intimation that war and revolution were games played for keeps, unlike the casual street brawls with which they were familiar.[113]

The engineers had not fired, not because of sympathy for the Putschists or because, as Röhm claimed, their weapons were un-loaded by order of Captain Otto Will, but because First Lieutenant Richard Gutmann restrained them, on the grounds that no fire order had been received. Staff Sergeant (Unterfeldwebel) Xaver Moosbeck's remark at a subsequent Reichswehr investigation that he had removed his safety makes it clear that his weapon was loaded and that he was prepared to use it.[114] The Putschists later claimed that the return of their fire by the Reichswehr was a viola-tion of the cease-fire order, but Captain Konrad testifies that the cease-fire order reached him only after the firing had taken place.

Apparently as a result of the firing, a portion of the garrison of the Wehrkreiskommando, primarily or exclusively composed of Kampfbund München men, began to surrender to Braun on their own initiative, although Röhm on his return managed to hold some of them in line at pistol point. Therefore, Braun was able to pene-trate the defenses of the building without further bloodshed, and the Putschists' position became even more hopeless from a military viewpoint. Fortunately for Röhm, just at this time Captain Wilhelm Wimmer of the Reichswehr arrived with the terms of surrender, which were essentially those he had been offered before: the sur-render of the building and arms of his unit and the arrest of Röhm himself. The rest of his men could go home. Since Wimmer also brought a message from Ludendorff advising surrender, Röhm agreed and the Putsch was to all intents and purposes over, since the only other Putschist force had already been smashed.[115]

The Putschists were then disarmed by Captain Bergen's com-pany of Landespolizei and Braun's company. During the process,

[113] NA, T79, 53, pp. 1152-56, 1164, 1167-68, 1174; B, II, MA103476, pp. 1362-63; IV, HSIV, EE7, Endres MS, pp. 52-53; GP, B, Archivdirektor Gerhard Böhm; Röhm, *Geschichte*, pp. 244-45.

[114] NA, T79, 53, p. 1164.

[115] NA, T79, 53, p. 1154; NA, EAP 105/7a, Meldung: Konrad an von Wenz, 2:15 p.m., 9.11.1923; GP, B, Archivdirektor Gerhard Böhm; Röhm, *Geschichte*, pp. 246-47; Ludendorff, *Feldherrnhalle*, p. 69.

there were several minor clashes between Braun and members of the Kampfbund. Braun, however, kept tight control of the situation and these did not develop into anything beyond muttering, bickering, and a slap in the face for one Putschist. In the end, the RKF marched off bearing the corpse of Faust before dispersing to their homes. Despite their boast of fighting to the last man, they had not fought at all, although adroit propaganda was, almost immediately, to make them paladins beside whom Roland and his friends were cowards. Here at least the pen was to be mightier than the sword.[116]

The other government offensive went off even more smoothly. It was, in fact, a success long before it reached its objective. The Police Basic School (Polizei Vorschule) had arrived in München at 6:00 a.m. and then proceeded to the Max II Kaserne, from which they were dispatched to the Türkenkaserne. At about 10:30 a.m. they were ordered to advance on trucks through the Ettstrasse, Neuhauserstrasse, and Marienplatz to the Bürgerbräukeller and arrest the Putschists there. After the usual delays attendant upon getting a military force into proper marching order, the school set out. At approximately 1:00 p.m. their column reached the Marienplatz to learn that the mountain had come to Mohammed. Here they met the erstwhile garrison of the Bürgerbräukeller, recoiling in shock from the "battle" at the Feldherrnhalle, and were able to accomplish the bulk of their mission with ease and dispatch. Josef Lehmann, who commanded one of the companies or "classes" (Lehrabteilungen) of the school describes the encounter vividly:

. . . We sprang from our trucks and faced the Freikorps [Oberland], forming a line of skirmishers at the south end of the square. The Oberländer did the same. They came directly from the fighting at the Feldherrnhalle. Oberland was very nervous. They feared, apparently, that here as at the Feldherrnhalle they would be met by fire. Both sides had removed the safeties of their weapons. A bloodbath was prevented when I jumped between the lines shouting: "Don't shoot!" Spontaneously Class "C" disarmed the Oberländer who did not resist. . . .[117]

Other Police School units disarmed Putschist groups in the Tal (between the Isartor and the Marienplatz) and near the Ludwigs-

[116] NA, T79, 53, pp. 1137-75; GP, A, General von Kiliani, 18.9.1960.
[117] GP, A, General Lehmann, 13.8.1955.

brücke, where the Kampfbund bridge guards fled at their approach. The result was that they reached the Bürgerbräukeller between 2:30 and 3:00 p.m. to find it almost deserted. They captured a number of National Socialists and some truckloads of weapons and ammunition, and freed a number of Lapo prisoners. From the beer hall they then proceeded to the East Railway Station where a small group of rebels was making trouble.[118] They met no resistance from the Putschists, but were overwhelmed by abuse from the rabidly partisan citizenry. Captain Johann Salbey of the Landespolizei Landshut gave a vivid description of the temper of the crowd:

> . . . As we marched through the Maximilianstrasse [after capturing the beer hall] we were showered with names: "Pfuie! Jew defenders! Betrayers of the Fatherland! Bloodhounds! Heil Hitler—Down with Kahr!" etc. As we crossed the Odeonsplatz, the passers-by roared, whistled, howled, and threatened with their fists, so that I ordered [the men] to take out their night-sticks and undertook an arrest.[119]

VI. *The Kampfbund Counteroffensive*

As word of the government offensive against the Wehrkreis headquarters reached the Bürgerbräukeller, the Kampfbund leaders realized that they would have to take some action or simply sit where they were until they were surrounded by troops and must surrender ignominiously. This prospect was not one that appealed to men of their stripe, nor was it calculated to find favor with their followers. They had to take some positive action. Since they had already ruled out the alternatives, there remained only the possibility of a "counteroffensive" within the city, and it was this course that they adopted, although they never worked out a systematic plan of procedure. In typically Hitlerian manner, they launched an ad hoc attack in the hope of being able to exploit a favorable situation when it developed. Their preparations were half those one would make for a military operation and half those one would make for a parade, and they never seem—until after the event—to

---

[118] B, I, SA 1, 1494, pp. 174-75; II, MA103476, p. 1223; MA104221, PDM, Lapo Kdo. M., A Nr. 500 Geh./2300, 17.12.1923; Bomhard an Chef, Abschnitt IV, Lapo M., 13.11.1923; Kretzer Bericht 14.11.1923; NA, EAP 105/7a, Official Reichswehr Bericht, Lapo in Putsch; GP, A, General Lehmann, 13.8.1955.

[119] B, II, MA104221, Salbey Bericht, 10.11.1923.

have been sure which they envisaged. It is probable that, like Vikings of old, they planned to fight if the enemy was weak enough and to demonstrate if he were too strong. Essentially, they operated much like the SDS at Columbia University in 1968. The tactics of political dissidents don't change much over the decades or even centuries. The Gracchi would have understood the situation in the beer hall and probably would have reacted in the same manner, and Robespierre's last hours of freedom were roughly similar, except for his inability to work himself up to the point of marching.

It is clear that the rebels operated on a number of premises that proved to be false. Ludendorff and Hitler both believed that neither Reichswehr nor Landespolizei troops could be brought to fire on the "strategist" of World War I or any column of which he was a part. Ludendorff later claimed that only Hitler nourished this delusion, but in fact Ludendorff was a strong proponent of the theory, as is attested by Graf Helldorff, no foe of the Kampfbund or friend of the triumvirate:

> . . . I asked Ludendorff [on 8 November] whether he was certain of the Reichswehr in Bavaria and whether there was not a danger that the Reichswehr or at least portions of it would oppose the action. Ludendorff replied: "The heavens will fall before the Bavarian Reichswehr turns against me!" . . .[120]

Hitler believed in the magic of the Ludendorff name, just as in the election campaign of 1968 George Wallace seemed to believe that the name of Curtis Lemay might work wonders for him. A sign that Hitler still held this belief in the days of the Putsch is his insistence that the Kampfbund troops in the beer hall swear a solemn oath of allegiance to Ludendorff. Hitler himself was casual about oaths and promises alike—although he was bound by emotional commitments—but he had already learned the lesson he was to use with great effect in the future, the binding to him of men who did take oaths and promises seriously by formal and impressively stage-managed public oaths.

The oath undoubtedly helped, but it was not enough. Inaction is hard on the nerves in times of stress. It opens the door to doubt and fear, especially among irregulars. Something was clearly needed to change the spirit of defeat in the Bürgerbräukeller. Ludendorff testified to the depression and unrest that reigned there.

[120] B, II, MA103476, p. 750.

Men were beginning to seep away to their homes. The march on the city—the Feldherrnhalle was never the planned objective, but merely the high water mark of the counteroffensive—was a tonic that revived hope and gave the restless men a chance to take part in the winning of the day.[121]

Even afterwards the leaders were not entirely agreed on the specific goal of the march, although naturally enough then they strongly stressed its pacific and propagandistic aspects and shrugged off the more bellicose manifestations clearly present in the preparations and in some of the actions of the marchers. Dr. Weber said at the Hitler Trial that the aim was to encourage popular enthusiasm for the Putsch and to learn what the situation was in the inner city.[122] Ludendorff suggests that he was thinking of a "relief" of the Putschists penned up in the Wehrkreiskommando. Such an aim in the face of the army and police seems folly at first glance, but from the Putschists' point of view there was much to recommend it. Germans had all been profoundly influenced by the revolution, whether they had been in favor of it, neutral, or against it, and the revolution had seen much more forlorn hopes succeed for sheer lack of opposition. Hitler makes it clear that he thought of the revolution in his assessment of the resistance he might meet.

". . . We said to ourselves that the officers around Lossow (who had once without hesitation removed the old Cockade of Honor, under which thousands had fought, . . . in order to adopt another) had had, God knows, experience in cockade-changing and perhaps would again don the old Cockade of Honor as easily as they had once adopted the worse one, without tradition, with the single tradition of the unholy 8 November 1918. That was the reason why we also hoped even in this moment that a change was possible. . . ."[123]

The men in the Bürgerbräukeller envisioned Eisner and his 700 marching down the same München streets to overthrow the king in the face of the Bavarian army; they may also have had in mind the melting away of General Arnold Lequis' troops in Berlin before the blandishments and threats of a hostile crowd in the bleak December days of 1918.

[121] B, II, MA103476, pp. 1268-69, 1274-75, 1281-82; Ludendorff, *Feldherrnhalle*, p. 65.
[122] NA, EAP 105/7, II, p. 37; Ludendorff, *Feldherrnhalle*, p. 67.
[123] NA, EAP 105/7, I, pp. 106-07.

November 1923 was not November 1918, but it is understandable that the Putschists believed that it might be and advanced against the well-drilled, disciplined professionals of the Landespolizei and Reichswehr with more confidence than Eisner and his workers had probably felt when facing worn-out, sullen, and dispirited draftees, tired of a long and bitter war and thoroughly alienated from their officers. The long tradition of an effective army had lent the appearance of invincibility to a force that was a mere shadow of its former self, while the memory of the revolution distorted the image of the effective new armed forces. Both Eisner and Ludendorff marched against a phantom, but behind Ludendorff's phantom stood the reality of cold steel and hot lead. Afterwards the Putschists claimed to have had forebodings, but these clearly alternated with dreams of golden triumph.

The columns that were to march into the city were formed and organized in the same casual and careless manner that marked the military activity of the Putschists throughout the rebellion. For example, one company of Oberland was out to lunch and was left behind. Generally, the force was organized with three forces in columns of four, side by side, an impressive sight as their twelve columns filled the streets, but awkward and inflexible from a military viewpoint. Seeming was obviously more important than being. Stosstrupp Hitler was on the left, SA Regiment München in the middle, and Oberland on the right. In front marched the leaders in a double file behind skirmishers and standard bearers.[124] The Infantry School students, having warned that they would fight neither Reichswehr nor Landespolizei, fell in behind, as did Fürst Wrede's SA Cavalry Corps, to whom nobody bothered to give orders at any time during the Putsch.[125]

The Kampfbund leaders later insisted that they never thought of fighting and that if they had they would have adopted a different formation. This, however, need only be taken as an honest and convincing argument if one thinks that they were planning a pitched battle of the type that two armies meeting in the field might fight. This they were certainly not planning to attempt. However, there is every evidence that they hoped for the sort of confused,

[124] Ludendorff, von der Pfordten, Kriebel, Göring, Brückner, Reiner, Dr. Weber, Streck, the Kolb brothers, Dr. von Scheubner-Richter, von Graefe, Feder, Streicher, etc. Röhm, *Geschichte*, p. 249.

[125] B, II, MA103476, p. 1329; NA, EAP 105/7, II, pp. 66-68; 105/7a, WKK VII Abt. Ib 1582 Geh.; NA, T79, 82, pp. 209-10.

close-quarters, half-hearted battle with a demoralized, infiltrated, and feckless foe that would possibly bring them victory, and in each of the two skirmishes that they entered, they used just the sort of tactics that the Bolsheviks used in Petrograd in 1917 or the Blues and Greens in Byzantium a millennium earlier.

Similarly, the Kampfbund leaders claimed at their trial that they gave orders for the troops to march with unloaded weapons. Needless to say, it was important for them to make this point. If they did give this order, they did not try to make sure that everyone received it, nor did they do what any experienced commander does in such circumstances, which is to check each individual weapon before moving off. There is always some fool or hothead who has not followed orders. In this instance, the testimony of considerable numbers of Putschists indicates that many heard nothing of such an order, and there is evidence from several stages of the march that at least some Putschists had their weapons loaded from the outset. Furthermore the arms carried were not merely those that any military marching and chowder association might be expected to carry. Many Putschists carried assembled machine guns and, by and large, men don't carry such heavy and awkward loads unless there seems to them an urgent reason for doing so. Any machine-gunner can testify that a machine gun is carried broken down on the march and is not carried at all in parades. It is too unsightly as well as too heavy.[126]

Initially, Göring gave the order to include the captured city councilors in the column, and they were duly impressed, with the exception of one who was lame. Göring also gave the order that they should be shot if the column was fired upon, and Heinrich von Knobloch embroidered this order by assuring them that they would be beaten to death rather than shot. This charming scheme was, however, brought to naught by Hitler, who, coming along, decided that he did not want to take the chance of creating martyrs for the other side and ordered them returned to the beer hall.[127]

It was almost noon before the column, some 2,000 men strong, finally began to move, marching down the Rosenheimerstrasse towards the Ludwigsbrücke. At the river's edge, near the Müllersche Volksbad, they encountered a small force of Landespolizei, under

[126] B, I, SA 1, 1494, p. 41; M. Inn, 73695, Stenglein Bericht, 2.6.1924; II, MA103476, pp. 1344-45, 1350, and Putschist testimony passim; NA, EAP 105/7, II, p. 46.
[127] B, II, MA103476, pp. 1330, 1343; Kallenbach, *Mit Hitler*, pp. 154-55.

Lieutenant Georg Höfler, which was, although the Putschists did not know this, part of the foremost outpost line of the covering force of Detachment "A" (Pflügel).[128]

The police were at a considerable disadvantage, since, although they had been briefed regarding the situation,[129] they were clearly bound to a considerable extent by their normal procedures in times of civil unrest. They were also hampered by the inadequacy of the force sent to hold the bridge. Höfler had only two infantry squads and one machine-pistol squad to hold the bridge, although a force of three or four companies would have been no more than adequate if the Putschists were in earnest. The Ludwigsbrücke defense was also rendered extraordinarily complex by the fact that the police had, as usual, not closed the bridge to civilian traffic and a fair was being held on the island in the middle of the river. Finally, again in accordance with the normal reluctance of the police to use firearms, Höfler had not ordered his men to load their weapons.[130] Höfler was not really expecting trouble, since several small columns of Putschists had obeyed his orders to halt when they reached the bridge. However, ominously as it proved, they had not withdrawn but had halted in place and a little to one side, forming another problem for the tiny Lapo force.[131]

Now, as the main column arrived at the bridge, at about 12:15, Höfler sent a messenger to warn his company commander, while he, himself, went forward to order the column to halt. The leader of the advance guard (apparently drawn from Stosstrupp Hitler) ordered the troops to march slowly, whereupon Höfler warned that if they did not halt he would open fire. He then turned to his men

[128] B, II, MA104221, PDM, Lapo Kdo. M., A Nr. 500 Geh./2300, 17.12.1923; NA, EAP 105/7a, Reichswehr Official Bericht, Anlage 5.

[129] This orientation had been very necessary, since they had arrived from Landshut in company with the local SA and under the impression that they were both on the same side.

[130] This reluctance to use firearms or even bayonets is reflected in the reaction of Lieutenant Colonel Otto Muxel, a Lapo officer of considerable experience, when Lieutenant Colonel Lagerbauer told me that he had been with a unit that had charged a crowd with levelled bayonets during the aftermath of the Putsch. Muxel asked Lagerbauer to repeat his statement and then remarked that in his entire career he had never seen or heard of such weapons being used against civilians. Even in this instance they were not actually used, for the crowd broke before the threat.

[131] B, II, MA104221, Höfler Bericht, 10.11.1923; Schnitzlein Bemerkungen zu Höfler Bericht, 24.11.1923.

and ordered, "Load with ball ammunition,"[132] but it was too late. At a bugle signal, Putschists from the column and from the smaller detachments he had halted earlier fell on his men before they could finish loading, shouting, "Don't shoot at your comrades." Then, having reached the policemen the Kampfbündler threatened them with loaded weapons, and in some cases beat them up. The policemen were threatened with immediate execution and then led away as prisoners to the Bürgerbräukeller.[133]

Since the Putschists claimed that the Lapo refused to fire and welcomed the Putschists as brothers, it is fortunate that we have independent testimony regarding the affair. Patrolman Georg Kirchner of the blue police, standing post on the bridge, testified that the "Hitler people" approached with leveled bayonets and confirms Höfler's account fully.[134] Another trained and independent observer saw the end of the encounter. Captain (Ret.) Karl Hofberger of Bund Bayern und Reich, who had himself once been a National Socialist but now disliked them, was riding a streetcar that passed right through the fray. Here was a man of intelligence who was as well-informed on military and paramilitary matters as one could desire. His description makes it clear that there was no such "fraternization" as the Putschists so lovingly described:

". . . As the streetcar arrived at the Ludwigsbrücke the column had just marched over the bridge. On the bridge, besides the column, other groups stood to one side especially on the eastern bank. Beside the Müllerbad was about a company of Oberland, approximately a company of Nat[ional] Soc[ialists]. The end of the column was already on the bridge. Among the aforementioned two groups were a number of Landespolizei soldiers. The attitude of these Kampfbund men towards the Landespolizei was violent. He saw from the streetcar, which had partially stopped at this point, partly moved slowly forward, how the Landespolizei were disarmed and how they had to surrender their arms and bayonets. During this disarming a whole group of National

---

[132] "Mit scharfen Patronen laden!"

[133] B, II, MA103476, pp. 1344-45; MA104221, Höfler Bericht, 10.11.1923. Needless to say, the Putschists told a somewhat different story when interrogated by the Prosecutor's Office. For example, see Konard Linder's account of the skirmish. MA104221, Linder Aussage (Linder sometimes appears in the documents as Lindner, but it is almost certain that the former is the correct spelling of the name). See also Pölnitz, *Emir*, p. 129.

[134] B, II, MA103476, p. 1344; GP, B, Emil Maurice.

Socialists and Oberländer stood with rifles and pistols ready to shoot, in part with fixed bayonets, covering the police, although he did not see the policemen try to resist or to act in a recalcitrant manner. On the contrary, they had remained cool. These Kampfbund men must have had loaded rifles, too, for he had seen a number switch their safeties off. He did not, however, see any actual assault on the policemen. . . ."[135]

Captain Salbey, Höfler's company commander, was in no position to aid his platoon leader. He had only an understrength company at his disposal and had been informed at the same time as he heard of the bridge incident, that eight truckloads of National Socialists were advancing towards him from the Isartorplatz. In fact, this was a portion of the Police School coming to capture the Bürgerbräukeller, but by the time Salbey realized this the chance to act, if it had existed, was gone.[136]

In the course of the confusion, Lieutenant Rudolf Deisinger, one of Salbey's platoon leaders, was fired on by the Putschists and an attempt was made to capture both Salbey and Deisinger. After the barn was empty, Salbey, angered at the way the Landespolizei had been treated, and probably now aware of the identity of the troops in his rear, set up roadblocks facing both ways in his sector and manned them with his small force and the cavalrymen of the blue police. At the same time, reinforcements arrived in the form of Captain Georg Becher and his company. Had they arrived slightly sooner and had the arrival of the Police School either been earlier or correctly reported, the main conflict might well have occurred at the Ludwigsbrücke. And it was, the Putschists had evaded nemesis for only a few brief moments.

The column now continued along the Zweibrückenstrasse to the Isartor and into the Tal. It then debouched into the Marienplatz through the old City Hall. Here, although a car bearing a machine gun went straight forward up the Kaufingerstrasse, the marching men turned right into the Weinstrasse to the Theatinerstrasse. Then, seeing Landespolizei pickets in front of them, they turned right again into the Perusastrasse and entered the Max Josef Platz. Thence they marched along the Residenzstrasse towards the Odeonsplatz. Everywhere in the center of the city they were accompanied by throngs of civilians filling the sidewalks, many of them

---

[135] B, I, SA 1, 1494, p. 41.
[136] B, II, MA104221, Salbey, Weitere Bemerkungen, 22.11.1923.

shouting encouragement and waving them on. Marchers and on-lookers sang patriotic songs.[137]

Now the column was about to run into the main body of the covering force of Detachment "A." Fortunately for themselves, they hit it just after a number of movements had rendered its forward elements less dangerous to them. Shortly before the column entered the Residenzstrasse, Lieutenant Rasp and his machine guns moved out of the mouth of the Briennerstrasse, crossed the Odeonsplatz, entered the Hofgarten and marched on towards the Army Museum. This took them off the scene of the coming action. First Lieutenant Heinrich Greiner of the Eighth Company (Machine gun) of the Nineteenth Regiment had also passed through the Hofgarten gate along with the infantry unit he was accompanying. Therefore, the last machine guns which might have fired on the Putschists moved out of the square, although one was set up in the small gate just north of the main gate at the time of the fighting at the Feldherrn-halle. This meant that the Putschists faced only a small body of Landespolizei armed with rifles instead of two companies of infantry, a full machine gun company, and a machine gun platoon.[138] These troops could and undoubtedly would have been committed had the fight lasted even a few minutes. Since it was so shortlived they might as well have been on the moon for all the impact they had on events.

The Putschist leaders have often described the column as being "unarmed" and have spoken of it as being essentially civilian in nature. This description is deliberately misleading. Of all the Putschist leaders, apparently only Ludendorff could not have been tried by court-martial for armed revolt, for that canny and cautious soul was in civilian clothes and unarmed, another of those "lucky coincidences" that dotted his revolutionary career. Practically everyone else, including most of the leaders, was not merely in uniform but armed. A few, like Hitler or Streicher, were not in uniform but were armed. Hitler was rarely far from his Browning, and Streicher has been described by witnesses as marching along pistol in hand. A description of the leading echelons by Karl Brokesch, himself clearly a Putschist, provides a valuable corrective to the

137 B, ii, MA104221, Muxel Bericht, n.d. (ca. 9.11.1923); NA, EAP 105/7, I, p. 114; II, pp. 37-38; NA, T79, 82, pp. 209-10; Müller, *Wandel*, p. 166.

138 NA, EAP 105/7a, Greiner Bericht, 14.11.23; GP, A, General Heinrich Greiner, 20.2.1961; General Siegfried Rasp, 22.3.1960.

picture of the casual Sunday stroll of harmless people: "Men with rifles sat in the auto that moved in the column, and a machine gun was also up there. Behind the standard bearers was a line of armed men, each of whom held a pistol ready to fire. . . ."[139]

The situation just before the clash is clearly illustrated by the report of Police Lieutenant Max Demmelmeyer:

> The company advanced as the right flank cover of the Detachment Pflügel. Its mission was: "Block Ludwigstrasse [and] Briennerstrasse and secure the right flank." When I reached the Ludwigstrasse, I cordoned off first the Briennerstrasse and then pushed back the spectators around the Ludwig statue and then cordoned off [the street] at the statue. I sent some men into the Theatinerstrasse to block it at the level of the Theatinerkirche. . . . Then I went to the picket line at the Theatinerstrasse and saw a column advancing which bore Hitler standards. I dashed into the Residenz[140] and collected several squads for cordon duty, since I had only five or six men for this purpose. I distributed the men of the Second Company and went back to the Theatinerstrasse. Now I saw that the column was turning into the Perusastrasse. I hurried over to the Residenzstrasse and saw an endless Hitler column, the front of which was already in the middle of the Residenzstrasse. I rushed into the Residenz and alerted [them]. The Second Company came out in a short time, but in the meantime, the column was already at the level of the Preysingstrasse.[141] The policemen advanced with riflebutts forward, with rifles held across their bodies and with night sticks against the column, in order to halt it. . . .[142]

Here, for the first time, the Putschists were coming into contact with a large government force with a clear mission that it was in a position to execute. However, having gained false confidence at the Ludwigsbrücke, they had no intention of halting for anyone. Dr. Weber, the leader of Oberland, said flatly at the Hitler Trial:

---

[139] B, ii, MA103476, pp. 1349-50. This account is confirmed by a spectator on the sidewalk, Hans Friedrich, who was a member of the NSDAP. Friedrich also states that Hitler held a pistol in his hand. See p. 1347. Kuhn's testimony is on p. 1349.

[140] The headquarters of the I. Abschnitt (Btl.) of the München Lapo was in the Residenz.

[141] Now the Viscardistrasse.

[142] B, ii, MA104221, Demmelmeyer Bericht, 12.11.1923.

> Naturally we intended to march through the city and after the encounter at the Ludwigsbrücke we did not even consider [the possibility] of being halted by the Landespolizei. There the Landespolizei had given way after the merest pretence of resistance in that they stepped aside. We assumed that this would happen elsewhere.[143]

Aside from the distortion of what had happened at the bridge, Weber's statement indicates clearly the readiness of the Putschists to defy the authorities and their continued confidence that this could be done with impunity.

However, although the policemen now facing them were commanded by Captain Rudolf Schraut, who had right radical sympathies, and included National Socialists, the unit obeyed its orders, as had those at the bridge fifteen minutes earlier. To avoid bloodshed, as Demmelmeyer noted, they advanced as was usual with policemen in crowd-control situations, with their firearms held to form a barricade or to be used as clubs rather than in position to fire. It is therefore most unlikely the first shots could have come from the forward elements of the Landespolizei. They could not have fired had they wished to do so, for they were engulfed by the advancing column and pushed, wrestling and arguing with the Putschists, back along the Residenzstrasse. A crowd of civilians advancing with the Putschists along the sidewalks made the police task even more difficult and the situation more confused. Both the Hitlerites and the police were shouting.[144]

Meanwhile, under the leadership of Lieutenant Michael Freiherr von Godin elements of the Second Company of Landespolizei, which in answer to Demmelmeyer's summons had just taken a position to hold the Theatinerstrasse, rushed back. Godin's account, written with the event fresh in his mind, brings the scene vividly to life:

> . . . I dashed with my platoon [which was] in the Theatinerstrasse back around the Feldherrnhalle and realized that the counterattack of the Hitler troops, who were armed with every kind of weapon, had easily broken through the cordon in the Residenz-

143 NA, EAP 105/7, ii, p. 64.

144 B, i, M. Inn. 73695, Stenglein Bericht, 2.6.1924; SA 1, 1494, pp. 308-09; ii, MA104221, Muxel Bericht, n.d. (ca. 9.11.1923); MA103476, pp. 1352-56; GP, B, Lieutenant Colonel Otto Muxel; Lieutenant Colonel Max Lagerbauer.

strasse. I went over to the counterattack against the successful breakthrough of the Hitler people, with the order: "Second Company, double time, march." I was received in their ranks with leveled bayonets, unlocked rifles, and leveled pistols. Some of my men were grabbed and had pistols held against their chests. My men worked with rifle-butt and night-stick. I myself had taken a rifle so as to defend myself without going over too soon to the use of my pistol, and parried two bayonets with it, overturning the men behind them with rifle at high port. Suddenly a Hitler man who stood one step half left of me fired a pistol at my head. The shot went by my head and killed Sergeant Hollweg behind me. For a fraction of a second my company stood frozen. Then, before I could give an order, my people opened fire, with the effect of a salvo. At the same time the Hitler people commenced firing and for twenty or thirty seconds a regular firefight developed. We were fired on from the Preysing Palace and from the Rottenhöfer Bakery by the Hitler men. . . .[145]

While there may be minor inaccuracies in Godin's account—and he naturally altered it somewhat during the Third Reich, according to various Landespolizei officers—the bulk of it is supported by evidence from other sources on both sides as well as by neutral observers.

A classic question in such clashes is: Who fired the first shot? Here, as in most instances, it is far easier to ask than to answer and is, in any case, not really very important for the historian. What is important is that an irresistible force met an immovable object with the usual results. However, while the question cannot be answered with absolute certainty, there is definite evidence as to the first shot. Unfortunately, this evidence is confusing. Godin's report suggests, but does not absolutely state, that the bullet fired at him was the first one. Sergeant Hermann Ruhland, standing by Godin, testifies that he saw a Putschist in the uniform of a Jäger or artillery officer of the old army fire the first shot from a doorway in the Preysing Palace.

The Putschist leaders claimed that the first shot came from the police. In fact, on more than one occasion they stated that no one in the column fired at all and that the slain policemen were all killed by the bullets of their fellows either by error or as

[145] B, II, MA104221, Godin Bericht, 10.11.1923.

richochets.[146] The police believed that the Putschists fired the first shots and at least some of the Putschists and bystanders also supported this contention. Karl Brokesch and Hans Friedrich both testified that they believed the first shots to have come from the column, and Friedrich was certain that it was a pistol shot. Freiherr von Gebsattel, a resident of the Preysing Palace who watched the affair from his window, also testified that the first shot came from the column, but claimed that the first shots were all from rifles. He was certain that none of the troops, whom he, like other witnesses, calls Reichswehr, had not fired up to this time.[147] August Allgaier, watching from a window in the Theatinerstrasse, testified that a policeman fell as the first shot rang out, which also indicates that the shot came from the Putschists.[148] Lieutenant Bruno Ritter von Hauenschild of the Reichswehr, who calmly looked out on the fight in the security and comfort lent one by an armored car, testified that the front ranks of the Putschists (probably Stosstrupp Hitler) advanced with leveled bayonets, but apparently he could not make out who fired the first round. Interestingly enough, some professional military testimony suggests that the first shots came neither from the police nor from the column. Lieutenant Heinrich Greiner who was standing just outside the little gate in the Hofgarten wall on the Odeonplatz, reported at the time that Sergeant Gutmann of the Seventh Company of the Nineteenth Regiment had nearly been hit by the first bullets—which would indicate that they came from the column. First Sergeant (Feldwebel) Seufert (Eighth Company of the Nineteenth Regiment) however, stated flatly that the first rounds came from the upper stories of the Preysing Palace. He clearly saw puffs of powder there. Greiner, years later, confirmed this statement: "On the other hand, I saw clearly that the first shot came from a window under the roof of the Preysing Palace. I saw powder smoke and heard the crack."[149] Ruhland was scratched by a round that could only have come from the upper stories of the

[146] See, for example, EAP 105/7, ɪɪ, pp. 39-40; ɪ, pp. 114-16; GP, B, Sergeant Hermann Ruhland. The best single account is the thorough and critical compilation written by the chief prosecutor, Stenglein: B, ɪ, M. Inn. 73695, Stenglein, 2.6.1924.

[147] B, ɪɪ, MA103476, p. 1348. Perhaps some extra weight should be given to this report, since the Gebsattels were mostly professional soldiers. However, I have been unable to identify this man more closely.

[148] B, ɪ, SA 1, 1494, pp. 308-9.

[149] GP, A, General Heinrich Greiner, 20.2.1961. See also NA, EAP 105/7a, Greiner Bericht, 14.11.1923.

Ministry of the Interior (to judge from trajectory), though this was almost at the end of the clash. Another enlisted man even believed that one of the first shots came from the southern tower of the Theatinerkirche. Wherever they came from, they signified the end for the Putschists.

In view of the claims of Putschist leaders that their men marched with unloaded weapons and that all or almost all of the firing came from the police, it is perhaps well to indicate some of the evidence that this was not the case. Much of this evidence comes from Putschists themselves. The student Walter Hewel, who was the standardbearer of Stosstrupp Hitler and later played a role in National Socialist foreign policy, admitted under interrogation that he hit the ground when he heard the first shots and fired at the police. Robert Kuhn, an SA man, testified that he marched with his rifle under his arm, ready to fire, and that the Putschists fired on the police in the melee. Hans Krüger of Stosstrupp Hitler testified that men behind him—hence Putschists—were firing. Anton Reitlinger, a student who claimed to be an innocent bystander, believed that the first shot did not come from the side of the column he was on or from behind him, but did state that the Putschists then fired on the police.[150] Hauenschild claims that five rounds hit his armored car, and these could scarcely have come from anyone but the Putschists. Demmelmeyer reported that the Putschists opened fire immediately after the first shots and other policemen confirm these statements. A Lapo squad leader claims that at least one of the Putschist machine guns was fired during the fight and the court found evidence at the trial of the members of Stosstrupp Hitler that they too had put a machine gun into action. However, according to Fräulein Gertrud Rommel, who was caught in the midst of the battle, the Landespolizei also committed at least one machine gun. Finally, Sergeant Ruhland of the Landespolizei, who unloaded and collected Putschist weapons after the firing had ceased, stated that he found many weapons that had been fired, many with fixed bayonets, and many that were loaded and unlocked.[151] Whoever may have fired first, the Putschists were certainly not shy thereafter.

The firing was heavy, but lasted only a very short time. Within two or three minutes at the outside, there was not a Putschist to be seen except for a few dead and wounded. They had no stomach for

[150] B, I, SA 1, 1494, pp. 234-35, 302ff; II, MA103476, pp. 1346-49.
[151] B, I, SA 1, 1494, pp. 301-2; II, MA103476, pp. 1353-55; Kallenbach, *Mit Hitler*, p. 29.

a serious fight, although—had they taken to the buildings, to the windows, and the roofs, and had their reserves come up, formed lines of skirmishers, and advanced in small groups against the foe —a serious battle could have developed in which, at first, the conditions of street fighting would probably have reduced the immediate effects of the superior training and organization of the armed forces. As usual, though, the irregulars showed no interest in a knock-down and drag-out battle, and most of them, including the bewildered Reichswehr cadets and Wrede's Reiterkorps, faded away without even hearing a shot whistle over their heads. The Putsch was over.

Ludendorff refused to take shelter and marched right through the firing policemen, accompanied by Major (Ret.) Streck, who had a bloody nose from a grazing round. This merely led the general into the arms of Lieutenant Demmelmeyer, who escorted him to the Residenz where he behaved like a spoiled child. His "courage" has often been praised as a contrast to the "cowardice" of Hitler and the others, who hit the ground as soon as the firing started.[152] In actual fact, Ludendorff showed merely foolhardiness, pride, or confidence in his destiny. I have never heard a man who had been in combat criticize Hitler for dropping, but many have criticized Ludendorff for not doing so. After all, only if you fall down do you have a chance to fight back effectively.[153]

With the bulk of the marchers fleeing into the hands of the Police School and Ludendorff in the hands of the authorities, there was time to count the cost of the Putsch. Police Captain Schraut and three enlisted men of the Landespolizei, all of whom had been more or less close to the National Socialists, had been slain. On the other side, fourteen Putschists, who were later immortalized as martyrs of the movement, were slain. They were a cross-section of the Putschists—rich and poor, educated and ignorant, worker and noble, leader and follower—but the bulk of them, like the bulk of the National Socialists, were young. Although a high percentage of those killed were leaders of the party, of the sixteen men slain

---

[152] Almost from the beginning the Putschists claimed that Hitler had been pulled down by Scheubner-Richter when the latter was slain. This may well be true, but I suspect that Hitler would have dropped anyway. Such reflexes become automatic in a front soldier. However, some Putschists claimed, on other grounds, that Hitler lost his nerve during the clash.

[153] B, II, MA104221, Demmelmeyer Bericht, 12.11.1923; GP, B, Minister a. D. Hans Ehard; Lieutenant Colonel Erhard; Sergeant Hermann Ruhland; NA, T79, 82, pp. 209-10.

in both encounters only five were over thirty years of age and nine were below twenty-six. Some of them were men whose loss may well have been significant; others were men who could have done nothing as valuable for the party in life as they did in dying for it.[154] They became the kernel of a myth that played a significant part in bringing the party to power. Through them, ignominious failure was made into glorious defiance of tyranny. To us, looking back on the event, they, like those nameless Spartacists who died in Berlin in January 1919, were the men who paid for the miscalculations of their leaders, although at least this time the leaders took the risk themselves and paid part of the price.

VII. *Conclusion*

At midnight the Putschists had still been confident, or, at least, hopeful. By mid-afternoon their venture was a thing of the past—although this was not entirely clear to the Bavarian authorities. The rebels' main hope had lain in controlling the triumvirate or in a breakdown of the discipline of the armed forces, and neither of these bets on which they had placed so much political capital paid off. Once out from under Hitler's thumb, the members of the triumvirate had returned to business as usual, and the fond belief that the armed forces would never fire on men led by Ludendorff had died in the gunsmoke that rolled across the Odeonsplatz. Hitler's first serious attempt to seize power had been a one-day wonder, an illustration of the rapidity of tempo that later enabled him to cram a thousand-year Reich into twelve years.

[154] One of them, Kuhn, was probably only an innocent bystander. See Hofmann, *Hitlerputsch*, p. 211.

13.

THE PUTSCH OUTSIDE MÜNCHEN

I. *Introduction*

Accounts of the Putsch have normally considered only the situation in München itself, ignoring not only the rest of Bavaria but the remainder of Germany as well. Yet it is not possible to appraise the potential of the Putsch and the capabilities or limitations of the Putschists without at least some knowledge of what happened in Bavaria and, to a lesser extent, what happened beyond the border. The Putsch was crushed in München, but the question arises as to what its prospects in Bavaria were had it succeeded in winning a strong foothold in München or in taking over control of the city. This question is of particular importance because München was not Paris or Vienna, or even Berlin, as the leftist revolutionaries of 1919 learned to their sorrow.[1] It was not necessarily even a political bellwether. With some 630,000 inhabitants it was not an overwhelming segment of the population in a state where approximately seven million lived. The bulk of the citizenry still lived in small towns and villages,[2] and had attitudes, beliefs, and leaders far dif-

[1] They found that holding München was no guarantee of success in Bavaria. It is true that the popular base of the revolutionary Left in 1919 was far smaller than that of the Putschists in 1923, but their political-power situations within Bavaria were roughly similar. The USPD, Eisner's ruling party, spoke of being the party of the masses, but won less than one twentieth of the popular vote in München at a time when the party was in power, whereas the successor party to the NSDAP won a plurality in the München communal elections following the Putsch with thirty-five percent of the vote. In either case, the party's hold on the countryside was far smaller than that on the capital, and the populace outside the capital was not swayed by currents there to a decisive extent, nor were there sufficient armed forces in the capital to check those outside it. For the election figures see *Das Statistische Jahrbuch Bayerns*, 1919, pp. 584-85; 1926, p. 616.

[2] *Statistisches Handbuch des deutschen Reiches*, 1924-25, pp. 1, 4.

ferent from those of the capital. It is therefore not safe to assume that Bavaria would go as München went.

Furthermore, most of Bavaria's armed forces, whether regular or irregular, were outside München. The Reichswehr was carefully scattered throughout the state, mostly in smaller towns, as it was throughout Germany, at least in part to avoid the political "contagion" of the large city. While this arrangement had been adopted with the radicals of the Left in mind, it was a similar barrier to the radicals of the Right who were, in this period at least, primarily urban in habitat.[3] This meant that defeating or winning over the München garrison did not give one military control of Bavaria, especially since a very large portion of the Landespolizei was also stationed outside the capital, although this proportion was by no means as high as that of the army.[4] Beyond Bavaria, it was also crucial for the long-term success of the Putsch that the reaction in the Reich be not too unfavorable and that there be no foreign intervention. Yet, on this score, too, there is practically no information in most accounts of the Putsch.

II. *Oberbayern*

The situation in Oberbayern was complicated by the fact that the communications of the Putschists were much better than those of the government. This was partly because the Putschists, having the initiative, were able to give out sealed orders well in advance of the Putsch's outbreak, and partly because they used motor vehicles and special couriers sent out early in the evening to inform other groups. In eastern Oberbayern, the government "communications gap" was not too serious, since couriers brought word of the situation and orders for the officials during the course of the night of the Putsch. In western Oberbayern, on the other hand, it was days in some cases before reliable information filtered down to the local level because of the cutting off of telephone communication with München.[5] In many of the small towns of Oberbayern, the heart was taken out of the Putsch by the calling of the local Sturmabteilungen and Oberländer to München for the big show. For exam-

---

[3] *Rangliste*, 1923, pp. 17-18, 47-51, 65, 77-78, 82, 85, 88, 92, for the disposition of the Bavarian Reichswehr. See Chapters III and IV, above, for the Verbände.

[4] Sagerer & Schuler, *Landespolizei*, pp. 14-15, for indications as to the disposition of Landespolizei forces.

[5] B, II, MA103476, pp. 1208; IV, BuR, Bd. 36, Akt 2, Item 5, Reg. Präs. Obb. U41/1285, 3.12.1923.

ple, seventy Oberländer went to München from Garmisch, and others went from Oberau. Similarly, the Kampfbund "soldiers" from Bad Tölz went to München, leaving the town quiet in their wake.[6]

More serious problems arose in some towns, usually as the result of Kampfbund activity, but sometimes as a result of the actions or unrest of their sympathizers in other organizations. In Aibling, for example, news of the Putsch brought to a head a long-smouldering feud between the local leadership of Bund Bayern und Reich and the district administrative officer of the Ministry of the Interior. Even before the Putsch the Verbände in Aibling were demanding action and insisting that, in view of the many unemployed men in their ranks, their units should be mobilized. Otherwise many of the men might drift away into the camp of the leftist parties. Then, around 3:00 a.m. in the morning of 9 November, the local Bund leadership received the following enigmatic account of the Putsch from Dr. Pittinger:

> Hitler-Ludendorff Putsch in München. Kahr has declared himself regent for the monarchy. Government and Parliament set aside. Reichswehr and Landespolizei behind Kahr. Generalstaatskommissariat apparently in Rosenheim after this morning. Chiemgau Regiment to mobilize. Take security measures in Aibling immediately to ensure that autos with Putschists cannot go through. Knilling arrested.[7]

Pittinger had left München well after midnight and must have fully understood the situation there, since his instructions came from Freiherr von Freyberg, whose stand had from the beginning been hostile to Hitler. Nonetheless, Pittinger gave Oberregierungsrat Merz the impression that he was overjoyed at the overthrow of the parliamentary government, while it is equally clear that he ordered, in Kahr's name, the establishment of roadblocks against the Putschists. This juxtaposition suggests that Pittinger hoped that Kahr had finally seized power in his own hands and that he, rather than Hitler or Ludendorff, would retain it after the defeat of the Putschists. This was a course which some of the less radical, minor Verbände had been urging for some time.[8] The Aibling affair did

---

[6] B, I, GSK 44, pp. 75-76, 80-81, Reg. Präs. Obb., 19.11.1923.

[7] B, I, GSK 99, pp. 30-31.

[8] B, I, GSK 44, pp. 20-21; GSK 99, pp. 14-16, 28-29. See also Chapter IV above.

not result in any action against the government, and exhausted itself in a squabble over a placard announcing the overthrow of the government and the Diet, but it revealed basic differences of attitude and potential hostilities between the local representatives of Bayern und Reich and the local officials that could have become crucial had the Putsch in München been more successful.

In Ingolstadt, a town with a strong National Socialist Party supported by the local military commander, Lieutenant Colonel Hofmann, the situation remained surprisingly quiet, primarily because the local SA was called to München for the Putsch and because Hofmann was himself involved in complicated negotiations and machinations. Unlike his friends and later party comrades Röhm and Hühnlein, he did not irrevocably commit himself to the Putsch. On the other hand, when ordered by the irate Ritter von Pflügel to march with his battalion to München to help put down the Putsch, Hofmann refused to go, saying that he had recently spoken with Captain Daser who had said nothing of such an order and claiming that there were too many workers in Ingolstadt for him to denude the town of troops. Pflügel reiterated his order and informed Hofmann that it came from General von Ruith. Hofmann stood by his guns. Later, when the order was renewed by Major Doehla, Hofmann finally dispatched one company of Lapo and one company of Reichswehr.[9] Hofmann's real views are revealed by his completely different reaction to a summons from the Putschists. About 8:00 a.m., Marschall von Bieberstein brought an "order" from Ludendorff for Hofmann to present himself at the Bürgerbräukeller, whereupon the obedient "Trotsky" abandoned his battalion and returned posthaste to München with Marschall.[10] Here Hofmann played an active, if not very significant, role in the negotiations for Röhm's surrender.[11] This was a good example of one of the problems that always face rebels. Even some of their best friends are unwilling to burn their bridges behind them and take a clear stand before the fate of the Putsch is decided or at least until the first battle is won. Hofmann obviously did everything that he

[9] B, ii, MA103476, pp. 1316, 1327.

[10] Captain Emil Leeb and Lieutenant Commander (Ret.) Ehrhardt, who had just arrived in Ingolstadt from Nürnberg, journeyed to München with Hofmann and Marschall, but, in more ways than one, were not of their company. See below under Nürnberg.

[11] B, ii, MA103476, pp. 1327-28; iv, HSIV, EE7, Endres ms, p. 52; GP, A, General Emil Leeb, 18.1.1960; Ludendorff, *Feldherrnhalle*, pp. 148-50; Pölnitz, *Emir*, pp. 127-28.

could possibly cover by excuses, including disobeying or sabotaging direct orders, but he would not and did not declare openly for the Putschists.

Apparently most of the Reichswehr garrison in Ingolstadt was favorably disposed towards Hitler, a situation that undoubtedly reflected in part the plain predilections of the commandant, and partly the belief that Lossow and the München Reichswehr favored the movement. However, not all officers and former officers felt this way. For example, Major (Ret.) Adolf Gabler, who was in charge of the Reichswehr's cache of illegal arms in Ingolstadt, refused to release weapons to the SA on the evening of the Putsch, while Captain Wilhelm Stemmermann, an active officer, provided weapons but no ammunition. The city commissar of Ingolstadt was also hostile to the Putschists and towards Hofmann.[12] Thus, as a result of the preoccupation of the rebels and potential rebels with München and, to a lesser extent, as a result of local opposition, Ingolstadt, a major danger center, remained completely passive during the Putsch.

In Landsberg am Lech there was a good deal of excitement but no real trouble on the morning of 9 November, with sentiment generally favoring the Putschists at first, apparently at least partially on the basis of the laudatory early editions of the München newspapers. It was fortunate that things remained quiet, for the garrison had moved out during the night to reinforce the authorities in München, leaving only a skeleton force behind to hold the barracks.[13]

In Mühldorf, the Oberländer reacted to the Putsch in a manner that must have been most annoying to Dr. Weber and the other Kampfbund leaders. The Ortsgruppe duly sent its armed contingent to München. However, as soon as they learned that Kahr did not support the Putsch, they turned on their heels and marched back home. Here was a clear case of a local organization that disagreed with the revolutionary policy of the central leadership.[14]

In Miesbach practically all able-bodied National Socialists and Oberländer went to München for the Putsch, but no one else, and,

[12] B, I, M. Inn. 73696, 7094, BA Ingolstadt; GSK 44, p. 110, HMB, Obb., 4.1.1924; II, MA103476, p. 1328; GP, A, Eberhard Dennerlein, 29.2.1960.

[13] B, I, GSK 44, pp. 76-77; GP, A, General Franz Halder, 23.5.1960; General W. Hauser, 5.5.1960.

[14] B, I, GSK 44, p. 78; IV, BuR, Bd. 34, Item 151, Reg. Obb. an GSK, 11.11.1923.

according to the local officials, there was little local sympathy for the enterprise despite the violently right-radical tone of the local newspaper, the *Miesbacher Anzeiger*. Surprisingly, even this newspaper came out for Kahr against Hitler. On the other hand, the district administrative officer noted with some bitterness and a touch of xenophobia that all the north-German former officers in his area were aligned with the Putschists.[15]

The Pfaffenhofen SA was alerted in the middle of the night of the Putsch by the Ingolstadt SA as it passed through. Some twenty Pfaffenhofen SA men then took a private truck and, in accordance with orders passed on by the Ingolstadt unit, went to München. The rest of the SA and the Oberländer set up a guard room in a brewery and prepared to open a recruiting office the next day. The Bayern und Reich leader was cool towards the news from München and suspected that it might mean only a Putsch rather than a new national government, and he remained aloof from both sides. First he offered his services to maintain order, but, on learning that his men might have to disarm the right radicals, withdrew the offer. Events here underscored the problem of using the Verbände as auxiliary police in any situation where they might possibly have to be employed against right radicals. The Oberland leader was also suspicious of the affair. There was bad blood between SA and Oberland in any case because, on learning of the Putsch, the National Socialists had stolen arms from an Oberland cache.[16]

In Rosenheim Dr. Pittinger, still playing Paul Revere, informed the Bezirksamt of the Putsch and of Kahr's opposition to it. The district administrative officer—who had warned the Generalstaats-kommissariat on the morning of 8 November of the tense situation in Rosenheim and of the danger that it would pass under the leadership of Hitler—reported that, although the Chiemgau Regiment of Bund Bayern und Reich had assembled in the hope of marching on Berlin, or at least München, to "throw the rascals out" of office, the men took their disillusionment well, at least partly because the practical problems of feeding and housing 3,000 men kept them busy. The regiment was also involved in the liquidation of the Putsch, disarming those Putschists who got as far as Rosenheim, and maintaining order in the streets.

According to Rosenheim Bayern und Reich sources, Pittinger

[15] B, I, GSK 44, pp. 76-77; Bennecke, "*Röhm Putsch*," p. 88.
[16] B, I, GSK 44, p. 18; IV, BuR, Bd. 36, Akt 1, Item 37.

was far less communicative with them than he was with the Bund leadership in Aibling or the Bezirksamt in Rosenheim. After arriving and alarming the Chiemgau Regiment he was silent as to what their mission would be and as to the situation in München. The picture they paint of an uncertain and cautious man slumped over his beer as he talked twaddle is striking and unlike Pittinger. It suggests either that he was unsure of the Chiemgau leaders and therefore wished to paralyze them by denying them a clear picture of the situation, or that he was himself playing for time before committing himself clearly to either side in the Putsch. Whichever his aim, it seems to have succeeded in the short run, for there was no trouble in Rosenheim during the Putsch, although he seems to have disenchanted the local leaders still further.[17]

In Schrobenhausen the first news indicated a combined effort of the Bavarian Right and led to great enthusiasm. Some 200 men from Bayern und Reich and the Blücherbund, mostly former front soldiers, assembled in the square awaiting further news or orders. The account of the events of the morning in München was a heavy blow to thousands in the area. There was, though, no trouble during the Putsch.[18]

III. *Schwaben*

In Schwaben, which was the least unruly of the Bavarian provinces "right" of the Rhine, there were only about 1,500 members of the Kampfbund all told. Even here there were, nonetheless, some difficulties. In Augsburg itself the trouble was delayed because someone did not get the word, and seven truckloads of Augsburg SA men went to Mehring in Oberbayern to guard a National Socialist assembly. Thus 300 of the Kampfbund's troops wasted an evening when their presence in München would have seemed imperative. As a result it was only the next morning, when the civil authorities were on their guard, that the Kampfbund organizations assembled their men under arms to march on the capital. This merely brought them together and made their arrest simpler. Practically all of the leaders and many of the "soldiers" were gathered up and spent the

---

[17] B, I, GSK 43, p. 149, 131, Reg. Pr. Obb. an GSK, 3.12.1923; GSK 44, pp. 78-80, 221-22; M. Inn. 73696, *Rosenheimer Anzeiger* 68; GSK 99, pp. 14-15.

[18] B, I, GSK 44, p. 80.

day in durance vile, being released only when the news of the collapse of the enterprise arrived in Augsburg.[19]

In two or three smaller towns such as Memmingen and Ottobeuren, there was more difficulty, because the authorities had far less force at their disposal than they did in Augsburg, but even here the various groups of National Socialists were prevented from getting far. In Schwaben, as in Oberbayern, the authorities found the auxiliary police unreliable, even when made up of Bayern und Reich members. Some groups flatly refused to move against Kampfbund men. The bonds of sympathy and a common background were too strong. The United Patriotic Bands of Augsburg (Vereinigte Vaterländische Verbände Augsburgs) did come out in favor of the legally constituted authorities, making it clear that they supported not only Kahr but also the elected Bavarian government. This was a clear example of the moderate tone of political life in Augsburg, as opposed, for example, to München or Nürnberg.[20]

General von Ruith had come to Augsburg during the night and shipped off the Reichswehr garrison to München, except for a skeleton force to hold the Kaserne. He also ordered the troops in Kempten and Lindau to the capital. Their battalion commander, Lieutenant Colonel Wilhelm List, had been at the commander's conference in München on 7 November and was therefore more or less aware of what the order portended. He had had no chance, though, to tell his subordinates, especially those in Lindau, of Lossow's warning regarding the political situation, so that they were completely in the dark. However, Ruith himself boarded the trains carrying List and the Kempten contingent in Kaufbeuren, and the one carrying the Lindau garrison in Buchloe, so that they had the latest word well before they reached München.

The Lindau garrison had been contacted only with great difficulty. The telephone was out and telegraph service was routed by way of Ulm-Friedrichshafen while heavy snow made any other means of communication unthinkable. As a result the troops were simply ordered to proceed to München.[21] The story of the trip and

[19] *Ibid.*, pp. 75-76; SA 1, 1490, p. 6; II, MA102140, HMB 2282, Schw., pp. 1-2; MA104221, Kdo. B, Lapo Augsburg, Abt. B, 44/Geh.

[20] B, II, MA102140, HMB 2282, Schw., pp. 1-2; MA103472, VVVA an Graf von Spreti, 9.11.1923.

[21] NA, EAP 105/7, XI, p. 006697; Z, Hpt. Arch. d. NSDAP, Mappe 125,

the misunderstandings attendant on it is vividly recounted by General Endres:[22]

> . . . An episode during these transports is revealing regarding the attitude of the troops. Captain Ritter von Schobert . . . was shipped off with his troops by railway telegraph and without further explanation. During a halt in Kempten[23] he learned the first rumors of the Putsch and the creation of a new government. Schobert then ordered the troops out on the station platform, informed them of this news and called for cheers for the new government and for Hitler. The train then proceeded on its journey. In Buchloe, the infantry commander, General von Ruith, awaited the transport to explain the real situation, and prevent them from being misled by Hitler followers. Schobert fell from the clouds: "Now I have just ordered them to cheer for Hitler in Kempten and now we must fight him!" But he carried it off. The troops, [again] brought into the picture followed their popular leader without question on the opposite tack and did their duty fully. An excellent example of military discipline and a warning that one must keep politics away from the troops. . . .[24]

In fact, it would seem that the troops, while obedient, were still sorely puzzled, for List attests that there were difficult explanations necessary when the Lindauer arrived at their München quarters in the Hohenzollern School.[25]

IV. *Niederbayern*

In Niederbayern, Landshut was the key to Putschist activity. Although the National Socialists in Niederbayern had not been given orders to proceed to München before the Putsch, Julius Schaub was dispatched to summon their Storm Troops at 7:30 p.m. on 8 November. Meanwhile the Landshut SA had gone to Freising—well along the road to München—where Hitler was supposed to speak

---

Telegramm: Pflügel an Kempten, 9.11.1923; GP, A, Marshal Wilhelm List, 29.10.1960.

[22] Endres sometimes embroiders his stories for impact, but this one is generally confirmed, in drier prose, by Field Marshal List.

[23] Marshal List, who was then Schobert's immediate superior, says Kaufbeuren.

[24] B, IV, HSIV, EE7, p. 62.

[25] GP, A, Marshal Wilhelm List, 29.10.1960.

that evening. On Schaub's arrival, the Landshut SA collected the Freising unit, and the two proceeded to München in company with the Landshut Landespolizei which had been summoned by Doehla.

The Regierungs-Präsident took precautions against trouble by calling out the auxiliary police and arresting the local Communist leaders, although, as in Rosenheim, there seems to be no evidence that they had any plans for action. The only resistance encountered was that of postal authorities loyal to the Reich, who refused to allow the confiscation of Putschist propaganda or to interdict all non-official telephone messages because they had no orders from Berlin to this effect and would not accept the authority of Kahr. Only when a Reichswehr officer arrived and officially warned that he would take over the Post Office by force in case of resistance did they comply, a surrender undoubtedly made easier by the fact that they accepted the orders of another federal authority, rather than a state one.[26]

The only other flurry of Putschist activity in the province was in Passau, where Theodor Sailliez, a National Socialist activist, tried to organize a mass meeting in support of the Putsch for the evening of the 9 November. The local authorities, who had been confused by the conflicting information they had received during the course of the previous night, were aware of the true situation by dawn and prevented the assembly. The Passau Reichswehr battalion and the Landespolizei were ordered to München during the night of 8-9 November, but in the end only the Reichswehr went, leaving shortly before 8:00 a.m., too late to play any serious role in the events in the capital.[27]

v. *The Oberpfalz*

The Putsch in the Oberpfalz was essentially the Putsch in Regensburg. The Putschists appear to have made more grandiose plans for a Putsch than elsewhere outside München, and Hitler seems to have had high hopes—probably on the grounds of assurance from the local National Socialists—that the city would fall into his hands. When told at dawn on 9 November that the free members of the Bavarian government had fled to Regensburg, he replied: " '. . . furthermore, Regensburg is solidly behind us and the gentle-

[26] B, I, GSK 44, p. 74; SA 1, 1494, pp. 294-95; II, MA102140, HMB 1102, N/B, p. 1; HMB 1174, N/B, pp. 1-2; MA103476, p. 1052; MA104221, p. 3; GP, B, Lieutenant Colonel Max Lagerbauer.

[27] B, I, GSK 44, p. 60; NA, EAP 105/7, VII, p. 006267.

men would suffer a disappointment.' "[28] On this point, as so often on that fateful night, Hitler was badly misinformed. Harold Loeser, the leader of the local SA, was a man with a very spotty military background. He had been a simple soldier in a Thüringian Freikorps, from which he deserted. He later tried to join the Reichswehr as an officer candidate, claiming that he had been an Austrian cadet. Rejected because of his lack of documentation for his claims, he turned to the National Socialists. On the day of the Putsch he traveled to München and received orders from Göring, already in the expansive and destructive mood that characterized him that night. Loeser was to arrest Dr. Heinrich Held, the leader of the Bavarian People's Party, and to destroy the press of the Social Democratic newspaper[29] in Regensburg. At the same time, by means of a telegram reading "Aunt Bertha has died," Loeser ordered the SA units from the entire Oberpfalz to Regensburg.

Loeser led his men to the Reichswehr Kaserne for training as usual that evening. At the end of the training period, instead of turning in their arms and equipment, the SA unit marched out of the Kaserne and onto the Galgenberg, where they set up an impromptu camp. Then, according to Loeser, he returned to the Kaserne to turn his unit over to the Reichswehr in accordance with his orders. According to Lieutenant Max Josef Pemsel, the officer of the guard in the Kaserne, Loeser tried to seize control of the installation, but Pemsel was able to thwart him and placed him under arrest.[30]

Meanwhile, the Regierungspräsident of the Oberpfalz, Dr. von Winterstein, called Lieutenant Colonel Walter von Unruh, the commander of the First Battalion of the Twentieth Infantry Regiment, the main force stationed in Regensburg, to ask if all was quiet in the barracks. Unruh went immediately to the Kaserne to investigate, encountering en route several small parties of storm troopers that had been ordered to arrest Winterstein, the Oberbürgermeister, and other prominent persons. He persuaded these men to accompany him and then ordered them held in the barracks area.

About 2:00 a.m. Loeser, resplendent in a uniform richly embel-

28 B, I, SA 1, 1493, ca. p. 28, Bericht of Herbert Müller on telephone call he monitored.

29 Volkswacht.

30 B, I, GSK 90, p. 312; II, MA103476, pp. 1253-55; GP, A, General Max Josef Pemsel, 9.4.1957; General Walter von Unruh, 13.3.1955.

lished with gold braid on the sleeves, was brought to Unruh. Loeser took a strong line, despite being a prisoner:

This man . . . presented himself to me as plenipotentiary of the new government. He refused to give me any further information. He only said that the move was against Berlin. He did not wish to take the Reichswehr with him [on this campaign] because it was not dependable enough. Perhaps he would use it for rear echelon duty on the northern frontier of Bavaria. For this impudence I locked him up.[31]

Loeser had no greater luck with the regimental commander, Colonel Johann Etzel, who kept him in custody and made him give orders for his men to surrender. When they marched docilely into the Kaserne and laid down their arms, the rising on which Hitler had set such high hopes was ended without a shot being fired or a blow being struck. Here, as in München, the Putschists showed far more bark than bite.[32]

By the time General von Kress and Dr. Matt arrived in Regensburg the excitement, such as it was, was long since over, and they could send the bulk of the garrison off to München without any fear of difficulties in the Oberpfalz.

VI. *Unterfranken*

In Unterfranken as elsewhere, the local authorities complained of the unfortunate effects of the blanket ban on telephone traffic, indicating that it did as much harm as good by keeping those who should enlighten the public either in ignorance or incommunicado. Generally speaking, there was little Putschist activity in the province, although during the afternoon of 8 November the Karlstadt Oberländer received sealed orders to proceed under arms to Würzburg, the provincial capital. Despite preparations for the trip, they never marched.[33]

In Würzburg itself the night passed quietly and at 6:00 a.m. the Regierungspräsident, Dr. Julius von Henle, assembled the civil, military, and police officials and the political leaders for a conference. He informed them of the situation and issued a proclamation telling the populace that the civil and military authorities stood

---

[31] GP, A, General Walter von Unruh, 13.3.1955.
[32] B, II, MA103476, p. 1255; NA, 105/7, IX, pp. 006504-5.
[33] B, II, MA102140, HMB 1740, Ufr., p. 2; IV, BuR, Bd. 36, Akt 1, Item 17.

firmly behind the Knilling government. Even the local leaders of the Verbände agreed not to undertake any action in view of the confused situation. The army and police troops were alerted, but this proved to be an unnecessary precaution. One of the leaders of Bund Frankenland, which had close ties with the Kampfbund, did attempt to mobilize its forces on the frontier but was thwarted by his own "regimental commander," who was really a Wiking man.[34]

The only unpleasantness that arose was peripheral to the Putsch. During the night, the Heeresleitung in Berlin sent a radio message to Lt. Col. Franz Feeser, the garrison commander, forbidding him to obey orders from the Seventh Division. Feeser, who was a strong supporter of Bavarian rights, informed the Heeresleitung that he could not and would not take himself or his unit out of the Seventh Division without undermining military discipline.[35] This affair had no repercussions on the situation since the Heeresleitung and the Seventh Division were in fact on the same side, but it did very possibly contribute to the subsequent side-tracking of Feeser's career.[36]

In essence, there was no Putsch in Unterfranken, a fact which not only underscores the weakness of the Kampfbund in northern Bavaria but also indicates the extent to which the government could have afforded to denude this area of troops in order to bring the Putsch under control if it had achieved initial success in München.

VII. *Mittelfranken*

In Mittelfranken, Nürnberg and its satellite, Fürth, were the obvious centers where trouble could be serious, since there were strong Verbände and allied organizations in both towns and in Nürnberg there were also large and vigorous Communist and socialist organizations. However, even here no trouble developed, and Captain Heiss, who was in a position to know, later claimed that the Kampfbund organizations in the north were not even alerted for the Putsch. Be this as it may, no serious plans were made for a takeover in Nürnberg, as is indicated by the summoning of the key

---

[34] B, IV, BuR, Bd. 36, Akt 1, Item 17.

[35] B, II, MA102140, HMB 1740, Ufr., p. 2; GP, A, General Fritz Hengen, 28.11.1963; General Max Siry, 2.5.1960.

[36] Feeser was later refused promotion to brigadier general (Generalmajor) because of his hostility towards Seeckt and the Heeresleitung in the fall of 1923. See Chapter XX, Section II, below.

Nürnberg leaders of the NSDAP—Walter Kellerbauer, Streicher, and Klotz—to München. Police Director Heinrich Gareis, though, took no chances. He summoned the Verbände leaders to the Berg at the first word of trouble and kept them under his eye until 4:00 a.m. Nürnberg did, however, see the only visible Marxist reaction to the Putsch. The Communists plastered the walls with calls for armed attacks on the bourgeoisie and for a general strike. The Communist "action" never proceeded further than this, and Police Director Gareis was justified in claiming that his headquarters remained in clear control of the situation throughout the night.[37]

The Reichswehr picture was at first unclear, as a result not of the local situation but of changing orders from München. Initially— some time before 11:00 p.m.—the garrison was ordered to march on München. Shortly before midnight a radio message apparently modified this order by calling for a "red alert,"[38] and at 3:45 a.m. the garrison commandant, Colonel Georg Freiherr Loeffelholz von Colberg, was still attempting to find out whether his troops were to be sent south. In the end, they stayed at home. Their entire posture and the conduct of their commander makes it clear that they were prepared to carry out any orders they received. It was the confusion in München that caused uncertainty.[39]

Loeffelholz, who was hostile to right radicalism and loyal to the Reich, took other measures to ensure quiet in northern Bavaria. One of the most important of these was the neutralization of Lieutenant Commander Ehrhardt. Ehrhardt was in Nürnberg when word of the Putsch arrived, and Loeffelholz felt that it would be wisest if the commander were given no opportunity to repeat his Kapp exploits. Between 3 and 4 a.m., therefore, Loeffelholz ordered Captain Emil Leeb to bring Ehrhardt to General von Lossow "in such a manner as to prevent him from committing any follies en route."[40] This order separated Ehrhardt from his troops on the northern border and kept him out of contact with all parties until the fate of the Putsch was decided, for—traveling by way of Ingolstadt—Leeb and his charge did not arrive in Lossow's headquarters

---

[37] B, I, GSK 44, p. 217; GSK 90, p. 370; SA 1, 1494, p. 171; II, MA103476, pp. 1243-44; IV, BuR, Bd. 36, Akt 1, Items 14/3 and 35.

[38] "Erhöhte Bereitschaft."

[39] B, I, GSK 43, pp. 180-81; IV, Lapo, Bd. 17, Akt 4, "Funksprüche," 8-9.11.1923; NA, EAP 105/7, VII, p. 006267; 105/7a, Funkspruch II. ab Nürnberg, 9.11.1923.

[40] GP, A, General Emil Leeb, 18.1.1960.

until approximately 10:00 a.m.[41] Lossow welcomed Leeb for the news he brought of quiet in Nürnberg, but showed no interest in Ehrhardt, whom he sent to see Kahr.[42] Like similar measures elsewhere, Loeffelholz' actions were overshadowed by the events in München, but his firmness and that of Police Director Gareis, who apparently never let his sympathy for the right radicals extend to countenancing activities against the state, underscore the fact that winning München would not have been enough to give the Putschists control of Bavaria.[43] Without action in Nürnberg, even restless Fürth remained quiescent. Mittelfranken only reacted to the Putsch after its collapse.

VIII. *Oberfranken*

In Oberfranken the story was much the same as in the rest of Bavaria north of the Danube. The only exception was the Coburg-Hof area, where the bulk of the irregular troops of Bavaria's border defense force (Grenzschutz) against Thüringia and Saxony were gathered. Regierungspräsident von Strössenreuther, although usually sympathetic with the Verbände, moved unhesitatingly to assure his control of the province. He arrested the leading National Socialists in Bayreuth and in the early morning hours informed the authorities in the other cities of the province that the triumvirate denounced the Putsch. Bayreuth remained quiet throughout the affair.[44]

In Bamberg, Major Anton Freiherr von Hirschberg, acting commander of the Seventeenth Cavalry Regiment in the absence of Colonel Max Zürn, took counsel with the infantry battalion commander in Bayreuth; both expected that they would be called to München with their well-disciplined units. Hirschberg then placed the Bamberg Oberland leader under arrest, apparently partly to

[41] The latter part of their journey was made together with Lieutenant Colonel Hans-Georg Hofmann, who gave Leeb the impression that he favored the National Socialists but was not prepared to renounce his military obligations overtly.

[42] Emil Leeb's presence in the Lossow headquarters probably explains why Röhm, who was, of course, not present himself, later believed that Ritter von Leeb, who was again in Stettin, was with Lossow. See Röhm, *Hochverräter*, p. 249.

[43] NA, EAP 105/7a, Reichswehr Official Bericht, Vorgänge beim Stab; GP, A, Field Marshal Ritter von Leeb, 8.3.1954; Pölnitz, *Emir*, pp. 128-29.

[44] B, I, GSK 90, p. 323; II, MA102140, HMB 1797, Ofr., 19.9.1923; IV, Lapo, Bd. 17, Akt 4, "Fünksprüche," 8./9.11.1923.

prevent him from undertaking foolish moves and partly to protect him from arrest by the civil authorities.[45] The National Socialist leader, Heinrich Bauschen, was arrested by the Stadtkommissar. Both civilian and military authorities in Bamberg opposed the Putsch and took swift measures to ensure that it would not spread into their jurisdictions.[46]

In the area around Coburg the situation was much more dangerous, at least potentially. Here, too, nothing happened, although a fire-fight nearly broke out between the Landespolizei and a Jungdo unit as a result of a misunderstanding. The Wikinger were called out by Kautter on behalf of Kahr at 10:55 p.m. on 8 November. Major Kurt Kühme, the local Wiking commander, was put in charge of the Wiking, Blücher, and Frankenland troops until the anticipated arrival of Ehrhardt.[47] In general, these Verbände obeyed the orders of the Landespolizei, although at Heiligersdorf in Unterfranken First Lieutenant Franz Stiegler of the Lapo, in ignorance of Kahr's consent to the mobilization of Wiking and its allies, arrested a Jungdo officer and the two forces faced one another in arms. As a result of caution on the part of local officers and as a result of the intervention of higher authority on both sides, the threatening clash was avoided. The Jungdo men relaxed at their machine guns, and Stiegler withdrew his force.

Still, all trouble could not be avoided. In the belief that they were being fully mobilized for active operations, the irregulars had requisitioned food and transport. As soon as the purely defensive nature of their mission became clear, the great bulk of the goods and animals were returned intact to their owners. The only unpleasantness arose where north Germans of Ehrhardt's forces or National Socialist refugees from Saxony and Thuringia had taken advantage of the situation to loot the homes of local Jews in order to get food and other goods that they were lacking.[48]

---

[45] Oberland, but not the SA, had been assigned to the Bamberg Reichswehr for training as part of the Bavarian mobilization program.

[46] B, I, GSK 90, pp. 25-27; GP, A, General Freiherr von Hirschberg, 20.4.1962.

[47] Ehrhardt was, of course, diverted to München by Colonel von Loeffelholz and therefore never arrived. His impending presence must have been a paralyzing factor for Kühme in the early hours of 9 November 1923 and his unexplained absence an increasing source of unease and irritation in the later ones.

[48] B, IV, Lapo, Bd. 17, Akt 4, Abschnitt Kühme: Abend-Meldung, 9.11.1923 (?); Bd. 26, Akt 1, II/2 an Regt.-Stab (Jungdo-Regt.), 9.11.1923;

In the Bayern und Reich battalion at Coburg, some difficulties arose between men favoring the Putschists and those opposing them. The battalion commander, Major (Ret.) Arno Buttmann took a strong stand, however, and easily carried the day. Buttmann personally was sympathetic towards the National Socialists and had given his son permission to join the party. On the other hand, he had a strong sense of duty and stated flatly that he and his men would, when in the service of the state as auxiliary policemen, fire on rebels from either Right or Left. He then called for his troops to stand either for the Bund or for Hitler. Several men apparently left, but the majority stood by their commander, who then called in the local National Socialist leaders and read them the riot act. They were bitter, particularly because Buttmann's lecture was emphasized by the arms in the hands of his men, but they did not try to cause trouble. Buttmann also warned his men against Ehrhardt whom he called an adventurer who planned some sort of enterprise in the next few days. In the course of these comments he remarked, "The Wiking people are only good for rushing around in automobiles spraying mud on the populace, while the Jungdo men are [only] able to shoot one another. . . ."[49] Buttmann's bluntness and loyalty to the state undoubtedly alienated some former friends, but it set the seal on local Bayern und Reich policy in the Putsch.[50]

In Hof, the same pattern developed: the authorities arrested the National Socialist leaders, and the other Verbände supported the government, even if with reservations in some cases. All motor vehicles were requisitioned for the use of the Landespolizei and the auxiliary police units operating under their control. The National Socialists of the area sought to assemble at Hof. The Hof SA leader, Captain (Ret.) Hans Wolf von Winkler cooperated with the authorities by ordering units under his control to give up this plan. Units from Selb and Selbitz, apparently over 200 men, did arrive at Hof but were calmed and eventually led away by Lieutenant (Ret.) Lustig, the SA leader in Haidt. Other SA units assembled at Berg but broke up on learning that the Putsch had been a failure.

Bd. 26a, Akt 3, Stiegler Bericht, 10.11.1923; Akt 5, Gr. Sch. IIIc, Beilage 1, Chef 361 g., 24.11.1923.

[49] B, IV, BuR, Bd. 36, Akt 2, Item 33/4, Bericht von Besprechung, 11.11.1923 (Hitler orientiert).

[50] B, IV, BuR, Bd. 36, Akt 2, Items 33/5 and 33/9.

Their leader assured the authorities that he and his men would never fight the Landespolizei or Reichswehr.[51]

IX. *The Reich*

To all intents and purposes there was no Putsch in the Reich outside of Bavaria. However, it is a mistake to think that, because there was no Putsch in the Reich, there were no Putschists and no Putsch potential. In truth, there were surprising numbers of people in the Reich who had some knowledge of the impending Putsch and were anxious to support it, as well as many others who did not know of it but who would have been glad to take part. Beyond these men were the many more who would have been glad to participate if they had thought it had a chance of success.

Although the Verbände in the north were far less developed and popular than in Bavaria, there were a number of points where they had considerable strength despite their illegality and the constant attempts of the authorities to eliminate them. One of the most important of these strongholds was the capital itself. Berlin had five right radical battalions; only one of them was National Socialist, but the others certainly had no sympathy for the Republic. Even if they were each only some 300 men strong, as was often the case with "battalions" of irregulars, their combined strength was enough to cause serious trouble if they meant business.[52] Yet on 9 November 1923 Berlin lay quiet.

Another concentration lay in Upper Silesia where Peter von Heydebreck, the later SA Gruppenführer, claimed to have had five battalions of miners under his command. This "Freischar" was well armed and anxious to take part in any right radical assault on the Republic. Heydebreck even had contacts with some of the most activist Communists and hoped that they would join him when the time came.[53]

Ehrhardt's Wikingbund and its allies were also apparently preparing for a rising during the fall of 1923. They were particularly strong in northwest Germany and in Saxony-Thuringia. These groups had reached agreements with Rossbach's north German

---

[51] B, IV, Lapo, Bd. 26a, Akt 5, Gr. Sch. IIIc, Erlebnisbericht, St. V. 1 33, Lapo Hof, 20.11.1923, pp. 1-6.

[52] B, II, MA104221, Second Seisser-Landbund Conversation, p. 5.

[53] Heydebreck, Peter von, *Wir Wehrwölfe*, Leipzig, 1931, pp. 180-93. Hereafter cited as Heydebreck, *Wehrwölfe*.

organization, which was always ready for trouble. Their plans included feigned cooperation with the Reichswehr so that when the crisis came they could seize the barracks and matériel after the troops left for active service. Major Buchrucker's "Arbeitskommandos"[54] were loosely associated with the Wikinger and such units of this force as survived the Küstrin Putsch[55] by "going underground" were also ready to begin a new insurrection.

Minor organizations along the northern coast were alerted at the time of the Putsch and wished to take part in it. In Celle, a company of would-be Putschists formed up on the orders of their commander, but when he ordered them to prepare to march south, half of the force melted away, and the entire enterprise came to nothing.[56]

Besides the organized units, there was also a great deal of enthusiasm for the Putschists in at least some universities outside Bavaria. A National Socialist claimed in a meeting shortly after the Putsch that "thousands" of students in Göttingen were enthusiastic supporters of Hitler. This may well have been an exaggeration, but there is much supporting evidence for the attraction that Hitler and his movement had for students. In Mannheim, for example, the corps (Burschenschaften) of the Handelshochschule marched as a unit to join the Putschists.[57]

It is therefore clear that, as the Reich government was well aware, there were many discontented and armed men in the north, and it is equally clear that the Putschists to all intents ignored these

[54] Irregulars employed by the Reichswehr primarily to repair and maintain materiel beyond the limits imposed by the Treaty of Versailles, and expanded somewhat as part of the mobilization preparations undertaken after the French invasion of the Ruhr.

[55] An attempt by Buchrucker to take over several garrisons in the vicinity of Berlin. Apparently he hoped to set off the clearly impending right radical revolution by a bold and successful action. The immediate collapse of the Putsch led to the dissolution of the Arbeitskommandos and the retirement of the Wehrkreiskommandant, who had let them get out of hand. See NA, T120, 1748, p. D756906; Seeckt Papers, Stück 289, Selchow, II, p. 8; Pölnitz, Emir, pp. 122-23.

[56] B, I, GSK 43, p. 243; II, MA103476, pp. 861, 1072; Blome, Dr. Kurt, Arzt im Kampf, Leipzig, 1942, pp. 159-73 (hereafter cited as Blome, Arzt); Schirmer, Friedrich, Das Celler Soldatenbuch, Celle, n.d. (ca. 1937), p. 138; Krüger, Alf, 10 Jahre Kampf um Volk und Land, Berlin, 1934, pp. 15-18.

[57] NA, T81, 89, pp. 102650-51; B, II, MA104221, Bericht von Lichtenberg Waffenring Versammlung, 23.11.1923.

men, despite belated gestures in their direction such as the dispatch of Röhm's friend Captain Seydel to Berlin to act as liaison with the Verbände there. Moreover, they did not merely ignore the northerners; if Heydebreck is to be believed, the Kampfbund leaders actively discouraged cooperation:

Had I been able to half-way accept the party activity in Berlin, my battle group and I would at least be sure of a friendly reception and broad support. The situation was different in München where indeed much German idealism and a good dose of Prussian self-control was required to swallow in good spirit the manner in which I was initially greeted.

It was in October. The general [Ludendorff] received me. Like every true leader he always had time for his faithful ones. He directed me to Hitler and Kampfbund, which was preparing the outbreak of the German revolution. I should not let myself be badly treated; he also gave me battle maps and a short evaluation of the combat value of the München Verbände.

I could not reach Adolf Hitler. Granted, he had much to do. Therefore Captain Göring, the leader of the München Kampfbund [sic] received me.[58] Our conversation was very short. He, the typical Bavarian, exuding power and uncouth; I, rooted entirely in the old Prussian tradition, reserved and acid. We were far too different by nature to find common ground quickly. He believed that the Verbände that wandered around north Germany were of no interest in München, Rossbach and others had already been there. He could only say that the states up there would later finally be brought back into order by Bavaria. Only when I pointed out to him the strength and combat value of the München Verbände—a reckoning which came out three to one in favor of my Freischar—was he convinced that I was surprisingly well informed and asked me to talk with his chief of staff, Lieutenant Senior Grade Hoffmann. This I was glad to do, for Hoffmann was no stranger. I had dealt with him gladly in other days. A short conversation between us forged the last link in the chain that bound my Freischar and myself for good or evil to the National Socialists. We were now, as a portion of their combat troops committed to cooperation in the loosing of the German revolution.

[58] Göring was actually the commander of the SA of the NSDAP.

I was not the only man out of the north who received similar cool treatment in München. In Lower Silesia an officer [Höfer?], a proven Upper Silesian fighter, had created a useful force based on Görlitz. He then went to München and placed himself at the disposal of the NSDAP. There he was, as he told me, rejected. In order to have some sort of relations he then joined the Stahlhelm.[59]

Although Heydebreck indicates that he finally succeeded, through his old friend Hoffmann, in having his troops integrated into the National Socialists' plans for the German revolution, typically nothing of the sort actually occurred. Hoffmann, who was clearly not in Göring's favor, was a fifth wheel on the wagon throughout the Putsch and, despite his assurances to Heydebreck, the latter received word of the Putsch from München at the same time that he learned of its collapse.[60] The men running the Putsch informed no one in north Germany of the precise timing of the Putsch. Duesterberg, the leader of the Stahlhelm in central Germany, apparently was not informed, despite his sympathy with the movement.[61] Only Ehrhardt, then in München, was informed of the Putsch, and even he was alienated, either by the unwillingness of Hitler to give him a "place in the sun" or by Hitler's refusal to share Ehrhardt's reservations regarding foreign policy repercussions.[62]

x. Conclusion

The course of events in Bavaria outside München and in the rest of the Reich during the day of the Putsch indicates how limited it was in scope and how little hope of success it had outside the capital. It revealed both the comparative weakness of the movement

---

[59] Heydebreck, *Wehrwölfe*, pp. 191-92. For Höfer see B, ıı, MA103476, pp. 947-48.

[60] Heydebreck, *Wehrwölfe*, p. 202.   [61] B, ıı, MA103476, p. 735.

[62] We do not know precisely what happened at the meeting between Hitler and Ehrhardt that took place on 6 or 7 November, but we do know that it resulted in flat disagreement between Hitler and the Viking leader. Hitler said that the disagreement was a question of "persons." Ehrhardt later told at least some of his own followers that the difference had been with regard to foreign repercussions. Very possibly both factors contributed to the breakdown of the negotiations between the rivals, as did the circumstance that they were after all scarcely mutually attractive personalities. See NA, EAP 105/7, ıı, pp. 69, and 90; Blome, *Arzt*, pp. 171-73.

beyond the München area and the startling casualness and optimism of the Putschist leaders.

The Putschists were so weak in numbers that in order to raise enough troops to make a serious showing in München they had to denude much of southern Bavaria of SA and Oberland units. Even then, the force they fielded was composed to a large extent of untrained or semi-trained youths and was almost totally lacking in the artillery and technical and supply units that would be essential for any sort of serious campaign beyond the city or for merely maintaining their force beyond the first forty-eight hours.

In northern Bavaria they lacked sufficient strength to undertake any sort of serious action against the legal authorities. Even in those areas, such as Hof and Coburg, where they were strong, Kampfbündler were faced by far stronger opposing forces and by civil authorities who were not only determined to keep control of the situation but who were difficult to attack directly because of their popularity in conservative and even right radical circles. Only in Regensburg was a Putsch attempted and it was a farce.

In northern Germany, although there were scattered groups of determined activists, the organizations were not integrated and many of the leaders were at odds with one another. They were also in ignorance of the specific plans of the Putschists, although they had a general knowledge of what was coming.

Finally, the Kampfbund leaders clearly did not care about what happened anywhere but München. They gave up the south without a qualm in order to be stronger in the city. They wrote off the north in similarly cavalier fashion, summoning the Nürnberg leaders to München rather than ordering them to make trouble at home. At the same time, they cold-shouldered all Bavarian right radical organizations that did not belong to their group. Rossbach they allowed to remain in München and scribble busily but futilely at a desk in the headquarters of the SA when he would have been far better employed in preparing a diversionary action in Mecklenburg where most of his strength lay. They actively discouraged other northern Verbände from joining them, and despite the obvious value of his force as a diversionary element or even as a second column for the march on Berlin, they ignored the one group whose leader had forced himself upon them. Their only gesture towards the northern Verbände during the course of the Putsch was made, typically, in München. Ludendorff's son-in-law, Lieutenant Heinz Pernet, was sent to find Ehrhardt at the home of his München host, a right radical manufacturer named Theodor Heuss,[63] but the bird had flown. Having given up on cooperation with the Kampfbund, Ehrhardt had set off to visit his troops, possibly with some scheme for an attack on Saxony and Thuringia still in mind, only to find himself shipped ignominiously back to München.[64]

With the legitimate government in full control of at least ninety per cent of Bavaria and of more than seventy-five per cent of its armed forces, it is hard to see how even a triumph in München could have meant more than a delay in the wiping out of the insurgents. Furthermore, with northern Bavaria in the hands of loyal troops, the border was open for the entry of Reichswehr troops from other states, which had already been offered to Lossow and the government.

Largely as a result of their own actions or lack of action, the Putschists could look for no serious accretions of strength in the immediate future either from within Bavaria or from the rest of the Reich. The entire situation indicates the character of the right radical leaders and particularly of Hitler, revealing both his greatest strengths and weaknesses. He was incapable of weighing the odds against him carefully and coldly. He was contemptuous of all who were not on his side. He was sure of victory for the right and of the triumph of the spirit over material obstacles. He was absolutely opposed to compromise on essentials. These qualities led him into a trap in 1923, led him to triumph over the next decade, and sealed his fate during World War II. He might and did learn tactical lessons from the Putsch, but he did not change his stripes. The man who believed with blind faith in April 1945 that Wenck's army could relieve Berlin was the same man who had believed that Regensburg was in the hands of his forces on the morning of 9 November 1923—and nowhere in between did his primitive faith in ultimate victory desert him for long, borne up as it was by his massive egotism and iron will.

[63] Apparently no relation of the later Bundespräsident and historian.
[64] B, I, SA 1, 1494, H. Pernet, pp. 367-69.

14.

THE PUTSCH IN THE BALANCE

In view of the many legends, rumors, and conflicting stories that have so long surrounded the Putsch, a closer examination of the events and of their meaning is necessary to clear away the smoke of speculation and reveal the events and their significance.[1]

I. *The Coming of the Putsch*

Why was there a Putsch? This question calls for many answers, some general, some specific. Where general answers are concerned, the first is undoubtedly the general course and tendency of Hitler's activities since 1921. As the police warned the government at the beginning of 1923, Hitler was sailing a collision course with the authorities. He preached revolution and clearly believed his own propaganda. This meant that, as long as the "system" he hated existed, he could be expected to take action against it as soon as he felt strong enough to do so. In turn, Hitler's propaganda had a terrific impact on his followers. Even had he not believed in the proposals he made and the revolution he promised, the mass of his followers did believe. This meant that sooner or later, he would be forced to revolt or lose them. He had only the choice between following Napoleon III or Boulanger—and the one course led by way of Putsches to a throne, while the other led by way of lost opportunities to a lonely suicide.

Another strong force working towards a Putsch was the success of the Revolution of 1918. The Left had succeeded in overturning the existing government with a handful of activists—in München no more than seven or eight hundred. This appeal to violence on the part of a minority, even though it was claimed that the minority represented the wishes of the majority, was a provocation to all

---

[1] The need for such an examination of the Putsch is intensified by the fact that this account has concentrated on what happened and not on what various people claimed had happened.

who did not accept the new state of affairs and an invitation to go and do likewise. It is always amusing in the study of history to see how horrified former revolutionaries, who have gotten control of a state by violence, become when there is a possibility that violence will be used against them. The legitimacy of any government established by revolution is always questionable until it has been in existence for at least a generation, and only rarely is it not challenged by both dissenting revolutionaries and counterrevolutionaries. Summed up briefly, the question was, if Eisner could make a successful revolution in the face of the opposition or passivity of the great bulk of the population of München, why couldn't Hitler with much of the population of München behind him make a successful revolution?

A final general cause of the Putsch was the increasing desperation of the population in general and of Hitler's followers in particular. With the value of the mark spiraling downward at a dizzying rate, with stores and factories shutting daily, with hunger stalking many persons to whom it was normally a stranger, pressures for action were increasing at a geometrical rate—especially since the government in Berlin seemed to be doing nothing at all to relieve the situation. Particularly in circles hostile to the Weimar Republic this tragic economic disaster was seen not just as the result of passive forces; it was seen as the active work of Germany's enemies, both foreign and internal, and the demand for the seeking out and punishment of the traitors and profiteers was popular at many levels of the population. Beyond the clamor for the identification and punishment of the guilty lay the bald demand for a strong man to introduce new policies and save Germany. Democracy is always at its worst in a serious crisis, and the demands for a strong man soon follow disaster. In the Germany of 1923, where the existing system was unpopular and identified in the eyes of many citizens with foreign oppressors, the demand was particularly strong. In Bavaria where there was always suspicion of the "manipulators" and "capitalists" in Berlin, a city that offended not only by being "Red" but also by being Prussian, the demand for violent change was loudest and most heartfelt.

Besides these basic and general reasons for the Putsch, there were specific reasons why the leaders of the Kampfbund should revolt. First of all, despite all their talk at the trial—and even before —of wanting Kahr to act so that they could go along with him, they lived in constant fear that Kahr or the government might act and steal their thunder. This fear they stated clearly in September, and it is easy to read it in their later actions. If Kahr moved, neither they nor their policies would receive serious consideration. They apparently did not really believe he would move, but they realized that all of their plans would come to nought if he did. They were undoubtedly deeply disturbed by Kahr's negotiations with the Landbund and the northern Verbände, because, having little understanding of the situation outside München, let alone outside Bavaria, they greatly overestimated the strength of these groups and the possibility that they could strike a successful blow in Berlin.

Hitler was also under very serious pressure from his followers to act. He had been promising, in general terms, a revolution against the revolution. Now his followers—disturbed, frightened, and increasingly impatient—were demanding that he seize time by the forelock. Moreover, the economic crisis had radicalized great numbers of Germans who would normally be opposed to violence and revolution. The great majority of any population is essentially passive, unless stirred up by great events, constant irritation, or nagging economic and social pressures. Here was a crisis situation that might never occur again. To let it pass without an effort to capitalize on it was scarcely in the nature of the "true-believer" or the political gambler in Hitler. Finally, Hitler was one of those great leaders of men who are closely attuned to the masses that they manipulate. In building up the expectations of his followers to fever pitch, he built up his own, and by the time of the Putsch he was a dangerously overloaded human generator of violent emotions that must unload itself in the near future.

These, then, were reasons why the Putsch came. Why was it timed when it was? Here there seem to have been several factors at work. One was the symbolism of the national revolution. Since the aim of the new revolutionaries was to replace the old, corrupt, and treacherous Marxist revolutionaries with pure and noble nationalist revolutionaries, it was only proper that the action should come on the day when the treachery of the Left had brought defeat and disaster to Germany. The day of infamy should be followed by the day of glory. Throughout his life, 9 November had a mystical influence in Hitler's eyes, and it is not chance that great events were unleashed on this date on several occasions. Further, it was quite clear that something was brewing in Berlin, and there was the danger that the Stresemann government might pull an economic rabbit out of its hat—as it soon did—and thus release harmlessly much of the tension in the atmosphere. Other minor factors probably contributed to the decision, including the return of the students to the University, which had swollen the ranks of the SA noticeably. These young men were full of enthusiasm for the cause and anxious for action. Not only would they chafe at delay, but the pressures of the semester's work might soon reduce the political activity of many of them. Finally, and probably very significant regarding timing were the clear indications that the Bavarian authorities were beginning to take a much harder line with regard to Hitler and the Kampfbund. One way or another it is easy to see why Hitler, brooding over the situation, might come to the conclusion that it was now or never.

II. *The Putsch*

Once the Putsch began, its course and its outcome were clearly going to be the result of the effectiveness with which the contenders met the problems it posed them. The Putschists' problems were simple to state, if not simple to solve. They had to win over or coerce Kahr, Lossow, and Seisser, since they had decided to make the Putsch under cover of their names and authority. They had to confuse or neutralize all other opposition until that first aim was accomplished and then swiftly root out those centers of resistance that did not accept the authority of the triumvirs. They must also win over a large percentage of the many waverers who are found in the early stages of any civil struggle that is not fought out on an essentially regional basis.

Hitler undertook to solve these problems by seizing Kahr and his colleagues at the Bürgerbräukeller, where he could also lay hands on most of the members of the Bavarian government. To confuse the opposition, the rebels issued orders in the names of the triumvirs long before they confronted them with the Putsch—although the desire to dupe those of their own followers who would not wish to fight the Reichswehr and Landespolizei or who might be loyal to Kahr also seems to have played a part in this ploy.[2] To eliminate possible centers of counteraction, they ordered the capture of the Generalstaatskommissariat and other key government buildings and installations as well as the occupation of the Wehrkreiskommando and the telephone and telegraph building. To get

---

[2] This was a double-edged sword, though, and to some extent worked against the rebels once Kahr began to move to quell the insurrection, since his orders were sometimes believed by Putschists to be valid for themselves.

weapons and to ensure that the troops could not be used against them, their men were ordered to infiltrate barracks, to steal weapons from official caches, and to fraternize with the troops of both army and police. If, by these measures, they could win effective control of München by dawn they had achieved the first step in a successful revolution. If they failed, the odds would be increasingly against them. Time was both their greatest ally and their worst foe, depending upon how well they were able and ready to exploit it.

On the other hand, the government faced quite different problems. The first of these was surprise and, its natural complement, unpreparedness. Key officials were at home or out on the town when the Putsch broke. The bulk of officers and men of the armed forces were scattered throughout the city. A second major problem was that resulting from the capture of so many of the leaders of the government in the initial act of the Putsch. With the heads of the Bavarian government, the dictator, the commanders of the armed forces, and the München police all in the bag at the Bürgerbräukeller, the opposition lacked any single person who had full authority and a clear understanding of the existing situation—let alone knowledge of the attitudes of his superiors regarding the Putsch. Finally, since it soon became clear that at least some officials were involved in the Putsch, and since many others were suspected by one official or another of being sympathetic to the Putschists, an air of suspicion permeated the government ranks, and the lack of coordination imposed on the authorities by the loss of key leaders was multiplied by the unwillingness of various groups to reveal to others the fact that they were taking action against the Putsch. The result was that several centers of resistance developed separate plans of action and started to put them into effect before a central coordinating headquarters was established. For example, because of Frick's activities early in the Putsch, the Generalstaatskommissariat and the Landespolizei regarded the Police Directory as suspect and therefore did not keep it abreast of the situation. Similarly, because of suspicion of other agencies and fear of misuse of these agencies or their names by the Putschists, not only the Putschists but most officials were denied the use of telephonic and telegraphic facilities during the night of the Putsch, so that not only Putsch activities but anti-Putsch activities were seriously hampered. All of these government problems, however, were ones that, given time, would clear up of themselves. Therefore, while time worked against the Putschists, every minute of delay worked for the government, since with the passage of time more information could be gathered, the scattered men and troop units could be concentrated, and mutual suspicions could be resolved.

The resulting situation was an apparent Putschist triumph which resolved itself into disaster during the coming day. The success of the first Putschist measures was so overwhelming and impressive that it translated them into a state of euphoria that was as dangerous as it was pleasant. The result was that they left undone much that should have been done and paid dearly for this laxity as the situation developed. Vigorous and continuous action on the part of the Putschist leaders was particularly necessary because their planning for the Putsch had been spotty and poorly coordinated. Both Hitler and Göring were men who, while capable of stretches of hard work, were anything but methodical. Lacking access to well-trained, methodical staff personnel, they hit only the high spots in their planning for the Putsch, especially in view of the short time involved and the need for secrecy. Having scorned proffered aid from the north and made only the most casual arrangements for action outside of München, they stood or fell with events in that city. Yet, faced with this situation, they wasted most of the night in haphazard activities, many of which were at best peripheral to the basic problem.

Another reason for Putschist failure was the hesitance of both sides to indulge in bloodshed. Caution in starting a fight is normal in the first stage of civil wars. No one wishes the onus of firing the first shot and no one is certain what repercussions may occur. Firing on a foreign invader is a reflex. Firing on a fellow citizen, whether loyalist or rebel, is something different; it opens Pandora's Box with a vengeance. In the Putsch situation, this reluctance was even greater than usual, because the members of the two opposing forces were frequently not fully aware that they were opponents. The Putschists had been told by their leaders that the Reichswehr and Landespolizei were on their side, while at least portions of the armed forces had heard from various sources stories that the triumvirate was behind the Putsch. Also, the government troops had orders to avoid conflict as far as possible during the night, because their leaders wanted to wait until they had gathered overwhelming strength before acting. This would not only preclude an embarrassing, if not dangerous, initial setback, but provided the best chance to prevent bloodshed. The Putschists might take on a handful of policemen or soldiers—as they did at the Ludwigsbrücke—but they would be unlikely to engage in a fight which would pit them against thousands of trained troops.[3]

In the end, both sides held their initial strongholds throughout the early hours of the Putsch. This meant the collapse of the Putsch, for fresh troops were pouring into the city by dawn and the local units were at strength and alert. Planning methodically and moving in overwhelming strength, the army proceeded against Röhm's forces in the Wehrkreiskommando, while the Landes-polizei defended their flanks. The result was the surrender of the Reichskriegsflagge without a fight and the collapse of the "relieving force" from the Bürgerbräukeller when it came into fleeting contact with the outer edge of the defensive screen. It is doubtful that the Putsch could have had a long run under any circumstances, but the failure of the leaders to cope with the most vital and elementary problems facing them resulted in a premature collapse of the enterprise.

III. *Obstacles in the Path of Truth*

The prelude to the Putsch and the Putsch itself have been veiled in uncertainty and subjected to serious dispute because of a number of factors. The first and most important of these factors is the tissue of legends that the Putschists themselves wove about the circumstances and happenings involved. It was naturally to their advantage to portray themselves in the most favorable light—as their followers and admirers would see the matter—and to discredit their opponents as far as possible. This process began immediately after the Putsch and, to some extent, may have grown out of actual misunderstandings and errors. By the time of the trial of Hitler and his chief associates, the legends had taken on clearer form, and, largely through the agency of the presiding justice, the trial became a platform for the promulgation of these legends.[4] This end was achieved, whether by intent or negligence, not only by giving the Putschists their heads in court, so that they could tell their side of the story, but also by the failure of the court to defend the govern-

---

[3] Another indication of Putschist caution is the fact that, despite blood-thirsty ranting, they slew no hostages or opponents except in the fire-fight at the Feldherrnhalle.

[4] The more important legends will be considered critically in Section IV, below.

ment witnesses from insult and accusations of perjury, even though these accusations were not supported by serious evidence. Whether the justice minister, the presiding judge, or the chief prosecutor was responsible for the fact that a number of damaging witnesses for the prosecution were never called has never been clarified. The upshot was that Hitler, with his gift of tongues, dominated the trial and gave it its tone.

The impact of the Putschist legends was greatly increased by the fact that they were taken up not merely uncritically but gleefully by the political Left. Hitler and his colleagues had set themselves the task of blackening the triumvirs and casting as much mud as possible on innocent bystanders of the other camp, while protecting everyone in their own ranks. This tendency is to be seen in Pöhner's refusal to implicate Frick, although Frick was clearly involved, as well as in the refusal of Putschists to name unidentified comrades and in Hitler's refusal to say who the two men were with whom he consulted at the time of his decision to move. On the other hand, he and others went out of their way—ignoring the fact that they had arrested his right-hand man—in their attempts to implicate the crown prince of Bavaria. All of these targets of the "embarrassing embrace" were political opponents of the SPD. The result was that the accusations were reiterated with gusto by men who normally claimed that Hitler had never said a true word in his life. To be fair, the Social Democrats probably believed these stories or portions of them, for they fitted in with their own suspicions of conspiracy and dishonesty in high places. The result was that the lies were embalmed along with the truth in accounts from the radical Right and all shades of the Left, and thence passed into the historical literature.

Inconsistencies in the legends were ignored, although these were to be found in plenty. For example, the National Socialists claimed, correctly, that Kahr was dealing with north German right radical circles regarding the establishment of some sort of authoritarian regime in Berlin. At the same time, they accused him with equal vehemence of being a Bavarian separatist who was seeking to create, with the aid of the Papacy and France, a Danube monarchy consisting of Austria and Bavaria. In other words, on the one hand Kahr was identified with nationalist Prussians who wanted to establish centralized control of all Germany from Berlin, and on the other he was accused of trying to separate Bavaria from Germany to please Poincaré. One needs a strong stomach to swallow both of these stories at one sitting, and yet both of them were used again and again by the Left and by right radicals.

Another major factor in the uncertainties regarding the Putsch was the official policy of secrecy. Governments are, in general, inclined to secrecy and the Bavarian government was more secretive than many. Even where no very good reason existed, the Cabinet often refused to release government officials from their oaths of secrecy to testify in court because it was a bad precedent. In the Hitler Trial they had much better reason to worry. The Allies were about to begin a major military inspection in Bavaria, seeking to find and expose violations of the Treaty of Versailles. The Putschists knew of a good number of such violations and, using patriotism as a veil, successfully hinted that the government had a great deal to hide with regard to cooperation with them, when more often the real aim of the government was to maintain secrecy vis-à-vis the Allies. The Putschists made every accusation they could think of against the triumvirs, and a good number against the government, in open court and then pretended to think better of the matter when the question of proof came up. They then took refuge in "secret sessions," where they revealed little they hadn't already said and made statements that clearly conflict with the bulk of the pre-Putsch evidence. The Allies thus provided the defenders with a perfect device for safely smearing their opponents.

Finally, there really was a good deal of confusion regarding the events of the pre-Putsch and Putsch period, and it is only by the most painstaking and detailed detective work that one can learn—if one can—what really happened in a number of instances. Onlookers differed in their testimony; different people heard the same man say somewhat different things at the same time; individuals were misidentified. The result is that some relatively minor questions will probably never be entirely settled. As a result of all these factors enough uncertainty remained that everyone believed what he wanted to believe and used the story that best suited him for his own ends. The truth was the principal victim of this confusion, for partisans almost always find an excuse for the excesses of their heroes and see villainy in the good deeds of their foes.

IV. *Examination of the Open Questions*

In view of the controversy surrounding some of them and the mystery involved in others, it seems worthwhile to look briefly at some of the questions raised before, during, and even after the trial.

The evidence regarding these matters has largely been indicated earlier, but in a few instances, where this is not the case, the evidence will be cited here.

The first question is: Were Kahr, Lossow, and Seisser planning a "march on Berlin" in company with Ehrhardt, Hitler, and the other Verbände? Hitler and Kriebel claimed at the trial that this was the case. Evidence that seemed to support this accusation at least in part was introduced at the trial. However, the bulk of the pre-Putsch evidence and common sense unite to oppose this idea. Whatever Kahr's military abilities, both Seisser and Lossow were extremely capable general staff officers. It seems incredible that they could have thought of marching against the bulk of the Reichswehr, plus the riot police of Prussia at the head of a single division plus a rag tag and bobtail of irregulars. The idea becomes ludicrous when one realizes that, although the Bavarian forces had less than five days' supply of ammunition for the Reichswehr alone, Lossow had throughout the fall refused to support a scheme of J. H. Lehmann's that would have given him a considerable supply of Bavarian manufactured ammunition.[5] The situation was no better regarding food and was far worse regarding even the most essential supplies for the irregulars. According to the Landespolizei most of these men could not have marched ten miles without new shoes. Again, no preparations had been made for movements; key officers were on furlough; there were no maps for the troops to use. Finally a "march on Berlin" flies in the face of Kahr's negotiations with the Landbund and other north German groups calling for action *in Berlin*.

The second question is: Were the Putschist leaders telling the truth when they said that they had no intention of opposing the triumvirate or of fighting the Reichswehr and Landespolizei? They were bitterly opposed to Kahr and made no bones about it. Hence it is unlikely that they wanted to serve under him. Further, they turned out false statements signed with Lossow's name, Kahr's name, etc., before the Putsch had actually begun and continued to try to distribute such false documents during the period when they were, according to their own account, the allies of the triumvirate. A good example is the poster that Klotz tried to have distributed during the night of 8-9 November. Clearest of all, they attacked and overran the Landespolizei at the Ludwigsbrücke. Röhm, him-

---

[5] NA, Epp Papers, EAP 1-e-16/4, 20.11.1923.

self a Reichswehr officer even if he was awaiting discharge, was ready to fight at the Wehrkreiskommando by his own testimony and that of his men. Despite all of their contradictions and occasional denials, almost all of the Putschists admit that there were serious preparations made for fighting and that only the order of Ludendorff persuaded Röhm to give up. These are only isolated indications from among dozens that could be cited. The Putschists wanted to win, and if fighting would bring victory they would fight.

Were Kahr, Lossow, and Seisser really persuaded by Hitler that they should join him in the Putsch or were they, as they later claimed, only play-acting in the Bürgerbräukeller? We will never know the true answer to this question unless in some way we receive an insight into the minds of these men during the crucial few minutes involved. The impressions of others are widely varied, and their own later testimony is, of course, suspect either way. What can be clearly proven is that, from the moment they came into contact with their key advisors, at least two of these men were committed against the Putsch. By the time Kahr arrived at the GSK Freiherr von Freyberg had set in motion the machinery of government against the Putschists. Kahr did not countermand these orders. Lossow arrived in the headquarters of the city commandant, spoke with his subordinate generals, and immediately began issuing orders against the Putsch or confirming those they had issued. Seisser was inscrutable, but, since he was in constant touch with each of the other two, his refusal to commit himself openly in the presence of line officers smacks more of security and uncertainty regarding the reactions of some of his subordinates than it does of any sympathy with or cooperation with the Putschists. Therefore it can be said that these men made their promises to Hitler under threats and at gun point and clearly moved over to the other side as soon as they were free of his orbit.

The Putschists claimed that they believed the Putsch to be legal because Kahr, Lossow, and Seisser were behind it. This was their statement and, interestingly enough, does not seem to have been questioned by anyone at their trial. Yet, after all, Kahr, Lossow, and Seisser were not the legal government of Bavaria and had no right to make a Putsch. Therefore, their participation would make it no more legal than would Hitler's. A group of Putschists including prominent judges like von der Pfordten and Pöhner could scarcely have believed such nonsense even if they spouted it to their credulous supporters and the audience in the courtroom. Therefore, no matter what position the triumvirate had taken, only the least sophisticated of the Putschists could have believed that their actions were legal.

Another question that arose was whether the Putschists knew at the time of the march on the Feldherrnhalle that Kahr, Lossow, and Seisser were arrayed against them. The answer to this question is clearly yes, based on the testimony of Putschists and of official witnesses alike. The actions of the Putschists are mute testimony to this knowledge even when their words deny it, and their words are not consistent. In any case, the question really has no serious significance. Whoever was opposed to them, they were rebels and the decision to continue the rebellion carried with it responsibility for the ensuing bloodshed.

First Lieutenant Braun of the First Battalion, Nineteenth Infantry Regiment, was later made a major scapegoat of the National Socialists and was hounded first out of the army and then out of Germany because they claimed that he had "murdered" two of their comrades at the Wehrkreiskommando. The campaign against Braun seems to have begun as a result of a sincere error of identity in the confusion of the short clash at the Wehrkreiskommando. It was carried on first as part of a campaign against loyal officers in the Reichswehr, then as an example of the rare and villainous officer who opposed the good cause, and finally as a personal vendetta. This means that long after they knew that their original accusations were untrue, the National Socialists carried on their persecution of Braun because he had been opposed to their penetration of the army.[6]

The next two questions are closely related. Was the column that marched to the Feldherrnhalle an unarmed and peaceful demonstration to win popular support or was it an armed attempt to carry on the revolt and to relieve the Wehrkreiskommando? Who fired the first shot at the Feldherrnhalle? The answers to the first of these questions are mixed. The column was not unarmed and clearly hoped to carry on the Putsch by means of armed force, if necessary. On the other hand, it seems that the leaders were not planning a formal battle with the opposing troops. The Putschists' claim that their troops did not have loaded weapons and that even in the firefight in front of the Feldherrnhalle they did not fire is flatly untrue.

[6] For evidence regarding the events involving Braun see NA, T79, 53, pp 1137-90; and Chapter III, Section V, above.

Most of the Putschists carried some sort of arms; Ludendorff was one of the few exceptions. Many of them carried loaded arms, and, if orders were given to unload, as has been claimed, these orders did not reach many Putschists. One unit, Stosstrupp Hitler, even marched with fixed bayonets. Machine guns were carried in the column and on vehicles. Putschists prepared to fire at the Ludwigs-brücke.

The question of the first shot is wreathed in mystery and has been since the day of the Putsch. The accounts of the participants on both sides are highly contradictory, and not merely on the basis of partisanship. It is unlikely that anyone really knew, except possibly the man who fired the shot. What is clear is that the Putschists fired back and with a promptness that indicates that their weapons were loaded and ready. Only one Putschist, Walter Hewel, admitted to the police that he had fired on them, but other Putschists testified that their fellows did so. In any case, since the firing only started after the Putschists had not only refused demands to halt, but also brushed aside one line of police and become involved in a hand-to-hand struggle with the next, the Putschists were clearly resisting the police in the execution of their duty. The superior discipline of the police, the training that instilled in them the idea that the firearm was a weapon of last resort, and their use of their weapons as staves, all suggest that the police were less likely to fire without orders than the Putschists, but the best estimate is still a guess.

Another question often asked in those days, but ignored today, is: Who led the Putschists, Hitler or Ludendorff? As late as 1927, Deputy Wilhelm Hoegner (SPD), of the parliamentary committee that investigated the Putsch, believed that Ludendorff was at the very center of the affair, although he has now come to believe that this was not the case.[7] All the evidence indicates that, while Hitler was careful not to oppose Ludendorff clearly and directly on purely military matters during the Putsch, he ran everything himself. Ludendorff, belonging to no organization and having no political or military machine behind him in any direct sense, was far more a father figure of the type so often found in youth movements, rather than a mover of men and director of events. Ludendorff, already quite ill, was still infatuated with Hitler. Hitler, outwardly

[7] B, II, MA103476, p. 1361; GP, A, Minister Präsident a. D. Dr. Wilhelm Hoegner, 9.8.1966.

friendly and even obsequious, as he would later be with Hindenburg, in private made no bones of his contempt for the hero of World War I. According to Seisser, Hitler told him that he needed Ludendorff because no soldier would fire on him. Hitler's remarks to Lieutenant Colonel von Berchem, however, are even more revealing of Hitler's views of himself as well as of his famous colleague:

> "When I was present at a conference with Hitler at the beginning of October he demanded an *active* attack on Berlin with all Bavaria's forces. Hitler now had definite Napoleonic and messianic ideas. He declared that he felt the call within himself to save Germany and that this role would fall to him, if not now then later. He then drew a number of parallels with Napoleon, especially with the return of Napoleon from Elba to Paris.
>
> To my interjection, as to how he could burden his project with the name Ludendorff, which was possible neither at home nor abroad, he declared that the policy would be made by him alone and that Ludendorff, for whom only an exclusively military role —especially the winning over the rest of the Reichswehr—was planned, would not have the slightest influence. He added further that Napoleon in building his directory [*sic*] had surrounded himself only with unimportant men."[8]

Here, if Berchem, considered a most upright man by those who knew him, is to be believed, the mask really slipped and Hitler indicated his true opinion not only of Ludendorff but of his other associates in the proposed directory. If Lossow remembered and understood this remark, he must have winced on hearing his name among the directors.

The last question to be considered is the honesty of the Putsch leaders themselves. In the trial and in their post-Putsch propaganda they were scathing in their attacks on Kahr, Lossow, and Seisser for breaking their promises to support the Putsch—ignoring the fact that in law, both lay and ecclesiastical, an oath extorted under threat of violence is not binding.[9] Almost all comment has centered

[8] B, II, MA103476, p. 1151.

[9] The fact that the promise was not legally or morally binding does not change the fact that much of the propaganda against the triumvirs would have been impossible had they not made this promise. Therefore it would seem that they were tactically in error, if, as seems probable, they so acted merely to escape captivity. To quote the cynical Fouché: "It was worse than a crime; it was an error!"

on this meaningless question, while the question of the extent to which the Putschist leaders themselves held to the stern rules they wished to apply to others has been largely ignored. Yet the Putschists are most vulnerable on this score. They had long since passed, emotionally and intellectually, out of that world in which personal honor is vital, and into a frame of reference where the end justifies any means, including lies and perjury.

Hitler, in the course of the altercations following the Putsch, made the remark that he had "only one word of honor." There seems to be some truth to this statement, and the indications are that he had lost it somewhere very early in his political career, perhaps in Dr. Schweyer's office, since that gentleman reports that in a conversation one day in the summer of 1922 "Hitler sprang from his seat, struck his breast with his right hand, and said in an emotional tone: 'Herr Minister, I give you my word of honor, I will never in my life make a Putsch.' "[10] Hitler also apparently promised Seeckt early in 1923, during their one meeting, that he would never act against the Reichswehr, and Lossow assured Seeckt that Hitler had taken this stand.[11] In October, Hitler gave his word to Seisser to the same effect, only to withdraw it later. Seisser claimed, while admitting this withdrawal, that Hitler had then renewed the promise to Lossow.[12] By all accounts, Hitler gave his word to a good number of people but only remembered to withdraw it in one case. The least one can say is that he was lamentably casual with his promises, and this is a very charitable view of the situation.

In Dr. Weber's case, one cannot be so charitable. Whatever one may think of the extent to which Hitler's assurances should bind his associates and subordinates, Dr. Weber is on record personally. Oberland, unlike the SA, was a part of the Bavarian Auxiliary Police and everyone in this organization had to take an oath of allegiance to the Bavarian government. Oberländer also, as part of the military reserve, took an oath to follow Lossow—although before the Putsch Dr. Weber told at least some of his troops that this oath was no longer binding. There is no indication that he told the authorities anything or that he ever repudiated his obligations to the government. Dr. Weber was also fully aware of the obligations

---

[10] B, II, MA103476, p. 1373.

[11] GP, A, Oberst a. D. Hans-Harald von Selchow, 22.7.1959; B, Colonel Ernst Schultes.

[12] B, II, MA103476, p. 1141; IV, BuR, Bd. 34, Item 133, Bomhard Lagebericht; NA, EAP 105/7, II, Dr. Weber, p. 19.

he owed the government, for Seisser reminded him of them on 9 October, and Weber acknowledged them, and said that in a conflict between Hitler and the government he would consider his obligations to the government to be primary and those to Hitler secondary. Therefore, Dr. Weber knowingly and deliberately violated his oath and led his men to violate theirs, despite his horror at the "baseness" of Kahr, Lossow, and Seisser. Weber later claimed that he had warned Seisser that he would not fight Hitler, but he did not deny his obligations. During the Putsch, of course, he did not merely refuse to fight Hitler, he fought at Hitler's side against the government. Yet no Kampfbund leader was in the least upset by such dishonesty.[13]

Ludendorff told so many different stories to so many different people that it is hard to believe that he himself was always sure what the truth was. In fact, he seems to have been incapable of recognizing clear contradictions in his own statements. Not only did he on one occasion admit writing comments on a document and then deny having seen it at the only time when he could have written these comments,[14] but he also denied any interest in a revolution to the editor of the *Münchner Neueste Nachrichten* at the very time he was pressing Lossow in favor of a Putsch and explaining to Admiral Reinhard Scheer how vitally necessary a national revolution was. During his interrogation, Ludendorff denied having made any commitment to Lossow and then said that he had promised him "loyal cooperation" in return for a counterassurance. Apparently taking part in a Putsch against Lossow fell under this heading in Ludendorff's mind. Again, Ludendorff stated flatly that he did not know that the triumvirs had turned against the Putschists, whereas the evidence indicates clearly that if he didn't know it was only because he refused to believe what he was told by responsible persons. Finally, Ludendorff claimed that he only joined the Putsch after he knew that Lossow had agreed to go along. Yet Ludendorff was one of those who pleaded with Lossow to change his mind and accept the fait accompli. In the case of the old man from the Ludwigshöhe, it must be said that his view of the truth was peculiar.[15]

[13] B, ii, MA103476, pp. 1035, 1049-50, 1154-55, 1157.

[14] GP, B, Minister a. D. Hans Ehard.

[15] B, ii, MA103476, pp. 701, 1139; NA, EAP 105/7, I, passim; Müller, *Wandel*, p. 155; Ludendorff, *Feldherrnhalle*, passim; Chapters X-XII, above, passim.

Hermann Göring, while not foresworn before and during the Putsch, cheerfully gave his word of honor that he would not escape when he was interned by the police in a clinic in Garmisch. He then slipped across the border.[16] Röhm and Hühnlein were active officers and therefore violated their oaths in taking part in the Putsch, as did many other individuals who were policemen, officials, and employees of the government. Some SA units that had taken an oath of loyalty to Lossow could also scarcely claim that their honor was entirely unsullied.[17]

In view of the clear vulnerability of the Putschists on the score of honesty and honor, it is surprising that the government did not make strong use of this weapon against them, especially in view of the successful use of it by the Putschists against the triumvirs. Fumbling references to the Putschists' lies were made from time to time, but in a casual and defensive manner, and no serious effort was made to document them. This failure was a major error and a basic cause of the Putschists' propaganda victory after the Putsch. After all, the great majority of officers, officials, and former officers were still gentlemen of the old school to a greater or lesser degree. The worst reproach one could bring against the Putschists in their eyes would be that they were liars and knaves, yet even the Left made very little play with this accusation. The leftists framed their accusations in such general terms and in such provocative language that they could have very little impact on anyone but other leftists. Also, few nationalists were prepared to take lessons in honor from Marxists or indeed ever saw any Marxist propaganda. Therefore only the authorities could have wielded this sword effectively, and they did not do so.

v. *The Significance of Negative Factors in the Putsch*

No analysis of the Putsch can claim to be complete without considering the negative factors, because what did not happen was in many ways almost as important as what did happen. These negative factors are not, as one might assume, what are known as the "ifs" of history; things that did not happen in this sense are more in the realm of romance than history. Here, however, the question is one of things that did happen but happened in a negative sense.

The most important negative factor in the Putsch was the pas-

[16] B, I, M. Inn. 71770, Garmisch, 5085; Bericht, Leutnant Meier [*sic*], 12.11.1923; Bennecke, "Röhm-Putsch," p. 86.

[17] B, II, MA102140, HMB 3073, Ofr., p. 1.

sivity of Bund Bayern und Reich. Here was an organization with some 60,000 members, of whom at least 35,000 were organized into military units. On the night of the Putsch this organization did nothing, except in the Rosenheim area, where Regiment Chiemgau was alerted and—although kept in the dark as to developments in München—used to prevent Putschists from going to the capital. Dr. Pittinger, the leader of the Bund, spent part of the night driving from München to Rosenheim and the rest of the night soothing and confusing the leaders of the local Bund, which was close to both Ehrhardt and the Kampfbund. The result of his official decision to support Kahr and not to call out the Bund was crucial for the Putsch. Had Pittinger's Bund stood for the Putchists the situation would have been radically changed. Their strength would have been swollen almost tenfold, and their weaknesses in higher-ranking and specialized officers would have been compensated for by the surplus in the Bund.

However, one of the greatest lessons of the Putsch for the historian and for the government, although the Cabinet may have only partially understood it, was that Bayern und Reich could only be used effectively in one of two specific situations. In case of a Left insurrection there can be no question but that Bayern und Reich would have rallied to the support of the government to a man. The same is true of a national war against a foreign foe. However, the months that followed the Putsch made it clear that Bayern und Reich, in the form in which it existed on 8 November 1923, could be used by neither side in case of a right radical revolt against the Bavarian government. The central leadership, most of the responsible officers and officials of the Bund, and a great number of the veterans in its ranks would flatly refuse to act against a Bavarian government of even moderately conservative and national hue. On the other hand, a considerable number of the younger officers and enlisted men in the organization would not fight against men they regarded as brothers in the Racist or Patriotic Movement under any circumstances. The result of this situation was that a general call to arms against the Putschists would have meant the collapse of the Bund, while a call to arms on behalf of the Putschists would have been even more lamentably unsuccessful. This analysis indicates that the Bund was of real value only for two situations, both of which the Bavarian government feared might arise, but which in fact were not imminent and did not arise during the Weimar years. It is therefore not surprising that the government's interest in and support of the Bund declined markedly after the Putsch, despite its negative loyalty.

The VVM's situation was very similar to the Bund's, although, operating in right radical München, this Verband was far more sympathetic towards the Kampfbund than was Bayern und Reich. Its members were, however, mostly a good deal older and more solid citizens, with larger stakes in society, than the Kampfbündler. This meant that, although they might roar approval of Putschist slogans, when the night of decision came, their organization remained neutral. Here were hundreds more men—since a far smaller percentage of this group was apparently organized in military units—who could be used by neither side.

Less important for Bavaria but significant for the Putsch's repercussions in the Reich was the fact that Commander Ehrhardt, who had been preparing his own Putsch in the north for months and who had two regiments—seriously understrength and very badly equipped and armed—on the Bavarian-Thuringian border, refused to take part in the Putsch. Had Ehrhardt joined this Putsch he could, at the very least, have created diversions elsewhere that would have been disconcerting and alarming to the military and political authorities of Bavaria and the Reich. These repercussions would have given isolated right radical paramilitary organizations like Peter von Heydebreck's Upper Silesian regiments a chance to enter the fray and would therefore have given the entire affair a new dimension. It is probable that the outcome would still have been the same, especially in view of the speed and completeness of the Putschist defeat in München, but the possibilities for serious civil war and for foreign intervention would have been multiplied. Therefore, Ehrhardt's decision to support Kahr and not Hitler was an important negative development.

The other significant negative development was what may be called that of the "Silent Left." Sherlock Holmes once remarked that the important thing about the dog in the night was that he had not barked. This was certainly what was important about the Left in the Putsch. If the Left could crow in November 1918 at the way in which the German "Spiessbürger" had crouched in his burrow when the proletarian lion roared, the radical Right was entitled to exult in the fact that when they took to the streets under arms no Communist or Socialist dared raise his head in protest, let alone oppose the Putsch either in arms or by a strike. There is little evidence of what leaders of the Left did. Certainly there was no action in München. Even in such proletarian strongholds as Schweinfurt and Nürnberg there was no leftist reaction beyond a few KPD placards in Nürnberg. Yet in some areas official observers reported that there was a good deal of sympathy for the Putschists among the frightened and desperate workers and even more among the unemployed. Hitler might be a nationalist and a foe of Marxism but at least he was trying to do something about the situation, and no one else was doing anything but talk. If the Left, both moderate and radical, was silent and passive during the Putsch of 1923, can one be surprised that it fell so swiftly and easily in 1933? Here was an omen that passed unnoticed then and has, by and large, not been noticed since. Yet, it must be considered to be one of the negative aspects of the Putsch, since a massive reaction by the Left would certainly have modified the situation drastically, although it is very doubtful if this modification would have been fortunate from the viewpoint of either the Left or the government.

VI. *Conclusion*

In summary, then, one must say that the Putsch was long abrewing but that it was triggered by immediate and critical factors: a combination of ambition, dissent, and popular desperation. The Putschists played their hand badly, failing to realize the need for speed and determination if they were to have a chance of even temporary success. They were doomed when they failed to neutralize or win over the triumvirate, the government, and the armed forces. Suppression of the Putsch at an even earlier hour was only delayed by surprise, confusion in the government camp, and the determination of the authorities to have overwhelming force at their disposal before they acted.

Since the authorities kept their heads and the bulk of the armed forces remained loyal, the Putsch could not succeed and, ironically, it was probably best from the viewpoint of the Putschists that it should fail, as Hitler himself came to realize. Since the Putsch was so much his Putsch, it is perhaps only fitting to let him pronounce its epitaph. In 1933, shortly before dismissing General Pirner from his post as the head of the Landespolizei, Hitler said to him:

"It *was the greatest good fortune* for us National Socialists that this Putsch collapsed, because

1.) cooperation with General Ludendorff would have been absolutely impossible, . . .

2.) the sudden take-over of power in the whole of Germany would have led to the greatest of difficulties in 1923 because the essential preparations had not been even begun by the National Socialist Party, and

3.) the events of 9 November 1923 in front of the Feldherrnhalle, with their blood sacrifice, have proven to be the most effective propaganda for National Socialism."[18]

In his own cynical and shrewd manner the triumphant dictator looked back on the Putsch as a step in his and his party's careers and placed his finger both on the fatal weaknesses and on the potential advantages that he later exploited so effectively. The handful of men who lay on "eternal sentry duty" on Arcisstrasse helped to bring millions of youths to Hitler. If ever dead heroes have earned their keep, Scheubner-Richter and his comrades did.

[18] GP, A, General Christian Pirner, 26.9.1960.

12. Hitler marshalling his followers for a commemorative rerun of the march on the FHH after he seized power

Part Three

The New Political Milieu

13. Landespolizei Cavalry clears the Odeonsplatz of Putschist sympathizers in the afternoon of 9 November 1923

15.

THE POPULAR REACTION
TO THE PUTSCH

I. *München*

Public opinion in München and in most of the other larger Bavarian cities clearly favored the Putschists in the days immediately following their defeat. Turbulent crowds surged through the center of München again and again, vilifying Kahr and cheering Hitler. Broken up by the police, they soon reformed and reappeared elsewhere. At 4:00 p.m. on 9 November a violent crowd was cleared from the Odeonsplatz by the Landespolizei. In the next few hours other threatening crowds were dispersed in the vicinity of the Türkenkaserne, in the Max Josef Platz, in the Maximilianstrasse, in the Marienplatz, and in other locations. Around 9:00 p.m. a large mob was cleared out of the Stachus and another from the Tal, and both areas were cordoned off by the police. In all of these encounters, the crowd fought back, spat on the police, and called them names. As the police bitterly noted in their reports, some of the most violent individuals were members of the "so-called better classes." Women as well as men shouted, kicked, and threw various objects at the police. Individual soldiers and policemen who appeared on the streets were abused and sometimes beaten up.

The next three days were little better. On the tenth, a rowdy mob gathered in the Promenadeplatz within earshot of the assembled Bavarian Cabinet. Other mobs had to be cleared out of the Odeonsplatz and the Stachus on several occasions, and a mob in the Max Josef Platz was so violent and hostile that First Lieutenant Karl Koller, the later Luftwaffe general, ordered his company to advance with levelled bayonets—the only time in his life that one career police officer ever saw bayonets used against a mob. At the last moment, the crowd broke and ran, but for several tense minutes serious bloodshed seemed certain. On the eleventh, rumors of a Kampfbund assault from the southeast kept the defenders of München on edge, although in the end nothing happened. Then on the twelfth came the student assault on Unruh's Reichswehr column, which marked both the climax and the end of the popular violence.[1] Thereafter the crowds thinned and shouts became mutters. The right radicals were emotionally exhausted after days of operating at fever-pitch, and they were temporarily dejected by their failure to make any impact upon the government or the armed forces.[2] It was 14 November, though, before Haniel could make this report to Berlin:

> The emotions here are gradually beginning to calm down and the city has returned to something like its usual appearance. Even the fanatical adherents of Hitler, mostly students and youths of the same age, insofar as they have not fled because of their participation in the Putsch, no longer appear in public in the aggressive manner of the past few days. University and Infantry School are closed. The burial of the victims of the street fighting has also gone off without clashes. Serious breaches of the peace are no longer to be feared. The movement has lost its leader with the arrest of Hitler. None of his lieutenants are capable of replacing him. . . .[3]

The days following the Putsch had seen senseless, hopeless paroxysms of rage on the part of the many citizens who had identified themselves with the Putschists, but these were just the waves that continue to rage for a time after the passage of the storm. The failure of the Putsch had altered the entire political atmosphere. Just as the authorities who had tolerated or encouraged the Kampfbund and other right radical groups—in the belief that they were young men of good will who wished to reform society and the state in a generally acceptable manner—had now been roused from their complacency, so too had the right radicals. Many of them were very badly shaken by the realization that revolution means serious bloodshed and that not all of this blood would be that of the "bad

---

[1] See Chapter XVI, Section III, below.

[2] B, I, Kahr MS, pp. 1369, 1376; SA 1, 1490, Police Timetable; II, MA99521, 10.11.1923, p. 5; MA104221, PDM, Lapo Kdo. M., A Nr. 500 Geh./2300, 17.12.23; IV, HSIV, EE7, Endres MS, p. 65; GP, A, General Heinrich Greiner, 20.2.1961; General Walter von Unruh, 19.4.1955; B, Lieutenant Colonel Max Lagerbauer; Lieutenant Colonel Otto Muxel.

[3] NA, T120, 5569, p. K591591.

guys." They were used to seeing bloodied heads and broken bones as a result of street fighting with the "Reds," but these were no more than what one might expect in a vigorous sport. Death was something else again, and it was not only the young men who bore Faust's body home in silence who were shocked and unnerved. Later perhaps they would face the police again, just as they would make heroes of the "martyrs" of the movement. Some of them would come to believe that they even envied these martyrs. Temporarily, however, much as they might rage, few of the right radicals wished to face the rifles of the army and Lapo. On 7 November München had been a city waiting to explode. On 10 November the city was still reeling from the impact of the explosion. By 14 November it was limp and enervated. The crisis was over.

II. *Oberbayern*

Although the Verbände were very strong in Oberbayern and many of the leaders and men alike favored drastic action—preferably a march on Berlin and vigorous measures against profiteers—most of the Verbände remained loyal to Kahr during the Putsch and helped to disarm and disperse the Putschists. In the next few days, though, not only the Verbände but also many of the townspeople were won over to the Putschists because of the successful propaganda spread by the Kampfbündler and because of disappointment at the collapse of their hopes for action. For a time Kahr was very unpopular and Hitler's stock rose steadily. Then, however, official propaganda of all sorts and second thoughts as to the probable consequences of a successful Putsch in München began to take hold. The result was a general improvement of Kahr's image throughout the province and increasing calm among the people. There were still pockets of resistance, and there were places where public opinion veered like a weather-cock between the two positions.[4]

The most difficult situation in many ways was the disaffection of Regiment Chiemgau of Bund Bayern und Reich. This unit was the most important single paramilitary organization in southeastern Bavaria, and both Kahr and Pittinger were most anxious to keep it from drifting into the Kampfbund or Ehrhardt camps. Through the efforts of the civil authorities and such senior Bayern und Reich leaders as General Franz von Schultes a half-success was achieved: Regiment Chiemgau moved away from the groups hostile to the Bavarian government and the Reichswehr but also left Bund

[4] B, I, GSK 6, p. 17; GSK 44, pp. 22-85, 111, 183.

Bayern und Reich. From Pittinger's viewpoint this was, naturally, a serious defeat, but the retention of Chiemgau and its influential leaders within the circle of those who more or less accepted the status quo was a victory for the government that greatly eased the situation in Oberbayern.[5]

In the countryside things were different. The Racist Movement had been, throughout 1923, largely an urban development, affecting the towns and the middle-class and non-farming elements of the villages but leaving the farmers cold. As a result the peasantry in most areas was either disinterested in the entire affair or stood firmly behind Kahr or the legal government or both. For example, although Starnberg itself was the scene of some unrest, the peasantry voted full confidence in Kahr through their local organizations. In the Aibling district, the peasants included Bund Bayern und Reich in their suspicions and demanded that its local leaders explain to the peasant leaders the aims of their organization. However, this does not mean that the peasants were content with the existing situation. They were extremely anxious for an improvement of the economic situation and the return of the "good times" they had been enjoying in recent years. Some of them demanded that Kahr take drastic steps to improve their condition and, in general, the support of the peasantry for any and all authorities was clearly predicated upon the authorities' success in coping with the economic crisis.[6]

III. *Schwaben*

Schwaben probably had the smallest percentage of Putsch sympathizers of all of the Bavarian provinces right of the Rhine. Spreti said of their power and influence:

> Anyone who follows the racist press might well believe that the Kampfbündler and their satellites had the entire population behind them. The Bavarian government has also credited to these organizations a far greater strength than they really possess. If one would ascertain how many people support the Hitler Putsch, one could not credit them, in Schwaben, with even *one percent* of the population. . . . One can hardly believe that such a rela-

[5] B, II MA100411, Brief: H. Jäger an Knilling, 21.2.1924; MA102141, HMB 390, Obb., p. 4; IV, BuR, Bd. 34, Item 151.
[6] B, I, Kahr MS, p. 1378; GSK 44, pp. 74-85, 110, 221-23.

tively small number of people could win so much influence and power as they did simply because they adopt a radical stance. . . .[7]

The National Socialists remained unhappy and restless and clearly did not accept their dissolution. They even tried to make difficulties for the authorities, and Commander Ehrhardt made common cause with them here, but, as the Regierungspräsident noted, they were not strong enough to be more than a very minor nuisance. They rioted briefly in the center of Augsburg but were swiftly dispersed.

Public opinion was as concerned with the problem of Bavarian relations with the Reich as it was with the Putsch, and even before the Putsch the majority was opposed to the Verbände's plans for a march on Berlin. In Augsburg there was far more criticism of the failure of the authorities to suppress Hitler's pretensions before he broke loose than there was criticism of the "harshness" of their measures against the Kampfbund after the Putsch. Clearly Augsburg was not a smaller München. Naturally enough, in this atmosphere, Kahr's stock sank measurably. Indeed, in Donauwörth, the feeling went so far that the populace looked on all authority, whether state or federal, with marked coolness and suspicion. The problem of unemployment also reduced the interest in purely political matters.[8]

iv. *Niederbayern*

In Niederbayern, the Regierungspräsident identified Putschist sympathies with the "now generation:"

> . . . The circles that stand in contact with the national movement, that is, the younger, more educated people, including members of "Bayern und Reich" as well as the Notpolizei, appear at first to be inclined to stand sulkily aside and no longer to place themselves at the disposition of the authorities. . . .[9]

As was the case elsewhere, the hard-core Kampfbündler were undaunted by the suppression of the Putsch, but they remained

[7] B, I, GSK 44, p. 194.

[8] *Ibid.*, pp. 22, 94; II, MA102140, HMB 2150, Schw., p. 2; HMB 2399, pp. 2-3; HMB 2282, pp. 1-3; NA, EAP, 105/7a, II, I.R. 19, 11.11.1923, Pflügel an Reinwald.

[9] B, II, MA102140, HMB 1102, N/B, p. 2.

quiet, awaiting better times. The leftist parties were also quiet, and the workers seemed interested only in bread-and-butter questions, although the extreme Left was making progress among the unemployed.

While the peasants were strongly behind the legal government, the workers were divided between those who welcomed the neutralization of a force that they feared far more than the authorities, and those who felt sympathy with the Putschists. Friedrich von Chlingensperg noted in this regard: ". . . In workers' circles—even in a large portion of the Left-oriented—sympathy for Hitler exists, since they had hoped that this action would bring an improvement of the cheerless economic situation."[10] However, because the basic power of the government and its hostility towards the Left remained unaltered, and because the bulk of the workers were far more concerned with keeping themselves and their families fed in this desperate situation than they were in any political developments, the leaders of the Left found themselves unable to profit from the Putsch. Therefore Niederbayern lay quiet, though far from content, in the post-Putsch period.[11]

v. *Unterfranken*

In Unterfranken the bulk of the population was surprisingly disinterested in the Putsch. The shadow of starvation and chaos lay heavy over the land and drained even the radical workers of Schweinfurth of their interest in politics and of the energy to take radical action. The Verbände, however, responded vigorously, as did all rightist circles, although they did not all respond in the same way. The Kampfbündler attacked Kahr viciously, while leaders of Bayern und Reich, like General Hans von Mieg, defended him. The Knilling government was generally unpopular, even after it had been slightly reshuffled—at least in theory—in the middle of December. Indeed, many people looked on the ritual reshuffle as another indication of the bankruptcy of the parliamentary system itself. As a result, even though most people believed that the Putsch had to be put down, neither the government nor Kahr were popular enough to profit from having done so. They were tolerated simply because there was no real alternative. The one positive result was that all ideas of putsches and the leaders of the Kampfbund were

[10] B, ii, MA102140, HMB 1102, N/B, p. 3.
[11] B, i, GSK 44, pp. 60-61; ii, MA102140, HMB 1102, N/B, pp. 2-3; HMB 1174, pp. 1-3.

discredited in the eyes of many persons who had looked hopefully to them earlier.

Only the Verbände maintained a shadow life of apparent vigor. Although their teeth had been drawn, they continued to quarrel among themselves and to rail against the authorities, for the impact of the Putsch on their members was different than it was on the rest of the population, even among their sympathizers. The continuation of the ban on the NSDAP and Oberland was deeply resented, even by many members of Bayern und Reich. The result was that Kahr was the greatest loser. The bulk of the population blamed him not only for the Putsch but also for the distress they suffered, and the Verbände withdrew their support because of the Putsch and Kahr's post-Putsch "hard line" policy towards them. By the end of the year, it was clear that few tears would be wept at the passage of any of the more prominent political figures from the scene.[12]

VI. *Mittelfranken*

Mittelfranken suffered far more from violent reactions to the Putsch than did either of its neighboring provinces, and these disturbances continued longer than elsewhere. The Verbände were strongly entrenched in Nürnberg and were kept highly militant by the existence of a large, active, and hostile leftist movement. Thus, nerves were more tightly stretched, tempers were more edgy, and resentments ran deeper even than in München, where the Left was proportionately both weaker and more chastened.

In Nürnberg, as in München, the Putschists got their version of the events into circulation in rightist circles well before the official version was known, with the result that passions soon ran high against the triumvirate. This made it very difficult for the more moderate leaders, like Major (Ret.) Karl Winneberger of Bayern und Reich to keep their men in hand. As a further result, the Verbände sent an ultimatum to Kahr on 10 November.[13] On 11 November, large crowds of unruly right radicals gathered in the streets, and the irrepressible Julius Streicher made at least one speech to them. However, the recent events in München seem to have had their impact on him, for, aside from a few slurs directed at Jews or policemen, he held a moderate tone and advised the demonstrators not to clash with the police. Despite the size of the

---

[12] B, I, GSK 44, p. 180; II, MA102140, HMB 1740, Ufr., pp. 1-2; HMB 1810, pp. 1-2; IV, BuR, Bd. 36, Akt 1, Item 17; Schwend, *Bayern*, pp. 570-71.

[13] B, IV, BuR, Bd. 36, Akt 1, Item 14/3, Winneberger an Truspeck.

crowd, the blue police were able to handle it without too much difficulty.[14]

In the following days, the situation became more tense as increasing numbers of Verbände members were to be counted among the unemployed, probably partly through recruitment of the jobless and partly through the workings of the continuing economic crisis. In fact, the economic corner had already been turned, but this was not visible from the "frog perspective" of those who still suffered under earlier blows or were struck down in the death struggles of the inflationary monster. Most of the population was depressed and lethargic, but the members of the Verbände and the students remained vigorous and militant. There was therefore the possibility of serious riots in Nürnberg well after other towns and areas had returned to normal.[15] In the end, however, there was actually only one minor flurry, which occurred on 9 December. Streicher was stirring the pot, both below and on the surface, as were many other agitators. The result was a demonstration by a large crowd led by National Socialists after a Sunday concert. The police were ready, and aside from one man wounded by a saber thrust, there was no bloodshed, although the National Socialists spread the usual rumors of police brutality and spoke of "streams of blood."[16] In Nürnberg as elsewhere, the crowds wanted no serious trouble and there were no further demonstrations after this abortive one.

In the countryside, there were, in the days immediately following the Putsch, several attacks against Jews by National Socialists. In one case the home of a Jewish merchant was burned. In another, National Socialists and Jews exchanged shots—apparently without hitting anything. In both cases, the offenders were caught and indictments prepared. Thus, despite the greater unrest and the higher potential for trouble, no serious outbreaks occurred in Mittelfranken, probably at least partially because the Kampfbündler knew that Police Director Gareis was determined to maintain order at any and all costs.

VII. *Oberfranken*

The situation in Oberfranken was more complex than in most of the other provinces because of the special problems posed by the

[14] B, I, GSK 90, pp. 573, 578-79, 590.

[15] B, II, MA102140, HMB 2074, M/F, p. 2; IV, BuR, Bd. 36, Akt 1, Item 35.

[16] B, I, GSK 44, p. 217; GSK 90, p. 590.

existence of the Border Defense Force against Saxony and
Thuringia, by the fear of these "Red" strongholds, and by the tensions between Catholics and Protestants. As a result, the divisions
in the populace seem to have gone even deeper and the unrest continued far longer than elsewhere. From the beginning, there was
much difference of opinion in different parts of the province. In the
northwest, for example, the Putsch was frowned upon even within
the Verbände, while in the northeast, Kahr was widely blamed for
the events in München. After the Putsch the tide of resentment
ebbed and waxed and ebbed again. On 14 November the Verbände
still buzzed like bees. On 16 November Strössenreuther believed
that the worst was over, but a few days later he had to admit that
a new wave of Kampfbund propaganda had once again raised feelings against Kahr. It was nearly Christmas before he could report
that the bulk of the middle class was behind Kahr and approved of
his actions. Even then, he warned that many people remained stub-
bornly "wrongheaded:"

> Everything that Hitler and his followers say is obviously correct.
> They show the deepest distrust for official pronouncements, on
> top of which long reading of the *Völkische Beobachter* with its
> long-term one-sided reporting must have a deleterious effect on
> the critical faculties of the reader. A major role is also played by
> the fact that the Protestant population feels strong distrust for
> certain tendencies in the Bavarian People's Party. This distrust
> leads, unfortunately to far too much generalizing, especially in
> this regard, and the most incredible rumors are believed. The en-
> lightenment [of the people] is to a considerable extent also made
> more difficult by the fact that they believed, as a result of the
> more or less tolerated [paramilitary] concentration on the
> frontier, that a march on Berlin really was planned.[17]

All in all, Kahr could look for little comfort in this direction. The
moderates would favor the Volkspartei and the legitimate government while his support among the rightist elements was badly
undermined.[18]

Despite strong Putschist propaganda, especially on the part of
upper class women, Bayreuth was relatively free of riots. The
Lieb'sche Wirtschaft, which was the chief gathering place of the

[17] B, II, MA102140, HMB 3073, Ofr., p. 1.
[18] B, I, GSK 44, pp. 17-19, 21, 53, 57; II, MA102140, HMB 2201, Ofr.,
p. 1; IV, Lapo, Bd. 26a, Akt 3, Items 77, 79-80.

National Socialists, had to be cleared and closed and crowds had to be cleared from in front of it twice, but this was apparently the extent of the disturbances in the city.

In Bamberg there was more trouble. Dr. Friedrich Amende, a Balt, and Christian Roth stirred up a large crowd to violent action on 12 November. A mob of 2,000 tried to storm the city hall, and the Landespolizei as well as the blue police had to be used to restore order. The Reichswehr was also alerted, but not used, partly perhaps because Colonel Zürn, not keen on police duties, warned that if the Reichswehr came out, it would come out shooting. A few persons were injured but none seriously. This affair apparently drew the fangs of the Kampfbündler, for there were no more large demonstrations.[19]

In the border defense area around Hof and Coburg the situation immediately after the Putsch was tense, since the events in München shattered the high hopes of the Verbände that there would be a march on Berlin. Both the National Socialists and the members of the other Verbände were bitterly opposed to the dissolution of the NSDAP and other Putschist organizations. On 11 November, the National Socialists led a large mob in a public demonstrations which the police let run its course since they had insufficient forces to halt it effectively. Later, however, they broke up several smaller demonstrations and the public expression of indignation withered away. The tide continued to run against Kahr, though, and Putschist propaganda was widely distributed.[20]

VIII. *The Oberpfalz*

Despite the usual excitement and unrest following the Putsch in the Oberpfalz there were no formal demonstrations against the government. The only resistance appeared in the form of nocturnal destruction of official proclamations in Regensburg, its suburbs, and in Neumarkt. Some National Socialist propaganda was also pasted up at night. As a result of a methodical campaign by local officials, the government soon won the upper hand in the eyes of the bulk of the population and a marked relaxation of tensions followed. At the same time, the enthusiasm of the younger generation for the

[19] B, I, GSK 50, pp. 34-35; GSK 90, p. 417; IV, Lapo, Ed. 26a, Akt 3, Items 77, 79, 90.

[20] B, I, GSK 43, pp. 265-67; SA 1, 1492, 2482/23 Bahnüberwachungsstelle Hof; II, MA102140, HMB 3073, p. 2; IV, Lapo, Bd. 26a, Akt 3, Item 70; Akt 5, Gr. Sch. IIIc, Erfahrungsbericht St. V. 1, Hof 33, pp. 3-8.

Patriotic Movement was thoroughly dampened, a fact which Regierungspräsident von Winterstein deplored. As was the case everywhere, the bulk of the National Socialists remained sullen and hostile to the government, while Reichsflagge was sharply divided on the proper stand to take. Bayern und Reich stood clearly for the government, but only vigorous action on the part of officials and prominent local leaders had prevented large-scale defections by younger members. The parties of the Left remained quiet throughout the period.[21]

IX. *Conclusion*

The aftermath of the Putsch in Bavaria outside München made it very clear that there was, despite widespread dissatisfaction with the economic and political situation, very little base for a serious revolutionary movement. However, the base that did exist was determined, hard-working, and optimistic, characteristics that suggested that the movement would not easily be stamped out even though it could be held to a minimal level of overt activity. The Putschist support was strongest among young people, especially those with a Gymnasium or university education, but the Putsch appealed to younger workers and even to some younger peasants as well. In general, though, the peasantry was still very cool to the Putschists and their strength centered in the larger towns, with peripheral groups in the villages consisting primarily of non-farming elements.

The reaction to the Putsch also made it clear that any serious action against rightist Putschists would have to be taken by the government. In many cases the Verbände opposed to the Putsch and friendly towards the government would not carry their support so far as to clash with their "brothers" of the Kampfbund, while the average citizen expected the government to protect him. The Left, whether moderate or radical, had failed to produce any serious opposition to the Putschists and failed to take any effective action to profit from the discomfiture of the radical Right and the government in the period after the Putsch. The Left was simply not a serious political force in Bavaria in 1923.

Finally, the Putsch completed the destruction of the myth of Kahr as the savior, the man of action who would lead the people out of the wilderness, that had been strong in rightist circles, and

[21] B, II, MA102140, HMB Opf., 12.11.1923, pp. 1-2; HMB 875, Opf., pp. 1-3.

it added to the heavy burden of distrust with which he had been regarded for years in moderate circles. Only in portions of the peasantry and of Bund Bayern und Reich, as well as in some elements of the bureaucracy did he still have any real support, and this support was not strong enough to make up for the many powerful enemies he had found, the people he had disillusioned, and, most of all, the fact that he had destroyed the need for himself as a buffer between the government and the people by breaking the Putsch. The government, in touch with the popular mood through the parties and the bureaucracy, could therefore proceed against him with impunity, and it did so.

The Putsch showed that National Socialism had a long way to go before it could claim to be a major political force, but it also showed that it had a leadership cadre that was determined to achieve this goal.

16.

THE IMMEDIATE REACTION OF THE VERBÄNDE, THE PRESSURE GROUPS, AND THE LEFT

1. *The Kampfbund*

The Kampfbund, naturally, found the collapse of the Putsch a bitter pill to swallow, and the immediate reactions of its members to defeat and disappointment were often vigorous and violent—particularly where the local leadership remained relatively unscathed, as was often the case outside of München. The reaction was, however, not entirely uniform. Some Kampfbund members, and even some groups of members, opposed the Putsch and left their organizations, while others merely pretended to do so.[1] Many dropped out of all political activity in disgust. Some of these apparently returned soon, but often the others did not reappear until the National Socialists came to power in 1933, if at all.[2] The bulk of both leaders and followers seem, however, to have stood by their guns in the period immediately after the Putsch. This was clearly the case in München, where they made themselves only too apparent to the authorities, but it was also true throughout most of Bavaria. Even in Schwaben, where the National Socialists had the lightest

[1] It is not always easy to tell which defections were genuine and which were a mere sham, undertaken to throw dust in the eyes of the authorities. This is especially true because some of the genuine defections were only temporary. See in this connection, Chapter xxii, Section 1.

[2] Hans Kallenbach, for example, complains of the "others for whom the march was too tiring, for whom it was too long before we reached our goal." Kallenbach, *Mit Hitler*, p. 215. One example was Heinrich Himmler's old friend Heinrich Gärtner, who only called himself to Himmler's attention again when he asked for a job in November 1933. NA, T175, 99, p. 2621015.

hold of any province, the Regierungspräsident wrote on 11 December 1923:

> The National Socialists and Kampfbündler are not prepared to accept the dissolution of their organizations and appear to be working, quietly, for a new Putsch. . . . The *Schwäbische Volksstimme*, which formerly appeared in Neuburg and has since been banned, wrote in its last number: "National Socialists! They can, naturally, dissolve us and ban us, but no power in the world is in a position to make us break our oaths or be dishonorable. We have sworn our loyalty to the fatherland and to our leader, Hitler—our oath still exists."[3]

The Regierungspräsident of Niederbayern agreed, saying:

> The local organizations of the Kampfbund Verbände have apparently accepted their dissolution; their members, however, are, as before, convinced of the correctness and strength of their movement. Most of them are not to be moved to join other patriotic Verbände, but clearly only await favorable times in order to reappear upon the scene.[4]

These evaluations receive strong support not merely from later developments but from statements made by Putschists and other National Socialists right after the Putsch. A National Socialist on a steamer for Mexico at the time of the Putsch wrote to assure Hitler of his loyalty and his firm faith in eventual victory. The leader of a National Socialist Ortsgruppe in Austria wrote a very similar letter to Hitler a few days later. On 16 November a National Socialist speaker in Hof was already openly preaching that Hitler would soon be free again and that they would finally be triumphant. Fürst Wrede, whose Reiterkorps had been the "orphan" of the Putsch, nonetheless held staunchly to his convictions and proclaimed that the triumvirate was ruined and that in the end all would be well. Meanwhile, he and his men would carry on as before the Putsch. J. F. Lehmann also testified to bitterness and determination in Putschist circles.[5]

Not all voices in the NSDAP sang this tune, though. Such Infan-

---

[3] B, II, MA102140, HMB 2399, Schw., p. 2.

[4] B, II, MA102140, HMB 1174, N/B, p. 1.

[5] B, IV, Lapo, Bd. 26a, Akt 5, Gr. Sch. IIIc, Bericht Lochner-Gruber, 16.11.1923, pp. 1-3; NA, T79, 82, p. 211; T84, 4, pp. 3473-76, 3754-55; NA, Epp Papers, EAP 1-e-16/4, Brief: Lehmann an Epp, 20.11.1923.

try School Putschists as Robert Wagner and Siegfried Mahler were soured on the men who had led them into the Putsch and lied to them during it.[6] Karl Beggel, the commander of the First Battalion of SA Regiment München, came to the conclusion that his leaders were not capable of supporting their pretensions.[7] Many of the wounded Putschists were bitter against Hitler.[8] In Kronach the local NSDAP went over to Bayern und Reich immediately after the Putsch and before various Kampfbund leaders issued orders to take refuge in, and take over if possible, other Verbände. In Teuschnitz National Socialist members of the PNB remained loyal and later renewed their oaths to support the government without question. Moreover, some National Socialists from other parts of Germany still wished to join the Bavarian Landespolizei and Reichswehr in the north, and at least some of the workers who had been won over by Hitler tended to return to the SPD or the Communist Party after the collapse of the Putsch.[9]

The activists, those with faith in the future and determination to carry on the fight, adopted a number of tactics in following their goal. They spewed forth propaganda of all sorts by all available means; they organized and reorganized National Socialist groups or created new organizations under new names; and either directly or through sympathizers they protested loudly and bitterly about their treatment by the authorities. Originally the organizational attempts were focused on maintaining or reviving the NSDAP as such, but these activities provoked immediate police action and placed the activists clearly on the wrong side of the law. Anton Ritter von Bolz was arrested in Nürnberg; Walter Bernhardt, in Regensburg; and Dr. Albert Niemes was forced to flee to Austria. Meanwhile attempts to build a unitary leadership in München had broken down as much because of personality conflicts and the lack of a strong and recognized chief as because of official harassment. Similar problems, compounded by money shortages, resulted in the

[6] See above, Chapter XII, Section III.

[7] B, I, SA 1, 1493, PDM via-F-2703/23, 18.12.1923.

[8] Nissen, *Helle Blätter*, p. 84: "Der grösste Teil kam auf meine Station. Die späteren 'Unsterblichen' waren nicht zurückhaltend in der Kritik der Flucht des Mannes, der sie zu dem Blutbad geführt und feierlich geschworen hatte, dass der Tag der Revolution ihn siegreich oder tot finden werde. . . ."

[9] B, II, MA102140, HMB 3073, Ofr., p. 2; IV, Lapo, Bd. 26a, Akt 3, 2524 Ofr., 11.11.1923; Item 73 J.N. 30 II/2, Tagesbericht, 9.11.1923; Akt 5, Gr. Sch. IIIc, Erfahrungsbericht, Lapo Bamberg, Stat. *V.* Süd., p. 2; Lapo Hof, 1. Stat. V. 33, pp. 3, 7.

collapse of the attempt to establish a general headquarters in Salzburg.[10]

The result was that the National Socialists went over to the recipe that had already been used successfully by Verbände in the north. They adopted camouflage, depending on the slowness of legal procedures and the complex legal safeguards that tend to characterize justice in a democratic state. Rossbach expressed the basic idea behind this technique in an interview in December 1923, during which he also voiced a favorite notion shared by both the extreme Right and the extreme Left with the liberal Left: the imperviousness of ideas to physical force.[11] In a sense Rossbach sums up two eternal axioms of the discontented in any society. They are, however, axioms which have proven to be true only in cases where the society attacked has been permissive, or seriously ill, or both.

> ". . . Rossbach also said that he no longer became unduly upset by the dissolution of any Verband in which he was active. He had already been 'dissolved' more than twenty times.
>
> He is of the opinion that any suppression of an idea by force can only aid it and does not understand the super-clever people who again and again commit the absurdity of forbidding a party. . . ."[12]

In short, an organization can be formed in ten minutes by ten determined men—or fewer—while in a democracy it takes hundreds of highly trained men and months of effort to prove it illegal and ban it, leaving aside the right of appeal and difficulties of proof. Therefore a democratic state can rarely win a complete victory over determined opponents, no matter how small in number, although it can keep them reasonably well in hand as long as they do not have too much support in the population at large. What the National Socialists did was to make the most of this tactic after the Putsch. As early as 16 November a National Socialist speaker in

[10] B, I, GSK 90, pp. 45c, 57; GSK 4, p. 14; GSK 43, p. 128; II, MA103473, Bericht, PDM, Abt. VI/N, 15.1. 1924.

[11] The idea that physical force cannot stamp out an idea lives on, especially in the minds of political dissidents and intellectuals, despite the disappearance of Nestorian Christianity, Albigensianism, and even National Socialism itself—although all of these ideas died when their carriers were effectively smashed by combined military and police action, as have many others.

[12] B, I, GSK, ca. p. 287.

Hof urged his listeners to join other Verbände and await the moment when they could re-emerge into the light. In Ansbach the National Socialists took over a small local group of the Deutschvölkische Schutz- und Trutzbund; in Kronach they formed an Ortsgruppe of Wiking; in Schmölz/Kronach they joined Jungdo; in Coburg they joined a Wiking group; and so the game began. The National Socialists joined existing organizations or formed new ones. The authorities found them out and banned these groups, but in the meantime the National Socialists had formed bowling clubs and similar organizations or had founded still more political groups.[13]

However, in view of the alertness of the authorities, the splintered conditions of the party, and the shortness of funds—which had been a problem at the best of times and was now catastrophic—the main effort was, naturally enough, on the propaganda front. Leaflets, placards, clandestine newspapers (and later new newspapers, which operated legally until banned), and, at the beginning, speeches in the streets were all used. Leaflets were handed to passers-by, thrown into barracks, dropped from airplanes. Newspapers with false (and harmless) front pages were distributed. Some newspapers were printed in Austria and smuggled into Bavaria until the money for this operation ran out. Placards of all sorts were pasted up at night in defiance of the authorities, and it was extremely hard to find the persons responsible. With time the National Socialists were arrested regularly and illegal activity became less and less important as the Putschists found new and legal means to carry on their movement, but in the period immediately after the Putsch they were a constant annoyance to all law enforcement agencies.[14]

In their propaganda the National Socialists played all the chords that were to be used in the elaborate mythology they built up around the Beer Hall Putsch in later years, although often in crude

[13] B, I, GSK 43, p. 149; II, MA102140, HMB 2287, M/F, pp. 1-2; IV, Lapo, Bd. 26a, Akt 3, Reg. Ofr. 2837, 1.12.1923; 2800, 28.11.1923; Item 65; Bd. 17, Kdo. Lapo Coburg, Chef 350 Ig, 16.11.1923; Akt 5, Gr. Sch. IIIc, Bericht Lochner-Gruber, 4, Anlage Hof, 16.11.1923, p. 3; Kallenbach, *Mit Hitler*, pp. 213-14.

[14] B, I, GSK 43, pp. 130-33, 144, 147, 163-66; GSK 90, pp. 327, 409; II, MA100425, R. M. Inn. P6043, p. 153; MA102140, HMB 1271, N/B, pp. 1-2; IV, BuR, Bd. 36, Akt 2, Item 6; NA, EAP 105/7a, 5/I.R. 19. Offz. v. D., 15.11.1923. See Chapter XXII, Section I.

form and with significant dissonants. Nonetheless, much of this propaganda was shrewdly conceived, and some of it was tellingly and cleverly presented. Perhaps the most significant theme was the vilification of Kahr, Lossow, and Seisser as traitors who had led the Putschists to believe that they would side with them but who lost their nerve and stabbed the noble völkisch leaders in the back. In one poem the day of the Putsch was referred to as "Kahrfreitag," a play on the German term for Good Friday (Karfreitag). The Bürgerbräukeller was nicknamed the "Kahrwandelkeller," a similar play on words ("Karwendel" is the name of a mountain range in southern Bavaria). In another the triumvirate was blamed for the prevailing economic chaos and disastrous unemployment, even though the situation was clearly not of their making and was, in any case, already beginning to improve markedly. Other pamphlets, articles and leaflets harped on the "lies" of Kahr, Lossow, and Seisser. Lossow was accused of wishing to shoot the Putschist leaders out of hand. A leaflet claimed that units of the Reichswehr had mutinied in favor of Hitler and been shot down. It was also claimed that Kahr was calling for help from Communist Saxony (where the left socialist government had been hamstrung by the Reich government). Fürst Wrede called on his men to help to drive the triumvirate out of the veterans organizations in which they might have influence or hold membership. He was also one of those who began the trend by which in one way or another the authorities were blamed not only for the deaths of the Putschists but also for those of the police when he claimed that Kahr had basely forced Captain Schraut to fight his old comrades.[15]

The government and the coalition parties were also attacked by the Putschists. Dr. Heim was accused of being a profiteer. The authorities were accused of using the methods of the Spanish inquisition, and it was strongly hinted that key figures in the Fuchs-Machhaus affair[16] had been murdered by the government. Dr. Matt was flayed for having spoken disparagingly of the "Prussian Ludendorff," even though he had avoided the usual opprobrious Bavarian synonym for Prussian.[17] The Catholic Church and Jews were often

[15] For examples see B, I, GSK 43, p. 245; GSK 44, pp. 236-38; GSK 71, p. 13; NA, T79, 82, p. 211; EAP 105/7a, 9.11.1923ff, passim; Koerber, Adolf-Viktor von, *Der völkische Ludendorff*, München (1924), Einführung.

[16] See above, Chapter VIII, Section III.

[17] GSK 43, pp. 43, 122; GSK 44, pp. 60-61; NA, T120, 5569, p. K591590.

seen by the National Socialists as co-conspirators, and at least one National Socialist leaflet saw a Jesuit-Jewish plot as the cause of the failure of the Putsch.[18] In Nürnberg, because of the failure of the Putsch, Major (Ret.) Walter Buch, the later senior magistrate of the Supreme Party Court, called for a pogrom in revenge against the Jews, although there is no evidence to indicate that the Jewish community either could or did react actively in any way to the insurrection. Kahr and Cardinal Faulhaber were accused of conspiring with Poincaré, the French president, to create a separatist south German state. Another National Socialist source claimed that Kahr consulted with Papal Nuncio Eugen Pacelli, the later Pope Pius XII, both before and after the meeting in the beer hall. Taken together, these accusations present us with very interesting and, one would guess, uncomfortable, intellectual bed-fellows. Yet, it is clear that many persons then and later believed one or more of these stories.[19]

The Reichswehr and the Landespolizei did not escape scot-free, either, although here the National Socialists seem to have been divided on tactics from the very beginning. The first reaction was bitter indeed, but later some propagandists were prepared either to admit that the army had only done its duty or to deny that they had had any intention of opposing the army. These men warned their party comrades that success at home and victory abroad could only be won with the army's cooperation.[20] There was less attempt to defend the Lapo, and to some extent Putschists vented on the police the wrath they felt it impolitic to unleash on the army. Interestingly, one of the charges laid against the Reichswehr officers in a leaflet circulating in the university was:

Kahr set his bloodhounds on the carriers of the idea of German freedom, and Reichswehr officers ordered the salvos against Hitler and his men without batting an eyelash. From a sense of duty? No, because of conscious or unconscious hatred against the common man from the people, of whom Hitler is one, because of arrogance, because of conceit, because of baseness.[21]

[18] This pamphlet circulated widely among the students in München.

[19] B, I, GSK 43, p. 293; IV, Lapo, Bd. 26a, Akt 3, Reg. Ofr. 2644, 17-18.11.1923; BuR, Bd. 34, Item 175; NA, T120, 5569, pp. K591648-49.

[20] B, IV, Lapo, Bd. 26a, Akt 5, Gr. Sch. IIIc, Bericht Lochner-Gruber, 16.11.1923, p. 2; RV, 361, p. 12208, von Graefe (DvFP), 22.11.1923.

[21] B, IV, BuR, Bd. 34, Item 175.

Here the officers represent the classes against the masses. Another set of rumors claimed that the Reichswehr and Lapo officers were bribed by Kahr.[22] Most of the propaganda against the army, however, centered about Lieutenant Braun, who became a symbol of the brutal officer who viciously opposed the movement as compared to other soldiers who received the National Socialist imprimatur then or later.[23]

Despite some efforts to claim the support of the crown prince for the Putsch and to claim personal monarchism on the part of some individuals, the National Socialists made little effort to hide their distaste for the monarchy and the crown prince.[24] In this connection a Nazi leaflet distributed in Bayreuth is clear and to the point:

Fellow Germans!

Hitler had to act in order to forestall the proclamation of the Danube monarchy on that evening, which would have brought us deepest misery.

Fellow Germans! Do you now want kings and princes or bread!

Do you want pomp and ceremony at gay courts or do you want to secure your own existence, your future?

Hold out! Hitler lives![25]

Even Prince Wrede claimed that Kahr wished and planned only to restore a clerical, separatist monarchy.[26] Yet the Nazis also claimed that he had cooperated with Hitler and then betrayed him. Such inconsistencies are hard to reconcile.

These attacks on the existing fabric of the state and society comprised the negative side of National Socialist propaganda after the Putsch. The positive side was given less stress, under the circumstances, but was by no means neglected. The faithful and the public were given not merely an enemy to hate and despise, but a vision of the New Jerusalem and a situation report on the pilgrimage there. Walter Buch's order of the day for 11 November presents these positive elements clearly:

[22] B, i, SA 1, 1490, Police Timetable.

[23] For data on the National Socialist attacks against Braun see Chapter xx, note 38, below.

[24] B, ii, MA103476, pp. 1403-09.

[25] B, iv, Lapo, Bd. 26a, Akt 3, Reg. Ofr. 2644, 18.11.1923, Beilage.

[26] NA, T79, 82, p. 211. See also B, iv, BuR, Bd. 34, Item 175.

"The first period of the national revolution is over. It has brought the desired clearing [of the air]. Our highly revered leader, Adolf Hitler, has again bled for the German people. The most shameful treachery that the world has ever seen has victimized him and the German people. Through Hitler's blood and the steel directed against our comrades in München by the hands of traitors the patriotic Kampfverbände are welded together for better or for worse. The second phase of the national revolution begins [now]. . . ."[27]

Here are assembled the positive elements of the Hitler myth in clear, if possibly unintentional, parallelism to the Christian tradition. The martyr bleeds for his people as a result of treachery, but he and his work remain intact. Unfortunately, Hitler could not die and rise on the third day, but the implication is that he did his best. Also very much in both the Christian and the world-wide tradition of political radicalism is the prompt use of the blood of martyrs, whose sufferings and example will inspire the faithful to greater sacrifices and more vigorous efforts. In Weilheim, shortly after Hitler's arrest, an alleged message from him to his followers was circulated: " 'Germans, be united and faithful. Do not desert the Fatherland! Hitler.' Written in the moment of his arrest." Here was the father of his people, whose every thought was of them, even in adversity. The admirers of Frederick the Great and of John Kennedy could both understand and approve the symbolism here—if not the man to whom it was applied.[28]

Another significant theme that is most important for any revolutionary movement was also played strongly. Hitler and Ludendorff were portrayed as men of action who tried to save the people from agony and hunger by bold action while the "old men in power" looked on callously or wasted precious time and lives by meaningless debates in their equally meaningless parliaments. This is another timeless accusation. Stresemann and Knilling find themselves in the company of Nero and Marie Antoinette, while the National

[27] B, I, GSK 90, p. 575.

[28] There is no supporting evidence for Hitler's having written or spoken any such message, and there is some evidence, such as "Putzi" Hanfstaengl's slightly malicious account of his surrender, that makes its authenticity seem dubious. Here, though, the impact of the "message" is more important than its origin. See Chapter XVIII, Section I, below.

Socialists play the role of the persecuted Christians and down-trodden peasants.[29]

Oberland and Reichskriegsflagge followed the same general policies after the Putsch as did their major ally. Dr. Weber, whose men had broken the oath they had taken as members of the PNB when they joined the Putsch, took a high moral line:

> "Broken promises and treachery have triumphed over those who believed in the German oath and loyalty. This defeat is an honor for us.
>
> We are dissolved and banned. That which has sealed its loyalty with blood and death is, however, not dissoluble!
>
> Our loyalty to our Racist Movement, which we and Germany have praised, can only be eradicated by our deaths, not by means of paper decrees.
>
> [Even] if we have suffered a defeat, we yet know that [the] honorable German cause will be carried through to victory.
>
> Our seed is fertilized with blood and will bear fruit manyfold.
>
> We remain faithful, brave, free!"[30]

As in the case of the National Socialists, however, some Oberländer did not approve of the Putsch and either did not take part in it or did so in the belief that they were taking part in a legal action ordered by Kahr. At least one such group, from Mühldorf, turned around and went home as soon as they learned the true state of affairs. Dr. Weber seems, however, to have spoken for the bulk of his followers and certainly for those who remained in the Bund after the Putsch.[31]

The spirit which animated Reichskriegsflagge is illustrated by Röhm's message to his men from prison and by the RKF directive issued on 3 December 1923. Röhm said:

> Victory was denied the first assault of the Racist Freedom Movement on the anniversary of the November revolts of 1918. We have lost a battle, but not our cause. The RKF, like its comrades of the NSDAP and of Oberland had to lay down its arms on 9 November 1923. It was, with its fellows, dissolved and forbidden by Generalstaatskommissar von Kahr. Two noble com-

[29] NA, EAP 105/7, I-II, passim; T120, 5569, p. K591646.

[30] B, I, GSK 43, p. 93.

[31] B, IV, BuR, Bd. 34, Item 151, Reg. Obb., an GSK, 11.11.1923, p. 2; Bd. 36, Akt 1, Item 27.

rades have sealed their faith in death, the unforgettable assault troop leader Lieutenant Casella, the best one of us, and our friend Faust. They will witness before God that there yet remains a young Germany, which is ready to make the supreme sacrifice for the freeing of the fatherland. I thank all of you, dear comrades, for the loyalty, discipline, and bravery which you, in fulfillment of your pledges, have shown, [and] which even our heavily armed opponents had to recognize. Our shield of honor gleams brighter than ever. Pride in you, comrades, will allow me to be happy within the walls of the jail in which I have now been thrown.[32]

The RKF directive on conduct reveals the bitterness which many Putschists, felt towards the officers who had crushed their insurrection:

... Cooperation with the RW and LP is, as a result of the events of 8 and 9 November, no longer possible as long as Lossow and Seisser lead these organizations. Every tie with the RW and LP which has not already been sundered is to be severed immediately, including any training that is possibly still being performed by these organizations. Every man of the Verbände is forbidden to accept any obligation no matter how alluring it may be. All officers of the LP and RW who still serve today under a foresworn Lossow and company must be simply ignored by us. This applies also for private relations. Beyond this, the behavior towards officers and enlisted men of the RW and LP must be left to the tactfulness of the individual in each case. This should not be very difficult, if everyone always clearly remembers that these people, whether under orders or on their own initiative, fired on our comrades and our leaders and shot down a great number of our best. It is obvious that the future armed forces and we must and will again stand shoulder to shoulder. It is clear to us all, though, that this can only occur after a thorough purge of the armed forces to remove all those elements that today give them their tone....[33]

Thus the Kampfverbände remained basically unrepentant and confident in the future triumph of their movement. Crushed and officially disbanded they clung together and breathed defiance against

[32] Röhm, *Geschichte*, pp. 281.
[33] B, I, GSK 4, p. 10.

their foes. Ludendorff, who always played Wilson to the "Big Three" (Hitler, Dr. Weber, and Röhm) of the Kampfverbände, danced a pas de seul, but the tune was the same except for his stronger emphasis on the "guilt" of the Catholic Church and a tone that was perhaps more petulent than confident.[34]

II. *The Other Verbände*

Bund Bayern und Reich, the most powerful of the Bavarian Verbände, was not invited to take part in the Putsch, nor would it have done so had it been invited. On the other hand, although the high command of the Bund stood firmly on the side of Kahr, the members and even the local leadership did not always take up the same firm posture. In no case did Bund members take a stand against the government,[35] but a number of local groups refused to defend the authorities from the Putschists, and in still other groups there was a greater or lesser degree of dissension on this point.[36]

Apparently in reaction to pressures from the Bund membership, although the members' sentiments may also have been used as an excuse for pressing a policy desired by Dr. Pittinger and his closest associates, on 10 November the Bund sent a letter to Kahr pressing for the resignation of the government and the passing of full powers to Kahr. In this missive, Pittinger stressed that the Bund had stood loyal and united behind Kahr during the Putsch but that, unless a real dictatorship was established promptly, Pittinger could not guarantee that this unity or support would continue. On the next day, in a letter to Seisser, Pittinger disavowed the ultimatum to Kahr issued by Hermann Bauer and his friends, and warned that he thought Commander Ehrhardt was behind it. Pittinger was thus a loyal supporter of Kahr's authority and a foe of the legal government.[37]

[34] For Ludendorff's activities after the Putsch see Chapter XVIII, Section I, below.

[35] They were accused of doing this in Bad Aibling, but, after much squabbling, the local Bezirksamtsvorstand admitted that a misunderstanding had existed. B, I, GSK 42, p. 255; GSK 43, pp. 254-55, 257, 268; GSK 44, pp. 20, 74-75, 221-22; GSK 99, pp. 28-30.

[36] B, I, GSK 44, pp. 12-13; II, MA102140, HMB 2282, Schw., p. 2; IV, BuR, Bd. 36, Akt 2, Item 33/4-9, Buttmann an Bundesleitung, Anlage 5.

[37] B, I, GSK 43, pp. 150-51; II, MA104221, Pittinger an Seisser, 11.11 - 1923.

During this period the Bundesleitung turned out a stream of propaganda in support of Kahr directed at the membership of the Bund. Whatever reservations Pittinger or Tutscheck may have had about Kahr were not reflected in either the political orientation issued by the former or the latter's letter to the military leaders of the Bund. Both directives of 12 November placed the full responsibility for betrayal and bloodshed on the heads of the Putschists and announced the Bund's unequivocal loyalty to Kahr. Propaganda in favor of the Putschists was denounced and Marxists were accused of being behind part of this campaign. Characteristically, no mention was made in either document of the legal Bavarian government.[38]

On the whole, the Bund seems to have followed the path of its leaders. At least twelve local or district groups expressed their firm support for Kahr, while only two, one of which (Chiemgau) had remained loyal during the Putsch,[39] took a clear stand against him. However, a number of those groups that supported Kahr also pressed for amnesty for the Putschists and future cooperation with them. These groups took the viewpoint that the Putschists had made an error but that they had done so with the best of intentions and that their aims were the same as those of Kahr and the Bund. Therefore they should be forgiven, and all racists should go on together to better things. At this level there were also demands for Kahr to take full power in Bavaria and act vigorously. In Eichstädt the bulk of the officers of the PNB contingent (provided by Bayern und Reich) announced that they would no longer guarantee to fight against rightist rebels, even though they did not approve of the Putsch, and the Lichtenfels Bund echoed this stand. At the other end of the scale, Baron Franz von Gagern, the Kreisleiter for Oberfranken, resigned from the Bund because it was too "soft" towards Hitler, a move that was greeted with enthusiasm by a number of his key subordinates and by dismay on the part of Dr. Pittinger.[40]

[38] B, I, GSK 99, pp. 17-20. For other propaganda see IV, BuR, Bd. 36, Akt 1, Items 16, 20, 24.

[39] The Chiemgauer had disarmed those Putschists who got as far as Rosenheim. See Chapter XIII, Section II above.

[40] Shortly thereafter, Gagern withdrew his resignation at Pittinger's insistence, despite Tutschek's desire to let it stand. B, I, GSK 43, pp. 308-13; GSK 44, pp. 12-13, 105; II, MA102141, HMB 476, Ofr., p. 1; IV, BuR, Akt 1, Item 18. See also Chapter XXIII, Section III.

The entire Putsch episode made it clear that the government could not possibly depend on the Bund for active support against the Kampfbund, a lesson that was clearly read by Knilling and his colleagues. However, it would seem that they read into this passivity a threat of active hostility, which really wasn't there, and feared a Putsch by the Bund. In fact, such a Putsch was even more out of the question than Bund action against the Kampfbund.[41]

The position of Ehrhardt's Wikingbund and its allies was not as clear-cut as that of Pittinger's Bund. Ehrhardt had certainly told Duesterberg in late October that he would not oppose Kahr and had refused to go along with Hitler's Putsch plans. During the Putsch he had been neutralized, and his München deputy, Kautter, had cooperated with Kahr.[42] After the Putsch, though, Ehrhardt seems to have scented an opportunity to replace Hitler as the head of the potentially powerful Racist Movement and charted a course for himself that could only be regarded by the authorities with suspicion. As early as the night of 9 November, Ehrhardt began encouraging right radical students at München University to pass a resolution attacking Kahr and supporting the Putschists. Ehrhardt and Kautter both claimed that Kautter had sought to persuade Kahr to take over and direct the Putsch and that their men were not mobilized against Hitler but for the "march on Berlin"—as though Kahr would have had either time or interest to spare for this project on that hectic and uncertain night, even if he had ever thought of such a scheme.[43] At the same time, the Putschists leaders were characterized as naive and unfit; Ehrhardt's propaganda was meant to cut both ways. Throughout the rest of November Ehrhardt followed this double line, on one hand promising to aid the Putschists in their time of troubles and to unleash a bigger and better Putsch shortly, and on the other seeking to persuade members of the dissolved organizations to forsake their previous allegiances and join his organizations or at least accept his leadership. In pursuit of this aim he continued to cultivate the students and wooed individual

[41] B, I, Kahr MS, pp. 1433-34; GSK 99, pp. 10-11, 21, 36; GSK 101, p. 28; IV, Bd. 26a, Akt 3, Reg. Ofr., 2827, 1.12.1923; Akt 5, Gr. Sch. IIIc, Erfahrungskericht, Lapo Hof, 1. Stat. v, 33, 20.11.1923; BuR, Bd. 36, Akt 1, passim. See also Chapter XIV, Section V.

[42] B, II, MA103476, p. 736. See also Chapters X-XII and XIV above.

[43] This claim also disagrees with the evidence from both GSK and Kampfbund witnesses regarding Kautter's activities on the night of 8-9.11.23. See also Chapter XII, Section I, and Chapter XIV, Section V, above.

local groups of Kampfbündler. Again and again he put himself forward as the man behind whom the entire movement could unite.[44] Ehrhardt's policy and the activities of his men in the weeks after the Putsch backfired. The authorities became both suspicious and hostile; Bayern und Reich neither trusted nor liked Ehrhardt; and the Kampfbund organizations were furious at his failure to support the Putsch and at his attempts to raid their organizations afterwards. By the end of November it was pretty clear that Ehrhardt was not going to succeed in his attempt to replace Hitler as the "völkisch" man of the hour. It was not yet clear whether he would, nonetheless, make gains as a result of his campaign.[45]

The remaining Verbände are less important than Bayern und Reich and Wiking, but some of them played a very active role in the days immediately after the Putsch. Central to these developments was Professor Hermann Bauer of the VVVB who always sought to offset the weakness of his organization by personal energy but who never quite brought it off. On 9 November, Bauer called on Kahr to take the bit in his teeth and unleash an all-out assault on the Weimar Constitution, Marxism, and the Bavarian government. The next day Bauer (for VVVB), Kleinhenz, Ehrhardt, Heiss, and Jäger (for Chiemgau) presented an ultimatum to Kahr in which, after briefly disavowing the Putsch, they demanded—in view of the fact that a national revival and the fulfillment of Kahr's stated program must depend on the Verbände rather than on the Reichswehr—the following concessions: an immediate general amnesty for all patriotic Verbände, the dissolution of the Social Democratic Party, the closing of all socialist newspapers, and the abrogation of the Weimar Constitution for Bavaria. Kahr was also to agree to recognize no Reich government except a dictatorship that would adopt the same measures. This document, issued on Saturday, demanded a reply by Sunday and threatened that the Verbände that the signers represented would choose new and radical leaders if these terms were not adopted. By this time-honored device, Bauer and his associates avoided direct threats that might possibly rebound against them in favor of a formula that would enable them to dodge direct responsibility if they were successfully defied.

[44] B, I, GSK 49, p. 46; II, MA103476, pp. 1286-88; MA104221, passim; NA, T120, 5569, pp. K591596-97.

[45] B, I, GSK 73, p. 40; GSK 90, p. 14; II, MA104221, Ehrhardt Erlass, 15.11.1923; IV, Lapo, Bd. 26a, Akt 3, Item 74; BuR, Bd. 36, Akt 1, Items 35, 52, 54; Akt 2, Item 20. See also Chapter XXIII, Section II, below.

When Kahr and the government more or less ignored the ultimatum and proceeded with their measures against the Kampfbund, there were no repercussions. The signers took no action and none of them, except Kleinhenz (who had, apparently, resigned from leadership of the Hermannsbund before signing) left their posts. On 11 November Bauer still hoped for a march on Berlin. A week later, having abandoned his hectoring tone, in the name of his organization he sent Kahr a plea for the unification of the Racist Movement and for action to save the fatherland, but his reference to Kahr as the man who had rescued the state showed how the times had changed since the Putsch and how little real power Bauer represented.[46]

The VVV had always been a loose organization, and in this crisis most of the organizations in the München VVV did not support Bauer. Some, like Pittinger and the leaders of the major veterans' organizations, took an opposite tack, as did the VVV groups in Aschaffenburg, Regensburg, Nürnberg, and Augsburg. Fritz Geisler, the national leader of the VVV strongly supported both Kahr and Seeckt, which must have taken still more wind out of Bauer's sails. The entire episode indicates how fragmented the nationalists were and how little their various factions agreed on fundamentals.[47]

In northern Bavaria, the powerful Reichsflagge was generally hostile towards Kahr and close to Ehrhardt in the immediate post-Putsch period, and in München at least portions of the VVM cut their ties with the police and Reichswehr to express their bitterness at the suppression of the Putsch. This, however, was as far as their hostility led them.[48]

The truth of the matter was that the Putsch had created such a disarray among these Verbände that they could neither act independently nor place effective pressure on authorities suddenly rendered cold to their advances. Until their leaders worked out their own positions and established an understanding regarding the new situation with their followers, the Verbände were hamstrung, even in the absence of opposition.

[46] B, I, GSK 100, p. 24; GSK 101, pp. 2-24; Kahr MS, p. 1384; II, MA103476, pp. 974-75, 1392; MA103473, Ultimatum.

[47] B, I, GSK 101, pp. 21-28; GSK 102, pp. 18, 30-40; II, MA103472, VVV Augsburg an Graf Spreti, 9.11.1923; MA104221, Pittinger an Seisser, 11.11.1923; IV, BuR, Bd. 36, Akt 1, Item 36.

[48] B, I, SA 1, 1450, Aufkl. Bl. d. Kampfbund, Dec. 1923; II, MA103476, p. 1054; IV, BuR, Bd. 36, Akt 1, Item 35.

III. *Other Special Interest Groups*

The most shrill and unruly of the pressure groups was, not surprisingly, the university and Hochschule[49] students. Student passions often do not run deep, but they usually run loud, and they also often run to minor violence, particularly where the students take an interest in politics. Certainly this was the case in Bavaria in the period following the Hitler Putsch. World War I had drastically changed the outlook of the student generations of the war and postwar years. Being both national and inclined to accept the idea of a welfare state—which they, as children of their time, identified exclusively with socialism—at first (during the immediate postwar months) they wavered between Left and Right, until the tactical inflexibility and alien doctrines of Marxism threw them decisively to the Right. One of their number describes the early stages of the process as he observed it vividly:

> . . . The increasing decline in the value of money created an academic society that was easily accessible to political demagogy. Nevertheless radical movements had at first only a limited following among the students. Reactionary conservatism, which was characteristic for the German prewar student generation, had given place to an honorable longing for socialism. It was a tragic failure that the German social democracy did not understand [how] to win the cooperation of a receptive, influential, and, for the future, important portion of the population. The Social Democratic Party lacked powerful leaders. The functionaries, who determined its policy, were not in a position to free themselves from the old preconceptions concerning a reactionary student body and saw in the university students the obstinate foes of their regime, until they really succeeded in strangling the "socialist longing" with their prejudice. When I transferred in the summer of 1919 to Marburg, which was associated for me with the pleasant memories of a convalescence during the war, the right radicalization of the students was already in full progress.[50]

Nissen clearly overstates the possibilities for serious cooperation between students and socialists of the old school and blames the

---

[49] University-level, special technical, business, or other specialized institutions.

[50] Nissen, *Helle Blätter*, p. 41.

latter too much for their failure to find each other. After all, the students were nationalists first and socialists afterwards, whereas the internationalism of the socialist leaders, at least, had been recently infused with new energy by the experiences of defeat—which they blamed on nationalism—and revolution. On the other hand, he sketches clearly the students' inclination towards a socialism that could be united with nationalism, an inclination that goes far to explain the enthusiasm with which many students followed Hitler and the readiness of many others to look on the actions of these radicals complacently.

In Bavaria great numbers of university students and even Gymnasium students had been active in the Verbände throughout 1923. Kampfbund leaders, such as Ernst Röhm and Gerhard Rossbach, moved in student circles and talked to student groups, operating in part through some of the student corporations. Some key Kampfbund leaders like Dr. Weber, Rudolf Hess, and Karl Osswald, were themselves students or instructors at the university or the Technische Hochschule, as were such Wiking leaders as Lieutenant Kautter and Walther Hemmeter (who was also closely associated with the Kampfbund). Only the Catholic student organizations supported the legal government.[51]

As a result of this orientation of the most active students, a wave of unrest and violence swept the bulk of the students into violent demonstrations, while the faculty, hopelessly divided among sympathizers with the activists, disapproving but permissive moderates, stern disciplinarians, and political opponents of the activists, made no serious attempt to master the situation. In any case, even if they had been solidly united in favor of maintaining order, the faculty would have found that the disciplinary organs and procedures that operate within a normal university community in normal times are completely inadequate for meeting major crises and massive disorder.

On 10 November crowds of students roamed the streets shouting threats against "Judas Kahr" and "Treacherous Lossow." Between two and three thousand students marched into the Odeonsplatz and passed a resolution against Kahr. Some of them planned,

---

[51] Evidence on this score has been presented earlier in many instances. For evidence regarding the stand of the students in general see B, I, Kahr MS, p. 1387; GSK 6, p. 28; II, MA103476, p. 1190; NA, EAP 105/7a, WKK VII 4365/Ib 6285; GP, B, Colonel Ernst Schultes; D, passim. See also Chapters III-IV, and XV above.

the authorities believed, to try to disarm and disband the police. Later, between three and four thousand students marched on the Stachus.[52] Again on the eleventh large mobs of students gathered in the vicinities of the University and the Technische Hochschule, but it was 12 November that saw the climactic clash between students and troops that ended the period of violent demonstrations.

On the morning of the twelfth, the radical students of the university and the Technische Hochschule assembled in the great entry hall (Aula) of the university for a mass meeting. A National Socialist convert from socialism, Adolf Schmalix, dominated the scene although he was not a student.[53] Commander Ehrhardt was also present and spoke to the students. Any student who dared to raise a dissenting voice was shouted down or threatened, sometimes by non-students. Finally, after two such meetings, the students came boiling out of the building and marched around the block. At the beginning there were only a few hundred of them but other students and passers-by joined in so that by the time they reached the square in front of the university again their numbers were greatly swollen, and in the square they became mixed with other students who were standing there in crowds.[54]

Meanwhile, the operations officer of the Bavarian Division of the Reichswehr, Lieutenant Colonel Endres, had persuaded Lossow that the right radicals and their sympathizers needed a lesson in deportment. He therefore chose a battalion commanded by the highly intelligent and tough-minded Prussian, Walter von Unruh, to make a sortie through the streets, reinforced by seven Lapo companies. The troops had orders, in case of trouble, to use their rifle butts but not fire, and the toughest company in the battalion was given the task of rearguard. The first pass through the center of the city, with band playing, met no overt resistance, despite dirty looks from many passers-by. Even at the university, where the streets were deserted because of the meeting inside, all went quietly, and Unruh, less anxious for a tussle than Endres, decided to avoid the university on his return journey. His drum sergeant-major, how-

[52] B, I, GSK 44, p. 7; SA 1, 1490, Police Timetable, 10.11.1923; IV, BuR, Bd. 36, Akt 1, Item 36; Müller, *Wandel*, p. 168.

[53] Apparently, like so many youthful—or would-be youthful—radicals, Schmalix was also an advocate of free love, for he was in difficulties with the authorities for transmitting a venereal disease. The causes change with the times, but their advocates do not seem to change much.

[54] B, I, Kahr MS, pp. 1387-88; GSK 73, p. 51; GSK 90, p. 545; SA 1, 1490, Police Timetable, 11-12.11.-1923; Müller, *Wandel*, pp. 172-74.

ever, did not know München[55] and blundered into the square in front of the university where the right radical students were gathered. The students, intoxicated with revolutionary phrases, saw the presence of the troops as a provocation and swarmed to the attack without hesitation. The troops, largely workers with a strong admixture of peasants,[56] having suffered a deluge of abuse for days without a chance to reply, welcomed the opportunity to teach the spoiled brats of the upper classes a good lesson. The result was a brief but heated skirmish in which a good number of students were bruised and battered and in which the inevitable activist professor —in this case the famous surgeon Sauerbruck—received a crack on the head that increased his great popularity still further.

The right radicals were now further enraged and there was much muttering about atrocities, but, significantly, there were no more attacks on troops by students. The rumor that students would attack the barracks that night came to nothing, possibly in part because the news undoubtedly leaked out that Endres had received permission to repulse any attack with all available weapons.[57] The most radical students subsided into reluctant quietude, but soon attacked the triumvirate in a student newspaper and in other direct and indirect ways that were on the safe side of violence, while the bulk of the students turned to more pressing matters.[58]

The student activists elsewhere in Bavaria took the same tack as those in München. In Erlangen they demonstrated vigorously

[55] The battalion was from Regensburg.

[56] Despite the popularity, especially among Marxists and generals, of the belief that most German enlisted soldiers in the days of the Weimar Republic were peasants and therefore naturally reactionary, the available— rather scanty—statistics clearly demonstrate its fragility. In mid-1920 an official survey of the Bavarian Division of the Reichswehr revealed that two-thirds of the enlisted men were workers and that the remainder were drawn from the peasantry and all other social groups. In 1924, a Communist source quoted official figures to indicate that the same proportions were applicable to the entire Reichswehr. B, II, MA99517, 7.5.1920, p. 14; MA101248, Anlage 2, PDN-F 6100/II "Vom Bürgerkrieg," Heft 15, 15.10.1924.

[57] B, IV, HSIV, EE7, Endres MS, pp. 66-67; NA, EAP 105/7a, Reichswehr Official Bericht, Anlage 8; GP, A, General Walter von Unruh, 19.4.1955; Müller, *Wandel*, pp. 174-75; Nissen, *Helle Blätter*, p. 84.

[58] B, I, Kahr MS, p. 1424; M. Inn. 73696, Bomhard Bericht, 22.11.1923; 73694, PDM VI/N 8.1.1924; II, MA103458, Kleophas Pleyer; IV, BuR, Bd. 34, Item 169; NA, EAP 105/7, III, p. 1; 105/7a, WKK 34365/Ib 6285, 27.11.1923; NA, T79, 82, p. 211; T120, 5569, p. K591657; Müller, *Wandel*, pp. 182-83.

against Kahr on 11 November, and the slate of officers overwhelmingly elected by the students in late November took a strong stand
for Ludendorff. Radical students in Nürnberg petitioned the government on behalf of Hitler and were unrepentant when admon-
ished. Many of the students at the Agricultural Hochschule at
Weihenstephan were not only racist in attitude but also members of
the Kampfbund. If winning over the most articulate students means
winning the next generation, the Weimar Republic was clearly in
trouble in Bavaria and Hitler was in clover, but fortunately there
is much evidence to suggest that this is not necessarily the case, as
Bismarck's Germany attests.[59]

The reaction of Crown Prince Rupprecht and the royalists to the
Putsch was hostile. Some Putschists, like Max Neunzert and
Walther Hemmeter, claimed that the crown prince sympathized
with them initially, and Neunzert's testimony, at least, probably impressed some people, since he had ties with the prince and had been
the Kampfbund's envoy to Rupprecht during the Putsch. However,
the evidence is overwhelmingly on the side of those who state that
Rupprecht stood aloof but was hostile to Hitler and his friends—
and logic lends added weight to this position. Dr. von Kahr was, in
many ways, the crown prince's "man" in München in the fall of
1923. Hitler was scarcely the type to appeal to Rupprecht, and
Ludendorff was bitterly hostile towards the crown prince even before the Putsch. There was therefore no good reason for the prince
to side with them, even if he disregarded their clear preference for
a republican form of government.[60]

On the other hand, the crown prince, as always, prudently remained in the background during and after the Putsch. On 8 and
9 November, he was visited by two and possibly three envoys with
news of the events in München. Freiherr von Fürstenberg came on
behalf of Kahr, although he was not sent by him; Lieutenant
Neunzert came on behalf of Hitler; and there is some evidence indicating that a Landespolizei officer was sent by Seisser.[61] Rup-

---

[59] B, I, GSK 3, p. 20; GSK 44, p. 74; SA 1, 1490, Police Timetable,
11.11.1923; 1492, III, p. 37; II, MA102140, HMB 2287, M/F, p. 2;
MA103474, Hassfurter an Bayr. Regierung, 4.4.1924.

[60] See also the discussion in Chapter XIV, Section III, above.

[61] Graf Soden, the crown prince's right-hand man, doubts if such a visit
was made, because no mention of it is made in the crown prince's diary
and Rupprecht never mentioned such a visit to Soden (who was, of course,
at the time a prisoner of the Putschists). On the other hand, Max Neunzert,
the Putschist's envoy to the crown prince, mentioned the prior visit of a

precht did not take a public position himself that day, but shortly thereafter he did publicly express his opposition to the Putsch and called for an end to strife and the cooperation of all nationally minded men, while in a letter to Kahr he referred more frankly to the "mad act of 8 November."[62] An equally clear indication of Rupprecht's opposition to the Putsch is to be found in the overt hostility towards the Putschists of organizations in which he had overriding influence. The Heimat- und Königsbund denounced violent solutions to Bavaria's problems; all three major organizations of former Bavarian officers[63] attacked the Putsch verbally on 9 November; and some were actually called up against the Putschists. Many younger monarchists and former officers may have been torn by diverging loyalties, but their organizations took a firm stand.[64]

After the Putsch, Rupprecht continued to stay out of the limelight, but began to put pressure on Kahr to resign in the interest of re-establishing harmony. When it became clear that Kahr would not resign, the crown prince tried to guide his hand, especially with regard to drastic economic measures. Kahr, however, was no longer as responsive to Rupprecht's nudges as he had once been, so that their relationship cooled somewhat. In any case, Kahr was no longer in a position to take vigorous action as a result of his relations with the Cabinet.[65]

In the days following the Putsch difficulties developed inside the officers' organizations. In München the leaders succeeded in holding the bulk of their followers behind the triumvirate, but only by

---

Lapo officer in his interrogation and National Socialist–inclined Lapo officers believed in this mission. B, II, MA103476, p. 1407; GP, B, Colonel Ernst Schultes.

[62] B, I, Kahr MS, pp. 1395-96; SA 1, 1493, pp. 209-10; II, MA103476, pp. 1406-10; IV, HSIV, EE7, Endres MS, p. 62; Gengler, Ludwig, *Die deutschen Monarchisten, 1919-1925*, Kulmbach, 1932, p. 157; Sendtner, Karl, *Rupprecht von Wittelsbach, Kronprinz von Bayern*, München, 1954, p. 534; Zimmermann, Werner G., *Bayern und das Reich, 1918-1923*, München, 1953, Chapter VII, passim.

[63] DOB, NVDO, and VBORV—Deutscher Offiziersbund, National Verband Deutsche Offiziere, Verband bayer. Offizier- und Regiments-Vereine.

[64] B, I, Kahr MS, pp. 1411a-c; II, MA103476, pp. 1090, 1411-12; IV, BuR, Bd. 36, Akt 1, Item 36; Ludendorff, *Feldherrnhalle*, pp. 64-65; Röhm, *Geschichte*, pp. 261-64; GP, A, Graf Josef Maria von Soden-Fraunhofen, 6.8.1966.

[65] B, I, Kahr MS, pp. 1394-96; NA, T120, 5569, p. K591603.

creating an escape-hatch for Ludendorff, whom many former officers, such as Captain Gustav Luppe (a former naval officer and the brother of the leftish democratic mayor of Nürnberg), insisted upon seeing as a man betrayed by Hitler—although why the role of dupe is preferable to the role of rebel is not entirely clear, except with the coming trial in mind.[66] In order to do this, however, the leaders had to repulse the vigorous efforts of the more radical officers to take over the organizations. For example, in the Nationalverband Deutscher Offiziere (NVDO) the dissidents tried to pass a resolution ousting the triumvirate from membership.[67]

In Bamberg a similar struggle was set off by the attempt of Dr. Christian Roth to take over a meeting of the united officers' organizations from General (Ret.) Hermann Freiherr von Gebsattel, who had convened it. When Gebsattel attempted to present to the assembled officers a directive from the "highest war lord" (i.e., Crown Prince Rupprecht), he was hissed and booed by a good portion of the audience, not all of whom were members of the officers' organizations. Roth spoke for the dissenters when he refused to accept directives from above, saying that the future belonged to youth and those who did not understand this would be trampled. Roth then gave his own spirited rendition of the events of the Putsch in München in the course of which he blamed Kahr for the bloodshed which had occurred. When General Konstantin Freiherr von Gebsattel tried to reply to Roth he was at first simply shouted down. When he could finally make himself heard, the general gave a simple and logical refutation of Roth's position and deplored his raw and violent emotionalism: Hitler and Ludendorff had made a serious error, and a march on Berlin was dangerous nonsense. Roth seized the floor again and defended his views to the accompaniment of cheers and applause. The upshot of the meeting was a sharp division of the former officers in Bamberg into mutually hostile camps. The Putsch had led to the collapse of the Burgfrieden, between conservatives and moderates on the one hand and right radicals on the other, within the officers' organizations. For many on each side it was a permanent parting of the ways.[68]

[66] In any case, a quarrel between these organizations and General Ludendorff soon arose over his bitter attacks on the crown prince.

[67] B, II, MA104221, Auszug aus Protokoll d. . . BORV, 11.11.1923; NA, T79, 82, p. 210.

[68] B, I, GSK 50, pp. 31-34; GSK 90, pp. 407, 417, 423, 439; IV, Lapo, Bd. 26a, Akt 3, Item 90, VI Nachtrag.

As an institution the Catholic Church in Bavaria, led by the staunchly monarchist Cardinal Archbishop of München, Michael von Faulhaber, stood behind the government, the crown prince, and the Bavarian People's Party in opposition to the Putsch. Even the Papacy, clearly concerned over the anti-Catholic overtones of the Racist Movement, allegedly supported Kahr. Faulhaber, who had just been preaching against the antisemitism of the National Socialists and their allies, found his hostility accepted and returned with interest by the Kampfbündler, many of whom bracketed Rome with "Juda" as a foe of Germany. However, in any institution where extremely tight discipline is not practiced, deviations from the official "line" are to be found, and this was true in the Bavarian clergy. Individual priests, such as Abbot Alan Schachleiter and Josef Roth of München, were strongly in favor of the Racist Movement despite the disapproval of their superiors.[69]

Other priests were just as vigorously opposed to the Kampfbündler. The clergy in Hof, for example, complained to the civil authorities about a Nazi parade held on 11 November. Father Sextl of Bamberg sent a hostile report to the government on Dr. Roth's tirade at the officers' meeting called by General Freiherr von Gebsattel. Father Michel, the director of a Schülerheim in Rosenheim, told his assembled charges that Hitler was a "bandit, scoundrel, and traitor." The dislike of the right radicals and the bitterness over their attacks on the Church spilled over the borders of Bavaria and led to demonstrations against the Kampfbund by Catholics elsewhere, as was reported by the Bavarian envoy in Stuttgart. The feeling against the Putschists and the determination not to be involved in their politics proved not to be a transitory phenomenon. In November 1924 Kampfbündler were refused permission to celebrate a mass for the souls of those slain in the Putsch. The pastor had agreed to officiate but was forbidden to do so by his superiors. In general, the Church made clear its basic position but attempted to avoid direct involvement in politics. This sort of activity was left to its close ally—or secular arm—the Bavarian People's Party.[70]

[69] B, I, Kahr MS, pp 1382, 1411; II, MA103474, passim; Ludendorff, *Feldherrnhalle*, pp. 76-77, 154; *SZ*, 64, 16.3.1966, p. 10.

[70] B, II, MA101248, PDM 19, pp. 9-10; MA104393, B.G. in St., 105 T255, 28.3.1924; IV, Lapo, Bd. 26a, Akt 5, p. 4; Akt 3, Item 90; BuR, Bd. 36, Akt 1, Item 34; Akt 2, Item 60; NA, T175, 99, pp: 2620754-55; EAP, SA Rgt. München, 230-a-10/4 3, ca. 10.6.1923; Müller, *Wandel*, pp. 129ff; Röhm, *Geschichte*, p. 208; Maser, *Frühgeschichte*, p. 421.

IV. *The Left*

Despite the fact that both the Communist Party and the Social Democratic Party had armed forces theoretically available—although they had just been banned by Kahr—there is no report of a single armed leftist appearing anywhere in Bavaria during the Putsch. Also, there was no general strike. It is perhaps natural that the pacifist and law-abiding workers of the SPD should be passive, but even the fire-breathing activists of the Communist Party, the comrades of those who had fought so bitterly and futilely in the streets of Hamburg in October, dared do no more in Bavaria than paste up a few placards in the dark of night. A different wind blew south of the Main, and especially south of the Danube, than blew along the Wasserkante, a wind that was destined to blow farther and farther north as the years went by.

As soon as the Putsch was over, the leftist parties turned to politics as usual. They were torn between joy at the troubles of the Right and bitterness at the effective campaign mounted against them by Kahr. The Social Democrats demanded and hoped for, but did not expect or receive, aid from the Reich government. They also hoped to widen the gap between Kahr and the government, and they feared that Ehrhardt would start a new and more dangerous Putsch. On the other hand, the SPD, which—according to the minutes of a district leaders' meeting passed on to the Nürnberg police—felt that "the true guilty [parties] are neither Hitler, Ludendorff, nor Kahr, but the BVP," was not prepared to join any united front against the right radicals even if an opportunity had been offered them.[71] At the same time, they suspected both the "capitalists" and the governments of Bavaria and the Reich of plots against the workers. Whatever they believed, however, they were helpless to do more than carp in view of the voting pattern in Bavaria.[72]

And carp they did, often showing themselves to be either ill-informed (which was sometimes clearly the case), or simply malicious, or both. They tended to pick up and repeat every accusation made by the National Socialists against the government, Kahr, the Reichswehr, and the police. Of course, it was the true accusations that drew the loudest cries of rage, from the BVP at least. For example, while the government was debating how to get rid of Kahr, the BVP press denied that it was not on excellent terms

[71] B, I, GSK 43, pp. 170-72.
[72] B, I, GSK 43, pp. 170-73, 207-09; GSK 44, pp. 12-14, 150, 175, 229; NA, T120, 5569, pp. K591602-03.

with him. Only Lossow, always the political outsider, was upset at being accused of involvement in supplying arms to the Putschists on the basis of the "revelations" of "Hitler-Officer Götz" (who turned out not to have been an officer at all), while the SPD not only unwittingly acted as a National Socialist propaganda agency but also caused the death of one of its own agents, since the details of the story, being false, could have come only from one source.[73] The Social Democrats tried to arouse anger against the Reichswehr on the grounds that the troops were being allowed to profit by the crisis—by receiving many special benefits because they were "mobile"—while workers were starving. They also, of course, accepted and spread a good number of National Socialist legends about the Putsch and created some of their own.[74]

The Communists, most of whose upper- and middle-range leadership even at the local level was either under arrest or surveillance, did their best to profit from the reverses of the right radicals and from the generally chaotic political-economic situation. Their efforts, however, were neither coherent and coordinated, nor effective. Each local group seemed to go off on its own tack, and the programs planned by the central committee in Berlin, which were to some extent followed up by those local groups that knew about them, were alien to the realities of the German as well as the Bavarian situation. Rumors of revolt to come were passed about. General strikes were called, as were mass meetings of work councils and the unemployed. Workers were told to steal arms and prepare to fight the Reichswehr and police; the workers of Pirna and Hamburg should not be left to bleed for the cause alone.[75] The lack

---

[73] With malice aforethought Götz apparently fed the "revelations" to a man whom he believed to be an SPD agent in the NSDAP. He thus hit the foes of the party on both Right and Left with one blow. After the "revelations" were published in the SPD press, the alleged informant was murdered. Lossow was pilloried in the Socialist press, and the police, although certain that Götz was the murderer, had no evidence to bring him to book. The incident helped to lead to his social downfall, though, for the police investigations of his background eventually revealed that he had never been commissioned, and many doors were thereafter closed to him as a fraud. See B, ii, MA103472, Abt. ic 1712 Geh., 7.2.1924.

[74] *Ibid.*, B. i, GSK 43, p. 141a; iv, Lapo, Bd. 17, Akt 4, *Bamberger Volksblatt*, 16.1.1924; NA, T120, 5569, pp. K591621, K591648. See also Chapter xiv, Section iii.

[75] References to the Communist insurrection in Hamburg and to a clash between soldiers and Marxist workers in the Saxon town of Pirna. See

of reaction to these appeals strongly suggests that the Communists of Bavaria were quite prepared to let others bleed in the face of overwhelming force if they so desired—but, in the phrase of a later day, "ohne mich." The explosion of a dynamite capsule near Füssen was the only event that could possibly have been construed as a response to the clarion call to battle.[76]

v. *Conclusion*

Kampfbund members might spread propaganda against the government and the armed forces; their sympathizers might roam the streets, cursing, shouting and manhandling individual soldiers and policemen; leaders of other Verbände might seek to intimidate the government or to incite the discontent to new revolts; but it was all in vain, an anguished expression of impotence. When the vaunted "Storm Troops" of the Kampfbund clearly demonstrated at the Feldherrnhalle that they might be fit for street tussles with the "Reds," for parades, and for harassing Jewish shopkeepers, but that they had no stomach for serious fighting, the myth of the Verbände's "power" was destroyed. Since the status of the Verbände in Bavaria and their influence on policy had depended very largely on the myth that they represented a serious military power, this status had vanished before the powder mist had cleared from the Odeonsplatz. The Verbände had marched imposingly; they had weapons; they had said that they were fit for combat and would fight to the death; and many Bavarians had believed them. Many more had not dared to disbelieve them. Now everyone knew what Lossow and Seisser had known all along, and what, to be fair, many leaders of the Verbände had known: as long as the armed forces were loyal, there could be no successful Putsch in Bavaria. Since the armed forces had just clearly demonstrated their loyalty, dissidents on both Right and Left could mutter or even shout. It would do them no good.

Hartenstein, *Kampfeinsatz*, pp. 38-82; Gordon, H. J. Jr., "Die Reichswehr und Sachsen, 1923," *WWR*, Dec. 1961, p. 685.

[76] B, I, GSK 43, pp. 62, 74, 84-86, 101, 140; GSK 44, pp. 70, 162, 172, 194ff, 217; IV, Lapo, Bd. 26a, Akt 5, Gr. Sch. IIIc, Erlebnisbericht, St. V. 1, Hof, 33, p. 1.

17.

THE PUTSCH AND THE REICH

I. *The Federal Government*

The government of the Reich reacted swiftly to the news of the Putsch in Bavaria. The ministers had been worried for some time by the ominous concentration of paramilitary organizations along the northern frontiers of Bavaria and by the hostile attitude of the Bavarian government. They were therefore not taken entirely by surprise and wasted little time.

Chancellor Gustav Stresemann heard the news while dining with Hjalmar Schacht, the president of the Reichsbank, and rushed to the Chancery. He then summoned the Cabinet to a meeting. By midnight the Cabinet had assembled, together with President Ebert and General von Seeckt, who was accompanied by his ubiquitous political advisor, Kurt von Schleicher, and his aide, First Lieutenant Hans-Harald von Selchow. Minister-President Otto Braun and Interior Minister Carl Severing of Prussia were, as was so often the case, there among the Reich ministers.[1] Ebert and Seeckt remained calm, but most of the ministers were highly excited. Selchow remarked of Stresemann that he was "beside himself."[2] The ministers did not lose their nerve, though. They were determined not to flee again from Berlin as had happened in 1920. Riot Police (Schupo) were alarmed to defend the government quarter. All news not passed by the Reichswehr Ministry was forbidden. All Wehrkreis commands were notified. Passenger and freight service to Bavaria was halted as well as all financial transactions. Stresemann meanwhile wrote a proclamation to the German people nullifying Hitler's proclamation and warning all those who followed

[1] Seeckt Papers, Stück 289, von Selchow, II, pp. 10-11; Stresemann, *Vermächtnis*, I, pp. 203-4.
[2] "Ganz aus Häuschen."

the Putschists that they would be liable for prosecution for high treason and national treason.[3]

Finally Ebert, with the consent of the Cabinet, transferred the dictatorial powers previously vested in Reichswehrminister Dr. Gessler to General von Seeckt in more extensive form and at the same time gave Seeckt the right to exercise Ebert's powers as commander-in-chief of the Reichswehr. Seeckt then calmly gave orders for Lieutenant von Selchow to get in touch with München and went home to bed, since there was nothing more to be done until the situation was clearer.[4] As a result, Lieutenant Colonel Joachim von Stülpnagel, the chief of the operations branch of the general staff (Truppenamt), carried the burden of the "hot line" to München during the critical period of the Putsch. Meanwhile Ebert closed the Cabinet meeting with a final remark that belies the allegation that the civilian leaders had succumbed to panic: " 'We've forgotten the most important item. We have neglected to inform the federal envoy in München, von Haniel, of the developments there.' " This was a reference to the fact that Haniel was at a party and couldn't be located.[5]

The government then turned its attention to the most important foreign powers. The British ambassador, Edgar Viscount D'Abernon, was awakened at 2:00 a.m. by a senior foreign office official, Baron Ago Maltzan, who told him of the Putsch and assured the ambassador that the government would put down the rebels. D'Abernon was fearful of civil war, but his worries were soon put to rest by the news of the collapse of Hitler's enterprise.[6] Whether or not the French were as promptly informed as the British, they reacted very swiftly, issuing a démarche on 9 November, which warned that France could not look with indifference on a change of government that left Germany ruled by a nationalist military dictatorship. There were, indeed, a good number of indications that the French intended to take advantage of the situation to march

[3] German law distinguished between treason against the existing government (Hochverrat) and treason against the German state (Landesverrat), which implied cooperation with external foes.

[4] Seeckt Papers, Stück 289, von Selchow, pp. 8-9; II, pp. 10-11; *Reichsgesetzblatt* 1923, I, p. 1084; 1924, I, p. 152; *RV*, 361, 23.11.1923, Dr. Gessler (RWM), p. 12260; Dr. Stresemannn (Kanzler), pp. 12189ff.

[5] GP, E, Gessler Papers, IIId, p. 11.

[6] D'Abernon, Viscount Edgar Vincent, *Ambassador of Peace*, London, 1929, 3 vols., II, pp. 270-71. Hereafter cited as D'Abernon, *Ambassador*.

still deeper into Germany, and the German government was aware of this problem, for the German ambassador in Rome had reported on 6 November that the French had requested the Italian government to make preparations to march into Bavaria. On 10 November 1923 the Bavarian government's listening post in the Pfalz reported on the French military reaction to the suppression of the Putsch:

> "Between 11:00 and 12:00 Oberregierungsrat Riederer was called to the first adjutant of General de Metz in Speyer. This [officer] made the following statement to Riederer:
> 'I have two questions to ask you. One: Who is now your government?' When Riederer replied, 'the Bavarian government, presently represented by Minister Matt,' the second question was dropped and Riederer dismissed. [That] afternoon Riederer was again called in by the French and told that this dispatch was false. The French were extremely excited and obviously very disappointed when Riederer assured them most emphatically that the Putsch had collapsed."[7]

Such clear warnings of French intentions to profit from the Putsch must have exerted considerable extra pressure on the government to settle the Putsch and to end the impasse between Bavaria and the Reich, although the tremendous internal pressures were the main impetus behind their actions.

After the collapse of the Putsch, the Cabinet left the security measures in Bavaria, as elsewhere, to Seeckt. They turned to the Bavarian question only when they had to do so, for they were preoccupied by even more complex and vital problems in the post-Putsch period. Financial questions, both on the domestic and reparations fronts occupied a large portion of their time and energy, as did the closely related question of the Rhine-Ruhr area. Once the shooting on the Odeonsplatz had ended, much of the immediacy of the Bavarian problem faded, and the Cabinet had neither interest nor time in those days of crisis for any problem that was not absolutely imperative. There were far too many other problems that simply could not be ignored, either because they were so important, or—as in the case of some trivial matters—because legal deadlines or crucial interest groups were involved. With the threat

---

[7] B, ii, MA103476, p. 1393. See MA103472 for a report on the French démarche and on the French approach to the Italians.

of a right radical revolution banished, the Bavarian question became a recurrent and irritating ache rather than a dangerous disease of the body politic.[8]

Nonetheless the Bavarian question could not be entirely ignored and from time to time the Cabinet did reluctantly turn its attention to one or another aspect of this complex of issues in the months following the Putsch. In several cases their discussions dealt only with specific minor points. At first, the Cabinet expressed a determination not to turn the trial of the Putschists over to the Bavarian Volksgericht, with only Minister of the Interior Karl Jarres dissenting. Yet, in the long run, they permitted just this disposition of the case, giving way to the insistence of the Bavarian government and, very possibly, the advice of Haniel that the Bavarian government not be placed in an impossible position. The fact that the Staatsgerichtshof in Leipzig was already burdened far beyond its capacity by the trials of the Communist rebels from Hamburg may also have played a role in the decision which left the rebel leaders to a court far more sympathetic than the Leipzig tribunal. The silent abandonment of a position strongly supported by the vast majority of the Cabinet on 19 November suggests that for most of the ministers the matter was not one of principle.[9]

The Cabinet also agreed to keep up the economic pressure on Bavaria to seek an accommodation with the Reich. On 9 November, the Cabinet agreed to a temporary suspension of all payments to Bavaria until it was certain who ruled there. More significant was their vote a week later to hold up grain shipments to Bavaria as long as the Bavarians maintained transport barriers against the Reich.[10] Finally, the Cabinet pursued negotiations, largely through the Reichswehr Ministry, concerning the regularization of Reich-Bavarian relations and the liquidation of the Lossow affair. In February 1924 these negotiations led to an agreement far more favorable to the Reich than could have been dreamed of before the Putsch when even the chancellor and other ministers talked seriously of making broad concessions to states' rights sentiment. Here, too, the Putsch was a catalyst that altered the relative strengths of the opposing sides, since it reduced the pressure Bavaria could

---

[8] See NA, T120, 1749-52, passim.

[9] Cabinets changed in the meantime, but the ministers were mostly the same.

[10] NA, T120, 1749, pp. D757710-11; 1750, pp. D757779, D757817-20; 1751, pp. D758913, D759463-64; 5569, pp. K591588-90 and K591602-04.

exert on the federal government and increased the Bavarian government's need for federal aid and support.[11]

II. *General von Seeckt*

On the day of the Putsch itself, Seeckt told General von Ruith, who had requested orders, that the Bavarian troops should, if necessary, fire on the rebels.[12] Thereafter Seeckt used his dictatorial powers to consolidate the strength of the state and to undermine that of its foes. He gave his divisional commanders the task of supervising public order and issued a series of decrees dissolving both the Communist and the right radical parties, press, and other organizations.[13]

Where Bavaria was concerned, Seeckt left the maintenance of law and order to General von Lossow and the Bavarian Reichswehr and police. He did offer further troops to Lossow on 9 November, but, although there was some backing and filling, they were not needed.[14] Things went less smoothly with regard to the question of the Lossow affair. Despite attempts by Stülpnagel and General von Möhl of Group Command 2 to mediate between Lossow and Seeckt, there could be no real settlement reached through military channels, since, although the quarrel was technically military, it

[11] B, II, MA99521-22, 23.11.1923-24.2.1924, passim; NA, T120, 1749-52, passim.

[12] Stülpnagel, *75 Jahre*, p. 212.

[13] In his biography of Seeckt, General von Rabenau stated that Seeckt only banned the NSDAP because Ebert would only agree to the dissolution of the KPD if the National Socialists suffered the same fate. (Rabenau, *Seeckt*, p. 390.) This statement would seem to be one of those alterations of fact that Rabenau undertook to get his manuscript through the National Socialist censors, for his own notes for the biography (Seeckt Papers, Stück 281, Rabenau Notes, p. 59) indicate that Seeckt was moved by an honest opposition to all radical and revolutionary groups. This conclusion is further supported by the Reichswehr memorandum regarding the dangerous political parties (Stück 153) and Seeckt's inclusion in his ban of not only the basic right radical parties but also all their readily identifiable satellite organizations. See also in this connection B, I, M. Inn. 71536, C.d.H. Nr. 678, 2.24, T.1.III. v. 25.2.1924; C.d.H. 442.24 T.1.III. v. 9.2.1924. For an interpretation hostile to Seeckt see Caro, Kurt, and Oehme, Walter, *Schleichers Aufstieg*, Berlin, 1933, pp. 170-71.

[14] B, II, MA103476, pp. 1316-17; NA, EAP 105/7a, 9.11.1923ff. Goerlitz' statement that Seeckt empowered General von Kress to suppress the Putsch is incorrect. For this statement see Goerlitz, Walther, *Der deutsche Generalstab*, Frankfurt am Main, 1950, p. 353.

was in fact being waged between the two governments. Seeckt, however, could and did put pressure on Lossow to achieve a settlement by adamant refusal to promote Bavarian officers until the matter was closed. Seeckt also acted as one of the chief representatives of the Reich in the final confrontation which resulted in the settlement of the dispute in mid-February.[15]

With the accord between the Reich and Bavaria, the only military problem outstanding was that of the Infantry School, and here Seeckt was absolutely immovable. On the day after the Putsch he closed down the Infantry School and the attached Engineer School. He might be prepared to forgive the officer candidates for their folly because of their youth, but he was not prepared to forgive the city which he believed to have infected them with the spirit of insubordination. He therefore moved the school first to the Ohrdruf training area in Thuringia and then, in 1926, to Dresden. The Bavarians fought hard to oppose the transfer, but were unable, even with the support of the Prussian government and the chancellor, to carry the day. Seeckt was inflexible on this score. The officer candidates must not be trained in halls that had seen mutiny and in a state that had ordered a German general to disobey his superiors.[16] The Reichswehr Ministry did, however, make one important concession to Bavaria after the settlement of the Lossow affair. Although it rejected all attempts to obtain federal funds to pay for the unauthorized Bavarian pre-mobilization activities during the fall of 1923, the Heeresleitung picked up the bill for all military costs associated with the suppression of the Putsch.[17]

III. *The Reichswehr Outside Bavaria*

The officers of the Heeresleitung, even the Bavarian ones, seem to have stood firmly behind Seeckt before and after the Putsch. Certainly the key figures did, and none of them record any instances of dissension or insubordination among their colleagues or subordinates.[18] Even at the time, there were no allegations to this

---

[15] B, I, GSK 59, p. 21; II, MA103476, pp. 1316-17; MA103458, Niederschrift, 14.2.1924; NA, T120, 1751, p. D759556; T79, 82, pp. 147-48, 217.

[16] B, II, MA99522, 24.7.1924, p. 17; 14.11.1924, pp. 2-3; NA, T79, 82, p. 178; 56, p. 637; 65, pp. 460-61; Seeckt Papers, Stück 281, Rabenau Notes, p. 64; GP, A, General Walther Leuze, 11.4.1960.

[17] B, I, GSK 59, p. 5; NA, T79, 48, p. 947.

[18] Seeckt Papers, Stück 281, 289 (Rabenau, Liebers Notizen, Selchow, Stülpnagel, etc.); GP, E, Heye Memoiren; Rabenau, *Seeckt*, pp. 365-66.

effect. The position of the senior commanders[19] was more controversial and unclear.

General Richard von Berendt was often alleged, in left and in right radical circles, to have been prepared to eliminate Seeckt in order to replace him with a man—probably Berendt—more prepared to overthrow the Republic. These allegations, which seem to stem from a single Landbund source were based on wishful thinking and are clearly contradicted by Berendt's actions during the prolonged crisis, and even before it began. On 20 October 1922 Otto Hasse was informed by General von Berendt and Lieutenant-Colonel von Hammerstein-Equord[20] of Bavarian attempts to interfere in the affairs of the Reich. Later, during the Lossow affair, Berendt publicly assured Seeckt of his support, and Rabenau notes that it was Berendt who warned Stresemann that the Reichswehr would be displeased by the replacement of Seeckt. These were scarcely the actions of a schemer who was seeking to overthrow his superior.[21]

General Ritter von Möhl has usually been ignored in evaluations of the higher commanders at this time, but he was not idle. Although he pretended to be neutral and even offered his services on several occasions as an intermediary between Lossow and Seeckt, he was secretly committed to the Bavarian side. In early October[22] Lieutenant Colonel von Unruh was apparently called to München and sounded out by Möhl and Lossow about the possibility of a "march on Berlin."[23] Later, when the conflict between Lossow and Seeckt deepened, Colonel Feeser told his officers that Möhl had said to Lossow: " 'If you go now, you perform a minor service for the Reichswehr but deliver a crushing blow to the national cause.' "[24] Möhl, however, could do little more than provide moral support to his Bavarian friends, surrounded as he was in Kassel by Prussians and Württembergers.

[19] Group commanders and division commanders.

[20] Kurt rather than Günther.

[21] B, ii, MA103476, p. 1145; MA104221, Seisser Besprechung-Notizen, Seisser-Landbund (I); Item 3; Seeckt Papers, Stück 281, Lieber-Hasse, pp. 30, 64; BT, 52 Jhrg., Nr. 500, 24.10.1923, p. 1. For a differing view see Carsten, *Reichswehr*, pp. 192ff.

[22] General von Unruh dates this interview in September, but other evidence indicates October.

[23] Seeckt Papers, Stück 281, Lieber-Hasse, 1923, pp. 31, 46; 1924, p. 3; GP, A, General von Unruh, 13.3.1955.

[24] NA, T79, 73, p. 398; GP, A, General Fritz Hengen, 28.11.1963.

The remaining divisional commanders seem clearly on Seeckt's side, although some of them, like General Rudolf von Horn, would have liked to see him more closely aligned with the political Right. General Walther Reinhardt of the Fifth Division was very much oppposed to Lossow and Bavaria. Kahr claims to have contacted General Alfred Müller, the commander of the Fourth Division (Saxony), and to have received from him assurances that he was entirely in agreement with Kahr and Bavaria and that he would never undertake any action against Bavaria. On the other hand, Müller had the full confidence of Reichswehrminister Gessler, a very shrewd judge of men, and stood with the other northern Reichswehr generals when they announced their support for Seeckt. Perhaps the best indication, however, that none of the northern division commanders was prepared to support Lossow seriously is to be seen in Lossow's own belief that he could not count on them.[25]

While there is not much evidence of sympathy with Bavarian particularism in the Reichswehr outside Bavaria, there was some sentiment in favor of the Racist Movement, particularly at lower levels. This sentiment was apparently strongest among the enlisted men, whom both Otto Hasse and Stresemann characterized as strongly rightist, but it also influenced some junior officers. It was the existence of this sentiment that worried the political and military leaders of the Reich and encouraged the Kampfbund leaders, although neither side had any real information on the extent or depth of this feeling before the Putsch. All the contemporary judgments regarding Reichswehr sentiment were based on extrapolation from extremely fragmentary evidence.[26]

It is also clear that there was a good deal of Reichswehr sentiment in favor of the performance of duty even if this entailed combat against Bavaria. General Endres, at that time a key officer on Lossow's general staff, was strongly behind the Bavarian government's position but was equally sure that the northerners would

---

[25] B, I, Kahr MS, p. 1322; II, MA103476, pp. 746, 1075-76; Seeckt Papers, Stück 281, 1923 Lieber Notes on Hasse Diaries, pp. 30, 52; *BT*, 52 Jhrg., Nr. 500, 24.10.1923, p. 1; Nr. 522, 6.11.1923, p. 3; GP, E, Gessler Papers, IIIc, p. 35.

[26] B, I, GSK 98, Bund Wiking Intelligence Report, 16.10.1923; II, MA103476, pp. 734, 739, 749, 1075-76, 1081; IV, BuR, Bd. 35, Akt 5, Baring an Schad, 20.9.1923; Seeckt Papers, Stück 281, Lieber-Hasse, 1924 (?), p. 11; D'Abernon, *Ambassador*, III, p. 56; GP, Reichswehr, Aussagen und Briefe, passim.

fight, if necessary. In speaking, much later, of the possibilities for a successful Putsch he said:

> . . . A possible participation of the Reichswehr and Landes-polizei in the Putsch could not, if one weighs [the problem] coolly, alter this outcome[27] except, at most, to raise the casualty figures by several zeros. The north German divisions, which General von Seeckt would undoubtedly have committed, would have swiftly suppressed the miniscule Bavarian revolt, with the applause of the entire Red riffraff.[28]

There is other fragmentary evidence supporting the readiness of northern Reichswehr units to fight against Bavaria if necessary. Apparently the Mecklenburg Reichswehr, in recruiting Zeitfrei-willige to fill up the ranks and to hold the barracks should it be called out for active service, asked the candidates if they were pre-pared to fight Bavaria. Another straw in the wind was the visit of a Hanoverian Reichswehr officer to Major Doehla in the General-staatskommissariat. This man, a captain, warned that if the Ba-varian Reichswehr marched on Berlin the northern troops would obey the orders of their superiors. A Bavarian ex-officer, on return-ing from Thuringia shortly before the Putsch, agreed with this diagnosis. His impression was that if General Ernst Hasse ordered his division to march against Bavaria, it would do so. In another instance, a northern regimental commander, when asked by a stu-dent officer of the Infantry School as to what stand he should take in the Seeckt-Lossow controversy, minced no words in ordering him to stand firmly by Seeckt.[29] It is further very clear that such re-luctance as there was to fight Bavaria was to a very large extent reluctance to fight the Bavarian Reichswehr and did not spill over to protect the Verbände. Even Lieutenant Colonel (Ret.) Duester-berg, who was anxious to see Lossow march on Berlin, warned Seisser on 28 October 1923 of this situation:

> "I went then with Helldorff to Colonel von Seisser in the Gen-eralstaatskommissariat and declared [that] I was definitely in-formed that the Reichswehr in Thuringia had orders to fire on members of the Patriotic Bands in case they should invade

[27] The collapse of the Putsch.

[28] B, IV, HSIV, EE7, Endres MS, p. 31.

[29] B, II, MA103476, pp. 1080, 1191; IV, Lapo, Bd. 17, Akt 4, Melzer Bericht, 10.11.1923; BuR, Bd. 34, Item 137.

Thuringia, and that the Thuringian Reichswehr would unquestionably execute these orders. I added that an attempt to solve the political question could only be successful if it were made by Bavaria, that is, only with the Bavarian Reichswehr. . . ."[30]

Here, too, the Putsch cleared the air and forced men to make up their minds, and there was no question where the Reichswehr stood. Soldiers and officers everywhere quietly obeyed their orders, giving no indication of support for the Putsch or the Putschists, whatever sympathy individual soldiers and officers may well have felt. The situation might have been somewhat different had the Bavarian Reichswehr come out strongly for the enterprise—but this was, practically speaking, impossible, even had Lossow wished to take such a stand. Far too many of his officers would have refused to go along for him to have delivered the Bavarian Reichswehr to Hitler. The most he could have done would have been to immobilize it, and there is good reason to believe that even this would have been beyond his powers, especially since he was not the sort of charismatic personality who could sweep men off their feet but one who depended on his post to ensure him respect and obedience.[31] Even if we move into the realm of conjecture so far as to accept the adherence of the Seventh Division to the Putsch, the weight of the evidence concerning the rest of the Reichswehr indicates that it would have remained loyal. This assumption is underscored by the fact that General von Seeckt, in summing up the reaction of regimental and battalion commanders to the activity of the Infantry School personnel in the Putsch, felt obliged to indicate that many of them were too harsh in their judgments on individuals as a result of knowing only a portion of the story.[32]

IV. *Political Parties and Pressure Groups*

By and large, the parties never came seriously to grips with the problem of the Putsch, since it was so swiftly and painlessly sup-

[30] B, II, MA103476, p. 736.

[31] See above, Chapter VI, Section II.

[32] B, II, MA103473, 666 T1235, 9.11.1923; MA103476, p. 1190; Seeckt Papers, Stück 281, 1923, Lieber Notes on Hasse Diaries, pp. 45-46; Rabenau, *Seeckt*, pp. 57-58, 64; Stück 289, Selchow, II, pp. 10-11; NA, T79, 65, p. 461; *BT*, 52, Jhrg., Nr. 528, 9.11.1923, p. 1; GP, A, General Gotthard Heinrici; General Ernst Köstring; General Bernhard von Lossberg; General Oskar Munzel; Gerhard Rossbach; General Kurt von Tippelskirch.

pressed and because there were so many other vital problems clamoring for their attention. In general, the government parties supported the stand of the Cabinet and General von Seeckt. The Social Democrats, as usual, were divided, with Ebert the decisive figure in giving full powers to Seeckt and Minister-President Braun of Prussia opposing the decision, while other leaders took even more divergent views. They were all, of course, hostile to the Putschists.[33]

The pressure groups associated with the various parties took the same stands as their parent organizations. Some of the right radical groups, however, did not go along with the right radical parties but supported Kahr and Seeckt. The most prominent among these organizations was the VVVD. Later their leader, Fritz Geisler, even went so far as to advocate the release of Hitler on the grounds that this would injure the Racist Movement and thus aid the German People's Party (of which he was a deputy) and the German nationalists.

To some extent, the response differed from state to state. While there was no serious echo of the Putsch anywhere, Württemberg, as Bavaria's neighbor, reacted most vigorously. The government, already uneasy before the Putsch, arrested the National Socialist leaders, as did the Badenese. Anti-Putsch proclamations were issued in Baden, Württemberg, and Hessia. In the north, where the NSDAP was already outlawed, there was practically no active response to the Putsch, although in some areas, such as Hamburg, it was believed throughout much of 9 November that the Bavarian Reichswehr had gone over to the rebels. It was only later that the authorities used the atmosphere following the collapse of Hitler's enterprise to clean up such strongholds of right radical activism as Upper Silesia.[34]

[33] *RV*, 361, passim; Braun, Otto, *Von Weimar bis Hitler*, New York, 1940, p. 59 (hereafter cited as Braun, *Von Weimar*); Severing, *Lebensweg*, I, pp. 446-47; GP, E, Gessler Papers, IIId, pp. 8-11.

[34] B, I, Kahr MS, p. 1326; GSK 102, pp. 18-20, 30-40; II, MA103458, B.G. in St., 592 T 1119; MA103472, 713 T 1293; MA103473, 666 T 1235; MA103474, Preger an M. Äuss., 28115; MA103476, p. 960; W, L, E131, S16/2, pp. 1-4; Seeckt Papers, Stück 281, Hasse, 1924, p. 4; Rabenau Notes, 1923, p. 56; *Hamb. Correspondent*, Nr. 524, Morgen Ausgabe, pp. 1-2; *BT*, 52 Jhrg., Nr. 528, 9.11.1923, pp. 1-2; Noske, Gustav, *Erlebtes aus Aufstieg und Niedergang einer Demokratie*, Zürich-Offenbach/Main, 1947, p. 259; Stresemann, *Vermächtnis*, I, p. 205; Heydebreck, *Wehr-Wölfe*, pp. 202-04.

v. *Summary*

Looking backwards, the student of Weimar Germany sees the Hitler Putsch as an event that looms large in the development of the NSDAP towards power. At the time, it seemed to most people, and especially to the leaders of the Reich, rather an end than a beginning, and was, at the most, a problem solved at a time when many pressing problems remained unsolved. Just as Napoleon III's Boulogne Putsch was a joke that discredited him with the "knowing ones" in France, and seemed to dispose of him as a serious menace to Louis Philippe, so did the Beer Hall Putsch, as seen from Berlin or Stuttgart, seem to dispose of Hitler and to leave the governments of Germany, Württemberg, or Baden the opportunity to devote their attention to the demands for economic action. Hitler had been a Bavarian phenomenon. Now he was passé.

14. Chief defendants in the Ludendorff trial, in bemedalled uniforms.
Left to right: Counsel Holt, Dr. Weber, Dr. Kriebel,
General Ludendorff, Adolf Hitler

18.

THE FATE OF THE PUTSCHIST LEADERS

I. *Flight and Pursuit*

By the time the echoes of the last shots fired at the Feldherrnhalle had died away, the Putschist leaders were in full flight. The order of the day was clearly: "Sauve qui peut!" All of them, except Ludendorff who was clad in the invincible armor of his arrogance, obeyed it.

According to the chief surgeon of the SA, Dr. Walter Schultze, Hitler was the first of the Putschists to get back on his feet. He then, apparently wounded in the arm, started to make his way towards the rear of the column. Schultze hurried on before him and brought forward a yellow auto in which Hitler and Schultze fled the scene. Driving down the Burgstrasse towards the Marienplatz, they ran into machine gun fire and turned away. They then tried to cross the river at the Isartor but again were met by automatic fire. Finally, they escaped from the closing ring by way of the Sendlingertorplatz and Thalkirchnerstrasse only to run into fire again near the southern Friedhof. Changing directions once more, the party fled due south out of München without any specific goal. Meanwhile, since Hitler was in considerable pain, Dr. Schultze examined his arm, and found that he was suffering not from a bullet wound but from a wrenched shoulder,[1] which, while painful, was not particularly dangerous. In the end, after an interim stop, the patient was brought to Uffing, a village on the road to Garmisch-Partenkirchen, where he took refuge in the house of Ernst Hanf-

---

[1] There has been some dispute about how this injury occurred, but the question is not of any significance. The wound was insignificant in itself, and the legend that arose around it was never more than a semiquaver in the National Socialist propaganda symphony. See Chapter XII, note 152, above. For Hitler's own account see NA, EAP 105/7, I, pp. 115-16.

staengl. His hosts spread the story that he was hiding in Starnberg, even to such close friends and sympathizers as Professor Karl-Alexander von Müller.[2]

At first, the authorities were completely at a loss regarding Hitler's whereabouts, but he was too well known and too controversial a figure to remain hidden for long. Within forty-eight hours, his presence in the Hanfstaengl house had been reported to the police and a force was sent to arrest him, arriving in Uffing about 4:30 p.m. on 11 November. At first the police searched the villa of Frau Hofrat Hanfstaengl but found no trace of Hitler. They then went to the house of Ernst, where they ran their quarry to earth. "Putzi" Hanfstaengl himself was not at home, being a fugitive from the police himself, but he later claimed, on the strength of his wife's testimony, that Hitler fell into a frenzy when he realized that he was cornered and tried to shoot himself. Since he was half-crippled by his bad shoulder Frau Hanfstaengl managed to wrestle the pistol away from him.[3] At the time Putzi's sister, Erna, told a quite different story to Karl-Alexander von Müller, claiming that the rumors of a suicide attempt were completely false: Hitler had been calm and surrendered to the Reichswehr[4] without melodramatics. However, the rest of her tale does not entirely tally with other information, and she had been a source of the earlier story that Hitler was in Starnberg.[5]

Whether or not he had been in a frenzy earlier, Hitler was calm, if subdued, when the police entered the house. Police First Lieutenant Rudolf Belleville, Rudolf Hess's wartime observer and a former friend of Hitler, found the latter in his bedroom in pajamas and informed him that he was under arrest. Hitler shook hands with Belleville and declared that he was ready to go along. He remarked that he had not broken his word and that it was only because of this fact that he was ready to be arrested. At about 8:45 p.m. Hitler arrived in the Bezirksamt, where he was again formally informed of his arrest. That same evening, he was escorted by Belleville and a soldier of the Landespolizei to the prison at Landsberg on the Lech. Having fallen into the depressed and sullen

[2] *Ibid*; B, II, MA103476, pp. 1357-59; Müller, *Wandel*, pp. 168-69.
[3] Hanfstaengl, *Hitler*, pp. 107-09.
[4] A natural error, since he was arrested by Landespolizei, whose field uniforms laymen could not easily distinguish from those of soldiers.
[5] Müller, *Wandel*, pp. 174, 181.

silence that he maintained for some time, Hitler was quiet throughout the trip, except for a question as to Ludendorff's well-being.[6]

From the very beginning, the National Socialists began to embroider the story of Hitler's arrest and to build it into a tale of dauntless courage on Hitler's part and correspondingly cowardly and vicious behavior on the part of the police. An account spread in late November told the following tale:

> "He [Hitler] was brought there [Uffing] by his faithful companions by auto and lay stricken with fever when two truckloads of green police (Pfui!) surrounded the village and literally dragged the half-conscious man from his sick bed. . . ."[7]

In December a different version was being circulated:

> "On 11 November 1923 about 5:00 p.m. green police began slowly to surround the house where Adolf Hitler lived. In the course of two hours an ever larger force of green police was assembled in order to be able to enclose the house more securely. Hitler watched these bloodhounds of the men who had betrayed him in a fateful moment and shouted to the police: 'Have you still not enough for one man?'
>
> As the police then came up the steps and informed him of his arrest, he said to them: 'I have only contempt for you!' Then the betrayed man was loaded on a truck and he, who entirely alone had worked in these last five years against Marxist betrayal and for Germany's freedom with untiring, glowing patriotism, was treated like a criminal, here in allegedly national Bavaria! . . ."[8]

Here again, the National Socialists, in accordance with Churchill's dictum that the truth should never spoil a good story, presented two clearly contradictory accounts of the same event for the delectation of Hitler's followers and the general public. One could have one's choice between a tortured and delirious man dragged off by pitiless monsters or a noble and defiant spirit—a sort of male Barbara Fritchie—facing his cruel foes with taunts in deathless prose. The

---

[6] B, I, GSK 44, pp. 18, 22; M. Inn. 73696, Reg. Obb., Betreff d. Verhaftung Adolf Hitlers, 13.11.1923; GSK 90, p. 211; IV, BuR, Bd. 34, Item 156; NA, EAP 105/7, I, p. 116; GP, B, Lieutenant Colonel Max Lagerbauer.

[7] B, I, GSK 43, p. 122.   [8] B, I, GSK 43, p. 100.

Hitler who shook his captor's hand and sat in sullen silence as they drove through the chill night over winding, deserted roads was not sufficiently romantic for the purposes of the movement and had to be replaced by legends better fitted to the new Siegfried.

Captain Göring cut an even less romantic figure than his leader —and later liquidated the man who revealed his true behavior. His vaunted sense of humor didn't cover authenticated attacks on his "honor."[9] Göring was wounded in the conflict at the Feldherrnhalle and was then carried to the private hospital of Professor Alwin Ritter von Ach, where his wound—a bullet in the upper thigh—was cleaned and dressed. Then, to escape from the police, Göring and his wife went by car to the house of Major (Ret.) Schüler van Kriecken, a party comrade. Here he lay hidden for two days before attempting to slip across the border into Austria. His car was halted at the border, however, and he was returned to Garmisch under guard, since an order for his arrest had arrived by telegram.[10]

After arriving in Garmisch, Göring was turned over to Lieutenant Nikolaus Maier of the Landespolizei. Maier called Captain von Bomhard, in Regierung Oberbayern, for orders. Bomhard said that there was no arrest order for Göring but that he would enquire at the GSK as to what disposition should be made of the SA leader. Maier said that he would, meanwhile, in view of Göring's wound, release him under his word of honor to go to the Kurhaus Jeschke. Bomhard concurred and Göring readily promised not to leave the Kurhaus until his fate had been decided. Maier then released him, but took the precaution of calling the hotel to make sure his charge had arrived. Assured that this was the case, the policeman felt that the situation was well in hand. About 10:00 p.m. Maier received new orders from Bomhard. Kahr had still not made up his mind about Göring, but he was to be placed under unobtrusive surveillance. When Maier asked for more precise directions, he was told to put guards at the door of Göring's room. Maier had no policemen available and asked if it would be all right to use auxiliary policemen. Bomhard agreed. Since the auxiliary police in Parten-

[9] Fritz Gerlich, the chief editor of the *MNN* in 1923, was the victim. He was slain during the "Blood Purge" of June 1934. See Bennecke, "*Röhm Putsch*," p. 87. For his quarrel with Göring in 1932 see B, I, M. Inn. 71770.

[10] B, I, M. Inn. 71770, 934, 12.11.1923, Zollamt Griessen-Landstrasse; Pölnitz, *Emir*, pp. 133-34.

kirchen were the most reliable in the vicinity, Maier ordered them to undertake this task, but by the time the guards arrived—11:00 p.m.—the bird had flown. Since there was no telephone service in the town after 10:00 p.m. and the postmaster, careful to side with the Reich in the dispute between Reich and Land, would not provide emergency service without authorization from higher postal authorities, nothing could be done. The result was that Göring was over the frontier to Innsbruck before an effective pursuit could be organized.[11]

The National Socialist version of this episode was somewhat edited for the benefit of those whose outmoded sense of honor might keep them from appreciating the true heroism of the *Führer* of the SA. Both his official biographer, Erich Gritzbach, and Götz Freiherr von Pölnitz painfully avoid any allusion to Lieutenant Maier or to Göring's promise to remain in the Garmisch hotel. Here, as in the case of Hitler, the National Socialist stories do not entirely agree. Gritzbach sees the motive for Göring's flight solely in the danger of arrest, while Pölnitz claims that only by escaping could the wounded man get proper treatment of his wound, which was rapidly getting worse. The important point for both was showing Göring to their audience as a noble soul pursued by vindictive villains rather than a man who escaped by violating the confidence of men who assumed that his sense of honor was still that of an officer of the German army rather than a political adventurer.[12]

Immediately after the Putsch Hermann Kriebel began to sink into the relative obscurity that swallowed him up in later years. He fled from Germany initially but returned in January 1924 to stand trial with Hitler. After his release from prison he joined Bund Oberland and remained associated with the National Socialist movement, but he never again came to occupy any central position. He ended his active career as consul general in Shanghai.[13]

Dr. Fritz Weber of Bund Oberland was another for whom the Putsch was the apex of his political career. Arrested, he was tried, convicted, and imprisoned with Hitler. After his release he was, for

---

[11] B, i, M. Inn. 71770, BA Garmisch 5085; Bericht, Lieutenant Meier [*sic*], 12.11.1923; Pölnitz, *Emir*, pp. 133-34.

[12] *Ibid.*; Gritzbach, *Göring*, p. 189.

[13] B, i, SA 1, 1756, 20323; GSK 4, p. 14; Röhm, *Geschichte*, pp. 256-57; NA, EAP 105/7, iii, passim; *Handbuch für das Deutsche Reich, 1936*, Berlin, 1936, p. 39.

a time, active in trying to revive Oberland and his own political career. He then withdrew into private practice as a veterinarian, but was not too prosperous. Despite dropping out of political life, he remained on good personal terms with Hitler, Ludendorff, and other old comrades. As a result, when the National Socialists came to power, Weber was called first to a responsible post as a veterinarian in München and then to Berlin. Despite having Hitler's ear, he devoted himself exclusively to veterinary matters. Then, when the need for manpower in the armed forces became acute in the latter part of World War II, Weber turned over his administrative post to his assistant and became a military veterinarian. After the war he never got back on his feet financially and died in reduced circumstances in 1954.[14]

Ernst Röhm, the leader of Reichskriegsflagge, was arrested when he surrendered the Wehrkreiskommando. He was tried and convicted with Hitler. Released on parole, he served briefly in the Reichstag, sought to revive the Kampfbund, and then became an officer in Bolivia, where he helped to engineer a student-military coup that unseated the president and his own German superior. Returning to Germany in the last years of the Weimar Republic, he became the leader (chief of staff) of the recreated Sturmabteilungen and a minister without portfolio in Hitler's government. In the end, he died at Hitler's orders during the Blood Purge of 1934.[15]

General Ludendorff, arrested as he walked across the Odeonsplatz in the wake of the skirmish there, was taken into the Residenz, where he behaved like a small child deprived of a favorite toy. When Lieutenant Colonel Wilhelm Muxel offered to inform Ludendorff's family that the general was safe and sound, Ludendorff shouted that he wanted no favors from Muxel and then launched into a violent tirade against his captor. Muxel must not call him "Excellency," but only "Herr Ludendorff." Ludendorff would never wear the uniform again as long as Muxel wore it.[16]

[14] B, ii, MA99523, 9.3.1925, p. 17; *Handbuch für das Deutsche Reich, 1936,* p. 117; GP, B, Dr. Walter Schulz (Tierarzt und ehemaliger Mitarbeiter Dr. Webers).

[15] See above Chapter iv, Sections i-ii; Röhm, *Geschichte,* pp. 300-364; Bennecke, *"Röhm-Putsch,"* pp. 87-88.

[16] In fact, Ludendorff wore the uniform again at the funeral of his former orderly and personal servant, Neubauer, a few days later.

Sergeant Wilhelm Baier testified shortly afterward: " 'In the battalion headquarters I heard Ludendorff shouting wildly. He continually shouted "Pfui!" and reviled my chief, Lieutenant Colonel Muxel.' "[17] Later, when he wanted to go to the bathroom, Ludendorff insisted that, as a prisoner, he must be escorted. First Lieutenant Oskar Erhard, Muxel's adjutant, refused to escort him, and in the end nature triumphed. The general swallowed his pride, took the proffered key, and went alone.[18] Later in the afternoon the chief prosecutor, Ludwig Stenglein, arrived with his newly assigned assistant, Dr. Hans Ehard. Stenglein briefly introduced himself and Ehard, muttered something about business elsewhere, and left Ehard to hold the baby, no simple task. Ludendorff was similarly gracious to Lieutenant Colonel Oswald Lutz of the Reichswehr, who had been sent by General von Danner, as a courtesy, to assist Ludendorff in any way he could. Ludendorff met this gesture with a stream of loud abuse in the course of which he referred to Lutz as a "perjured Reichswehr officer" with whom he wished no dealings. Although he had spurned Lutz and Muxel, he received Lieutenant Colonels Hans Georg Hofmann and Friedrich Haselmayr—both sympathetic to the Kampfbund—warmly.[19]

Despite his show of berserk rage, Ludendorff did not lose the caution that made him one of the most successful rebels against the Weimar Republic. He carefully washed his hands of serious Putschist activity by disavowing having given Röhm orders to hold the Wehrkreiskommando. This was his first step in creating the impression of the innocent bystander which had been so useful in the Kapp Putsch. In the late morning, the general had shown no hesitation in giving orders or even regally silencing Hitler when the latter disagreed with him. In mid-afternoon he was surprised that Röhm could think that the poor old man from the Ludwigshöhe could give anyone orders. There were no flies on Ludendorff.[20] Possibly impressed by Haselmayr's insistence on Ludendorff's essential innocence, but more likely impressed by the unpopularity they would earn if they imprisoned a national hero of the Right, the

[17] B, ii, MA103476, p. 1354.

[18] GP, B, Lieutenant Colonel Oskar Erhard.

[19] B, iv, HSIV, EE7, Endres ms, p. 54; Ludendorff, *Feldherrnhalle*, pp. 68-69; GP, B, Minister a. D. Dr. Hans Ehard; Lieutenant Colonel Oskar Erhard.

[20] NA, T79, 82, pp. 96-97.

triumvirate allowed Ludendorff to go free on his word of honor, a concession as grudgingly received as given.[21]

Thereafter, until the trial and beyond, Ludendorff and the authorities indulged in desultory and indecisive guerrilla warfare. Ludendorff believed himself free to attack the triumvirate and the government in print and by word of mouth, while they believed that he was under obligation to stay out of politics. They cut off his telephone service; they restored his telephone service. They confiscated political contributions sent to him and gave them to the poor. He wrote condemnatory political tracts about them and complained of their treachery to anyone who would listen. However, like Weber and Kriebel, Ludendorff had played his last major role on the historical stage. He now drifted, complaining vigorously, to the wings, from which he continued to maintain a querulous commentary on the viciousness of Catholics, Jews, and Freemasons, while becoming increasingly estranged from his one-time partner, Adolf Hitler. Their relationship unquestionably reached its nadir when Hitler offered Ludendorff a field marshal's baton only to have it contemptuously rejected on the grounds that field marshals are made on the field of battle and not at the whim of a politician,[22] but long before this event Ludendorff had become a Banquo's ghost for the Führer.[23]

Gerhard Rossbach was another Putschist whose name lost much of its nimbus of glory in the course of the Putsch and its aftermath. Rossbach's name had been one to conjure with among nationalist youths in the years following the Revolution of 1918. Handsome, a front officer with a fine combat record, a daring and effective Freikorps leader, and an outspoken foe of the "petit-

[21] *Ibid.*, B, ɪɪ, MA103457, GSK Denkschrift in Rothenbücher Affair, 8.2.1924.

[22] Dr. Sauerbruch, who reports that he was present on this occasion, states that Ludendorff was outraged and that Hitler, for once speechless, turned bright red and stalked out of the house, his rejected commission under his arm. Sauerbruch, Dr. Ferdinand, *Das war mein Leben*, München, 1960, p. 295.

[23] B, ɪ, SA 1, 1490, Police Timetable, 12.11.1923; GSK 44, p. 74; ɪɪ, MA99521, 12.11.1923, p. 13; 13.11.1923, pp. 3-4; MA103473, Dr. Matt, 21.11.1923; Kahr an Knilling, 18.12.1923, Min. Präs. 1896; Zezschwitz an Knilling, 24.12.1923; MA104221, GSK an VBORV, 14.11.1923; ɪᴠ, HSIV, EE7, Endres ᴍs, pp. 56-57; NA, T79, 82, pp. 96-97, 208; Stülpnagel, *75 Jahre*, p. 213.

bourgeois" Republic, Rossbach had built up a broad national following, while holding the hard core of his old Freikorps together in one form or another. He was, in a sense, the Ché Guevara of his generation, appealing largely to the same sort of audience and launching the same sort of guerrilla attacks against the existing society and the "rotten old men" as do the New Leftists of today.[24]

By 1923, he had struck many a shrewd blow against the Republic, but he had not, himself, gone unscarred. Years of hit-and-run struggle, of uncertainty, of lies and evasions, of hiding and fighting, of imprisonment, and—if his foes are correct in their accusations —of homosexual activity had changed him radically. By 1923 the guileless and reckless Gerhard Rossbach of 1919 had been replaced by a shrewd, devious, calculating political warrior who was in some danger of becoming an unreliable braggart, as is clear from his actions in the Putsch. One thing the student leaders of the Infantry School were agreed on after the Putsch was that they trusted neither Rossbach's courage nor his honesty.[25] Fritz Teichmann, one of the young lieutenants who was swept along into the Putsch by the infectious fever of that November night, testified to the speed with which suspicions of Rossbach arose among the older Schüler:

> On the march of 8 November through the city, I was, because of my seniority (I was classroom senior of an officer class) assigned to lead a company. There were a number of longish halts, which the other company leaders and I used to obtain informations from the leader of the column about the many obscure questions which had meanwhile arisen. I met First Lieutenant (Ret.) Rossbach in this manner. He astonished us by his overbearing and excitable manner and by the evasive and contradictory answers that he gave. He impressed me as being a professional agitator.[26]

This generally unfavorable impression of Rossbach was greatly strengthened by his actions after the Putsch. Following the fight at the Feldherrnhalle, he and a small force (probably members of the "Rossbach" units of the SA) had withdrawn to Rosenheim. Here First Lieutenant Schörner, a courier from Lossow, found him and persuaded him to cross the border to Austria. Unfortunately for

---

[24] For a general sketch of Rossbach's career see his autobiography, *Mein Weg durch die Zeit*, Weilburg/Lahn, 1950, passim.

[25] See above, Chapter XII, Section IV, for Wagner and Mahler on Rossbach.

[26] GP, A, Oberst Fritz Teichmann, 17.3.1969.

Rossbach, many of the men with him construed this move as a betrayal and abandonment of his men. Reportedly they voted to reject him as their leader for the future and accused him of "cowardly flight."[27]

Taken together, Rossbach's flight and the unfavorable impression he made on his subordinates in the Putsch provided a very poor base for future political activity. Beyond this, however, he was already outmoded. The day of the "political guerrilla" was at an end in 1923, although this was not yet apparent. Rossbach had played his role in keeping enmity to the Republic alive, but no movement which is based entirely on negative values can hope to get far in practical politics—or at least none has succeeded in doing so to date. Rossbach had no positive program. He was a wrecker, not a builder. It was therefore in the nature of things that he should eventually have to give ground before Hitler, who had a positive as well as a negative program and who sought to build a mass following rather than a guerrilla band. Here, to paraphrase Napoleon, the future was on the side of the bigger battalions. At best Rossbach's talents had been for fighting and organizing. They were no match for those of Hitler, who, added to all that Rossbach possessed, had a charismatic influence over those close to him and a gift of oratory that could hold masses enthralled. Rossbach, isolated and obscure in Austria while Hitler made himself into a national figure for the first time by his masterful manipulation of his trial for treason, was clearly outclassed and, apparently recognizing the writing on the wall, deserted politics at first for a boys' choir and then for the Civil Air Defense Organization. After World War II he conducted an import-export business. The coolness of his relations with Hitler in later years is indicated by his imprisonment at the time of the Blood Purge.[28] Like the Abbé Siéyès he had joined the revolution early and been excluded from any real influence in it early. However, unlike many of his temporarily more successful rivals, Rossbach could boast of having lived through and beyond the great upheavals.

Pöhner's career also reached its last high point in the Putsch, for he died in an automobile accident in 1925. Even in death he caused trouble for the Bavarian government, for the affair resulted in rumors that he had been murdered which were so persistent that

---

[27] B, II, MA103473, Anon. Brief. an *Bayer. Kurier*, 29.10.1924; GP, A, Field Marshal Ferdinand Schörner, 17.12.1963.

[28] Rossbach, *Weg*, pp. 87-88, 142-73.

the authorities secretly exhumed his corpse to ascertain if there was any possibility of truth in the accusations. On the other hand, it could not be said that the Putsch had done him any serious harm, for despite conviction by both the Volksgericht (People's Court) and a disciplinary court the only long-term penalty he paid was early retirement from the bench and the reduction of his pension by five percent, since he fought off imprisonment with claims of illness until the end of his life.[29]

A number of National Socialists, who had played major roles in the early development of the party, took almost no part in the Putsch and fell by the wayside thereafter. Dietrich Eckart, an early patron and showpiece of the movement, apparently spent the evening of 8 November at the Fledermausbar, ignorant of the Putsch and increasingly oblivious even of his immediate surroundings. Having slept late the next day, he took part in the Hitler march in a car. He was nonetheless arrested and died in prison of a long-standing disease, protesting to the very last against his imprisonment.[30] Anton Drexler, the founder of the party, was also apparently on the very edge of the Putsch. He had been slated to speak, together with Hitler, in Freising and later claimed that he only learned en route to the station that the speech had been called off. Invited to the Bürgerbräukeller, he apparently sat quietly through the stirring events of the evening, for no one either in the party or outside it so much as mentions his name in connection with the plans or actions of the Kampfbund. This was another step towards the "honorable obscurity" that increasingly enveloped him until his death in 1942, when his corpse was suddenly deluged with honors.[31] Alfred Hoffmann, the Stabschef of the SA, had been on the way out even before the Putsch and was pretty clearly cold-shouldered during it, though probably not to the extent that he claimed afterwards. He fled to Austria, where for a short time he was an active leader of the exile group in Salzburg. After a quarrel with Hermann Esser, he allegedly dropped out of both the SA and the party, and certainly he does not appear again in its higher ranks.[32]

[29] B, ii, MA99522, 8.7.1924, p. 7; MA99523, 13.5.1925, pp. 14-15; NA, T120, 5570, pp. K591919, K592176.

[30] B, i, GSK 44, p. 111; GSK 90, pp. 118-27; Röhm, *Geschichte*, p. 227.

[31] B, i, GSK 90, p. 103; Phelps, Reginald H., "Anton Drexler—Der. Gründer der NSDAP," 87 Jhrg., Nr. 12, Dec. 1961, pp. 1134ff.

[32] B, i, SA 1, 1493, pp. 223-26; ii, MA103476, pp. 1045, 1252.

Many other lesser lights among the Putschists fled or went underground for a time, although a few managed to carry on more or less as usual. Alfred Rosenberg, never a man of action, tried first in Salzburg and then in München to hold the party together, a major service to the legal authorities in view of his total lack of both organizing ability and the gift of manipulating men.[33] Esser went to Salzburg, where he soon made more enemies than friends in party circles. Heinrich Himmler apparently toyed with the idea of going to Turkey but in the end opted to be a political agitator in Niederbayern, a step that gave him his first real opportunity to climb in the movement. Himmler's friend, Eduard Heines, fell on very bad times in the absence of a viable paramilitary movement. Rudolf Hess fled to Austria but then returned and was sent to Landsberg to join Hitler.[34]

Altogether, the München authorities arrested 216 persons as a result of the Putsch or violently pro-Putsch activities thereafter. A good number more were arrested and held for short periods in the provinces. Few of these persons were ever formally charged and far fewer actually came to trial. Among those against whom indictments were prepared but later dropped were Klotz, Streicher, Lembert, "Putzi" Hanfstaengl, the Kolb brothers, General Ächter, Moulin-Eckart, Captain Weiss, and Wrede.[35]

II. *The Trials*

The decision had clearly been made very early that only the most important leaders would be tried, aside from persons who had committed definite crimes. Altogether there were four trials. The first and most important was the trial of Hitler and the other members of the top leadership group. The other three were trials of the members of Stosstrupp Hitler for their attack on the *Münchener Post*, the trial of several Putschists for the confiscation of banknotes from the official printing plants, and the trial of those responsible for the theft of weapons from the St. Anna Monastery.[36]

Aside from the struggle with the Reich as to where the main trial should be held and under whose auspices,[37] there were several

[33] B, I, GSK 4, p. 12; Pölnitz, *Emir*, p. 136.

[34] B, II, MA103473, PDM, Abt. VI/N; MA103476, pp. 1386-88; NA, T175, 99, pp. 2620015-17, 2620234; Kallenbach, *Mit Hitler*, pp. 67-68.

[35] B, II, MA103476, p. 1456; MA104221, PDM Nr. VIA 2503/23, Pol. Dir an GSK, 13.11.1923.

[36] B, II, MA99522, 27.3.1924, p. 4.

[37] See Chapter XVII, Section I, above.

hurdles to clear before the trial could be held. The first was the need for clear agreement on the matter in Bavarian government circles. The second was the completion of the necessary preliminary negotiations, interrogations, and other preparations. Last, but by no means least, came the completion of the necessary arrangements for the security of the government, the city, and the courtroom.

There were, even in official circles, some objections to having a trial at all. Not surprisingly, Kahr was one of those who was none too keen about a public airing of Bavaria's dirty linen. He therefore favored an arrangement by which the Putschists would admit their guilt but claim patriotism as a mitigating circumstance. In this manner the trial could be cut off at its very beginning. Needless to say —although Kahr later avoided the question—the accused must have been offered leniency or the proposal would never have been considered. The idea never got off the ground, though, because at least some of the Putschists would not agree.[38]

The location of the trial was also a hot potato. The judges and the Justice Ministry wanted the trial to be held in München. The Generalstaatskommissar, Knilling, and the minister of the interior wanted it held elsewhere for security reasons. Dr. Held, the leader of the most important political party, agreed with Knilling, Kahr, and Schweyer, forming an unlikely and powerful coalition. In the end, though, they were defeated, if Kahr and a secret Reichswehr report are to be believed, by the plea of inconvenience by the defense attorneys, who claimed that they simply could not go elsewhere because of their other professional commitments. Haniel notes, however, that strong objections to moving the trial were raised in the Landtag. Originally, it was intended that the trial be held in the regular municipal court building, but, probably for security reasons, it was transferred, over Lossow's objections, to the now-deserted Infantry School on the Blutenburgstrasse (at the Marsplatz). Dr. Matt, the acting minister-president, and the federal government both wanted the trial to be held in secret, since the proposed interspersion of open and secret sessions would result in the worst of all possible situations, especially in view of the notorious indiscretion of Hitler and Dr. Weber. Nonetheless, the original scheme was retained.[39]

[38] B, I, Kahr MS, pp. 1447-48.

[39] B, I, Kahr MS, p. 1450; GSK 49, p. 10; II, MA103474, Aufzeichnung: Dr. Matt an Gürtner, 28.2.1924; NA, T120, 5569, pp. K591654, K591673; EAP 105/7, I, pp. 5-30; 105/7a, WKK VII Ib 1665 Geh.

Meanwhile, the prosecutors interrogated the prisoners and other witnesses. In view of the hostility of many of these men this was no easy task, and Stenglein, at least, complained of being badly battered before the trial was over. Röhm admits that he worked at cross purposes to the interrogator. Müller wished to learn as much as possible about the Putsch and Putschists. Röhm wanted to implicate the triumvirate as deeply as possible, but he undermined his own argument and that of the other Putschists—that the fullest exposure of evidence would clear them and destroy Kahr, Lossow, and Seisser—when he admitted that he successfully concealed many of the most important documents from the authorities (who apparently never thought to search in the Wehrkreiskommando-gebäude for Putschist documents) and later burned them. If his conscience was so clean and that of the triumvirate so dirty, why did he not either make sure that the documents were publicly disinterred or, if that seemed unwise at the time, why did he not later merely remove them to a more secure hiding place for later publication? "Burn this letter!" is usually assumed to be prima facie evidence of an uneasy conscience.[40]

Hitler was equally uncooperative. First he demanded that he be interrogated and protested at being held prisoner. Then, when the interrogators arrived, he refused to speak at all. An interrogating judge tried to persuade him to talk, as did Martin Dresse and Ludwig Stenglein, but to no avail. Finally, Stenglein sent his newest assistant, Dr. Hans Ehard, to try his hand. Ehard established himself in the visiting room complete with typist and files. Hitler was brought in and sat in sullen silence. In Ehard's words: "He glared blankly like a sheep."[41] None of the standard tricks of interrogation worked. Finally, in desperation, Ehard banished his typist and his files and pointed out to Hitler that he was just doing his job. Wouldn't Hitler at least talk to him? In this unofficial and personal atmosphere Hitler suddenly broke down and began to talk. Soon his voice was rising and he was making speeches for an invisible audience. His voice grew louder and his face turned bluish. When asked an embarrassing question, he would sink again into silence only to erupt into a veritable torrent of words when a theme of interest was broached. When Ehard reported to Stenglein and Neithardt, the presiding judge assigned to the Hitler Trial, the judge suggested that Hitler was saving his "big guns" for the trial.

[40] Röhm, *Geschichte*, p. 275.
[41] GP, B, Minister a. D. Dr. Hans Ehard.

Ehard warned that Hitler was unquenchable and that he doubted that the man could possibly say anything more than he had already said. Neithardt looked dubious, but during the trial, having faced Hitler's eloquence for four solid hours, he admitted to Ehard, "I believe you were right."[42]

Meanwhile, letters and petitions on behalf of the Putschists poured into the court and the government. Most of them demanded that there be no trial and that the Putschists be freed. The letters came from members of the Racist Movement, but also from more or less innocent bystanders, among whom were several university professors, ex-officers, a railway worker, a representative of a group of north German industrialists (who may have been acting for them or for himself), a clergyman, and a teacher. More direct attacks were also launched. Gottfried Feder sued the minister-president for libel, and the lawyers of various prisoners demanded their release, as did some prisoners acting on their own. The old magic, however, did not work as it had before the Putsch; the trial was held on schedule.[43]

The security measures for the Hitler Trial were the responsibility of the GSK. The basic security forces were provided by the Landes-polizei, but München Reichswehr units were alerted for use in an emergency, and arrangements were made for calling in police and Reichswehr units from the provinces in case severe disorders developed. At the same time, the police watched the defense counsels carefully and kept a finger on the pulse of traffic within Bavaria and into München. However, no trouble developed except for minor flurries on the day the verdict was announced, and even this problem was foreseen. The Putsch had made it clear that the police and army would fight. The preparations to maintain the peace were sufficiently impressive to indicate that they were strong enough to do so. As a result, only a carefully planned and determined strike by a well-organized guerrilla force could have made real trouble, and the Kampfbündler had neither the leaders, the spirit, the organization, nor the arms to mount such an effort at this time.[44]

[42] B, I, GSK 90, p. 212; GP, B, Minister a. D. Dr. Hans Ehard.

[43] B, I, GSK 7, p. 11; GSK 43, p. 165; GSK 49, pp. 72, 77; GSK 90, pp. 207, 609; Kahr MS, p. 1446; II, MA103458, *Fränk. Kurier*, 23.11.1923; MA103473, Kahr an Knilling, M. Pr. 1896, 13.11.1923; MA103474, Stauder an Knilling, 3.5.1924; Feder Akten; MA103476, pp. 790-95; NA, T120, 5569, p. K591609.

[44] B, I, GSK 3, p. 44; GSK 43, p. 285; GSK 60, pp. 1-4; II, MA99522,

Besides the physical security problem, the authorities were also faced with the problem of the security of government secrets with reference to both Bavaria and the Reich. The first problem to be solved was that of official secrecy. Bavarian and federal employees were, like those of most governments, bound to secrecy regarding many of their official functions. The question therefore arose to what extent the respective governments should relax the official secrecy rule for those of their officials and officers called as witnesses in the Hitler Trial. In the end, the decisions made were remarkably liberal and suggest that, whatever the case may have been with regard to members of the triumvirate, the Bavarian government felt that it had nothing to hide, and the federal government followed the same policy. Lossow was given permission by Gessler to testify fully on anything dealing with the Putsch and its background, and the Bavarian government added its imprimatur, largely to indicate their claim to control over him as Bavarian Landeskommandant. Landespolizei officers, officials of the Ministry of the Interior who had served with the GSK, and Ministers Matt and Oswald were given freedom to speak if called as witnesses. However, with an eye to the future, and because of a general distrust of the accused men and their attorneys, the idea of a blanket release of officials from their secrecy obligation was rejected.[45]

The trial itself, which lasted from 26 February to 1 April, soon became a National Socialist propaganda display as Hitler took control of the proceedings again and again, dominating the judges and the courtroom with his oratory.[46] There is no question that Hitler's grasp of the tactical situation and his spell-binding gifts would have made for difficulties under any circumstances, but there was no need for the entire trial to have gone the way that it did. Much of the fault was to be found on the bench and some among the prosecutors. The presiding judge was absolutely determined not to find Ludendorff guilty. Dr. Schweyer said on 4 March 1924: ". . . He

---

14.3.1924, p. 8; NA, EAP 105/7a, 20.2.1923–1.4.1924, passim; T79, 33, p. 1160; 56, pp. 11, 98-99; T120, 5569, p. K591733.

[45] B, I, GSK 50, p. 21; MA, MA99522, 11.2.1924, pp. 6-7; 22.2.1924, p. 12; 26.2.1924, pp. 14-15; 4.3.1924, p. 5; MA103474, RWM (Heer) Nr. 23/24 T 1, III pers. 212.24; Staatsanwalt b. d. Landgerichts M. I zu 6480 Anz. Verz. Nr. XIX 421/23; Schmelzle, 13.2.1924; Justizmin. 10911 G. an Knilling, 18.3.1924; Justizmin. 6847 G an Oberstaatsanwalt, 19.2.1924; IV, Lapo, Bekanntmachung 18, 9.2.1924.

[46] NA, EAP 105/7, passim.

[Neithardt] said to Ministerialrat Zetlmeier even before the trial [that] Ludendorff was still the only ace which we in Germany possessed. Rumor has it that he has also said that Ludendorff would be acquitted."[47] Kahr reported a similar conversation with Neithardt. Dr. Ehard describes Neithardt as a strong nationalist and a well-meaning man, who believed that the Putsch was a "national deed." He was neither capable of keeping a tight rein on the accused men nor anxious to do so. In the case of Ludendorff, Neithardt even went so far as to scrap the record of the first interrogation, because it was too damaging, and to substitute for it a record in which Ludendorff studiously indicated ignorance of everything about the Putsch.

The lay judges on the court, however, made Neithardt look like Justice Jeffries of the "Bloody Assizes" of 1685. They were clearly partisans of the Putschists.[48] Taken together, the judges' attitudes ensured that the trial would take a peculiar course, and it did. The prosecutors also left something to be desired. Stenglein, the senior prosecutor, was a man who, by nature, wanted no trouble with anyone and very possibly was sympathetic with the accused men. Further, he apparently found the trial so physically exhausting that he talked of not being able to carry on. The most vigorous and capable of the prosecutors, Dr. Hans Ehard, was kept under wraps by his seniors to such an extent that he could not seriously influence the conduct of the trial.[49]

The results of this weakness in the prosecution and the bias of the judges appeared in other, more serious forms than the loose rein on the defendants. The most significant of all the fruits of this situation was the selection of witnesses. A number of men who had played key roles in the Putsch and could have added greatly to the clarification of many issues were simply ignored. Freiherr Hubert von Aufsess, Freiherr von Freyberg, Major von Hösslin, and Majors Hunglinger and Doehla were among the "invisible men" whom the prosecutors failed to locate and call. Lieutenant Colonel Endres was removed from the courtroom at the request of the defense, on the grounds that they were going to call him as a witness. Yet, when they did not call him, the judges and prosecutors asked

[47] B, II, MA99522, 4.3.1924, p. 3.

[48] B, I, Kahr MS, p. 1450; NA, T120, 5570, p. K591746; GP, B, Minister a. D. Dr. Hans Ehard.

[49] B, I, Kahr MS, p. 1449; II, MA99522, 4.3.1924, p. 7; GP, B, Minister a. D. Dr. Hans Ehard.

no questions. It is difficult not to believe that Endres was correct in thinking that the entire affair was simply a ploy to get a hostile personality out of the courtroom. Captain von Bomhard, the police and intelligence expert of Regierung Oberbayern was not called, nor was the chief of staff of the Landespolizei, nor even Lieutenant Colonel Muxel. It was suggested at the time that the government and the triumvirate did not wish these men to testify, but the documentary evidence does not support such a contention and, if the defense had been anxious to dig out the truth, they could have called these men themselves.

Nor was the failure to call witnesses the only failure of the prosecution and its investigators. Why, for example, did they not search for incriminating documents in the Wehrkreiskommando after its surrender by the Putschists? The leaders of the Putsch had spent much of their time there, and even a fairly cursory search should have turned up the incriminating documents hidden in a safe there. It is true that the military authorities might have been sensitive about a search of their premises, but a joint check would have been in the interest of all concerned. However, the failure to find documents is explainable; the failure to call obvious witnesses is not.[50]

Beyond these matters, the presiding judge influenced the trial in many minor ways. He referred to allegations by the defendants as "facts." He called witnesses in an order that gave subtle advantages to the defense. He allowed Lieutenant Wagner to insult General von Lossow without interference and only chided him mildly when Lossow complained. As a result Lossow walked out of the courtroom and refused to return, despite being held in contempt of court. Lossow's successor, General Freiherr Kress von Kressenstein, was moved to a formal protest against the attacks on the Reichswehr that were allowed to pass unchallenged by the bench. All to no avail. When the members of the Bavarian Cabinet complained and threatened to interfere, Gürtner soothed them and persuaded them to wait until the trial was over before judging the manner in which it had been conducted.[51]

[50] B, II, MA103476, pp. 673-74; IV, HSIV, EE7, Endres MS, pp. 4-5; NA, EAP 105/7, p. 007589; Röhm, *Geschichte*, p. 275.

[51] B, II, MA99522, 4.3.1924, pp. 4-5; 17.3.1924, pp. 11-12; MA103474, WKK Abt. Ic Nr. 1799 Geh., 29.2.1924; Min. Präs. Nr. C.O. 6329, Matt an Gürtner; Justizmin. 9851, 12.3.1924; Min. Präs. Nr. C.O. 7479, Knilling an Gürtner, 14.3.1924; IV, HSIV, EE7, Endres MS, pp. 69-73.

The tone of the trial, the extent to which it was dominated by Hitler, and the attitude of the Putschists is nicely summed up in the following statement that Hitler made on the first day of the trial:

> . . . I have not entered the courtroom to deny anything or to avoid responsibility. No, I protest at the declaration of Lieutenant Colonel Kriebel [that] his is the responsibility for the course of events. He has no responsibility. I carry it alone. I alone have, in the last analysis, desired the event. The other gentlemen have only cooperated with me at the end. I am convinced that I wished nothing evil. I bear the responsibility for all the consequences. But this I must say. I am not therefore a criminal and I do not feel myself to be a criminal; quite the contrary.[52]

Shrewder than Ludendorff, who sought to shake off all responsibility, Hitler realized intellectually or instinctively that the man who shouldered the responsibility would be the man who would become the hero of all those to whom the Republic was or would become anathema, and it was these men and women who were, after all, his constituency in the present as well as the future. Beyond all such considerations, there can be no doubt that the same terrible sincerity spoke here that would speak again and again in the future. Hitler did not feel himself to be a criminal in 1924, and he did not feel himself to be a criminal in 1945. He was the archetype of the "true believer," and his belief was in himself and his heaven-ordained mission. At least in part, it was the terrible sincerity within him that reached out and held his listeners in thrall. The bugles, the banners, the searchlights, the marching thousands, and the thundering chorus of "Sieg Heil" were useful and impressive like all of Goebbels' stage settings, but in the end, they were only trimmings. Even without them Hitler dominated the courtroom in 1924, just as without them he would dominate the Führerbunker in Berlin in April 1945.

A strong judge might have muzzled Hitler temporarily at least. An even-handed judge and stronger prosecutors could have changed the tone of the trial and could have brought forward evidence that was never presented. Even then Hitler would doubtless have made a strong impression, but he could not have had the floor on his own terms or without serious opposition. The presiding judge, however, was neither strong nor unbiased, while the senior

[52] NA, EAP 105/7, ɪ, p. 118.

prosecutors were reeds in the wind. As a result, the courtroom became a battlefield—and battles are won by the strongest and most determined protagonists. Here, Hitler was the victor.

The verdict was an anticlimax. Hitler, Pöhner, Kriebel, and Weber were sentenced to five years' fortress detention—minus six months of pre-trial imprisonment. Röhm and most of the others received sentences so short that they were released on parole immediately. Ludendorff was acquitted and—perhaps as a gesture of solidarity and perhaps because he belatedly recognized the implication of insignificance—heatedly protested his acquittal, much to the embarrassment and annoyance of the presiding justice. Perhaps he merely wished, as usual, to have the best of both worlds. Hitler's victory was consolidated with a martyr's crown of thorns; Ludendorff's departure from center stage was marked by a childish outburst. The act was over, and Hitler went to Landsberg for the intermission.[53]

The minor trials were not merely overshadowed by the "great trial," they were engulfed. The pattern was the same, however, as in the Hitler Trial. Most of the members of Stosstrupp Hitler were convicted in the *Münchener Post* case but were then turned loose on parole. A combination of a prosecution appeal, pressure from the SPD, and popular outcry resulted in a reconsideration that sent a good number of the convicted men to Landsberg to join Hitler. Meanwhile, the *Münchener Post* sued members of Stosstrupp Hitler for civil damages, apparently having little hope of restitution or punishment in any other manner. However, the National Socialists managed to postpone the trial with legal maneuvers for such a long time that in the end a compromise settlement favorable to the culprits was reached. On the whole, the lesser trials would seem to have been no more of a serious deterrent to political crime than the Hitler Trial itself, although his stint in prison, short and mild as it was, did seem to help persuade Hitler to avoid military adventures in the future. It is, however, equally possible that what impressed him was the sight of his Kampfbund dissolving before the rifle muzzles of the Landespolizei rather than the thought of his spartan room in Landsberg.[54]

[53] NA, T120, 5570, pp. K591738-40; Röhm, *Geschichte*, pp. 300-306; Ludendorff, *Feldherrnhalle*, pp. 79-90.

[54] B, II, MA103476, pp. 497, 1234; IV, OPA 73930, Urteil v. Volksgericht, passim; NA, T120, 5570, pp. K591856-57, K591811; Kallenbach, *Mit*

III. *Conclusion*

Aside from those who died in the Putsch itself, the rebels of November 1923 came off very well. Most of them were simply turned loose to go home. Others spent shorter or longer periods in protective custody. Fifty or so were tried on one charge or another, and most of these received very light sentences. Even some cases of actual theft—or requisitioning—went completely unpunished. Only a handful of the top leaders and some of the men who gutted the *Münchener Post* served much time.

It can be argued, and with some justice, that the small fry should have gone relatively free—although many persons who felt this way in 1923 had felt differently about the "Red" rebels of 1919—in view of the tremendous economic and social pressures during the fall of 1923 and the contagiously nationalistic atmosphere in München at that time. With a world tumbling down around them and their state apparently at the edge of war with the federal government, it is not surprising that many men clutched at straws in the hope of salvation.

It is probable that one of the reasons the Putschists were so gently handled was that, despite all their threats, they had killed no one except in the confused fight at the Feldherrnhalle, and they had apparently not injured any of their various victims seriously, although they had certainly handled some of their hostages roughly and beaten up several persons. The result was that there were no atrocities to rouse popular opinion against them, as the Geiselmord of 1919 had roused München against the "Reds." The Putschists had violated the law, but few people become emotional over such offenses. All of the dead, except for policemen—and the public usually seems to expect and accept the death or crippling of policemen without a qualm[55]—had been on the side of the Putschists, which undoubtedly aroused sympathy for them and justified leniency in the eyes of many neutrals.

Such considerations may help to explain the outcome, but they do not effectively defend the conduct and result of the Hitler Trial

---

Hitler, pp. 19-48, 152; *Kürschners Volkshandbuch Deutscher Reichstag, 1933*, p. 472.

[55] For example, note that all the sympathy of the press and the most vocal elements of the American intelligentsia was with the students who were injured by the police in the Columbia University riots of 1968. Yet, apparently no student was seriously hurt, while two policemen were so crippled that they will probably never recover.

of 1924. A state must defend itself against persons who seek its overthrow by violence if the state hopes to survive. The courts of a state must administer justice through the existing law. Justice may well be tempered with mercy—although the occasions and extent to which this should be done are a matter of debate—but no court or judge has a right to evade the laws of the land or allow persons standing trial to make a mockery of court and laws alike. Nor do judges have the right to conduct their courtrooms in such a manner as to aid one of the disputants at the expense of another or to fly in the face of evidence and the law alike. Yet the judges did all of these things in the Hitler Trial, and here they bear a share of the responsibility for the bill that Germany had to pay later as a result of the success and activities of Adolf Hitler.

The responsibility was not entirely that of the judges and the senior prosecutors; behind these men stood the Minister of Justice. He was responsible for the conduct of justice and the conduct of the persons who made up the judicial system. He could have interfered to provide a different judge. He could have seen to it that more vigorous prosecutors were selected. He did not need to defend the judge before the Bavarian Cabinet. It could be argued that he had no right to interfere in the workings of justice. Certainly, he should not interfere to prevent justice—though there is strong evidence that he had done just that in the case of the May Day affair[56] —but there was every reason for him to intervene to the extent of his powers and abilities where justice was not being done and the law was being defied. Here he can justly be faulted, whether the fault be of omission or commission, whether it was blindness or guile.

[56] See Chapter VIII, Section III, above.

19.

THE GOVERNMENT AND THE AFTERMATH OF THE PUTSCH

I. *The Cabinet and the Triumvirate*

The Putsch brought to a head the conflict implicit in the division of political and military power in Bavaria during the fall of 1923. In theory the Cabinet had been supreme all along. In fact, however, it had tended to make explicit or implicit concessions to the Generalstaatskommissar right up to the time of the Putsch. Kahr, or more properly the triumvirate of which he was at least the titular head, took full advantage of these concessions on the part of the government and increasingly tried to wring further concessions from Knilling and his associates. The Putsch now led both parties to insist upon a clear division of authority.

At the same time, the Putsch had changed the relationship between government and triumvirate. After all, Kahr had been appointed Generalstaatskommissar for the purpose of preventing or suppressing an insurrection of the Verbände. Once this insurrection had taken place and collapsed, the basic hold that the triumvirate had had on the government was removed. At first, it would seem, neither the government nor the triumvirate recognized this elementary fact. For one thing, they were too absorbed in the day-to-day problems of liquidating the Putsch and, for another, they were not certain for several days that the Putsch was definitely dead. However, when the light did dawn, it apparently dawned first for the Cabinet. The ministers might have been shaken by their imprisonment or their hurried flight to Regensburg, but they were in no very conciliatory mood when they met on the morning of 10 November to discuss the events of the past forty-eight hours.

Minister-President Knilling opened the Cabinet meeting with the question of whether or not Kahr should be continued in office in view of the Putsch. He clearly favored dispensing with the services of all three members of the triumvirate and nominated General

Franz Ritter von Epp to replace Lossow, with Colonel Josef Banzer heading the Landespolizei.[1] In his presentation he mentioned rumors that the Reichswehr no longer stood behind Lossow because he had shown himself afraid of the threats of the Putschists. Assistant Secretary of State Georg Schmidt, who had remained in München during the Putsch, reported, with obvious disapproval, that Kahr had flatly refused to accept directions from him on the ninth.[2] Krausneck did not believe that it would be possible to keep Kahr at his post and clearly resented his failure to take prompt action on behalf of the imprisoned ministers, although he himself belonged to the Regensburg group. He was also critical of Kahr's stand at the beer hall, whatever his motive might have been. Von Meinel took the same line: he had no faith in Kahr; if they left him at his post he would soon be a dictator. Dr. Schweyer and Oswald both clearly stated their mistrust of Kahr but were not sure that this was the moment to drop him. Schweyer felt that Kahr's fall might seem to be a victory for Hitler, while Oswald's grounds are less clear. Only Gürtner, who was generally considered to be the member of the Cabinet most friendly towards Hitler, defended Kahr, saying that "a man who acted as Hitler had could not expect to be treated like a gentleman. What Kahr had done had contributed to the re-establishment of peace in Bavaria."[3] In the end it was agreed that Knilling and Gürtner should go to speak with Kahr, who had refused to come to Knilling when summoned that evening. The question of Kahr's fate remained open, but the fact that only one Minister had defended him did not augur well for that gentleman's political future.[4]

The conference with the triumvirate—for Lossow and Seisser were with Kahr during the conversation—did not run smoothly. The three launched an offensive without waiting for Knilling to bring his guns into position. Kahr, Lossow, and Seisser saw no cause for embarrassment in their conduct during the Putsch. They had merely adopted a ruse in order to maintain their freedom. They did not believe that they could be replaced. Instead they judged that the time had come to turn over full powers to Kahr. He must not be dependent on a parliamentary government. Seisser spoke of a "supreme power"[5] in this connection. When Knilling asked Los-

---

[1] During the course of the meeting, Epp—in a private conference with Knilling—agreed to take on at least the military duties of the GSK.

[2] B, II, MA99521, 10.11.1923, p. 2. Schmidt was a Staatssekretär.

[3] *Ibid.*, p. 3.   [4] *Ibid.*, pp. 1-6.   [5] "Übergewalt."

sow flatly if the Reichswehr and the Landespolizei supported the constitutional government, Lossow's reply was evasive. When Knilling said that he must then assume that the troops were not unreservedly loyal to the government, Lossow said that that was not what he had meant. The general then added: "The Diet will not enjoy our protection. It will, if it convenes, be driven away with curses and disgrace."[6] Kahr carefully disassociated himself from any desire to do anything illegal, but even Gürtner admitted that Kahr's military associates did not seem able to distinguish between the power of the state and the right to execute the directives of the holders of power:[7] what they clearly wanted was to free Kahr from any commitments to the Diet. Since the minister-president demurred sharply, they finally agreed merely to ask for a public reaffirmation of the powers that the Generalstaatskommissar had initially been given.

What the triumvirate achieved was the deep hostility of the minister-president, who demanded on 12 November that the Cabinet take a clear stand on the question. He said he would like to ask for the resignations of all three on the grounds of the unpopularity of their actions on Thursday, 8 November, but he warned that, in his opinion, all three would refuse to resign. He also noted that some members of Parliament wanted to make an end of Kahr and his friends. Finally, he raised the question of whether or not the government had the authority to enforce its decision should the three refuse to go. At the same time, Knilling threw a new bone of contention into the political cauldron by demanding the resignations of Dr. Schweyer and Wutzlhofer because they were unpopular with the people—by which he clearly meant the extreme Right. Wutzlhofer said that his party had wanted him to resign some days before but that he had persuaded them to wait. Schweyer said that he would leave it up to the leaders of his party to decide if he should resign. Knilling threatened to resign himself if Schweyer did not. The other speakers ignored the Knilling-Schweyer fight and spoke to the Kahr issue. They were generally divided between those who wanted to get rid of Kahr now and those who wished to keep him

[6] B, II, MA99521, 12.11.1923, p. 3. Gürtner reported Lossow's comments in a far milder form: "Im weiteren Verlaufe der Unterredung habe er gesagt, die Reichswehr und Polizeiwehr hätten in den letzten Tagen schwerste Belastung aushalten müssen, man könne den Truppen nicht noch zumuten für den Landtag ihr Leben einzusetzen" (p. 10).

[7] "Staatsgewalt" and "vollziehenden Gewalt."

on for a while to prevent aiding Hitler. Gürtner remained alone in his support of Kahr.[8]

In the afternoon the Cabinet met with the leaders of the coalition parties and it became clear that while, in everyday matters, the government might go its way without too much interference, when the chips were down, the parties took a decisive hand in the game. Government sentiment was in favor of dropping Kahr, come what may, especially in view of the recently issued public proclamation —written by the historian Karl-Alexander von Müller—which used language that suggested dictatorial plans and was couched in the phraseology of the extreme Right.[9] Dr. Held of the Bayerische Volkspartei and Hilpert of the Mittelpartei were, however, determined to avoid public recriminations and to show a united face to the Putschists and the general public. They insisted on no resignations in the government and the retention of Kahr and his colleagues if they were prepared to accept an ultimatum to be delivered to them by representatives of the parties. This proposal carried the day.

On the thirteenth, despite some muttering on all sides, the Cabinet accepted Kahr's answer to the party ultimatum, and the various members agreed not to resign in view of the critical situation and the pressure on them from their parties to remain. Knilling was the most reluctant of all to accept the compromise solution and was, if anything, more annoyed at the decision in favor of Dr. Schweyer and Wutzlhofer than he was at the salvation of the triumvirate.[10]

These decisions were, of course, temporary, for the Cabinet was living on borrowed time in view of the coming elections and Knilling's determination to get out as soon as was decently possible. Also, reading between the lines of the party-government agreement, one could clearly see the determination that the triumvirate would be unloaded as soon as practicable. Meanwhile, the Cabinet and Diet alike kept a jealous eye on Kahr. He was forced by the Cabinet to give up his attempt to dismiss Police President Mantel of München and by combined government-Diet insistence to submit copies of his decrees to the Diet—a bitter pill. When he com-

[8] *Ibid.*, pp. 1-10.

[9] For this Aufruf see NA, EAP 105/7a, Aufruf, 11.11.1923; Müller, *Wandel*, pp. 170-71.

[10] B, II, MA99521, 12.11.1923, Nachmittag, pp. 11-18; 13.11.1923, pp. 4-6; NA, EAP 105/7a, WKK VII, Abt. Ib 1471 Geh.; NA, T120, 5569, pp. K391593-602.

plained of not being informed about important legislation, the Cabinet replied that it lay outside his competence and added, significantly, that in any case his office was not a permanent one.[11] In December, faced by rumors that the triumvirate was thinking of a new Putsch, the government even sounded out General Freiherr von Kress and Colonel Banzer as to their positions if the rumors should prove to be true. This incident showed how far the suspicions of the Cabinet had grown.[12] Such guerrilla warfare was the overture to the removal of the triumvirate, which the government seriously undertook in the new year. Here things went relatively smoothly where Kahr and Lossow were concerned, despite the struggles of the men involved, but Seisser proved to be a match for even the shrewd, alert, and none-too-scrupulous Knilling.

Lossow was in one way the easiest to eliminate, since he was also unpopular with the military authorities in Berlin. He was in another sense the greatest problem, since, while the Cabinet wished to get rid of Lossow the man, it wished to retain Lossow the general until Berlin had bowed to Bavaria's terms in the conflict centering around him. In the end, Lossow, apparently sick and tired of the complex game in which he was a pawn and under pressure from his subordinates, surrendered to Berlin, a decision that helped to force the Bavarian government to accept a compromise solution to the conflict.[13] Lossow thus shuffled off into the wings before the Hitler Trial began, and, despite rumors that he was to enter the Turkish service, he did not again tread the political stage, although he was destined to live well into the Third Reich. Despite the accusations that rained down on him from various sides, Lossow suffered no sanctions for his stand during either the Lossow affair or the Putsch. In the spring of 1924 both the Bavarian and the federal prosecuting attorneys reported that there was no evidence to warrant action against him, and in the Third Reich he encountered no legal or official persecution, although on at least one occasion young Nazi firebrands apparently planned to humiliate Lossow and the other members of the triumvirate in public.[14]

[11] B, I, M. Inn. 73694, Reg. Obb. 701, 16.7.1924; II, MA99521, 12.11.1923, pp. 2-3; 27.11.1923, pp. 7-12; MA103458, 37913, Knilling an Kahr, 4.1.1924; GSK Pol/Nr. 6057, 10.1.1924; GSK Pol/Nr. 5344, 21.12.1923.

[12] B, I, GSK 6, pp. 26ff.

[13] B, II, MA99522, 16.2.1924, pp. 3-11; NA, T79, 49, pp. 343-46.

[14] B, II, MA103476, p. 1554; IV, HSIV, EE7, Endres MS, pp. 71-72; NA, T79, 72, pp. 605-6; T120, 5570, pp. K591803, K591841.

With regard to the other two men, the Cabinet members betrayed that politicians like other mortals can find the veil of even the near future too thick to penetrate, for that body took the following position on 17 April:

> The Cabinet is of the opinion that the two men must be prevented from taking up their official duties again. In the case of Colonel von Seisser no difficulties will arise. Regarding Excellency von Kahr the question arises as to whether he should be asked to visit the minister of the interior who would explain the situation and the position of the Cabinet to him and suggest that he should make the necessary decision himself or whether Dr. von Kahr should be approached through his close friend President of the Insurance Chamber Dr. von [sic] Englert.[15]

The Kahr problem was a two-stage one, the first stage of which had been achieved by the time the Cabinet reached the optimistic appraisal above. Kahr had clearly found his post as Generalstaatskommissar less attractive after the Putsch. On the day of the Putsch itself he had given up his plans for a national directory and dropped negotiations with the "northerners."[16] Shortly thereafter he was forced to give the government written assurances that he would not exceed his authority and was made increasingly aware of their general distrust and disapproval of him and his policies. Too, he was clearly unpopular with large segments of the populace of München and with the right radicals throughout Bavaria. One Cabinet member, for example, doubted if Kahr dared show his face in the streets during the troubled days following the Putsch.[17] The result was that when Kahr was pressed in February by Knilling—who had clearly forgotten his own friendly relations with the Kampfbund—to resign because he had been too soft regarding Hitler, Kahr did not fight too vigorously. Indeed, he fell in with the Cabinet's desire that he resign before the Hitler Trial began and timed his resignation to coincide with Lossow's.[18]

This resignation, however, automatically returned him to his pre-

---

[15] B, II, MA99522, 17.4.1924, p. 10.

[16] B, II, MA103476, p. 743.

[17] B, I, GSK 6, p. 24; II, MA99521, 13.11.1923, pp. 2-3; MA103456, Nr. M. Pr. 1704, Knilling an Kahr, 4.12.1923.

[18] B, I, Kahr MS, p. 1438; II, MA99522, 21.1.1924, p. 5; 9.2.1924, pp. 5-6, 8; 16.2.1924, pp. 7, 11; MA103457, Kahr an Knilling, 17.2.1924; NA, T120, 5569, pp. K591621, K591692.

vious post of Regierungspräsident of Oberbayern, and therefore made him responsible for the political security of München and much of southern Bavaria. The majority of the Cabinet was of the opinion that public security considerations and his unpopularity with many citizens of various political complexions both made his return to this post most undesirable. Therefore, despite the fulsome praise they had showered on him in the letter which had, with almost unseemly haste, accepted his resignation, the Cabinet also wished him to resign from his permanent post. It was here that Kahr dug in his heels, although he agreed to take a prolonged vacation and they agreed to leave the problem to be solved by the new government which would soon follow them.[19]

The new government of Dr. Held found the problem no simpler than had its predecessors, and Kahr tried to force their hand by returning to his duties. The new interior minister, Dr. Karl Stützel, immediately ordered him back on furlough, and the government turned its attention to the festering question. Like the old government, Dr. Held and his colleagues decided that Kahr must go but that he should not be thrown out in the cold, and therefore they began the search for a post that would be acceptable to him and safe from their point of view. Meanwhile, rumors that Kahr would survive resulted in a wave of attacks on him in the right radical press to which Kahr reacted by demanding once again his return to duty. In the end, by bribing the incumbent, the government made available for Kahr the post of President of the Administrative Court (Verwaltungsgerichtshof), the same post in which his father had ended his career. He lost power but gained in salary and rank by the change. Like Lossow he had played his last political role.[20]

The case of Seisser, which seemed to be the simplest and easiest to handle—since he was, unlike Lossow, a Bavarian rather than a federal appointee and was without an independent political base—turned out to be the knottiest of all and was the only one in which government had to accept defeat. Seisser was already on cool terms

[19] B, I, Kahr MS, pp. 1463-75; II, MA99522, 17.3.1924, p. 8; 28.4.1924, p. 13; 24.5.1924, p. 8; MA103457, 5104, Dr. Matt an Kahr, 18.2.1924; NA, T120, 5570, p. K591802.

[20] B, II, MA99522, 8.7.1924, pp. 4-6; 27.9.1924, p. 5; 8.10.1924, p. 6; MA103458, M. Äuss. 18766, Dr. Held an Dr. von Kahr, 9.7.1924; 1289, Reg. Obb., Dr. von Kahr an Dr. Held, 20.9.1924; NA, T120, 5570, pp. K592001, K592027; Wulz, Georg, *Die Familie Kahr, Aus Archiv für Rassen- und Gesellschaftsbiologie*, Bd. 18, Heft 3 (Sept. 1926), p. 253.

with his minister and on bad terms with Oberregierungsrat Pirner, the Lapo specialist of the Ministry of the Interior. The Putsch and a subsequent quarrel with a Regierungspräsident were additional factors in the decision to remove the colonel from his post. The anger, however, was not all on one side: Seisser complained officially to Kahr when Knilling approached Colonel Banzer behind Seisser's back with questions that seemed to impugn Seisser's loyalty to the government. Furthermore, Seisser made it very clear that he had no intention of resigning or of asking to be relieved of his duties as Chef des Landespolizeiamts. On 18 February 1924, the government decided to wait until after the Hitler Trial to act in this matter. Should Seisser be incriminated in any way the Cabinet could reconsider his case.[21]

In early March the question was raised again by Permanent Undersecretary Dr. Hans Schmelzle, probably at the instigation of the minister-president, whose senior aide he was. Schmelzle claimed that the Landespolizei should not be burdened with the leadership of a man who had been accused—by the Putschists—of high treason. Dr. Schweyer noted that Seisser had been furloughed and in any case, because of the administrative nature of his office, was not a commander but an administrator. Two weeks later, Dr. Krausneck demanded that Seisser be dismissed along with some other Landespolizei officers and that the Police Directory be thoroughly purged. Colonel Josef Ritter von Reiss, the commander of the Landespolizei in Nürnberg, was suggested as a successor to Seisser, since Banzer's conduct had also been questionable.[22] However, it was not until the last day of March that the Cabinet decided finally that Seisser must go.[23]

The government then demanded Seisser's resignation, and this action was reported in the press. Interestingly, while most newspapers passed over it without comment, the organ of the Bavarian

---

[21] B, I, GSK 6, pp. 26-28; II, 99522, 18.2.1924, pp. 2-3; MA103457, P/Nr. 5330, 10.12.1923; M.I. 2005a 152; 37201 Min. Pr.

[22] This suggestion indicated how little the Cabinet members really knew about the Landespolizei, since Reiss was not a man of the same format as Seisser, but a good, sound, troop commander at the regimental level. Seisser's successor, in view of his responsibilities, should clearly have been a highly talented officer, preferably with general staff experience, but it is easy to see why Schweyer would prefer a plodding workhorse after his experiences in dealing with the wily and vigorous Seisser. GP, A and B, Landespolizei officers.

[23] B, II, MA99522, 4.3.1924, p. 6; 17.3.1924, pp. 5, 8; 31.3.1924, p. 3.

People's Party, the *Bayerische Kurier*, lamented the decision. Seisser simply refused to resign and defied the government to remove him. The Cabinet supported Dr. Schweyer. Seisser then appealed to the courts, and his friends stirred up sympathy for him in the Diet. The Cabinet was enraged and reiterated its determination that he must go after such actions. Gürtner stated that there were no grounds here for the intervention of any court; he felt that it would be better to leave the question to be settled by the new government. The Cabinet decided to uphold Schweyer in the dismissal of Seisser and the appointment of Reiss.[24]

In the end the new government (almost all holdovers from the old one) was left to hold the baby after all. Although it agreed that it was impossible to rescind the dismissal of Seisser, the Supreme Judicial court found in favor of Seisser. Dr. Held was of the opinion that the Supreme Court had no jurisdiction in the question. However, squirm on the hook as they might, there was no escape. Attempts to persuade Seisser to leave of his own free will or to restore him to duty but not to his post all broke down. Seisser returned to his office and remained there until he reached retirement age in 1930. The only consolation his enemies had was that his powers were somewhat reduced and that he was consistently denied the general's title which was soon accorded his successor.[25] Seisser would never again play the central role that he had carried off in 1923. Most of his hats were gone, and in the comparative quiet of the middle Weimar years he functioned simply and effectively as a senior bureaucrat and police chief. Yet perhaps he is inclined to feel that he has enjoyed one final triumph, for of all the senior figures in those crisis years, he alone was still alive in 1970. His opponents and friends alike are gone to the grave.[26]

Tactical errors on the part of the Cabinet, which had chosen illegal grounds for his dismissal—since only inefficiency or physical disability were proper legal grounds—and the fact that Seisser had provided no clear evidence for his foes to use against him combined to save him. To make the Cabinet even more embittered, Ritter von

[24] B, II, MA99522, 24.5.1924, p. 7; 20.6.1924, p. 7; NA, T120, 5570, p. K591802.

[25] The government, however, continued to consider him a general and to accord him a general's pay and allowances.

[26] B, II, MA99522, 14.2.1924, p. 9; 12.8.1924, p. 7; 28.8.1924, pp. 2-8; 5.9.1924, pp. 8-20; 5.9.1924, pp. 21-22; 3.11.1924, p. 24; MA103476, p. 587; GP, A, General Christian Pirner, 26.9.1960; B, Colonel Ernst Schultes.

Reiss had to be bribed into returning to Nürnberg, since there was no way of removing him from Seisser's post without his consent. This concession enabled Banzer, whom the government loved little more than Seisser, to insist that he be given the same terms as Reiss. If democracy is, as some would claim, government by frustration, the Bavarian government could claim that they had achieved democracy.

Thus the members of the triumvirate were robbed of much of their power early in 1924 by the resignation of Kahr and the end of the Generalkommissariat. All of them were out of power during most of the year, and only Seisser returned to his old post in the end. The legal government had eliminated the extra-legal rival it had created to defeat its illegal opponents.

II. *The Problem of Internal Security*

Much as the government and the triumvirate quarreled among themselves, they turned a united front towards the Kampfbund, the other Verbände, and the general public after the Putsch. Even Kahr said: "The experiences that I have had recently with men who acted as though no one in the country could equal them in patriotic fervor, have been so unfortunate that by now one is sickened by the sound of the patriotic and racist phrases."[27] Here spoke a new Kahr, suspicious and hostile towards the Verbände he had so long sponsored. The Putsch had been a nasty shock to the government, and it was determined that the right radical threat should not be revived. The state of emergency in München was maintained in full force until 21 November and at a lower level thereafter. Reichswehr and police troops from outside the city were retained in München for weeks after the Putsch, and until 22 November they were held ready for immediate action. The troops were apparently provided with tear gas and smoke grenades, and official buildings were carefully guarded as were bridges and other key points. Another sign of the seriousness with which the possibility of further armed revolt was taken is the fact that on 11 November the newly appointed commander of the Nineteenth Infantry Regiment, Colonel Martin Ritter von Dittelberger, was "requested" not to take over his new unit until the situation was calmer. To the great amusement of Knilling, the one security step the authorities could not take was to punish a playwright who planned to murder Kahr. The only applicable law was the Law for the Protection of the Republic,

[27] B, I, GSK 99, p. 41, Kahr an Tutschek.

which Kahr had declared null and void in Bavaria.[28] The authorities took now a firm hand with hostile demonstrators.[29] New regulations were developed for more effective use of the army and Landespolizei in civil emergencies and for better control of their relationships with local authorities. The government's political intelligence system was reorganized and reporting was made more methodical.[30]

More important from the point of view of long term policy was the decision to draw the teeth of the Verbände by means of a firm disarmament policy applied to all Verbände and an equally firm policy of repression aimed at the Kampfbund organizations. On 16 November 1923 Kahr issued a decree through Seisser which read in part:

> The Bavarian state government has up to now, for good reasons, allowed patriotic Verbände which were recognized as being loyal to the state to hold a portion of the arms that are the property of the Bavarian state for the purpose of security and protection.
>
> This privilege is withdrawn from the National Socialist Workers' Party, the Verbände Oberland, Reichskriegsflagge, the Seventh and Twelfth Districts of the V.V. München, and the Group Rossbach immediately as a result of the recent developments. In the same manner, all other weapons that have not yet been reported to the Landeskommandant in accordance with the agreement made with the Verbände are to be taken into the custody of the Reichswehr and the Landespolizei.[31]

This decree was not allowed to become a dead letter, as had earlier ones. Time and again Kahr or Seisser refused to permit exceptions to it and prodded the provincial authorities to take prompt and vigorous action to disarm the Kampfbund and to collect all unreported weapons caches. On 27 November Kahr and Seisser refused permission for Oberländer in Mittelfranken to retain their arms. On 7 December Kahr complained to the Regierungspräsidenten about the slow pace at which the disarmament and dissolution of

---

[28] B, I, GSK 3, pp. 24, 29, 38; GSK 60, p. 8; Kahr MS, p. 1401; IV, BuR, Bd. 34, Item 156; NA, EAP 105/7a, 10.11.1923ff, passim; T120, 5569, p. K591654.

[29] See Chapters XV-XVI above for evidence on this point.

[30] B, I, GSK 3, GSK/Abt. A/Nr. 2724, 19.11.1923; GSK 4, 11; NA, EAP 105/7a, 10.11.1923ff, passim.

[31] B, I, GSK 3, p. 61.

Kampfbund organizations was being conducted. On 19 December Kahr assured the Verbände loyal to the government that their caches would be left alone if they had been reported to the Reichswehr by 1 September 1923.[32] In mid-January Kahr stood firm on his demand that all weapons be reported and available to the government, and he struck to the root of the problem in defending this position:

> That it was a fateful error that must not be repeated always to give way to this feeling [against government control of weapons] was indicated on 8 November 1923.
>
> I cannot see why a Verband that is in every respect loyal to the government should not be willing to entrust the weapons to the government for storage and maintenance.
>
> The demand of the Verbände for free disposition over the arms springs primarily from the wish to make themselves independent of the government and, if the occasion arises, to emerge as a power in the state. This situation is unacceptable for an ordered state.
>
> Furthermore, the storage and maintenance of the weapons in the unregistered caches, which were withdrawn from the supervision of the RW and LP, was, by past experience, extremely inadequate. The weapons were mostly in a completely useless condition.
>
> Thus the security of the state and the preservation of valuable war materials both demand that the state take into its hands the storage and maintenance of at least the bulk of the weapons.[33]

He made it clear that he was not interested in small arms held in the homes of individuals or even in small caches of weapons, but in the large caches that had a military potential.

During the same month, all of the official and semi-official agencies involved in the arms question[34] came to a basic agreement by which all war materials were the property of the Bavarian state and were placed under the administrative control of the Landeskommandant, to whom they would be made available on the day of mobilization. As much materiel as possible over and above the

[32] B, I, GSK 3, pp. 31, 36-37, 41.   [33] B, I, GSK 101, p. 5.

[34] The Ministries of the Interior, Finance, and Justice, the Landeskommandant, Epp (as leader of the Deutsche Notbann), and the GSK. The leaders of the major Verbände had previously been consulted.

Reichswehr's official table of materiel would be kept on army property, especially small arms and ammunition. Heavy weapons and equipment would not be kept on a post if they would be too hard to remove in case of a surprise Allied inspection. However, a key part of any weapon that was not held on a post would be removed so that it could not be fired. The Deutsche Notbann[35] would assist the Reichswehr in carrying out this mission.[36]

After the dissolution of the Generalstaatskommissariat the same policy was followed by the Ministry of the Interior. On 16 August 1924 Stützel ordered the rigid enforcement of the ban on all military exercises and the confiscation of all weapons that appeared. This he saw as the best policy to protect the state from new insurrections.[37] The Beer Hall Putsch had ended the "herrliche Zeiten"[38] for the Verbände in Bavaria. They might continue to exist; they might continue to hold some weapons; but they could not operate in the open as they had once done, and their activities were greatly reduced in scope.

This disarmament program was more than a matter of policy or a sterile plan. As is always the case, the authorities failed to collect all of the weapons they tried to confiscate, but that they collected many is indicated by the reports of police and officials and by the protests of the Verbände. In the Passau Bezirk 143 military rifles were collected. In Rosenheim forty rifles and a machine gun had been surrendered by the National Socialists by the middle of December. In Niederbayern many machine guns and much ammunition had been collected by the end of November. Four communities yielded 213 rifles. In Oberbayern Captain von Bomhard of the Landespolizei noted in December that a great deal of war materiel had been collected from the dissolved organizations, including two batteries of artillery with ammunition, a searchlight, and much infantry ammunition. He noted that the local citizenry had in some cases informed the police where Oberland caches of artillery pieces were located. When the drive was over the problem was reduced to far more manageable proportions, and the price of maintaining arms was strict concealment.[39]

---

[35] See below. [36] B, IV, BuR, Bd. 36, Akt 2, Item 35.

[37] B, IV, Lapo, Bd. 26, Akt 1, M. Inn. 2015 d a 1.

[38] Wonderful times.

[39] B, I, M. Inn. 73694, Notiz für Akt 2004 kaa (ca. May 1924); GSK 44, pp. 22-23, 148, 183-84, 190-91, 214, 224; GSK 60, p. 10; SA 1, 1634, p. 603; II, MA102140, HMB 917, Opf., p. 1; HMB 1174, N/B, p. 1; IV, BuR,

The greatest emphasis in the battle against the Kampfbund, aside from the disarmament of the paramilitary units, was on the destruction of the organizations themselves and the elimination of their propaganda. The authorities were never completely successful in either of these endeavors, but they kept both organizations and propaganda down to a modest level.

It was, of course, easy enough to ban the organizations that had taken part in the Putsch. It was something quite different to keep them dissolved and to prevent successor organizations with the same aims and personnel from being formed. This task was made doubly difficult because the authorities wished to separate the leaders from the led and to prevent thousands upon thousands of citizens from being permanently alienated from the existing government. Therefore, Kahr in particular wished to see the former Kampfbund members enter competing Verbände, as long as they entered as individuals or in groups small enough to be successfully absorbed. However, since in some places entire Kampfbund organizations were going over to other Verbände, the danger of a "take-over" of the infiltrated Verband was very real, because such take-overs were part of the policy of the Kampfbund leadership. Therefore it was necessary to blow hot and cold and to deal with each situation individually.

The organizations dissolved initially were the NSDAP, Oberland, and RKF. All of their discoverable assets were confiscated, but these did not amount to much, partly because the organizations had operated on a hand-to-mouth basis and partly because they seem to have spirited away their most valuable possessions before the police arrived to take over their various premises.[40] Later Reiterkorps Wrede and Gruppe Rossbach, both sub-organzations of the NSDAP, were added to the list, as was Kampfbund München (formerly Seventh and Twelfth Districts of VVM) which—probably to the indignation of the vainglorious Zeller—tended to be ignored by the authorities in much the same manner that Liechtenstein was forgotten by the Prussians when making peace with their enemies in 1866. Finally, in January 1924, the Kampfbund Deutscher Offiziere, a right radical protest organization of veterans, was dissolved, although this organization was more one of the new

---

Bd. 34, Item 169, Bomhard Rund-Schreiben, 23.11.1923; Item 172, 27.11. 1923.

[40] B, I, GSK 3, p. 60; GSK 88, pp. 13, 18, 21; II, MA103458, GSK R/Nr. 6472, 18.1.1924.

wave of racist organizations which characterized the year 1924 than one of the "old line" right radical groups. It was, however, early enough to be banned with the old organizations rather than with its own generation.[41]

The campaign against Kampfbund and other right radical propaganda was energetic, if not frenetic. The main National Socialist organ, the *Völkischer Beobachter*, was seized, together with its printing shop, as property of a dissolved organization, but this was only the beginning. New papers and old ones were constantly printing attacks on the government and praise of Hitler. As a result, at least sixteen newspapers were banned or, in the case of those printed outside Bavaria, forbidden to sell within the state in the course of the months immediately following the Putsch. This leaves out the clearly illegal "underground" press, which appeared from time to time and place to place, and the illegal newspapers smuggled in from Austria. Most of the burden of suppressing hostile propaganda fell on Kahr, but Knilling also took a hand when necessary. On 30 November, for example, he threatened to fire the chief editor of the official Bavarian government organ, the *Bayerische Staatszeitung*, if he persisted in printing false reports of the Putsch.[42] Kahr also appealed to outside authorities for assistance in the battle against Kampfbund propaganda. He asked Seeckt to keep the north German press in rein and prevent the spread of lies, but he received cold comfort from that quarter in view of the unsettled Lossow affair. Knilling requested that the Austrian authorities take similar action in their jurisdiction, but he was rebuffed on the grounds that no legal basis for such action existed.[43]

The press was relatively easy to police, though, in comparison to the waves of virulent poster and leaflet propaganda that periodically deluged portions of Bavaria, especially in the early weeks after the Putsch. The police were ordered to proceed energetically against this menace, and Bavarian soldiers had standing orders to seize any person who tried to press propaganda on them. Finally,

[41] B, i, GSK 88, pp. 11, 19; M. Inn. 71536, GSK Nr. 2737, 20.11.1923; GSK R/Nr. 5898, 5.1.1924; ii, MA103458, GSK R/Nr. 6542, 18.1.1924.

[42] B, i, GSK 43, p. 145; GSK 44, p. 56; GSK 83, pp. 42, 53, 66, 74; SA 1, Polizeizeittafel, 12.11.1923; ii, MA103458, GSK R/Nr. 4467, 7.12.1923; MA103473, 35590 M. Äuss. vom 30.11.1923; NA, T120, 5569, pp. K591646, K591657, K591727, K591732.

[43] B, ii, MA103472, Abt. R/Pr. R/Nr. 4468; 871 Knilling an Landeshauptmann, Salzburg; Brief: Landeshauptmann, Salzburg an Knilling, 28.1.1924; i, M. Inn. 73695, Nr. 706/23, T 1, iii, pers. Abschrift.

a highly respected professor at München University wrote a pamphlet on the Putsch that amounted to a scathing assault on Kahr. After much debate and passing the buck, the pamphlet was banned—too late to have any real effect—and a wordy but unimportant struggle over whether or not the ban was an infringement of academic freedom developed.[44]

In the course of enforcing the regulations against the Kampfbund the authorities arrested or sought to arrest many individuals who were seeking to revive or maintain illegal organizations or to spread Kampfbund propaganda. Among the prominent leaders who were arrested for their activities in the period immediately after the Putsch were Gregor Strasser, Anton Drexler, Dr. Christian Roth, Julius Streicher, Dr. Fritz Weiss, and Anton Ritter von Bolz.[45] In addition to the arrest of various Kampfbund leaders for seeking to carry on their organizations, others were expelled from Bavaria as undesirable aliens under the regulations that had been used earlier in Kahr's era against Poles and Jews. It must have been doubly annoying to Putschists to know that they were the victims of a weapon that they had forced into Kahr's hands. Among the expellees were a Major (Ret.) Hans Braune, who had attacked Kahr in meetings of a veterans' organization; Franz Kleophas Pleyer, a National Socialist student leader who was later to bloom as a National Socialist historian; and Arno Schickedanz, a White Russian friend of Scheubner-Richter. This weapon seems to have been used sparingly, however, probably because any expulsion of large numbers of German citizens from Bavaria would have made for serious difficulties with the other states, while very few Putschists were citizens of foreign countries.[46]

In view of the sudden change of front made by the government and the Generalstaatskommissariat, they encountered difficulties in enforcing their new policies from some of their own officials who either sympathized with the Kampfbund or believed that there was a sound and salvageable core within the movement. Evidence on this score is elusive and partially negative, since from the begin-

[44] B, I, GSK 6, p. 20; GSK 43, p. 148; GSK 83, p. 71; II, MA103457, GSK R/Nr. 7291; GSK R/Nr. 2675; NA, EAP 105/7a, I.R. 19, 15.11.1923.

[45] B, I, GSK 43, p. 145; GSK 44, p. 89; GSK 49, p. 1; GSK 90, pp. 108, 118, 417, 563, 594; II, MA103457, 6068/II PDN-F an M. Inn.; PDN-F 1301/II 24; 6181/II; NA, T81, 116, p. 136782.

[46] B, II, MA103458, Dr. O. Rutz an Gesamtministerium, 8.1.1924; A. Glaser an Knilling, 15.1.1924; M. Inn. 2088 a 4, 29.1.1924; NA, T120, 5569, p. K591657.

ning of recorded time bureaucrats have been masters of the art of "planned inefficiency" when faced by policies of which they disapprove. However, Oberregierungsrat Stauffer, the government's liaison man with the Verbände during 1923, admittedly wished to save Oberland from dissolution despite the Putsch. In January, in response to laxness in executing those of his decrees aimed against the Kampfbund, Kahr had to explain to the Regierungspräsident of Mittelfranken that it was necessary to place the government's needs above the wishes of the Verbände. At least a portion of this laxness doubtless stemmed from laziness or timidity on the part of various officials. A portion, though, undoubtedly represented intentional foot-dragging. Specific complaints of official toleration of Kampfbund activities were sent to the Generalstaatskommissariat from time to time.[47]

Other complications arose because of the complexities of the problems raised by the various bans and by the constitutional limitations that hampered action against the former Kampfbund organizations and their sympathizers. For instance, it was against the law for a group of former Kampfbündler to meet for political purposes. On the other hand, they had a perfect right to meet as individuals to discuss economic matters. The problems this situation posed for the police are clear and not susceptible to a fully satisfactory solution. There were even problems caused by the refusal of the postal authorities, who were in the federal service, to take orders from state authorities.[48]

The general attitude towards the Verbände did, however, become markedly cooler. Kahr ordered the Landespolizei to cease providing military training for any and all Verbände until the creation of a new system for the reinforcement of the armed forces was completed. This new attitude is also reflected both in Kahr's suggestion to the Regierungspräsident of Oberfranken that Jungdo should perhaps be dissolved in that province, in view of difficulties encountered with it in Bamberg, and in his ban on Verbände membership for students of grammar or high schools.[49] Similarly, at the end of November the Generalstaatskommissariat not only refused to give money to the Wikingbund but ordered all authorities to oppose the collection of money from the general public by any and all Verbände. Finally, both local and central authorities were far

[47] B, I, GSK 3, p. 36; GSK 44, p. 71; GSK 6, p. 21; Müller, *Wandel*, p. 168.

[48] B, I, GSK 44, pp. 214, 230.   [49] Volks- und Mittelschulen.

less ready to permit parades and public demonstrations by the Verbände, and in cases where they permitted such activities they insisted on far more restrictions than formerly. The days when armed men could frequently be seen marching down the streets of Bavarian towns had passed.[50]

In Bavaria, however, no public security program was complete if it looked only towards the Right. Just as a north German socialist could say, while fighting Communists, "The enemy is on the Right," so did the Bavarian leaders of 1923-24 believe that the true foe was on the Left. Certainly Knilling and Kahr were at one in this belief if in nothing else. They therefore adopted measures to ensure that the Left would not be able to take advantage of the quarrel on the Right.

The campaign against the Left was directed primarily against the Communist Party, which Kahr banned on 11 November 1923, nine days before it was banned by the Reich. He did not ban the Social Democratic Party, but he did ban their press during the month of November, after which they were again permitted to publish, although the local authorities were given permission to set up conditions governing the appearance of individual papers. These could thereafter be banned for cause. Since the Communist Party was banned, all of its press and institutions were suppressed as well. Only the Independent Social Democratic Party seems to have been ignored, a clear indication of the extent of its collapse. Not even the hyper-sensitive Kahr could see the USPD as a menace.[51]

The campaign against the Left was, like that against the radical right, not just a paper campaign. While Socialists were generally not molested, known Communists were watched carefully and arrested on any provocation. The police were especially vigilant in arresting those Communists who were collecting firearms and high explosives. A tailor in Aubingermoos was arrested for possession of firearms and explosives as was another Communist in Neuhaus. Karl Albrecht of Altmühldorf provided a real Wild West chase: cornered by the police, he drove them off by pistol fire and escaped, only to be picked up the next day in a nearby town. Other Com-

[50] B, I, GSK 3, pp. 23, 33; GSK 6, p. 19; GSK 71, pp. 2-3, 7, 38; GSK 98, p. 8; GSK 99, p. 37; II, MA103457, Gerken an Knilling, 28 and 31.1.1924; MA104221, GSK N/Nr. 4489; IV, BuR, Bd. 36, AKT 2, Item 7.

[51] B, I, GSK 145, *passim*; GSK 44, pp. 111, 184-85; GSK 83, p. 35; M. Inn. 71537, Staatsanzeiger, 11.11.1923 and 20.11.1923; NA, T120, 5569, p. K591615.

munists were arrested when they returned to Bavaria after sojourns with the "Red army" in Thuringia. Some were arrested for spreading propaganda or attempting to carry on the party. The result was that Niederschönenfeld prison, which housed imprisoned Leftists, received in one day in November forty-four prisoners to be held in protective custody.[52]

In view of Bavarian fears of the militant Left and of the desire to maintain reserves for the armed forces in case of civil or foreign conflicts, the Bavarian government included in its public security program a new state-sponsored paramilitary organization, which was intended to replace the sometimes unreliable or dangerous Verbände with an apolitical force under direct, if tastefully concealed, state control. This new organization, the Deutscher Notbann, was to provide all of the benefits brought by the Verbände while eliminating the perils so clearly underlined by the Putsch. It would be given a monopoly on the right to military training and the use of arms and would be closely supervised and largely paid for by the state. The Notbann was headed by General von Epp, always popular in nationalist circles, and was to accept only individuals rather than organizations. Moreover, each individual was to be carefully scrutinized before being admitted. Kampfbund members were not to be rejected. Indeed, they were to be welcomed with open arms if they came individually and were genuinely prepared to support the Bavarian government.[53]

The Bavarian authorities thus established a complete program to cope with the aftermath of the Putsch and to prevent recurrence of such phenomena. The Putschists were scattered and their organizations prohibited. The leaders were jailed or placed under surveillance. All Verbände were largely disarmed, and a new organization with direct governmental sponsorship and subsidies was created to lure the potential military reservists from the Verbände, whether disloyal or loyal. The Bavarian government could be said to have learned its lesson late, but learn it did.

At the provincial level, officialdom did not always read the lessons of the Putsch quite as clearly as did the central authorities who had the advantage of loftier perspective and who had been far more

[52] B, I, GSK 44, pp. 4, 22, 83, 172, 194-96, 214, 217, 229; GSK 90, p. 21; II, MA102141, HMB 333, Obb., p. 3; IV, BuR, Bd. 36, Akt 1, Item 45.

[53] B, I, M. Inn. 72449, passim; B, II, MA99521, 28.12.1923, pp. 2-3; MA104221, Bomhard an Baron Freyberg, 26.11.1923; IV, BuR, Bd. 34, Item 174; Bd. 36, Akt 2, Item 57.

clearly the targets of the rebels. The attitudes of the Regierungspräsidenten ranged from the belief of Dr. Johann Baptist Loritz
(who was standing in for Kahr in Oberbayern) and Otto von
Strössenreuther of Oberfranken that the Putsch had to be crushed
but that the Racist Movement and the Verbände were basically
sound and should be preserved,[54] to that of Heinrich Graf von
Spreti of Schwaben, who said:

> . . . Agitation of the people and revolution must, however, be
> fought with all severity and if the organizations practice agitation
> and revolution they must be ruthlessly destroyed, even if they
> call themselves patriotic. The state owes itself this [duty]. If the
> state does not destroy the organizations, the organizations will
> destroy the state. Armed organizations sooner or later will al-
> ways seek political power.
>
> Armed organizations can therefore be tolerated by no state.
> Power belongs to the state alone, and to it alone the weapons.
> A state which deviates from these principles betrays itself.[55]

Officials at lower levels were similarly divided regarding the nature
and value of the Verbände. In Lichtenfels, the district chief favored
coming to terms with Hitler and his followers: Hitler was too popular to drop, and he had performed too many services for Germany, but he must be prevented from running amok again. An official of comparable rank in Ansbach condemned Kahr hotly for
having invited the Putsch by his patronage of the Verbände. Yet,
whatever their general stance regarding the Verbände, the overwhelming majority of the officials were clearly loyal to the government and prepared to execute its orders, just as they condemned
the Putsch as folly and an offense against law and the authority of
the state.[56]

III. *Summary*

The Putsch, by eliminating the possibility of armed revolt for the
foreseeable future, made it possible for the legal government to
eliminate its rivals for control of the state. The Generalstaatskommissariat broke the Putsch and removed the Verbände as major

[54] B, I, GSK 44, pp. 74-75; IV, Lapo, 2672, Ofr. an Chef, Lapo Bayreuth,
19.11.1923; BuR, Bd. 34, Item 149.
[55] B, I, GSK 44, pp. 193-94.
[56] B, I, GSK 43, passim; GSK 12-13 passim; GSK 50, pp. 2-6; II,
MA102140, passim.

contender for power. This action in turn made the Generalstaats-kommissariat superfluous and, because of its unpopularity even on the Right, vulnerable. The government then dismantled the GSK and took the reins back into its own hands, holding them firmly until some months after Hitler had taken power in the Reich. Partly by luck and partly by skill, Knilling and his colleagues guided the ship of state through some very treacherous rapids indeed and emerged at the far end slightly battered but clearly afloat. The triumvirate had been replaced by the single collective executive characteristic of parliamentary democracy at far less cost in blood and gold than might have been anticipated at any time during the troubled autumn.

20.

THE REICHSWEHR AND THE POLICE AFTER THE PUTSCH

The Hitler Putsch was a very serious shock for the armed forces, since both the Reichswehr and the Landespolizei had had various ties at all levels with the Kampfbund as well as with the more moderate Verbände. These official or semi-official ties with the organizations themselves were reinforced by personal ties based on familial relationships, former associations, or social encounters. The Putsch obviously carried with it the disruption of these relationships and called for the establishment of new policies and relationships. This readjustment was as necessary for individuals as for the organizations themselves, and obviously could not be painless in either sphere or at any level. Yet it could not be avoided. Humpty Dumpty could not be put together again—and full trust could scarcely be re-established easily between men and organizations that had stood face to face over smoking rifle barrels on 9 November 1923.

I. *Reichswehr Policy*

Reichswehr policy after the Putsch fell into two phases. The first phase lasted until the resignation of General von Lossow and was clearly an interim period, in the course of which primary attention was given to the immediate problems raised by the Putsch. The second was the "new course" established by the new Bavarian Landeskommandant, General Friedrich Freiherr Kress von Kressenstein, which far more clearly represented the wave of the future.

During the first period, the relations of the Bavarian Reichswehr with the Bavarian government were dominated by two problems, which complicated an otherwise improved relationship. These problems centered on the person of General von Lossow. The government distrusted him as a result of the events of 8-10 November[1] but could not rid themselves of him without discarding their

[1] See Chapter XIX, Section I, above.

only trump in the very tense card game they were playing with Berlin over states' rights. They had every intention of letting Lossow go, but not until they had tried to gain concessions from the Reich for so doing.

On the other hand, the staunchness of the other generals and the troops in the Putsch resulted in Knilling taking a far more favorable view of the army than he had on occasion during the fall. On 22 November he wrote to Dr. Held, the key leader of the Bavarian Volkspartei, that "the Hitler Putsch, which in case of even temporary success would have plunged Bavaria and Germany into measureless disaster, was crushed thanks to the impeccable stand of the Reichswehr and Landespolizei."[2] His view seems to have been that of the Cabinet in general to judge from the tenor of Cabinet meetings and from the fact that, when they feared that a new Putsch was brewing in which Lossow and Seisser could be implicated, the Cabinet approached the city commandant and the commander of the München Landespolizei regiment.[3]

While an uneasy truce between Knilling and Lossow continued until Lossow's dismissal, the distrust of Lossow's political activities seems to have been unjust. He had learned a lesson from the Putsch, although overtones of the old softness towards the Patriotic Movement and of his belief in the value of political understanding for the soldier lingered on.

His chief of staff, Lieutenant Colonel Freiherr von Berchem, on 15 November, laid down the new ground rules for Reichswehr cooperation with "national forces" in the civilian population:

> The task which now lies before us is to gather the national forces together again under the national authorities. They must, however, subordinate themselves unconditionally to the authority of the state. The civilian authorities, the army, and the schools must assume the leadership. The army will further national ideas and especially the defensive power of the people in every way in the future. It will, however, no longer tolerate the formation of armed bands. Training will be given in the future only to individ-

[2] B, II, MA103473, Knilling an Held, 22.11.1923.

[3] Neither Banzer nor von Danner was enthusiastic about this approach behind the back of his superiors, but the move indicates the extent to which the government had transferred its confidence from those top military and police leaders whom it had "sensitized" to politics to those professionals who had remained outside the realm of politics. B, I, GSK 6, pp. 26-27; II, MA99521-22, 9.11.1923–19.2.1924.

uals who place themselves unreservedly at the disposal of the army and who are bound to no other leaders.[4]

A few days later he voiced the disenchantment of most senior officers (and many junior ones) regarding the actions of those former officers who had taken part in the Putsch. In the anger of the moment he even seems to have been guilty of the same sort of generalized attack on former officers which so often marked the political speeches of the Left, for he ignores the fact that the great bulk of the former officers did not side with the Putschists; and that a number of key Putschists did not fall into the former officer category.

> ... It is regrettably true that the driving force behind the Putsch was those inactive officers without fixed employment who [have] for years been active in political or patriotic organizations and hoped to alter their destiny in this manner. One need not wonder that they showed such poor political and economic judgment, but [it is surprising] that they completely misunderstood the military situation and attacked.
>
> Besides the many unemployed former Bavarian officers in München and Bavaria there are also many former Prussian officers, who enjoy hospitality and [political] asylum here. They are a standing danger. Ehrhardt receives large sums of money, for example, from sources who earlier gave to Hitler and the Kampfbund. . . .[5]

Berchem, who, after all, had never been a friend of the National Socialists or of politics in the army was not the only representative of this determination to sail a different course. Even Lossow, whose friendship with Hitler had played a part in the coming of the Putsch, had come to see some of the problems involved in the introduction of the soldier into politics. He did not cease to believe that the soldier should be politically aware, but whereas he had previously alternately encouraged or tolerated political activity, he now frowned upon it. In his official farewell to the Officer Corps Lossow wrote:

> The officer and the older soldier must have an understanding of political matters and [make] judgments in political matters. He must stand firmly on his own feet with [regard to] his political

[4] NA, EAP 105/7a, WKK vii 32789/Ib Nr. 6089, 15.11.1923.
[5] *Ibid.*, WKK vii, 33710/Ib Nr. 6190, 20.11.1923.

views, and have a definite set of convictions. The view that the soldier and the Reichswehr should be absolutely apolitical and above the parties, ought not to mean that officer and soldier should not think politically at all and have no judgments, in short that they should be in political matters sexless beings, which characterlessly and thoughtlessly change their political coloration according to need.

On the other hand, the officer and soldier should and must renounce every *active* involvement in political life; it is always an error when he himself steps into the arena of political struggle. This applies also to every sort of active participation in the patriotic organizations. Deviation from this ground rule is only to be pardoned when an officer or soldier in an impasse must make a decision which can have political consequences. Such dilemmas can develop more easily in our times, where we live always under the influence of the Revolution, than in the more peaceful times before the war. The Wehrkreis commander and Landeskommandant [and] then the Garrison Commandants (Standortältesten) can find themselves in situations when they must make decisions with weighty political consequences on their own responsibility. Even the individual soldier can be forced to judge and then to decide whether he can remain in a public assembly, which takes on a political coloration, or whether he must leave it.[6]

Obviously torn here between his experience in the "Lossow affair" and the somewhat contradictory experiences of the Putsch days, Lossow shows himself to have realized, at the very least, that any active dabbling in politics must be denied the soldier.

Meanwhile, on 15 November the first steps in executing the new policy and towards a return to normal peacetime military policies were taken, in the form of an order ending the preparations for the so-called "Herbstübung" (fall maneuver), forbidding the training of members of the Verbände and stopping new enlistments. This order made it clear that Lossow's change of heart was not merely a matter of words. It closed a chapter in the history of the Bavarian Reichswehr.[7]

It was only with the change in leadership of the Bavarian divi-

6 NA, T79, 49, p. 345.

7 B, ɪɪ, MA103476, pp. 987-90; Seeckt Papers, Stück 281, Rabenau Notizen, p. 64.

sion, though, that the permanence and extent of the post-Putsch changes became defined. The first change, and one which had long been pending, was the replacement of Berchem by Ritter von Leeb as chief of staff. This concession to Berlin, which had tried in vain to effect the shift earlier, was a sign of the times and placed Lossow in a difficult position, not only because he had fought against this appointment, but because it carried with it the implication of his own replacement. It also gave him as his chief advisor an officer who was not interested in a duel with Berlin. The appearance of Leeb at the desk in Lossow's antechamber was as much a harbinger of Seeckt's victory over Lossow as a crocus is the harbinger of spring's victory over winter.[8]

Then, with the Reich-Bavarian agreement regarding the Lossow affair, the General himself departed. The Heerlesleitung immediately appointed General Freiherr von Kress to be acting division commander and at the same time gave Colonel Georg Freiherr Loeffelholz von Colberg the post of artillery chief on the same basis —a clear indication that the Berlin authorities saw these appointments as being permanent in all but name.

The Bavarian government, still sore at its defeat, huffed and puffed but quickly gave way. It had no alternative candidate and its opposition to Kress was based only on the grounds that he was being forced down the throats of the Bavarians by Seeckt and Gessler. The only possible alternative, General Ritter von Epp, had been very carefully excluded by the Heeresleitung (which had just succeeded in getting him out of the army) when it refused to allow the consideration of retired officers. Therefore, on 15 March 1924, Knilling himself, with rather bad grace, nominated Kress as Landeskommandant. Seeckt had won. The Bavarian division was now in the hands of men who believed in a German rather than a Bavarian army, and in Seeckt's rather than Lossow's or Möhl's concept of the relation of the army to politics.[9]

Kress was a capable and very hard-working man, who drove himself even harder than he drove his subordinates. Considered one of the very brightest officers of his generation in Bavaria, he was an artilleryman who, like his predecessor and Seeckt, had

[8] NA, EAP 105/7a, WKK vii, Lageberichten, 27.11.1923–12.12.1923; Seeckt Papers, Stück 281, Lieber-Hasse, p. 46.

[9] B, ii, MA99522, 10.4.1923, p. 4; NA, T79, 49, p. 0347; 72, p. 737; Seeckt Papers, Stück 281, Rabenau Notizen, 1924, p. 1; Gordon, Harold J. Jr., "Ritter von Epp und Berlin," *WWR*, June, 1959, passim.

served in Turkey during World War I. A good friend of Seeckt's, he was a Grand Seigneur of the old school and a moderate conservative. He had served in the Heeresleitung in Berlin during the early Reichswehr years. His entire background gave him a broader viewpoint than that of many Bavarian officers, and his firm character assured that there would be in the future a much stronger hand on the helm than there had been during Lossow's brief but turbulent regime.[10]

Even before Kress took the reins in hand, the atmosphere regarding the least connection with politics had become extremely cool. For example, all officers were ordered to remain aloof from Ludendorff until after the Hitler Trial in early January and about the same time, Lieutenant Colonel von Wenz was refused permission to attend a patriotic celebration organized by the Bavarian People's Party. Once Kress was in the saddle, the screws were tightened still farther. The army suggested to the government a ban on the wearing of the Red-White-Black cockade of the imperial army by civilians and later pressed for similar controls on the wearing of uniforms by civilians.[11] Perhaps Kress' basic attitude is best summed up in the comments with which he closed a directive ordering Reichswehr personnel to stand aloof from a number of political organizations in the spring of 1926:

> The more the political differences within Germany grow sharper, the more the Reichswehr must cling resolutely to its supraparty position. It serves the state and the entire people. Free of every political obligation and subversion it is alone in the position to prevent civil war in Germany by the weight of arms and of law.[12]

Unlike his predecessor, Kress was also primarily interested in military problems rather than police problems, with the result that there was a shift in emphasis in military matters. Whereas during Lossow's term of office as division commander almost all of the army's attention was directed to the question of maintaining order

[10] *Stellungsbesetzungsliste des Reichsheeres vom Jahr 1920* [Sept.], Berlin, 1920, p. 9; Kress von Kressenstein, Friedrich Freiherr, *Mit den Türken zum Suezkanal*, Berlin, 1938, passim; GP, A, General Schwandner, 23.1.1960; B, General Emil Leeb.

[11] B, II, MA99522, 5.5.1924, p. 4; 5.12.1924, p. 3; NA, EAP 105/7a, WKK VII, Abt. Ib Nr. 1572 Geh., 3.1.1924; Wenz und B. Vp., 15-16.1.1924.

[12] NA, T79, 53, p. 1024.

at home, under Kress the problem of the defense of the borders became central. In the fall of 1924 Kress made a "general staff ride" along the Bavarian-Czech border and returned appalled at the situation there. He was badly worried about the apparent lack of patriotism among the border population and by the absolute lack of defenses in this area, which had been, of course, in the hands of Germany's staunchest ally before the war, but which was now held by a hostile state. He therefore proposed the organization of a border security system, an intelligence system, and preparations for guerrilla operations in case of an attack, either by regular or irregular Czech forces. This concern with border problems was a far cry from Möhl as well as Lossow and indicated to what an extent he was a soldier's soldier rather than a civilian's soldier.

As a result of this change of emphasis and of the agreement on the dangers of dealings with the Verbände which had emerged as a result of the Putsch, government-army relations were generally smooth, despite the persistent government belief that the Reichswehr should really be an arm of the Bavarian government.[13] Such difficulties as arose in 1924-25 were largely outgrowths of the Putsch or of the turbulent months preceding it. One thorny problem was the payment of the costs for the various mobilization measures of the Reichswehr in 1923. The Reich was prepared to pay the costs involved in the suppression of the Putsch, but not various other police costs arising from the use of troops for public security purposes. Similarly, the Reich refused to pay for "Herbstübung" since this was entirely a Bavarian project which had been neither ordered nor approved by Berlin.

Another issue which soured relations between the Bavarian government and the army was the perennial question of the rights of ownership and use of the weapons and other materiel of the old Bavarian army. But even this thorny problem was finally solved by a judgment of Solomon. The disputing parties agreed first that the Bavarians could have that materiel which they already held in April 1924 and secondly, that a detailed and mutually satisfactory agreement regarding the rest of the loot would be worked out. A similar quarrel broke out over possession of the building of the

---

[13] B, II, MA99522, 27.10.1924, pp. 2-11; MA102141, HMB 789, Opf., p. 5. See MA103476, p. 116 for Dr. Schweyer's statement, in 1925 or 1926, that the Reichswehr and Landespolizei were exclusively executive organs of the Bavarian police authorities. "Hie München, hie Berlin!"

former Infantry School. All of these matters were, however, handled in a casual and dilatory manner indicating that they were far from burning issues. Both sides were just picking up any advantage they could. Thus these little disputes were evidence of the extent to which the real problems had been dissolved by the Putsch and the Homburg Agreement between Bavaria and the federal government which grew out of it. As a result, General von Seeckt could visit München in April 1924 and receive an exceedingly warm welcome despite the fact that three months earlier many of his hosts had been screaming for his political scalp.[14]

II. *The Purge in the Reichswehr*

Even before the Putsch, the Heeresleitung had been continuing the policy of gradually weeding out right radicals from the Bavarian officer corps which it had initiated in 1922. The Putsch greatly accelerated this process, since it removed the opposition of both the Bavarian government and the Bavarian military authorities, which had hitherto operated as inhibiting factors.

The only two active officers who took part in the Putsch were Major Hühnlein and Captain Röhm, both of whom had already fallen victim to the "bloodless purge," since they were on terminal leave at the time of the revolt. However, a good number of other officers were now eliminated from the service, either because they had too clearly sympathized with the Putschists or because they had fought too vigorously against Berlin during the course of the Lossow affair.

Captain Ritter von Krausser, an outspoken advocate of the Kampfbund, was discharged from the Reichswehr in February 1924, allegedly at his own request, but probably under pressure: a long step towards his rendezvous with an SS firing squad in June 1934. Captain Albert Seekirchner was apparently dismissed for paying his respects to Hitler in Landsberg. Colonel Konstantin Hierl was dropped as a bad example because of his influence with younger officers. Lieutenant Erich von dem Bach-Zelewski,[15] the later SS General, was also dismissed from or left the army at this time.[16]

---

[14] B, I, GSK 59, pp. 1-5; M. Inn. 72449, 2503 c 7, 20.6.1924; 2503 c 9, 16.2.1925; II, MA99523, 17.4.1925, p. 16; Rabenau, *Seeckt*, pp. 401-2.

[15] Called von Zelewski in the Reichswehr. See *Rangliste 1923*, p. 30.

[16] B, IV, HSIV, EE7, Endres MS, p. 59; Seeckt Papers, Stück 281, Lieber-Hasse, 1923, p. 55; Hierl, Konstantin, *Im Dienst für Deutschland, 1918-*

A number of other officers were not dismissed outright but found themselves on "dead spurs" as far as their careers were concerned. Colonel Haselmayr was retired in 1928 and promptly joined the NSDAP. Major Otto Baumann was dropped from the general staff and transferred to Regensburg for a number of reasons, including National Socialist sympathies and a botched job as an intelligence officer. He was then retired prematurely in 1927.[17]

The most important of the side-tracked officers was Lieutenant Colonel Hofmann, the later National Socialist Staatssekretär. By all of the normal rules of the game, he should have gone the way of von Krausser and the other dismissed officers, for he was not only in bad odor as a political meddler before the Putsch, but had flatly disobeyed orders to march his men to München during the Putsch while obeying a summons from Ludendorff without question. Nor were his troubles entirely on the military side. Colonel Seisser complained of his activities shortly after the Putsch and the Stadtkommissar in Ingolstadt was extremely hostile to him. Later, in November 1924, an incident involving an attack on a number of Allied officers brought the unfavorable attention of the Bavarian Cabinet upon him. Finally, even in his own political camp his reputation was not enviable. Dr. Pittinger, long his superior in Bund Bayern und Reich, believed that he was mentally unstable and Hierl allegedly confirmed this judgment. Yet, despite all of these formidable foes, Hofmann succeeded in hanging on in the Reichswehr until 1926, a circumstance that suggests a powerful patron in the background—perhaps General von Epp. In any case, of all of the officers who had acted in any clearly culpable way in the Putsch, he was the only one not to suffer immediately.[18]

A number of other officers who came under suspicion or attack as a result of their activities or sympathies during the Putsch were retained. First and foremost of these survivors was Captain Eduard Dietl. Dietl's conduct was examined by a special investigating board, and he was given a clean bill of health. The presiding offi-

1945, Heidelberg, 1954, p. 21; Röhm, *Geschichte,* p. 260; *Heeresverordnungsblatt, 1924,* 26.1.1924; 29.2.1924, p. 26; *Kürschners Volkshandbuch 1933,* p. 106; NA, T79, 31, pp. 1053-54.

[17] B, II, MA103476, pp. 1072-73, 1078-79; IV, HSIV, EE7, Endres MS, pp. 1, 23, 38, 56-58; *Führerlexikon 1934-1935,* p. 174.

[18] B, I, GSK 44, p. 118; B, II, MA9522, 10.11.1923, pp. 31-32; MA104221, Seisser, 24.11.1923; NA, T79, 31, p. 1057; 72, pp. 1083-85, 1094-95; *RV,* 389, Schneller (KPD), 3.3.1926, p. 5899; *Rangliste 1927,* p. 22.

cer's charge to the board suggests strongly that it approached its task with the expectation of finding him innocent of the charges against him. However, it would seem that their finding was basically correct. The available evidence, from persons on both sides of the fence, indicates that Dietl carried out every direct order given to him on the night of 8-9 November 1923, including the order that he disarm the SA units gathered at the barracks of the First Division of the Nineteenth Infantry Regiment. He was thus technically innocent. The court did not, however, dwell on the fact that it was probable that he was innocent only because his commanding officers—primarily Lossow and Schönhärl—carefully refrained from ordering him to march against the Putschists. The same careful handling saved Lieutenants von le Suire, Vogler, and Rossmann from open mutiny, although they made their feelings far more public than did Dietl. Dietl seems to have been a personally popular officer, and his superiors were also aware that his duties had called for him to fraternize with the SA units of München over a considerable period of time, so that a sense of responsibility for his difficulties undoubtedly played a role in determining their consideration for him. He had, after all, been "infected" in the line of duty. The only action taken against Dietl was the transfer of the regimental officer candidates, who had previously trained within his company, to that of First Lieutenant Braun, whose conduct in the Putsch had been vigorously loyal.[19]

Lieutenant Colonel Freiherr von Berchem was the chief victim of the Lossow affair. Closely identified with his commander and considered more or less co-responsible for his actions, Berchem was not merely transferred from his post as chief of staff but was retired almost immediately. He had apparently foreseen this outcome, for at the time of his transfer he requested permission to become a political advisor to Kahr, but the request was rejected by the Heeresleitung. Nor was this his only burden in the days after the Putsch. Röhm challenged him to a duel, which led, perforce, to an enquiry and a settlement dictated by a court of honor. Despite his caustic tongue and blunt manners, many Bavarian officers felt that Berchem deserved far better treatment than he received, and it does, at this date, seem that he was punished, as have been so

---

[19] B, IV, HSIV, EE7, Endres MS, pp. 63-64; NA, EAP 105/7a, Schönhärl an Wenz, 16.11.1923; Dietl Protokoll, 19.11.1923; I.R., 19, ia Nr. 300/23 Geh., 19.11.1923; NA, T79, 53, pp. 1064-65, 1141; 56, pp. 647, 713.

many other men throughout history, not for what he had done and represented, but for his associations.[20]

Lieutenant-Colonel Feeser of the Seventh Artillery Regiment can be seen as another white-blue victim of the Putsch period, in that, like Berchem, he suffered not for being friendly to the rebels but for being unfriendly to Berlin. The bitter words he used regarding Seeckt in a conference with his officers just before the Putsch had no immediate effect, since he was promoted to colonel and given a regiment. When he was considered for promotion to brigadier general, however, General Wilhelm Heye, Seeckt's successor, quoted Feeser's words in rejecting the recommendation.[21]

Apparently a number of enlisted men were also dismissed or requested discharges after the Putsch. Some apparently took part in the Putsch and at least one was arrested among the Putschists in the Wehrkreiskommando. However, such mutinous behavior seems to have been rare and therefore each case was probably treated individually at the company level, but the evidence on this score is fragmentary.

Some enlisted men also were dismissed before the Putsch for their loyalty towards the Reich, when they refused to take the special oath to Bavaria administered in Bavarian units in the course of the Lossow affair. North German officers had been allowed to go on furlough if they did not wish to take the oath, and, in Augsburg at least, this was the solution reached with regard to north German enlisted men, while Lossow took the line that they could continue to serve if their presence would not make obvious difficulties. Bavarian enlisted men, however, were handled differently. Lossow ordered that they could be dismissed without ceremony, and at least some commanders made use of this authorization. Two of these men appealed their cases to Berlin and General Friedrich Ritter von Haack, the chief of Seeckt's personal staff and a Bavarian, took up the case with Ritter von Leeb, warning that if they were not reinstated, the matter could lead to new difficulties for Lossow. Since the correspondence ends on this note, it would appear that Leeb and Lossow took the hint.[22]

[20] Seeckt Papers, Stück 281, Lieber-Hasse, p. 46 (1923); NA, T79, 53, pp. 1206-23, 1249; *Rangliste 1925*, p. 48; GP, A, General Franz Halder; General Josef Kammhuber; General Emil Leeb; Field Marshal Wilhelm List.

[21] NA, T79, 73, pp. 398ff; GP, A, General Fritz Hengen, 28.11.1923.

[22] B, I, GSK 59, p. 16; II, MA103476, p. 1220; NA, T79, 49, pp. 361-64,

The purge in the Infantry School, and even in the tiny Engineer School, was, naturally enough, a good deal more ruthless than that in the Bavarian units. Not only had a very large proportion of the school personnel—primarily students—clearly sided with the Putschists, but most school officers did not have the excuse that they were "sensitized" to revolt by having taken part, under orders from their military superiors and their civil authorities, in a "bloodless revolt" against Berlin.

Basically, Seeckt took the position that officers in responsible positions and with seniority were to be held fully responsible for their actions, whereas allowances could be made for youth, inexperience, and the general atmosphere of München in judging the student officers and cadets. With considerable justice, he believed that had the senior officers of the schools taken a strong stand, they could have brought their students around. Most important of all, he believed that whether they could have brought their students around or not it was a grave dereliction of duty not to make every attempt to do so.

The result was that—after a thorough investigation based on the testimony of all officers and cadets concerned—heads rolled. General Tieschowitz von Tieschowa, the commandant of the school, and his deputy commander, Colonel Johannes Kretzschmar, were relieved from their assignments and then retired in April 1924. Their primary offense was inactivity during the Putsch and failure to foresee and prevent trouble. Lieutenant Colonel Gehre, the commander of the Engineer School, went the same way, as did Major Emil Baumann, one of his senior assistants. Colonel Ludwig Leupold of the Infantry School was also dropped. He had not done anything clearly actionable during the Putsch and had, indeed, done much more than General von Tieschowitz to dampen the ardor of the students. However, he was well known to be a sympathizer of Hitler's and had also failed to carry out Lossow's order of 7 November to warn all officers against the Kampfbund.[23] Taken

---

369, 381; 82, p. 172; Röhm, *Geschichte*, pp. 234, 260; *Kürschners Volkshandbuch 1933*, p. 235.

[23] In fairness to Leupold, this order was not an easy one to execute, since the school officers were scattered throughout the city and did not necessarily appear at the school at any one time. He claims that he therefore planned to warn each of them on Friday, 9 November, when they came for their pay. Assuming that he was telling the truth here, he took a calculated risk that didn't pay off.

together, these factors weighted the scales against him, especially since he was suspected of knowing trouble was coming. Major Hans Fischach, one of the instructors at the Infantry School, was also retired, apparently because he had been a vigorous Hitler-Ludendorff partisan before the Putsch and aided the Putschists during it.[24]

The students, both officers and cadets, came off very lightly, and most of them seem to have learned their lesson pretty well, for they don't seem to have taken an aggressive interest in politics thereafter. Indeed, several of them have testified to the strong impression made on them by Seeckt's speech in Ohrdruf after the Putsch, particularly since it was coupled with severe dressings down from their unit commanders on their return to their basic troop units. Since at least some of them had scarcely hoped to avoid dismissal from the service, they were also grateful for Seeckt's forbearance. Only the ringleaders among the students, Lieutenants Robert Wagner[25] and Hans Block,[26] were dismissed from the service. Apparently Lieutenants Siegfried Mahler and Friedrich Hubrich[27] were also requested to leave, as was Cadet Friedrich Winkler, because of vigorous participation in the uprising.[28] Thus the most culpable activists were excluded from the general amnesty.

[24] B, iv, HSIV, EE7, Endres ms, pp. 38-40; NA, T79, 31, p. 1053; 65, pp. 460-61, 532-33; *Heeresverordnungsblatt, 1924*, pp. 32, 37, 46, 50; GP, A, General Martin Dehmel; General Walther Leuze; General Otto Ottenbacher.

[25] Later NSDAP Gauleiter of Baden. Executed as a war criminal.

[26] Block was reinstated in the army when Hitler came to power and was killed in action as a general in 1945. Keilig, Wolf, ed., *Das deutsche Heer, 1939-1945*. Bad Nauheim, 1957ff. 211, p. 31. Hereafter cited as Keilig, *Heer.*; GP, A, General Walther Nehring.

[27] The grounds for Hubrich's resignation are not entirely clear. Despite hints that he was compromised in the Putsch, he may have left the army voluntarily. If so, the coincidence of timing is striking.

[28] B, i, SA 1, 1635, p. 758; ii, MA103476, p. 1264; NA, EAP 105/7a, WKK vii Haupt Nr. 1459 Geh. iia Nr. 11 pers., 9.1.1924; NA T79, 56, p. 637; 65, pp. 460-61; 73, p. 468; Rabenau, *Seeckt*, pp. 379-80; Heusinger, Adolf, *Befehl im Widerstreit, 1923-1945*, Tübingen und Stuttgart, 1950, p. 14; *Rangliste 1925*, passim; GP, A, Colonel Richard Baur; General Walther Leuze; General Walther Nehring; General Josef Pemsel; Gerhard Rossbach; Colonel Otto Schaeffer; Colonel Fritz Teichmann; B, Archivdirektor Gerhard Böhm; E, Leuze Bericht, 11.11.1923.

III. *The Reichswehr and the Verbände*

The relationship between the Reichswehr and the Verbände was drastically altered by the Putsch. This alteration applied particularly to the Kampfbund organizations, but there was a very clear carry-over to other groups. The change resulted in part from orders issued by Lossow after the Putsch and the new policies that marked the accession of Kress von Kressenstein, but it also reflected modifications of views at all levels on both sides of the fence. The Putschists were livid with rage because the Reichswehr had opposed them—"betrayed" the national cause as they put it—while the soldiers were bitter about the manner in which the Putschists had acted during the Putsch, as well as about their slurs on the army afterwards. A number of the members of the Verbände that had not taken part in the Putsch nonetheless scored the willingness of the soldiers to shoot down their "national brothers" in the interests of the "Reds," and the army resented this criticism deeply. On each side, though, the bitter resentments were tempered by the hope of winning over elements in the other camp. Particularly on the side of the Putschists, this hope resulted often in divided counsels and contradictory policies. Essentially there were three policies pursued to a greater or lesser extent by Kampfbund propagandists and leaders.

The first policy was that of an all-out attack on the Reichswehr and was particularly apparent in the first days after the Putsch, while passions were still at fever heat and thoughts of policy had not yet asserted themselves. Street orators, leaflets, and student demonstrators heaped abuse on soldiers indiscriminately.[29] The Reichswehr reaction was prompt and clear. General von Danner, the commandant of München, ordered: "The soldiers can go into the city in large groups when off duty. They are to be informed that they must avoid [showing] a provocative manner. If they are cursed, abused, or attacked, however, they [will] act decisively, seizing the attackers etc. and bring[ing] them to the barracks. The unit is responsible for secure delivery to the Police Directory. Firearms are to be used only in self-defense as a last resort."[30]

The second policy was one of attacking the higher officers and a few carefully selected scapegoats among the younger ones—such

[29] NA, EAP 105/7a, Kommandantur Befehl Nr. 3, 12.11.1923; II/I.R. 19, 11.11.1923; T79, 82, p. 212; B, I, GSK 43, pp. 79-80. See also Chapters XV and XVI above.

[30] NA, EAP 105/7a, Kommandantur Befehl Nr. 1, 15.11.1923.

as First Lieutenant Braun—while praising the younger officers and enlisted men and seeking to win them over to the cause, a policy that called for close cooperation with friendly officers, such as Lieutenant Colonel Hofmann in Ingolstadt. Here again the accent was on youth and a call for cooperation against the old men. This policy appeared after the first few days and was pursued vigorously especially by students and former officers. The right radicals thus, neither for the first nor the last time, adopted a program similar to that of the Communists and one that they could follow with far more hope of success since their goals were far more acceptable to soldiers and their personal relations with the soldiers had been far closer and more friendly.[31] That they had some success is indicated by scattered reports about individual soldiers. However, the great bulk of the officers and soldiers stood by their leaders, and the key field grade officers—on whose cooperation successful military revolts against the "old generals" have normally depended—remained adamantly loyal to their superiors. This is clearly indicated by the reports and other communications of these officers during the critical period. Captain Günter Rüdel's remark of 12 November was representative of the view of his superiors as well as his peers: " 'There is no true word in the matter [rumors]. The entire officer corps stands solidly behind Herr von Lossow. . . . We are officers and not politicians.' "[32] Colonel Albert Ritter von Beckh in Nürnberg, Lieutenant Colonels Hilmar Mittelberger in Bayreuth and Wilhelm Hofmann in Landshut all reported in tones that indicated their coldness towards the Kampfbund and their confidence in the loyalty of their officers and men. Indeed, nowhere in the many reports and comments, military or political, is there any indication of disaffection in the Reichswehr at any level.[33]

The third Kampfbund policy was that adopted by Röhm after his first pique at the failure of the Putsch was over. Like a number of other former Putschists, he came to realize that the active hostility of the generals must be avoided if possible, since it was clear that the generals controlled the army. This policy appears so much

[31] B, i, GSK 43, pp. 79-80; GSK 44, p. 110; NA, EAP 105/7a, WKK vii 33710/ib Nr. 61-90; WKK vii ib Nr. 1505 Geh.; WKK vii, ib Nr. 1530 Geh.; WKK, ic Nr. 1779 Geh.

[32] B, ii, MA103458, Sommer Vormerkung, 12.11.1923.

[33] B, i, GSK 90, pp. 561, 572, 574; NA, T79, 49, p. 333; NA, EAP 105/7a, Lindau, 4.1.1924, Lagelbericht. See also Reg. Präs. Berichten in B, II, MA102140 and MA102141, passim.

later that it really belongs to a new and different era. Still, it should be mentioned here because it is clearly an organic growth resulting from the bankruptcy of the earlier policies and is therefore a strong attestation to the unity of the army and the failure of the Verbände to make perceptible inroads on this front. Nothing but desperation could have brought Röhm to swallow his hatred for Kress and the Bavarian government and approach the very men who had suppressed the Putsch and the movement itself to propose cooperation in a new paramilitary effort, or to defend in public the stand of the Reichswehr in the Putsch. Yet by August 1924 he had gone so far as to make this desperate, indeed hopeless, attempt.[34] The only result of these efforts to win over the military authorities was the issuance of new orders, not only in Bavaria but throughout the Reich, for the Reichswehr to stay away from Röhm's new "Frontbann" and for the Reichswehr to beware of the spreading of rumors by the Frontbann that the organization had Heeresleitung support. The regular soldiers would not so readily fall into new traps set for them by the "political soldiers."[35]

Other factors also operated to make the relations between the Reichswehr and those Verbände that had not taken part in the Putsch much cooler. The arms and training question played a major role in increasing this estrangement. Partly because of the lessons of the Putsch and partly because of the tighter control exercised by Berlin after the accession of von Kress, the Reichswehr was no longer prepared to cooperate with the Verbände, and particularly not regarding arms and training. As early as 25 November, the Nürnberg Reichswehr received orders to halt all training of members of Wehrverbände, and several days earlier Colonel Zürn, in Bamberg, had reported adopting the same policy regarding Brigade Ehrhardt on his own initiative. At the same time, the Zeugamt was vigorously collecting weapons in the countryside. This policy, which paralleled that adopted by the Bavarian government after the Putsch, was further reinforced by General von Seeckt's renewed emphasis on the absolute severance of all ties with Verbände. In Bavaria the day of military permissiveness towards paramilitary organizations was over.[36]

[34] B, ɪɪ, MA100423, Geh. Bemerkungen (Zetlmeier) an Stützel 2019 h 4, p. 53; MA103473, PDN-F 8190/ɪɪ, 19.12.1924, p. 9; NA, EAP 105/7a, Standortälteste Kempten, 61 Geh., 14.2.1924.

[35] B, II, MA100423, RWM (Heer) 447/24 Geh. T. 1. III, p. 28.

[36] B, I, GSK 3, p. 31; II, MA104221, Besch an Lapo Augsburg, 29.1.1924;

IV. *The Landespolizei*

The transition to post-Putsch policies in the Landespolizei was very similar to the transition in the Reichswehr and was considerably simpler since, despite the efforts of the government to dislodge him, Seisser remained in his post and kept essential control.[37] The man might remain but the policies had to change. Seisser was one of the chief targets of the Putschists and therefore could do no less than oppose them. In any case, it seems clear that he had had his fill of them. He therefore executed the government's policies regarding the Putschists with vigor.

The main tensions that existed between the government and the Landespolizei leadership in the post-Putsch period dated back to the days of the Putsch and before or were the result of the obvious support given Seisser and Kahr by the Landespolizei officer corps after the minister-president and his colleagues had become disillusioned with these men.

The government was also perturbed by the fact that there were officers and men in the Landespolizei who sympathized with the Putschists, even though they had performed their duties during the Putsch. The minister of the interior was even more upset to learn that it was very difficult, if not impossible, to get rid of these men under existing civil service regulations. Political opposition to the specific government or party in power was not legal ground for dismissal from the service.

All of these discordances were minor, though. Essentially, the Landespolizei and the government were at one as to both means and ends. Seisser and Pirner might fire paper bullets at one another, and Stützel might complain of Seisser's independent attitude, but these petty rivalries were kept within the "house" and did not alter the course of policy or reduce the determination and consistency with which it was pursued.

v. *The Purge in the Landespolizei*

Like the Reichswehr, the Landespolizei purged itself of those members who had failed to perform their duties during the Putsch or who had been guilty of breaches of discipline during its aftermath. And, in the case of at least one higher officer, the minister of the

---

IV, BuR, Bd. 36, Akt 1, Item 48; Lapo, Bd. 26a, Akt 1, Coburg Lapo, Chef 94 Ew.; NA, T79, 82, p. 177.

[37] See Chapter XIX, Section I, for discussion of the Seisser affair.

interior himself took a hand. Neither Schweyer nor Pirner had been pleased by the equivocal responses of Colonel Banzer to their directives during the Putsch, and Banzer was therefore passed over when a "successor" to Seisser was selected so that, while he held his post, he temporarily lost the pay and perquisites of a brigadier general which went to Colonel Ritter von Reiss with his accession and which he held when Seisser returned to duty.[38] However, no more could be done, since Banzer had not disobeyed orders at any time and in the latter phases of the Putsch had acted decisively against the rebels.

As in the case of the Reichswehr, only a very few Landespolizei officers and men sided clearly with the Putschists, and these men were either dismissed or resigned from the service in the days immediately following. The best example was First Lieutenant Gerhard von Prosch, who had left his hospital bed without authorization and clearly identified himself with the Putsch, acting as a sort of bodyguard-jailer for Colonel Banzer. Prosch was cashiered and, despite a series of appeals, was unable to win favorable reconsideration of his case.[39] Lieutenant Heinrich Hierthes, who apparently tried to kill his battalion commander with a howitzer because of his opposition to the Putsch, was also dismissed from the service. Captain Wilhelm Stark, a strongly nationalistic and antisemitic officer was also dropped,[40] although he claimed to have resigned of his own free will. He immediately became active in the NSDAP and its cover organizations. First Lieutenant Hugo Alleter was another officer who was apparently eliminated, although he may have succeeded in resigning before his superiors acted.[41] Captain Karl Schweinle was dismissed for having taken a pro-Putschist attitude after the fight at the Feldherrnhalle, while First Lieutenant Wilhelm

[38] In the end, the government had to make this concession to Banzer also to keep peace in the family. B, II, MA99522, 17.3.1924, pp. 7-8.

[39] Ironically, Major Doehla, who chaired the committee that confirmed the justice of Prosch's dismissal, was also destined to preside over Prosch's reinstatement in 1933.

[40] Stark claimed that he was one of 6 Landespolizei officers who cast their sabers at Seisser's feet after the Putsch.

[41] B, I, M. Inn. 73696, v. Bomhard an Stuhlreiter, 10.11.1923; GSK 7, pp. 6-7, 13; SA 1, 1633, pp. 491-93, 497; II, MA101235, Nachrichtenblatt 13, 15.8.1924; MA103476, pp. 1219, 1315; B, IV, OPA 73930, passim; GP, B, Colonel Ernst Schultes.

von Grolman, who was in Sweden at the time of the Putsch, apparently fell victim to the purge simply because he had been officially assigned to act as Ludendorff's adjutant during the year prior to the event. Here was another case of guilt by association.

Some enlisted men and employees of the Landespolizei were also quietly discharged from the service, but there is little trace of them, except where, like Emil Hamm or Johann Niederreiter, they had played flamboyant roles in the Putsch. In general, the enlisted men had done what they had been ordered to do, and those few who had joined the Putschists had exercised no real influence on events and would not do so in the future. They had been "faceless men" in the Putsch and they would remain "faceless men" whether they had been loyal or disloyal, whether they left after the Putsch or remained. In the aggregate they had been of crucial significance. Individually they were lost in the anonymity of the ranks.

The subsequent dismissal of First Lieutenant Freiherr von Godin from the Landespolizei has, on occasion, been associated with his leading role in halting the Putschists on the Odeonsplatz. However, this event came much later and was ordered by Colonel von Seisser, scarcely a friend of the Putschists, on the grounds of repeated dereliction of duty.[42]

The reaction of the Landespolizei officer corps to the Putsch can perhaps be best summed up in the words of Captain Johannes Bernhardt, the chief of the Landespolizei in Coburg:

> . . . The Hitler Putsch teaches [us] that the patriotic bands must disappear as a political factor, since the authority of the state was seriously impaired by the multiplicity of their goals. Had there existed a unified, apolitical defense organization, the Hitler Putsch would not have occurred, the bands would have continued to be a strong tool of the government, and here on the border [we] also would have been spared many difficulties and unpleasantnesses.[43]

In the police "army" as well as in the Reichswehr the bulk of the regular officers were disenchanted with the political amateurs.

[42] B, I, M. Inn. 73694, 2004 kaa 90; II, MA103476, pp. 1373-75, 1380; MA104221, Lapoamt Abt. Pol./Nr. 1993; GP, B, Lieutenant Colonel Max Lagerbauer; Lieutenant Colonel Otto Muxel; Sergeant Hermann Ruhland; Kallenbach, *Mit Hitler*, pp. 22, 34.

[43] B, IV, Lapo, Bd. 26a, Akt 5, Gr. Sch. IIIc, Beilage 1, Chef 361g, p. 7.

vi. *The Police Directories*

The Police Directory in München was, next to the Landespolizei, the police organization most involved in the Putsch and its suppression. It was also the center of political control and intelligence for the capital, a responsibility that had brought it into closer contact with the Putschist organizations before the Putsch than any other organization. Naturally enough, it was not entirely unscarred by the tumultuous events of 8-9 November.

The Cabinet, ever sensitive to the security of the capital, pressed for a purge and greater efficiency in the Police Directory, and Dr. Schweyer assured them that action was being taken. Police President Mantel, however, opposed any broad purge, although he was ready to sack men who had been derelict in their duty or who had joined the Putschists. Since Mantel's loyalty credentials were impeccable in view of his arrest and internment with the Cabinet members, he not only remained in office but carried the day on policy.[44] He set forth his policy clearly some months after the Putsch in a statement that also discussed the background of the personnel problems he faced and placed at least a portion of the responsibility for these problems in the laps of his superiors:

> I am now permitted to speak out briefly regarding the doubts that have been raised in various quarters regarding the political positions of a portion of the officials of the Police Directory. It is true [that] under Pöhner's leadership the National Socialist activities were encouraged in every way and that this [fact] was not without influence on the attitudes of a number of officials. It is also true that a large number of officials were members of the dissolved NSDAP and that on 8 November a number of these marched out with the Kampfbund. A conversion of this portion of the officials cannot be accomplished overnight. The attempts of the government to preserve the worthwhile elements of the Patriotic Movement [found] in the racist camp, attempts which found particular expression in the extended negotiations

[44] The chances of the success of any large-scale purge were poor in view of the civil service laws and the unwillingness of the disciplinary courts to find officials guilty of offenses that would cost them their tenure and pensions. Dr. Wilhelm Frick, for example, was acquitted by the Disziplinhof despite having accepted the post of police president under the rebels. (NA, T120, 5570, p. K592076.) In the end, three men were dropped from the PDM for carrying on Kampfbund activity after the Putsch. (B, I, M. Inn. 71771, PDM 2176/vid.)

with the Kampfbund after the creation of the Generalstaatskom-missariat, were also a barrier against strong action [in this matter]. Nonetheless a number of officials, who took part in National Socialist activities to an extent that damaged the reputation of officialdom were discharged from police service. Mere membership in the NSDAP before 8 November did not appear to be sufficient grounds for such action. The same [reasoning] applies with regard to those officials who on 8 November, in ignorance of the aims [of their leaders] followed the summons to arms of the Kampfbund. The conduct of these last officials is, now that the trial is over, to be re-evaluated in accordance with Order No. 1051 b 15 of the State Ministry of the Interior [issued] on 27 January 1924. In any case, the conduct of the officials of the Police Directory is now, as I can definitely assure you, entirely in the direction of the state policy laid down by the government.[45]

In fact, Mantel did take measures against at least those men who had most clearly compromised themselves. Dr. Frick, who had long before been transferred from the political section, of which he had been chief under Pöhner, was immediately suspended and temporarily replaced by Regierungsrat Graf August von Soden, until he was reinstated by court action. Josef Gerum and Konrad Linder (who promptly emigrated to the United States) were dismissed from the police after being convicted of criminal activity in the course of the Putsch, while some other minor officials, like Fritz Glaser and Karl Hermann Rau, against whom no clear charge could be brought, remained in the service, although under a cloud of suspicion.[46]

In Nürnberg, Gareis rode out the storm far better than had Mantel. By sitting firmly on any possibility of illegal action within his bailiwick, he disarmed possible critics. At the same time, he prevented any purge of his establishment. He might sympathize with the National Socialists, but, unlike Pöhner, he apparently had no interest in joining them in a political adventure and was determined that there should be no such adventures within his sphere of influence.

The situation in Nürnberg was typical in many ways of the situ-

[45] B, II, MA103473, Mantel Bericht, 5.4.1924, pp. 5-6.
[46] B, I, M. Inn. 73694, 2004 kaa 90; II, MA103476, pp. 1194, 1219, 1540; *MNN*, 12.11.1923, p. 4; Kallenbach, *Mit Hitler*, pp. 23, 34.

everywhere outside the capital. The senior police and mili-
uthorities had acted so swiftly and so firmly that every at-
at rebellion was smothered before the soldiers were faced
.... he difficult decisions that the individual policemen and their
opposite numbers in München had faced. The Putsch had been
born and died in München, and it was there that official authority
had been severely threatened and undermined. It was therefore also
in München that the new policies and the proscriptions were
centered.

Finally, the government was unenthusiastic about the effectiveness of the political intelligence service, which they believed had
not given the government sufficient warning of the Putsch.[47] At the
same time, the police were pointing out that the government had,
after the Putsch, sharply cut the budget for the Police Directory in
München and therefore for the political police and its intelligence
system, which embraced both the Landespolizei—especially in the
provinces—and the police directories of München and Nürnberg.
The Bavarian government, like many others before and since,
wanted to spend very little money on its police and yet expected
ever more effective police measures. The ministers wanted reports
on what the political parties and splinter groups were doing, but
they did not wish to pay policemen for attending these meetings
to make reports. They then blamed the police for inefficiency when
they did not report on the activities of all suspicious parties.[48]

VII. *Conclusion*

The Beer Hall Putsch brought an end to the dangerous dualism of
loyalty and division of power that had created an atmosphere of
uncertainty within which the Putschists could hope to operate successfully and without which they could scarcely have operated at
all. With the passing of Lossow and the coming of General von
Kress, the Bavarian division became a division like any other in the
Reichswehr, rather than a force that wavered between the rival au-

[47] On this point the ministers were unfair, since the political police of
München and the police specialists in the Ministry of the Interior had all
warned of the dangers of an NSDAP Putsch on a number of occasions in
the year preceding 8 November 1923. It is true that the precise moment of
the outbreak was not accurately predicted, but warnings that it would
surely come if preventive measures were not adopted had not been lacking.
See V, X-XII.

[48] B, I, GSK 6, p. 26; GSK 43, p. 137; GSK 50, p. 26; GSK 57, p. 1;
M. Inn. 71708, Nr. 2005 a 47, 17.4.1924; II, MA99522, 17.3.1924, pp. 7-9.

thorities in München and Berlin. At the same time, Seisser not only lost much of his independent power, but also seems to have lost the desire to exercise such power, so that the Landespolizei was now an instrument in the hands of the government rather than a semi-autonomous organization which was half police force and half Bavarian army and which, in alliance with the Verbände, could possibly have dictated policy to the government. A clear and definite chain of command was established and accepted. The great majority of soldiers and police officers had come to see the dangers to the armed forces and the state of flirting with indiscipline and politics. In effect, the day of the Putsch was over; as it is always over wherever the armed forces are clearly loyal to the legal authorities. Putsches are expressions of political instability, and like all other threats to order and peace they can only exist where there is serious political strife, political weakness, or political chaos. These conditions had existed in München on 8 November 1923. Two months later they had disappeared.

21.

THE NEW GOVERNMENT AND ITS POLICIES

I. *The Passing of the Knilling Government*

As a result of economic chaos and political stresses the Knilling government had been increasingly disunited and increasingly unpopular well before 8 November. The Putsch made it even less united and far more unpopular. Knilling now seemed genuinely exasperated with politics. He was particularly unhappy about the composition of his Cabinet and complained bitterly to Haniel about Schweyer and Wutzlhofer, whom he saw as foreign elements disrupting the unity of the government.[1] In February the minister-president carried his grievances to a key figure in Bavarian politics. In a letter to Dr. Heinrich Held, the most important single leader of the Bavarian People's Party, Knilling said that he could not understand the failure of the two ministers to resign when he requested them to do so. Wutzlhofer was ready to go, but Schweyer was defiant. Nowhere but in Bavaria could ministers defy their chief with impunity. He then came to the heart of the matter, requesting Held's aid in ousting the recalcitrants. If they would not go, Knilling would. In any case, he wanted to leave office as soon as possible. In support of his request he stressed his belief that the two ministers in question were so unpopular with broad groups in the population as to make his government ineffectual.[2] It is clear that Held did not exert himself seriously in this matter, for his influence in the party was certainly great enough to eliminate Schweyer easily in view of the latter's many detractors within the BVP. Thus, the continuance of Schweyer in office was another sign that the days of the government were numbered, whatever its members might do. Without the full support of the strongest party in

[1] NA, T120, 5569, p. K591607.
[2] B, II, MA103473, Knilling an Held 22.2.1924.

Bavaria they could scarcely hope to rule effectively in such troubled times.

Besides the Schweyer-Wutzlhofer quarrel with Knilling, the Cabinet was plagued by other tensions. Finance Minister Krausneck resigned on 3 December 1923 over the failure of the Diet to vote Knilling and Krausneck full economic powers under a special enabling act. Krausneck was persuaded to withdraw his resignation, in return for changes in the draft of the Enabling Act, but the failure of the Diet to approve the act left him disgruntled.[3]

The spring elections themselves undermined the Knilling Cabinet still further.[4] The old coalition on which it rested was shattered and its majority destroyed. The timing of Knilling's resignation suggests that this was the crucial question, although the Cabinet, meeting right after the Landtag elections, agreed not to resign because resignation would be a farce; the same politicians would have to remain as a caretaker government, there being no triumphant coalition in sight. Less than a month later the Cabinet, clearly under pressure from the minister-president, reversed itself by announcing its resignation on the constitutional grounds that the elections had destroyed its legal basis. The Cabinet would stay on until a new one was elected but only in a caretaker capacity. It thus fell as a delayed casualty of the Putsch, as much its victim as the policemen who fell before the Feldherrnhalle.[5]

With the Cabinet ended the political lives of the two major protagonists within it. Dr. Schweyer was taken care of by promotion to the senior rank in the civil service, Staatsrat,[6] while Knilling became president of the Administration for the Liquidation of the State Debt, an organization that seems guaranteed eternal life in modern states. In Bavarian politics political casualties were not left to fend for themselves but were provided with secure posts in the administration when they lost office—a procedure rendered comparatively easy by the fact that many of them had risen through the career civil service and still had a claim to tenured positions.[7]

However, before they passed from the scene Knilling and his colleagues had wrestled with a number of problems and taken a

---

[3] B, II, MA99521, 3.12.1923, p. 7; NA, T120, 5569, p. K591637.

[4] For the elections see below, Section II.

[5] B, II, MA99522, 5.5.1924, p. 2.

[6] Roughly equivalent to Staatssekretär in Prussia and the state secretary or undersecretary in the United States or Great Britain.

[7] B, II, MA99522, 8.7.1924, p. 16; 8.10.1924, p. 7.

number of actions, some of them significant for later developments. The most important of these was, of course, the re-establishment of normal and friendly relations with the Reich government, the major step towards which was ending the Lossow affair.[8] Next came the acceptance of the Law for the Defense of the Republic (RSG) after considerable soul-searching within the Cabinet. At the end of January, the Ministry of the Interior had requested that Kahr's order suspending the execution of the RSG be withdrawn, but the Cabinet had not acted on the question. Surprisingly, the matter was raised seriously in the Cabinet by the enigmatic Gürtner. Despite his close ties to the National Socialists and their hysterical opposition to the RSG, the justice minister introduced the question on 16 February, pointing out that since the execution of the law had been suspended Bavaria had become a refuge for many undesirable characters. At the same time he indicated that the only proper solution in the case of Commander Ehrhardt was an amnesty from Berlin. In fact, what he did was more to indicate the problems that arose from the situation than to suggest that the law be enforced. He had, however, set the ball rolling, and pressure from Berlin kept it in motion. By the middle of March the ministers agreed that, although they were as opposed to the law as ever, they could scarcely hold out long. In view of the unpopularity of the RSG, though, they were agreed that no move should be taken until after the elections.[9] A few days later, Gürtner brought up the question again, and this time he specifically asked for the withdrawal of Kahr's order,[10] but with the elections still to come the government dragged its feet. By the middle of April, when Gürtner and Schweyer—odd allies—again pressed for action, the Cabinet went so far as to send a confidential letter to the Regierungspräsidenten informing them that after 1 April the ban on execution of the RSG was no longer in effect. It was not until after the Landtag elections had been held, though, that the lower authorities were informed of the change of front. The Bavarian government had finally removed one of the most serious barriers to friendly relations with the Reich

[8] See Chapter xix, Section i, and Chapter xx, Section i, above.

[9] B, ii, MA99522, 16.2.1924, p. 9; 14.3.1924, pp. 15-16; MA103161, M. Inn. 2093 d 1 an M. Äuss., 29.1.1924.

[10] It is possible that the Machiavellian Gürtner wished to discredit the BVP and the government and thus aid the right radicals and the Mittelpartei by saddling the Cabinet with such a decision on the eve of the elections.

government, but only after its foes had been denied effective use of the concession as a weapon.[11]

Another concession to northern sensibilities was the abolition of the People's Courts, which had long been promised. Now that the criminal courts reform was complete, no grounds remained for postponing the measure, and Gürtner pressed for action. The Cabinet agreed to abolish all People's Courts except that of München[12] as of 27 March, while München would be granted until 15 May to complete trials in process. This decision was of more than regional significance, because it not only brought Bavaria into line with the other states in judicial matters but also meant that in the future Bavarian political crimes would be handled by the highest federal political court, the Staatsgerichtshof in Leipzig, since with the demise of the People's Courts there would be no Bavarian courts with jurisdiction in political matters. Here again the Bavarian Cabinet had made a major concession, but only after the immediate question in dispute, the Hitler Trial, had been handled according to their specifications, although certainly not to their satisfaction. In return for immediate political concessions which they felt to be vitally necessary for the welfare of the Bavarian state and the ruling parties, the Bavarian Cabinet recognized the basic jurisdiction of the Reich in future instances. Knilling and his colleagues had taken another reluctant step deeper into the Reich.[13]

To some extent, the path for these Bavarian concessions had been cleared by the willingness of the Reich government to cooperate with Bavaria in the question of the state of emergency. By the middle of February, the Reich government was planning to replace the military state of emergency under Seeckt with a milder civilian form under the Reich minister of the interior. In general the Bavarian Cabinet agreed with the plan, as long as Bavaria was excluded. The Bavarian ministers were determined to maintain their own state of emergency and did not plan to give an inch. Some of them saw this new threat as being essentially the same as that of 27 September.[14] All the elements for resumption of the old battle on the old lines were present. This time, though, the federal

---

[11] B, II, MA99522, 27.3.1924, pp. 5-6; 12.4.1924, p. 7; MA102141, HMB 629, Obb., p. 7.

[12] The delay in this case was to permit completion of the Hitler Trial, which was still in progress.

[13] B, II, MA99522, 27.3.1924, pp. 4-5; NA, T120, 5569, p. 591731.

[14] See Chapter IX, Section I, above.

authorities arranged a compromise by which the Reich minister of the interior would delegate his authority under the state of emergency to the Bavarian government. The Bavarians did not like this acceptance of crumbs from the Reich's table, when they felt that they were well within their rights. However, neither side wanted trouble and this compromise gave the essentials of their positions to both sides. As a result it was accepted and the smoothness with which it operated doubtless did much to persuade the Bavarians to make their later concessions.

The growing warmth was further illustrated by Schweyer's willingness in the middle of March to arrange for joint action with the Reich against the racists, although he had, a month before, been violently up in arms against the Reich.[15] At home, the government retained its policy of repression against the Communists and the racists, in so far as was possible in view of the legal problems raised by the election campaign.[16] Thus the ban on the NSDAP and Bund Oberland was retained. At first the Ministry of the Interior was empowered to make up its own mind about the NSDAP's central organ, the *Völkische Beobachter*, but later the Cabinet decided to retain the ban so as to allow the new government to reach its own decision on the question of the racist press.[17]

Aside from economic matters, always in the fore during this period of hardship and slow recovery from runaway inflation, the government gave the rest of its attention to defending itself against hostile propaganda and to proposals for the reorganization of the Bavarian political system. Knilling was forced to issue dementi in rapid succession in reply to both serious and frivolous accusations, that the government was dealing with Poland or the government was dealing with France. None of these accusations could be left unanswered in the feverishly tense atmosphere following the Putsch. The most serious and dangerous accusations, though, were those levelled by responsible persons and based on something more solid than mere imagination. Knilling and his colleagues therefore found themselves in the position of devoting an inordinate amount of time to the Rothenbücher Case.

Karl Rothenbücher, a professor of law at München University,

---

[15] B, ii, MA99522, 18.2.1924, pp. 2, 4-5; 22.2.1924, pp. 5-10; 26.2.1924, pp. 6-11; 14.3.1924, pp. 9-10.

[16] See Section iii below.

[17] B, i, GSK 4, pp. 87-88; ii, MA99522, 14.2.1924, p. 10; 12.4.1924, p. 5; 28.4.1924, pp. 12-13; 24.5.1924, p. 6; NA, T120, 5569, pp. K591653-54.

had been a thorn in the flesh of the government even before the Putsch because he supported the Reich position in the Lossow affair. Then in February his brochure "The Kahr Case" was circulated in Bavaria. In this pamphlet Rothenbücher attacked Kahr, and Kahr promptly ordered the suppression of the essay in Bavaria. The Cabinet was drawn into the matter because of the subsequent uproar in right radical circles. The ministers were agreed that the pamphlet was essentially a tissue of lies, but they felt that it would be very difficult to refute many of the lies and that, in any case, the booklet had already been circulated so widely that a ban would be practically useless. The ministers therefore agreed on 9 February, that if General von Seeckt did not uphold the ban in the Reich and the courts did not uphold the seizure of the pamphlet, the Cabinet would insist on the withdrawal of the decree.[18] Two days later, the Cabinet came back to the matter. Kahr claimed that he had opposed the ban but had been overpersuaded by his subordinates in the GSK. Dr. Matt stood strongly for ending a ban that was both illegal and ludicrously ineffective, but Gürtner pointed out that there was no need for specific Cabinet action because the prosecutor's office had categorically refused to order the confiscation of the pamphlets. Thus, the entire matter came to nothing, but had taken up much of the Cabinet's attention during two meetings. It is a good example of the non-essential but painful problems that the ministers faced after the Putsch and also of the difficulty of successfully fighting hostile propaganda directed against public officials, whether true or false, in a democratic state. In this game the odds are all with the sniper and against his victim. The most the government could do was to annoy the publisher by dragging its heels on the question of releasing confiscated copies of the essay.[19]

The Cabinet had no better luck with the positive side of its political program after the Putsch than it had had with the defense of its reputation and that of its agent, Gustav von Kahr. At the end of December 1923 the Landtag refused to give the government the special economic powers it had requested. The deputies were even less prepared to give the government extraordinary economic powers after the Putsch than they had been before it. Equally sterile was the scheme for altering the Landtag election law. It is indeed hard to imagine why the government—or, more likely, the Bavar-

---

[18] B, II, MA99522, 9.2.1924, pp. 3–8; NA, T120, 5569, p. K591652.
[19] B, II, MA99522, 11.2.1924, p. 9; 14.2.1924, p. 14; MA103458, Rothenbücher an Knilling, 21.10.1923; GSK R/Nr. 7291.

ian People's Party—put forward this proposal at such a moment. The Landtag was asked to vote for a reduction in its membership which was to be accomplished by raising the number of voters per member. At the same time, the number of districts was to be reduced from eight to four. It is hard to persuade deputies to vote for a law that will clearly cost some of them their seats. It is, practically speaking, almost impossible to persuade them, on top of reducing the number of seats, to scramble the electoral districts so drastically that not even the safest and most popular member could be sure what sort of electorate he would face in the future. When such a proposal is made just before an election that is clearly going to be bitterly fought by forces of uncertain strengths, only obstinate optimism or desperation can explain its presentation. In this case it was, naturally enough, quietly shoved under the carpet.[20] The deputies went into the election with an unchanged and familiar political system to give them what comfort it could in the face of a sullen and unpredictable electorate.

On the whole, the Knilling government had gone out well. It could perhaps be said that it died better than it had lived, but even this was unfair to a Cabinet that had faced a most complex and unstable situation and brought the state through it with little loss of life and considerable political profit. When the Cabinet had come into office, it seemed possible that Bavaria would drift away from the Reich and that the entire economic fabric of the state would collapse, while it seemed more than probable that civil war might break out at any minute on one of several fronts. When the government resigned there was no more talk of secession and Bavaria had made its peace with the Reich within the bounds of the existing Constitution. On the home front, revolution had been avoided and a dangerous coup d'état had been contained with the loss of only a handful of lives. It was very clear that neither the radical Right nor the radical Left were able to make a revolution and equally clear that no one else wanted to do so. No one could have safely prophesied such a favorable scene when Knilling was sworn into office or on 7 November 1923. On balance, the Knilling government, despite all its errors and weaknesses and admitting that some of its successes were a matter of luck rather than skill, had done better than many other governments in Germany or elsewhere that have faced similar problems. In politics as well as in horse races,

[20] B, II, MA99521, 27.12.1923, p. 12; NA, T120, 5569, p. K591661.

the payoff is on the final result. By the struggles and death of his government, Knilling had helped to create a situation that enabled his successor to stay in office for the remaining years of the Weimar Republic.

II. *The Spring Elections*

The spring elections took place at a time and under circumstances that placed the governing coalition at a tremendous disadvantage and was embarrassing to most of the other traditional parties. Yet to avoid the elections was scarcely possible because of the Putsch and its aftermath.

Initially, it would seem that the Bavarian People's Party saw the period immediately following the Putsch as a fortunate one for it and called for the dissolution of the Landtag and new elections. Elections at that time might well have favored the BVP. The Landtag, however, would not accept dissolution, and the BVP was forced either to give up the idea or to go to the people with a referendum proposal. The party decided in favor of the second alternative and presented not one but two proposals to the voters. The first called for the immediate dissolution of the Landtag. The other called for a change in the Constitution to permit the passage of laws altering the Constitution by a simple majority. Despite the efforts of its foes, the BVP handily won enough votes to place their resolutions on the ballot and at the same time helped to generate such popular pressure for elections that the Landtag capitulated. It rejected the BVP proposals, but it agreed to its own dissolution.[21]

By 6 April 1924, the situation was considerably different from what it had been in late November 1923. Inflation was at an end, slain by a drastic national currency reform. However, once the people had recovered from the immediate threat of starvation, the initial gratitude of those who had had any savings was blunted by the realization that these had gone down the drain. The peasants, the heart and soul of the BVP, were groaning under the weight of the new taxes and forced mortgages supporting the new currency, and smarting at the loss of the favorable economic position they had enjoyed since the war. The consumer was pleased that prices had come down drastically, but unhappy because they were still much higher than in "peacetime" and because he had so little money. The Hitler Trial had left a bad taste in the mouths of many people, who

[21] Ibid., pp. K591650-714.

did not believe that Hitler's accusations against Kahr and the government could be all lies. Officialdom was under the pressure of wage cuts and the threat of a reduction in force. The unemployed and the underemployed numbered many thousands; they had not enjoyed any of the fruits of the incipient economic recovery and were sullen, restless, and desperate. Finally, the right radicals and the left radicals and their sympathizers were even more discontent and rebellious than they had been before the Putsch. Many people blamed their plight on the government and the coalition parties. How serious these resentments were and how they would be expressed was unclear, but it was no secret in political circles in the early months of 1924 that the elections might well bring unpleasant surprises for the coalition.[22]

There was, though, a general feeling that the basic situation would not change much despite these factors; many voters might change allegiance, but the bulk of them would follow their normal pattern. Knilling, a shrewd observer with the best available evidence before him, believed just before the elections that the racists would get twelve to fifteen seats, while the SPD would take losses that could be credited to the KPD. He was apparently not afraid that his party would take any losses but admitted that its left wing would very probably not support him and his government. For this reason the new Landtag might well be incapable of forming a new government.[23]

Another factor working against the government and the coalition parties was the fact that the elections reopened the road to political activity for their most virulent opponents. Even before the elections, Kahr had gone too far with his political proscriptions. When, after the Putsch, he banned the Social Democratic press,[24] he found he had stirred up a hornets' nest: not only the political Left but also the political Right's radical edge was opposed to this move, and every newspaper felt threatened. Dr. Schweyer also opposed a

---

[22] This paragraph is based on a great number of sources, a sampling of which follows: B, I, GSK 7, pp. 60-63; GSK 43, p. 71; GSK 44, pp. 984-85, 89-92, 99, 121-23, 140, 148-51, 214; II, MA102140, HMB 1174, N/B, 4.12.1923; HMB 1810, 11.12.1923; HMB 3073, Ofr., 18.12.1923; HMB 1271, N/B, 18.12.1923; MA102141, HMB, Ufr., 7.3.1924 [No. torn away]; IV, BuR, Bd. 36, Akt 2, Item 14; NA, T120, 5569, p. K591682.

[23] *Ibid.*, 5570, p. K591747.

[24] This ban led the SPD to bring forward strong legal arguments in favor of private property, which must have made Marx squirm in his grave. B, II, MA103458, SPD Appeal, 17.11.1923.

broad, long-lasting ban on SPD sheets. The result was that Kahr
was forced to back down and accept limitations on his policy in
this matter, which left only the Communist press under a general
ban; other papers would be judged individually on their actual published material. Thereafter Kahr was under pressure for further
loosening of the gag.[25] Once new elections were announced most
restrictions on political activity went by the board:

> The Order for the Security of Elections re-establishes, in prepa-
> ration for the elections, freedom of assembly, speech, and the
> press. Assemblies in the open air, processions, etc. are still for-
> bidden. Former members of dissolved organizations may form
> combinations for election purposes. The ban on the parties and
> organizations remains in effect. . . . The order also demands that
> the arrest of persons who are put forward as candidates, etc. will
> be canceled (release of Communist leaders!).[26]

This meant, in essence, that the right and left radicals could operate
with little hindrance for the election period. They would have all
of the advantages and few of the disadvantages of political martyr-
dom and for the first time since the Putsch they were in a position
to rally their forces openly and safely.

The most active element in the election campaign was, not
surprisingly, the racist groups, which had organized themselves
loosely for the campaign under the name "Racist Block"
(Völkischer Block). The provincial authorities were in agreement
that the racists showed more vigor and held more meetings than
any of their competitors. One Regierungspräsident noted that they
also seemed to have more money to spend than any of the other
parties, and several commented on the unpleasant tendencies they
showed in their propaganda and in their interference with the campaigns of other parties. In public meetings the racists avoided direct attacks on the government and calls for rebellion, but in closed
meetings they seem to have been less circumspect.[27]

The government coalition—primarily the BVP, the Mittelpartei,

[25] *Ibid.*; GSK R/3603, 25.11.1923; Org. d. Münchner u. Bayer. Verleger u.
Redakteure, 26.11.1923; M. Inn. 2004 kaa 54, 26.11.1923; NA, T120,
5569, p. K591613.

[26] NA, EAP 105/7a, WKK vii, Abt. ic Nr. 1779 Geh. See also B, ii,
MA103458, GSK R(?)/Nr. 6378, 12.1.1924.

[27] B, i, GSK 7, p. 60; GSK 44, p. 9; GSK 90, p. 572; SA 1, 1756, PDM
1278/VId; ii, MA101235, PDN-F 2743/ii 24; MA102141, HMB 222, Opf.,

and a number of splinter groups[28]—coordinated its election tactics but ran a rather relaxed campaign, which was, to judge by the acid comments of the Regierungspräsident of Schwaben, characteristic of the approach of the leaders of the middle-class parties.[29] The BVP, the chief target of the parties outside the coalition, played its cards close to the chest as well as casually. As the representative of the most Bavarian-oriented portion of the population, its campaign centered on the theme of Bavaria for the Bavarians and blamed the recent radicalism of both Right and Left on the intervention of "foreigners" from the north. The party also took a less nationalistic and patriotic line than had previously been the case. Not only was it hostile to the NSDAP, but it was definitely cool and critical regarding other Verbände, including the "echt bayrisch" Bund Bayern und Reich as well as the "foreign" Commander Ehrhardt. The BVP pressed hardest for constitutional reforms of a nature that would give a party with a simple majority control of Landtag and the state, while the Mittelpartei seems to have rested on its laurels.[30]

The German Democratic Party (Deutsche Demokratische Partei) allied itself with the Peasants' League (Bauernbund) for election purposes, forming the "German Block" (Deutscher Block). The Democrats found enough financial support—allegedly from the Aufhäuser banking interests—to open a newspaper (*die Allgemeine Zeitung*), but their campaign activities were relatively limited and low key. They stood for the basic liberal-democratic principles of their party and opposed the program of reform suggested by the BVP. The Peasants' League was both more active and more radical than its ally. It opposed the heavy new taxes levied on the farmer and sought to discredit the government and Kahr. At one meeting, held despite the disapproval of the authorities, the Bauernbund speaker went so far as to demand the trial of Kahr and the Cabinet for "betrayal of the people." However, even

---

1.4.1924; HMB 689, Ofr., 2.4.1924; HMB 440, N/B, 3.4.1924; HMB 459, Schw., 8.4.1924; NA, T120, 5570, p. K591747.

[28] Nationale Landespartei Bayerns plus a number of Catholic and patriotic organizations. NA, T120, 5569, p. K591712.

[29] B, II, MA102141, HMB 523, Schw., p. 1.

[30] B, I, GSK 7, p. 60; GSK 44, pp. 184-85, 194-95; II, MA99521, 27.12.1923, p. 13; MA102141, HMB 440, N/B; IV, BuR, Bd. 36, Akt 2, Item 6; NA, T120, 5569, pp. K591686, K591695-97, K591708-9, K591712.

during the campaign, neither party showed any evidence of having the kind of energy, leadership, or popular support that would make the block a serious force.[31]

The SPD clearly should have been "running scared" in view of the tense and desperate economic situation, which tended to radicalize the workers and cut their willingness and ability to contribute to the party's coffers. The crisis underlined the fact that unions, like other political and economic organisms, are strongest when they least need strength and weakest under just those conditions where they need strength most. The SPD also suffered from the fact that the existing crisis increased the hostility between its left and right wings and weakened the hold of the middle over both. As a result of this increasing dissent within the party, the right wing, which had control of much of the party apparatus and which was more flexible and adroit tactically, managed to get its candidates nominated, although at least in northern Bavaria it was not at all certain that many rank and file members and hangers-on would vote for these men. The SPD election campaign was less than inspired. Despite the Putsch and the opportunity it presented for building up fear of the right radicals, the SPD concentrated on national issues, socialist dogma, and old bugaboos, apparently assuming that the Putsch had settled the right radical issue. On one of the few occasions when the right radicals were mentioned, Endres attacked Seeckt as being insincere in banning their parties and organizations. The right radicals were thus merely a stick for beating the army, which had crushed their bid for power. Similarly, at a time when the restoration of the monarchy was, by admission of the pretender himself, not likely in the foreseeable future, Auer concentrated his considerable oratorical powers on the monarchy and on the government as its tool. At a time when most workers feared unemployment or were actually unemployed, the party's major effort on the labor front seemed to be the drive to retain the eight-hour day—a boon of little aid to those who were working only four hours a day or enjoying unlimited leisure without pay. For the SPD leaders the campaign was obviously just one more routine operation, despite the dangers and opportunities it presented to them. They clearly expected the bulk of their followers to accept them on the basis of their traditional program and approach despite the economic and

[31] B, I, GSK 44, pp. 114-15, 151, 194; II, MA102141, HMB 254, Schw.; HMB 425, Ufr.; HMB 222, Opf.; NA, T120, 5569, pp. K591679, K591722.

social pressures kneading the worker as well as the other elements of society into new and sometimes tortured political forms.[32]

The KPD, despite the fact that every Bavarian's hand was against it, tried to make up for lack of numbers and lack of popular support in many areas by feverish activity. Like the Social Democrats, the Communists stuck to their well-worn slogans, but since these were revolutionary, they were nearer to the tastes of many desperate workers than were the pacifist and gradualist slogans of their rivals. Also, since they had no hostages in the existing order, either in the form of union control or an expensive and elaborate party apparatus, the Communists were able to make the most of their position of opposition. They concentrated on the unemployed, with a few sporadic attempts to appeal to rank and file policemen and soldiers as proletarians. Although most of their known leaders were under arrest, the Communists were able to use their enthusiastic younger members to distribute leaflets, to organize the unemployed, and to make difficulties for the government and the SPD on all fronts.[33]

The other parties and political groups were, at best, "also walks," since they scarcely ran in any serious manner. The result of the Landtag elections which were held on 6 April 1924 (in Bavaria east of the Rhine) and 4 May 1924 (in the Pfalz) was:

	Bavaria East of the Rhine	*Pfalz*	*Total*
Bavarian People's Party	919,587	61,104	980,691
Racist Block	491,862	15,683	507,545
Social Democratic Party	433,821	80,778	514,609
Peasants' and Mittelstand League	207,422		207,422
Communist Party	203,017	42,641	245,658
United National Right	197,509	80,589	278,287
German Block	73,818	20,968	94,786

None of the other parties received enough votes to elect more than a single deputy and are therefore not included in the table.[34] The result in terms of seats in the Landtag (total, 129) was:[35]

[32] B, I, GSK 43, pp. 170-71, 269; GSK 44, pp. 114, 117, 134-36, 165, 172; II, MA102141, HMB 425, Ufr.; HMB 333, Obb.; HMB 130, Opf.; HMB 251, Ufr.; NA, T120, 5569, pp. K591726, K591717.

[33] B, I, GSK 44, pp. 89, 121, 133-34, 136-37; II, MA102141, HMB 425, Ufr.; HMB 222, Opf.; NA, EAP 105/7a, WKK VII Lagebericht 9, Beilage.

[34] NA, T120, 5570, pp. K591752, K591796.

[35] *Statistisches Handbuch Bayern, 1924*, p. 476.

Bavarian People's Party	46
Racist Block	23
Social Democratic Party	23
Peasants' and Mittelstand League	10
Communist Party	9
United National Right	11
German Block	3
Miscellaneous minor parties	4

The elections were catastrophic for some parties and cheering for others. In general, they had proven the axiom that critical times foster radical parties and hurt moderate ones. The Democrats lost some seventy percent of their former voting strength; the SPD lost about a third; the Mittelpartei lost some twenty percent; the BVP lost almost fifteen percent of its voters, which was better than some people had anticipated; and the Peasants' League held up best of all. Thus the two traditional parties that had the largest peasant following felt the impact less than those based in the cities, despite the current unhappiness of the peasant regarding the economic situation. The Racist Block achieved the greatest, indeed startling, gains, largely at the expense of the more leftist middle-class parties and apparently also as a result of attracting large numbers of youths of all classes, including peasants. In at least some areas the racists also gained a good portion of the Protestant vote. The BVP tried to lay most of the blame for the Völkisch success on the impact of the Hitler Trial, but it is clear that far deeper and more permanent forces were at work. The trial certainly introduced Hitler to many people for the first time, but had his message not carried weight with them the introduction would have been of little significance. The racist success was a symptom of a deep unrest in Weimar Germany,[36] as well as a reflection of the more ephemeral developments stressed by contemporary observers.

The racists' success in München was especially spectacular, for they received a plurality, with 105,000 votes. München, where Hitler had operated for years, was the cornerstone of their success, whereas in the Pfalz, where Hitler was personally unknown and his ideas could not be presented in an election campaign because of the French presence, the racists made their worst showing. Whatever else the racists had succeeded in doing, they had clearly destroyed

[36] For a discussion of some of the forces working for the success of the Racist Movement and the NSDAP as its cutting edge, see Chapters I and III above and XXII below.

any factual basis for the SPD claim that it represented the "masses" in the capital. The Social Democrats might control certain workers' quarters, but they did not dominate the city by numbers as they would have liked one to believe.[37]

The KPD had also made sizable gains, many of them clearly at the expense of the SPD—although there is evidence that some of the SPD losses were to the NSDAP and not to the KPD.[38] The desperation of the workers was clearly expressed in this migration to the Left and extreme Right; they were possibly as much alienated by the SPD's failure to tackle the questions of the moment squarely and provide possible solutions for them as they were attracted by the specific solutions offered by the KPD or racists. A drowning man is more likely to grab a floating toy thrown to him than to give heed to swimming instructions in a monotone from the safety of the bank. The KPD and racists at least promised to do something for the working man—and the non-working man—immediately if they got into power. The SPD's primary promise was the continuation of a system and a situation that the worker found uncomfortable, if not disastrous. Its appeal was to the faithful of the party, the unions, and particularly those who had jobs to protect. It offered little to the man on the fringes or to the youths in search of jobs.

The *Münchener Post* explained away the disaster blithely. The SPD's losses must not be taken tragically. The solid phalanx of the faithful had stood fast. The losses were only the fair-weather socialists. It took comfort in claiming that, taken together, the Marxist parties had lost few votes to the racists, although the middle-class parties had entered the elections with a solid front against the Marxists. It then went on to explain that the elections had proven that no recovery in Bavarian political life could take place until the BVP recognized the meaning of the elections and adopted an honorable, republican, and democratic social policy in true alignment with the German Republic. This was a very interesting interpretation of an election in which the party most closely identified with the Republic—the Democrats—almost disappeared, and in which the Marxist party favoring the Republic—although sometimes grudgingly—lost heavily to the Marxist party that wished to

---

[37] B, II, MA102141, HMB 459, Schw.; HMB 764, Ofr.; HMB 505, N/B; NA, T120, 5570, pp. K591754-56, K591762; *Statistisches Handbuch Bayern, 1924*, ca. p. 470; Bennecke, *SA*, p. 106.

[38] See Chapter XXII, Section I, below.

overthrow it by violence. The same complacency that marked the BVP analysis of the election stares forth from every line of the *Post*'s analysis, and the argument that losses to the KPD were not really too bad because it was also Marxist closely parallels the argument of the German nationalist *München-Augsburger-Abendzeitung* that the Mittelpartei's losses to the racists were compensated for in part by the votes the racists won from the Marxist parties. Neither in the major parties of the Right nor in those of the Left does one find a real attempt to spike the enemy's guns or even a recognition that the enemy closest to one is often the most dangerous. Both were clearly intending to go on with politics as usual.[39]

Undoubtedly, the traditional parties took considerable comfort from the fact that in the Reichstag elections, which followed close on the heels of those for the Landtag, both the racists and the Communists took some losses as compared to their earlier showing. The campaign had been lackluster, at least partially because the parties were all financially exhausted and partially because the Landtag campaign had used up much of the nervous energy of the protagonists. It had generally been assumed in political circles that the racists and Communists would show even greater strength than in April. Instead there was a moderate come-back by most of the major losers except the Democrats. The SPD, the BVP, and the National Right all won more votes for the Reichstag than for the Landtag. The tide of radicalism was clearly receding somewhat in Bavaria, although this development was overshadowed by the overall achievement of the racists and Communists in the Reich as a whole. The racists, in particular, had been practically unrepresented in the Reichstag and now won thirty-two seats. In Bavaria, however, they were some 50,000 votes below their peak. This decline left them still far stronger than they had been before the Hitler Putsch and very possibly aided them by increasing the complacency of their foes.[40]

The elections showed a shifting of the political scene in Bavaria, and the divergence between the first election and the second indicated that the situation was still fluid. However, no matter how much the traditional parties might whistle in the dark, a serious

---

[39] NA, T120, 5570, pp. K591754-56.

[40] B, II, MA102141, HMB 307, Opf.; HMB 595, Schw.; HMB 327, Opf.; HMB 959, Ofr.; Bennecke, *SA*, pp. 106, 113; *Statistisches Handbuch Bayern, 1924*, p. 458.

new factor had appeared on the political scene. The extreme edge of the Patriotic Movement was developing from a disorganized force with a hydra-headed leadership into a single political party with serious appeal to a wide spectrum of voters. The atmosphere and balance of Weimar politics was changing, and the change appeared first in Bavaria. The "nationalist opposition" was becoming organized and abandoning Putsches for the ballot box.[41]

III. *The Held Government*

The new government, which succeeded Knilling's on 5 July 1924, was the first since Hoffmann's government fell in March 1920 to be headed by a reigning party leader. Dr. Heinrich Held, the most important single figure in the BVP and long a decisive influence from behind the scenes, now moved into the open as minister-president. With the exception of Knilling's foes, Wutzlhofer and Dr. Schweyer, Held's Cabinet was that of his predecessor. Gürtner stayed as justice minister; Dr. Matt, as Kultusminister; Dr. Krausneck, despite his earlier threats of resignation, reappeared in charge of finances; while Oswald and Dr. von Meinel retained their portfolios as social and trade ministers. Dr. Karl Stützel, a professional bureaucrat who had served in the Social Ministry in recent years, was the new minister of the interior. Professor Anton Fehr of the Bavarian Peasants and Mittelstand League was agriculture minister and the league's watchdog in the Cabinet. A former Reich food minister and a peasant leader, he brought the same kind of expertise to his task as had his predecessor—and represented the same general interests. Like his predecessor, he was also an outspoken foe of the NSDAP.[42]

The new government, like the old, was dominated by the BVP, but included representatives of those parties allied with it. Most of the ministers were still former career civil servants, whose party affiliations were clear but whose main energies had been devoted to administrative rather than political life. The minister-president, however, was a politician and newspaper man, who, although not even a Bavarian, had risen under the aegis of Dr. Georg Heim, a Bavarian of the purest water. Having married into the publishing family whose newspaper he edited, he made the *Regensburg Anzeiger* his personal organ in the postwar years and used it to

[41] For a discussion of this shift see Chapter XXII.
[42] B, II, MA99518, 5.1.1921, p. 7; MA99520, 4.4.1922, p. 6; MA99522, 5.7.1924, p. 1; MA102140, HMB 3, Opf.; MA103457, 3064 a 7, 27.9.1923.

consolidate his power and influence in the party. As a "Zugereister" he was more "weissblau" than many born Bavarians and, like his patron Dr. Heim, was suspected of having carried particularism to the point of separatism at the end of World War I, a suspicion given at least some support by his refusal to support the Landtag resolution of October 1918 expressing loyalty to the Reich. He was the first minister-president since World War I to last more than two years in office and the last minister-president before the National Socialists took over Bavaria by force in 1933. He was both a product and a symbol of the more stable and moderate atmosphere that dominated Bavaria after the Hitler Putsch, and clearly his brand of moderate conservatism suited the majority of Bavarians or he and his party could not have held power for so many years in a democracy where political heads rolled unexpectedly and often.[43]

From the beginning, the Held government was secure, although it had a majority of only seven seats, because there was no serious substitute for it. No possible alternative majority existed that would not have included both the SPD and the racists, a most unlikely combination and one of the few that never did emerge, except in the most negative sense—cooperation in the overthrow of a government—during the Weimar period. On the other hand, with an opposition mustering 61 of the 129 seats in the House, the grand schemes for constitutional revision had to be jettisoned. Thus, Held, who had pressed for this scheme and who had wanted in the fall of 1923 to proceed with a Bavarian currency reform without reference to the Reich,[44] found himself in power but bound by the very rules and regulations he had sought to alter. His government therefore worked within the realm of the possible, dealing primarily with the problems of the slowly convalescing economy and those political problems left over from the Putsch.

On the political scene, the government's primary attention was given to the larger elements of the opposition, particularly the left and right radicals. Typically, Dr. Held seemed more worried about the Left, including the SPD, than he did about the Right radicals. His anxiety regarding the KPD was certainly justified by their intentions, since they would gladly have launched a bloody revolution in Bavaria—as they had earlier in Hamburg—had they had

[43] B, II, MA99522, 5.7.1924, p. 1; NA, T120, 5569, p. K591469; T175, 99, p. 2620749; Held, Dr. Joseph, *Heinrich Held*, Regensburg, 1958, passim.
[44] B, I, Kahr MS, p. 1310.

the strength to do so. However, the police were in firm control of the situation and kept the Communists off balance and disorganized, so that there was little danger in fact from that quarter.

In view of the events of 1919 it is easy to understand, of course, why the shadow of the KPD loomed so much larger and more dangerous than the actuality. It is far harder to understand and to accept as logical or practical the inordinate fear and distrust of even the moderate conservatives in the SPD. That Dr. Held shared this fear is indicated by the fact that in commenting on one of the early police reports that he received from Nürnberg-Fürth, the minister-president singled out as especially important those matters concerning not only the KPD but also the SPD and its new paramilitary organization, Reichsbanner Black-Red-Gold, while passing over in silence the discussion of the right radical movement.[45] In fairness to Held it must be added that the creation of Reichsbanner at the very moment when the right radicals had been disarmed and effectively dispersed could suggest an aggressive aim. It was also true that the organization was, on paper, exceedingly formidable, being by far the largest paramilitary organization to be created in the Weimar Republic, aside from the loosely organized, politically disunited, and relatively inactive Stahlhelm. Since it was not yet clear to what an extent this organization was primarily a "chowder and marching club," passive in nature and defensive in aim, the authorities would necessarily watch it carefully in a state where its founders were in vigorous opposition to the government. There was, however, an edge of fear in the official attitude towards Reichsbanner that certainly would not be justified by its subsequent history. Nonetheless, Held was determined not to repeat Knilling's error. He would certainly oppose Reichsbanner, but he would not proceed only on the Left:

> On the basis of the biweekly reports (HMB) of various Regierungspräsidien, the minister-president drew attention to the dangers that threaten from the Reichsbanner Black-Red-Gold. The question of a ban on this organization is not simple. As long as it has not been established that one is dealing with a military organization (successor to the SA) one can hardly intervene. It is therefore necessary to assemble the appropriate evidence. A move against this organization must also not proceed in a one-sided manner. The government must rather suppress all armed

45 B, II, MA101235, PDN-F 3822/II, 31.7.1924.

organizations outside the Wehrmacht and the Landespolizei. He would like to request that the question be considered from all angles so that the Cabinet can make a decision in this question in a few weeks.[46]

This viewpoint was a long way from Knilling's pre-Putsch policy of suppressing the Left and encouraging the Right Verbände.

The Cabinet took an even stronger stand against the right and left extremists. It flatly refused a demand by the KPD faction in the Landtag to end the ban on the KPD and NSDAP, and Stützel, with the assent of his colleagues, was prepared to quash demonstrations from either side. At the same time, he was also firm in handling new racist paramilitary organizations, such as the Front Fighters League (Frontkriegerbund) and Front Force (Frontbann) with which the former was affiliated.[47] Held even went so far as to attempt to prevent—by means of behind-the-scene negotiations—the Landtag from allowing racist deputies to act as reporters on the government budget.[48] He was, however, careful to stay within constitutional bounds in handling the racists in the Landtag, informing Jewish protesters against antisemitic proposals made by racists in the House, that the government had no power to muzzle the deputies, but only to oppose their positions—and, expressing a typical middle-class Bavarian resentment, added that there would be far less antisemitism in Bavaria if the radical left movement were not led by Jews.[49] It is also interesting to note that for Dr. Held the National Socialist danger was, to a considerable extent, a threat from the Left. In discussing the question of whether or not the ban on the NSDAP could be lifted, he referred to "the dangers that, in his opinion, threatened from the left radical wing of the NSDAP. The desire for the revocation of the ban against the party could only be met if absolute guarantees were given that certain persons would be held in check in the future."[50]

With regard to all of the Kampfbund organizations, Held took the viewpoint that the bans against them could not be ended as long as the organizations continued to seek to carry on paramilitary activities. On the other hand, the authorities were prepared to per-

[46] B, II, MA99522, 9.8.1924, pp. 6-7. See Chapter XXIII, Section v, for further data on Reichsbanner.
[47] See Chapter XXII, Section II.
[48] B, II, MA99522, 5.12.1924, p. 13.
[49] B, II, MA99522, 31.7.1924, p. 6; 2.8.1924, p. 5.
[50] *Ibid.*

mit individual members of former Kampfbund organizations to join the new semi-official defense organization, Deutscher Notbann, on the same terms as other recruits: unquestioned acceptance of government authority, subordination to Notbann leaders, and no military activities outside of Notbann.[51] This policy was in line with both the general attempt to win over as many of the rank and file members of the right radical groups as possible and the desire to continue to maintain some form of military reserve in defiance of the Versailles Treaty.

Besides these direct measures, the government encouraged Crown Prince Rupprecht to undertake many more public appearances than he had in the recent past so as to counterbalance Ludendorff. By setting a highly popular figure combining royal authority and a field marshal's rank against the former first quartermaster general the government not only prevented many former Bavarian soldiers from following the Pied Piper of Ludwigshöhe but also encouraged Ludendorff to indulge in those personal attacks on the crown prince that played a significant role in the decline of his influence in Bavaria.[52]

The Cabinet was also cool towards those Verbände that had not taken part in the Putsch. When Dr. Held indicated on 2 August 1924 that he planned to call together the leaders of the loyal Verbände and talk turkey with them, Oswald warned against accepting mere assurances of loyalty from the leaders. Experience indicated that this was by no means satisfactory. Gürtner, no less, insisted that all Verbände, whatever their names, had only a qualified loyalty to the state. Therefore one must not make terms with them.[53] In this respect the change introduced by the Putsch was clearly a lasting one. Never again would the Bavarian ministers be as trusting towards the militant Right as they had been before 8 November 1923.

With regard to the Reich, Held also inherited a position considerably more comfortable than those that had confronted his predecessors. Not only had the recent agreement, based on mutual compromises, brought about at least an armistice in the long quarrel

---

[51] B, I, M. Inn. 72449, Aktenvermerk (Ref. 17), 20.5.1925; Zu No. 2004 k z 19, 22.5.1925; II, MA99522, 28.8.1924, pp. 16-17.

[52] B, II, MA99522, 24.7.1924, p. 17.

[53] *Ibid.*, 2.8.1924, p. 6: "Minister Gürtner weist darauf, dass eben alle Verbände, gleich viel wie sie heissen, nur eine bedingte Einstellung zum Staat haben. Daher könne man sich mit den Verbänden auf nichts einlassen."

over states' rights, but also he faced a chancellor who was Catholic and moderately conservative in attitude. Ironically, the one question now at issue between Bavaria and the Reich was the treatment of the right radicals. Whereas previously the right radicals had been under ban everywhere in Germany except Bavaria and the Reichstag and Reichsregierung had tried to bring Bavaria into line with this policy, the situation was now reversed. The Bavarians had outlawed the National Socialists and their allies, while in the north such bans had largely been relaxed and questions were asked in the Reichstag about the continued "persecution" in Bavaria. At first, the Reich government was privately anxious for the Bavarians to hold the line. In answer to a Bavarian query the Reich replied that the Ausnahmezustand there could not be ended because of the Communists and that it did not wish the Bavarians to end their state of emergency either. Within ten days, though, when an attack was launched against the Bavarian state of emergency in the Reichstag, the Bavarians felt that the defense of the Bavarian position by the Reichsregierung was lukewarm at best. They suspected that they were being sold down the river by Chancellor Marx and were determined to hold firm, not merely because they believed they needed emergency measures to control the right radicals and Communists but because this was one of the last rights left to the states and they were not prepared to see it disappear by default.[54]

In the end, it was February 1925 before the Cabinet agreed to an end to the ban on parties and organizations, on the grounds that ideas couldn't be effectively forbidden and that the general ban against paramilitary activities would cover the really dangerous activities of most of the radicals. Held noted the pressure that Bavaria was under because the Reichstag could also take action in this field and might if Bavaria did not. As he put it: "We must summon up the courage to return to normal relationships, and seek to control the things that are dangerous to the existence of the state by normal means."[55] Even then, the state of emergency was not completely abandoned. The government retained a number of special powers. It was only in December of 1925, in the face of a probable Reichstag demand for its end that the Bavarians reluctantly gave up the last scraps of special authority to which they had clung for so long.[56] It was therefore more than two years after the Putsch be-

[54] B, II, MA99522, 8.7.1924, pp. 2-3; 14.7.1924, p. 9; 24.7.1924, pp. 5-8.
[55] B, II, MA99523, 9.2.1925, p. 10.
[56] *Ibid.*, 7.11.1925, pp. 4-5; 1.12.1925, p. 20; 12.12.1925, pp. 2-8.

fore Bavaria returned completely to that theoretical condition of "normalcy" that she had scarcely known since 1914.

IV. The Fall Elections

The new elections in the fall, which followed the dissolution of the Reichstag, were an anticlimax after the spring elections and their tumultuous and fateful prelude. In at least some areas, the communal elections that were coupled with them aroused more interest than did the Reichstag contests. There was also apparently a good deal of monarchist activity and enthusiasm, parallel with, but separate from, the election campaign, which reached down even into workers' groups. This activity may well have been aimed at increasing the popularity of the BVP and reducing that of the racists.[57]

From the economic point of view things in general were considerably better than they had been in the spring, and the pressures and resentments of that period had been blunted both by the passage of time and by greater prosperity. In Schwaben the peasants were prosperous again despite the new taxes, and beer consumption was up. The workers and lower officials were still suffering, especially from a squeeze between low wages and rising prices. Nonetheless, the lack of interest in the elections in the countryside was a sign of relaxation. In the cities there was a good deal more interest, but even here it was muted, according to all the Regierungspräsidenten.[58]

As far as the parties were concerned, there was little change from the spring. The BVP and the Bauernbund agreed not to attack one another. The KPD, apparently hoping for some swing votes from the right radicals, printed a leaflet explaining that they believed the Putschists to have been motivated by high ideals. The SPD coupled a campaign against war and officers with an attempt to win over the enlisted men of both the army and the police, an attempt that, as usual, went no further than empty words. The racists made a play for Catholic votes, but were too torn by their

---

[57] See Cabinet remarks regarding the increased activities of Rupprecht as evidence of this cooperation and its objectives. See also B, II, MA101235, PDN-F 3822/II; MA102141, HMB 1301, Ofr.; HMB 1458, Ofr.; HMB 1145, Schw.; HMB 1610, Ofr.; HMB 974, N/B.

[58] B, II, MA101248, PDN-F 6100/II; MA102141, HMB 494, Opf.; HMB 1145 Schw.; HMB 789, Opf.; HMB 1390, Schw.; HMB 1347, Ufr.; HMB 1904, Ofr.; HMB 1547, Obb.; HMB 1319, Schw.

internal feuds to give these elections the attention and enthusiasm that they had to the earlier ones,[59] so that several senior officials predicted that the movement would suffer sharply at the polls. Otherwise the campaign was normal if quiet.[60]

The results of the elections confirmed the trend that became noticeable between the Landtag and Reichstag elections of the spring. The "crisis vote" that had swollen the ranks of the racist and Communist parties melted away, leaving them larger than they had been in mid-1923 but shadows of their crisis selves. The results of the elections to 55 Reichstag seats were:[61]

Bavarian People's Party	19
Racist Block (including GVG)	4
Social Democratic Party	11
Peasants' and Mittelstand League	5
Communist Party	3
United National Right	9
Democratic Party	2

The result was especially chastening for the racists, who saw the bulk of their Reichstag mandates melt away. While the Racists retained their Landtag seats despite these losses, the pressure that they exerted on the government was greatly reduced now that it was certain that new elections would cut their representation drastically. In practical terms, the election gave the Held government a far firmer basis than it had enjoyed earlier, so that it was no longer merely safe but also sound. There was no growing threat to cause it concern on either the left or the right horizon.

v. Conclusion

The year and a half following the Putsch saw the transformation of the National Socialist Movement into a political party calculated to receive the votes of those non-Marxists who were discontent with the existing parties, the existing government, and the existing society. The same period saw this party rise on a crest of disillusionment in the populace and enthusiasm on the part of its sup-

[59] See Chapter XXII, Section III, for a discussion of the quarrels in the racist camp.

[60] B, II, MA101235, PDN-F 3822/II, pp. 14-15; 5614/II, pp. 15-16; MA101248, Anlage 2 zu PDN-F 6100/II; PDM Nachrichtenblatt 19, pp. 9-11; MA102141, HMB 1189, N/B; NA, T175, 99, p. 2620760.

[61] *Statistisches Handbuch Bayern, 1926*, p. 610. The Zentrum and a minor middle-class party also each received one seat.

porters, especially young men. It also saw the breaking of the wave and the decline of the new party to a much lower but ominously stable level. For the time being it was helpless, but it existed as a cadre for future development should conditions again turn large numbers of voters violently against the Republic.

Meanwhile, the traditional parties reasserted their control over the bulk of their usual followers, and the most powerful of them, the Bavarian People's Party, resumed its hegemony in Bavaria. The traditional forces had won the battle of the Putsch and the campaign for control of Bavaria, and had won them decisively. The war for control of Germany was, however, still unsettled, and the final battles would be fought and lost far from Bavaria by forces over which the Bavarians would have little influence and no power.

In the Bavarian battles the conservative forces had proven themselves still capable of holding the loyalty of the bulk of the population and of exerting sufficient attraction for the more moderate elements of the Patriotic and Racist Movement to isolate the extremists of the latter. Theirs had been a victory essentially of strategy, although even in tactics they had proven themselves superior to the racists once they had recovered from the surprise attack on 8 November 1923. The Marxist and bourgeois Left played no significant role in the battles or the campaign. They could scarcely have hoped to play a decisive role under any circumstances, but they might well have exerted some influence had they been tactically more adroit and vigorous. As it was, they were content to sit on the sidelines and criticize all of the active forces on both sides bitterly and futilely.

Held and Hitler were both victors, each in his own way. Held kept Bavaria, while Hitler had learned valuable lessons and won for himself a national foothold. Each had eliminated many of the other's rivals. Hitler's advantages, however, were still merely opportunities to be exploited, opportunities highly dependent upon factors beyond his control. Held's victory was immediate and solid, and only the boldest and least rational of prophets would have ventured to say in 1924 that in the long run Hitler would play Edward IV to Held's Earl of Warwick.

22.

THE INTERIM RACIST MOVEMENT

1. The New Situation

When the excitement generated in Völkisch circles by the Putsch and its suppression had died down, the Kampfbündler who were still free found themselves in a new and difficult situation. The Putsch had failed and the government was in firm control of both the police and the army. The mob actions that had developed more or less spontaneously in the wake of the Putsch had been exhilarating as well as exhausting for the participants, but they had in no way threatened the post-Putsch political equilibrium. The enthusiasm and rage from which these demonstrations were born could not be maintained indefinitely. The movement must either find other ways to meet the new situation or perish.

The most serious of the problems facing the Kampfbund and its sympathizers was, as became increasingly clear during the following year, the loss of key leaders. Some of these men like Scheubner-Richter and von der Pfordten, were dead. Others, like Göring and Hess, had fled abroad. Many of the remainder, including Adolf Hitler, were incarcerated.

Almost as disastrous as the loss of leaders was the new-born active hostility of the Bavarian authorities. Before the Putsch, the authorities had been of two minds regarding the movement. Some high officials had been openly favorable towards the broader movement; and a smaller group, towards the Kampfbund itself. Far more saw positive as well as negative elements in it and did not believe that it could be dispensed with in view of the threat of leftist violence and northern encroachment on Bavarian rights. Even those members of the government firmly hostile to the NSDAP and its allies had not wished to risk a direct confrontation with all its uncertainties and unpleasantness. The Putsch changed this situation overnight. Thereafter, as a simple measure of self-preservation, the government had to take strong measures against the Kampf-bund. Instead of being a legal entity, which was alternately condemned and courted by the government, the Kampbfund and its component organizations became outlaws, and very few days passed before the Putschists learned how much less comfortable it was to be on the wrong side of the law than it was to be merely on its edge.

Moreover, these fundamental difficulties were not the only ones with which the Kampfbund had to cope. Outsiders within the broader movement sought to harvest the bewildered and disorganized "foot soldiers." Commander Ehrhardt and Captain Heiss were particularly active in seeking to take advantage of Hitler's absence from the scene and the demoralization of many of his followers to improve their own positions or even to supplant him as the messiah of the right radicals.[1]

Another serious problem arose out of the sudden increase in the movement's popularity. At the very moment when its head was, at least temporarily, cut off, the movement gained large numbers of new members, and from this group new leaders arose naturally on the basis of local selection. These new leaders were, in many cases, neither in close contact with nor under the direct control of the remaining Kampfbund leaders. Thus they and at least the new elements among their followings were an unknown factor in all calculations, and it was not at all clear how they would fit into the new movement or to what extent they would modify or determine its nature.

Next came the rivalry among the old leaders themselves, another problem that had to be solved if the movement was to prosper. These rivalries were twofold in nature. To a very considerable extent they reflected the personal dislikes and ambitions of the leaders themselves, for in Hitler's absence the temptation to be his chief representative—if not his successor—was as great for insiders as for outsiders. However, these rivalries also reflected strong differences of opinion regarding the development of the movement and the tactics that it should employ.

Finally, the movement faced increasing financial problems as the months went on, despite its surprising initial successes at the polls and substantial permanent gains in membership and adherents. In the period immediately after the Putsch and through the elections

[1] See Chapter xiv, Section ii, above.

in May and June, the movement seems to have been able to tap local sources of revenue effectively, so that various officials reported that it seemed to have more money to spend than any other political group. As early as July, though, this situation was changing, and by the end of the year reports indicated that the financial pinch was serious. Völkisch newspapers were folding for lack of cash. Part of the early prosperity seems to have been the fruit of loans and of press profits from both advertising and paper sales. Probably individual contributions were also larger at this time, as they tend to be in times of crisis when personal sacrifices are made that are not easily maintained on a voluntary basis over any long term, as many a political party has discovered to its sorrow. This financial problem continued to plague the party throughout the years until it obtained a monopoly position after the Machtergreifung, but it seems to have been especially acute at this time when the movement was operating without the benefit of Hitler and his skill at collecting money.[2]

Set off against these critical problems were several major advantages over the situation before the Putsch. The first of these advantages was psychological. The movement had clearly shown its flag. Previously it had seemed to waver between working with the "old" authorities and within the framework of the existing state and society and adopting a clearly revolutionary program. As late as the eve of the Putsch, and during its early phases, Hitler had maintained the fiction that he was only seeking to push Kahr and the government into doing what they really wished to do anyway. For propaganda purposes this claim was still made at the Hitler Trial. In fact, though, the party was now officially committed to fighting on both flanks—against both "the Reds and reaction"—in favor of a revolutionary solution to Germany's problems. Having given up hope of using the government to destroy itself, the movement could and did enjoy to the hilt the advantages of a vigorous—if not violent—opposition in the same untrammeled away that the New Left enjoys these advantages today. Ironically, the abandonment of violence as a means had been coupled with the clear adoption of revolution as an end. None of the basic tenets of the National Socialist program were changed, but it could now be admitted that

[2] B, I, GSK 43, pp. 308f; II, MA101235, PDM, NB1. 10, pp. 9-11; NB1. 12, p. 5; MA101248, PDM, NB1. 20, p. 11; MA102411, HMB 317, Schw., 8.3.1924; HMB 684, Opf., pp. 2-3; HMB 1993, Ofr., p. 1.

they applied to conservative Bavaria as well as to Red Berlin. This might and clearly did cost the National Socialists much conservative aid, but it also won for them the support of many other elements that wanted a right radical revolution and greeted the breach with "reaction" with enthusiasm.

It was here that the greatest of the tangible gains was to be found. The Putsch acted as a catalyst. Many persons who had wavered between the moderate and radical wings of the Patriotic Movement made their decision in favor of radicalism as a result of the emotional pressures unleashed by the Putsch. Others, who had hardly heard of the right radicals or who knew little of their program, learned through the furor in the press and by means of the grapevine how closely the aims of the Putschists corresponded to their own. Some were led to join the National Socialists because they accepted the allegation that Kahr had betrayed Hitler and broken his word. Others clearly lost faith in Kahr as a man of words and pledged their allegiance to Hitler, who had proven himself to be a man of deeds. The election returns alone prove the strength of the radical Racist Movement in the months following the Putsch.[3]

Who were these supporters? The answer to this question must, of course, be partial at best. Nonetheless there are clear indications as to the groups that made up this following. They can be divided into four major categories: former National Socialists who remained loyal to Hitler and the movement, members of allied or parallel organizations who clearly recognized Hitler as their leader, groups that remained loyal to the Kampfbund ideal and the radical Völkische program but refused to accept Hitler unreservedly, and new elements from outside the Kampfbund.

The reports of the district officers and other administrative officials show that a high percentage of the members of the NSDAP remained doggedly true to their leaders after the ban on the party. The report of the provincial president in Niederbayern on 3 January 1924 is typical:

> The National Socialists, who do not indeed appear as a party in any form in the public eye but feel themselves at heart more bound together than ever before, persist in their hostility towards the present form of government. They are now, as before, permeated by the unshakable belief in the truth and impact of

[3] See Chapter XXI, Sections II and IV.

their [political] course. With various exceptions they are at present superficially quiescent.[4]

These official reports are at least partly confirmed by available fragmentary statistical data: at least 352 persons belonging to the pre-Putsch NSDAP reappear in the post-Putsch movement, mostly as leaders or activists.[5]

Many members of other Kampfbund groups now moved directly into the camouflaged NSDAP, including a large percentage of the members of Röhm's Reichskriegsflagge. Some of these men entered the new political organizations, but others were primarily active in one of the new paramilitary organizations, such as Frontring or Altreichsflagge.[6] Karl Osswald, Röhm himself (previously a National Socialist only in name), and Heinrich Himmler (the later SS leader who was destined to be the nemesis of his old chief) were among the RKF converts.[7] Another organization that went the way of Reichskriegsflagge was Kampfbund München. Instead of returning to legality and the VVM fold, its component organizations (the Seventh and Twelfth Ward Organizations) remained true to Hitler and evaded the ban on their continued existence by adopting new names.[8]

The primary group that remained loyal to the Kampfbund but maintained or even increased its distance from Hitler was Bund Oberland. The Oberländer sought to maintain their organization and remained dedicated to their old goals and methods. Unlike Reichskriegsflagge and Kampfbund München, however, they remained aloof from the new, common Völkisch organizations, both civilian and military. Supporting Hitler and Ludendorff against Kahr, they were loyal to Dr. Weber, who showed himself increasingly ready to reach an accommodation with the Bavarian author-

[4] B, I, GSK 44, p. 165. See also GSK 43, 44, 95, passim; and II, MA102141, passim.

[5] These figures exclude a good number of members of the early party who were probably—but not demonstrably—active in this interim period. Therefore, the number of persons from the statistical sample of the early party who were also active in the interim organizations is undoubtedly far higher than the confirmed figures above indicate. GP, D (Personalities).

[6] See below, Section II, for information on these groups.

[7] B, I, GSK 4, p. 14; SA 1, 1493, pp. 6-9; II, MA100423, N/Nr. 16, pp. 41-42; IV, OPA 73930, Urteil, pp. 3-7; NA, T175, 99, p. 2621263; Röhm, *Geschichte*, pp. 323-24.

[8] "Brückenwinkler" and "Gemütlicher Zwölfer." See B, I, M. Inn. 73694, 1051 b 10; GSK 3, p. 61.

ities during the course of 1924 and early 1925.[9] Oberland thus occupied an uneasy position between the two camps and had, by the time Hitler emerged from prison, largely passed out of his orbit.

The new elements from outside the Kampfbund seem to have been as diverse as those that made up the original party. They included both converts from other political camps and newcomers to politics. They came from every conceivable background and represented a wide spectrum of occupations. Indeed, the picture that they formed so successfully defied interpretation on conventional class and political lines that the officials reporting on the development of the movement were sometimes reluctant to accept the results of the evidence they themselves had assembled. However, they are almost all in agreement that the most obvious trend was that of young men into the movement and that another strong group of newcomers was workers. In this respect the new movement is a clear extrapolation of the old one. The main difference is the emphasis that is placed by several reporters on the heavy influx of women after the Putsch, although increasing interest on the part of the peasantry is another new factor.[10]

Besides these complete outsiders, there was a drift of younger elements from the center organizations of the movement, especially Bayern und Reich, into Hitler's wake. In April 1924, the provincial president of Oberfranken reported succinctly:

> The racists have made inroads into [the followings of] not only the left parties, but even more the existing right parties. When one examines the situation, one can see that not only the younger people out of middle-class, worker, and official circles, but also the peasants in the country communities, especially on the Protestant side, have voted for the racists.[11]

In Niederbayern, the story was the same:

> ". . . The Völkische Block, which has found many followers within middle-class circles as well as in a portion of the working class and the rural population at the expense of the Bavarian

[9] B, I, GSK 4, p. 14; GSK 95, pp. 2-3; M. Inn. 72449, Aktenvermerk, Ref. 17, 20.5.1925; Zu No. 2004 k z 19, 22.5.1925; II, MA100423, pp. 35, 40; MA101235, PDN-F 5614/II, p. 24; PDN-F 3822/II, p. 34; Röhm, *Geschichte*, pp. 323-26.

[10] B, I, GSK 44, pp. 106, 159; GSK 101, Ofr.; IV, BuR, Bd. 36, Akt 2, Item 14; II, MA101235, PDN-F 5614/II, p. 21.

[11] B, II, MA102141, HMB 764, Ofr., pp. 1-2.

People's Party and the United Socialists, is indeed the most active [party]. Former members of the Peasants' League are also [found] among them. It is reported that the farm workers of the large estates in Gauböden, who were previously inclined to socialism, will soon move over to the Racist Block. . . . The free peasantry came out for the racist candidates. . . ."[12]

In much of Bavaria a large-scale transfer of Communists to the Racist Movement marked the end of 1923, and the speakers for the movement frankly wooed the Communists as well as other workers. In some areas the tide was so strong that police and political authorities believed that it represented an attempt by the Communists to get weapons or to take over the movement, since they could not believe that such a concerted surge of leftists to the right radicals could be genuine.[13]

The extent to which suspicion of and hostility towards ordinary middle-class values had penetrated the movement is indicated by the remark of the district officer in Kronach regarding the relations of the National Socialists and Bayern und Reich:

> . . . an amalgamation with "Bayern und Reich" has not, in so far as can be seen at present, proven possible in the Kronach district. This Verband is seen by the former NSDAP as too tame, too friendly towards the government, and as the Verband of the possessing classes. . . .[14]

On the other hand, especially in Oberfranken, many members of Bayern und Reich deserted to the Kampfbund successor organizations, and in Bayreuth the Jungdo Ortsgruppe followed the same path. In Nürnberg the Bayern und Reich Ortsgruppe split, with the smaller portion, some thirty to forty men, going over to Hitler.[15]

A number of the newcomers soon carved out niches for themselves as leaders. In Ingolstadt, the local leader of the Democratic Party, who had been negotiating with the NSDAP through Lieu-

[12] *Ibid.*, HMB 440, N/B, p. 1. See also B, II, MA102141, HMB 505, N/B, 17.4.1924.

[13] B, I, GSK 43, p. 135; GSK 44, p. 190; II, MA101235, PDN-F 2425/II 24, p. 10; MA102141, HMB 254, Schw., p. 2; HMB 568, Ofr., p. 1; HMB 529, M/F, p. 1; HMB 286, N/B, p. 2; HMB 344, p. 1; IV, BuR, Bd. 36, Akt 1, Item 55; Lapo, Bd. 26a, Akt 5, Item 90/Sop. Geh., p. 9.

[14] B, I, GSK 44, p. 229.

[15] B, I, GSK 43, p. 284; GSK 44, pp. 190-91, 229; II, MA100424, Anlage zu M. Inn. 2020 t 17; MA102141, HMB 568, Ofr., p. 1; IV, BuR, Bd. 36, Akt 2, Item 8, Winneberger Bericht, 7.12.1923.

tenant Colonel Hofmann even before the Putsch, brought his Ortsgruppe over with him and became the local leader of the NSDAP.
In Augsburg two prominent local leaders were men who had been
violent left activists during the Republic of Councils in 1919. In
Bamberg, the leaders of the Völkische Ortsgruppe were men who,
until a short time before, had been conspicuously democratic in
their political coloration. In Hof the leaders were men who had not
hitherto been involved in politics, as was true of one of the key men
in Bayreuth. In Thurnau/Oberfranken, former Bayern und Reich
leaders shared equally with National Socialists in the leadership of
the Völkische Ortsgruppe.[16]

Finally, the significance of youth must again be noted. The
student elections in Erlangen were swept by the racist groups. The
students at the Hochschule in Nürnberg were also strongly
Völkisch, as was noted by Gareis and made manifest in their reactions to the Putsch. The Bezirksamt Freising was of the opinion
that the bulk of the students at the Hochschule in Weihenstephan
were Hitler sympathizers, and the München students left no doubt
about their views after the riots of 9-12 November. Furthermore,
the students were not the only youths attracted to the movement.
In Staffelstein members of the local socialist youth group moved
over to the National Socialists, and in Traunstein the son of a
prominent left radical was arrested for distributing National Socialist propaganda.[17]

A last word on the social composition of the party comes from
Haniel, who reported to Berlin in March:

> The German racist *Augsburger Tageszeitung* published in to-
> day's edition the candidates that the Racist Block has put up for
> the Diet elections in Bavaria. The list, . . . , in which all occupa-
> tions and groups are represented among the candidates provides
> a true reflection of the manifold composition of this party.[18]

This impression of the social composition of the party and espe-

[16] B, I, GSK 7, p. 60; GSK 43, pp. 264, 284; GSK 44, pp. 102, 109, 222;
GSK 73, p. 1; II, MA102141, HMB 254, Schw., p. 1; NA, T84, 4, pp.
3349-50.

[17] B, I, GSK 43, pp. 143, 308-309; GSK 44, pp. 5, 117-18, 222; II,
MA101249, PDN-F 1357/II, p. 15; MA102141, HMB Obb., 18.3.1924, p. 2;
HMB 1993, Ofr., p. 1.

[18] NA, T120, 5569, p. K591728.

cially of the newcomers is, at least in part, confirmed by fragmentary materials regarding individuals. Out of 291 newcomers to the movement between November 1923 and mid-1925, most of whom were leaders, activists, or future leaders of the NSDAP, 42 were clearly typed by their occupations as middle class, 28 were workers (mostly skilled), 30 were officials of various ranks and categories (including grammar school teachers), 46 were members of the free professions (including all branches of the law and professors at the university and Gymnasium level), 17 were students, 8 were journalists or writers, 7 were farmers, and the remainder were scattered through a spectrum of jobs ranging from foremen and chief clerks to Protestant clergymen.[19] Out of 120 persons for whom specific age data are available, 12 were younger than 21, 45 were between 21 and 31, 37 were between 31 and 41, 22 were in their 40's, and 4 were over 50. This means that approximately one-half, including many of the new leaders at both the provincial and local level, were under 31, while only slightly over a fifth were over 40 years of age.

Where political background is concerned, many of the newcomers were so young that they had not hitherto been active in politics or, in other cases, had never interested themselves seriously in political matters. For many others there is no indication as to their political background. It can, however, be established that 15 came from other racist groups, 3 came from the SPD, 3 from the Democratic Party, 3 from the radical Left (KPD and USPD), and one from the BVP, while another was considered by the district officer who reported on him to have been "democratic" in the past.[20] It is clear from this evidence that the movement was growing rapidly and that it drew its support from all groups and classes of the population, but especially from younger people.

The picture was not all one of roses and wine for the National Socialists, for they had losses as well as gains to record, and in some areas they found elements of the population, especially the peasantry, to be still very cool towards them. Finally and most painful, by the end of 1924 they had seen a fair portion of their newfound strength leak away. Some of the losses the National Socialists suffered were persons who went over to their opponents. Others simply dropped out of politics, disgusted or discouraged by the events of early November 1923. Among those who were pre-

---

[19] GP, D (Personalities).   [20] *Ibid.*

pared to cut their ties with the party were Ortsgruppenleiter Entmoser in Moosburg/Pegnitz, who dissolved his Ortsgruppe after the Putsch and began negotiations to join Reichsflagge, and Georg Quindell, a leader of one faction of the NSDAP in Hanover. He dissociated himself from the Putsch, stating that he disapproved of violence, and said that he would drop out of the movement.[21]

Throughout Bavaria, individuals and often entire Ortsgruppen of the NSDAP went over to other Verbände. In some instances, at least, this switch represented a genuine retreat from the party and its program. However, since the party itself issued orders for its members to adopt a policy of mass transfer so as to be able to take over legally recognized organizations of all kinds as camouflage, it is not easy to be sure which mass transfers represent a shift of loyalties and which are indications of "piracy."[22] Some cases seem quite clear-cut, though. For example, four local National Socialist leaders assured the district officer in Weilhelm on the evening of 9 November 1923 that they stood staunchly behind Crown Prince Rupprecht and refused to accept Ludendorff as a leader. This attitude, adopted at the height of the post-Putsch hysteria, indicates that here were round pegs in square holes. In Staffelstein, a number of the older adherents of the Kampfbund dropped out of the movement. Late in October 1924 an even clearer case came to light when the Ortsgruppe of the Frontkriegerbund[23] declared itself politically neutral and cut its ties to the central racist organization in München.[24]

Schwaben was the area least attracted to right radicalism, and the movement encountered comparatively little success there, although in absolute terms it made considerable gains, especially in the early months of the year 1924. In Oberbayern the peasants were suspicious of a movement that had so long been based in the towns and that included so many "foreigners" (non-Bavarians) among its leaders. After the end of June, resistance everywhere stiffened and many persons who had listened to the racist siren song in the cold, dismal, and hungry spring were no longer prepared to do so. Reports from all kinds of sources agree that the movement

[21] B, I, GSK 44, p. 190; FH, Allg. Akten 1923, Quindell an Oberpräsident von Hannover, 12.11.1923.

[22] See Section II below for further discussion of "piracy."

[23] One of the new camouflaged organizations. See Section II below.

[24] B, I, GSK 44, pp. 21, 80-82, 183-84, 190-92; GSK 101, BA Kronach, 3.1.1924; II, MA102141, HMB 1443, Obb., p. 3.

was clearly ebbing by July and that the ebb continued throughout 1924 and into 1925.[25]

Nonetheless, the Racist Movement had grown astonishingly during 1924. In a report of 1 December 1924, based on open and secret reports from all over Germany, the Reichskommissar for the supervision of internal order summed up the situation briefly:

> Within the right movement one may discern recently a [tendency towards] an abandonment of Verbände oriented towards National Socialism into those with no clear political ties or to groups close to the German Nationalist Party. However, even if the racist Verbände are badly shaken and reduced [in numbers] as a result of party squabbles, a marked increase in strength of the total movement of the right Verbände is established. The appearance of the republican organization Reichsbanner Schwarz-rot-gold has led to a counter-movement within the right Verbände in the form of a consolidation and the reduction of internal quarrels. The Verbände have also become more specific and more determined in their political demands and are striving vigorously to become a political power factor in the state.[26]

In short, despite the drop from the high point of membership it had reached in the late spring of 1924, and despite the manner in which internal quarrels had divided it, the Hitler Movement was far stronger and more effective at the end of 1924 than it had ever been before, and it was potentially much more susceptible to unification, since all of its basic elements except Oberland now accepted Hitler as the senior leader of the movement.

II. *The Illegal Movement*

In the face of the difficulties and opportunities presented by the new situation, the racist leaders were far from united on tactics. Particularly in the early weeks after the Putsch, this difference of opinion centered around the question of whether to continue the old organizations in the old way, under either their old or new

[25] B, I, GSK 43, p. 308; II, MA102141, HMB 1228, Ofr., pp. 1-2; HMB 1010, Obb., p. 2; HMB 1078, Schw., p. 1; HMB 459, Schw., pp. 1-2; HMB 578, Obb., p. 3; HMB 1004, Schw., pp. 1-2; HMB 1217, Ufr., p. 3; MA104221, Hans Besch an Kdo. d. Lapo, Augsburg, 29.1.1924; NA, T175, 99, p. 2620235.

[26] B, II, MA101248, Rk. O. In. 108, p. 32.

names, or whether to create a new legal organization to carry forward the fight in a new arena—Parliament—as well as among the people themselves. To some extent this quarrel found the SA leaders and the more military-minded of the party leaders on the side of illegality and a fight to the bitter end with the authorities, while the civilian-minded leaders were on the side of new departures and at least superficial legality. However, civilian-minded activists sided with the proponents of illegality, while more sedate soldiers sided with the civilians.

Since there was no effective central control mechanism, each group went its own way. Also, since in real life, as opposed to political fiction and theoretical studies, political theory is often warped in practice by the forces to which it is exposed, the "purity" of the two movements was soon diluted, especially in the case of the militant and illegal movement. Its leaders soon found that pure and complete illegality was not only uncomfortable but decreasingly effective. As a result, they sought, in various ways, at least partial legality, although they never gave up their militancy or seriously thought of accommodation with the existing state. Furthermore, as time went on, the same man might play roles in both the illegal and legal movements. For example, Ernst Röhm was at the same time the leader of the banned and illegal SA, the leader of the semi-legal paramilitary organization Frontbann, and a member of the Reichstag for the Völkischer Block, the legal successor organization. However, one can best achieve an orderly overview of the situation, by considering the two aspects of the Racist Movement separately.

The militants' first efforts were concentrated on simple defiance of Kahr and the government. The largest-scale and most ambitious efforts were centered in München and Nürnberg. In München, Amann, Drexler, and Rosenberg formed a committee to continue the party and appointed Major Buch to take over Göring's functions as leader of the SA. According to a National Socialist account, a shadow SA organization was kept alive all winter by Buch. If so, that is all that it was, for the police kept at their heels and nearly caught them on several occasions, despite alleged assistance from friends in the Landespolizei. Röhm, meanwhile, received authority from Hitler and Göring to build a new SA, but he too seems to have made little real progress. It is almost impossible to destroy completely the underground organization of an outlawed political organization if the underground's members are determined and reasonably intelligent, even where the police have unlimited powers. It is far less possible to do so under a democratic system with guarantees of personal rights and strict limits on the authority of the police. On the other hand, it is equally true that it is nearly always impossible for the underground to maintain any elaborate organization or undertake broad action if the authorities are moderately alert. The result is the suppression but not the extirpation of the illegal organization. This is what happened in München in 1924.[27]

In Nürnberg an even more ambitious program was undertaken which called for the creation of a "national army" under the newly-created "Northern Command" (Kommando Nord). This organization, which was largely the work of Dr. Fritz Weiss and Major (Ret.) Anton Ritter von Bolz, failed to win over the uncommitted Verbände and soon attracted the unfriendly attention of the authorities. It may well be that Bolz and Weiss had believed that Police Director Gareis would protect them, but Gareis was an effective policeman and a man who rarely exposed a flank to his foes. Despite the use of various cover names, the organizations were dissolved and Bolz, Weiss, and an indignant Streicher were placed under "protective arrest." By the time they were released, it was clear that an attempt to revive the "Kommando" was futile and that there were far more profitable channels for activity. The attempt to maintain the old central and regional headquarters was abandoned.[28]

The authorities had little luck, though, in completely suppressing National Socialist activities or in preventing small groups from continuing to exist as entities. Locating such groups was extremely difficult, and it was even harder to prove that a superficially innocent new organization was really a continuation of a portion of a banned one. For this reason, the Twentieth Company of SA Regiment München survived throughout the period of illegality as the "Falcon's Nest" (Horst der Falken), which was later called "Company Käss." The police were well aware of its existence and its identity and were able, from time to time, to make things hot for its leaders and members. In the end, though, the solid core was kept together and entered the new SA as a unit. Those remnants of Stosstrupp

[27] B, I, SA 1, 1493, A. Rosenberg, p. 216; II, MA103473, Bericht, PDM, VI/N, 15.1.1924; Röhm, *Geschichte*, pp. 323-24; Pölnitz, *Emir*, pp. 134-40.

[28] B, I, GSK 4, p. 14; GSK 43, p. 128; GSK 90, pp. 57, 563, 594, 634; GSK 95, p. 2; II, MA103457, PDN-F 6181/II, 27.12.1923.

Hitler that escaped the vigorous police investigation into the destruction at the *Münchener Post* also succeeded in maintaining their unity by claiming to be first a bowling club and later a Turnverein. Here, too, the police cannot be accused of negligence, for on some occasions the "Bowling Club" had to change its meeting place two or three times a week.[29]

Such racist organizations appeared everywhere and, when suppressed, promptly reappeared under a different guise. In Günzburg a racist organization adopted the name "Reichsbanner," either in an attempt to confuse the authorities by its nominal similarity to the leftist paramilitary organization or simply by chance. In Halbermoos, it was a "Racist Singing Club." In Würzburg the "Freischar Körner" was formed by National Socialist and Communist youths. In Regensburg Rudolf Loyer, an indefatigable National Socialist organizer, formed a "Racist Pathfinder Detachment." In Forchheim and Hof, the name was "Bund Schill" (after the Prussian officer who had been martyred by Napoleon). In Bamberg a group of racist women formed the "League of True German Women." In Naila it was a Turnverein; in Augsburg, a "Schlageterbund." These activities kept both the police and the Kampfbündler busy, without bringing either side a decisive victory.[30]

In general, the purely illegal organization was of little serious importance, except insofar as it helped to keep cadres together and sharpen the members' determination. The semi-legal movement and the legal movement were far more important in terms of retaining public attention and collecting and integrating new members. The semi-legal movement consisted largely of organizations that the authorities planned to ban, when enough evidence against them was collected. They were also organizations that the racist leaders hoped to palm off on the authorities as harmless or even apolitical. One of the most important of these semi-legal organizations was

[29] B, I, GSK 71, pp. 8-10; M. Inn. 73433, PDM 1001/1050/25, VI/N, 5.9.1925; II, MA100423, N/Nr. 17, 17.10.1924, p. 34; Kallenbach, *Mit Hitler*, pp. 213-14.

[30] The organizations mentioned above represent only a fraction of those that appeared in Bavaria alone in the period when the NSDAP was under ban, but even this short list gives some idea of the problems the authorities faced in their fight against the right radicals. An equally truncated list of sources follows. B, I, GSK 44, pp. 106, 116; II, MA100425, N/Nr. 16, 1.10.1924, p. 42; MA101235, PDN-F 2907/II, pp. 8-9; PDM, NBl. 8, 3.6.1924, p. 8; NBl. 13, 15.8.1924, pp. 6-7; IV, BuR, Bd. 36, Akt 1, Item 55; Lapo, Bd. 26a, Akt 3, Item 91.

the German Rifle and Hiking League (Deutscher Schützen- und Wanderbund). This league was particularly irritating to the authorities, because they were absolutely sure that it was a successor organization to Bund Oberland. However, proving this in a court of law was extremely difficult, even though the leaders of the two groups were identical, for the simple reason that the league had been formed well before Oberland was dissolved. It is not clear whether the league was formed with the possibility of dissolution in mind, or whether it was originally intended to be an auxiliary youth movement. In either case, it stood Oberland in good stead, providing a more or less secure shelter for its reconstitution.[31]

Central to the Kampfbund survival effort on the paramilitary front was the organization Frontring and its chief subsidiary Frontbann. These Verbände were established with a dual purpose. First of all they were to provide a substitute for the dissolved SA, and secondly they were to act as a counterbalance to the Bavarian government's new paramilitary organization, Notbann.[32] Originally, Frontring had a serious rival in the north Bavarian Wehrring, but this organization—which was sponsored by Oberland—was finally dropped as a result of a meeting of Völkisch paramilitary leaders at which Ludendorff presided. Frontring was to be the umbrella organization for all Verbände in the Reich that recognized Hitler, Albrecht von Graefe, and Ludendorff as the leaders of the Racist Movement. Ernst Röhm was its commander, and the Frontbann was its principal subordinate and executive Verband. In fact, Frontring lay very much in the shadow of Frontbann during their short term of existence.[33]

Frontbann was constructed, in theory at least, on a grandiose scale. In reality it does not seem to have ever developed beyond a very thin cadre. It was apparently entirely Röhm's idea and was frowned on by Hitler, Kriebel, and Weber. Röhm, with characteristic energy and that independent attitude towards Hitler that was to seal his fate in later years, went ahead anyway, and the three prisoners dropped their opposition—very possibly because they did

[31] B, I, GSK 44, p. 106; GSK 95, pp. 2-5; II, MA100423, N/Nr. 17, p. 35; MA100428, *MAA*, 23, 24.1.1925.

[32] For information on Notbann see Chapter XXIII, Section IV.

[33] B, II, MA100423, PDM, NBl. 16, p. 42; 17, p. 35; Brief: Röhm an Stützel, 27.8.1924. Abschrift zu "2019 L4, p. 52; MA101235, PDN-F 2425/II 24, p. 9; PDM, NBl. 14, 29.8.1924, pp. 11-12; PDN-F 5614/II, 25.9.1924.

not wish to reveal how helpless they were as long as they were in Landsberg prison. It was better to see a scheme of which they disapproved carried out with their implied consent than to see it carried out over their explicit veto.[34] However, Frontbann was stunted because Röhm was unable to win official support or even tolerance for his creation, and because he encountered suspicion and opposition even within the movement. In vain Röhm tried to persuade Seeckt and the Reichswehr that his new creation should be protected as a valuable adjunct to the army. At the same time, he tried to persuade Stützel that Bavaria needed the Frontbann to counter the Communists, but the Putsch had taught the Bavarian authorities a lesson, and Stützel refused to accord Röhm the legality he sought. Instead Stützel jailed as many Frontbann leaders as he could find and crippled the organization in Bavaria.

Röhm was prepared to fight on this front if he had to do so, and he managed to maintain his organization on the national level, partly openly and partly covertly, keeping a cadre active even in Bavaria. He could not, however, win the battle with his own colleagues and allies. From the beginning, Oberland wished to know nothing of Frontbann. All of the Völkisch parliamentarians and both civilian factions of the Racist Movement looked on it and Röhm with suspicion if not enmity, and in the end even Ludendorff distanced himself from it. The result was that when Hitler was released from prison he was able to eliminate Frontbann and its embarrassingly independent leader with one blow by appointing Röhm to head the new SA and ordering him to dissolve and absorb Frontbann. Röhm, predictably, resigned both as SA Führer and as Frontbann Führer, since he could scarcely lead an organization dedicated to Hitler into sudden opposition to him or destroy one he himself had created. As Röhm retreated to Bolivia to sulk, Hitler could be well satisfied with himself. Röhm had done much to keep the paramilitary cadre of the Racist Movement alive and active, but both the man and the organization had become too independent. In one swift operation, Hitler demonstrated his appreciation to Röhm, drove him from the movement, and gathered in the men Röhm had saved or won over. It was a master-stroke, whether Hitler acted with Machiavellian skill or simply at the prompting of the amaz-

[34] B, I, SA 1, 1633, Ludendorff, p. 519; II, MA100423, PDM N/Nr. 16, 1.10.1924, pp. 41-42; MA101235, PDM, NB1. 15, 17.9.1924, p. 7; MA101248, PDN-F 8160/II, pp. 9-10; Röhm, *Geschichte*, pp. 321-27.

ing political instinct that led him again and again to eliminate any person or factor not completely under his control.[35]

The battle of the illegal and the semilegal organizations—for Frontbann itself was not banned in Bavaria, although all its member organizations were[36]—had been inconclusive. Both sides had won victories and suffered losses. Had the fight gone on, the odds were with the government. However, the fight did not continue because developments on other political fronts brought it to a premature end.

III. *The Legal Movement*

Originally, the new, legal successor organizations to the NSDAP were local or regional in nature. However, in the face of the oncoming elections, they soon united under the name "Racist Block" (Völkischer Block). Into this block went the German Workers' Party (Deutsche Arbeiterpartei), the German League (Deutscher Bund), and the Racist League (Völkischer Bund), while more specialized organizations like Wilhelm Stark's "Catholic League for National Politics" (Katholikenbund für nationale Politik) were affiliated with it, as were racist parents' groups, medical groups, pharmacists' groups, and racist trade unions among others.[37] The candidates chosen by the new block clearly indicated its character. Dr. Roth and Graf Treuberg represented the "old" NSDAP; Pöhner represented the monarchical wing of the radical Racist Movement; Dr. Alexander Glaser and Dr. Rudolf Buttmann were recruits from the German Nationalist Party; and Walther Hemmeter came from Bund Wiking by way of the Kampfbund. Here was a strong admixture of new and old that indicated the way in which Hitler's following had grown and changed in the wake of the Putsch.[38]

Originally, almost all former NSDAP leaders more or less accepted the block's program and turned their attention to the fight

[35] B, I, SA 1, 1627, p. 90; 1633, Ludendorff, p. 520; Adolf Ächter, p. 575; II, MA100423, pp. 11-12, 28, 29, 53-54; MA103473, PDN-F 8160/II, p. 9; Seeckt Papers, Stück 281, Rabenau Notes, p. 23; Röhm, *Geschichte*, pp. 322-43.

[36] Frontkriegerbund, Altreichsflagge, Deutsch-Völkischer Offiziersbund, etc.

[37] B, II, MA100423, N/Nr. 17, p. 34; MA101235, PDN-F 2907/II, pp. 9-10; PDM, NB1. 10, p. 10; PDN-F 3822/II, p. 27; 1531, p. 8; 4668/II, pp. 14-15; PDM, NB1. 14, p. 11; MA101248, PDM NB1. 18, p. 12; PDN-F 6100/II, pp. 19-21.

[38] B, I, M. Inn. 73694, PDM VI/N, 8.1.1924.

for political survival and influence. At this stage the fight against external foes overshadowed all internal quarrels.[39] Once the elections were over, however, this superficial unity was shattered in a struggle over policy and power. Aside from lesser quarrels and early sparring around in the middle of the ring, two serious contenders developed. The first was the Völkischer Block and those subsidiary organizations that remained loyal to it. The other was the Grossdeutsche Volksgemeinschaft (GVG). The Völkischer Block was, in general, more moderate and gradual in approach and more parliamentary in outlook than the GVG. Its leaders were mostly drawn from the outspoken "civilians" of the party and seem to have included a high percentage of the leaders drawn from outside the old NSDAP. The GVG, headed by such rabid activists as Hermann Esser and Julius Streicher, centered in the major cities of München and Nürnberg. It struck not merely a more violent, but also a more egalitarian, tone and scorned the leaders of the Völkischer Block as being "doctors and academics" who were alien to the NSDAP and had embraced parliamentarianism. The two factions fought bitterly and with varying success, while many followers dropped out of the movement altogether. Pöhner went his own way in solitary splendor, but in the end, together with Dr. Ottmar Rutz—another new recruit who found the National Socialists too radical for his taste—he joined the German Nationalist Party, where he was far more at home in most respects.[40]

The upshot of this long and involved feud was that no single figure emerged who could effectively control the movement, although most members of both factions, and of the Frontbann, paid at least lip service to Ludendorff. They clearly did not see him as their political leader, however. This situation meant that when Hitler, whose support all factions claimed and on whom none could depend, came out of Landsberg, he was accepted by all groups as their leader—although each hoped that he would side with them against their foes.[41]

[39] B, II, MA103473, PDM, Abt. VI/N, 15.1.1924.

[40] NA, T120, 5570, p. K592133.

[41] The struggle within the party is treated at length, if not always clearly, in official reports, although more "inside" information would be helpful. The general outline of the fight and the ups and downs of the two sides are illustrated in the documents cited hereafter. B, I, GSK 4, p. 14; II, MA99522, 14.3.1924, p. 8; MA100423, N/Nr. 17, 17.1.1925, p. 34; MA101235, PDN-F 4906/II, p. 14; PDN-F 2907/II, p. 8; PDM, NB1. 9, p. 10; NB1. 10, pp. 9-10; NB1. 11, pp. 7-11; PDN-F 3822/II, pp. 25-29;

IV. *Hitler's Return*

From the moment of his arrest, Hitler became a burning question for all factions of the Racist Movement, for the Bavarian government, and to a lesser extent for every political party in Germany. For the racists he became the symbol of their hates and hopes. For the Bavarian authorities he became a man who had taken the wrong turn and changed from a national leader to a nihilist demagogue. For the other political parties he became, on the Right, a man to watch with suspicion and fear but not to provoke unnecessarily, and, on the Left, a whipping boy to be trotted out on all occasions where he could be used as a bad example or identified with their foes. Neither the Right nor the Left, nor even the Bavarian government, however, saw him as a really serious political factor. He was Napoleon III after Boulogne or Napoleon I after Thermidor. Only in the eyes of the faithful was he more than a warning of the dangers inherent in right radicalism or a useful weapon in the daily skirmishes between Right and Left. In his own eyes, Hitler remained the man of destiny, and he wrote his personal political manifesto and creed, *Mein Kampf*, during his enforced retirement. At the same time, after a tentative essay in controlling the movement from prison, he wisely withdrew from all political action.

Outside the walls his stature increased daily as no one arose to take advantage of his eclipse. Every little quarrel, every petty jibe at a comrade made it clear that the movement could not spare him. Even had the leaders wished to forget this fact, their followers drove home the point at meeting after meeting by their insistence upon loyalty to Hitler, by their cheers when his name was mentioned. Here and there a leader of strong personal ambitions, like Streicher, may have toyed with the possibility of independence, but nothing came of such stray thoughts, if they existed. The very existence of the Völkischer Block made loyalty to Hitler an absolute necessity to the GVG, and the same was true in reverse. Esser stressed again and again that his policy was Hitler's, and Streicher

---

PDN-F 4906/II, p. 14; PDM, NB1. 14, pp. 9-10; NB1. 15, p. 6; PDN-F 5614/II, pp. 18-22; MA101248, Rk. O. In. 107, pp. 26-28; PDN-F 6100/II, pp. 18-20; PDM, NB1. 18, pp. 10-12; NB1. 20, pp. 10-13, 16; PDN-F 8160/II, pp. 2-4; MA102141, HMB 261, M/F, p. 2; HMB 1458, Ofr., p. 2; HMB 1145, Schw., pp. 1-2; HMB 1291, Obb., p. 2; HMB 1195, Schw., pp. 1-3; HMB 1263, Schw., p. 3; Röhm, *Geschichte*, p. 328; Pölnitz, *Emir*, p. 138.

claimed to be Hitler's anointed deputy for northern Bavaria. Ernst Woltereck, one of GVG's Münchner deputies, called for public avowal of loyalty to Hitler and won a unanimous vote of confidence. On the other side of the fence, Dr. Buttmann, the archetype of the new, parliamentary National Socialist, was always careful to take a firm "Hitler" line, defending the Putsch staunchly and indicating that he had cleared all of his moves with the "martyr." Major Bolz, in attacking Streicher, accused him of disloyalty, even lèse majesté, in regard to Hitler.[42] As the representative of the "third force" in the movement, Röhm chimed in with the pithy statement: " 'If even a General Ludendorff can place himself under the Corporal Hitler, so can everyone else accept Hitler as a leader.' "[43] Much as they might belabor one another, none of his paladins so much as whispered a word against Hitler. The freeing of Hitler was a major topic in the racist press. The mere rumor that he was to be freed was enough to send a ripple of restless energy through the little racist organizations throughout Bavaria. The tension of waiting built up the sense of expectancy and the spirit of loyalty to Hitler in much the same manner that the stage-managed delay in his appearance at public functions was later to drive crowds into a frenzy. The stage was set. The delay in the appearance of the star only added to his lustre.[44]

Meanwhile, the Bavarian government found itself in the unenviable position of having to decide what to do about Hitler. Anything they did was sure to bring down the roof over their heads in the form of bitter denunciation from one side or the other. The Knilling government, secure in the knowledge that it was not long for this world, had been able to ignore the problem and refuse to consider racist petitions and demands for Hitler's release. In fact some ministers wished to appeal portions of the verdict. The matter then slumbered during the spring and summer, except for Bavarian inquiries in Austria regarding Hitler's citizenship and the possibility of expulsion, which resulted in an agreement with the provincial

---

[42] B, I, *GSK* 44, pp. 107; II, MA101235, PDM, NB1. 9, p. 10; PDM, NB1. 11, p. 7; PDN-F 3822/II, pp. 25-29; PDN-F, 5131, "Extrablatt"; MA101248, PDM, NB1. 18, pp. 10-11; PDN-F 8160/II, p. 4; Jochmann, Werner, *Nationalsozialismus und Revolution: Ursprung und Geschichte der NSDAP in Hamburg, 1922-1923*, Frankfurt, 1963, pp. 77-78. Hereafter cited as Jochmann, *Nationalsozialismus*.

[43] B, II, MA102141, HMB 1301, Ofr., p. 1.

[44] B, II, PDM, NB1. 8, p. 7; MA102141, HMB 1291, Obb., p. 6; HMB 1365, Obb., p. 3.

government of Oberösterreich to accept Hitler as an Austrian citizen if Bavaria deported him.

In September, the question flared up again when Penal Chamber I of the Landesgericht München took up the question of whether or not Hitler, Weber, and Kriebel were eligible for parole as of 1 October 1924.[45] The court decided that Hitler and Kriebel were eligible, but that the decision about Dr. Weber would have to wait until it was clear whether or not he was incriminated by evidence in a current trial against former Oberländer for illegal continuation of their organization. The Cabinet then opened up the question of whether or not an appeal should be made against this decision and whether or not the deportation of Hitler should be pressed. Dr. Matt favored an appeal if there was a fair chance of its being successful. He believed that the question of deportation should not be raised now, for fear of pulling together the opposition. Gürtner told the Cabinet that he intended to appeal. The three chief offenders must be held at least until the Frontbann Trial was settled.[46] He would use as grounds the flagrant violation of visiting privileges of which the three were guilty. The Cabinet then empowered Gürtner to proceed with his appeal on the basis of post-Hitler Trial evidence, and asked him to let them know if rejection was pending so that they could consider other action.[47]

By early November it was clear that the government was fighting a rear-guard action, for Held informed Haniel that there would be no decision on Hitler until after the Reichstag elections, so that his interference in these elections was out of the question. Held planned that, should the courts not grant parole to Hitler, the government would offer to pardon him if he would agree to leave Bavaria. Should the courts free him, however, the government could not deport Hitler in view of the Austrian refusal to accept him.[48]

[45] B, II, MA99522, 12.4. 1924, pp. 3-5; MA100427, Landesregierung für Oberösterreich A/2 Z1. 2335/2, 20.4.1924; NA, T120, 5570, pp. K591745, K591989.

[46] Before the Staatsgerichtshof in Leipzig. In the end, the trial was never held, probably because of lack of firm evidence. Röhm, *Geschichte*, p. 334.

[47] B, II, MA99522, 27.9.1924, pp. 2-4; NA, T120, 5570, p. K592011.

[48] The Bavarian government had meanwhile been informed that, despite the acceptance of Hitler as an Austrian citizen by the Oberösterreichische Landesregierung, the Austrian federal government had ordered its border police to reject him or expel him as a stateless person. (B, II, MA100423, [M. Inn.] 2032 z 93, 10.10.1924 an M. Äuss.) The final rejection of Hitler by the Austrians came on 18.6.1925, when the Austrian government in-

The Bavarian government could not be responsible for his being interned as a stateless person. Held also believed that the movement had declined enough to have greatly reduced its danger and that Hitler would not be able to put it back together again—a view which was, to be fair to Held, shared by the Reichskommissar for public security.[49]

On 18 December, the Cabinet again considered Hitler's release, this time in a manner that made it clear that the ministers now accepted it as an accomplished fact. Their primary attention was devoted to ensuring that there would be no public demonstration on his behalf and no upsurge of racist activity. Almost immediately thereafter the Bavarian Supreme Court (Oberste Landesgericht) justified the Cabinet's attitude by rejecting the chief prosecutor's objections to the paroling of the Putsch ringleaders. The Putschists were promptly set free on Saturday, 20 December, and returned quietly to München, where Hitler, after a brief vacation on the Baltic, settled down to the task of cleaning out the Augean stables, while Kriebel sank back into the obscurity of private life. Dr. Weber, still involved in controversy over his responsibility for the revival of Oberland, was not released until more than a month later.[50]

The Bavarian government had, however, been preparing for some time a Parthian shot to dampen the joy of the right radicals. In a clearly calculated move, aimed partly at disarming leftist criticism of Hitler's release and partly at showing that the government put Hitler on a par with other political offenders, the government released along with Hitler the last leftists still held on general political charges stemming from the Republic of Councils period. Hitler's face must have been a study in horror and rage when he learned that Mühsam, Olschewski, and Fechenbach would accompany him on the road to freedom. The Bavarian government could scarcely have thought of a scheme that would more effectively curdle

---

formed the Bavarian government that, at Hitler's request, the Upper Austrian government had released him from Austrian citizenship. (MA100427, Bundeskanzleramt A.A. 13. 985-17.)

[49] B, II, MA101235, Rk. O. In. 106, pp. 14-15; NA, T120, 5570, p. K592071. Colonel Kuenzer (Rk. O.), however, also recognized that the mass of the racists looked to Hitler to perform just that task. See MA101248, Rk. O. In. 109, p. 34.

[50] B, II, MA99522, 18.12.1924, p. 23; NA, T120, 5570, pp. K592158, K592161, K592170, K592211.

racist joy. Yet, for this cuckoo's egg Hitler could thank primarily his old—if sometimes unreliable—patron and future Reichsjustizminister, Gürtner, who was pursuing his usual inscrutable and unpredictable course between practical support of the racists and oral disapproval of their activities.[51]

Hitler soon found that he might be free, but that he was not untrammeled. At first the Bavarian government clung to the state of emergency, which enabled it to ban not only the NSDAP but also the KPD. This meant that in his early months of freedom, Hitler could only work underground. The state of emergency, however, became an albatross around the neck of the Bavarian government. When the socialist-dominated governments of Prussia and Saxony dropped their bans against the NSDAP, the nationalist Bavarian government could hardly do less than follow suit—even if the Reichstag had not been threatening to override it on this matter. The result was that in order to save elements of the Ausnahmezustand, the Bavarians gave way on the parties, and the NSDAP was refounded by Adolf Hitler on 28 February 1925.[52]

Having given way in theory, the government continued to hold its line in practice, at least where Hitler was concerned. Held made his attitude plain during the debates on the state of emergency:

"... Hitler himself cannot be trusted very far despite his solemn protestations. He will return to his old ways if certain influences become active, which seek to push him into the old path. He is making efforts to find financial patrons in any case. In this regard he has declared that his goals are only to be reached by way of a civil war.[53]

The result of this evaluation, which encountered no opposition in the Cabinet, was a swift crack-down on Hitler when he gave way to the temptation to attack the government in a speech in the Bürgerbräukeller on 27 February 1925. Held had, earlier that day, expressed the hope that Hitler had become "wiser" as a result of his imprisonment, adding that if this were not the case, future appearances must be prevented. Hitler was not "wiser" and the gov-

[51] B, II, MA99522, 27.3.1924, p. 2; 18.12.1924, p. 23; NA, T120, 5570, pp. K592163-64.

[52] B, II, MA99523, 23.1.1925, pp. 21-29; MA101248, pp. 37-38; *Führer Lexikon*, p. 376.

[53] B, II, MA99523, 23.1.1925, p. 22.

ernment promptly muzzled him. A directive was issued to the local authorities to ban each Hitler speech individually.[54] Needless to say, the National Socialists wept bitter tears and insisted upon their rights to freedom of speech. Frick, in an impassioned letter to the Bavarian government, asserted that the ban was illegal. The Reich Ministry of Justice did not seem perturbed by this violation of Hitler's rights, and the Reich Ministry of the Interior had already—in a case involving Soviet agents—taken the view that the free speech rights of the Constitution only protected citizens and not foreigners. On the grounds that not only rallies where Hitler himself was to speak but also other National Socialist rallies were forbidden, Gürtner changed tack again and questioned the justice of preventing National Socialist meetings and muzzling Hitler, while allowing the Communists free rein. However, at least partially because of an indiscretion on his part, Gürtner did not make any progress. The ban remained in effect.[55]

As time went on, Hitler was clearly working hard and with considerable success to rebuild his party. His hostility towards the government was also unabated and was expressed with increasing freedom and violence in the *Völkischer Beobachter*. As a result the government of Oberbayern and the minister of the interior both wished to revoke his parole, since a trial for treason would only give him a broader audience for his tirades. These proposals never got off the ground, but neither did further attempts to allow Hitler to speak in public. He therefore found himself free, but deprived of one of his most effective political weapons, his own persuasive tongue.[56]

In early 1927, however, the Social Democrats came hurrying to Hitler's assistance. It is a trifle surprising, if not amusing, to see the doughty socialist Reichstag Deputy Alwin Saenger as a St. George rushing to defend the maiden Hitler from the Bavarian dragon, but the maneuver was certainly successful. The Bavarian government could fight off the demands of the radical Right and Left, even when the former were supported by the moderate Right, but when

[54] It is interesting that one reason advanced for muzzling Hitler was the damage he did to the tourist trade. B, II, MA99523, 27.2.1925, p. 19; MA100427, M. Inn. 2251 ab an M. Äuss., 4.5.1927; MA103476, p. 18.

[55] B, II, MA99523, 27.3.1925, p. 22; 20.4.1925, p. 7; MA100427, Frick an Min. Rat, 24.3.1925; M. Äuss. (?) 7954; Gürtner an Held, 24.4.1925.

[56] B, II, MA100425, Reg. Obb. 328, 19.11.1925, p. 161; MA100427, M. Inn. 2032 z 1, Abdruck an Min. Justiz, 8.1.1926.

the weight of the SPD was added to that of the Communists—who had begun their campaign as early as August 1924—they found their backs to the wall. The racist Deputy von Graefe introduced a proposal in the Reichstag against the speech ban, indicating that the Social Democrats also disapproved of it. One of the Bavarian envoys to the Reichsrat reported as follows on the subsequent developments:

> Then the Social Democratic Deputy Saenger spoke against Bavaria and went rather far back, insofar as he reviewed the Hitler Putsch and its preparations. In conclusion he also then declared the ban was inadmissible and spoke in favor of phrasing the proposal so as to [declare] that all such preventive bans should not be issued.[57]

On 27 March 1927, the Reichstag passed the von Graefe proposal, as amended in committee, so that Saenger—who with the best of intentions had insisted that "Captain" Oestreicher, the Oberland leader, be commissioned—had now won the dubious honor of unleashing Hitler's flaming oratory. The Bavarian government was forced to make the best of a bad bargain: it agreed to allow Hitler to speak in public again in return for his promise that the party would follow no illegal goals, that Hitler and the party would cause no disruption of public order, that the first rally at which Hitler spoke would be outside of München, and that the government would be justified in taking action against Hitler if any of these conditions were violated. Thus Hitler's last shackles were stricken off over the vehement objections of the Bavarian government, and the new Siegfried was able to march off into the future with the aid of those who considered themselves to be his most effective foes.[58]

[57] B, II, MA100427, Imhoff an M. Inn., 13.1.1927, p. 3 (Antrag 2620, Reichstag, III Wahlperiode, 1924-26).

[58] It is true that the ban could probably not have been maintained much longer under any circumstances, but the SPD, which has often been most unkind to others of Hitler's unconscious or reluctant "promoters," should not forget that it, too, gave him a hand on at least this one occasion. Certainly, the SPD acted with its own interests in mind—but so, too, did others who have been castigated for similar actions. If nothing else, this incident indicates clearly to what an extent Hitler was underestimated by everyone, on Right and Left alike. Had he been seen in 1926 as the greatest menace ever to the SPD and the Republic, it is doubtful if Saenger would have spoken his piece, much as the SPD might treasure free speech and believe that its own virtue would eventually be rewarded by success.

The new National Socialist Party and the new Hitler were on their way to success, glory, and disaster.

v. *Conclusion*

The period after the Putsch was highlighted by Hitler's increasing significance. The inability of the party's satraps either to cooperate with one another or to hold the "foot soldiers" of the movement behind them became painfully clear. Some of them were effective speakers, and some were talented organizers. A handful even united these two characteristics to a considerable degree, but none approached Hitler in either sphere. Most important of all, none had the personal magnetism needed to dominate his fellows without alienating them or the passionate belief in his own invincibility that marks the true wonder-worker and empire-builder. Hitler's absence from the movement sealed its dependence upon him.

The interim period also showed that no existing institution was prepared to make the kind of appeal to the mass of the racist followers that would bring them into a different and less radical path. Only an organization that placed nation above class could appeal to these people, and there was no such organization available on the government side of the fence, except those which for one reason or another were moving into eclipse.[59] During this same period the Putschists learned that they could no longer deceive the Bavarian government into helping destroy it, so they dropped all pretense of anything but hostility towards it. This change is reflected in the drop in interest in national defense, which had once been a very important element in all groups within the Patriotic Movement, in favor of an essentially internal program. The SA was no longer to be a portion of a national army to defend the fatherland, but a tool to conquer the fatherland.[60]

At the same time, the failure of the German authorities to cooperate against the movement was made painfully clear and boded ill for the future. While the Prussians, Saxons, Württembergers, and Badenese banned the party, the Bavarians tolerated it. When the Bavarians banned the party, the Prussians, Saxons, and others tolerated it. When the SPD was attacking the party vigorously, the Bavarian government was acting against the SPD. When the Bavarian government sought to muzzle Hitler, the SPD came to his aid. In any case, the attacks on the right radical Verbände that

[59] See Chapter XXIII.
[60] NA, EAP 105/7a, WKK VII, Ib 1505 Geh.

marked late 1923 and 1924 were an aid rather than a hindrance to the NSDAP, for it could claim to be just another political party and thus was more or less immune to accusations of "secrecy" (Geheimbündelei). This meant that, since it offered all the advantages and few of the disadvantages of the Verbände, it tended to pick up the human chips.

Two other crucial facts were established at this time. The first was that, in a democracy in a time of peace, the right radicals were correct when they argued that an idea and its carriers could not be suppressed by force, although it could be forced underground and its carriers reduced in numbers. The movement reacted to suppression like quicksilver. It broke instantly into thousands of individual fragments. As soon as the pressure was eased, however, these fragments tended to flow together to form a unit. Finally, the rise and fall of the radical Right's voting strength clearly followed the rise and fall of passions regarding the Putsch and, far more significantly, the state of the economy and the hopes or despairs of the masses. It was clear from the immediate aftermath of the Putsch that there was a reservoir of people who, under pressure, would seek salvation in the Racist Movement, while the decline in voting strength that marked the latter portion of the year indicated that the removal of such pressures would result in the return of these people to less activist political positions. The new NSDAP was the cadre for a revolution, but only a serious economic crisis or crises could flesh out its divisions and make the party's menace to the existing state more than a potential one.

23.

THE VERBÄNDE BEYOND
HITLER'S ORBIT

I. *Introduction*

After the Putsch there were three basic reactions within those Verbände that had not joined the Kampfbund or supported the Putsch. The first reaction was a general search by the senior leaders for balance in the new political situation. This search did not take the same form or direction in each Verband, nor did it result in the same new stance, but the process occurred in all of them. Either a restatement of existing policy in new terms or a new policy was necessary. The second development or reaction was what might be called the sifting of souls. Those persons who favored the Kampfbund tended to leave organizations that were not clearly identified with Hitler, even though they might be friendly towards him, while those who disliked Hitler tended to leave those Verbände that moved nearer to him. Some members of most Verbände seem to have dropped out of the movement because they were sick and tired of what they considered to be useless squabbling among the leaders or because they disapproved of the introduction of politics into the Verbände. Closely associated with the attitude of the drop-outs was a third phenomenon found in most of the Verbände: the demand for an end to politics and the unification of all paramilitary organizations under a single apolitical leadership—although even this apolitical organization would have had definite political overtones, to judge by the remarks of at least some of its proponents.[1]

Aside from these general internal reactions, two major questions of external policy affected the Verbände decisively. These were their relations with the Bavarian government (including the

---

[1] See the discussion of the individual Verbände below.

Reichswehr) and their relations with the Kampfbund. Here again, the reactions to the Putsch, to the policy of the government, and to the policy of the Kampfbund's successor organizations was far from uniform, but no Verband could ignore the two poles of the active political spectrum.

The government posed a particularly knotty problem for the so-called neutral or loyal Verbände.[2] Whereas before the Putsch, the government had looked on the Verbände with a reasonably complacent, if not always approving eye, this was no longer the case. The new attitude of suspicion resulted in two serious blows against the entire Verbände system. The first of these was the disarmament of the Verbände, and the second was the creation of a new organization, Notbann, to take over their paramilitary functions.[3] Each of these actions called for reactions on the part of the Verbände, and these were forthcoming.

However, for most of the Verbände, relations with the Kampfbund were almost as serious a problem as relations with the government. This was particularly true because the Putsch resulted in an immediate and instinctive hostility on the part of the Kampfbündler for those who had not supported them. A sharp line was now drawn between "us" and "them" at all levels, whereas before the Putsch it had normally been confined to the higher echelons. Even more serious, the Putsch enabled the Kampfbund to pre-empt the label "racist," not only by claiming it for themselves because they were the most advanced, vociferous, and activist carriers of this doctrine, but also because it was thrust upon them, as a term of opprobrium, by their foes. The Putsch had been an action of the Racist Bands. Therefore those who carried it out were racists, and those who did not take part in it or who opposed it were not racists. This was superficial and inaccurate thinking, but it was simple, clear, and therefore appealing to the masses on all sides. The end result was that, since the racists were identified with the Putsch and the Putsch in turn was identified with Hitler—for in Germany it was always the Hitler Putsch rather than the Beer Hall Putsch—Hitler became the embodiment of the Racist Movement for most Germans. Needless to say, this development raised major problems for organizations that considered themselves to be "Völkisch" but

[2] Some claimed to be one; some claimed to be the other; some claimed to be both. See below.

[3] See Chapter XIX, Section II.

did not accept Hitler's leadership and rejected at least some of his ideas.

The result was the struggle for souls mentioned above, which paralleled the struggle that plagued primitive Christianity after its initial triumph within the Roman Empire or the new Protestant churches after the first phases of the Reformation. The Verbände that did not belong to the Kampfbund had to fight to hold their own members against the lure of the Kampfbund and its clear-cut activism, even if they did not try to attract Kampfbündler. In this struggle the dissenting Verbände suffered the disadvantages of a defensive position. Hitler had proven his orthodoxy and militancy by seeking to create a racist government. His opponents had the far more difficult task of proving that they were racist or even patriotic after having either refused to support Hitler or opposed him. The history of the Verbände during 1924 is very largely the story of how they adjusted to the new situation and new pressures. The way of the moderate or neutral is often harder than that of the transgressor.

II. *Radical Verbände*

In many ways Reichsflagge faced the most difficult problems after the Putsch, although it enjoyed some advantages the other radicals lacked. On the shadow side was the stress on the group because of its previous membership in the Kampfbund and the sympathy many of its members felt for its former leader Röhm, and for Hitler. On the positive side was the fact that Reichsflagge was well dug in throughout much of northern Bavaria and enjoyed the support of both the director of police in Nürnberg and the provincial president of Mittelfranken. Equally important was Heiss' access to the business and industrial community. This access gave him a practical monopoly on financial support from these circles in Nürnberg but apparently depended in large part on his remaining estranged from the Kampfbund.

It is clear that there were pressures on Heiss from both directions and that he wavered among various policies during the days immediately following the Putsch. Initially, borne forward by the indignation of his followers and racist and patriotic circles in Nürnberg, Heiss signed the hostile ultimatum of the city's Verbände to Kahr. On 16 November he officially withdrew his support of Kahr. After the first wave of emotionalism subsided, though, Heiss sang a different tune, and by October-November 1924 he was stoutly defending Kahr's stand in the Putsch.[4] Similarly, Heiss originally opposed any attempt to establish a new umbrella organization to control all paramilitary activities but later agreed to support the Notbann. Equally characteristic was the fact that he then attempted to maintain full autonomy within this organization to the exasperation of Ministerialrat Pirner, the Ministry of the Interior's Landespolizei and military expert, without, however, taking any overt action that could be read as direct defiance of the government.

At no time, not even immediately after the Putsch, did Heiss intend to sacrifice his independence to Hitler, and he even seems to have attempted to take over at least the SA at that time. Thereafter came a political Watschentanz in which Heiss and the Kampfbündler both attacked Kahr while missing no opportunity to pummel one another with words or even fists. Their relations never improved much, with the result that Heiss found himself in an extremely awkward situation after the Machtergreifung.[5] The tension between Reichsflagge and Kampfbund is most clearly indicated by their struggles for members. The powerful Reichsflagge Ortsgruppe in Nürnberg, the group's headquarters, lost some 500 members to Altreichsflagge, a new organization that was closely related to the Kampfbund, and recognized Hitler's primacy.[6] The same thing happened in Würzburg, and in Hof the Ortsgruppe was divided in half by the reactions to the Putsch. Major (Ret.) Albrecht Jahreis, who was personally very popular, was able to prevent an open break, but the organization was clearly seriously weakened by the bitter differences of view. In some other localities, National Socialists joined Reichsflagge, whether because of differences with their leaders or to preserve some semblance of their organization. At the same time, Reichsflagge managed to form some new Ortsgruppen during 1924 and absorbed the bulk of the

[4] B, I, GSK 100, p. 24; SA 1, 1450, PDN-F, Abt. II, 7.10.1924; 6.11.1924; BuR, Bd. 36, Akt 1, Item 35.

[5] B, I, SA 1, 1450, passim; II, MA100411, M. Inn. zu Nr. 2020 u 2, Abschrift; Aktenvermerk, 4407, 7.4.1925.

[6] Apparently the Putsch precipitated a break that had been in the making ever since Röhm had left Reichsflagge in October 1923 and that was based not only on political differences but also on a personal clash between Heiss and Dr. Karl Braun, a local leader in Nürnberg. The break also apparently reflected a reaction of the younger and less socially elevated members of the Ortsgruppe against the many former officers who belonged to and dominated the organization there. B, II, MA101235, PDN-F 3822/II, 22.7.1924.

Nürnberg Bund Bayern und Reich in the late spring. The upshot of the contest was that Reichsflagge endured but was in reduced strength. It had lost its base south of the Danube when Röhm defected, and it was now weakened within its major sphere of operations and had lost most of its appeal to racist activists.[7] By 1925, Reichsflagge seemed safe but static, with sufficient political support in conservative circles not only to prevent the government from taking direct action against it, even at Pirner's urging, but also to discourage the federal government from action against Heiss.[8]

Next to Reichsflagge, Wiking was probably the most significant of the unaffiliated radical Verbände, although it had always been comparatively weak in Bavaria. In the period immediately following the Putsch, its power was temporarily enhanced by the presence along the Bavarian-Thuringian border of considerable elements of Brigade Ehrhardt (as its mobilized units were called) from north Germany. Ehrhardt's influence was still further increased by the fact that the Jungdo Regiment in the Grenzschutz was very largely commanded by his followers. Finally, Ehrhardt had succeeded, in the months leading up to the Putsch, in allying himself with several Bavarian Verbände: Blücherbund, Regiment Chiemgau of Bund Bayern und Reich, Frankenland, and Jungdo's Bavarian elements.[9]

The Putsch jolted Ehrhardt, spoiling his schemes for a general German rising. It is obvious that he did his best to fish in troubled waters afterwards, but the precise nature and scope of his plans is unclear. Despite having refused to take part in the Putsch, he subsequently sought to persuade the members of the Kampfbund, and especially the students of München, that he was the man to take the torch from Hitler's hand. Even after it was reasonably clear that he was not going to succeed in this bid to take over the Racist

[7] B, I, SA 1, 1450, PDN-F 4253/II, 21.7.1924; Aufklärungsblatt d. Kampfbundes; GSK 43, pp. 308ff; GSK 44, pp. 102, 138ff, 153, 229; GSK 90, p. 561; II, MA101235, PDN-F 2907/II, pp. 8-9; IV, BuR, Bd. 36, Akt 1, Item 48, Truspeck an Bundesleitung, 25.11.923; Akt 2, Item 8; Item 16; NA, EAP 105/7a, WKK VII 34365/Ib Nr. 6285.

[8] B, II, MA100411, PDN-F 319/II, Abschrift; M. Inn., Zu Nr. 2020 u 2, Abschrift, 16.3.1925; Aktenvermerk, 4407, 7.4.1925; M. Äuss. 8823, Abdruck, 24.4. 1925.

[9] B, IV, Lapo, Bd. 17, Akt 4, Jungdo Rgt., B.E.J. Nr. 29/23; Bd. 26a, Akt 5, Gr. Sch. IIIc, PNB Ofr., Abschnitt Kühne, 221/23, pp. 1-3; NA, EAP 105/7a, Reichswehr Lagebericht, 12.12.1923; GP, A, Fritz Warnecke, 2.12.1954.

Movement, he told a group of Wiking leaders from all of south Germany that his goals were the same as those of the National Socialists and that he would, in good time, unleash a far better prepared Putsch than theirs. His sincerity in this regard is given added weight by the preparations his organization had been making in north Germany since the late spring of 1923. In the same direction lay the patching-up of his long-standing quarrel with Ludendorff and his claim that he failed to appear at the Hitler Trial because his testimony would have been damaging for the defendants. At the same time, Ehrhardt worked hard to keep his lines to Kahr, Seisser, and the Bavarian government open, despite their increasing suspicion of him. He also sought to persuade financial and industrial circles in Nürnberg of his reliability and moderation in order to obtain money from them.[10]

None of his twists and turns saved Ehrhardt from serious losses of manpower, and they may, indeed, have caused some of these losses. The Bayreuth Ortsgruppe went over to Hitler immediately after the Putsch. Sometime later, the Bamberg Ortsgruppe dissolved itself, most of its members going over to a newly-founded Frankenbund. Even within the national and Bavarian headquarters there were defections. Lieutenant (Ret.) Friedrich Friedmann, who had long been active as a leader in München dropped out of Wiking and out of politics, and in mid-summer, Lieutenant Senior Grade (Ret.) Kautter, a key Ehrhardt deputy, broke with his leader. The end result was that by early 1925, Bund Wiking was moribund in Bavaria. It never recovered from this decline, for soon afterwards Commander Ehrhardt dissolved his organizations and abandoned politics, a decision that seems to have been as much the result of a turn towards moderation in his personal views as of his distaste for Hitler who increasingly dominated right radical politics.[11]

---

[10] B, I, GSK 43, p. 230; GSK 44, pp. 184, 190ff; GSK 73, pp. 40-41; GSK 100, p. 24; SA 1, 1490, Police Timetable, 13.11.1923; II, MA100424, R. M. Inn. VII 1038, 24.2. 1924; Kahr, R/Nr. 7016, 1.2.1924; Knilling, 2114, 27.1.1924; MA101249, Rk. o. In. 99, pp. 23-24; MA102141, HMB 172, Obb., p. 3; HMB 629, p. 5; MA104221, Pittinger an Seisser; IV, BuR, Bd. 36, Akt 2, Item 20; Lapo, Bd. 26a, Akt 3, Item 74; NA, EAP 105/7a, WKK VII 32784/Ib 6064; 33425/Ib 6123; 34365/Ib 6285; NA, T120, 5569, pp. K591591, 591596-97, K591608. See also Chapter XVI, Section II.

[11] B, I, GSK 43, p. 307; GSK 44, p. 106; II, MA100424, Anlage zu M. Inn. 2020 t 17, 3.12.1924; MA101235, PDN-F 4906/II, p. 15; MA101248,

In 1924, Bund Blücher was in many respects just an appendage of Wiking. It remained small and limited largely to northern Bavaria. Rudolf Schäfer, its leader, continued to be at least superficially loyal to the government, although he was accused by one former Bund member of singing a different tune in private. There was certainly a good deal of sympathy with Hitler at lower levels, which probably led to some loss of membership. In any case, neither before nor after the Putsch was Blücher strong enough to play a serious independent role as either a political or a paramilitary organization, and after the Putsch it seems to have been rather inactive.[12]

Bund Frankenland, another Ehrhardt satellite, was shattered by the Putsch. The bulk of the organization under its leader, the National Socialist Dr. Otto Hellmuth, went over to Hitler, while a rump group led by Lieutenant Senior Grade (Ret.) Walter Heyn remained loyal to Ehrhardt. Frankenland became part of the Völkischer Block, and Hellmuth went on to be a Gauleiter in the NSDAP, while Heyn's men formed an Ortsgruppe of Wiking in Würzburg.[13]

Jungdo, the most important Ehrhardt ally in the fall of 1923, moved away from him after it became clear that the rank and file racists would not accept him as a substitute for Hitler. Jungdo's key Bavarian leaders, Pastor Hellmuth Johnsen and Hans Dietrich, were both much closer to Hitler than to Ehrhardt and brought their organization into the Völkischer Block. The extent to which Johnsen, who was considered the more moderate of the two, represented right radicalism rather than any form of conservatism is clearly indicated by a quotation from a speech he made in December 1923:

". . . To recognize and to eliminate this purely reactionary danger, as much in Prussia, (return of the crown prince, entry of nationalist youths into the Reichswehr of Seeckt who has a Jewish wife) as in Bavaria (von Kahr regent for the king, order for the expulsion of Jews revoked), must be our next task."[14]

Rk. O. In. 108, pp. 33-34, Anlage 18; MA104221, 438 DJ, Bamberg, 2.12.1923; GP, A, Carl Tillessen.

[12] B, I, GSK 43, pp. 303-5; GSK 44, pp. 102, 115; GSK 90, p. 561; NA, EAP 105/7a, WKK VII 34365/Ib 6285.

[13] B, I, GSK 44, pp. 138ff; MA101235, PDN-F 3822/II, p. 32; MA101249, PDN-F 1357/II, p. 14; MA102141, HMB 350, M/F, p. 2.

[14] B, IV, Lapo, Bd. 26, Akt 1, Jungdo Bayern, p. 1.

Dietrich made no attempt to conceal his sympathy for the Putschists and his hostility towards the government, while Johnsen drew
only a light veil over his similar attitudes. Both wanted to move
closer to the NSDAP and to see the creation of a racist state "on
a national, social, and Christian [read Protestant] basis." Neither
was prepared to give up the organization's weapons—including
those received from the government—despite the agreement, accepted by all Verbände involved in the PNB and Grenzschutz, that
all military arms were the property of the Bavarian government.
On this score Johnsen said flatly: " 'The rifles remain the property
of the order. No one has [any right] to dispose of them except myself and persons who have an identity card signed with my
name. . . .' "[15]

Johnsen also emphasized the importance of maintaining the
paramilitary activities of the organization and continuing military
training so as to be prepared for all eventualities. On the other
hand, for the near future he clearly put more faith in victory at the
polls than he did in an appeal to arms. He also thought of the paramilitary forces of Jungdo primarily in terms of an inner mission,
rather than as a force to strengthen the army in conflict with a foreign foe, and he referred to the government's attempts to reorient
the paramilitary activities in the latter direction as "the end of all
our hopes."

Finally, the order was seen by its leaders, and by a good number
of Protestants outside its ranks, as a force to maintain the rights of
Protestants against the black reaction in München. The district
officer in Coburg warned that a ban on the order would be interpreted locally as a Catholic blow against Coburg. Nominally Catholic, Hitler had become a Protestant hero against Protestant Kahr.
In politics everything is not only possible but probable if it is
absurd enough.

In the new atmosphere after the Putsch, Jungdo not only divorced itself from Ehrhardt but also declared open war on Bund
Bayern und Reich, which offended not only by its political moderation but by its primarily Catholic membership. Here again, though,
Johnsen tried to play both sides of the street. At the same time that
he attacked Bayern und Reich, he tried to prevent counterattacks
by complaining to General von Tutschek of Major Buttmann's unfriendly attitude towards Jungdo. Johnsen then came out in favor

[15] *Ibid.*, p. 2.

of the cooperation of all Racist Bands, apparently including Wiking, but pointedly excluding Bayern und Reich.[16]

Despite its closeness to Hitler, or more likely because of it, Jungdo lost some adherents to the Hitler organizations after the Putsch. The Ortsgruppe in Bayreuth, for example, went over en masse. In Lichtenfels, according to the very nationalistic district officer, the Ortsgruppe leaders favored Kahr. On the whole, the order seems to have held its own, partially by means of a vigorous recruiting campaign to replace its losses. However, its expansion was limited by its identification with militant Protestantism to non-Catholic regions, and even here it had an uphill fight as a racist organization outside the Hitler fold. In December 1924 the authorities estimated that the order had some 4,500 members in Bavaria, of whom 3,000 were to be found in the immediate vicinity of Coburg. It is therefore fair to say that Jungdo survived but did not thrive in the new political atmosphere.[17]

Of the other radical organizations only VVM deserves special mention, and that because of its size and sloth. The leaders, at least at the middle and lower levels, seem to have been strongly sympathetic towards Hitler, which is surprising, since the VVM was composed of older men than were to be found in most other Verbände. However, since it represented radical and racist München, and since the military leader of the Kampfbund himself and many of his deputies had come up out of the old Einwohnerwehr, of which VVM had been a major component, this exception to the rule that the Kampfbund appealed primarily to the young is not surprising.[18] It is also important to recognize that, in the case of the VVM, political sympathy did not readily translate into active support during the period of the interim Racist Movement. Impressed by Hitler, the leaders of the VVM were still not prepared to expose themselves on his behalf, nor is there much evidence that the organization was very active in any respect. It can be characterized as being both local and sedentary and therefore not a serious factor in the Movement.

[16] B, ɪ, GSK 4, p. 14; GSK 43, pp. 128, 209, 211, 214, 218, 307-308; ɪɪ, MA104221, 438 DJ, Bamberg, 2.12.1923; ɪv, BuR, Akt 2, Item 12; Lapo, Bd. 26, Akt 1, Jungdo Bayern, p. 3.

[17] B, ɪ, GSK 43, pp. 210, 217-18; GSK 44, p. 220; GSK 101, HMB, Ofr., 3.1.1924; ɪɪ, MA100424, Anlage zu M. Inn. 2020 t 17, 3.12.1924; MA101235, PDM, NBl. 8, p. 8; MA102141, HMB 1610, Ofr., pp. 1-2.

[18] B, ɪ, GSK 43, p. 135; ɪɪ, MA101248, PDM, NBl. 20, p. 15.

III. *Bund Bayern und Reich*

Bayern und Reich was the embodiment of the broad middle stratum of the Patriotic Movement. Standing between the conservative (or reactionary), class-bound, Christian, and monarchist right wing and the racist, anticlerical, anti-monarchist, and classless left wing of the movement, it embodied elements of both. In many ways it had formed a bridge between these wings, until this bridge was blown sky high by the Putsch. Bayern und Reich occupied the same position within the Patriotic Movement as did the SPD in the Marxist Movement, and it therefore had at least some of the same advantages and disadvantages. Like the SPD, in the calmer times of 1922 and early 1923 it had attracted the bulk of the members of the movement, while the two wings trailed behind it. Moderates of both wings, repelled by the stark intolerance and bigotry of the extremes—by the narrowness and rigidity of the Right and the vulgarity and brutality of the Left—merged with the adherents of a compromise policy in a practical if sometimes uncomfortable alliance within the Bund. By the time of the Putsch, the Bund had created a consensus within itself and had secured a solid position within the movement.

The Putsch destroyed the consensus and the Bund's assured place in the movement at one blow; it also warped the Bund's relationship with the government. Members at all levels were forced to re-evaluate their positions within the Bund and with regard to other institutions and organizations. The tensions created throughout the tragic year 1923 by differences of political and social outlook, by differences of age, by differences of environment (especially between town and countryside), and by differences of economic position had reached dangerously high levels by November, so that the additional pressure exerted by the Putsch released powerful and long-suppressed forces that threatened the Bund's very existence. Equally important was the chasm between the military- and civilian-minded elements of the Bund. Was military preparedness or political action to set the tone?

At the top, these pressures resulted in a fight for the control of policy that was more a conflict of views than one of personalities. Dr. Pittinger, the political leader of the Bund, wished to carry on along the same political line as before the Putsch. For him, the Bund was essentially a political tool for holding the government on a conservative course and a military tool for holding down the threat of a Marxist revolution. The political goals were paramount and the military organization existed only to reinforce them. It seems clear that he did not realize the extent to which his weight in the councils of the state depended upon this military organization, or he would not have sacrificed it as readily as he did.

Pittinger stood at the right edge of the Bund, openly expressing his support for the monarchy and the existing society. Strongly Bavarian, he represented the Bismarckian compromise, not ultramontane particularism. In fact, he was cool towards the altar despite his loyalty to the throne. Given his choice in late 1923, he would have liked to see a conservative, nationalist dictator in control of Bavaria, one who would thrust parliamentarians of all stripes back into their boxes. He expressed these views very precisely on 22 December 1923:

> The Generalstaatskommissar is offered a favorable opportunity to assume the necessary measure of political freedom of action that he needs in order to be more than the police bailiff of a government dependent on parliamentary forces. If he seizes this opportunity to assert himself he will have, by one blow, public opinion on his side, as well as those forces that can and will effectively support him in the practical work in the economic sector.
>
> The possibility of mastering fate in this sense will perhaps be measured only in hours. If Knilling moves first by utilizing Article 48 of the federal and 60 of the Bavarian Constitution, then he makes himself dictator in practice, and the game is lost for the present. Even the reduction in the number of ministries will then be undertaken in a form that follows the old plan of the Bavarian Volkspartei, which is certainly awkward, but brings the most important activities of the state still more firmly into their hands. . . .
>
> The situation has not been so favorable for the Generalstaatskommissar since 8 November as in this moment. There are positive indications that he will win an unprecedented success if he acts swiftly and drastically. However, in the tension with which the general public awaits his or Knilling's next moves, one can foresee the degree of disillusionment that will result from a failure to take such measures, and that can only be described as crushing.[19]

[19] B, IV, BuR, Bd. 36, Akt 2, Item 22.

However, when Kahr did not act, Pittinger resigned himself to operating within the existing system and to recognizing the existing government. He was in no position to launch a revolution of his own and was well aware of this fact, despite the suspicions of the government, which had apparently gotten wind of his plans for Kahr. He therefore flatly—and truthfully—denied the rumors, for, like Kahr in early November, Pittinger had not planned a Putsch but had hoped to support a coup.[20]

After Kahr disappointed him, Pittinger's policy paralleled that of the government in many ways. He was, of necessity, hostile to the Kampfbund, favored a policy of a strong Bavaria within a strong Germany, and supported the BVP plan for amending the Bavarian Constitution. When faced with a choice between Hitler and the legitimate government, Pittinger obviously preferred the government, and the Bund officially supported the government against the racist radicals throughout 1924. The result was that, although they neither liked nor trusted one another even to the limited extent that they had in 1923, the government and the Bund tolerated one another, despite the issues that exacerbated their relations.[21]

The most important of these issues was the government's insistence on the disarmament of the Verbände and the creation of the Notbann as a substitute for independent paramilitary organizations. The disarmament problem caused much bad feeling between the authorities and the Bund, especially at the local and provincial level where Bund attitude toward the alien Reichswehr, with its ties to "Red" Berlin, was one of general distrust. The military leaders of the Bund at all levels wished to keep their weapons and were particularly unhappy because their weapons, largely reported to the government during 1923, were taken into official custody, while the Kampfbund, which had generally refused to report its caches, was able to retain, at least temporarily, a considerable proportion of its arms.[22]

Overshadowing the question of arms was the far more central

[20] B, I, GSK 6, p. 26; II, MA103457, Pittinger an GSK, 19.12.1923.

[21] B, II, MA102141, HMB 948, Obb., p. 3; IV, BuR, Bd. 36, Akt 1, Item 38; Anon. Memorandum (Schad?), p. 3.

[22] B, II, GSK 3, p. 40; GSK 43, p. 149; GSK 44, pp. 191-92, 233; GSK 101, BA Lichtenfels, 3.1.1924; BA Kronach, 3.1.1924; II, MA104221, Besch an Lapo Augsburg, 29.1.1924; IV, BuR, Bd. 36, Akt 1, Ortsgr. Augsburg an Mil. Oberleitung, 29.11.1923; Akt 2, Item 32; Item 42/2-3.

issue of the future of the Verbände in Bavaria. It is significant that here the military leaders of the Bund found themselves in a dilemma that grew as they saw the way in which the Notbann was developing. Within Bayern und Reich there was surprisingly strong sentiment in favor of a "non-political" paramilitary organization—although the Verbände were by this time so politicized that what they thought of as being apolitical was really strongly tinged with politics. The extent to which some of them nonetheless recognized the difficulties of the government and the need for a more reliable force is indicated by General (Ret.) Wilhelm Kaiser, the Bund's troop inspector:

> The state cannot yet *directly* take the *non-legal defense organization* into its *own hands* in the present situation, although it is dependent upon it and must work with it.
>
> It [the state] also cannot leave it [the defense organization] to private corporations (Wehrverbänden) fully *independent* of the state, if such serious abuses as those we have just experienced are to be avoided.
>
> There remains only the state supervised and loyal private defense organization, . . . privileged and subsidized by the state as the only possible solution.[23]

Yet, even as he emphasized the need for state control and for loyalty on the part of the Verbände, Kaiser revealed the extent to which he himself partook of the demi-world mentality of the Verbände that he denounced by leaving the door open for the new defense organization to refuse to obey the summons of a government that did not represent "German national interests"—with the determination to be made, naturally, by the leaders of the Verbände. Here indeed was the eye of a needle through which a camel could be driven. If even Kaiser, who was incensed by the "playing soldier which is ruining an entire generation for serious military activity"[24] could make such reservations, it is not surprising to find them on every hand. As the district officer in Lichtenfels warned, one could not simply turn the clock back overnight and ignore the developments of the past three years.[25] Despite reservations, there can be no doubt that many of the military leaders of Bayern und Reich, including Kaiser, were sincerely sick of the continual splin-

[23] B, IV, BuR, Bd. 36, Akt 1, Item 39.
[24] B, IV, BuR, Bd. 36, Akt 1, Item 14/2.
[25] B, I, GSK 101, BA Lichtenfels, 3.1.1924.

tering of the Verbände, of the squabbles among leaders, and looked with longing towards a return to orderly and predictable procedures, clear and regular promotion policies, regular training, and better pay and allowances, not only for their own benefit, but also in order to create a viable military reserve. They wished to escape from the "Freikorps spirit" as more than one of them expressed it —yet they were not ready to return to unconditional obedience to orders. The government had its dilemma; the military leaders of the Bund had their own.[26]

There was a solid base of support for a single organization subordinated to the government, and it is probable, given the nature of the Bavarian government of the period, that the reservations of the Bund's military leaders could have been assuaged and then eliminated as they grew into the new organization. However, the Notbann leader, General (Ret.) Ritter von Epp, never a tactful personality, made it very clear that he was going to bring in his own team to run the new organization and that there would be little if any room for the cadre of Bayern und Reich.[27] As a result, the incipient enthusiasm for Notbann was nipped in the bud as far as the Bund's military personnel were concerned. Pittinger, on the other hand, seems to have been increasingly annoyed at his military opposite number and the entire military hierarchy of the Bund after the beginning of December 1923. Therefore, ignoring the implications for his own position, he was prepared to go along with the government's demand that all paramilitary training be carried out through the Notbann. This was one of two questions that precipitated a serious crisis in the Bund.

The other question that led to the estrangement of Pittinger and General von Tutschek was a matter of political and personnel policy. Freiherr Franz von Gagern, the provincial leader (Kreisleiter) of the Bund in Oberfranken, had long been unpopular with many of his more racist and activist subordinates because of his personal identification with the BVP and his vigorous hostility towards the NSDAP. The matter came to a head when Gagern re-

---

[26] For demands for a unitary apolitical organization see: B, I, M. Inn. 73696, Ruef an Tutschek, 16.11.1923; II, MA104221, Besch an Lapo Augsburg, 29.1.1924; IV, BuR, Bd. 36, Akt 1, Items 27, 35, 41, 52; Akt 2, Items 9, 17; Anon. Denkschrift (Schad?), pp. 3-4; Lapo, Bd. 17, Akt 4, Jäger-Kp. Coburg an Lapo Coburg, 12.11.1923; Bd. 26a, Akt 5, v. Conta an Obstlt. Ritter von Häublein, 23.11.1923.

[27] B, IV, BuR, Bd. 36, Akt 2, Item 24, Schad an Allweyer.

signed on 11 November 1923 on the grounds that the leaders of the Bund were too soft on National Socialism. Tutschek welcomed the resignation. Pittinger and Kahr, the Bund's official arbitrators, were ready to admit that Gagern had been right about National Socialism and insisted that he be persuaded to remain. A see-saw battle ensued, in the course of which Gagern withdrew and resubmitted his resignation, while a good number of other former officers in Oberfranken resigned rather than serve under him.

At the München level the struggle became increasingly a question of the relative positions and powers of Pittinger and Tutschek. The general claimed that they were equals, while Pittinger insisted that Tutschek was merely his military advisor and assistant. It was in the climate created by this conflict that the decision over the Bund's relationship to Notbann was made. The leaders of the organization had reached a major fork in the road. They could support Tutschek and reject cooperation with the Notbann, which very possibly meant an eventual move into illegality, and sharp opposition to the government, or they could support Pittinger, civilian control of the Bund, and cooperation with the government. At a meeting on 16 January 1924, Pittinger carried the day despite the number of former professional soldiers among the Bund leaders, and Tutschek resigned on 31 January.[28]

On the question of the Kampfbund there was no serious conflict. Taken as a whole, the leaders of the Bund above the Ortsgruppe level, and even most Ortsgruppe leaders, stood against the radicals and for the Bund's middle position. Even those who opposed Gagern and Pittinger and demanded a softer line towards Hitler and his followers did so as a matter of tactics rather than political conviction. For example, one of them, Gymnasium Professor Richard Reinhardt of Bayreuth, wrote on 28 November:

> . . . The nationalists and youths, [who] had been brought, by means of National Socialist agitation, which has had great success here for months, into a state of political intoxication, for which one can, indeed, generate a certain psychological understanding, acted almost like lunatics at first. Soon, though, I made the shattering discovery that also national [-minded] men and women of all classes and occupations, who had previously been

[28] B, I, GSK 43, p. 313; GSK 99, pp. 40-42; IV, BuR, Bd. 36, Akt 1, Items 18, 40, 52; Akt 2, Items 15, 21, 25, 27, 28, 29, 42, 47; Akt 5, Tutschek Denkschrift, 21.12.1923.

highly regarded by me, had also succumbed to this regrettable hysteria.[29]

These are not the words or attitudes of a crypto–National Socialist, but for Reinhardt and many others the unity of the Patriotic Movement was of paramount importance, and he did not wish to estrange the bulk of the Kampfbund rank and file by too harsh a stand towards their organizations. Here, too, he did not stand alone.[30] A good number of Bayern und Reich leaders demanded action of their own Bundesleitung and of Kahr, although they were usually vague as to what sort of action they wanted. There is very little doubt, though, that their representations were, like those of Pittinger himself, aimed at pushing Kahr into making himself a real dictator at the expense of Landtag and Cabinet.[31]

In the Ortsgruppen the situation varied from place to place. Each Ortsgruppe faced at least a slightly different situation than its fellows with a different leader or leaders. Nevertheless, some patterns can be identified. Generally speaking, the attraction of the Kampfbund and Hitler was greatest for younger men, and membership losses were heaviest in those areas with the most youths, in those with relatively radical leaders, or in those where the general sentiment was inclined towards radicalism. Furthermore, two provincial leaders reported that almost all non-Bavarians had gone over to the Kampfbund, which indicates the susceptibility of refugees from the Red north to National Socialism and confirms the truism that refugees tend to activisim. On the other hand, even where youths were concerned, strong leaders could keep most of them in line. The best example here is Professor Johannes Reinmöller, the leader of the Wanderverein, a radically inclined youth organization with heavy student membership. Reinmöller took a strong stand in defense of Kahr, accused Hitler of folly, and ruthlessly expelled the most active opponents of Kahr from his organization. The result was that, at least for the time being, he carried the day, although he had admitted as early as February 1923 that most of his followers leaned towards National Socialism.[32]

A number of Ortsgruppen went over to the Kampfbund intact, among them those in Weiden and Helmbrechts. Others, like those

---

[29] B, I, GSK 43, p. 157.

[30] See the materials regarding the Gagern controversy.

[31] B, I, GSK 44, p. 19; IV, BuR, Bd. 36, Akt 1, Item 17 and *passim*.

[32] For Reinmöller in action see: B, I, GSK 43, pp. 157-63; IV, BuR, Bd. 35, Akt 3, Item 9/2.

in Memmingen, Nürnberg, and Traunstein were so shattered by the reactions to the Putsch that they disintegrated, at least temporarily. In other localities, the bulk of the members remained loyal but larger or smaller defections occurred. Most of the youths left the Bund in Staffelstein. In Bayreuth a small group dropped out. The same pattern held in Aichach and other towns or villages.[33] Some losses, especially in Oberfranken, reflected the quarrel among the local leaders (Gagern versus his deputies) which predated the Putsch but was aggravated by it. Here, Gagern's second and final resignation helped to smooth things over and led to the return of some of the other defectors. Other losses were men who dropped out of the Bund and the Patriotic Movement because of general disenchantment with the atmosphere of bickering and distrust that permeated inter-group relations.[34]

Some Ortsgruppen seem to have fallen on hard times because they had never been very robust and were therefore seriously weakened by even minor repercussions from the Putsch. This is the gist of a report regarding Marktleuthen and seems to apply to Kronach as well. In Starnberg, according to the local Lapo chief, the problem was that the Bund leaders were mostly teachers and teachers were held in low esteem in this vicinity.

The Putsch also speeded up the general splintering process that had been a chronic ailment of the Bund ever since the departure of Möhl and its loss of the monopoly over training and weapons in Bavaria. Justizrat Dr. Grassmann led the Landsberg Ortsgruppe out of the Bund, but local officials of both Bund and government believed that the move expressed personal ambition more than political conviction. More important, the aftermath of the Putsch brought two large organizations within the Bund to the point of divorce. The bulk of the Bund organization in Niederbayern, long autonomous and hostile to Pittinger, now left the Bund entirely, becoming independent under the name Bund Unterland. Wilhelm Willmer and Hans-Georg Hofmann remained the key men in the new Bund. Similarly, the Bayern und Reich leaders in the Chiemgau, who considered Pittinger too civilian, too conservative

---

[33] B, I, GSK 43, p. 309; GSK 44, pp. 74-76, 87-88, 117, 184, 190-92, 229; GSK 99, pp. 22-26; GSK 101, p. 32; II, MA101235, PDN-F 3822/II, p. 32; MA102141, HMB 679, Schw., p. 1; HMB 568, Ofr., p. 1; IV, BuR, Bd. 36, Akt 2, Winneberger, 7.12.1923.

[34] B, I, GSK 43, pp. 308-309; GSK 44, p. 175; II, MA102141, HMB 359, Ofr., p. 1; MA104221, Besch an Lapo Augsburg, 29.1.1924.

and too passive, led their followers out of the Bund and moved closer both to Ehrhardt and the Kampfbund.[35]

These losses were heavy blows, but there was another side of the picture. Many Ortsgruppen remained steadfastly loyal to the Bund throughout 1924, and in the second half of the year its strength increased considerably. A number of the groups that had suffered heavily right after the Putsch revived themselves well before the end of the year. The troubles in Oberfranken were over by the beginning of spring, and in October the provincial president reported that the Bund there was waxing fat. In Bamberg and Hof it had gained its old position again. In Niederbayern, despite the defection of the old organization, more than 10,000 persons attended a Bayern und Reich rally in June.[36]

In summation, it may be said that the Bund took losses that transformed it into a much more conservative and passive organization than it had been during 1923. By the end of 1924 it seemed well on its way to becoming a patriotic marching and chowder association with political interests, rather than a paramilitary organization dedicated to serious military action in case of civil or national war. At the same time, it had ceased to be a part of the racist element of the Patriotic Movement in any significant sense and therefore was no longer really in competition with the Kampfbund for members. The separation of sheep and goats had proceeded far enough that the two camps were now clearly delineated.

iv. *Deutscher Notbann*

The decision of the Bavarian government to create the Notbann was a result of the Putsch, but pressure in favor of such a development had been building up much earlier in the politically crucial BVP.[37] Essentially, the forming of the Notbann was an attempt to go back to the Einwohnerwehr system, which had been given up under Allied and federal pressure in 1921. The new organization,

[35] B, I, GSK 43, pp. 237, 308-309; GSK 44, pp. 184-85; II, MA102141, HMB 333, Obb., pp. 3-5; IV, BuR, Bd. 36, Akt 1, Item 55; NA, EAP 105/7a, Reichswehr Lagebericht 7.

[36] B, I, GSK 43, pp. 161-62, 308-309; GSK 44, pp. 102, 111, 229; GSK 90, p. 561; M. Inn. 72449, DJ 708, Bamberg; II, MA101248, PDN-F 6100/II, p. 23; MA102140, HMB 1102, N/B, p. 2; MA102141, HMB 476, Ofr., p. 1; HMB 734, N/B, p. 1; HMB 948, Obb., p. 3; HMB 1458, Ofr., p. 2; HMB 1109, Ufr., p. 2; HMB 1802, Ofr., p. 1; IV, BuR, Bd. 36, Akt 2, Items 19-20; Lapo, Bd. 26a, Akt 3, 2837, Ofr., 1.12.1923.

[37] See Chapter II, Section I.

standing under the clandestine patronage of the Bavarian government, would re-establish the monopoly over paramilitary training and the use of military arms that the Einwohnerwehr, and later Bayern und Reich, had once enjoyed. At the same time, this organization would seek to win over the rank and file of the Kampfbund paramilitary units to the government camp.

Only individuals, not organizations, could join Notbann, although members of organizations that were not hostile to the government could join without giving up their other affiliations. Thus, if all members of an organization joined the Notbann, it could, to some extent, maintain its corporate identity within the new system. In theory, at least, any male over sixteen years of age could join if he was of good character.

The emphasis in Notbann, unlike that in Einwohnerwehr, was on the creation of a ready reserve for the Reichswehr in case of external conflict, rather than on participation in internal conflicts, although arrangements were made for calling up the Notbann in case of major disturbances or civil war. This shift of emphasis may have been partly the result of a desire to eschew political coloration that might well have repelled Kampfbund members or sympathizers, but it also reflected the desire of the soldiers, both active and out of service, for a reserve divorced from politics.[38]

In theory, the Notbann seemed a very good idea. In practice everything went wrong. For one thing, instead of hitting while the iron was hot, the government waited until the Verbände had recovered from the shock of the Putsch and the Kampfbund had been more or less re-established. Secondly, they chose as the leader of Notbann a man unlikely to understand or solve its problems. General Ritter von Epp was certainly a hero of the Patriotic Movement due to his role in the liberation of München in 1919 and his paternal attitude towards the movement in more recent years. On the other hand, he was a very difficult and autocratic personality with no trace of the bedside manner needed in his new post. He was also on cool terms with the Heeresleitung and probably with the new Reichswehr commander in Bavaria, General von Kress, whose outspoken rival he had been. Epp quickly made a hash out of the per-

[38] B, I, M. Inn. 72449, 68 DJ, Bamberg, 18.2.1925; 2503 c 12, Ref. 17, 24.2.1925 mit Anlage; IV, BuR, Bd. 36, Akt 2, Item 42, Notizen über Kreisleiterkonferenz, 16.1.1924; NA, T79, 82, pp. 67-68; Röhm, *Geschichte*, pp. 322-23.

sonnel question. Not only did he freeze out the great bulk of the leaders of all of the existing Verbände, but in many cases he replaced them with former officers who had none of the necessary ties and qualities for successful leadership in a complex situation. In the case of Niederbayern, where he clearly leaned on "Trotsky" Hofmann for advice, he practically took over Bund Unterland, while ignoring Bayern und Reich. In other instances he chose National Socialists as leaders, much to the annoyance of the government. The result was unhappiness and uneasiness both above and below him.

Even so, had the Bavarian government seriously and effectively supported Notbann, it might have taken hold. The government, however, as a result of pressure from Berlin and the Bavarian Left, wavered in its support and even attempted at times to pretend that Notbann did not exist. Meanwhile, it encouraged the organization in a desultory way. Although increasingly unhappy with Epp, the Cabinet made no move to replace him or to direct his policy more closely. Most important of all, the government failed to provide Notbann with the money it needed to operate efficiently. It gave just enough to keep it alive, but not enough to enable it to offer advantages that the Verbände could not. The entire enterprise suffered from all of the disadvantages of being a political stepchild at a time when only vigorous and consistent support could have made it viable.[39]

The result was that the project failed in its major goals. The racist leaders were able to hold most of their former followers away from Notbann. The military leaders of Bayern und Reich, resentful at being ignored, did little to encourage their followers to take an interest in Epp's child. Those Verbände that encouraged their members to join usually did so with the purpose of exploiting Notbann for their own advantage. Captain Heiss, for example, did so very successfully. Therefore, Notbann neither collected all available active volunteers into an effective reserve nor drew the teeth of the Putschists.[40]

[39] B, I, M. Inn. 72449, passim; M. Inn. 73433, PDM, 1001/1050/25 VI/N1, 6.9.1925; II, MA99522, 20.6.1924, pp. 8-9; 8.7.1924, pp. 7-11; MA99523, 20.10.1925, pp. 16-17; IV, BuR, Bd. 36, Akt 2, Items 24, 41.

[40] B, I, GSK 4, p. 14; GSK 44, p. 102; M. Inn. 72449, 3421, BA Wasserburg; 648 Verbandsleitung; V77, BA Straubing; II, MA99522, 18.12.1924, p. 22; MA100411, M. Inn. Zu Nr. 2020 u 2, Abschrift, 16.3.1925;

v. *The Leftist Organizations*

On the Left, the old paramilitary organizations were dead or moribund. After the Putsch the Communists created a new "Red Front Fighters' League," which was destined to gain strength and notoriety in later years, especially in north Germany, but in Bavaria in 1924, where the party was feeble and under constant pressure from the police, it was a power factor only in theory. The SOD was still active as election guards for the SPD but had no military potential. However, a new leftist paramilitary organization appeared on the Bavarian scene during the summer of 1924, which was watched with jaundiced eyes by the political authorities. This was Reichsbanner Black-Red-Gold. Reichsbanner was theoretically open to all republicans in Germany, but, in Bavaria at least, it consisted primarily of Social Democrats with a light frosting of Democrats and was officially supported by both the DDP and SPD.

The Bavarian Reichsbanner was concentrated in München and Nürnberg, although other industrial cities had sizable groups. In München, the leaders were all well-known Social Democrats, while in Nürnberg, the Democratic Oberbürgermeister and SPD leaders were the prime movers. The organization boasted a large number of former NCO's and some officers and displayed the same sort of paramilitary trappings and activities as had the Patriotic Bands. In August, Gareis, whose ears were close to the ground regarding the Left as well as the Right, estimated that Reichsbanner had some 20,000 members, of whom perhaps 10,000 were in Nürnberg-Fürth.[41]

Reflecting the attitude of the SPD, Reichsbanner made no bones of its suspicion of and hostility towards the Bavarian government. According to the provincial president of Mittelfranken, a Reichsbanner speaker in Nürnberg had the following remarks to make about the goals of the organization:

> "The Patriotic Bands are foes of the Republic, wish to overthrow it and restore the monarchy. In these efforts they are sup-

MA102141, HMB 247, Obb., pp. 4-5; HMB 333, Obb., pp. 3-5; HMB 392, Schw., p. 2; HMB 578, Obb., p. 5; HMB 629, Obb., p. 5; HMB 705, Obb., pp. 2-4; HMB 796, Obb., p. 2; HMB 860, Obb., p. 10; MA101235, PDM, NB1. 8, p. 10.

[41] B, ii, MA101235, PDN-F 2425/ii 24, pp. 7-8; 5614/ii, pp. 5-6; PDM, NB1. 11, pp. 4-5; PDN-F 3822/ii, p. 20; 4668/ii, pp. 7-11; MA101248, PDM, NB1. 19, p. 9; MA102141, HMB 1904, Ofr., p. 1.

ported by the government. Officials who are paid by the Republic did not shirk from working against it. The task of the Reichsbanner Bund is to train the republican workers so well that they will be in a position, in case of need, to replace the non-republican officials. The organization Black-Red-Gold is intended to defend the Republic against its enemies on the Right and Left, if necessary with force."[42]

Such words were unlikely to warm the hearts of the authorities, and the threat of the use of force was nicely calculated to arouse visions of the Republic of Councils in the eyes of the Cabinet members, just as it helped the Verbände in their recruiting campaigns. Reichsbanner was created to meet the threat posed by the Verbände as they were at their nadir. Its appearance on the scene, however, helped to revive the appeal of the Verbände and to mute their quarrels with one another.

The government took such steps as it could to curb Reichsbanner without actually banning it and was doubtless strengthened in this policy by a number of scuffles between rightist groups and Reichsbanner, in at least some of which the Reichsbanner men seem to have taken the initiative. Reichsbanner threats to ignore police restrictions did not improve relations between the Bund and the authorities. Therefore, although it was, as time soon revealed, not really an aggressive or even a very effective organization despite its great size, the appearance of Reichsbanner on the Bavarian stage right after the Hitler Putsch was enough to lead the government to think again about the possibility of civil war on the Left and therefore to count its forces and allies.[43]

VI. *Conclusion*

The Hitler Putsch eliminated from serious consideration as contenders for leadership of the Racist Movement those radical Verbände that were not associated with Hitler. These organizations found themselves in a very weak propaganda position. All they could say was "We can do it better!" when Hitler had already done it and they had stood aside. Such Verbände were also caught between two much larger, mutually hostile, groups—the Kampfbund

[42] B, II, MA102141, HMB 1631, M/F, p. 2.
[43] B, II, MA99522, 14.7.1924, p. 8; 31.7.1924, pp. 2-3; MA101235, PDM, NB1. 11, pp. 4-6; MA101248, PDN-F 7410/II, p. 19; 8250/II, p. 7.

and Bayern und Reich. If they moved towards radicalism, there was a tendency for their members to be attracted to the Kampfbund Verbände, while if they moved in the other direction, Bayern und Reich had more to offer. On the other hand, those members that Bayern und Reich or the Kampfbund lost were usually lost to one another. Thus the independent radical Verbände were in trouble whether they moved or stayed in their old positions.

The lesser Verbände also operated with the disadvantages of a small numerical base, at least in Bavaria. Those that were large organizations in their own right, had the bulk of their strength in other states where it could not be applied to assist them. Outside strength did them little good anyway, since the eyes of racists throughout Germany were now concentrated on Bavaria, and it was there that the battle for leadership was fought out. Those organizations that were essentially Bavarian were not only small in numbers but were confined to a limited geographical area even within Bavaria. All of them were too weak to thrive once government patronage or toleration was replaced by hostility.

Finally, all of these Verbände occupied a weak political position. They were essentially paramilitary in nature, and their political programs were both primitive and negative. None of them boasted a serious political organization, and none of them had leaders with the characteristics needed to make them popular political figures. In any case, since the fight was underway as soon as the Putsch was over, even had such leaders existed they would not have been able to catch up with Hitler overnight. The truth of the matter was that Hitler and his party had no need to fear serious competition within their own doctrinal camp once the post-Putsch situation had revealed the weaknesses of their potential rivals.

Equally significant for the political development of the NSDAP and for the political situation in Bavaria was the decline in the power and influence of Bund Bayern und Reich. The Bund was seriously weakened by the developments that followed the Putsch. The fall of Kahr removed its most powerful patron. The loss of so many activists to the Kampfbund reduced the Bund's vitality far more than its numbers. The loss of its military rights and the toleration accorded its paramilitary activities by the government divested it of much of its glamor for potential members, a development that Pittinger apparently had not anticipated. Equally serious, the loss of its military muscle reduced the Bund's lure for local patrons and supporters, since a good number of these supporters had looked to the Bund for protection from the Reds should revolution come again. A disarmed Bund was far less appealing than a Bund that could turn out armed men on a few minutes notice to defend home, shop, and factory.

The loss of government support hurt the Bund in other ways as well. Many of its members were more or less solid citizens who, while moderately adventurous, had no interest in entering on a career of real as opposed to apparent illegality or of courting imprisonment. The Bund could only retain the military apparatus that meant strength by illegality, and its members as well as its leaders eschewed illegality. Even had there been an interest in illegality, the Bund was too large and too vulnerable to go underground easily. Its leaders were readily identifiable men of position or property. A mouse can hide where an elephant cannot. Therefore, illegality was not really a practical alternative. In any case, the bulk of the members of the Bund had no intention of fighting the government and did not seriously envisage opposing under arms any government that was not Marxist.

This meant that by the end of 1924, the Bund had ceased to be the sort of organization that could win even mild racists away from Hitler. Forced to decide, the Bund had chosen to move towards moderation and conservatism rather than activism and revolution. This decision preserved it as an organization but changed its nature and potential drastically; this decision also left the National Socialists in full control of the Racist Movement.

Working at cross purposes, but at least partially recognizing the consequences of their actions, Hitler and the authorities, between them, had destroyed or reoriented the many apparently formidable competitors Hitler had faced in the early fall of 1923. This elimination had been, in part, the result of direct actions on the part of one or the other of the antagonists, but it was also partly the result of the impact of the emotions and controversies unleashed by the conflict between them. Since the leftist Verbände were a null factor, Hitler and the Bavarian government now faced each other across a battlefield that had been denuded of other figures. Hitler was winded and his forces scattered, but it can be argued that it was not he and his followers who had suffered most, but those groups that had sought to be bystanders in the struggle for power. The next time that desperation and outrage sent masses of normally passive adherents of the Patriotic or Racist Movements in search of a banner to follow, there would be only one banner unfurled and only one leader to bear it. The drummer of 1922 would be the standard-bearer of 1930, a role the Putsch had only temporarily wrested from his grasp.

24.

THE BALANCE SHEET

I. *The Pre-Putsch Period*

The situation that made possible the attempt to overturn the governments of Bavaria and the Reich was a complicated one that had developed over a number of years. Its origins were to be found in the pressures exerted by the Marxist Movement, the Patriotic Movement, the Räterepublik of 1919, and the Treaty of Versailles. Together, these factors led the government of Bavaria to adopt policies that proved to be unwise and dangerous, because they placed the temptation and the means to act against the government in the hands of unscrupulous men dedicated to sweeping away both the existing government and the state.

The Marxist Movement, of course, came first in time and was a causal factor in the development of the other elements in the situation. Initially, as a result of the make-up of the Bavarian population, the Marxists were more an annoyance and a potential threat than a real menace to the Bavarian state and society, especially in the period when the movement was dominated by moderates. After World War I, though, the movement and the milieu were both drastically altered. The revolution brought the most radical elements of the Marxist Movement briefly to the helm in Bavaria or, more accurately, in München and some of the other towns. The reign of the radicals who controlled the Räterepublik was brief, but it was long enough and they were radical enough to terrorize and anger large elements of the non-Marxist population and to lead the Bavarian government that succeeded the "Reds" to take vigorous steps—with popular approval—to prevent any recrudescence of the Red menace.

The terms of the Treaty of Versailles, however, put serious obstacles in the way of the Bavarian government's realizing its security objectives. In fact, the treaty limited the freedom of the government much as a set of manacles limit the freedom of an individual. Not only was the German army greatly reduced in size, but the Allies also placed very severe restrictions on the size of German police forces. The Bavarian government was far less worried by the first limitation than by the second, since in the Weimar Republic the control of the army passed to the federal government, which from the beginning was looked upon in München as dangerously "soft" on Marxism and vulnerable to legal or illegal Marxist influence or control. Since they had some influence over the Bavarian contingent of the Reichswehr, the Bavarian leaders were prepared to see a larger army than the treaty allowed Germany and, as German patriots, they would even welcome such an army—although there is very little indication that in the period 1919-23 any Bavarian politicians seriously considered the army as anything but a form of police force to be used against a Red insurrection. Even the Bavarian commanding generals of this period were interior-oriented, which was one of the reasons they were at odds with the chief of the army leadership, General von Seeckt, who thought of the army exclusively in terms of national defense against external enemies and fought any attempt to turn it into a police organization or assign it police missions.

Nearer by far than the army to the heart of the Bavarian government was the Bavarian Landespolizei, or riot police. This force, organized more tightly on military lines than any other police organization in Germany, formed to all intents and purposes a Bavarian division under Bavarian control. All indications are that, had they been able to expand this force to the size they believed necessary for internal security (and, perhaps, to balance the Reichswehr), the Bavarians would have been perfectly content to leave the battle for a larger army to the Berlin authorities. Far more significant for political developments in Bavaria, they would have had no interest in encouraging or permitting the development of the Patriotic Bands into paramilitary organizations. For that matter, had it even been permitted to create a reserve army or police force, the Bavarian government would probably have let matters lie, but because of the treaty none of these options was open to it. Determined to hold to its course, the Bavarian government threw its support solidly behind the Einwohnerwehr, which was a public corporation in much the same sense as is the Port Authority of New York or the Reichsbank (Bundesbank after World War II). Here, too, however, they soon reached an impasse. Despite their quite legitimate pleas that the Einwohnerwehr was intended only for local defense and was capable of accomplishing only a local defense mission, the Allies insisted on its abolition. At first the Bavarian government attempted to resist, but in the end, although Gustav von Kahr stepped down as minister-president rather than go along, the Einwohnerwehr was officially abolished.[1]

The government was now forced either to give up its insistence on the maintenance of a local defense force or to find a new and less official organization to fulfill this purpose. It decided that the question was one of life or death and that it would continue to maintain such a force. In view of the fact that the Einwohnerwehr itself, although originally much more broadly based (even including socialist elements), had fallen more and more into the hands of the adherents of the Patriotic Movement,[2] this movement or portions of it seemed the natural military reservoir for the defense of the state. The result was the creation of the organization that later came to be known as Bund Bayern und Reich. This was a private organization under state patronage with secret financial and military ties to the government and the armed forces, as well as official commitments to the local police authorities. For a time this arrangement seemed to establish a perfect symbiotic relationship. The government got what it wanted: an auxiliary force, to be used against Red revolution, that was not directly identifiable with the government. The Bund, its leaders and members, got political toleration, access to arms and ammunition, training at the hands of the armed forces, and a status that enabled it to prepare not merely to fight the hated Marxists, but also to defend Germany against foreign attack, if not to launch a war of liberation to reestablish Germany in her old European and world position. The government, always inclined to pinch pennies, soon realized with pleasure that this system was also cheap. It was only later—after painful lessons—that the Cabinet came to realize that a government controls its armed forces only so long as regulations, promotion, and pay proceed from this government.

When Hitler and his movement appeared on the edge of the Patriotic Movement, they, too, were initially tolerated because Kahr, Pöhner, and far more moderate men saw in them the sort of

---

[1] See B, ɪɪ, MA99518, 1921, passim.

[2] These elements had gained control partly by their greater enthusiasm and willingness to work in the organization and partly as a result of the increasing pressure they put on other elements to get out.

crude but effective politicians who could get the corn down where the hogs could reach it. They saw that Hitler was winning workers, especially young workers, away from Marxism, and this was, in their view, a healthy phenomenon. This optimistic view was especially easy to maintain in the early days when lines within the Patriotic Movement were not yet clearly drawn and insiders and well as outsiders were unaware of the extent to which differences of viewpoint and activism existed within the movement. Hitler was still simply the "drummer" who brought the masses in München into the nationalist fold.

However, in politics as elsewhere in life, nothing remains still. The Verband (later Verbände), which was called to arms for the defense of the government but represented the "new wind" in politics, moved further and further from the government politically, while the various leaders came more and more to think of themselves as independent figures rather than as mere instruments of official policy. This development, of course, went furthest on the radical fringe of the movement and was least noticeable among the conservatives on the right edge—although even they were affected.

Meanwhile, because of their involvement—at governmental insistence—in dealings with the Verband and in the question of the defense of the government against domestic foes, the personnel of the army and the police forces at all levels were "sensitized" to politics. Here again, the Bavarian government proved blind. Generally speaking, just as politicians who are given arms and permitted to form military organizations begin to think about using those arms to accomplish their political aims, so soldiers who are asked to take an interest in politics begin to think of using their arms to defend or support the political solution of their choice. Therefore, just as the leaders of the Verband and its component parts moved further away from government control, the Bavarian armed forces began to assume an increasing autonomy.[3]

By leaving the Verband largely to its own devices and forcing it to look to other sources for a good portion of its funds, the gov-

[3] The fact that this phenomenon did not occur elsewhere in the Reich is only one element in the chain of evidence linking the political activity of the armed forces in Bavaria with the policies adopted by the Bavarian government. Equally striking is the other side of the coin. Once the Bavarian government dropped the policies in question, the armed forces ceased playing a serious role in politics—without any major changes in personnel at any level within the services, aside from the retirement of Lossow, which would not have been long delayed in any case.

ernment was responsible, at least in part, for the divorce that followed. In the same way, by consulting the commanders of the army and Landespolizei regarding political policy, instead of its implementation, and by encouraging these officers to build bridges to the irregulars, the government fostered a sense of autonomy in Seisser and Lossow and in the forces these men commanded—especially the München garrisons of the army and the Landespolizei—which was to alarm the Cabinet at the time of the Hitler Putsch.

Finally, the government adopted a police policy regarding political rallies, demonstrations, and similar activities that positively encouraged the political activists to use violence against their foes. Since the most effective armed forces in politics were those belonging to the Verbände (including the NSDAP), this policy not only helped to further the move towards autonomy in these organizations but also led them into direct conflict with the police. Here again the impact of the Treaty of Versailles was felt. Because of the limitations on the size of police forces, there were not enough police readily available to handle large demonstrations or disturbances in many areas. Probably reasons of economy also played a role, as did the tendency of politicians everywhere and in every period to take the easy way out of a difficult situation. In any case, the government decided to ban or dissolve a political meeting that was threatened with disruption by its opponents rather than to undertake its defense. This meant that if rivals could cause enough disruption at any rally they could get the police to close it down. Thus the innocent were made to pay for the offenses of the aggressors, and both Left and Right took to disruptive action ranging from boos and catcalls to armed assault, according to relative strengths, local leaders, and local opportunities.

The natural result of this situation was that all political parties soon created defensive forces which, as they developed, increasingly took the view that an offensive was the best defense. Here, too, the Bavarian government learned the truth of a political axiom the hard way. A government that does not maintain law and order for the protection of its citizens soon finds that groups of citizens undertake to provide this law and order for themselves. In the Bavarian instance, those political groups—primarily the National Socialists—that were also associated with the Verbände and belonged to the militant wing of the Patriotic Movement profited most from the declaration of a political open season and from the weakness of the Bavarian authorities.

It was thus that the reins of power began slipping from the hands of the Bavarian government at an alarming rate during 1922 and much of 1923. As early as January 1923, a showdown between the right radicals and the government was in the wind. Equally clear was the fact that Hitler was the most determined and aggressive of the proponents of such a collision. The splintering of the Verband into a number of Verbände, which began at the end of 1922 and was greatly accelerated by the removal of Möhl from his post, liberated further radical elements from the dominance of the moderates who controlled Bund Bayern und Reich and brought them into the orbit of Hitler and Ludendorff. Hofmann, Heiss, and Röhm, the Reichswehr's prodigal sons, and their organizations were among the most significant recruits.[4]

Having succeeded in bearding the government in January—partly by guile and partly as a result of unauthorized concessions on the part of the München police president—Hitler and his colleagues moved on to a more serious confrontation on May Day. Here the government refused to back down, and the right radicals suffered a stinging humiliation. However, they succeeded in masking the humiliation from the public eye quite effectively, a success that was partly the result of SPD accusations against the government and armed forces for collaborating with the Arbeitsgemeinschaft. The leaders escaped effective legal retaliation despite the fact that they had clearly broken the law and defied the authorities. Their escape seems to have been largely the work of the justice minister, but there is also evidence that the minister-president worked to prevent a confrontation in his own capital with a political force that was so strong. Knilling's lack of enthusiasm was further enhanced by the fact that, if he acted, he would have to act on the basis of the Law for the Defense of the Republic, which the great majority of Bavarians abominated. The result was that relations between the Hitler circle and the government cooled markedly, but Hitler was encouraged to believe that no one dared to take direct action against him.

In the middle of September, the National Socialists seemed to

---

[4] This splintering can, in turn, be seen as a further reflection of the breakdown of governmental authority over the Verbände. Much of the authority of the leaders of Bund Bayern und Reich before 1923 had depended on their "official" position. The achievement of autonomy freed their subordinates from them, just as it freed the Bund from the government.

be on the verge of launching a Putsch. As a result Knilling gave way to demands from several quarters that he give Gustav von Kahr dictatorial powers to meet the crisis. Despite his initial opposition to the appointment, the wily Machiavellian soon saw that it had advantages from his viewpoint. In view of his character, Kahr was unlikely to do anything drastic. He ran more to talk than to action. At the same time, holding such a post at such a time was almost certain to destroy Kahr's popularity, since the bulk of the Patriotic Movement's adherents would expect miracles and not get them. On the other hand, he might just possibly be able to persuade the entire Patriotic Movement to support the government, which was especially important in view of the government's quarrel with the Reich and of its fear of a Red invasion from central Germany. Finally, should Kahr fail to lead the movement to the government, he should at least be able to divide it by using his ties with Dr. Pittinger and Bund Bayern und Reich. Here was a situation where the government could only win and one that would help it to squirm out of very tight spot in which its gradual abdication of practical power had placed it.

By November great numbers of Germans of all classes were frightened out of their wits by the galloping inflation that threatened the most unlikely people with ruin or even starvation. These frightened and desperate people were increasingly bitter against a federal government that seemed to be fiddling while Germany burned, and it is only fair to admit that the Reich Cabinet seems to have felt much less urgency about the situation than its catastrophic impact on the citizen would warrant.[5]

Had the government in Berlin been more obviously concerned with the plight of the citizen, it might not have faced so many citizens in arms during the course of the fall. In Bavaria, the hatred and suspicion of the Berlin government was particularly acute. After all, Bavarians were traditionally suspicious of the "Saupreissen," and great numbers of Bavarians in all walks of life were convinced that the increased economic centralism espoused by the Weimar Republic had been an active element in the economic collapse and in their sufferings during the inflation. Many Bavarians also saw in the Berlin government the agent of a greedy German capitalism, a vicious international capitalism, or an even more

[5] See the debates of the Reichskabinett during the fall of 1923: NA, T120, 1749-51, passim.

wicked Marxism—if not all three. These pressures and emotions provided both the impetus and the opportunity for the Putsch that Hitler had long preached and often contemplated.

II. *The Putsch as a Catalyst*

When Hitler moved, his action proved to be a catalyst that brought about far-reaching changes, some of which could hardly have been predicted with any certainty by the most astute seer.

The Putsch forced the Patriotic Bands and their members to take a stand. Because it was Hitler who made the Putsch, the choice was naturally made in terms of being "for" or "against" him, which in turn meant that, in the eyes of foes as well as friends, he became the focal point of the entire Racist Movement, the personification of the Kampfbund. The Patriotic Movement now dissolved into its component parts.

The Putsch forced the government to make up its mind regarding not only the Putschists but also the entire Verbände system. The result was the abandonment of the support of independent Verbände and the attempt to return to the secret public corporation system of 1919-21. By the time this scheme fell through, because of sloppy and niggardly implementation, the political situation was sufficiently stabilized that even the Bavarian government seems to have recovered from the fears generated by the events of 1919, and it is probable that mature reflection on the outcome of the clash at the Feldherrnhalle played a role in the soothing of its fears. Much of the fear that permeated the government and most of the middle class before November 1923 had rested on the inability of civilians to differentiate between exhausted, warweary rear echelon troops, such as those who had collapsed without a fight in 1918, and a well-trained, well-led, combat-ready force of young volunteers. It was clearly shown on 9 November 1923 that even the militant right radicals, despite some military training and experience, despite some heavy weapons and the advantage of sympathizers in the armed forces, simply melted away at the first "whiff of grape." If this was the case, what would be the fate of leftist rebels, who would enjoy none of these advantages?

Whether these considerations or others weighed in their minds, it is clear from the documents that the main consideration moving the government leaders after the Putsch was the realization that they had allowed a Frankenstein's monster to grow up in their midst. They therefore turned their attention to disposing of it. They not only dissolved the obviously hostile bands, they disarmed and demilitarized them all. Having seen where the dispersion of military power outside the hands of the state led, the ministers gathered it back to themselves. The era of Putsches was at an end, and the Verbände were destroyed or seriously weakened.

The Putsch also forced the Bavarian People's Party, which had dominated earlier Bavarian governments without openly leading them or taking public responsibility for their actions, to step out on the stage. Knilling, primarily a bureaucrat despite his official adherence to the BVP, was replaced by Dr. Held, the most powerful figure in the party. The Putschists, who had sought to end the "misrule of the parties" succeeded in placing the parties openly and frankly in charge of Bavaria for the first time.

Simultaneously the Putsch revealed vividly that the political Left in Bavaria, whether moderate or radical, was a "Paper Tiger." Its greatest political significance was a negative one which its leaders probably did not recognize. By its constant attacks on National Socialism, the Left kept the Nazis respectable despite all their vulgarities and lies, since many Bavarians thought that no one could be very bad who had enemies like that. This was the sort of unwisdom that led Americans in World War II to believe that Stalin loved democracy. After all, he was fighting Hitler, wasn't he? It was as easy for anti-Marxist Germans to forget Hitler's shortcomings—which at this stage of his career were still rather insignificant—as it was for Americans to forget that Stalin had officially been on Hitler's side until the day Hitler attacked the Soviet Union. In Weimar Germany the Left's accusations against the National Socialists were particularly easy to shrug off because the Marxists insisted on identifying the Nazis with monarchism and conservatism, thus helping to win for them friends they would never have had while sailing under their true colors.

III. *The New Political Situation*

When the many political reactions set in motion by the Putsch had come to a halt, the new situation was very different from the one that had existed on 8 November 1923. The old political parties, pressure groups, and political associations went their way much as before. They held most of their old members, but their ability to win new ones, especially among the members of the younger generation, was considerably reduced, as election statistics show. The right wing of the Patriotic Movement had been reabsorbed into these traditional political groups to a very high degree. Already essentially conservative and passive, it now became more so.

The broad center of the Patriotic Movement, as personified by Bund Bayern und Reich, suffered severely. Although it occupied a position in the movement similar to that which the SPD occupied in the Marxist Movement, the Bund was not as fortunate as the SPD. The break in the Marxist Movement came only after it was more than a generation old and the solid center had succeeded in getting control—on the basis of the great numerical strength it boasted in peaceful times—of much of the party apparatus and its parallel institutions, especially the free trade unions and the Marxist press. With the advantage of the ingrained loyalty of many socialists and with the aid of the posts and institutions it controlled, the SPD was able to ride out military, social, political, and economic crises, although, especially in the Third Reich, it did not go unscathed through these storms. Bayern und Reich met its great crisis when the movement was only four years old and the Bund only two. The crisis came in the midst of serious political, economic, and social disasters that intensified the strains within the movement. Moreover, the Bund had no large-scale auxiliary institutions to help it. As a result, it lost heavily in numbers to both wings of the movement. It also suffered from loss of energy and loss of spirit caused by the cessation of its paramilitary activities and its favored status with the government. The Bund therefore ceased to be a major power factor in Bavaria.

The left wing consolidated itself into an activist, revolutionary movement, most of whose elements owed allegiance to Adolf Hitler. Hitler was a man with a fine political sense and the ability to learn from an initial rebuff (although he usually proved unwilling to modify the solution to meet the problem when it reappeared in a somewhat different form). He was also a tenacious and powerful personality, whose spellbinding powers over both individuals and crowds have few parallels in history. Hitler kept his eye continually on the main chance. His revolution was essentially a political one, since he was not particularly interested in the social revolution that was bound to accompany the political changes he desired. He wanted to achieve a national revival, a national unification, and the full exploitation of the abilities of every loyal German for the welfare of the state and people. Therefore he stressed political loyalty, an almost Rousseauian or Leninist "General Will" of the Volk (of which he was the chosen interpreter), and the baton in every knapsack approach of Napoleon. In social and economic matters he was flexible, since they were secondary in his scheme of things. He would adopt any solution that seemed to fit his ends and give lip service to any that seemed likely to attract followers. The result has been that observers who think of all revolution in terms of outbreaks against colonial powers or in terms of essentially socioeconomic revolutions of a Marxist nature fail to recognize the essentially revolutionary aims and spirit of National Socialism as practiced by Hitler.

This very activist and revolutionary element made Hitler's party the strongest and most active opponent of the Bavarian government. However, this element also meant that it attracted primarily those who believed in a simplistic and violent approach to politics, a group that included then, as it does now, large numbers of people who had very little practical experience and who had faith in the solution of complex problems by rapid and drastic action. A high percentage of these people were very young, since the aging process usually reduces enthusiasm for such nostrums. Such youths were convinced that their elders had, through their folly, viciousness, and weakness, created an unholy mess which it was the duty and pleasure of the younger generation to clean up. These youths were vigorous, enthusiastic, and capable of hard work on a short-term basis. Hitler milked them of every ounce of energy with a skill that grew with the years. From them he built up the cadre that would eventually drive his party to triumph.

youth

This movement and these men have sometimes been seen as an expression of despair, but, in plain fact, they represented the opposite of despair. They were revolting violently against the despair that characterized the outlook of many members of the older generation in the Weimar Republic. The National Socialists were fanatically optimistic regarding their personal fates, their movement, and the future of Germany. During all of his years of struggle Hitler clearly never lost the belief that he was destined to be the leader of a revitalized Germany, nor did the hard core of his followers lose faith. This was a movement of unquenchable, almost mindless, optimism rather than despair. This optimism was both its greatest strength and its weakness, and it was Hitler and the young men clustered around him who were its carriers.

On the other hand, as the economic crisis ebbed, Hitler lost most of those consumers who had joined the movement as a last bitter protest against their sufferings at the hands of society and blind economic forces. He lost the apolitical elements who returned to their lethargy. He lost the faint-hearted and the hangers-on, who had been moved to activism only by the hope of speedy triumph. The result was fewer but better National Socialists than there had been at the high point of the movement's early growth in the first months of 1924. Hitler, however, had developed patience. He turned his attention towards preparing for the long haul. He built a more effective party machinery. He reorganized the shattered SA and the debilitated propaganda machine. He spread his version of the Putsch—and he waited for the new crises that he was sure would come and lift him to power. Like the Biblical Egyptians he tightened his belt and endured his seven lean years.

He was even kind enough and optimistic enough to give his opponents a sure formula for defeating him:

> In order to defeat the National Socialists one must remove the causes that brought them into existence, that is, the general despair, the economic and political poverty of Germany. Any government that eliminates these causes will be national socialist in a broader sense. The present National Socialists would then be superfluous.[6]

Here, with his usual skill, Hitler placed his finger on the root of the trouble. Hitler and National Socialism were a serious danger for Germany's government and society only if and when enough Germans lost faith in these institutions and were therefore ready to flesh out his political armies. In the meantime he was, at most, an irritant in the body politic.

It was here, in the months after the Putsch, that one finds the real Triumph des Willens. By sheer determination and sense of mission Hitler transformed himself from the frenetic revolutionary who had been shattered and silenced by the Putsch into a political leader ready to accept years of careful building and constant struggle as a prelude to power. Rossbach, Ehrhardt, and Ludendorff all failed to turn this vital corner and perished politically. Hitler took it in stride and left them far behind. The Putsch had transformed the old Hitler into the new, just as World War I and the revolution had turned the bohemian would-be artist of Vienna and München into a revolutionary leader—and of the two transformations it was perhaps the greater. Hitler's first crisis had made him a revolutionary. His second made him the undisputed leader of a serious

[6] B, II, MA100427, Kuenzer an Held, 9.2.1927, p. 4.

political movement. The third crisis brought him to the helm of Germany, while the fourth led him to conquest, defeat, and death. In 1925 he was therefore at the halfway point of his political career, although most Germans who had heard of him at that time would have guessed that his career was behind him.

15. Hitler, Maurice, Kriebel, Hess, and Weber in prison after the Putsch

Appendix

IA. BAVARIAN NSDAP ORTSGRUPPEN

Allach
Aschaffenburg
Augsburg
Bad Reichenhall
Bad Tölz
Bayreuth
Berchtesgaden
Berg
Bergen/Traunstein
Biberach
Birnbach
Burghausen
Busbach
Cham
Coburg
Deggendorf
Diesenhofen
Dingolfing
Eckersdorf
Eichstätt
Erbendorf
Erding
Erlangen
Forchheim
Freising
Fürstenfeldbruck
Fürth
Füssen
Grafing
Garmisch-
  Partenkirchen
Griesbach
Grossgrundloch
Günzburg
Gunzenhausen
Hassfurt

Hengersburg
Höchstadt
Hof
Hochkirchen
Ingolstadt
Kempten
Kirchbus
Kreising-Rothen-
  kirchen/Teusch-
  nitz
Kronach
Kulmbach
Landshut
Lichtenfels
Lindau
Ludwigstadt/
  Teuschnitz
Mainleus
Marktbreit
Markt Oberdorf
Memmingen
Mering
Moosburg
Münchaurach
Münchberg
Murnau
Naila
Neuhaus/Ulm
Neumarkt/Opf.
Neustadt a. A.
Neu-Ulm
Nördlingen
Nürnberg
Ottingen
Otterfing
Ottobeuren

Pappenheim
Pasing
Passau
Peesten
Pfonten
Prien
Regensburg
Rehau
Roding
Rosenheim
Rothenburg
Schliersee
Schwabach
Selbitz
Stadtstein
Staffelstein
Starnberg
Tegernsee
Thurnau
Traunstein
Vilsviburg
Wasserburg
Weiden
Weiding
Weissenburg
Weissendorf
Weissenhorn
Wemding
Westheim/
  Augsburg
Werting
Wrisberg/
  Kulmbach
Wörth
Würzburg
Zwiessel

IB. AGES OF NSDAP MEMBERS

(*National Socialists by Year of Birth*)

To 1853	4	1886	20
1854-63	14	1887	17
1864	2	1888	22
1865	1	1889	25
1866	1	1890	32
1867	1	1891	29
1868	13	1892	32
1869	5	1893	31
1870	2	1894	36
1871	4	1895	32
1872	7	1896	44
1873	8	1897	48
1874	5	1898	59
1875	12	1899	56
1876	11	1900	49
1877	12	1901	59
1878	6	1902	59
1879	7	1903	51
1880	11	1904	38
1881	13	1905	28
1882	21	1906	14
1883	15	1907	4
1884	19	1908	2
1885	13		

Ic. OCCUPATIONS OF NSDAP MEMBERS*

(Members before the Putsch)

Ärzte	17	Bildhauer	3	
Agent	1	Brauer	1	
Agitatorinnen	3	Brauereiarbeiter	1	
Amtsrichter	2	Brauereibesitzer	1	
Angestellte (no		Buchbinder	3	
further details)	9	Buchdrucker	3	
Antiquar	1	Buchhändler	7	
Apotheker &		Buchhändlersgehilfe	1	
Apothekebesitzer	8	Buchhalter (innen)	9	
Arbeiter (no		Bürodiener	1	
further details)	12	Bürogehilfe	2	
Arbeitslose	3	Bürovorsteher	1	
Architekte	10	Chemiker	1	
Archivrat	1	Dachdecker	1	
Assessoren	2	Dekorationsmaler	2	
Assistent	1	Dichter	3	
Aufkäufer	1	Diener		
Aufsichtsbeamter	1	(Dienstmädchen)	1	
Ausgeher	4	Diplom. Landwirte	4	
Automechaniker	2	Direktor	1	
Bäcker	9	Dreher	2	
Bäckersgattin	1	Druckereibesitzer	2	(+2?)
Bahnarbeiter	2	Einschaler	1	
Bahn Beamter	1	Eisenbahnober-		
Bandagist	1	sekretär	1	
Bank Beamte		Eisendreher	3	
(Angestellte)	29	Eisenhändler	2	
Bankgehilfe	1	Elektriker	1	
Bankinspektor	1	Elektromonteur	6	
Bankmetzger	1	Elektrotechniker	6	
Baumeister	1	Fabrikant	5	
Bauschüler	1	Fabrikdirektor	1	
Bergarbeiter	2	Färber	1	
Bergwerksdirektor	1	Fahnenschmied	1	
Berichterstatter	1	Fabrikarbeiter	5	
Betriebsleiter	3	Feinmechaniker	2	
Bezirksamtober-		Feinmechaniker-		
sekretär	1	lehrling	1	
Bezirksbaumeister	1			

* Where specific information (position/title) is available it is given. Otherwise, the general designation of the position is given.

Fideikommiss-		Kaufm. Lehrling	1
besitzer	1	Kellner	3
Filetstricker	1	Kesselschmied	1
Filmschauspieler	2	Klavierpolierer	1
Fläschner	1	Kleinfabrikbesitzer	1
Förster	4	Kleinkaufmänner	11
Freibankkünstler	1	Klempner	1
Friseur	11	Köchin	1
Garagebesitzer	2	Konditoren	3
Gastwirte	4	Konditorgehilfe	1
Geistliche	3	Kontorist (in)	4
Geometer	1	Kraftfahrer	18
Gerichtsassistent	1	Krankenpflegerin	1
Gerichtsbeamter	1	Küchenmeister	1
Gesangslehrerin	1	Kürschnergehilfe	1
Gesangsschüler	1	Kunstgewerbler	1
Geschäftsführer	4	Kunstglaser	1
Goldschmiede	3	Kunsthistoriker	1
Grosskaufmänner	4	Kunstmaler	13
Gutsbesitzer	2	Kunstschlosser	1
Gutspächter	2	Kunsttischler	1
Gymnasiast	8	Kupferschmiede	2
Haar- und Bartpfleger	1	Kutscher	6
Handlungsgehilfen	9	Laboranten	2
Handwerkmeister	1	Lagerhalter	1
Hartsteinfabrik-		Lageristen	3
besitzer	1	Landgerichts-	
Hausfrauen	14	inspektor	1
Hausverwalter	1	Landgerichtssekretär	1
Heeresangestellter	3	Landwirte	7
Heizer	1	Landwirt-	
Hilfsarbeiter	9	praktikanten	3
Holzhändler	2	Landwirtsch. Arbeiter	
Hotelangestellte	3	(Familienhof)	4
Hutmacher	2	Landwirtsch. Beamte	
Immobilien-Agent	1	(Privat)	2
Ingenieur	28	Lederhändler	1
Kalkulator	1	Lehramtskandidaten	2
Kaminkehrer	1	Lehrer (Oberlehrer	
Kanzleiassistent	1	usw.)	27
Kassenassistent	1	Lehrling	6
Kassierer (innen)	5	Lehrseminar Student	1
Kaufmänner	120	Leitungsaufsteher	1
Kaufmännische		Lichtpause & Plan-	
Angestellte	17	druckanstaltsbesitzer	1

Linierer	1
Lithographen	2
Lohnvorsteher	1
Magazinarbeiter	2
Magistratsdiener	1
Maler	6
Maschinenschlosser	2
Maschinist	8
Mathematiker	1
Maurer	6
Mechaniker	17
Messungsgehilfe	1
Metallarbeiter	1
Metzger	2
Ministerialrat	1
Mölkereibesitzer	1
Monteurs	
(Installateur)	5
Müller	1
Museumsbeamter	1
Musikdirektor	1
Musiker	4
NSDAP Angestellte	
usw.	20
Oberamtmann	1
Oberamtsrichter	1
Oberlandes-	
gerichtsrat	1
Oberpostdienstler	1
Oberpostsekretär	2
Oberrechnungsführer	1
Oberregierungsräte	3
Obersekretär	1
Oberverwal-	
tungssekretär	1
Ölmühlbesitzer	1
Operateur	1
Optiker	1
Packerin	1
Pensionsinhaber	2
Pferdehändler	1
Pförtner	1
Photographen	2
Pianolagerer	1
Pinselfabrikbesitzer	1

Postinspektoren	2
Postpraktikant	1
Postschaffner	5
Postsekretäre	5
Praktikanten	7
Privatiere	3
Professor, a.O.	1
Professoren (Dr.)	5
Professor emeritus	1
Professoren,	
Gymnasium	3
Professor,	
ordentlicher	1
Prokuristen	2
Propaganda	
(Reklam)	1
Rechnungsführer	1
Rechnungsgehilfe	1
Rechtsanwälte	6
Reedereiangestellte	1
Referendare	3
Regisseur	1
Reichsbankbeamte	
(Angestellte)	2
Reisender	1
Reizer	1
Reklamebewerber	1
Revisor	1
Sattler	3
Schäffler	1
Schauspieler	4
Schiffbauer	2
Schlosser	21
Schmiede	3
Schneider (meister)	12
Schreiner (meister)	17
Schriftleiter	16
Schriftsteller	8
Schuhmacher	4
Schriftsetzer	5
Sekretäre (innen)	6
Senatspräsident	1
Silberarbeiter	1
Speditionsinhaber	1
Spengler	4

Stadtsekretär	1	Vereinssekretär	1
Städtischer Bauführer	1	Verkäuferinnen	4
Städtischer		Vermessungsassistent	1
Oberamtmann	1	Versicherungs-	
Städtischer		oberinspektor	1
Verwaltungs-		Versicherungsmänner	
assistent	1	(Angestellte)	9
Steinbruchbesitzer	1	Versicherungs-	
Steindrucker	1	mathemiker	1
Stenotypist	1	Vertreter	2
Stickerin	1	Volkswirtschaftler	1
Studenten	103	Voluntäre	6
Studienräte	4	Vulkaniseur	1
Syndiken	3	Wagner	1
Tapezierer	5	Werkmeister	2
Taxifahrer	1	Werkstudenten	3
Techniker	7	Werkzeugschlosser	1
Technikum Schüler	1	Wirtschaftspächter	1
Telefonisten (innen)	3	Witwen	3
Telegrapharbeiter	1	Zahnärzte	8
Telegraphen-		Zahntechkniker	2
facharbeiter	1	Zimmerer	1
Tierärzte	8	Zirkusgeneralvertreter	1
Tischler	1	Zolloberinspektor	1
Tonkünstler	1	Zollsupernumerar	1
Uhrmacher	2		

ID. OCCUPATIONS OF LOCAL NSDAP LEADERS

Ortsgruppenführer

Apotheker	1	Malermeister	1
Arbeiter	1	Maschinenhaus-	
Architekt	1	gehilfe	1
Arzt	1	Maschinenschlosser	1
Assessor	1	Maschinist	2
Aushilfslehrer	1	Mechaniker	2
Bäckermeister	1	Metzgermeister	1
Bahnarbeiter	1	Mölkereibesitzer	1
Bankbeamter	2	Monteur	1
Brandversicherungs-		Müller	1
kommissar	1	Notariatssekretär	1
Buchhalter	1	Oberpostbeamter	1
Diplom Ingenieur	4	Oberverwaltungs-	
Diplom Landwirt	1	sekretär	1
Eisenbahnsekretär	1	Ölmühlbesitzer	1
Fabrikarbeiter	1	Pensionsbesitzer	1
Fabriktechniker	1	Photographe	1
Feinkostgeschäfts-		Postsekretär	1
inhaber	1	Professor	1
Gastwirt	2	Rechtsanwalt	1
Gutspächter	1	Revierförster	1
Gymnasium		Schneidermeister	1
Professor	1	Stadtoberamtmann	1
Handlungsgehilfe	1	Städtischer	
Holzhändler	1	Bauführer	1
Immob. Agent	1	Student	1
Kaufmännischer		Studienrat	2
Angestellte	1	Telegraphen-	
Kaufmann	3	facharbeiter	1
Kunstmaler	1	Tierarzt	4
Kupferschmied	2	Verwaltungs-	
Landwirt/Gastwirt	1	oberinspektor	1
Lehrer	2		

S.A. Führer

Amtsrichter	1	Lehrer	1
Assistent bei Versorg-		Oberrechnungsführer	1
ungsamt	1	Pfarrer	1
Bankbeamter	2	Postsekretär	2
Eisenhändler	1	Referendar	2
Forstamtmann	1	Städtischer Beamter	1
Hilfpostschaffner	1	Steuerassistent	1
Holzhändler	1	Tierarzt	2
Kaufmann	3	Uhrmacherlehrling	1
Kürschnergehilfe	1	Verwaltungsinspektor	1
Landwirt	1	Wirtschaftspächter	1
Lehramtskandidat	1	Zollinspektor	1

List of Abbreviations

Abt.	Abteilung
a. D.	ausser Dienst
Äuss.	Äusseres
B, I	Bayerisches Hauptstaatsarchiv, Abteilung I
B, II	Bayerisches Hauptstaatsarchiv, Abteilung II
B, IV	Bayerisches Hauptstaatsarchiv, Abteilung IV
BA	Bundesarchiv Koblenz
BA	Bezirksamt
Batt.	Batterie
BBK	Bürgerbräukeller
BG	Bayerischer Gesandter
BLV	*Bayerischer Landtag, Stenographische Berichten*
BT	*Berliner Tageblatt*
Btl.	Bataillon
BuR	Bund Bayern und Reich
BVP	Bayerische Volkspartei
DDP	Deutsche Demokratische Partei
DNB	Deutscher Notbann
DNVP	Deutschnationale Volkspartei
DOB	Deutscher Offiziersbund
DR	*Deutsche Rundschau*
DSZ	*Deutsche Soldatenzeitung*
DvFP	Deutschvölkische Freiheitspartei
DVP	Deutsche Volkspartei
EW	Einwohnerwehr
FH	Archiv, Hansestadt Hamburg
FK	*Fränkischer Kurier*
FKB	Frontkriegerbund
FZ	Feldzeugmeisterei
Geh.	Geheim
GP	Gordon Papers
GSK	Generalstaatskommissar; Generalstaatskommissariat
GVG	Grossdeutsche Volksgemeinschaft
HC	*Hamburger Correspondent*
HMB	Halbmonatsbericht
IR	Infanterie Regiment (III./I.R. 19 = Drittes Bataillon, Infanterie Regiment 19)

Kdo.	Kommando
KDO	Kampfbund Deutscher Offiziere
KPD	Kommunistische Partei Deutschlands
Lapo	Landespolizei
LC	Library of Congress, Washington, D.C., Rehse Collection
Ldtg.	Landtag
MAA	*München-Augsburger-Abendzeitung*
M/F	Mittelfranken
M. Inn.	Ministerium des Innern (Bayerisches Staats-)
MNN	*Münchner Neuesten Nachrichten*
MP	*Münchener Post*
MSPD	Majoritäts-Sozialdemokratische Partei Deutschlands (= SPD)
NA	National Archives of the United States, Washington, D.C.
N/B	Niederbayern
NBl.	Nachrichtenblatt
NDO (NVDO)	Nationalverband Deutscher Offiziere
NSDAP	Nationalsozialistische Deutsche Arbeiterpartei
NSFP	Nationalsozialistische Freiheitspartei
Obb.	Oberbayern
Obltg.	Oberleitung
Ofr.	Oberfranken
Opf.	Oberpfalz
PDM	Polizeidirektion München
PDN-F	Polizeidirektion Nürnberg-Fürth
PNB	Polizei Nothilfe Bayerns
Pol. Komm.	Polizei Kommissar
PW	Polizeiwehr (Frühname der Landespolizei.)
Reg.	Regierung
Reg. Präs.	Regierungs-Präsident = Präsident eines Regierungsbezirks
Rgt.	Regiment
RK (Rk. O.)	Reichskommissar für die Überwachung d. öffentlichen Ordnung
RKF	Reichskriegsflagge
R.M. Inn.	Reichsminister (-ium) des Innern
RSG	Republik-Schutz-Gesetz
RV	*Reichstag, Stenographische Berichten*
RV	Reichsverfassung
RW	Reichswehr (Reichsheer volkstümlich oder Wehrmacht)
RWM	Reichswehrminister (-ium)

SA (NSDAP)	Sturmabteilungen der NSDAP
SA (SPD)	Sturmabteilungen der SPD
Schw.	Schwaben
SOD	Sozialistischer Ordnungsdienst
SPD	Sozialdemokratische Partei Deutschlands
Stadtkomm.	Stadtkommissar
St. V.	Stations-Verstärkung (Kompanie) (Lapo)
SZ	*Süddeutsche Zeitung*
Ufr.	Unterfranken
USPD	Unabhängige Sozialdemokratische Partei Deutschlands
VBORV	Verband Bayerischer Offiziere und Regimentsvereine
VB	*Völkischer Beobachter*
Vo	*Vorwärts*
VSPD	Vereinigte Sozialdemodratische Partei Deutschlands (= SPD)
VVV	Vereinigte Vaterländische Verbände
VVVA	Vereinigte Vaterländische Verbände Augsburgs
VVVB	Vereinigte Vaterländische Verbände Bayerns
VVVD	Vereinigte Vaterländische Verbände Deutschlands
VVM	Vaterländische Bezirksvereine Münchens
WKK	Wehrkreiskommando (Reichswehr)
W	Württembergisches Staatsarchiv
WWR	*Wehrwissenschaftliche Rundschau*
Y	Yale University Library
Z	Institut für Zeitgeschichte, München

Critical Bibliography

PRIMARY SOURCES

ARCHIVAL

I. National Archives of the United States, Washington, D.C.

Most of the materials used in the National Archives have since been returned to the custody of the German government and are now to be found in the Bundesarchiv Koblenz; the Bundesarchiv, Zweigstelle Freiburg, Breisgau (Militärarchiv); or in the Bayerisches Hauptstaatsarchiv, Abteilung I, München. Almost all of the materials formerly to be found in the National Archives are also available on microfilms in the American Historical Association–National Archives (AHA-NA) or Hoover Institution series.

AHA-NA Microfilm Materials. Materials included in this series and recorded from it are keyed to it. References commence with the file group number, followed by the roll number, followed by the page number. An example is: T120 (file group), 5570 (roll), p. K591455. The microfilm materials used for this book include: T79, Wehrkreis VII; T81, Hitler Correspondence; T84, Hitler Correspondence; T120, Gesandtschaftsberichten aus Bayern und Reichskabinettssitzungsprotokolle; T175, Heinrich Himmler Sammlung.

Epp Papers. These papers were included in the Miscellaneous Personalities (EAP) Group of the Military Documents Collection, which was sent to Freiburg. The Bekanntmachungen of SA Regiment München for most of 1923 are included in this collection; another copy is in the Institut für Zeitgeschichte in München. The Epp Papers references in this book are keyed to personal microfilm copies in the possession of the author but are almost identical with the identification symbols used in the AHA-NA microfilms.

Hitler Putsch File of the Nineteenth Infantry Regiment of the Reichswehr. The originals are in Freiburg and microfilms are available. References in the book are to a set of these microfilms purchased by the author before the AHA-NA team reached this material.

Hitler Trial Stenographic Report (including the secret sessions). This original (a carbon copy) of the NA document has been returned to Germany and is in Koblenz. A different carbon copy was uncovered several years ago in the Bayerisches Hauptstaatsarchiv, Abteilung II. The references to this series are, for technical reasons, of two kinds. References to the earlier days of the trial are keyed to the page numbers of individual daily sections. Later days are keyed to the rubber-stamped "run-through" pagination. This shift should cause no difficulty for the researcher since both sets of numbers are found on all pages of the NA-Koblenz copy of the report.

Landespolizei Bekanntmachungen. The references in the book were taken from the documents themselves and were made when the materials were still in the United States. These documents are now included in the Landespolizei Collection in the Bayerisches Hauptstaatsarchiv, Abteilung IV.

Seeckt Papers. These are now included in the Freiburg collections. Nearly complete microfilms of these papers are available in the United States.

II. Gordon Papers

A. Letters: Oberst a. D. Richard Baur, Generalleutnant a. D. Martin Dehmel, Herr Eberhard Dennerlein, Korvettenkapitän a. D. Hermann Ehrhardt, Generalleutnant, a. D. Heinrich Greiner, Generaloberst a. D. Franz Halder, General der Infanterie a. D. Hermann von Hanneken, Generalleutnant a. D. Eduard Hauser, Generalleutnant a. D. Wolfgang Hauser, Generaloberst a. D. Gotthard Heinrici, Generalleutnant a. D. Fritz Hengen, Oberst a. D. Karl H. Herschel, Generalleutnant a. D. Anton Freiherr von Hirschberg, Minister-präsident a. D. Dr. Wilhelm Hoegner, Brigade-General a. D. Max Ibel, Generalleutnant a. D. Josef Kammhuber, Generalmajor a. D. E. von Kiliani, General der Kavallerie a. D. Ernst Köstring, General der Artillerie a. D. Emil Leeb, Generalfeldmarschall a. D. Wilhelm Ritter von Leeb, Generalleutnant a. D. J. Lehmann, Generalmajor a. D. Walther Leuze, Generalfeldmarschall a. D. Wilhelm List, Freiin Anna Loeffelholz von Colberg, Generalmajor a. D. Bernhard von Lossberg, Generalmajor a. D. Oskar Munzel, General der Panzertruppe a. D. Walther Nehring, Generalleutnant a. D. Curt Osterroht, Generalleutnant a. D. Otto Ottenbacher, Generalleutnant a. D. Max Josef Pemsel, Herrn Kurt Pflügel, Generalmajor a. D. Christian Pirner, General der Infanterie a. D. Siegfried Rasp, Frau General Lise Renz, Generalmajor a. D. Gottfried Riemhofer, Herr Gerhard Rossbach, Generalleutnant a. D. Otto Schaefer, Generalfeldmarschall a. D. Ferdinand Schörner, General der Infanterie a. D. Max Schwandner, Oberst a. D. Hans-Harald von Selchow, Major a. D. Alexander Siry, Generalleutnant a. D. Maximilian Siry, Generalleutnant a. D. Friedrich Sixt, Graf Josef Maria von Soden-Fraunhofen, Oberst a. D. Fritz Teichmann, Herr Carl Tillessen, General der Infanterie a. D. Kurt von Tippelskirch, Generalmajor

a. D. Wilhelm Ullersperger, General der Infanterie a. D. Walter von Unruh, Generalmajor a. D. Günther von Uslar-Gleichen, Herr Fritz Warnecke, General a. D. Max Winkler, Oberst a. D. Hans Streck. *B. Depositions*: Anonymous Landespolizei Officer (later Bundeswehr), Anonymous Waffenschüler of I. Lehrgang which graduated in September 1923, Archivdirektor a. D. Gerhard Böhm, Minister-Präsident a. D. Dr. Hans Ehard, Oberstleutnant a. D. Oskar Erhard, Professor Hans Fehn, Oberstleutnant a. D. Max Lagerbauer, General der Artillerie a. D. Emil Leeb, Professor Karl Loewenstein, Herr Emil Maurice, Oberstleutnant a. D. Otto Muxel, Oberst a. D. Josef Remold, Herr Hermann Ruhland, Oberst a. D. Ernst Schultes, Dr. Walter Schulz.

D. Card File
1. Personalities
2. Organizations
3. Press

E. Documents
Gessler Papers. These include drafts of chapters of his autobiography (which differ slightly from the published version) and testimony of his adjutants, etc.

Heye Memoirs. Microfilms in the possesssion of the author. There is a copy in the Württembergisches Staatsarchiv, Stuttgart.

Leuze Report. This is a copy of the general's report of 11 November 1923 concerning his actions during the Putsch.

Kurt Pflügel Statement. His statement of 9 October 1963 regarding the Hitler Putsch.

Selchow Notes. Hans-Harald von Selchow's notes about the Hitler-Seeckt meeting of 11 March 1923.

Wenz Notes. Undated notes of Generalleutnant a. D. von Wenz zu Niederlahnstein regarding the Putsch.

PUBLISHED MATERIALS

Anker, Kurt. *Unsere Stunde kommt*: Leipzig: Leipziger Graphische Werke A. 1923.
    This work is valuable as an expression of the views and attitudes of racist circles in western Germany in the period before 1924.

Blome, Dr. Kurt. *Arzt im Kampf*. Leipzig: Johann Ambrosius Barth, 1942.

Bonnin, Georges. *Le Putsch de Hitler à Munich en 1923*. n.p. [Paris]: Bonin, 1966.
    Bonnin's slender collection of documents is useful in that he presents some items from collections not used by Hofmann and not included in Deuerlein's larger document collection, although these

documents have long been known to some American scholars. His work serves more as a supplement to Deuerlein than as an attempt to make a full presentation of the most significant Putsch materials.

Braun, Otto. *Von Weimar bis Hitler.* New York: Europa, 1940.

The Prussian minister-president's memoirs are helpful for general background and for the views of a moderate northern Social Democrat. The Bavarian scene and the Putsch period are peripheral to Braun's account.

D'Abernon, Viscount Edgar Vincent. *Ambassador of Peace.* 3 vols., London: Hodder and Stoughton, 1929.

D'Abernon's account of Berlin reactions to the Hitler Putsch are interesting, though brief and superficial.

Deuerlein, Ernst. *Der Hitler-Putsch.* Stuttgart: Deutsche Verlagsanstalt, 1962.

This extremely valuable document collection with a long introduction by Professor Deuerlein is a major contribution to our knowledge of the year 1923 in Bavaria. Despite the introduction, however, many of the documents need much interpretation and supplementation for foreigners and even for the present younger generation of Germans, so that it is perhaps of greatest value for those who already have a considerable knowledge of Bavaria in these critical years or for use in seminars and for other advanced student work.

Goebbels, Dr. Joseph. *The Goebbels Diaries, 1942-1943.* New York: Doubleday, 1948.

These diaries are primarily valuable as foreground for the student of the earlier period, since they enable him to check the development and ideas of the early leaders and party against the later period.

Hanfstaengl, Ernst. *Hitler: The Missing Years.* London: Eyre and Spottiswoode, 1957

Hanfstaengl's account is essentially light and journalistic. Nonetheless, he provides interesting sidelights and highlights regarding Hitler and his entourage in the critical years 1923-24. Hanfstaengl is not always accurate, though, and is especially likely to err when reporting events in which he took no direct part.

Heydebreck, Peter von. *Wir Wehr-Wölfe.* Leipzig: F. K. Koehler, 1931.

Heydebreck, a daring young officer in World War I, a famous horseman, and an independent-minded SA leader, was one of the victims of the Blood Purge of 1934. His autobiography, while colored by prejudice and exaggerating his own significance and that of his men, is a valuable window on the Racist Movement in Upper Silesia and reveals the extent to which Hitler and his colleagues failed to recognize their need for a national, as well as a Bavarian, power base.

Hierl, Konstantin. *Im Dienst für Deutschland, 1918-1945.* Heidelberg: Vowinckel, 1954.

Hierl, a Reichswehr officer who joined the NSDAP shortly after his retirement and became Hitler's labor service chief, says very little about the early years of his postwar career, but he does reveal the fact that he was squeezed out of the army because of his involvement with National Socialism.

Hinkel, Hans. *Einer unter Hundertausend.* München: Knorr and Hirth, 1938.

Hinkel's work is primarily valuable for the atmosphere it depicts and the attitudes it reveals. It helps to re-create the München of 1923 as the racist youths saw it.

Hitler, Adolf. *Es sprach der Führer.* Gütersloh: Mohn, 1966.

This work deals with a later period but includes a single parenthetical reference to Hitler on 9 November 1923 that could not be ignored.

Hitler, Adolf. *Mein Kampf.* München: Franz Eher, Volksausgabe, 1942.

Hitler's Landsberg autobiography and program is a vital document but one that must be handled with great care and circumspection, as is pointed out by Werner Maser (*Hitlers Mein Kampf*, München and Esslingen, 1966). It is, like Napoleon's memoirs and Napoleon III's prison writings, to be seen more as a revelation of the man and his ideas than as a full and truthful account of his and his party's past. As is always the case with Hitler, truth is tastefully adorned with myth, half-truths, and downright lies.

Hitler, Adolf. *Tischgespräche im Führerhauptquartier, 1941-42.* 2nd edn. Stuttgart: Seewald, 1965.

These monologues are most useful for an indication of how little his attitudes, aims, and methods had changed in the years since 1923, as well as for actual references to events of the Kampfzeit and evaluations and descriptions of persons within the party and without.

Hoegner, Dr. Wilhelm. *Der schwierige Aussenseiter.* München and Wien: Isar, 1959.

Hoegner's memoirs reveal the SPD's situation and the views and activities of its leaders, as seen by a vigorous and independent-minded Social Democrat. It is much less sound on what was happening in the "enemy camp," whether right radical or conservative.

Jünger, Ernst, *Jahre der Okkupation.* Stuttgart: Klett, 1958.

Although devoted to a much later period, Jünger's book contains a vivid flashback to the hectic days of late 1923 in München.

Kallenbach, Hans. *Mit Adolf Hitler auf Festung Landsberg.* München: Kress and Hornung, 1939.

A National Socialist breviary, this is heavily laced with official mythology but also contains some useful information and reveals something of the mood and personalities of the Putschists. It provides the best published account of the Stosstrupp Hitler, which has sometimes been seen as the precursor of the SS.

Kress von Kressenstein, Friedrich Freiherr. *Mit den Türken zum Suez-Kanal.* Berlin: Vorhut, 1938.

This work is useful as background for one of the most significant figures on the military stage in the crisis years in Bavaria.

Krüger, Alf. *10 Jahre Kampf um Volk und Land.* Berlin-Schöneberg: Deutsche Kultur-Wacht, 1934.

The first section of this National Socialist collective memoir deals with the attempts of the nascent National Socialist organization in Hamburg to prepare for the Putsch and with the arrest of its leaders when the situation became critical.

Ludendorff, Erich. *Auf dem Weg zur Feldherrnhalle.* München: Ludendorffs, 1938.

Ludendorff's account of the Putsch, its prelude, and its aftermath is highly personalized and suffers from his ability to remold the truth with a crystal-clear conscience. Nonetheless, it is revealing and, used with care and in comparison with other sources, contributes to our knowledge of the Putsch and the Putschists.

Müller, Karl Alexander von. *Im Wandel einer Zeit.* München: Süddeutscher, 1966.

Müller, a prominent München historian in the between-the-wars period, was not a National Socialist himself but had many ties with the party and its leaders. As a conservative with vague right radical leanings and as the brother-in-law of Gottfried Feder, the National Socialist economic theorist, Müller was close not only to the Putschists but also to the circle around Kahr. His memoirs are therefore both interesting and valuable for the student of Bavarian politics.

Nissen, Rudolf, *Helle Blätter, Dunkle Blätter.* Stuttgart: Deutsche Verlagsanstalt, 1969.

This fascinating and provocative autobiography of a famous surgeon who was an acute social and political observer is invaluable less for facts than for its rendition of the atmosphere and currents of feeling, especially among the youth, in Weimar Germany.

Noske, Gustav. *Erlebtes aus Aufstieg und Niedergang einer Demokratie.* Zürich-Offenbach: Bollwerk, 1947.

Noske's shrewd evaluation of the development of Weimar Germany has only background value for this study, except where it indicates the lack of reaction to the Putsch in Noske's province.

Röhm, Ernst. *Geschichte eines Hochverräters.* 1st and 5th edns. München: Franz Eher, 1928 & 1934

There are striking but minor differences between the first and later editions; the fifth is the one from which all citations in this book are drawn. Röhm's autobiography is central to the study of the years

1923-24 in Bavaria and particularly the Hitler Putsch. It is therefore indispensible. On the other hand, Röhm is much less frank, open, and reliable than appears to be the case at first glance. His account must be carefully checked against others and against the existing pre-Putsch documents before any particular fact or scene is accepted as rendered. Röhm's narrative both distorts and magnifies his role in events. It sometimes intentionally and sometimes unintentionally misleads by silence as well as by distortion.

Rossbach, Gerhard. *Mein Weg durch die Zeit.* Weilburg-Lahn: Vereinigte Weilburger Buchdruckereien, 1950.

Rossbach's *Weg* through life has been somewhat smoothed and repaved by this book. It is, however, very useful for its revelation of his personality and for a general description of his career. Written many years later, the book glosses over the Putsch and his role in it and completely ignores the controversy that surrounded some of his actions. Rossbach's radicalism is toned down and there are a good number of inaccuracies.

Sauerbruch, Ferdinand, *Das war mein Leben.* München: Kindler, 1960.

This autobiography of a famous surgeon who was inclined, in the early Weimar period, to dabble in politics occasionally was, according to Nissen, written well after Sauerbruch's memory had begun to fail badly. It was partly written by Sauerbruch himself and partly by a professional writer on the basis of notes and conversations with Sauerbruch. The events of the fall of 1923 are merely touched upon, but there are some interesting sidelights on the times and students as well as information on Ludendorff that may help to explain his peculiarities.

Severing, Carl. *Mein Lebensweg.* 2 vols. Köln: Greven, 1950.

Severing provides some background material and some sidelights on the events of 1923 in Bavaria but is essentially peripheral to the theme.

Speer, Albert. *Erinnerungen.* Berlin: Propyläen, 1969.

Speer's account of his youth provides valuable insights into the sort of mood and tone that was prevalent among many German youths and helped to lead them into the Racist Movement and the NSDAP.

Stresemann, Gustav. *Vermächtnis.* 3 vols. Berlin, 1932.

This biography has now been largely superseded by other and more balanced accounts and, most of all, by the availability of the Stresemann Nachlass. However, taken together with the minutes of the debates of the Reichskabinett, it provided materials sufficient for this book.

Stülpnagel, Joachim von. *75 Jahre meines Lebens.* Düsseldorf (private edn.), 1960.

The life of an officer who served in a key Heeresleitung post during 1923, this work is revealing for background as well as for attitudes of prominent officers. It also supplements the information on the Putsch and other matters that General von Stülpnagel made available to General von Rabenau for his Seeckt biography.

Toynbee, Arnold J. *Acquaintances*. London. Oxford University Press, 1967.

Interesting here only for Toynbee's thumbnail sketch of Hitler and his evaluation of the Führer's intelligence and ability.

United States Department of State, ed. *Papers Relating to the Foreign Relations of the United States: The Paris Peace Conference 1919*. 13 vols. Washington, Government Printing Office, 1944-46.

Dr. Georg Heim's separatist activities in 1919 are confirmed by a document in this series.

SECONDARY SOURCES

Alter, Junius [pseud. of Franz Sontag]. *Nationalisten*. Leipzig: K. F. Koehler, 1930.

Useful for its indications of the attitudes and disagreements within the Patriotic Movement and other nationalist groups.

Angress, Werner T. *Stillborn Revolution: The Communist Bid for Power in Germany, 1921-1923*. Princeton: Princeton University Press, 1963.

Professor Angress provides data on the activities of the Communists and their allies that helps to explain why the Bavarians were so afraid of a Red revolution in 1923.

Bennecke, Heinrich. *Hitler und die SA*. München and Wien; Günther Olzog, 1962.

Written by an SA leader who was active in the organization from early 1923 on, this account is weak on the early years. It does, however, contain some useful information. Bennecke practically ignores the struggle for the control of the SA and its internal difficulties, although he was himself involved.

Bennecke, Heinrich. *Die Reichswehr und der "Röhm Putsch."* München and Wien: Günther Olzog, 1964.

Useful here only for the subsequent fate of some of the protagonists.

Bronnen, Arnolt. *Rossbach*. Berlin: Ernst Rowohlt, 1930.

Helpful for atmosphere and attitudes. Often inaccurate.

Caro, Kurt, and Oehme, Walter. *Schleichers Aufstieg*. Berlin: Ernst Rowohlt, 1933.

This polemic against the army by two militant left-wing socialists, one of whom was subsequently an active figure in the DDR, provides the radical Marxist viewpoint and a few snippets of documents which, taken in context, prove to mean quite the opposite of what Caro and Oehme wish them to prove. Peripheral to the Bavarian problem.

Carsten, F. L. *Die Reichswehr und Politik*. Köln-Berlin: Kiepenheuer and Witsch, 1964.

A general account of Reichswehr policy and relations with the Weimar Republic by a hostile historian. With regard to the Bavarian problems in the crisis years 1923-24, Carsten leans heavily on Hofmann and picks up a number of factual errors from him. Carsten takes only a peripheral interest in Bavaria and does not fully understand the Lossow affair.

Coblitz, Wilhelm. *Theodor von der Pfordten*. München: Franz Eher, 1937.

Although it is an NSDAP propaganda tract, it does provide some information on this most elusive of the significant National Socialist leaders of the Putsch period.

Frank, Walter. *Franz Ritter von Epp*. Hamburg: Hanseatiche Verlagsanstalt, 1934.

A more or less official NSDAP biography useful for background and, to a lesser extent, for the mood in Bavaria at the time. Frank completely ignores the coolness between Epp and the Kampfbund leaders during 1923-24 as well his opposition to the Putsch. Must be used with care.

Freksa, Friedrich. *Kapitän Ehrhardt*. Berlin: August Scherl, 1924.

This is a revealing if inaccurate book based on interviews with Ehrhardt and partially written by one of Ehrhardt's chief aides. It is mostly interesting for background.

Gengler, Ludwig. *Die deutschen Monarchisten, 1919-1925*. Kulmbach, 1932.

Contains a few items of interest but is generally dated and peripheral to the special Bavarian problems and developments. The author also suffered from lack of access to many materials which are now readily available.

Goerlitz, Walther. *Der deutsche Generalstab*. Frankfurt, 1950.

Peripheral and contains a few factual errors that should be corrected.

Gordon, Harold J., Jr. *The Reichswehr and the German Republic, 1919-1926*. Princeton: Princeton University Press, 1957.

Peripheral, but provides some background material and some information on parallel developments in Berlin. It includes some errors in regard to the Bavarian scene. The German edition (*Die Reichswehr und die Weimarer Republik, 1919-1926*, Frankfurt, 1959.) contains a few corrections of minor errors in the English language edition.

Gordon, Harold J., Jr. "*Die Reichswehr und Sachsen, 1923*," *Wehrwissenschaftliche Rundschau*, December 1961.

Although peripheral this article provides background data to help explain Bavarian hostility towards Saxony and fear of a Red invasion.

———— "*Ritter von Epp und Berlin*," *Wehrwissenschaftliche Rundshau*, June 1959.

Useful for background information about Berlin-München relations on the military front and about Berlin's method of handling right radical dissidents in the Bavarian contingent.

Gritzbach, Erich. *Hermann Göring: Werk und Mensch*. München: Franz Eher, 1941.

Provides the official NSDAP account of Göring's activities after the Putsch. Very thin on the early period in general and very inaccurate.

Hartenstein, *Hauptmann der Schupo*. *Der Kampfeinsatz der Schutzpolizei bei inneren Unruhen*. Charlottenburg: Offene Worte, 1926.

Valuable for its account of the Hamburg Communist revolt of 1923 and for general information regarding the employment of riot police units.

Heiden, Konrad. *Der Führer*. New York: Houghton Mifflin, 1944.

Although this work is now largely superseded by Bullock and others, and contains many factual errors, its provocative theories and discussion of atmosphere are striking.

Held, Dr. Josef. *Heinrich Held*. Regensburg: "Zeit und Welt," 1958.

This brief biographical sketch of the most important single leader of the dominant BVP during the crucial years is useful for background. It was written by a son.

Heusinger, Adolf. *Befehl im Widerstreit, 1923-45*. Tübingen and Stuttgart: Rainer Wunderlich, 1950.

A fictionalized treatment of the history of the Reichswehr and Wehrmacht by means of individual episodes (basically personal confrontations), including one based on the return of an Infantry School student to his regiment.

Hofmann, Hanns Hubert. *Der Hitlerputsch. Krisenjahre deutscher Geschichte, 1920-24*. München: Nymphenburger Verlagshandlung, 1961.

Hofmann provides an interesting account of the Putsch, its prelude, and its aftermath, although the subtitle suggests much more attention to the earlier period than it receives. The treatment is essentially the traditional left-liberal one, which accepts the National Socialist narrative of events in general but says that what the National Socialists say is good is really bad. For this reason there is less critical examination of the alleged "facts" put forward by the Putschists at their trial and in propaganda statements than one might wish.

Hofmann has used far fewer contemporary materials than were available at the time he wrote, and there have been significant new materials turned up since that time. He depends too heavily on memoirs and on the trial statements of the Putschists in preference to pre-Putsch data, even where such information is readily available. Since the pre-Putsch information often differs sharply from the evidence Hofmann uses, this practice leads to obvious factual errors.

In view of the very sharp divergence of viewpoints and the many differences regarding facts between my book and that of Professor Hofmann, it is impractical to do more than try to note some key factual differences in footnotes. The reader will have to decide for himself where interpretations are concerned.

Jochmann, Werner. *Nationalsozialismus und Revolution: Ursprung und Geschichte der NSDAP in Hamburg, 1922-1933.* Frankfurt: Europäische Verlagsanstalt 1962.

Very useful, and contains a number of documents of interest for the study of the Putsch atmosphere in north Germany. Jochmann does not, however, always distinguish carefully among the adherents of Hitler, Ehrhardt, Rossbach, and other racist leaders, which reduces the book's value for the student of the early period of racist competition.

Kater, Michael H. "Zur Soziographie der frühren NSDAP" in *Vierteljahrshefte für Zeitgeschichte*, 19. Jhrg./Heft 2 (April 1971).

Klass, Gert von. *Hugo Stinnes.* Tübingen: Rainer Wunderlich, 1958.

Koerber, Adolf-Viktor von. *Der völkische Ludendorff.* München: Boepple, 1923 [1924].

A very interesting National Socialist Kampfschrift published shortly after the Putsch, this is a good example of Putschist propaganda at that time.

Kruck, Alfred. *Geschichte des Alldeutschen Verbandes.* Wiesbaden: Franz Steiner, 1954.

Useful for background.

Leverkuehn, Paul. *Posten auf ewiger Wache: Aus dem abenteuerreichen Lebens des Max Erwin von Scheubner-Richter.* Essen: Essener Verlagsanstalt, 1938.

Valuable for its general account of the life of Scheubner-Richter and his ideas. It includes a good dose of National Socialist propaganda and is thinner on hard facts regarding his activities in late 1923 than one might wish.

Löbsack, Wilhelm. *Albert Forster.* Hamburg: Hanseatische Verlagsanstalt, 1934.

This court history of the Gauleiter of Danzig's career includes a very brief account of his activity at the time of the Putsch and its aftermath.

Lohalm, Uwe. *Völkischer Radikalismus.* Hamburg: Leibniz-Verlag, 1970.

This book provides the first serious and effective study of one of the most important right radical and antisemitic organizations of the period immediately following World War I. Its propaganda helped significantly to create an atmosphere receptive to National Socialism. It is therefore very useful for the student of National Socialism as well as for anyone who is interested in the new political currents of the postwar years.

Maser, Werner. *Die Frühgeschichte der NSDAP: Hitlers Weg bis 1924.* Frankfurt: Athenäum, 1965.

The best of the available accounts of the early National Socialist Party. It concentrates on the internal development of the party, especially Hitler's struggle for control and the reconstruction of the party after his triumph. Maser pays little attention to the party's relations with other organizations of the state. Much weaker for 1923 than the earlier years.

Meier-Welcker, Hans. *Seeckt.* Frankfurt: Bernard und Graefe, 1967.

This is the most recent and best biography of General von Seeckt. It contains some useful information regarding his relations with Bavaria.

Nolte, Ernst. *The Three Faces of Fascism.* New York: Holt, Rinehart, and Winston, 1966.

A valuable discussion of National Socialism in relation to the Italian and French brands of Fascism. Nolte has valuable insights, perceiving clearly the extent to which Fascism is a mirror image of and reaction to Marxism, but he is inclined to "intellectualize" a movement that was in many ways strongly anti-intellectual and was led by men who were contemptuous of any but concrete goals. He also tries to place in the confines of the lower middle class a movement that used the word "bourgeois" as a term of opprobrium and that, as Hitler later noted with pride, ordered its members to avoid wearing suits and ties so as to frighten away the Kleinbürger who would alienate the workers.

Hitler and the men around him were men of action who subordinated ideas and theories not only to their emotions but also to such aims as the creation of a new order in Europe based on a greater Germany. It is therefore very difficult to explain them and their activities effectively in terms of doctrinaire political theories as Nolte tends to do.

Orlow, Dietrich. "The Organization, History and Structure of the NSDAP, 1919-1923," *Journal of Modern History*, xxxvii (June 1965).

This article provides very little concrete information on the organization of the NSDAP in 1923; it concentrates on the earlier years.

Phelps, Reginald R. "Anton Drexler—Der Gründer der NSDAP," *Deutscher Rundschau* 87 Jhrg., Nr. 12 (December 1961).

———— "Hitler and the Deutche Arbeiterpartei," *American Historical Review*, lxviii (1963).

These two articles are valuable for background information concerning the early NSDAP.

Pölnitz, Götz Freiherr von. *Emir: Das tapfere Leben des Freiherrn Marschall von Bieberstein*. München: Georg D. W. Callwey, 1938.

A very interesting and informative biography of a National Socialist activist. It is not always reliable in detail, since it incorporates much National Socialist mythology regarding the Putsch, but it contains information not readily found elsewhere.

Rabenau, Friedrich von. *Seeckt. Aus seinem Leben, 1918-1936*. Leipzig: von Hase und Koehler, 1941.

Although largely superseded by Meier-Welcker's more recent biography, this work still provides useful data for the careful researcher.

Reichsarchiv (later Reichskriegsministerium and Oberkommando der Wehrmacht), ed. *Darstellungen aus den Nachkriegskämpfe deutscher Truppen und Freikorps*. 9(+) vols. Berlin: E. S. Mittler und Sohn, 1936-1940.

An official history useful primarily for background information.

Sagerer, G., and Schuler, Emil. *Die bayerische Landespolizei von 1919-1935*. München: Selbstverlag, n.d. [1954].

This brief sketch of the history and organization of the Landespolizei contains a good deal of material not easily located elsewhere.

Schirmer, Friedrich. *Celler Soldatenbuch*. Celle: August Pohl, n.d. [*ca.* 1937].

Schirmer's little volume provides an interesting and suggestive account of the collapse of a small racist paramilitary organization when it was called upon by its leaders to take part in the Hitler Putsch.

Schuler, Emil. *Die bayerische Landespolizei, 1919-1935*. München: Selbstverlag n.d. [1964]

A more recent account of the short life of the Landespolizei that supplements the account in Sagerer and Schuler. Some of the material in the earlier work is not found here, and some new data is provided.

Schwend, Karl. *Bayern zwischen Monarchie und Diktatur.* München: Richard Pflaum, 1954.

Schwend provides us with a useful general account of the Bavarian political scene during the Weimar period from a moderate-conservative viewpoint and with strong white-blue overtones. It is therefore to be regarded as almost a court history.

Sendtner, Karl. *Rupprecht von Wittelsbach, Kronprinz von Bayern.* München: Richard Pflaum, 1954.

Another useful general account, centered around the pretender and his retinue. Useful for background and some detail.

Wulz, Georg. *Die Familie Kahr.* Archiv für Rassen- und Gesellschaftsbiologie, Band 18, Heft 3 (September 1926).

Wulz's pamphlet provides background material, including a sketch of the early life and career of Gustav von Kahr.

Zimmermann, Werner G. *Bayern und das Reich, 1918-1923.* München: Richard Pflaum, 1953.

A general account that focuses on relations between Berlin and München, this book also provides a good deal of insight into the interests and activities of Crown Prince Rupprecht.

REFERENCE WORKS

Das deutsche Führer-Lexikon, 1934-1935. Berlin, 1934.

Handbuch für das deutsche Reich, 1936. Berlin, 1936.

Heereseverordnungsblatt. Berlin, 1919ff.

Hof- und Staatshandbuch des Königreichs Bayern, 1890. München, 1890.

Keilig, Wolf, ed. *Das deutsche Heer, 1939-1945.* Bad Nauheim, 1957ff.

Kürschners Volkshandbuch Deutscher Reichstag, 1933. Berlin, n.d. [1933].

Militär-Handbuch des Königreichs Bayern, 1914. München, n.d. [1914].

Rangliste der Offiziere der Königlichen Bayerischen Armee, 1917. München, n.d. [1917].

Rangliste des deutschen Reichsheeres Nach dem Stande vom 1. April 1923. Berlin, n.d. [1923].

Reichsgesetzblatt. Berlin, ca. 1866ff.

Reichstags-Handbuch 1924. Berlin, 1924.

Statistisches Handbuch Bayerns, 1919. München, 1919.

Statistisches Handbuch für den Freistaat Bayern, 1924. München, 1924.

Statistisches Handbuch für den Freistaat Bayern, 1926. München, 1926.

Statistisches Handbuch des deutschen Reiches 1924/25. Berlin, 1924.

Stellenbesetzungsliste des Reichsheeres vom Jahr 1920 [September]. Berlin, 1920.

Wer Ist's. Leipzig, 1922-36.

PARLIAMENTARY PAPERS

Bayerischer Landtag, Stenographische Berichten
Reichstag, Stenographische Berichten

NEWSPAPERS

Berliner Tageblatt
Die deutsche Soldatenzeitung
Fränkischer Kurier
Hamburger Correspondent
Münchner Neuesten Nachrichten
Die Süddeutsche Zeitung
Vorwärts
Newspaper Clipping Book for Putsch Period—In the possession of Dr.
Walther Richter, Bremen.

Index